# Corporate Narrative Reporting

T0384264

This book presents a comprehensive and expert-led insight into the role, types, practises and determinants of corporate narrative reporting (CNR). It provides a detailed overview of the importance of narrative disclosure in understanding the full annual report and, consequently, company performance and future prospects.

CNR comprises integral information presented in the front half of the annual report, which helps to tell the full story of a business, providing a comprehensive overview and understanding of both its past and future performance. Supported with illustrative tables and figures throughout, this volume contains a plethora of carefully selected chapters, featuring the analytical insights of knowledgeable academics and researchers from all over the world. Using different data collection and analysis methods, it links and advances theory and practice in the disclosure and presentation of non-financial information in annual reports and other disclosure channels.

The book is logically structured into four parts:

1. Narrative Reporting: The State of the Art
2. Empirical Research on Narrative Reporting
3. Narrative Sustainability Reporting
4. Narrative Reporting in Times of Crisis

Providing a global insight into CNR in practice, Corporate Narrative Reporting is an invaluable resource for both students and practitioners interested or involved in preparing, reviewing/auditing, analysing and understanding annual reports. It should also be of particular interest to policymakers, regulators and investors.

**Mahmoud Marzouk**, PhD, is a Lecturer in Accounting and Finance at the University of Leicester, and a Lecturer in Accounting and Auditing at Menoufia University, Egypt (on leave). He completed his master's (MRes) and PhD degrees at the University of York. Marzouk has extensive teaching and research experience in Egypt and the UK. His research interests lie primarily in the areas of corporate risk disclosure and narrative reporting. Marzouk is a Certified Management and Business Educator and a Fellow of the UK Higher Education Academy. He has also acted as a reviewer for several journals, and an external examiner and reviewer for a number of UK universities.

**Khaled Hussainey** is a Professor and Research Lead of Accounting and Financial Management at the Faculty of Business and Law, University of Portsmouth. He has over 25 years of teaching and research experience at both undergraduate and postgraduate levels. Hussainey has a growing research reputation in the field of accounting and finance. He has been featured in the list of "World Ranking of Top 2% Researchers" in the 2021 database (published: 19 October 2021) created by experts at Stanford University, USA. He has published about 150 articles in peer-reviewed journals and has written a number of book chapters and edited a textbook on corporate governance in emerging economies.

# Corporate Narrative Reporting

Beyond the Numbers

**Edited by Mahmoud Marzouk and Khaled Hussainey**

Routledge
Taylor & Francis Group

LONDON AND NEW YORK

Cover image: Getty Images

First published 2023
by Routledge
4 Park Square, Milton Park, Abingdon, Oxon OX14 4RN

and by Routledge
605 Third Avenue, New York, NY 10158

*Routledge is an imprint of the Taylor & Francis Group, an informa business*

*British Library Cataloguing-in-Publication Data*
A catalogue record for this book is available from the British Library

*Library of Congress Cataloging-in-Publication Data*
Names: Marzouk, Mahmoud, editor. | Hussainey, Khaled, 1972-editor.
Title: Corporate narrative reporting: beyond the numbers/edited by Mahmoud Marzouk and Khaled Hussainey.
Description: 1 Edition. | New York, NY: Routledge, 2023. | Includes bibliographical references and index. |
Summary: "This book presents a comprehensive and expert-led insight into the role, types, practices and determinants of corporate narrative reporting (CNR). It provides a detailed overview of the importance of narrative disclosure in understating the full annual report and, consequently, company performance and future prospects. Providing a global insight into CNR in practice, Corporate Narrative Reporting is an invaluable resource for both students and practitioners interested or involved in preparing, reviewing/ auditing, analysing and understanding annual reports. It should also be of particular interest to policymakers, regulators and investors"–Provided by publisher.
Identifiers: LCCN 2022020053 (print) | LCCN 2022020054 (ebook) | ISBN 9780367558444 (hardback) | ISBN 9780367558338 (paperback) | ISBN 9781003095385 (ebook)
Subjects: LCSH: Corporation reports. | Report writing.
Classification: LCC HG4028.B2 C686 2023 (print) |
LCC HG4028.B2 (ebook) | DDC 658.15/12–dc23/eng/20220609
LC record available at https://lccn.loc.gov/2022020053
LC ebook record available at https://lccn.loc.gov/2022020054

ISBN: 978-0-367-55844-4 (hbk)
ISBN: 978-0-367-55833-8 (pbk)
ISBN: 978-1-003-09538-5 (ebk)

DOI: 10.4324/9781003095385

Typeset in Times New Roman
by Deanta Global Publishing Services, Chennai, India

# Contents

# Figures

# Tables

# Contributors

**Mahmoud Marzouk**, PhD, is a Lecturer in Accounting and Finance at the University of Leicester, and a Lecturer in Accounting and Auditing at Menoufia University, Egypt (on leave). He completed his master's (MRes) and PhD degrees at the University of York. Marzouk has an extensive teaching and research experience in Egypt and the UK. His research interests lie primarily in the areas of corporate risk disclosure and narrative reporting. Marzouk is a Certified Management and Business Educator and a Fellow of the UK Higher Education Academy. He has also acted as a reviewer for several journals, and an external examiner and reviewer for a number of UK universities.

**Khaled Hussainey** is a Professor and Research Lead of Accounting and Financial Management at the Faculty of Business and Law, University of Portsmouth. He has over 25 years of teaching and research experience at both undergraduate and postgraduate levels. Hussainey has a growing research reputation in the field of accounting and finance. He has been featured in the list of "World Ranking of Top 2% Researchers" in the 2021 database (published: 19 October 2021) created by experts at Stanford University, USA. He has published about 150 articles in peer-reviewed journals, has written a number of book chapters and edited a textbook on corporate governance in emerging economies.

**Cristina Florio**, PhD, is an Associate Professor of Accounting at the University of Verona. Her research interests include accounting, auditing, and enterprise risk management. Her articles are published in journals like *The British Accounting Review, Journal of International Accounting, Auditing and Taxation, Accounting Forum, Meditari Accountancy Research*, and *Journal of Management and Governance*. Florio serves the American Accounting Association as an International Council Member-At-Large, the International Accounting Section as chair of the International Relations Committee and the European Risk Research Network as a member of the Scientific Committee. She has been an invited speaker in several workshops worldwide.

**Giulia Leoni**, PhD, is an Associate Professor of Accounting at the University of Genoa. Her research engages with accounting and accountability in diverse settings, including the digital environment, risk management, audit reforms and accounting history. Leoni's papers have been published in journals including the British Accounting Review and Critical Perspectives on Accounting. She serves as an editorial board member for *Accounting, Auditing, and Accountability Journal* and *Accounting History*, and has acted as a guest editor for special issues of both journals. She is the convenor of the Special Interest Group of Accounting History of Accounting and Finance Association of Australia and New Zealand.

**Alice Francesca Sproviero**, PhD, is an Assistant Professor of Accounting at the University of Verona. Her research interests focus on integrated reporting, disclosure of social-environmental scandals, and corporate legitimacy. Sproviero has published articles in Meditari Accountancy Research, the Journal of Intellectual Capital, the Journal of Management and Governance and Financial Reporting. She was a visiting PhD student and visiting scholar at the School of Business and Management of Royal Holloway, University of London. Sproviero was invited to hold a research seminar at the Portsmouth Business School, Portsmouth University, UK.

**Khairul Ayuni binti Mohd Kharuddin** (FCCA, FHEA, PhD) is an Associate Professor in Financial Accounting and Reporting at Universiti Teknologi MARA, Malaysia. She formerly taught at Loughborough University and Aston University in the UK, and currently serves as the external examiner for the University of Sheffield and Birmingham City University. Mohd Kharuddin was also a Senior Auditor at Ernst & Young. She was recently appointed as Executive Committee member for the Audit Group of the British Accounting and Finance Association, and the Associate Editor for the *Asian Journal of Accounting Research*. Her research interests are in the areas of auditing, corporate governance and financial reporting.

**Ilias G Basioudis** is a Senior Lecturer/Associate Professor of Financial Accounting & Auditing and the Research Convenor in the Accounting Department at Aston University Business School, UK. He is the Chairman of the Audit Group of the British Accounting and Finance Association. Basioudis is also an Editor of the International Journal of Auditing. His research interests lie primarily within the areas of auditing and corporate governance and include the market for audit services in the private and public sectors, earnings quality and audit quality, corporate governance, accounting education and audit committees.

**Omar Al Farooque** is an Associate Professor of Accounting and Finance at the UNE Business School, University of New England, Australia. He holds fellowships and full membership of accounting professional bodies in Australia, namely CPA Australia, IPA Australia and CA ANZ. Al Farooque's teaching area is financial accounting, accounting project and auditing. His current research interests are in corporate governance, board diversity, executive compensation, auditing, financial reporting/disclosure, earnings management/quality, CSR/ESG/sustainability, finance and banking/Islamic banking, SME, FDI and institutional quality. Al Farooque has published extensively in mainstream accounting and finance (ABDC/ABS ranked) journals, and conference papers, books and book chapters.

**Mostafa Hassan** obtained his PhD in accounting and finance from the University of Essex, UK, in 2003. Since then, he has worked at the University of Hertfordshire, UK, the University of Portsmouth, UK, the University of Sharjah, UAE, and Alexandria University, Egypt. Currently, he is a Professor of Accounting at Qatar University and on leave from Alexandria University, Egypt. Hassan has many publications in highly regarded peer-reviewed academic journals and his research interests include the sociological analysis of accounting practices, institutional theory and accounting change, corporate governance, globalization, performance evaluation, risk disclosure, risk governance and narrative disclosures.

**Hany Kamel** is an Associate Professor of Accounting at the College of Business and Economics, Qatar University. He is also a Lecturer in Accounting at the Faculty of Commerce, Cairo University. He received his PhD in accounting and finance from Cardiff University, UK. His research interests lie in the areas of financial reporting, corporate governance and performance measurement. He has published articles in top academic journals such as *Managerial Auditing Journal* and *Journal of Accounting in Emerging Economies*. He also reviewed many papers for journals such as *Management Research Review*, *Journal of Cleaner Production*, and the *Managerial Auditing Journal*.

**Bassam Abu-Abbas** is an Associate Professor at the College of Business and Economics, Qatar University. Bassam received his PhD in Accounting from Kent State University, USA in 2002. Prior to joining Qatar University, he worked at different universities in the USA, Jordan and Bahrain. His research interests lie in the areas of financial performance, Islamic accounting and corporate governance. Abu-Abbas has published several articles in different academic journals and reviewed many manuscripts in his areas of interests.

**Chiara Demartini** is an Associate Professor in Financial and Management Accounting at the University of Pavia, Italy. Her main teaching activities relate to financial accounting (undergraduate) and performance management (master's and PhD level). Demartini is a Visiting Scholar to the University of Lancaster, UK and Associate Editor of the journal SN Business & Economics (Springer). Her principal areas of research are the design and use of performance management systems, with a specific focus on healthcare organisations; the use of non-financial disclosure for risk management and audit risk in for-profit organisations; sustainable performance management; and cultural and social ties in accounting history.

**Sara Trucco** is an Associate Professor in Financial and Management Accounting at the Università degli Studi Internazionali di Roma in Rome. Her main teaching efforts are focused on business administration (undergraduate) and international accounting (master's level). She received her PhD in business administration at the University of Pisa in 2011, where she was a research fellow from 2011 to 2014. Her main research interests are in the fields of financial accounting, auditing and management accounting.

**Valentina Beretta** is a Postdoctoral Researcher at the Department of Economics and Management of the University of Pavia and Adjunct Professor of Business Administration at the Department of International, Legal, Historical and Political Studies of the University of Milano. Beretta is Teaching Manager of the CEF Telecom project "eXplainable Artificial Intelligence in Healthcare Management" and she collaborates in many Erasmus+ projects. She was a visiting scholar at the Université Laval (Québec City, Canada), at the Hôpital Européen Georges Pompidou (Paris) and invited visiting scholar at CHU Sainte-Justine and INESSS (Institut national d'excellence en santé et services sociaux) (Montréal, Canada).

**Taslima Akhter** is an Assistant Professor of Management at the School of International Studies at Kwansei Gakuin University, Japan. She received her PhD from the Kwansei Gakuin University, Japan, on integrated reporting.

**Mohammad Badrul Haider** is an Associate Professor of Accounting at the Institute of Business and Accounting at Kwansei Gakuin University, Japan. His research interests include sustainability accounting, reporting and auditing.

**Toshihiko Ishihara** is a Professor of Accounting and Public Governance at Kwansei Gakuin University, Japan. He is also an Honorary Professor at Edinburgh Business School, UK, and at Kent Business School, UK.

**Fatima Yusuf** is a Lecturer in Accounting at The Open University, UK. Her research interests include auditing, environmental accounting, corporate disclosure, and accountability practices of corporate organizations. She has published in various accounting, finance and management journals.

**Jiaxu Du** is a third-year PhD student at the University of Leicester School of Business. He holds an MSc in accounting and international management from Henley Business School, University of Reading, UK. His research interest lies in the area of non-financial disclosure. His PhD thesis focuses on corporate social and environmental responsibility disclosure practices in China.

**Nader Elsayed** is an Associate Professor of Accounting at the College of Business and Economics, Qatar University. He received his MSc and PhD degrees in accountancy from Exeter University, UK, and a BCom (Hons) degree in accounting from Minufiya University, Egypt. Elsayed is a Certified Management and Business Educator (CBME) and a fellow of the Higher Education Academy (HEA) in the UK. His research focus both empirical and qualitative, is within the wider field of corporate governance, financial reporting and disclosure and accounting education.

**Mohamed Nurullah** is an Associate Professor/Reader and former Head of the Department of Accounting, Finance, and Informatics at Kingston University

London. Nurullah received his PhD from Cass Business School of City University London where he also started his full-time academic career in 1999. He then worked for Westminster University, Glasgow Caledonian University, and Glasgow University in the UK. Nurullah has published over 50 academic papers, book chapters and commissioned reports. He has published papers in leading academic journals, such as the *Journal of Economic Behavior & Organization, British Accounting Review* and *Journal of Financial Services Research* and has successfully supervised 18 PhD students.

**Walid Ben-Amar** is a full Professor and Telfer Research Fellow in Sustainability Accounting at the Telfer School of Management of the University of Ottawa, Canada. A chartered professional accountant (CPA) in Ontario, he holds a master's degree in Accounting from Université du Québec à Montréal and a PhD in business administration from HEC Montréal. His areas of research include corporate governance, corporate social responsibility and disclosure strategies. Ben-Amar has published his work in academic journals such as *Journal of Business Ethics, Journal of Business Finance & Accounting, European Accounting Review, British Journal of Management* and *Critical Perspectives on Accounting.*

**Mohamed Saeudy** is the Director of the Research Centre for Contemporary Accounting, Finance, and Economics (Res CAFE). His research area is sustainable accounting and finance. His research focuses on how business organisations use accounting and finance tools to manage the contemporary challenges of sustainable development such as climate change, modern slavery, UN SDGs and ecological biodiversity, with an ambition to develop organisational lenses through which to explore how sustainability may allow or help organisations to improve their triple bottom-line impact. He argues the possibility of creating innovative social and environmental impact from the economic activities of business organisations.

**Shraddha Verma** is a Senior Lecturer and Head of Department of Accounting and Finance at the Open University, UK. Her research interests relate to accounting history, and accounting and risk, and she has explored risk in historical contexts and risk disclosures in financial reporting. Verma is a member of the Institute of Chartered Accountants of England and Wales and the Chartered Institute of Taxation and has significant experience as an academic lecturer and researcher.

**Eleonora Maserio** is an Assistant Professor at the University of Trieste, Italy. Until March 2020, she worked as a Postdoctoral Research Fellow at the Department of Management of Ca' Foscari University of Venice, Italy. She obtained her PhD in management and holds a bachelor's degree in history from the University of Padua, Italy, and an MSc in marketing communications from Manchester University, UK. During her PhD studies, she was an Honorary Visiting Associate in the School of Accounting of RMIT University, Melbourne, Australia. Maserio's research interests are communication of non-financial information, accountability, accounting history, strategic innovation and business model innovation.

**Faozi Almaqtari** is an Assistant Professor of Accounting at the Universiti Malaysia Terengganu. Almaqtari holds a PhD degree in accounting from Aligarh Muslim University, India, and a master's of Commerce degree from Savitribai Phule Pune University, India. At present, he is on the Faculty of Business, Economics and Social Development, University of Malaysia Terengganu as a senior lecturer. He is currently supervising a number of PhD students as a co-supervisor. Almaqtari has authored or co-authored numerous papers, and reviewed articles for several journals cited by Scopus and ISI Web of Science. His research papers have been presented at international conferences and seminars in several countries.

**Issal Haj-Salem** completed her PhD in accounting at IHEC Carthage, Tunisia. Haj-Salem's main research area is concerned with risk disclosure, corporate governance, and firm value. Her publications appear in the *Journal of Accounting in Emerging Economies, International Journal of Disclosure and Governance, Journal of Risk and Financial Management* and *IGI Global*.

**Karen McBride**, PhD, is a Reader in Accounting and Accountability, at the University of Portsmouth. She has published on various areas of accounting history, as well as more contemporaneous issues in financial reporting and corporate governance. McBride is a founder committee member of the accounting history SIG - BAFA, believing that studying accounting in history provides insights into accounting's impact past, present and future and its wide reach, as social and moral practice. As a chartered accountant, McBride remains engaged with wider areas of reporting, accountability and governance. Her research projects ensure she keeps up to date with current developments and issues.

**Marwa Soliman** is a doctoral candidate at Telfer School of Management, University of Ottawa, Canada. Soliman has earned an MSc degree in accounting from the University of Memphis, USA, and she has been a Certified Management Accountant (CMA) since 2012. Her research interests include narrative disclosure, disclosure quality and corporate governance. Her work has been presented at internationally recognized conferences such as the American Accounting Association, the Canadian Academic Accounting Association, and the European Accounting Association annual meetings. Marwa won first place in the national capital region thesis competition in 2019 and third place in the Telfer Thesis Competition in 2020.

**Philip Linsley** is a Professor of Accounting and Risk at the York Management School, University of York, UK. His research interests are risk related and include investigating risk disclosure, and risk and culture. He is particularly interested in applying the ideas of Mary Douglas to accounting. Linsley is also a qualified chartered accountant and has significant experience as an academic lecturer and researcher.

**Sudipta Bose** is a Senior Lecturer in Accounting at the University of Newcastle, Australia. Bose was awarded his PhD in Accounting from the School of Accounting, UNSW Sydney. He is a Chartered Accountant and Certified Management Accountant. His research interests include capital market, cost of equity capital, carbon emissions and assurance, integrated reporting, sustainability reporting and assurance and corporate governance. Bose has published in the Journal of Corporate Finance, Accounting, Auditing & Accountability Journal, British Accounting Review, Abacus, Critical Perspectives on Accounting, Accounting & Finance, the Journal of Contemporary Accounting and Economics and the Journal of Business Ethics.

**Amir Hossain** is a PhD student in Accounting at the University of Newcastle, Australia. He has completed the Master of Research degree in Accounting and Corporate Governance from Macquarie University, Australia. He has also completed the Master of Science degree in Accounting and Finance from the University of Greenwich, UK and the Master of Business Administration from the University of Dhaka, Bangladesh. His research interests include corporate governance, sustainability reporting, integrated reporting and capital market. He has published in the Australian Accounting Review.

**Nandita Mishra** is Universitetlektor in the Department of Management and Engineering, Linköping University, Sweden. She is also an ambassador to IIRC (International Integrated Reporting Council), London. She is country director to HETL (USA). Mishra was awarded her PhD in the field of corporate governance in the banking sector in 2013. She has more than 20 years of experience in corporate and academic. She is also on the Sustainability Reporting Board of the Institute of Chartered Accountant of India. She has written more than 40 papers and book chapters. She has also completed three funded projects and is involved in consultancy with many companies.

**Muhammad Jahangir Ali** (CPA, FIPA, FCMA) is an Associate Professor of Accounting at the Department of Accounting and Data Analytics, La Trobe University. He was awarded his PhD from La Trobe University, Australia. His research interests include corporate governance, corporate financial reporting, corporate social responsibility, audit quality and capital markets. Ali has published a number of papers in international referred journals including Accounting and Business Research, Accounting & Finance, the Australian Journal of Management, British Accounting Review, the Journal of Accounting and Public Policy, the Journal of Accounting Literature, the Journal of Business Ethics, the Pacific-Basin Finance Journal, and the International Journal of Accounting.

**Muhammad Shahin Miah** is an Associate Professor in Accounting at the University of Dhaka. Miah was awarded his PhD in Accounting from the School of Accountancy, Massey University, New Zealand. He is a Certified Practising Accountant (CPA). His research interests include capital market, regulations impact, audit reporting and corporate governance. Miah has published in the International Journal of Finance and Economics, the Asian Review of Accounting, the Accounting Research Journal, the International Journal of Auditing, the Journal of Chinese Economic and Business Studies, the Journal of Corporate Accounting & Finance, and the Journal of Islamic Accounting and Business Research.

**Ahmed Hassanein** is an Assistant Professor of Accounting with international teaching and consulting experience. Dr Hassanein is a Certified Management and Business Educator (CBME) and an Associate Fellow of the Higher Education Academy (HEA) in the UK. Hassanein has published in international peer-reviewed journals. His research areas centre around the informativeness of firm reporting practices, risk governance, IFRS, sentiment analysis, market-based accounting research and bibliographic analysis.

**Heba Abou-El-Sood** (College of Business, Zayed University and Faculty of Commerce, Cairo University) is an associate professor of Accounting and Finance with international teaching and consulting experience. She has earned an M.Sc. in accounting (Cairo University), an M.Sc. in accounting and finance (Boston College), and a Ph.D. in accounting and finance (Lancaster University). She published papers in impactful academic journals and wrote articles for professional magazines. She is a research fellow/catalyst in BITSS University of California Berkley and an alum of Fulbright and Newton.

# Foreword

I have been invited to introduce the book entitled *Corporate Narrative Reporting: Beyond the Numbers* edited by Mahmoud Marzouk and Khaled Hussainey. An invitation that I delightedly accepted. As one of my supervisory team, I have known Khaled Hussainey since I pursued my PhD study at the University of Stirling back in 2009. I came to know Mahmoud when he started his PhD study on the quality of risk disclosure at the University of York. Khaled has worked extensively on narrative reporting since his first publication in *Accounting and Business Research* in 2003. Since then, he has published many key articles in this area of research. Mahmoud Marzouk is interested in narrative disclosure with particular attention to risk-related information.

I have been investigating the main topic of this edited book for more than a decade, looking at the underlying incentives and economic consequences of corporate narrative disclosures. I have witnessed significant changes in this area over the years in terms of methods that have been incorporated from different, but still related, fields such as computer science by employing, for example, machine learning and data mining. Along with such development in the implemented methods, another emerging line of research incorporates some well-developed theoretical foundations from other fields such as psychology and political science to provide additional insights into how managers use corporate reporting to convey their intended and unintended messages to outsiders' recipients. Additionally, several lines of research have started to tackle some recent topics to reflect stakeholders' needs. Therefore, the area of narrative disclosures has moved forward in terms of employed methods, foundations, and emerging issues, highlighting the importance of this edited book.

It has been argued for so many years that market participants are likely to perceive accounting information differently depending on whether such information appears inside financial statements (meeting recognition criteria) and is known as "hard information" or outside financial statements (does not meet the recognition criteria) and known as "soft information". The evidence from both empirical and analytical work shows that narrative disclosure sections are getting longer and more challenging to read. While reliability is the criterion that prioritizes hard above soft information, the relevance of information, however, is the criterion that places soft information higher than hard information—these two criteria for assessing where to recognize accounting information despite the broader use for fair value approach. The credibility and the nature of information, along with whether each type of this information is presented in an isolation or integration manner, might have different effects.

This edited book covers plenty of essential topics on narrative disclosures distributed in 19 chapters, all of which capture imperative aspects. The book's chapters cover several streams. Firstly, narrative disclosures include recent directions, the effect of regulations, and governance. Secondly, examples of the content of narrative disclosures comprising forward-looking disclosure, quantity and quality of risk disclosure, and sustainability. Thirdly, some features of narrative disclosure encompassing readability, digital disclosure, current pandemic effect, extended auditor report, integrated reporting, and climate change. The book represents a wide-ranging selection of nicely linked topics, serving the more prominent areas of narrative disclosures. The readers of this book would benefit greatly from the different aspects of narrative disclosures in one place.

Tamer Elshandidy
Professor of Accounting
Ajman University
Ajman, United Arab Emirates (UAE)

# Introduction

Financial accounting research shows that corporate financial statements have lost their relevance and hence the traditional accounting model no longer satisfies stakeholders' information needs. This highlights the need for a more comprehensive model of business reporting that includes corporate narrative reporting (CNR) to complement the information included in the financial statements. CNR serves as an important source of information for stakeholders to enhance stakeholders' decision-making. CNR comprises information presented in the first/front half of the annual report, which is an integral part of the annual report.

CNR puts into context the financial information (numbers) and addresses aspects and events that are difficult to monetise such as forward-looking information related to strategy and risks, non-financial performance measures, narrative information related to intangibles, climate change, Brexit, COVID-19, Fourth Industrial Revolution (IR 4.0) technologies, customer loyalty, retention of skilled labour and the value-creation process. Political instability and economic uncertainty present a challenge to companies to disclose non-financial information and ensure its quality due to its forward-looking and qualitative nature.

CNR encompasses significant information in addition to the financial statements and notes to the accounts including the strategic report, directors' report, chairman's statement, corporate social responsibility, risk information and corporate governance disclosures. There is a growing interest among researchers, regulators and information users in narrative/non-financial information due to its importance along with financial information in telling the full story of a business and gaining a comprehensive understanding of its past performance and future prospects. Likewise, recent significant events and risks such as Brexit, COVID-19, the Russian invasion of Ukraine, corporate failures and scandals, and regulatory pressure have increased emphasis on what companies report in the front half of their annual report rather than depending solely on financial information. Non-financial information complements financial reporting and hence has either direct or indirect impacts on financial performance and investors' decisions.

The growth in CNR literature is also motivated by the findings of prior disclosure research which offers interesting implications for policy, CNR practices and theory. One strand of the CNR literature shows the extent to which companies voluntarily disclose narrative information in their annual reports and the change/trend

DOI: 10.4324/9781003095385-1

of this disclosure over time. Other studies explore the determinants of CNR which could inform regulations in terms of what drives companies to voluntarily disclose more and higher-quality narrative information in their annual reports. A third group of studies explores the consequences of CNR and provides evidence on the benefits of enhanced narrative disclosure practices, while other studies focus on the potential costs of increasing narrative disclosure in annual reports. Therefore, this area of research offers a cost-benefit analysis of CNR that could be helpful for regulators and companies to inform disclosure regulations and enhance CNR practices.

This book is a collection of high-quality scrupulously gathered chapters that provide an insightful and analytical look at CNR in terms of its relevance and perceived usefulness, limitations of current practices and areas for improvement and the incentives and disincentives for disclosing non-financial information. This book draws on disclosure theories and takes account of the particular nature of CNR in terms of its predominantly forward-looking, qualitative and hard-to-audit nature. It also brings together theory and practice and covers some key themes that should be of particular interest to and essential reading for academics, investors, annual report preparers, auditors and policy makers, as well as students. We are delighted to have received contributions from 38 academics and researchers from all around the world which enrich CNR literature from both theoretical and empirical perspectives.

The theoretical perspectives focus on the concept of disclosure (voluntary *versus* mandatory), the type of disclosure (e.g., forward-looking, risk, risk management, corporate social responsibility, COVID-19, carbon and climate change, sustainability, integrated reporting, sustainable development, digital reporting, intellectual capital, governance reporting, external auditors' reporting) and/or disclosure theories (e.g., agency theory, signalling theory, stakeholder theory) and CNR literature review. These theoretical perspectives should enable readers to critically evaluate and explore the broader areas of CNR. The empirical perspectives offer empirical analysis of CNR in financial and non-financial sectors, which include the measurement of CNR (using the content analysis approach), the examination of the impact of firm-specific characteristics and corporate governance mechanisms on CNR and the economic consequences of CNR. These empirical chapters provide fresh evidence which has practical and theoretical implications in terms of contributing to informing disclosure regulations and improving CNR practices.

This book is structured into four parts. Part 1 offers some contextualisation by providing a state-of-the-art review of the prior literature on different areas of narrative reporting. Part 2 presents empirical research on narrative reporting and provides international evidence. Part 3 discusses sustainability reporting and climate-related disclosures. Part 4 addresses how companies use narrative reporting to respond to significant crises and corporate scandals and failures.

We hope that this book advances our knowledge and understanding of current CNR practices, challenges and research gaps, fosters further interest in and discussions of the different strands of narrative reporting, as well as encourages further research into this rapidly evolving research area.

Mahmoud Marzouk          Leicester, United Kingdom
Khaled Hussainey          Portsmouth, United Kingdom

**Part 1**

# Narrative reporting

The state of the art

# 1 Corporate narrative reporting

## Nature and related costs

*Ahmed Hassanein*

## 1.1 Introduction

The disclosure practices and the types of information that firms disclose have changed. In addition to the financial statements, firms disclose narrative disclosures through which corporate managers disseminate textual information to different market users (Merkley, 2014). Corporate narrative reporting (hereafter, CNR) represents soft-talk discussions and analyses disclosed alongside financial information and provides helpful context for understanding financial statements (Li, 2010). It allows corporate managers to describe and discuss the economic environment's corporate performance (Hassanein *et al.*, 2019). Furthermore, it offers corporate managers the possibility to disclose a piece of soft, qualitative information not recognised within financial statements, such as risk information, information about key performance indicators and future-oriented information (Beattie *et al.*, 2004).

Remarkably, CNR is analysed by market participants and is considered in their decisions. It helps them understand the meaning of figures in financial statements and to configure the economic reality of a firm (Merkley, 2014). CNR reduces information asymmetry, mitigates the risk of adverse selection and promotes the firm's values (Chen *et al.*, 2017). Likewise, it is documented that CNR increases the accuracy of forecasts by analysts (Vanstraelen *et al.*, 2003) and facilitates the prediction of future performance (Schleicher *et al.*, 2007). Moreover, Brown and Tucker (2011) indicate that the CNR is value-relevant and carries information indicative of the firm's performance. In addition, Muslu *et al.* (2015) find that providing earnings guidelines in a firm's Management Discussions and Analyses (MD&As) helps investors to anticipate future earnings.

There are no absolute benefits of CNR, and some costs are associated with this type of disclosure. In response, firms adopt a disclosure policy, and they may avert the disclosure of narrative information if its related costs outweigh its benefits. Hence, firms adopt disclosure policies to reduce disclosure costs. For instance, the production and preparation costs of CNR may constrain firms from providing it (Field *et al.*, 2005; Core, 2001). Likewise, corporate managers may be concerned with political considerations and take steps to reduce the political pressure by providing more or less narrative reporting. Also, the proprietary cost

DOI: 10.4324/9781003095385-3

hypothesis suggests that firms may be unwilling to provide CNR to maintain their competitive market position. Furthermore, firms may be likely to either provide more CNR to avoid the litigation costs of having withheld information from the market or decrease their CNR, which they may later be accountable for updating to avoid litigation costs (Hassanein and Elsayed, 2021).

Prior research heavily investigated the benefits of CNR regarding its impacts on current and future performance, stock liquidity and firm valuation. However, research is scarce, and little is known about the costs associated with CNR. This chapter aims to provide a wide-ranging review of literature on the costs associated with CNR. In particular, it explores different costs of CNR, reviews the theories and literature on these costs and highlights avenues for future research. We contribute to the research by providing an up-to-date review of the recent literature on CNR-related costs, a largely uninvestigated research area. We enrich the literature by identifying the existing research gaps and providing suggestions for future research to fill these gaps.

As a discussion background, this chapter starts by providing an overview of the nature, contents and claims for and against CNR. We then turn to the direct and indirect costs of CNR. Finally, we highlight some concluding remarks and suggest areas for future research.

## 1.2 Corporate narrative reporting (CNR): an overview

Nowadays, CNR has become an integral part of a firm's annual report. This section describes the nature and contents of narrative disclosure and highlights the claims for and against CNR.

### 1.2.1 Nature of narrative disclosure

Financial statements provide users with historical financial information. The historical nature of financial statement information is inadequate to fulfil the information requirements of different users in the market. In response, firms begin to change their disclosure policy and provide users with more textual discussions alongside financial statements to improve their understanding of a firm's financial position and performance (Beattie *et al.*, 2004; Hassanein and Hussainey, 2015).

The CNR is soft, textual discussions and analyses disclosed alongside financial information. It helps develop a picture of the firm's strategy, performance, risks, market position and future. It reviews the firm's operations and performance, describes the accounting outputs and provides expectations for the future (Clatworthy and Jones, 2003). It accompanies the financial results and allows managers to disseminate textual information to market users (Merkley, 2014). Additionally, CNR offers corporate managers the possibility to disclose a piece of soft, qualitative information not recognised within financial statements, such as information about key performance indicators, future-oriented information, corporate social responsibility and risk information (Beattie *et al.*, 2004; Hassanein and Hussainey, 2015; Elzahar *et al.*, 2015; Hassanein and Elsayed,

2021). Nevertheless, the CNR is analysed by different users in the market and is incorporated in their decision-making processes. In particular, it helps them to link the performance and financial position with the economic reality of a firm (Feldma *et al.*, 2010; Merkley, 2014).

There are different channels through which firms can disclose their narrative information. For instance, the statement of the board chairman (i.e., the president's letter) is a channel through which a firm can provide an overview about the past year's operations and performance and convey predictions for the firm. Another channel for narrative reporting is the Chief Executive Officer (CEO) statement, which ultimately supplements the firm's performance and operations statements from the chairman. The MD&A is a primary channel for narrative reporting required by the US Securities and Exchange Commission (SEC). It can be provided annually or quarterly and explains the comparisons of the firm's performance with previous years' and includes forecasting for the future year. Similarly, the operating and financial review (OFR) is required by the Accounting Standards Board (ASB) as a channel for narrative reporting in the UK. It provides textual analysis about a firm's strategy, risks, performance, financial and market positions. There is no standard title for narrative reporting, and firms provide narrative statements under different titles. Hassanein and Hussainey (2015) surveyed the narrative sections of the annual reports of FTSE all-shares firms over the period from 2005 to 2011. They revealed that 38% of their sample reported the narrative statement under either the "Operating Review" or the "Financial Review". While 31% of the firms used the title "Business Review", 19% used the title of "OFR". In addition, 8% of firms reported the narrative statement under the title of "Chief Executive Officer".

### 1.2.2  Contents of narrative disclosure

There are no restrictions on the information contents of CNR. Specifically, firm managers have flexibility in identifying the extent of the information content in the CNR. Nonetheless, they must adhere to the guiding principles of narrative reporting as suggested by the regulatory bodies (e.g., ASB and SEC). Hence, the CNR can be seen as a compulsory, discretionary reporting channel (Hassanein and Hussainey, 2015). The information content of CNR should be adequately detailed and framed in a transparent and readable way. Furthermore, CNR should be unbiased and should include both positive and negative news about the firm, while future-oriented information is desirable in the narrative contents.

The CNR covers the following topics: (i) "The nature, objectives and strategies of the business" discusses a company's objectives to generate long-term value, sets out the strategies of the board of directors to achieve the firm's objectives and describes the company and its external environment; (ii) "Current and future development and performance" analyses the substantial aspects of performance over the year from the point of view of its directors; (iii) "Firm financial position" covers analyses of the factors that influenced the firm's financial position during the current year and which may impact its future; (iv) "Capital structure, cash flow and liquidity" contains discussions on the firm's capital structure and funding plans: (v) "Key Performance Indicators (KPIs)" covers the definitions and measurement methods of financial and non-financial KPIs and their purposes; (vi) "Resources, principal risks and uncertainties" describes the available resources and analyses the principal risks and uncertainties facing the firm; and (vii) "Relationships" describes relationships, such as those with stakeholders, which may affect corporate performance and value.

### 1.2.3  Claims for and against narrative disclosure

The literature suggests various claims for and against CNR. On the one hand, financial statements cannot adequately fulfil different users' information requirements in the market. Therefore, CNR can be used to communicate to users, with textual discussions alongside financial statements, to improve their understanding of a firm's financial position and performance. It provides an essential context through which investors and other users can grasp financial information as financial statements alone cannot serve this purpose (Li, 2010). In addition, it links the financial information with the economic reality of the firm (Merkely, 2014). Thus, CNR provides a channel for describing, discussing and analysing the firm's financial information. CNR also helps managers disseminate their perceptions and views about their firm to market participants (Hassanein *et al.*, 2019). Through CNR, corporate managers can explain and justify the current level of earnings, the risks that their firms may face and how to manage these risks. Overall, CNR reduces the issue of information asymmetry. Furthermore, the proponents of CNR suggest that it is a valuable information source for financial analysts and institutional investors and supports investment decisions (Clatworthy and Jones, 2003; Arnold and De Lange, 2004). In addition, investors use CNR to interpret financial statements, evaluate current and future results and make rational investment decisions (ASB, 2005, 2006).

It is worthwhile mentioning that the disclosure of narrative information leads to some benefits to the firms. It enhances investors' valuation of companies (Hassanein *et al.*, 2019; Hassanein and Hussaieny, 2015). It also improves the liquidity of a firm's stock (Caglio *et al.*, 2020). Furthermore, narrative information in a firm's annual report mitigates the adverse selection risk (Elshandidy and Shrives, 2016). Athanasakou *et al.* (2020) reveal that narrative information from a firm reduces its cost of capital. However, this relationship holds true only at an optimal level of narrative disclosure, beyond which an increase in narrative disclosure increases the firm's cost of capital.

On the other hand, some claims exist which oppose CNR. Opponents argue that narrative disclosure may be used as a tool to mislead investors (Li, 2008). Specifically, the discretionary nature of CNR, alongside the flexibility given to managers in preparation of its contents, may induce firm managers to disseminate narrative information to mislead investors (Marquardt and Wiedman, 2005). Empirically, Li (2008) reveals that loss-making firms are willing to disseminate complex narrative statements (i.e., which are difficult to read and understand).

The author further indicates that corporate managers can use the discretionary nature of CNR to complicate the financial results to hide their practices (loss/earning management) from market participants. Thus, the CNR may induce managers to take part in impression management practices to mislead investors (Healy and Palepu, 2001). In turn, they may "strategically manipulate the perceptions and decisions of stakeholders" (Yuthas *et al.*, 2002, p. 142).

## 1.3 Costs related to narrative disclosure

The CNR is associated with costs, and firms may avoid disclosing narrative information if its related costs outweigh its benefits. Hence, firms adopt disclosure policies to reduce disclosure costs. These costs may prevent firms from providing full disclosure. Hence, it is argued that "It is now generally recognised that a cost–benefit analysis is required, weighing the benefits of additional disclosure to investors against the costs" (Bhushan and Lessared, 1992, p. 150). The optimal level of CNR is thus a trade-off between the benefits and the costs of this reporting. The corporate managers may choose between full disclosure to obtain economic benefits (e.g., to minimise the cost of capital) and partial disclosure to minimise the disclosure costs.

The costs associated with CNR can be categorised into two broad categories: direct and indirect costs. The direct costs are associated with the production and dissemination of CNR sections (i.e., preparation costs), whereas indirect costs arise due to the effect of CNR on companies' activities (Leventise, 2001). The indirect costs include political, proprietary and litigation. This section reviews the theories and related literature on CNR costs.

### 1.3.1 Preparation costs of narrative disclosure

There are some costs associated with the development of the CNR section. These costs are called direct costs or preparation costs. They include the costs of producing, preparing and disseminating CNR information to the public (Core, 2001; Field *et al.*, 2005). They also comprise the costs of collecting and gathering the required information, handling and displaying it, auditing CNR information if required, the costs of information technology equipment and the management time spent on disclosure activities by operators. Bethel (2007) indicates that the information system used by the SEC processes approximately three million pages every day, and each page costs $0.15. Furthermore, auditing costs have increased considerably in recent years, suggesting increased preparation costs of a CNR section.

The preparation costs are not spent only once by firms, but are incurred regularly to update the reporting section. Hassanein and Hussainey (2015) examined whether or not firms update their narrative disclosure statements from year to year. They argue that the direct costs of disclosure restrict corporate managers' decisions to update their narrative reporting statement regularly. Specifically, firms may be able to afford to cover the preparation costs, so they will be more likely to change their narrative reporting section yearly. Nonetheless, other companies may not have enough resources to update their narrative section and simply cut-and-paste narrative statements from previous years. Furthermore, they argue that some firms may be able to afford to acquire the services of Big Four external auditing firms, while others may not have enough resources for Big Four external auditors. The results of Hassanein and Hussainey (2015) suggest that only large firms can update their narrative reporting statements from year to year. In addition, clients of Big Four auditors can change their disclosure yearly. This indicates that large auditing firms are affordable for the preparation costs of CNR.

Another aspect of the direct costs of CNR are the costs of applying the accounting regulations and requirements from the stock market, such as corporate governance principles and requirements for cross-listing status. One of the core principles of corporate governance is transparency. This requires more disclosure by firms. However, this increase in the disclosure may result in two potential costs. First, it leads to opportunity costs due to the time spent by corporate managers and their management teams in preparing and producing more information for better quality disclosure and the additional auditing costs for this information, if required. Second, it leads to risk aversion of corporate managers due to the pressure to provide more information to comply with the narrative reporting requirements. The increase in disclosure helps corporate shareholders and their board of directors to supervise and monitor the corporate managers effectively. However, it may accelerate the turn-over of corporate managers who would like to avoid the risks of preparing information or may induce them to falsify information for their benefit and in their own interests.

The requirements for cross-listing status may also lead to additional preparation costs. Cross-listed firms have to comply with the foreign market disclosure requirements. Specifically, firms with stocks on domestic and secondary listing markets must fulfil the domestic and foreign market requirements regarding the international disclosure practices and the international investors' needs for information. In this situation, the firm incurs more costs to acquire and process information about foreign firms than about national companies.

### 1.3.2 *Political cost and narrative disclosure*

The political costs can be seen as a re-allocation of capital and wealth away from the firm to other special interest groups (Whittred and Zimmer, 1990). The interest group may include customers, employees, government, politicians and environmental groups. These interest groups may support or criticise a company for non-reporting accounting figures or for disseminating insufficient information (Lemon and Cahan, 1997). Hence, politically visible firms can be criticised or supported by these interest groups. These groups are willing to increase pressure on firms to favour their specific interests. This may result in impositions of regulations or taxes by governments on these firms. Thus, political power may influence the transfer of wealth between the firm and different stakeholders. Nonetheless, the time of corporate managers may be usefully taken up with political considerations and they may take steps to reduce the political pressure through media campaigns, government lobbying and utilising accounting procedures to minimise reported earnings (Watts and Zimmerman, 1978). Political groups can use the firm's reported accounting numbers and disclosures to criticise or support this firm. Thus, firms may react by managing their reported earnings and disclosures to reduce their exposure to political pressure during times of high public sensitivity (Mitra and Crumbley, 2003).

The disclosure of narrative information may be used as a medium by which to reduce the political costs. Thus, politically visible companies should disseminate more narrative discussions and analyses of their performances and operations to prevent any assertion of suppressing information from the public and other special interest groups. It is known from previous research that larger firms are seen as more "politically visible"; consequently, these firms are more subject to political costs than are smaller firms (Aggarwal and Simkins, 2004). Thus, CNR may support firms to avoid the political costs and help them to avoid criticism from the interest groups. Consistently, Al-Hatybat (2005) found that larger companies disclosed more information to avoid political costs, such as the imposition of more taxes. Similarly, Dey *et al.* (2018) found that larger companies disclosed more risk information to reduce the political costs.

In addition, Brown and Tucker (2011) reveal that larger companies are less likely to disclose fuzzy information and more willing to update their disclosure periodically to avoid political costs. Their empirical findings support the idea that these companies modify their CNR to a greater degree than smaller companies. Similarly, Hassanein and Hussainey (2015) examine the narrative reporting statements of the UK FTSE all-share firms. They find that large firms provide less boilerplate information and update their CNR yearly. Furthermore, their CNR is more indicative of the firms' value. Recently, Sankara *et al.* (2019) reported that firms disclosing more social responsibility information reduced the political costs and led to fewer adverse reactions from the markets. Other research suggests that firms with a political "patronage" disclose less value-relevant information to the public (Chen *et al.*, 2017). Furthermore, Lemma *et al.* (2020) argue that political costs are a function of a firm's carbon risk. They examined whether firms with high carbon risks produced high-quality reporting. They found that these firms provided low-quality financial but high-quality voluntary carbon disclosures.

### *1.3.3 Proprietary costs and narrative disclosure*

Luo *et al.* (2006, p. 506) have stated that the proprietary costs are "the costs associated with strategic decision-making by a competitor using all available information". Therefore, the degree of market competition may prevent firm managers from disclosing information. Notably, information with proprietary costs is largely undisclosed by firms to prevent competitors from using this information in a way that harms the firm's income-producing activities (Verrecchia and Weber, 2006). Narrative disclosure explains companies from the viewpoint of their board of directors (Hassanein and Hussaieny, 2015), which improves the ability of the firm's rivals to understand the firm's economic environment and hence to decide on whether to enter its market. Linsley and Shrives (2006) revealed that competitors are willing to enter markets on positive information from rivals. However, empirical research reports opposing results on how the proprietary cost hypothesis affects the firms' disclosure policy.

On the one hand, the literature confirms that firms are unwilling to disclose information, in order to keep their competitive market position. Cormier and Gordon (2001) have explored how competition could affect the soft-talk disclosure of corporate social responsibility. They suggest that disclosing narrative information about a firm's environmental performance depends on the degree of market competition. In support of this, Jones (2007) reveals that firms facing high (low) competition in the market are less (more) willing to disclose research and development (R&D) information. In addition, the author points out that firms with competitive market positions are willing to withhold information.

Furthermore, Huang *et al.* (2017) explore how market competition affects the behaviour of firms' disclosures. They reveal that firms reduce the disclosure of management forecasts in response to greater competition. Burks *et al.* (2018) also explore the effect of competition on the disclosure policy. Their results indicate that firms disseminate more negative information in press releases when competition increases. They further explain that firms use these practices to prevent competitors from entering their markets. Moreover, Aobdia and Cheng (2018) reveal that firms disclose less than their rivals in the market, and that this disclosure practice has negative consequences for the firm. Recently, Li *et al.* (2019) indicated that proprietory costs decrease the monitoring incentives for firms, leading to excessive tone management practices in the firm's annual report. They further explain that this practice helps firms to maintain competitiveness in the market.

Another stream of research investigates the value relevance of disclosure in response to market competition. For instance, Brown and Tucker (2011) claim that disclosure is not informative if it has not been updated regularly. They then examine whether firms cut-and-paste their narrative disclosures from previous years or update them regularly. Their results suggest that firms facing greater competition are more likely to copy-and-paste the narrative statements from year to year, suggesting that these firms disclose less informative narrative information. Similarly, Hassanein and Hussaieny (2015) examined the narrative disclosure of UK firms. They provided supporting evidence to Brown and Tucker (2011) that UK firms facing greater competition are likely to provide boilerplate and more run-of-the-mill narrative information.

On the other hand, market competition increases firms' willingness to provide disclosure. Firms feel that narrative disclosure is less harmful to their competitive position in the market and that disclosing this information increases shareholders' confidence (Shivaani and Agarwal, 2020). Empirical research supports this view and reports higher levels of disclosure when a firm faces more competition in the market (Birt *et al.*, 2006). A recent study by Shivaani and Agarwal (2020) suggests that firms facing greater competition in the market disclose higher levels of information to signal their strengths to stakeholders.

### *1.3.4 Litigation costs and narrative disclosure*

Litigation risk is also known as litigation costs, which refers to the lawsuits a firm may face and which may result in penalties against the firm (Lowry, 2009). In response, firms adopt a disclosure policy to reduce the costs associated with litigation (Christensen *et al.*, 2021). The literature reveals two primary effects of litigation on the firm disclosure policy (Bourveau *et al.*, 2018; Dong and Zhang, 2019; Houston *et al.*, 2019; Naughton *et al.*, 2019).

The first effect indicates that firms respond to expected litigation risks by increasing their disclosure. More disclosures will help the firms avoid claims that they hide information from market participants and reduce the litigation risk due to insufficient disclosures (Field *et al.*, 2005). Disseminating more narrative information serves to avoid this and reduces the litigation risk for firms. Prior empirical studies confirm this effect and indicate that disclosure has a positive function towards expected litigation risk. In an early study by Skinner (1994), the author indicates that, when firms face higher litigation risk, they disclose their negative news information early. The author further confirms that this disclosure practice reduces litigation costs. In support, Levy *et al.* (2018) find that a firm's litigation risks lead to significant changes in its disclosure policy. They argue that the disclosure of negative information is higher when firms face greater litigation costs. Recently, Naughton *et al.* (2019) found that disclosing the information has a positive function towards litigation risks, and that this disclosure is not likely to be affected by the type of information. Consistently, Field *et al.* (2005) indicate that more disclosures reduce litigation costs. Johnson *et al.* (2001) also reveal that disseminating more earnings and sales forecasts reduces the litigation risks. In Miller and Piotroski's (2005) study, the authors focus on soft-talk information to reveal that more future-oriented information is disseminated by firms facing greater expected litigation risk. Hassanein and Elsayed (2021) also reveal that firms operating in the technology industry (a highly litigious industry) provide more informative risk information than do non-technology firms.

Dong and Zhang (2019) also examine how litigation risks affect the voluntary dissemination of information. Their results suggest that volunteering information is a function of litigation risk. This reveals that firms disclose more voluntary information when it faces higher litigation risk. Furthermore, Bourveau *et al.* (2018) explore how the litigation risks can affect the firm's narrative reporting strategy in response to universal demand rules. They found that narrative reporting increased after the introduction of the universal demand rules. Firms have increased their narrative discussions in MD&A in particular and provide substantial information on earnings forecasts. They further find that firms facing more litigation risk apply the universal demand rule more restrictively.

Other research also supports the notion that firms update their disclosure to reduce the litigation risk. For example, Nelson and Pritchard (2007) reveal that firms update their future-oriented disclosure when they expect higher litigation risks. Furthermore, Brown and Tucker (2011) indicate that US firms facing (lower) ligation risk are more (less) willing to provide informative narrative disclosures. Hassanen and Hussainey (2015) also show that UK firms operating in the technology industry (i.e., subject to high litigation risk) report informative narratives. Houston *et al.* (2019) examined the extent to which firms' disclosure policy is changed in response to litigation risks. They find that firms update their disclosure practices because of litigations. The firm disseminates more earnings forecasts when higher litigation risk is expected and provides fewer forecasts when expected litigation risks are low.

On the other hand, expected litigation risks reduce a firm's willingness to provide disclosure. Firms may avoid providing earnings forecasts to prevent mistakes that may lead to litigation risk (Kasznik, 1999). They may also avoid disclosing more information in order to reduce their responsibility for updating such disclosures, for which they may be penalised if it is not updated (Cox *et al.*, 2001). Literature supports the negative relationship between litigation risk and disclosure. An early study by Kasznik (1999) suggests that firms reduce their earnings forecast to prevent litigation costs. Rogers and Van Buskirk (2009) reveal that firms reduce their narrative disclosures when they face a higher expected risk of litigation. Aboody and Kasznik (2000) also indicate that firms reduce their future-oriented information to avoid forecast errors, which could lead to litigation costs.

## 1.4 Conclusion and suggestions for future research

This chapter provides an up-to-date review of the literature about the related costs of CNR. It is observable that there are different media through which firms could provide CNR, such as chairman statements, MD&As, the OFR statements and management commentary sections. Research focuses heavily on examining CNR contents in developed countries such as the US, UK and France. However, little is known about CNR in developing economies. Examining the structure, contents and motivations of CNR in developing economies is an avenue for future research. Furthermore, investigating the impact of country-level characteristics, such as legal/ political systems and the degree of economic development on CNR, is a potential area for future research.

Literature reveals that large firms are more likely to provide CNR than are smaller firms. This may be because large firms find the preparation and dissemination costs of this type of information affordable. Future research could thus explore differences among larger firms in their CNR practices. Employing other research methodologies, such as case studies and semi-structured interviews with corporate managers, to explore the qualitative motivations in large firms for CNR are potential areas for future research. Future research could also explore the preparation costs of narrative information on social media alongside its value relevance (Hassanein *et al.*, 2021b). In addition, the extent to which firms' R&D (Hassanein *et al.*, 2021a) and gender diversity (Zalata *et al.*, 2019) affect the disclosure of value-relevant narrative information would be worthwhile avenues for research.

The CNR is also affected by political costs. The "political costs" hypothesis suggests that firms that face risk due to political scrutiny are likely to follow disclosure policies designed to reduce such risk. The CNR may be used as a medium by which to reduce the claim that firms are withholding information from the public in order to reduce political costs. Empirical studies report mixed findings, and thus more investigation is required. Furthermore, empirical research on how political costs affect CNR is limited and focuses on the US and UK; future research may investigate the direct linkages between CNR and political costs in developing economies. In addition, conducting cross-country analyses on how different political systems affect narrative disclosure is an area for future research. Furthermore, exploring how political costs affect the level of information in the CNR could be an avenue for future research. Future research should also examine the spillover effect between expected litigation risk and the stock market (Hassanein and Elgohari, 2020).

The literature also suggests contradictory arguments in terms of the effect of proprietary costs on CNR. Given the benefit of CNR to competitors, firms may be less willing to provide more narrative information in order to prevent competitors from using the firm's information in a way that harms their income-producing activities. Conversely, CNR is seen as being less harmful to firms; thus, they may provide more narrative information when competition increases in order to enhance shareholders' confidence. Empirical studies consistently report mixed findings of the effects of market competition on narrative information. Thus, more research is required on how market competition can affect the quality of narrative disclosure. The literature focuses on the examination of the impact of market competition on the firm-level characteristics. Future research should extend the current research design to include other countries, to observe the influence of country-specific characteristics on the CNR. Future research could also investigate how the demographic characteristics of top management could affect the quality of the CNR.

The literature also suggests that firms may be more likely to provide more narrative disclosure to avoid lawsuits as a result of inadequate disclosures. However, they may be reluctant to provide narrative disclosure to avoid the duty to update it, for which they may be sued. The empirical literature supports both views and reports mixed findings. Substantial research has used the type of industry as a proxy for the litigation risk. Adopting actual lawsuits against a firm as a measure of its litigation risk may be a potential avenue for future research.

# References

Aboody, D., and Kasznik, R. (2000), "CEO stock option awards and the timing of corporate voluntary disclosures", *Journal of accounting and economics*, Vol. 29, No. 1, pp. 73–100.

Aggarwal, R., and Simkins, B. J. (2004), "Evidence on voluntary disclosures of derivatives usage by large US companies", *Journal of Derivatives Accounting*, Vol. 1, No. 1, pp. 61–81.

Al-Htaybat, K. (2005), "Financial disclosure practices: Theoretical foundation, and an empirical investigation on Jordanian printed and internet formats", PhD Thesis, University of Southampton, UK.

Aobdia, D., and Cheng, L. (2018), "Unionization, product market competition, and strategic disclosure", *Journal of Accounting and Economics*, Vol. 65, No. 2–3, pp. 331–357.

Arnold, B., and De Lange, P. (2004), "Enron: An examination of agency problems", *Critical Perspectives on Accounting*, Vol. 15, pp. 751–765.

ASB. (2005), *Reporting standard (RS 1)*. The Operating and Financial Review. Reporting Standard, London: ASB Publications.

ASB. (2006), *Reporting statement*. The Operating and Financial Review. Reporting Statement, London: ASB Publications.

Athanasakou, V., Eugster, F., Schleicher, T., and Walker, M. (2020), "Annual report narratives and the cost of equity capital: UK evidence of a U-shaped relation", *European Accounting Review*, Vol. 29, No. 1, pp. 27–54.

Beattie, V., Mcinnes, B., and Fearnley, S. (2004), "A methodology for analysing and evaluating narratives in annual reports: A comprehensive descriptive profile and metrics for disclosure quality attributes", *Accounting Forum*, Vol. 28, pp. 205–236.

Bethel, J. (2007), "Recent changes in disclosure regulation: Description and evidence", *Journal of Corporate Finance*, Vol. 13, pp. 335–342.

Bhushan, R., and Lessard, D. R. (1992), "Coping with international accounting diversity: Fund managers' views on disclosure, reconciliation, and harmonization", *Journal of International Financial Management and Accounting*, Vol. 4, pp. 149–164.

Birt, J. L., Bilson, C. M., Smith, T., and Whaley, R. E. (2006), "Ownership, competition, and financial disclosure", *Australian Journal of Management*, Vol. 31, No. 2, pp. 235–263.

Bourveau, T., Lou, Y., and Wang, R. (2018), "Shareholder litigation and corporate disclosure: Evidence from derivative lawsuits", *Journal of Accounting Research*, Vol. 56, No. 3, pp. 797–842.

Brown, S., and Tucker, J. (2011), "Large-sample evidence on firms' year-over-year MD&A modifications", *Journal of Accounting Research*, Vol. 49, No. 2, pp. 309–345.

Burks, J. J., Cuny, C., Gerakos, J., and Granja, J. (2018), "Competition and voluntary disclosure: Evidence from deregulation in the banking industry", *Review of Accounting Studies*, Vol. 23, No. 4, pp. 1471–1511.

Caglio, A., Melloni, G., and Perego, P. (2020), "Informational content and assurance of textual disclosures: Evidence on integrated reporting", *European Accounting Review*, Vol. 29, No. 1, pp. 55–83.

Chen, J. J., Cheng, X., Gong, S. X., and Tan, Y. (2017), "Implications of political patronage and political costs for corporate disclosure: Evidence from the Shanghai pension corruption scandal", *Journal of Accounting, Auditing & Finance*, Vol. 32, No. 1, pp. 92–122.

Christensen, B. E., Lundstrom, N. G., and Newton, N. J. (2021), "Does the disclosure of PCAOB inspection findings increase audit firms' litigation exposure?", *The Accounting Review*, Vol. 96, No. 3, pp. 191–219.

Clatworthy, M., and Jones, M. J. (2003), "Financial reporting of good news and bad news: Evidence from accounting narratives", *Accounting and Business Research*, Vol. 33, No. 3, pp. 171–185.

Core, J. (2001), "A review of the empirical disclosure literature: Discussion", *Journal of Accounting and Economics*, Vol. 31, No. 1–3, pp. 441–456.

Cormier, D., and Gordon, I. M. (2001), "An examination of social and environmental reporting strategies", *Accounting, Auditing, and Accountability Journal*, Vol. 14, No. 5, pp. 587–616.

Cox, J., Hillman, R., and Langevoort, D. (2001), *Securities regulation: Cases and materials* (3rd ed.). New York: Aspen Publishers.

Depoers, F., and Jeanjean, T. (2012), "Determinants of quantitative information withholding in annual reports", *European Accounting Review*, Vol. 21, No. 1, pp. 115–151.

Dey, R. K., Hossain, S. Z., and Rezaee, Z. (2018), "Financial risk disclosure and financial attributes among publicly traded manufacturing companies: Evidence from Bangladesh", *Journal of Risk and Financial Management*, Vol. 11, No. 3, pp. 1–50.

Dong, H., and Zhang, H. (2019), "Litigation risk and corporate voluntary disclosure: Evidence from two quasi-natural experiments", *European Accounting Review*, Vol. 28, No. 5, pp. 873–900.

Elshandidy, T., and Shrives, P. J. (2016), "Environmental incentives for and usefulness of textual risk reporting: Evidence from Germany", *The International Journal of Accounting*, Vol. 51, No. 4, pp. 464–486.

Elzahar, H., Hussainey, K., Mazzi, F., and Tsalavoutas, I. (2015), "Economic consequences of key performance indicators' disclosure quality", *International Review of Financial Analysis*, Forthcoming, Vol. 39, pp. 96–112.

Feldman, R., Govindaraj, S., Livnat, J., and Segal, B. (2010), "Management's tone change, post earnings announcement drift and accruals", *Review of Accounting Studies*, Vol. 15, pp. 915–953.

Field, L., Lowry, M., and Shu, S. (2005), "Does disclosure deter or trigger litigation?", *Journal of Accounting and Economics*, Vol. 39, pp. 487–507.

Hassanein, A., and Elgohari, H. (2020), "The linkage between stock and inter-bank bond markets in China: A dynamic conditional correlation (DCC) analysis", *International Journal of Economics and Business Research*, Vol. 20, No. 1, pp. 80–99.

Hassanein, A., and Elsayed, N. (2021), "Voluntary risk disclosure and values of FTSE350 firms: The role of an industry-based litigation risk", *International Journal of Managerial and Financial Accounting*, Forthcoming.

Hassanein, A., and Hussainey, K. (2015), "Is forward-looking financial disclosure really informative? Evidence from UK narrative statements", *International Review of Financial Analysis*, Vol. 41, pp. 52–61.

Hassanein, A., Marzouk, M., and Azzam, M. (2021a), "How does ownership by corporate managers affect R&D in the UK?", *International Journal of Productivity and Performance Management*, Forthcoming. https://doi.org/10.1108/IJPPM-03-2020 -0121.

Hassanein, A., Moustafa, M. M., Benameur, K., and Al-Khasawneh, J. (2021b), "How do big markets react to investors' sentiments on firm tweets?", *Journal of Sustainable Finance and Investment*, https://doi.org/10.1080/20430795.2021.1949198.

Hassanein, A., Zalata, A., and Hussainey, K. (2019), "Do forward-looking narratives affect investors' valuation of UK FTSE all-shares firms?", *Review of Quantitative Finance and Accounting*, Vol. 52, No. 2, pp. 493–519.

Healy, P. M., and Palepu, K. G. (2001), "Information asymmetry, corporate disclosure, and the capital markets: A review of the empirical disclosure literature", *Journal of Accounting and Economics*, Vol. 31, No. 1–3, pp. 405–440.

Houston, J. F., Lin, C., Liu, S., and Wei, L. (2019), "Litigation risk and voluntary disclosure: Evidence from legal changes", *Accounting Review*, Vol. 94, No. 5, pp. 247–272.

Huang, Y., Jennings, R., and Yu, Y. (2017), "Product market competition and managerial disclosure of earnings forecasts: Evidence from import tariff rate reductions", *The Accounting Review*, Vol. 92, No. 3, pp. 185–207.

Johnson, M. F., Kasznik, R., and Nelson, K. K. (2001), "The impact of securities litigation reform on the disclosure of forward-looking information by high technology firms", *Journal of Accounting Research*, Vol. 39, No. 2, pp. 297–327.

Jones, D. A. (2007), "Voluntary disclosure in R&D-intensive industries", *Contemporary Accounting Research*, Vol. 242, pp. 489–522.

Kasznik, R. (1999), "On the association between voluntary disclosure and earnings management", *Journal of Accounting Research*, Vol. 37, No. 1, pp. 57–81.

Lemma, T. T., Shabestari, M. A., Freedman, M., and Mlilo, M. (2020), "Corporate carbon risk exposure, voluntary disclosure, and financial reporting quality", *Business Strategy and the Environment*, Vol. 29, No. 5, pp. 2130–2143.

Lemon, A. J., and Cahan, S. F. (1997), "Environmental legislation and environmental disclosures: Some evidence from New Zealand", *Asian Review of Accounting*, Vol. 5, No. 1, pp. 78–105.

Leventis, S. N. (2001), "Voluntary disclosure in an emerging capital market: The case of the Athens stock exchange", PhD Thesis, University of Strathclyde, Glasgow, UK.

Levy, H., Shalev, R., and Zur, E. (2018), "The effect of CFO personal litigation risk on firms' disclosure and accounting choices", *Contemporary Accounting Research*, Vol. 35, No. 1, pp. 434–463.

Li, F. (2008), "Annual report readability, current earnings, and earnings persistence", *Journal of Accounting and Economics*, Vol. 45, No. 2–3, pp. 221–247.

Li, F. (2010), "The information content of forward-looking statements in corporate filings—A naive bayesian machine learning approach", *Journal of Accounting Research*, Vol. 48, No. 5, pp. 1049–1102.

Li, X., Liu, J., and Wang, K. (2019), "Pledgee competition, strategic disclosure, and future crash risk", *China Journal of Accounting Research*, Vol. 12, No. 3, pp. 271–291.

Linsley, P. M., and Shrives, P. J. (2006), "Risk reporting: A study of risk disclosures in the annual reports of UK companies", *The British Accounting Review*, Vol. 38, No. 4, pp. 387–404.

Lowry, M. (2009), "Discussion of "shareholder litigation and changes in disclosure behavior", *Journal of Accounting and Economics*, Vol. 47, No. 1–2, pp. 157–159.

Luo, S., Hossain, M., and Courtenay, S. M. (2006), "The effect of voluntary disclosure, ownership structure and proprietary cost on the return–future earnings relation", *Pacific-Basin Finance Journal*, Vol. 14, pp. 501–521.

Marquardt, C., and Wiedman, C. (2005), "Earnings management through transaction structuring: Contingent convertible debt and diluted earnings per share", *Journal of Accounting Research*, Vol. 43, pp. 205–243.

Merkley, K. (2014), "Narrative disclosure and earnings performance: Evidence from R&D", *Accounting Review*, Vol. 89, No. 2, pp. 725–757.

Miller, G. S., and Piotroski, J. D. (2005), "Forward-looking earnings statements: Determinants and market response", *SSRN Electronic Journal*. https://doi.org/10.2139/ssrn.238593.

Mitra, S., and Crumbley, D. L. (2003), "Earnings management and politically sensitive environments: Another test of corporate response to political costs", *Petroleum Accounting and Financial Management Journal*, Vol. 22, pp. 1–24.

Muslu, V., Radhakrishnan, S., Subramanyam, K. R., and Lim, D. (2015), "Forward-looking MD&A disclosures and the information environment", *Management Science*, Vol. 61, No. 5, pp. 931–1196.

Naughton, J. P., Rusticus, T. O., Wang, C., and Yeung, I. (2019), "Private litigation costs and voluntary disclosure: Evidence from the Morrison ruling", *The Accounting Review*, Vol. 94, No. 3, pp. 303–327.

Nelson, K. K., and Pritchard, A. C. (2007), "Litigation risk and voluntary disclosure: The use of meaningful cautionary language", Working Paper, Rice University and University of Michigan, Available: http://papers.ssrn.com/sol3/papers.cfm?abstract_id =998590.

Rogers, J. L., and Van Buskirk, A. (2009), "Shareholder litigation and changes in disclosure behavior", *Journal of Accounting and Economics*, Vol. 47, No. 1–2, pp. 136–156.

Sankara, J., Patten, D. M., and Lindberg, D. L. (2019), "Mandated social disclosure: Evidence that investors perceive poor quality reporting as increasing social and political cost exposures", *Sustainability Accounting, Management and Policy Journal*, Vol. 10, No. 1, pp. 208–228.

Schleicher, T., Hussainey, K., and Walker, M. (2007), "Loss firms' annual report narratives and share price anticipation of earnings", *The British Accounting Review*, Vol. 39, No. 2, pp. 153–171.

Shivaani, M. V., and Agarwal, N. (2020), "Does competitive position of a firm affect the quality of risk disclosure?", *Pacific Basin Finance Journal*, Vol. 61, pp. 1013–1017.

Skinner, D. J. (1994), "Why firms voluntarily disclose bad news", *Journal of Accounting Research*, Vol. 32, No. 1, pp. 38–60.

Vanstraelen, A., Zarzeski, M. T., and Robb, S. W. G. (2003), "Corporate non-financial disclosure practices and financial analyst forecast ability across three European countries", *Journal of International Financial Management & Accounting*, Vol. 14, pp. 249–278.

Verrecchia, R., and Weber, J. (2006), "Redacted disclosure", *Journal of Accounting Research*, Vol. 44, No. 4, pp. 791–814.

Watts, R. L., and Zimrman, J. L. (1978), "Towards a positive theory of the determination of accounting standards", *The Accounting Review*, Vol. 1, pp. 112–134.

Whittred, G., and Zimmer, I. (1990), *Financial accounting-incentive effects and economic consequences*. Sydney: Holt, Rinehart and Winston.

Yuthas, K., Rogers R., and Dillard, J. F. (2002), "Communicative action and corporate annual reports", *Journal of Business Ethics*, Vol. 41, No. 1–2, pp. 141–157.

Zalata, A., Ntim, C., Choudhry, T., Hassanein, A., and Elzahar, H. (2019), "Female directors and managerial opportunism: Monitoring versus advisory female directors", *The Leadership Quarterly*, Vol. 30, No. 5, pp. 1048–9843.

# 2 Searching for regulation in corporate narrative reporting for charitable organisations in the past

## An historical exploration in Italy and the UK

*Karen McBride and Eleonora Masiero*

## 2.1 Introduction

Accounting practices are socially and historically contextualised. Hence, accounting techniques and practices are shaped by their social, political and legislative contexts (Carnegie, McBride, Napier and Parker, 2020). In recent decades, the harmonisation of accounting principles through International Financial Reporting Standards (IFRS) has taken into account influences deriving from historical, cultural and legal differences at country level (Saita, Saracino, Provasi and Messaggi, 2012). In the last decades of the 20th century there was progressive international adoption and harmonisation of narratives in corporate reporting. In parallel with this, there has been a "growing interest among researchers, regulators and information users in narrative/non-financial information" (Marzouk and Hussainey, 2020).

While researchers witness the growing interest on the part of government, regulators and practitioners towards the implementation and harmonisation of corporate narrative reporting (CNR), it may be asked whether governments paid attention towards this form of external communication in the past. To contribute to this fascinating and relevant theme, this chapter adopts a retrospective historical approach to explore *if* and *how*, at the end of the 19th century, the Italian and UK governments legislated for CNR, i.e., non-financial/narrative information. The authors focus on the end of the 19th century because, whereas this historical period represents a fervent period of reforms and scientific discoveries in Europe, it also provides the opportunity to observe approaches towards CNR during a period when differences among countries were much stronger than at present.

This chapter examines narrative reporting requirements at the end of the 19th and the early 20th centuries for two differently regulated European countries. In Italy, the government was focusing on regulation to align this newly United Kingdom, whereas, in the UK, there was more of a reliance on market forces, a "laissez-faire" approach and a deliberate lack of government regulation (Taylor, 1972). The chapter focuses on charitable hospitals in order to explore narrative reporting regulations in the United Kingdom and the kingdom of Italy. The methodology is an historic examination of the regulations, with a narrative account (Previts, Parker and Coffman, 1990) and a thematic analysis of the findings (Braun and Clark, 2006). Considering accounting requirements from a historical perspective enhances an understanding of accounting

DOI: 10.4324/9781003095385-4

practices currently and into the future (McBride and Verma, 2021). The chapter aims to provide an international comparison (Carnegie and Napier, 2002) of the requirements for narrative reporting, either by regulation in Italy, or by voluntary compliance to suggested best practice within the UK charitable hospitals' sector in the period and gives some background information to these requirements. The objectives of the research are to outline the differing regulatory requirements within each country, and to identify the similarities despite these differences in approach. We do this by studying the regulatory/voluntary guidelines for each country, firstly in general and then specifically for charitable hospitals. By exploring and comparing possible governmental approaches towards CNR in two different historical contests, the researchers contribute to the current international debate on non-financial disclosures, providing examples of how these themes were tackled previously.

Accordingly, the authors selected the last decades of the 19th century for study because this historical period follows the unification of the Italian peninsula, hence enabling a comparison between the two countries when their geographical structure was similar to the current time. Finally, this period also sees the development, harmonisation and implementation of accounting regulation at country level.

Although not exhaustive, this work aims to provide readers with an idea of the forms and purposes of regulation of CNR and how these were expected to be implemented within the two countries in the late 19th and early 20th centuries. The chapter is structured as follows. After this introduction, the second section focuses on contemporary issues to recount the growing interest, among practitioners and academics, towards narrative information. It follows an accounting history approach of providing a narrative which is then explained. The third and the fourth sections look back at the past to illustrate narrative reporting requirements and regulation in Italy and in the UK. The fifth section provides an analysis. Finally, section six is the conclusion including possibilities for future research.

## 2.2 Accounting narratives and accounting history

Narrative/non-financial information has been gaining increasing attention and interest, in recent decades, among academics and practitioners (Beattie, 2014; Beattie, McInnes and Fearnley, 2004; Hussainey, Schleicher and Walker, 2003; Hussainey and Walker, 2009). Since the 1950s, accounting researchers have been exploring the readability of the narratives in annual reports (Courtis, 1998), thus focusing on "a limited component of the overall picture" (Rutherford, 2005, p. 350) in an attempt to investigate the annual reports' clarity for stakeholders. During the following decades, accounting researchers broadened the spectrum of analysis, comparing and exploring the different roles played by technical accounting and accounting narratives (Boland and Schultze, 1996; Llewellyn, 1999; Llewellyn and Milne, 2007; Roberts, 1996). Accordingly, investigations considered accounting-related narratives through different theoretical frames such as impression management (Brennan and Vourvachis, 2011; Clatworthy and Jones, 2001; Merkl-Davies, ), rhetoric (e.g., Brennan and Merkl-Davies, 2014) and legitimacy (e.g., Brennan and Merkl-Davies, 2014; Lupu and Sandu, 2017).

From a practitioner's perspective, at the end of the 1990s, Courtis (1998, p. 459) observed that the communication trend in annual reporting was "for management to employ more narrative disclosures as part of the overall communication package". This trend, towards an increase of narratives in accounting, was progressively observed by scholars who highlighted how accounting narratives represented an "increasingly important component" of annual reports (Clatworthy and Jones, 2001, p. 495) and illustrated the companies' awareness of the necessity to tell a story about their value creation (Beattie and Smith, 2013; Holland, 2004; Lai, Melloni and Stacchezzini, 2018). Likewise, studies showed the relevance of providing stakeholders with integrated, additional and alternative non-financial information in order to enhance effective communication (Brennan and Merkl-Davies, 2018; Masiero, Arkhipova, Massaro and Bagnoli, 2019). Companies rely on sustainability reporting to preserve a positive relationship with stakeholders and to signal their sustainability performance (Simoni, Bini and Bellucci, 2020).

There has been an increased interest in exploring accounting not just as technical, but also as social practice (Carnegie et al., 2020) with an increase in the study of narrative accounts of the past, going beyond focusing on techniques for recording transactions (Evans and Pierpoint, 2015; Masiero, 2020; McWatters and Lemarchand, 2010; Oakes and Young, 2008).

The progressive, international inclusion in corporate communication of narrative and non-financial information took place over time through an increasing adoption and recognition of Integrated Reporting (IR) and recently through the implementation, at EU level, of the EU Directive (2014/95/EU) relating to mandatory reporting of non-financial, Environmental, Social and Governmental (ESG) topics and diversity information. However, most of these regulatory initiatives retain managerial discretion in respect of the content of the disclosures (Merkl-Davies and Brennan, 2007; Peters and Romi, 2013; Schneider, Michelon, and Paananen, 2018), so that the temptation to impression management could be reduced by prescribing how information is to be presented (Hooghiemstra, Kuang and Qin, 2017). The aim is to improve organisations' ability to broaden, integrate and enhance the information provided to the stakeholders (Christensen, Floyd, Liu and Maffet, 2017). Studies have shown that countries where a non-financial regulation is in place present a higher quality of disclosure than those without regulation (Crawford and Williams, 2010). Likewise, the mandatory EU Directive (2014/95/EU) enhanced the quality of companies' disclosure pertaining to non-financial information (Venturelli, Caputo, Cosma, Leopizzi and Pizzi, 2017).

## 2.3   Back to the history: sociopolitical, legal context and accounting narratives in Italy

### 2.3.1   *The post-unification Italian context: a background for this study*

At the end of the 19th century, the Italian Kingdom was a constitutional monarchy, the result of the unification of the different states of the Italian peninsula under the Kingdom of Savoy-Sardinia. Hence, the last decades of the 19th century, following the unification of Italy, were full of reforms aimed at developing and harmonising, under the centralising forces, various aspects pertaining to the administration of the newborn state. With respect to the state's systems of control, 1862 saw a unified monetary system, and the institution of departments pertaining to state property, taxes and the Audit Court (Sandulli and Vesperini, 2011). In 1862, the Chamber of Commerce was founded, aimed at representing the business and industrial interests of the government (Sandulli and Vesperini, 2011, p. 88).

Reforms included the harmonisation of the different accounting rules and standards. Accordingly, the second half of the 19th century represented a fervent and intense period of scientific debate about the accounting discipline, the study of which moved from the simple technical perspective to a holistic and more comprehensive discipline, the "Economia Aziendale" (the term may be translated as "business economics"). This new discipline, which comprised organisational and managerial perspectives (Borgonovi and Maggi, 2007; Lazzini, Lacoviello and Ferraris Franceschi, 2018), laid the foundation for accounting studies related to the state, provinces, municipalities and public charitable institutions (Borgonovi and Maggi, 2007).

### 2.3.2 The enterprises and the Code of Commerce

The Code of Commerce, approved in year 1882,[1] came into force in 1883 and provided dispositions for the preparation of the financial statements, while leaving preparers with ample discretion in relation to the content and evaluation of financial statements (De Gobbis, 1925; Melis, 2007; Panfilo and Saccon, 2018). At the time, the set of norms provided by the Code of Commerce became principles to be followed (Broglia, 1925). The preparation of the financial statements by commercial enterprises was driven by confidentiality in spite of the transparency required (Melis, 2007).

With respect to financial statements' disclosure, the Code of Commerce (Art. 180, Titolo IX, Sezione IV, Capo 6° Law n. 681/1882, Registro della Corte dei Conti, 1882) required the enterprise's administrators, to deposit a copy of the financial statements, a copy of the statutory auditors' report to the financial statements, and a copy of the shareholders' approval of the financial statements at the Registry of the Court. The provision of an explicative report of the financial statements and of the administrators' management report remained optional (Melis, 2007, pp. 241–242). In this regard, the Code of Commerce did not provide specific requirements for the provision of a management report, requiring the administrators to present, to auditors, the financial statements with supporting documents "coi documenti giustificativi" (Art. 176, Titolo IX, Sezione IV, Capo 6° Law n. 681/1882, Registro della Corte dei Conti, 1882, p. 58).

### 2.3.3 Public administrations: financial statements and narrative reporting in charitable institutions

A first legislative act towards the harmonisation of administration of the benevolent institutions resulted in Law n. 753/1862. About two decades later, Law n. 753/1862 was substituted by Law n. 6972/1890 that would have been repealed in 2001 (D. Lgs n. 207/2001).[2] Law n. 6972/1890, secularised charitable institutions, defining their governance, supervision and accountability (Detti and Gozzini, 2000). This section focuses on the requirement of Law 6972/1890 and on r.d. 5 Febbraio 1891, n. 99 for financial statements and narrative reporting.

With respect to financial statements' requirements, Law 6972/1890 Art. 20 required charities to provide, each year, the estimated budget "Bilancio Preventivo", the annual financial statements "Conto Consuntivo", inclusive of the treasurer's financial account "Conto del Tesoriere", and a management report on the results achieved, "Relazione sul Risultato Morale della propria Gestione".

In this regard, the estimated budget had to be approved by September of the previous year.[3] With respect to the other statements, the charity's treasurer had to present his financial account to the charity's administration not later than March of each year, leaving until May for it to be agreed upon.[4] Once approved, all financial statements had to be sent to the Prefect for approval[5] and a copy of the annual report had to be stored in the charity's archive.[6] In preparing the financial statements, the charity's administration had to explain any increase (or decrease) of income and expenses by comparing the current financial statements with those produced in the previous year. The administration also had to justify new income and expenses.

With respect to the management report, Art. 43 (R.D. 5 Febbraio 1891, n. 99) provided clear guidelines on the expected content of the narrative part. In this regard, the charity's administration had to narratively report on the income and expenses. The administration had to describe the financial condition of the institution, its moral conduct, the difficulties overcome during the year, the criteria followed and the expected and desired improvements. Furthermore, administration had to discuss the quality of income, the form and methods to increase the productivity yield and to simplify bureaucracy, and also to discuss the possibility or convenience of maintaining, reducing or suppressing some of the expenses.[7]

## 2.4  Back to the history: sociopolitical, legal context and accounting narratives in the UK

### 2.4.1  The UK context: background for this study

To understand the changes to accounting and reporting in charitable institutions such as hospitals in the UK, we need to study the social and economic background in which this accounting change took place. Edwards (2019) observes that corporate financial reporting did not become the reporting we know today in an orderly or even a linear way; change occurred as a consequence of changes to the new circumstances of each new era with its context and conditions placing differing demands on accounting and accountants. Likewise, the accounting developed for charities and for charitable institutions such as hospitals developed and became uniform. The development of uniformity in accounts can be seen in the development of accounting, outlined in 1849, for UK railway companies, with legislation introduced in 1868 (Parker, 1990). Parker (1990) notes that, despite uniform accounts being introduced in 1870 for life assurance and in 1871 for gas companies, uniform accounts were not widespread and indeed were not favoured by legislators. However, in charitable or voluntary hospitals, uniform accounting was advocated by the Institute of Chartered Accountants in England and Wales and the Charity Organisation Society in 1890 (Robson, 2006). This system was not implemented, but in 1893 Henry Burdett[8] introduced his uniform accounts (Burdett, 1893). At this time, the combined social and economic factors of a substantial growth in hospital care and the emergence of ideas of managerialism led to their adoption by most of the larger voluntary hospitals in the UK (Robson, 2006).

This adoption of uniform accounting can be studied in the context of accounting requirements elsewhere in the UK within that period, for example that required for companies where matters of accounting and accountability were deemed to be for the shareholders and the creditors to negotiate with the company and its directors (Day, 2000). The Joint Stock Companies Act of 1844 enabled the incorporation of organisations by registration, with a requirement to keep books of account and prepare a balance sheet. Auditors appointed from the shareholders were to be furnished with these books of account and a report prepared for the shareholders Annual General Meeting. However, the content or layout of these accounts were not specified and there was no requirement of a statement of profit or loss, or any details of narrative reporting. This lack of prescription can be explained by a general approach of government not to be too prescriptive in the affairs of private enterprise, but also a lack of development of accounting techniques and auditing guidance (Edey and Panitpakdi, 1956). The idea of the government not imposing regulation on private enterprise is one which has continued in UK accounting practice. Indeed, although the Joint Stock Companies Act of 1856 included some guidelines for a standard balance sheet, with analysis of capital, assets and liabilities, it removed the requirement for accounting and audit, despite limited liability for incorporated companies being introduced in 1855. This requirement for accounts was not brought back until the 1900 Companies Act.

Whereas the early to mid-19th century was about a "laissez-faire" approach to business to promote freedom of trade (Edwards, 2019), the 1870s saw a move away from this (Taylor, 1972). The 20th century and the popularity of the limited liability company led to a need for published accounting information for investors to ensure that their money was being used in an effective way. In the UK, it was accountancy bodies rather than the government that developed the regulation and ensured accountability, starting in 1942 when the Institute of Chartered Accountants in England and Wales introduced the first of their 29 Recommendations of Accounting Principles (Edwards, 2019).

The British voluntary (charity) hospital system was instituted in the period 1720–1860. This period saw hospitals being established by philanthropists (Jackson, 2012; Prochaska, 1997). Benefactors wished to improve the lives of others less fortunate, to add to the population and prosperity of the nation and to enhance their social position (McClure, 1981). Often hospitals were organised as associations, part of a Protestant practice of charitable action during life rather than legacies at death; the hospitals were often funded by subscriptions and depended on public support, following the example of the joint stock companies which had changed the financing of businesses. These hospitals were often more selective in the people and the illnesses they assisted with than the previously formed royal hospitals.

### 2.4.2  Burdett's uniform accounts

Henry Burdett published books on the operation and management of the voluntary or charity hospitals. Using his background knowledge of banking both in Birmingham and at the Bank of England, Burdett considered the implementation of uniform accounts for hospitals. Burdett had moved from banking and studied medicine; he did not qualify as a doctor but combined his skills as Secretary at Queens Hospital, Birmingham (1868–1874) and later at the Dreadnought Seamen's Hospital (1874–1880), which moved from HMS Dreadnought to the land when the Royal Navy Hospital, Greenwich, closed. The hospital at Greenwich had seen the first government implementation of double-entry bookkeeping in 1828 (McBride, 2020). Burdett commercially managed the hospital, by reducing costs and increasing revenue.

Burdett published a manual outlining his "uniform" system of accounts for hospitals and similar institutions. "The Uniform System of Accounts for Hospitals, Public Institutions, Missions and Charities of all Descriptions" (hereafter, "the uniform accounts manual") was published in 1893, with a further edition in 1903, a reprint with the addition of a new Index of Classification (in an appendix) in 1910 and the fourth edition was published in 1916 (Burdett, 1893, 1903, 1910, 1916). This research refers to the fourth edition.

In the uniform accounts manual, Burdett observes that, within the City of London, firms of size and importance will have a least one partner, if not all, as a member of a committee of a voluntary hospital or other important charity. He continues to note that these wealthy individuals wishing to invest in charity institutions/hospitals (he states "men" but women were also investors, see e.g., Chojnacka, 1998; Fregulia, 2015; Froide, 2015, 2016; Prochaska, 1980; Sharpe, 2001; Shepard, 2015; Walker, 2008) have rendered the necessity that accounts not only be accurately kept, but also published in a way in which the financial position can be determined and it can be ascertained how much that can be improved by a gift of money (Burdett, 1916, p. vi), suggesting that this can be achieved by use of the Uniform System, as this will enable enterprises to present themselves in the same way as the best-managed and -supported philanthropic organisations.

### 2.4.3  Other reporting or narrative reporting

In outlining the uniform accounts for voluntary hospitals, Burdett (1916, pp. 9–10) observes:

> It is the business of every charitable institution to make and keep friends, and the careful preparation and issue of the Annual Report is a good means

to enable this ideal to materialise. ... We should like therefore briefly to state what in our opinion is the minimum of information an Annual Report should contain, and in so doing we do not lose sight of the fact that the individuality of an institution is one of the most attractive things of a voluntary system, and should be expressed, within certain wide limits, as a means of obtaining public recognition and support.

It is clear that the intention of reporting is to seek and retain investors in the business of providing hospital services.

The uniform accounts manual goes on to advise careful printing, good-quality paper and an attractive cover, with a clear indication of the motivation behind these advices being that the annual report is similar to a shop window, "it should therefore tempt the beholder to proceed further and view the contents". The uniform accounts manual suggests starting the report with an attractive view of the main building or an illustration of the main work carried out. The manual suggests further narrative reporting in the form of background information about the hospital or charity and details of the numbers of beds, patients and staff, plus a list of officers with titles and degrees. It is observed that accuracy is important; all details should be checked carefully, so as not to cause any offence with misspellings or incorrect details, including not striking out those who have died! We can note that, like nowadays, narrative reporting offered an opportunity to show an appealing and attractive view of the organisation to differentiate it from others and to foster good relationships with current and potential investors or supporters.

Narrative reporting today describes the non-financial information which is included in the annual report to give a wider, more meaningful picture of the enterprise. The uniform accounts manual suggests the same. It is recommended that institutions include a description of the founding, history and "progressive development" (Burdett, 1916, p. 11) of the organisation, even if it is the same paragraphs included each year.

Current narrative reporting also aims to provide a picture of the enterprise in terms of its market position, performance, strategy and future prospects (Hussainey and Al-Najjar, 2011). The uniform accounts manual likewise recommends that the report of the committee or the Board should show the events of the previous year, the period covered by the published accounts and statistics. The reports for each year together will show the history of the charity. It is suggested that "The report, while avoiding verbosity, should present in a pleasant and readable style the recent business, care being taken to thank especially those who have given large benefactions or rendered important personal service" (Burdett, 1916, p. 11) and advises the recording of gifts, however small.

The uniform system manual advises the presentation of the numbers of patients and the cost of patients under different headings and suggests these may be

according to taste, supplemented by tables of admissions and out-patient attendances arranged over a series of years, and followed by a report from the Registrar on the Medical and Surgical work of the hospital for the year under review.

(p. 11)

There should also be tables detailing the activities of the organisation. The report should also contain, "mouths to feed" (p.12) and patients or other recipients of charity. There should be a statement showing the benefactors' privileges and the cost of naming or endowing beds, pensions or other items. Then, there will be a list of the subscribers and governors which should agree with the income and expenditure accounts.

The narrative reports of the voluntary or charity hospitals were informed that

It is now generally admitted that every hospital and every kindred charity supported by voluntary contributions ought to publish annually a duly audited statement of accounts, the items in which should agree with the lists of contributions received during the year, printed in the report.

(Burdett, 1916, p. 12)

On page 13 report preparers are reminded that the figures in every published account should agree back to the details in the annual report, observing that any organisation that does not do this should expect to be viewed with suspicion by the public. So, lists of contributions should always be disclosed, totalled and agreed with the sum received in the year. The manual observes that frauds are more likely to be perpetrated and are often discovered when the accounts published do not show the facts, where items are concealed and donations not disclosed in a timely fashion.

The uniform accounts manual outlines the requirement for account books to be inspected by the committee, so that those responsible for the management of the institution can see if the accounts are being kept according to the system, that they are up to date and appear in order. It repeats the importance of an audit for public institutions and those dependent on voluntary contributions. The next part of the manual explains the uniform system of accounts.

## 2.5  Analysis

Analysis of the study uses the qualitative method of thematic analysis. Braun and Clarke (2006) describe thematic analysis as a method for "identifying, analysing and reporting patterns (themes) within the data" (p.79). The current authors have used this approach in analysing data for other projects (e.g., McBride and Philippou, 2021) and use it innovatively here for analysing these regulations. We use a bottom-up approach (Braun and Clark, 2006), as "a rigorous thematic approach can produce an insightful analysis that answers particular research questions" (Braun and Clarke, 2006, p. 97). A theme is something which captures the key ideas about the data in relation to our research project and shows a pattern or meaning in the data (Braun and Clarke, 2006, p. 82). The objective of this inductive approach is to allow research findings to emerge from main, frequent or significant themes in the regulations of the two countries. Using this approach, we determined key areas of interest from the regulations which link with current narrative accounting areas, under the headings below.

### 2.5.1 Requirements for the contextualising of events

In Italy, the narrative management report included with the financial statements was required to explain increases and decreases in income and expenses for the previous year. A justification of any new expenses was also required.

In the UK, the uniform accounts manual also recommended that the report of the committee or the Board, should show the events of the previous year, the period covered by the published accounts, and include statistics. There was a contextualising of events *via* narrative reporting relating to further background information about the institution, with further statistics on the day-to-day running of the institution.

### 2.5.2 Requirements for accountability towards human resource management (from an internal perspective)

In Italy, a hospital's administration was required to include in the management report discussion about the quality and form of the income plus any methods leading to increased productivity and to simplify bureaucracy. They were also required to report the potential for maintaining and reducing expenditure.

In the UK, further details were required of the numbers of beds, patients and staff, plus a list of officers with titles and degrees. It is noted in the manual that accuracy is important and all details should be checked carefully.

### 2.5.3 Requirements for accountability towards the relationship/impact on the beneficiaries/'clients' and on the community in general

In Italy, the management report included a description of the charities' management for the year, including information about personnel, beneficiaries and the relationship with external stakeholders.

In the UK, the narrative reporting was clearly aimed at these stakeholders, or at least at those providing the financing. The objective cited as being that of making and keeping friends. With the requirements of narrative reporting being described as the minimum information that the annual report should include and with the distinctiveness of a charitable institution requiring reporting on to obtain public support and recognition, and to retain and find investors.

### 2.5.4 Requirements for accountability towards the governance of the institutes

In Italy, any changes in internal regulation, enhancements, problems and achievements of the charity had to be disclosed in the management report, plus any necessary changes in the charity. Ordinary and extraordinary events were disclosed with comparisons to previous years and all details pertaining to these.

In the UK, the manual notes that the report should present the recent business in a pleasant and readable style, without indulging in verbosity, ensuring that the large benefactors or those who have rendered service should be thanked and gifts should be recorded regardless of size.

### 2.5.5 Requirements for proving a narrative description of facts, achievements, gains and losses aimed at integrating the accounting information, but not substituting the explicative notes to the accounts

Just as current narrative reporting provides a view of the business in terms of performance, efficiency, market position, strategy and potential, again so did these early narrative accounts. Therefore, these findings indicate previous interest towards narrative reporting practices. In fact, findings show how, about a century ago, two different approaches to regulation had already understood and acted to incentivise the adoption of narrative reporting in both public and private entities.

The Italian case shows that the adoption of narrative reporting was mandatory and rules based, for the public entities, while for private entities, the government's requirement was closer to a guiding principle to be followed but without specific requirements. Furthermore, as explained in the findings the regulation for the charities never faded, being still active at the present day.

The approach in the UK driven by investors and directors for private entities was more flexible. Whereas the guidelines for uniform accounts in the charity hospitals were driven by similar motivations to raise income and attract investors, but were more prescriptive.

## 2.6 Conclusion

Although not exhaustive on an extremely interesting and still almost unexplored topic, this chapter considered the past, to explore if and how CNR were regulated by two different countries, Italy and the UK, a long time before the recent international attention towards corporate narratives.

Findings shows that, at the end of the 19th century, both the Italian government and the UK management perceived the relevance of requiring both private and public companies to corroborate their statements with narrative reporting practices. Hence, findings illustrate how, in both countries, accounting practices were already conceived by the governments as being much more than a set of techniques, acknowledging the social and ethical implications for stakeholders and, for the surrounding communities, related to the disclosure (Carnegie *et al.*, 2020).

With respect to private entities, the governments' guidelines left organisations with plenty of freedom. This is particularly the case in the UK where the approach was one of a "laissez-faire" attitude, in order to preserve the privacy and autonomy of organisations, leaving it to investors and directors to negotiate what was required of the accounts. Within the hospital sector, these charitable organisations were actually more closely regulated, *via* Burdett's uniform accounts.

In this regard, in the Italian case, the government required a similar common law configuration for companies (Panfilo and Saccon, 2018). However, in the Italian context for public institutions, and specifically for charities, the government provided detailed rules, to be followed in each part of the statements, and set up a process of external control to ensure that charities were compliant with them.

This research studied the regulations for public sector organisations, particularly charitable hospitals, with private sector requirements and compared the approach in two differing countries to assess these approaches. Further research could extend the analysis to the published financial statements of public and private organisations in the past to investigate the impact of the regulations on the quality and quantity of narrative reporting.

Despite the differences, in regulatory approach, in both countries there was a clear description of the "non-financial" information required. In Italy, this was in the form of a management report, part of the annual report, where the charity was required to report in a narrative form on the situation of the institution, with narrative reporting on the income and expenses of the hospital. The financial position of the institution was to be reported, along with its moral conduct, any difficulties during the year, the conduct followed and any necessary or required enhancements.

In the UK, this information appeared in the annual report, and the charity was required likewise to report in a narrative form on the situation of the institution. The uniform accounts included various additional background data about the charity, as a supplement to the income and expenditure account and the balance sheet and required additional statistics on the day-to-day running of the hospital.

Hence, in line with contemporary studies, focused on the present international regulation (Crawford and Williams, 2010; Christensen, Floyd, Liu and Maffet, 2017; Masiero, Arkhipova, Massaro and Bagnoli, 2019; Venturelli, Caputo, Cosma, Leopizzi and Pizzi, 2017), this research shows how, despite the differences between Italy and the UK were not solely related to contextual factors but also to the common and civil law systems (Carnegie, Mcbride, Napier and Parker, 2020), already at the end of the 19th century, both governments understood the necessity to set clear guidelines when it came to the public entities, in order to reach higher level of disclosure quality.

For current policy makers, the research highlights the success of providing clear, mandatory or regulated information, whether this be by government or other regulation, and clarifies that either form of regulation can achieve the objectives required from corporate narratives. Those requirements served for the contextualising of events and for providing a narrative description of facts, achievements, gains and losses, plus the narrative requirements served for governance of the organisations and accountability not only of human resources, but also for impact on beneficiaries and on the community in general.

## Notes

1 Law 2 Aprile 1882, n. 681 (Serie 3°), "Codice di Commercio Pel Regno d'Italia", Gazzetta Ufficiale, Martedì 11 Aprile 1882, n. 86. Available at: https://www.gazzettaufficiale.it/eli/gu/1882/04/11/86/so/86/sg/pdf (accessed: 27 November 2020). Law 2 Aprile 1882, n. 682 (Serie 3°) was modified and promulgated on 31 October 1882 (see: Registro della Corte dei Conti, 3 Novembre 1882, Reg. 12, Atti del Governo "Codice di Commercio del Regno d'Italia", Regia Tipografia, Roma. Digitalization by Matteo Pati, Università degli studi di Brescia. Available at: http://www.antropologiagiuridica .it/codecomit82.pdf (accessed: 27 November 2020). These documents are listed in the Primary Sources where the link is also provided.
2 Legislative Decree D. Lgs. 4 maggio 2001, n. 207 regulated the reorganisation of public charities previously regulated by the Law 17 luglio 1890, n. 6972 (please see: https://www.gazzettaufficiale.it/eli/id/2001/06/01/001G0265/sg).
3 (r.d. 5 Febbraio 1891, n. 99, Art. 26).
4 (r.d. 5 Febbraio 1891, n. 99, Art. 41).
5 (r.d. 5 Febbraio 1891, n. 99, Art. 41).
6 (r.d. 5 Febbraio 1891, n. 99, Art. 44).
7 For the original and complete article, please see: (Art. 43, Titolo III, Capo 1° "Archivio – Inventario – Bilanci – Conti") r.d. 5 Febbraio 1891, n. 99).
8 Sir Henry Charles Burdett (1847–1920), philanthropist and hospital reformer, worked in charity administration and fund raising, focusing on various aspects of hospital administration including medical education, nursing and hospital statistics and accounts.

## Bibliography

Beattie, V. (2014) Accounting narratives and the narrative turn in accounting research: Issues, theory, methodology, methods and a research framework, *British Accounting Review*, 46(2), 111–134.

Beattie, V., McInnes, B., and Fearnley, S. (2004) A methodology for analysing and evaluating narratives in annual reports: A comprehensive descriptive profile and metrics for disclosure quality attributes, *Accounting Forum*, 28(3), 205–236.

Beattie, V., and Smith, S. J. (2013) Value creation and business models: Refocusing the intellectual capital debate, *British Accounting Review*, 45(4), 243–254.

Boland, R., and Schultze, U. (1996) Narrating accountability: Cognition and the production of the accountable self, in Munro, R., and Mouritsen, J. (Eds.), *Accountability: Power, ethos and the technologies of managing*, International Thomson Business Press, London, 62–81.

Borgonovi, E., and Maggi, D. (2007) Dalla contabilità pubblica all'economia delle amministrazioni pubbliche, *Dalla Rilevazione Contabile All'economia Aziendale. Dottrina e Prassi Nell'Amministrazione Economica d'Azienda*. Atti Del IX Convegno Nazionale Della Società Italiana, Società Italiana di Storia della Ragioneria, Perugia, 31–48.

Braun, V., and Clarke, V. (2006) Using thematic analysis in psychology, *Qualitative Research in Psychology*, 3(2), 77–101.

Brennan, N. M., and Merkl-Davies, D. M. (2014) Rhetoric and argument in social and environmental reporting: The dirty laundry case, *Accounting, Auditing & Accountability Journal*, 27(4), 602–633.

Brennan, N. M., and Merkl-Davies, D. M. (2018) Do firms effectively communicate with financial stakeholders? A conceptual model of corporate communication in a capital market context, *Accounting and Business Research*, 48(5), 553–577.

Broglia, G. (1925) *L'azienda Industriale*, II., Tipografia Schioppo, Torino.

Burdett, H. C. (1893) *The uniform system of accounts for hospitals and public institutions, orphanages, missionary societies, homes, co-operations, and all classes of institutions.* The Scientific Press, London.

Burdett, H. C. (1903) *The uniform system of accounts for hospitals and public institutions, orphanages, missionary societies, homes, co-operations, and all classes of institutions,* 2nd edition. The Scientific Press, London.

Burdett, H. C. (1910) *The uniform system of accounts for hospitals and public institutions, orphanages, missionary societies, homes, co-operations, and all classes of institutions,* 3rd edition. The Scientific Press, London.

Burdett, H. C. (1916) *The uniform system of accounts for hospitals and public institutions, orphanages, missionary societies, homes, co-operations, and all classes of institutions,* 4th edition. The Scientific Press, London.

Carnegie, G. D., Mcbride, K. M., Napier, C. J., and Parker, L. D. (2020) Accounting history and theorising about organisations, *The British Accounting Review*, 52(6), 100932.

Carnegie, G. D., and Napier, C. J. (2002) Exploring comparative international accounting history, *Accounting, Auditing & Accountability Journal*, 15(5), 689–718.

Chojnacka, M. (1998) Women, charity and community in early modern venice: The Casa delle Zitelle, *Renaissance Quarterly*, 51(1), 68–91.

Christensen, H. B., Floyd, E., Liu, L. Y., and Maffet, M. (2017) The real effects of mandated information on social responsibility in financial reports – Mine safety, *Journal of Accounting & Economics*, 64(2–3), 284–304.

Clatworthy, M., and Jones, M. J. (2001) The effect of thematic structure on the variability of annual report readability, *Accounting, Auditing & Accountability Journal*, 14(3), 311–326.

Courtis, J. K. (1998) Annual report readability variability: Tests of the obfuscation hypothesis, *Accounting, Auditing & Accountability Journal*, 11(4), 459–472.

Crawford, E. P., and Williams, C. C. (2010) Should corporate social reporting be voluntary or mandatory? Evidence from the banking sector in France and the United States, *Corporate Governance*, 10(4), 512–526.

Day, R. (2000) *UK accounting regulation: An historical perspective.* Working Paper. Bournemouth University School of Finance and Law, Poole.

De Gobbis, F. (1925) *Ragioneria Privata*, VII., Dante Alighieri, Milano, Roma.

Detti, T., and Gozzini, G. (2000) *Storia Contemporanea I. L'ottocento*, Bruno Mondadori, Milan.

Edey, H. C., and Panitpakdi, P. (1956) British company accounting and the law 1844–1900, in Littleton, A. C., and Yamey, B. S. (Eds.), *Studies in the history of accounting*, Sweet and Maxwell, London, 356–379.

Edwards, J. R. (2019) *A history of corporate financial reporting in Britain*. Routledge, Abingdon.

Evans, L., and Pierpoint, J. (2015) Framing the Magdalen: Sentimental narratives and impression management in charity annual reporting, *Accounting and Business Research*, 45(6–7), 661–690.

Fregulia, J. M. (2015) Stories worth telling: Women as business owners and investors in early modern Milan, *Early Modern Women*, 10(1), 122–130.

Froide, A. (2015) Learning to invest: Women's education in arithmetic and accounting in early modern England, *Early Modern Women*, 10(1), 3–26.

Froide, A. (2016) *Silent partners: Women as public investors during Britain's financial revolution, 1690–1750*. Oxford University Press, Oxford.

Holland, J. (2004) Corporate intangibles, value relevance and disclosure content, *Institute of Chartered Accountants of Scotland*, September.

Hooghiemstra, R., Kuang, Y. F., and Qin, B. (2017) Does obfuscating excessive CEO pay work? The influence of remuneration report readability on say-on-pay votes, *Accounting and Business Research*, 47(6), 695–729.

Hussainey, K., and Al-Najjar, B. (2011) Future-oriented narrative reporting: Determinants and use, *Journal of Applied Accounting Research*, 12(2), 123–138.

Hussainey, K., Schleicher, T., and Walker, M. (2003) Undertaking large-scale disclosure studies when AIMR-FAF ratings are not available: The case of prices leading earnings, *Accounting and Business Research*, 33(4), 275–294.

Hussainey, K., and Walker, M. (2009) The effects of voluntary disclosure and dividend propensity on prices leading earnings, *Accounting and Business Research*, 39(1), 37–55.

Jackson, W. J. (2012) 'The collector will call': Controlling philanthropy through the annual reports of the royal infirmary of Edinburgh, 1837–1856, *Accounting History Review*, 22(1), 47–72.

Lai, A., Melloni, G., and Stacchezzini, R. (2018) Integrated reporting and narrative accountability: The role of preparers, *Accounting, Auditing and Accountability Journal*, 31(5), 1381–1405.

Lazzini, A., Iacoviello, G., and Ferraris Franceschi, R. (2018) Evolution of accounting education in Italy, 1890–1935, *Accounting History*, 23(1–2), 44–70.

Legge, 17 Luglio 1890, n. 6972, "Delle istituzioni pubbliche di beneficenza", Gazzetta Ufficiale, Martedì 22 Luglio 1890, n. 171. Available at: http://ww2.gazzettaamminis trativa.it/opencms/export/sites/default/_gazzetta_amministrativa/amministrazione _trasparente/_lazio/_centro_regionale_s_alessio_margherita_di_savoia_per_i _ciechi_roma/010_dis_gen/020_att_gen/2015/0001_Documenti_1430817820424 /1430818136671_legge_17_luglio_1890x_n._6972.pdf (accessed: 14 October, 2020).

Legge, 2 Aprile 1882, n. 681, "Codice di Commercio Pel Regno d'Italia", Gazzetta Ufficiale, Martedì 11 Aprile 1882, n. 86. Available at: https://www.gazzettaufficiale.it/ eli/gu/1882/04/11/86/so/86/sg/pdf (accessed: 27 November 2020).

Legge, 3 Agosto 1862, n. 753, "Sull'amministrazione delle Opere pie", Gazzetta Ufficiale, Lunedì 25 Agosto 1862, n. 201. Available at: Gazzetta Ufficiale del Regno d'Italia N. 201 del 25 Agosto 1862 parte ufficiale e parte non ufficiale (accessed: 30 November, 2020).

Llewellyn, S. (1999) Narratives in accounting and management research, *Accounting, Auditing & Accountability Journal*, 12(2), 220–237.

Llewellyn, S., and Milne, M. (2007) Accounting as codified discourses, *Accounting, Auditing & Accountability Journal*, 20(6), 805–824.

Lupu, I., and Sandu, R. (2017) Intertextuality in corporate narratives: A discursive analysis of a contested privatization, *Accounting, Auditing and Accountability Journal*, 30(3), 534–564.

Marzouk, M., and Hussainey, K. (2020) *Call for book chapters for corporate narrative reporting: Beyond the numbers.* https://tandfbis.s3-us-west-2.amazonaws.com/rt-files/ Call+of+Chapter+Proposals.pdf. Routledge, Abingdon.

Masiero, E. (2020) Accountability by the accountable self: The case of Leone Wollemborg, *Accounting History*, 25(1), 109–133.

Masiero, E., Arkhipova, D., Massaro, M., and Bagnoli, C. (2019) Corporate accountability and stakeholder connectivity: A case study, *Meditari Accountancy Research*, 28(5), 803–831.

McBride, K. (2020) A French connection; paths to a 'new system' of accounting for the Royal Navy in 1832, *The British Accounting Review*, 53(2), 100884.

McBride, K., and Philippou, C. (2021) "Big results require big ambitions": Big data, data analytics and accounting in masters courses, *Accounting Research Journal*, 1030–9616.

McBride, K., and Verma, S. (2021) Exploring accounting history and accounting in history, *The British Accounting Review*, 53(2), 100976.

McClure, R. (1981) *Coram's children: The London foundling hospital in the eighteenth century*. Yale University Press, New Haven, CT.

McWatters, C. S., and Lemarchand, Y. (2010) Accounting as story telling: Merchant activities and commercial relations in eighteenth century France, *Accounting, Auditing & Accountability Journal*, 23(1), 14–54.

Melis, G. (2007) L'evoluzione del bilancio d'esercizio durante il Codice di Commercio (1882–1942), *Dalla Rilevazione Contabile All'economia Aziendale. Dottrina e Prassi Nell'Amministrazione Economica d'Azienda*. Atti Del IX Convegno Nazionale Della Società Italiana, Società Italiana di Storia della Ragioneria, Perugia, 235–266.

Merkl-Davies, D. M., and Brennan, N. M. (2007) Discretionary disclosure strategies in corporate narratives: Incremental information or impression management? *Journal of Accounting Literature*, 27, 116–196.

Merkl-Davies, D. M., Brennan, N. M., and Vourvachis, P. (2011) Text analysis methodologies in corporate narrative reporting research, *23rd CSEAR international colloquium*, 1–45.

Oakes, L. S., and Young, J. J. (2008) Accountability re-examined: Evidence from hull house, *Accounting, Auditing & Accountability Journal*, 21(6), 765–790.

Panfilo, S., and Saccon, C. (2018) Bilancio e sistema guridi. Prime regole contabili in ordinamenti diversi, in Billio, M., Coronella, S., Mio, C., and Sostero, U. (Eds.), *Le Discipline Economiche e Aziendali Nei 150 Anni Di Storia Di Ca' Foscari, Edizioni Ca' Foscari*, Venice, 271–292.

Parker, R. H. (1990) Regulating British corporate financial reporting in the late nineteenth century, *Accounting, Business & Financial History*, 1(1), 51–71.

Peters, G. F., and Romi, A. M. (2013) Discretionary compliance with mandatory environmental disclosures: Evidence from SEC filings. *Journal of Accounting and Public Policy*, 32(4), 213–236.

Previts, G. J., Parker, L. D., and Coffman, E. N. (1990) Accounting history: Definition and relevance. *Abacus*, 26(1), 1–16.

Prochaska, F. (1980) *Women and philanthropy in nineteenth-century*. Oxford University Press, Oxford.

Prochaska, F. (1997) *Philanthropy and the hospitals of London: The king's fund, 1897–1990*. Oxford University Press, Oxford.

Regio Decreto, 10 Febbraio 1889, n. 5921, "Regio Decreto che approva il testo unico della legge comunale e provinciale", Gazzetta Ufficiale, 11 Febbraio 1889, n. 36. Available at: http://homepage.sns.it/pavan/Storia/1889%20-%20r.d.%2010%20febbraio%201889, %20n.%205921.pdf (accessed: 16 October 2020).

Regio Decreto, 5 Febbraio 1891, n. 99 "Approvazione dei regolamenti per l'esecuzione della legge sulle istituzioni pubbliche di assistenza e beneficenza", Gazzetta Ufficiale, Mercoledì 11 Marzo 1891, n. 58. Available at: file:///C:/Users/masie/Downloads/RG 1891_03_11_058_PM%20(1).pdf (accessed: 14 October, 2020).

Regio Decreto, 9 Ottobre 1889, n. 6442, "Sulla tutela dell'igiene e della sanità pubblica", Gazzetta Ufficiale, Lunedì 28 Ottobre 1889, n. 256. Available at: https://www.gazzettaufficiale.it/eli/gu/1889/10/28/256/sg/pdf (accessed: 14 October, 2020).

Registro della Corte dei Conti, 3 Novembre 1882, Reg. 12, Atti del Governo "Codice di Commercio del Regno d'Italia", Regia Tipografia, Roma. Digitalization by Matteo

Pati, Università degli studi di Brescia. Available at: http://www.antropologiagiuridica .it/codecomit82.pdf (accessed: 27 November 2020).

Roberts, J. (1996) From discipline to dialogue: Individualizing and socializing forms of accountability, in Munro, R., and Mouritsen, J. (Eds.), *Accountability: Power, Ethos and the Technologies of Managing*, International Boston Business Press, London, 40–61.

Robson, N. (2006) The road to uniformity: Accounting change in UK voluntary hospitals. *Accounting & Business Research*, 36(4), 271–288.

Rutherford, B. A. (2005) Genre analysis of corporate annual report narratives: A corpus linguistics-based approach, *Journal of Business Communication*, 42(4), 349–378.

Saita, M., Saracino, P., Provasi, R., and Messaggi, S. (2012) *Evoluzione dei principi contabili nel contesto internazionale*. FrancoAngeli s.r.l., Milano, Italy.

Sandulli, A., and Vesperini, G. (2011) L'organizzazione dello Stato unitario, *Rivista Trimestrale Di Diritto Pubblico*, 1, 47–95.

Schneider, T., Michelon, G., and Paananen, M. (2018) Environmental and social matters in mandatory corporate reporting: An academic note, *Accounting Perspectives*, 17(2), 275–305.

Sharpe, P. (2001) Gender in the economy: Female merchants and family businesses in the British Isles, 1600–1850, *Histoire sociale/Social History*, 34(68), 287–306.

Shepard, A. (2015) Crediting women in the early modern English economy. *History Workshop Journal*, 79(1), 1–24.

Simoni, L., Bini, L., and Bellucci, M. (2020) Effects of social, environmental, and institutional factors on sustainability report assurance: Evidence from European countries, *Meditari Accountancy Research*, 28(6), 1059–1087.

Taylor, A. J. (1972) *Laissez-faire and state intervention in nineteenth century Britain*. Macmillan, London.

Venturelli, A., Caputo, F., Cosma, S., Leopizzi, R., and Pizzi, S. (2017) Directive 2014/95/ EU: Are Italian companies already compliant? *Sustainability*, 9, 1385.

Walker, S. P. (2008) Accounting histories of women: Beyond recovery? *Accounting, Auditing & Accountability Journal*, 21(4), 580–610.

# 3 Forward-looking disclosure

## Nature, determinants and consequences

*Ahmed Hassanein and Heba Abou-El-Sood*

## 3.1 Introduction

Corporate disclosure is a primary pillar that minimises the information asymmetry issue between a firm's corporate managers and its shareholders and solves the agency problem (Healy and Palepu, 2001). It is essential in the corporate decision-making process because it gives users information about the amounts, timing and predictability of the company's future cash flow. However, disclosure practices are evolving, as are different types of information disclosed by businesses. Firms are beginning to disclose forward-looking (henceforth, FL)[1] information instead of merely disseminating backward-looking financial information to accommodate the needs of different market participants for information.

Professional bodies and standard setters (e.g., AICPA, FASB, IASB and ICAEW)[2] have long recommended disclosing FL information. It is stated that:

> *"management should include forward-looking information. Such information should focus on the extent to which the entity's financial position, liquidity and performance may change in the future and why and include management's assessment of the entity's prospects in the light of current period results. Management should provide forward-looking information through narrative explanations or through quantified data".*
>
> (IASB, 2010, p. 10)

This type of information helps to reduce information asymmetry and to enhance the investors' valuations of firms (Hassanein *et al.*, 2019). Likewise, it helps investors realise the firm's past financial performances and facilitate earnings predictions (Hussainey *et al.*, 2003).

Substantial research has examined the antecedents and benefits of FL information in developed and developing economies. One stream of studies suggests that the firm-specific characteristics and corporate governance are seen to affect the disclosure of FL information (e.g., Kılıç and Kuzey, 2018; Wang and Hussainey, 2013; Hassanein and Hussainey, 2015). However, results from empirical studies are mixed and report disparate conclusions. Another stream of research studies the economic consequences of FL disclosure and it reports some benefits that firms gain from disclosing this type of information.

DOI: 10.4324/9781003095385-5

This chapter seeks to provide a wide-ranging review of literature on the disclosure of FL information. We cover the literature on the determinants and consequences of FL disclosure. We contribute to the existing literature by conducting an up-to-date review of the recent FL literature. We enrich the literature by identifying the existing research gaps and providing suggestions for future research to fill these gaps.

The chapter proceeds as follows. First, it discusses the nature of FL disclosure. Second, it investigates relevant theories and reviews the literature about the factors impacting FL disclosure. Third, it reviews prior studies investigating the economic consequences of FL disclosure and embedded theories. Finally, it concludes, identifies gaps in prior studies, and provides suggestions for future research.

## 3.2  Nature of forward-looking information

### *3.2.1 Definition*

Information disclosed by firms can be categorised into two types. The first is "*backward-looking information*", which includes historical disclosures related to past results of a firm. This information is disclosed within the frame of the financial statements. The second is the "*forward-looking (FL) information*". IASB defines FL information as "*Information about the future that may later be presented as historical information*" (IASB, 2010, p. 17). In addition, the Vodafone group public limited company (Plc) states

> that "*By their nature, forward-looking statements are inherently predictive, speculative and involve risk and uncertainty because they relate to events and depend on circumstances that will occur in the future*".
> (Vodafone Plc, Annual Report, 2007)

This suggests that this type of information may include management's projections, financial forecasts (e.g., projected revenues, costs and cash flows), and estimation of risks and uncertainties of the firm.

FL information is disclosed in different forms, including financial/non-financial, qualitative/quantitative and good/bad news information, and information for one-year/multiple-year forecasts. First, financial FL information is related to the firm's performance and financial position, whereas non-financial FL disclosure is concerned with firm-specific information (e.g., vision, mission, strategy and risks). Second, quantitative FL disclosure is connected with numbers or units such as the firm's earnings forecast; however, qualitative FL information is a soft-talk disclosure. Third, good (bad) news FL information includes positive (negative) messages about the firm. Finally, the one-year forecast FL information provides estimated results for one year following the current year, and the multiple years forecast provides information for multiple years' forecasts following the current year. This chapter discusses the determinants and consequences of these FL disclosures either in soft-talk narratives or quantitative information (e.g., earnings forecasts).

Bujaki and McConomy (2002) report that FL information in the Management Discussion and Analyses (MD&As) part of the annual report of US firms is qualitative and non-financial information. In addition, this information is dominated by good news, representing 97.5% of FL disclosures, and the non-financial and qualitative FL information represents 58% of the analyst report, and 31% represents multiple years' forecasts. Also, good news FL information dominates the bad news and represents approximately 83% of the FL information. Furthermore, Hassanein and Hussainey (2015) argue that UK firms prefer to report positive FL, and that this information is not verifiable or auditable by an external party.

### 3.2.2 Arguments for and against

A firm's corporate disclosure practices have changed and FL information is disclosed to satisfy different users' needs. In support, the regulatory requirements (i.e., IASB and FASB) recommend disclosing FL information to decrease information asymmetry and to provide insights into a firm's future cash flows. In addition, it ensures the efficiency of capital markets and reduces the cost of external financing, as suggested by the capital markets transactions hypothesis (Healy and Palepu, 2001). Finally, FL information is associated with value-creation capital and improves readability and understandability at larger scales (Guthrie *et al.*, 2020).

Conversely, other arguments support non-disclosure of FL information. It is difficult to provide an accurate prediction for what might happen in the future. Therefore, FL information may be inappropriate for decision-making as it may lead to a wrong decision. Rogers and Stocken (2005) suggest that firms' managers are willing to misrepresent their forecasts. Likewise, firms are likely to provide biased forecasts (Li, 2008). Moreover, disclosure of inaccurate FL information increases litigation costs because companies are penalised for their inaccurate disclosures (Field *et al.*, 2005; Hassanein and Elsayed, 2021). In support, Aboody and Kasznik (2000) argue that corporate managers are unwilling to provide earnings forecasts in order to reduce the chance of a forecast error and subsequent litigation risk. Likewise, Rogers and Van Buskirk (2009) indicate that companies operating in highly litigious industries reduce their earnings forecasts. Overall, market participants perceive and prioritise the need for different types of information in a way that reflects a gap between their information needs and those of the regulators (Mohamed *et al.*, 2019).

### 3.2.3 Measures

FL information can be measured through either management forecasts or content analysis. Management forecasts are typically a type of FL information voluntarily disclosed by corporate managers as a point or range and include estimates of earnings, revenue and costs (Hassan and Marston, 2019). They could be either quantitative or qualitative forecasts (Hutton and Stocken, 2009). These forecasts are verified by comparing them with the actual results of the firm.

Content analysis is a means of categorising a text, and it can be conducted either manually, through the manual reading of the document, or automatically, by using computer software. It has been heavily utilised in previous studies to measure FL disclosure either manually (Schleicher and Walker, 2010; Bozzolan *et al.*, 2009; Menicucci, 2018) or using computer software (Hussainey *et al.*, 2003; Li, 2010; Hassanein and Hussainey, 2015; Hassanein *et al.*, 2019). The manual content analysis is precise; however, it is labour-intensive and limits the sample size, making it difficult to generalise the results (Hassan and Marston, 2019). Automated content analysis saves time and effort and helps scholars explore the disclosures of large samples, leading to generalised results and reliable inferences. There is no one-size-fits-all solution to enhancing FL disclosure. In their recent study, Scannella and Polizzi (2021) find that non-automated content analysis provides an enhanced measure of disclosures in financial institutions.

## 3.3  Determinants of forward-looking disclosure

FL disclosure is a substantial type of information used for making better decisions (Hassanein *et al.*, 2019). Hence, professional organisations and standard setters (AICPA, FASB, IASB, ICAEW) have long advised businesses to provide this type of information. Consequently, academic research has focused on the factors that influence FL disclosure. This section discusses the theories and related literature on how firm-specific characteristics, corporate governance mechanisms and other factors influence FL disclosure.

### *3.3.1  Firm-specific characteristics*

Agency, signalling, stakeholder and cost-of-disclosure theories all describe how business characteristics influence FL disclosure. Corporate managers disseminate more FL information to (a) mitigate the information asymmetry and agency costs; (b) signal good performance and management's resilience and ability to handle distress in the event of bad news; (c) alleviate pressure and respond to stakeholder information needs; and (d) optimise dissemination costs, eliminate under-disclosure litigation and increase visibility. As a result, numerous firm-specific characteristics influence the level of FL disclosure, as follows.

#### *3.3.1.1  Firm size*

Agency theory argues that larger firms have greater access to external financing, pressuring them to provide more disclosure. Similarly, stakeholder theory suggests that institutional stockholders and financial analysts urge larger companies to voluntarily disclose more information (Mousa and Elamir, 2018). In addition, because larger companies have consistent and stable performance, they are more likely to disseminate information about their future earnings for signalling purposes (Kent and Ung, 2003). Furthermore, cost-of-disclosure theory suggests that larger companies benefit significantly from economies of scale, making it easier for them to finance the costs of preparation and dissemination of information. Additionally, according to litigation theory, larger companies have an incentive to reduce political costs and litigation risks (Hassanein and Elsayed, 2021). These companies can avoid public scrutiny by disclosing FL information, allowing them to gain visibility and easier access to capital (Alsaeed, 2006). Regarding the impact of firm size on the disclosure of FL information, empirical investigations have shown mixed results (Alsaeed, 2006; Hassanein and Hussainey, 2015; Wang and Hussainey, 2013; Hassanein and Elsayed, 2021).

### 3.3.1.2 Leverage

Highly leveraged companies are willing to provide a higher level of FL information in their annual reports (Aljifri and Hussainey, 2007). This is because these firms are likely to face increased agency costs, higher costs of capital and information asymmetry issues resulting from the risks associated with leverage (Alsaeed, 2006). More voluntary FL information is anticipated to reduce these costs. As a result, leveraged companies are better equipped to minimise their capital and agency costs when disclosing more voluntary FL information (Barak and Brown, 2008). They eventually communicate more company information, which aids in the reduction of risk premiums (Aljifri and Hussainey, 2007).

### 3.3.1.3 Profitability

In both developed (Menicucci, 2013) and developing markets (Dey *et al.*, 2020), a direct association between profitability and FL information has been reported. Profitable companies voluntarily reveal FL information to promote a positive tone to stakeholders as part of impression management (Leventis and Weetman, 2004). Other limited evidence suggests an inverse association between profitability and FL disclosure. It demonstrates that investors of more profitable companies are satisfied with current levels of profits; hence, they do not demand that more information be disclosed. Subsequently, more profitable companies disclose less FL information (Abed and Bravo, 2018; Hassanein *et al.*, 2019). Furthermore, due to concerns about lawsuits and public scrutiny, loss-making companies are compelled to disseminate more information (Field *et al.*, 2005; Hassanein and Elsayed, 2021).

### 3.3.1.4 Firm age

Corporate voluntary disclosure is affected by the age of the firm. According to Hossain and Hammami (2009), the FL information in a firm's annual report is a positive function of firm age, meaning that older (younger) firms disclose more (less) FL information. The reason may be that younger firms voluntarily provide less information due to being at a competitive disadvantage by nature, resulting in greater information-processing costs and having a lower level of expertise. Conversely, older firms use their business expertise and financial resources to improve their image and build a positive reputation (Akhtaruddin, 2005). Li *et al*. (2012) argue that voluntary information is adversely associated with listing period/firm listing age because relatively young corporations seek to entice investors by voluntarily disclosing more information.

### 3.3.1.5  Dividend payout

The association between dividend payment and FL disclosure is explained by two opposing views. On the one hand, signalling theory argues that, when enterprises have higher levels of information asymmetry, which is defined as providing less voluntarily FL information, they are willing to pay higher dividends to signal their optimistic predictions to investors. On the other hand, in pecking order theory, investors tend to under-invest in those firms suffering from higher levels of asymmetric information, i.e., lower voluntary FL disclosure. Therefore, managers tend to respond by paying out fewer dividends. Therefore, FL disclosure is more likely to be positively associated with dividend payment.

### 3.3.1.6  Liquidity

Highly liquid firms are willing to provide more voluntary information to distinguish themselves from companies experiencing liquidity issues by providing signals to the market through increased levels of FL disclosure (Hassanein *et al*., 2019). However, empirical studies failed to identify a significant impact of firm liquidity on voluntary disclosure (e.g., Elzahar *et al*., 2015; Hassanein and Hussainey, 2015; Hassanein *et al*., 2019; Hassanein and Elsayed, 2021).

### 3.3.1.7  Industry type

Literature reveals that the type of industry or sector in which a firm operates influences its FL disclosure level. This is attributable to the differences in capital structure, competition, growth opportunities and risk management strategies across industries and sectors (Kılıç and Kuzey, 2018). Therefore, scholars control for industry type in their disclosure studies (Hassanein *et al*., 2019). The empirical findings show that industry type significantly influences the level of FL information (Qu *et al*., 2015). Moreover, earlier findings show that voluntary disclosures differ by industry type in non-financial firms, with manufacturing firms disseminating more voluntary FL information than service firms (Cohen *et al*., 2012)

### 3.3.2  Corporate governance

Corporate governance has received greater consideration from standard setters and academia, particularly in the aftermath of corporate collapses (e.g., Enron, Tyco and WorldCom). Corporate governance practices aim to provide companies with clear direction, control management actions and lay out a strong foundation for accountability and regulation (Hassanein, 2021). Agency theory suggests that managers use FL disclosure to alleviate the uncertainty that shareholders have about future information. These practices eventually aid in mitigating information asymmetry. Hence, providing more disclosure serves two purposes. First, companies ensure that shareholders perceive that corporate interests are aligned to serve shareholders' interests. Second, shareholders and other stakeholders view companies as conforming to accountability demands. In this regard, the goal is to reduce information asymmetry and agency costs. Accordingly, firms have devoted their resources to establishing robust governance mechanisms to better protect shareholders' rights (Al-Najjar and Abed, 2014) and mitigate information asymmetry between corporate insiders and shareholders.

Previous literature suggests that firms with robust governance practices are inclined to provide more FL disclosures to attract the following of financial analysts, show more responsive share prices and better predict future earnings (Wang and Hussainey, 2013). As determinants of FL disclosure, substantial studies on governance mechanisms are established on agency and signalling theories propositions. The argument is that, when well governed, firms disseminate substantial voluntary information to mitigate information asymmetry. We divide previous studies examining the nexus of corporate governance and FL disclosures into several strands, depending on the governance mechanisms examined.

### 3.3.2.1 Characteristics of the board of directors

The characteristics of the board are a vital proxy for its effectiveness (Jensen and Meckling, 1976). They include board independence, size, the duality/turnover of CEO and diversity among board members. Agency theory reveals that independent members in the board play a substantial role in controlling the opportunist behaviour of corporate managers (Jensen and Meckling, 1976). They are more effective in the monitoring process than other board members (Hassanein and Kokel, 2019). According to empirical findings, board members' independence is associated with higher disclosure quality (Goh *et al.*, 2016), although there are disparate results regarding the effect of board independence on FL disclosure (Wang and Hussainey, 2013; Hassanein and Hussainey, 2015). Other research supports the initial finding, showing that firms with more foreign directors disseminate more FL information (Elgammal *et al.*, 2018).

The size of the board can also drive the disclosure of FL information. Larger boards are ineffective in making decisions because of relative lack of coordination among members (Jensen and Meckling, 1976). However, Klein (2002) contends this, proposing greater effectiveness because of their greater diversity of expertise. Empirical findings report positive (Wang and Hussainey, 2013), negative (Elgammal *et al.*, 2018) and non-significant (Karamanou and Vafeas, 2005) associations between FL disclosure and board size.

Combining the roles of CEO and chairman (i.e., CEO/chairman duality) can result in one person dominating the board and hence reducing the board's effective control (Jensen and Meckling, 1976). Consequently, the monitoring quality of the board becomes less effective. Boards with CEO/chairman duality are unwilling to share corporate information with outsiders due to the desire for self-entrenchment. Prior empirical research suggests either negative (Wang and Hussainey, 2013) or no association (Elgammal *et al.*, 2018) between CEO/chairman duality and FL information disclosure. In addition to CEO/chairman duality, other studies have examined how CEO turnover affects firm disclosure. They find that CEO turnover positively influences disclosure quality (Pereira and Peterson, 2011) and the accuracy of management forecasts.

Gender diversity has attracted the attention of academic research as an influential characteristic of the board of directors (Zalata *et al.*, 2019). Evidence shows that greater gender diversity in boards is positively associated with providing more FL disclosure (Bravo and Alcaide-Ruiz, 2019). The rationale is that female directors in gender-diverse boards bring new perspectives, improve decision-making (Barako and Brown, 2008), encourage participatory culture and enhance effective communication practices among board members (Bear *et al.*, 2010).

### 3.3.2.2 Ownership structures

Agency theory suggests that ownership structures, such as blockholders, institutional and managerial ownership, act as disciplinary mechanisms and are expected to monitor management behaviour and its reporting practices. There are two opposing views about institutional investors. On the one hand, they are vital corporate governance mechanisms and significantly affect the corporate decisions and policies that affect the prospects and future of their investee firms (Chung *et al.*, 2019; Hassanein *et al.*, 2021a). On the other hand, they are myopic and inactive in corporate decision-making (Callen and Fang, 2013). Empirical studies report mixed findings for the effect of institutional ownership on voluntary disclosure. Karamanou and Vafeas (2005) indicate that companies with substantial institutional investors disclose more earnings forecasts. However, other research indicates either a negative (Celik *et al.*, 2006) or a non-significant relationship (Wang and Hussainey, 2013) between these variables.

Agency perspective reveals that managerial ownership would mitigate the agency cost as it supports the interests of managers with those of corporate shareholders (Jensen and Meckling, 1976). As a result, it induces firms to disclose more information and solves the information asymmetry issue. However, the management entrenchment hypothesis argues that executives with substantial portions of corporate shares are more likely to feel that their positions are secured when their private benefits are maximised and, as a result, this raises agency problems and, therefore, increases the information asymmetry issue, with less disclosure being expected. Empirical research contradicts agency theory and supports the entrenchment hypothesis. It finds that managerial ownership negatively affects FL disclosure (Wang and Hussainey, 2013).

Prior studies also argue that blockholders induce corporate managers to provide additional voluntary disclosure to increase the firm's value and to alleviate agency costs (Huafang and Jianguo, 2007). On the other hand, other research argues that ownership by blockholders reduces the incentives of corporate managers to provide additional voluntary disclosure to reduce the dissemination costs. Previous results have been mixed with respect to the impact of ownership by blockholders on FL disclosure. Literature suggests that FL disclosure is inversely correlated with blockholder ownership (Al-Najjar and Abed, 2014). Nonetheless, limited research finds no association between voluntary disclosure and blockholding (Eng and Mak, 2003). Another group of studies finds that FL disclosure is positively correlated with blockholder ownership (Huafang and Jianguo, 2007).

### 3.3.2.3 Audit committee

The audit committee has a critical role in reducing agency conflicts by improving the quality of board oversight (Klein, 2002), and firms with audit committees are less likely to face lawsuits. Audit committees on corporate boards enable companies to better monitor management activities and reporting practices, resulting in lower agency costs (Hassanein and Kokel, 2019). Prior research has consistently found a market response to management forecast disclosure for firms with the size of audit committees (Karamanou and Vafeas, 2005).

Other studies have focused on the characteristics of audit committees. For instance, prior research finds that companies with independent members on their audit committees provide FL disclosure (Karamanou and Vafeas, 2005; Al-Najjar and Abed, 2014). Moreover, board members who have overlapping audit committee roles urge companies to disclose more FL information (Al Lawati and Hussainey, 2020). Furthermore, the presence of members with financial expertise on audit committees leads to a higher FL disclosure (Abad and Bravo, 2018). Besides, greater gender diversity on audit committees is positively associated with providing more FL disclosure (Kılıç and Kuzey, 2018). Recently, Al Lawati *et al.* (2021) indicate that audit committee size, gender diversity and multiple directorships improve the disclosure quality. However, the existence of financial expertise or foreign directorship on the audit committee, and high meeting frequencies deteriorate the disclosure quality.

### 3.3.3 Other determinants

Literature identifies other determinants of FL disclosure, including security offerings, growth opportunities of the firm, cross-listing status, the language of reporting, audit quality, the level of corruption, proprietary costs and investment efficiency. Hossain *et al.* (2005) suggest that FL disclosure is positively correlated with new security offerings and investment in growth opportunities, whereas it is negatively associated with barriers to entry. Al-Najjar and Abed (2014) demonstrate that the cross-listing status of a firm positively affects FL disclosure. Moreover, Leventis and Weetman (2004) show that when companies are more visible due to having dual language reporting, they would be likely to provide more FL disclosure.

Audit quality is positively associated with FL disclosure as the auditing function provides an additional monitoring mechanism, inducing managers to provide additional information to shareholders while improving reporting quality (O'Sullivan *et al.*, 2008). Furthermore, audit firm type affects FL disclosure as internationally affiliated audit firms provide extensive guidance to clients to enhance corporate reporting practices (Dey and Faruq, 2019). These audit firms are more inclined to maintain international standards and ensure high-quality disclosure. Additionally, it is assumed that larger audit firms conduct higher-quality audits; hence they stimulate better quality financial reporting and disclosure (O'Sullivan *et al.*, 2008).

Corruption has also been examined in association with FL disclosure. In a comparative study of two countries in sub-Saharan Africa, Agyei-Mensah (2017) highlights that companies in the less corrupt country provide more FL disclosure and have a higher level of transparency. Finally, studies show that FL disclosure is inversely associated with the firm's competitive position. Therefore, when proprietary costs are high, managers reduce FL disclosure to avoid adverse effects from competitors (Healy and Palepu, 2001).

Investment efficiency is associated with corporate voluntary disclosure due to requirements of improved monitoring, increased internal control and higher quality of financial reporting. Elberry and Hussainey (2020, 2021) demonstrate that disclosure of corporate performance is significantly associated with investment efficiency. However, disclosing good news information is associated with having relatively lower levels of corporate investment efficiency. Therefore, firms that over- or under-invest are inclined to mask corporate investment inefficiencies by disclosing more good news.

## 3.4  Consequences of forward-looking disclosure

As the dynamic changes in economies worldwide make it too difficult to rely solely on historical information, FL disclosure has been vital for capital market participants and other stakeholders (Menicucci, 2013). Subsequently, this type of information enables stakeholders to predict firms' future financial and non-financial performances. The economic impact of FL disclosure can be broken down into themes that focus on predicting future performance, the accuracy of analysts' forecasts, expected stock earnings and corporate values.

### *3.4.1  Prediction of future performance*

Frequency and changes of FL disclosures are associated with more informative corporate annual reports, reflecting future corporate performance. FL disclosure is likely to affect the future performance of a firm. One reason is that this type of information reduces the uncertainty of corporate performance (Firmansyah and Irwanto, 2020). In this sense, the importance of FL disclosure lies in its ability to influence investors' expectations about the company's stock returns and future cash flows (Miller, 2010). Furthermore, informative disclosure enhances investors' perceptions of the firm's future performance (Hassanein and Hussainey, 2015; Hassanein *et al.*, 2019).

On the other hand, another stream of research examines how disclosure influences a firm's cost of capital. The argument is that investors invest in firms with lower costs of capital to gain higher cash flows. Hence, the cost of capital is a negative indicator of corporate performance (e.g., Mangena *et al.*, 2016). The literature supports the view that annual disclosure decreases the cost of equity capital, whereas quarterly disclosure increases the cost of equity capital (Botosan and Plumlee, 2002).

Notably, many prior studies have endogeneity problems; hence, there are concerns about the ability of the results to be interpreted causally. Therefore, empirical tests must control endogeneity and find suitable instruments (Hassanein *et al.*, 2019). In a recent study on an international sample of listed firms, Raimo *et al.* (2021) attempt to control common methodological issues in prior research. They find that environmental, social and governance (ESG) disclosure is inversely associated with the cost of capital. Hence, enhancing ESG disclosure provides firms with better access to financial resources.

### 3.4.2 Accuracy of analysts' forecasts

Research recognises the benefits of FL disclosure as a tool to mitigate adverse selection and how these benefits are linked to the coverage of financial analysts (Warren, 2020). Beretta and Bozzolan (2008) believe that the FL disclosure can improve the quality of analysts' forecasts. In addition, Muslu *et al.* (2019) contend that high-quality disclosure of corporate social responsibility (CSR) information is associated with more accurate analysts' forecasts. Additionally, FL disclosures lead to meeting the analysts' forecasts, reducing forecast errors and decreasing earnings volatility (Baik and Jiang, 2006). Further empirical research tests the relationship between voluntary disclosure and the accuracy and variation of analysts' forecasts (Bozzolan *et al.*, 2009). Their results show a substantial impact of FL disclosure on both aspects. Further evidence suggests that higher-quality FL information leads to minor forecast error and small variation in analysts' earnings forecasts (Bozzolan *et al.*, 2009). The literature has differentiated between verifiable and non-verifiable disclosures and found a significant association between verifiable disclosures and the accuracy of analysts' forecasts (Hutton *et al.*, 2003). However, the results are not always sustained. Tirado-Beltran and Cabedo-Semper (2020) break down risk disclosures of Spanish firms to their verifiable and non-verifiable components and find no significant association with the accuracy of analysts' forecasts. Further investigation is needed across cultures while controlling for omitted variables.

### 3.4.3 Share price anticipation of future earnings

FL disclosure enables investors to assess the level of uncertainty of future cash flows in a better way (Beyer *et al.*, 2010). In addition, according to signalling theory, firms voluntarily disclose information to convey the good news to market participants. Interestingly, managers may disclose bad news voluntarily to show their ability to deal with corporate losses. The literature suggests that greater corporate disclosure positively impacts on capital markets by reducing the cost of capital, information asymmetry and stock return volatility (Mousa and Elamir, 2018). Beretta and Bozzolan (2008) report that FL disclosure is essential to explain future earnings. Further evidence demonstrates that FL disclosure is associated with greater accuracy in predicting stock prices (Hussainey *et al.*, 2003). The results of Hassanein and Hussainey (2015) confirm the substantial correlation between change in FL disclosure (as a proxy for informative disclosure) and change in earnings.

### 3.4.4 Corporate values

Theoretically, disclosing information enhances investors' assessments, leading to higher firm valuation. Disclosure increases the value of a firm by reducing its cost of capital and increasing its expected cash flows (Hassan *et al.*, 2009; Hassanein and Hussainey, 2015). The investor expectation about a firm is built after considering all available disclosures (Hope *et al.*, 2016). Signalling theory suggests that firms disseminate value-relevant information to satisfy the investors' requirements for information and to signal a firm's strong position in the market. Patel *et al.* (2002) reveal that firms with improved disclosure policies have higher values. Elzahar *et al.* (2015) reveal that voluntary disclosure increases the firm's value. Hassanein *et al.* (2019) explore the impact of disclosing FL information on UK corporate values. They find an increase in the UK firm values after disclosing this type of information. Furthermore, their results suggest that FL information is seen as value relevant for firms with a large auditor and firms with low performance. Recently, Haj-Salem *et al.* (2020) explore a sample of Tunisian firms to find that voluntary disclosure and corporate governance are jointly associated with corporate value.

## 3.5 Concluding remarks and future research avenues

This chapter adds to the existing literature and provides a wide-ranging review of studies on the determinants and consequences of disclosing FL information. Theoretically, research emphasises FL disclosure based on managers' incentive theories. Empirical research reports variable findings, and therefore there are diverse conclusions in terms of the factors that motivate firms to disclose FL information. Corporate boards should therefore structure the corporate governance system to enhance the disclosure of FL information. Furthermore, studies report some economic consequences from disclosing FL information, including facilitating estimates of future earnings, enhancing analyst forecasts, improving share price expectation of future earnings and promoting corporate values.

We note that there are different definitions of FL information. US-based studies define it as quantitative management forecasts. However, other research on different contexts (e.g., UK) defines it as any information related to the future. We propose that future research should apply FL disclosure in a way that is coherent and comparable. Further research is also needed to identify how FL disclosure types can be produced conceptually from financial statement classifications. For instance, FL disclosure is related to the income statement (e.g., anticipated sales and expected costs) and FL disclosure related to the statement of financial position (e.g., expected liabilities and projected capital expenditure).

Prior empirical studies focus heavily on the influence of corporate governance attributes and/or firm-specific characteristics on FL disclosure. However, they ignore the impact of demographic characteristics of corporate managers on this type of disclosure. Given that the characteristics of top corporate managers play a substantial role in decision-making and influence the accounting outcomes, future research should explore how corporate managers' demographic characteristics (e.g., age, gender, education, functional track, tenure and financial experience) affect FL disclosure. Additionally, research has focused on internal corporate factors, such as firm-level governance and firm-specific characteristics. There are different challenges, opportunities and disclosure policies in different counties. Thus, examining how country-level characteristics such as legal system, culture, degree of investor protection and market conditions could affect FL disclosure may be a suggested area for future studies. Furthermore, there is a need to investigate how internal governance characteristics interact with the external factors (market or regulatory) and how these interactions interplay to motivate FL disclosure decisions.

Although empirical research has reported some economic consequences arising from FL disclosure, there are still some areas for future research. Future research can focus on the efficient market hypothesis to explore whether FL information affects the stock market return or stock liquidity. Apart from the annual report, examining the FL information of other disclosures, such as online reporting, disclosure on social media such as Twitter (Hassanein *et al.*, 2021b) or conference calls, may be an area for future research. Finally, since technology is progressing rapidly, future research may go beyond the examination of manual *vs.* automated content analysis to employ the potential use of artificial intelligence (AI) and robotics in enhancing the accuracy and relevance of FL disclosures.

## Notes

1 "Forward-looking" and "future-oriented" information are synonyms and are used interchangeably throughout the chapter.
2 AICPA denotes the "American Institute of Certified Public Accountants", FASB denotes "Financial Accounting Standards Board", IASB denotes "International Accounting Standards Board" and ICAEW denotes the "Institute of Chartered Accountants in England and Wales".

## References

Abad, C., and Bravo, F. (2018), "Audit committee accounting expertise and forward-looking disclosures: A study of the US companies", *Management Research Review*, Vol. 41, No. 2, pp. 166–185.

Aboody, D., and Kasznik, R. (2000), "CEO stock option awards and corporate voluntary disclosures", *Journal of Accounting and Economics*, Vol. 29, pp. 73–100.

Agyei-Mensah, B. K. (2017), "The relationship between corporate governance, corruption and forward-looking information disclosure: A comparative study", *Corporate Governance*, Vol. 17, No. 2, pp. 284–304.

Akhtaruddin, M. (2005), "Corporate mandatory disclosure practices in Bangladesh", *The International Journal of Accounting*, Vol. 40, No. 4, pp. 399–422.

Aljifri, K., and Hussainey, K. (2007), "The determinants of forward-looking information in annual reports of UAE companies", *Managerial Auditing Journal*, Vol. 22, No. 9, pp. 881–894.

Al Lawati, H., and Hussainey, K. (2020), "Disclosure of forward-looking information: Does audit committee overlapping matter?", *International Journal of Accounting, Auditing and Performance Evaluation*, Forthcoming.

Al Lawati, H., Hussainey, K., and Sagitova, R. (2021), "Disclosure quality vis-à-vis disclosure quantity: Does audit committee matter in Omani financial institutions?", *Review of Quantitative Financial Accounting*, Vol. 57, pp. 557–594.

Al-Najjar, B., and Abed, S. (2014), "The association between disclosure of forward-looking information and corporate governance mechanisms: Evidence from the UK before the financial crisis period", *Managerial Auditing Journal*, Vol. 29, No. 7, pp. 578–595.

Alsaeed, K. (2006), "The association between firm-specific characteristics and disclosure: The case of Saudi Arabia", *Managerial Auditing Journal*, Vol. 21, No. 5, pp. 476–496.

Baik, B., and Jiang, G. (2006), "The use of management forecasts to dampen analysts' expectations", *Journal of Accounting and Public Policy*, Vol. 25, No. 5, pp. 531–553.

Barako, D. G., and Brown, A. M. (2008), "Corporate social reporting and board representation: Evidence from the Kenyan banking sector", *Journal of Management and Governance*, Vol. 12, No. 4, pp. 309–324.

Bear, S., Rahman, N., and Post, C. (2010), "The impact of board diversity and gender composition on corporate social responsibility and firm reputation", *Journal of Business Ethics*, Vol. 97, No. 2, pp. 207–221.

Beretta, S., and Bozzolan, S. (2008), "Quality versus quantity: The case of forward-looking disclosure. *Journal of Accounting, Auditing and Finance*, Vol. 23, No. 3, pp. 333–375.

Beyer, A., Cohen, D. A., Lys, T. Z., and Walther, B. R. (2010), "The financial reporting environment: Review of the recent literature", *Journal of Accounting and Economics*, Vol. 50, Nos. 2–3, pp. 296–343.

Botosan, C. A., and Plumlee, M. A. (2002), "A re-examination of disclosure level and the expected cost of equity capital", *Journal of Accounting Research*, Vol. 40, No. 1, pp. 21–40.

Bozzolan, S., Trombetta, M., and Beretta, S. (2009), "Forward-looking disclosures, financial verifiability and analysts' forecasts: A study of cross-listed European firms", *European Accounting Review*, Vol. 18, No. 3, pp. 435–473.

Bravo, F., and Alcaide-Ruiz, M. D. (2019), "The disclosure of financial forward-looking information: Does the financial expertise of female make a difference?", *Gender in Management: An International Journal*, Vol. 34, No. 2, pp. 140–156.

Bujaki, M., and McConomy, B. (2002), "Corporate governance: Factors influencing voluntary disclosure by publicly traded Canadian firms", *Canadian Accounting Perspectives*, Vol. 1, No. 2, pp. 105–139.

Callen, J. L., and Fang, X. (2013), "Institutional investor stability and crash risk: Monitoring versus short-termism?", *Journal of Banking and Finance*, Vol. 37, No. 8, pp. 3047–3063.

Celik, O., Ecer, A., and Karahacak, H. (2006), "Disclosure of forward looking information: Evidence from listed companies on Istanbul stock exchange (ISE)", *Investment Management and Financial Innovations*, Vol. 3, No. 2, pp. 197–216.

Chung, C. Y., Cho, S. J., Ryu, D., and Ryu, D. (2019), "Institutional blockholders and corporate social responsibility", *Asian Business and Management*, Vol. 18, pp. 143–186.

Cohen, J., Holder-Webb, L., Nath, L., and Wood, D. (2012), "Corporate reporting of non-financial leading indicators of economic performance and sustainability", *Accounting Horizons*, Vol. 26, No. 1, pp. 65–90.

Dey, P. K., and Faruq, M. O. (2019), "Determinants of intellectual capital disclosure: An investigation on DS30 firms in Bangladesh", *Asian Journal of Accounting Perspectives*, Vol. 12, No. 2, pp. 27–48.

Dey, P. K., Roy, M., and Akter, M. (2020), "What determines forward-looking information disclosure in Bangladesh?", *Asian Journal of Accounting Research*, Vol. 5, No. 2, pp. 225–239.

Elberry, N., and Hussainey, K. (2020), "Does corporate investment efficiency affect corporate disclosure practice?", *Journal of Applied Accounting Research*, Vol. 21, No. 2, pp. 309–327.

Elberry, N., and Hussainey, K. (2021), "Governance vis-à-vis investment efficiency: Substitutes or complementary in their effects on disclosure practice", *Journal of Risk and Financial management*, Forthcoming.

Elgammal, M. M., Hussainey, K., and Ahmed, F. (2018), "Corporate governance and voluntary risk and forward-looking disclosures", *Journal of Applied Accounting Research*, Vol. 19, No. 4, pp. 592–607.

Elzahar, H., Hussainey, K., Mazzi, F., and Tsalavoutas, I. (2015), "Economic consequences of key performance indicators' disclosure quality", *International Review of Financial Analysis*, Vol. 39, pp. 96–112.

Eng, L. L., and Mak, Y. T. (2003), "Corporate governance and voluntary disclosure", *Journal of Accounting and Public Policy*, Vol. 22, pp. 325–345.

Field, L., Lowry, M., and Shu, S. (2005), "Does disclosure deter or trigger litigation?", *Journal of Accounting and Economics*, Vol. 39, pp. 487–507.

Firmansyah, A., and Irwanto, A. (2020), "Do income smoothing, forward-looking disclosure, and corporate social responsibility decrease information uncertainty?", *International Journal of Psychosocial Rehabilitation*, Vol. 24, No. 7, pp. 9513–9525.

Goh, B. W., Lee, J., Ng, J., and Ow Yong, K. (2016), "The effect of board independence on information asymmetry", *European Accounting Review*, Vol. 25, No. 1, pp. 155–182.

Guthrie, J., Manes Rossi, F., Orelli, R. L., and Nicolò, G. (2020), "Investigating risk disclosures in Italian integrated reports", *Meditari Accountancy Research*, Vol. 28, No. 6, pp. 1149–1178.

Haj-Salem, I., Ayadi, S., and Hussainey, K. (2020), "The joint effect of corporate risk disclosure and corporate governance on firm value", *International Journal of Disclosure and Governance*, Vol. 17, pp. 123–140.

Hassan, O. A. G., and Marston, C. (2019), "Corporate financial disclosure measurement in the empirical accounting literature: A review article", *International Journal of Accounting*, Vol. 45, No. 2, pp. 195–201.

Hassan, O., Romilly, P., Giorgioni, G., and Power, D. (2009), "The value relevance of disclosure: Evidence from the emerging capital market of Egypt", *The International Journal of Accounting*, Vol. 44, pp. 79–102.

Hassanein, A. (2021), "Corporate governance and cash holdings", In A. Alqatan, K. Hussainey, and H. Khlif (eds), *Corporate governance and its implications on accounting and finance*, pp. 305–321. Pennsylvania, PA: IGI Global.

Hassanein, A., and Elsayed, N. (2021), "Voluntary risk disclosure and values of FTSE350 firms: The role of an industry-based litigation risk", *International Journal of Managerial and Financial Accounting*, Forthcoming.

Hassanein, A., and Hussainey, K. (2015), "Is forward-looking financial disclosure really informative? Evidence from UK narrative statements", *International Review of Financial Analysis*, Vol. 41, pp. 52–61.

Hassanein, A., and Kokel, A. (2019), "Corporate cash hoarding and corporate governance mechanisms: Evidence from Borsa Istanbul", *Asia-Pacific Journal of Accounting & Economics*, pp. 1–18] https://doi.org/10.1080/16081625.2019.1617753.

Hassanein, A., Marzouk, M., and Azzam, M. (2021a), "How does ownership by corporate managers affect R&D in the UK?", *International Journal of Productivity and Performance Management*, Forthcoming. https://doi.org/10.1108/IJPPM-03-2020-0121.

Hassanein, A., Moustafa, M. M., Benameur, K., and Al-Khasawneh, J. (2021b), "How do big markets react to investors' sentiments on firm tweets?", *Journal of Sustainable Finance and Investment*. https://doi.org/10.1080/20430795.2021.1949198

Hassanein, A., Zalata, A., and Hussainey, K. (2019), "Do forward-looking narratives affect investors' valuation of UK FTSE all-shares firms?", *Review of Quantitative Finance and Accounting*, Vol. 52, No. 2, pp. 493–519.

Healy, P. M., and Palepu, K. G. (2001), "Information asymmetry, corporate disclosure, and the capital markets: A review of the empirical disclosure literature", *Journal of Accounting and Economics*, Vol. 31, No. 1–3, pp. 405–440.

Hope, O. K., Hu, D., and Lu, H. (2016), "The benefits of specific risk-factor disclosures", *Review of Accounting Studies*, Vol. 21, pp. 1005–1045.

Hossain, M., Ahmed, K., and Godfrey, J. M. (2005), "Investment opportunity set and voluntary disclosure of prospective information: A simultaneous equations approach", *Journal of Business Finance and Accounting*, Vol. 32, Nos. 5/6, pp. 871–907.

Hossain, M., and Hammami, H. (2009), "Voluntary disclosure in the annual reports of an emerging country: The case of Qatar", *Advances in Accounting*, Vol. 25, No. 2, pp. 255–265.

Huafang, X., and Jianguo, Y. (2007), "Ownership structure, board composition and corporate voluntary disclosure: Evidence from listed companies in China", *Managerial Auditing Journal*, Vol. 22, No. 6, pp. 604–619.

Hussainey, K., Schleicher, T., and Walker, M. (2003), "Undertaking large-scale disclosures studies when AIMR-FAF ratings are not available: The case of price leading earnings", *Accounting and Business Research*, Vol. 33, No. 4, pp. 275–294.

Hutton, A. P., Miller, G. S., and Skinner, D. J. (2003), "The role of supplementary statements with management earnings forecasts", *Journal of Accounting Research*, Vol. 41, No. 5, pp. 867–890.

Hutton, A. P., and Stocken, P. C. (2009), "Prior forecasting accuracy and investor reaction to management earnings forecasts", Working Paper, available at SSRN: http://papers .ssrn.com/sol3/papers.cfm?abstract_id=817108 (accessed January 15, 2020).

IASB. (2010), *Conceptual framework for financial reporting*. London: International Accounting Standards Board.

Jensen, M. C., and Meckling, W. H. (1976), "Theory of the firm: Managerial behavior, agency costs, and ownership structure", *Journal of Financial Economics*, Vol. 3, No. 4, pp. 305–360.

Karamanou, I., and Vafeas, N. (2005), "The association between corporate boards, audit committees, and management earnings forecasts: Empirical analysis", *Journal of Accounting Research*, Vol. 43, No. 3, pp. 453–486.

Kent, P., and Ung, K. (2003), "Voluntary disclosure of forward-looking earnings information in Australia", *Australian Journal of Management*, Vol. 28, No. 3, pp. 273–286.

Kılıç, M., and Kuzey, C. (2018), "Determinants of forward-looking disclosures in integrated reporting", *Managerial Auditing Journal*, Vol. 33, No. 1, pp. 115–144.

Klein, A. (2002), "Audit committee, board of director characteristics, and earnings management", *Journal of Accounting and Economics*, Vol. 33, No. 3, pp. 375–400.

Leventis, S., and Weetman, P. (2004), "Impression management: Dual language reporting and voluntary disclosure", *Accounting Forum*, Vol. 28, No. 3, pp. 307–328.

Li, F. (2008), "Annual report readability, current earnings, and earnings persistence", *Journal of Accounting and Economics*, Vol. 45, No. 2–3, pp. 221–247.

Li, F. (2010), "The information content of forward-looking statements in corporate filings—A naive bayesian machine learning approach", *Journal of Accounting Research*, Vol. 48, No. 5, pp. 1049–1102.

Li, J., Mangena, M., and Pike, R. (2012), "The effect of audit committee characteristics on intellectual capital disclosure", *The British Accounting Review*, Vol. 44, No. 2, pp. 98–110.

Mangena, M., Li, J., and Tauringana, V. (2016), "Disentangling the effects of corporate disclosure on the cost of equity capital: A study of the role of intellectual capital disclosure", *Journal of Accounting Auditing and Finance*, Vol. 31, No. 1, pp. 3–27.

Menicucci, E. (2013), "The determinants of forward-looking information in management commentary: Evidence from Italian listed companies", *International Business Research*, Vol. 6, No. 5, pp. 30–44.

Menicucci, E. (2018), "Exploring forward-looking information in integrated reporting: A multi-dimensional analysis", *Journal of Applied Accounting Research*, Vol. 19, No. 1, pp. 102–121.

Miller, B. (2010), "The effects of reporting complexity on small and large investor trading", *The Accounting Review*, Vol. 85, No. 6, pp. 2107–2143.

Mohamed, M. K., Allini, A., Ferri, L., and Zampella, A. (2019), "Investors' perception on the usefulness of management report disclosures: Evidence from an emerging market", *Meditari Accountancy Research*, Vol. 27, No. 6, pp. 893–920.

Mousa, G. A., and Elamir, E. A. (2018), "Determinants of forward-looking disclosure: Evidence from Bahraini capital market", *Afro-Asian Journal of Finance and Accounting*, Vol. 8, No. 1, pp. 1–19.

Muslu, V., Mutlu, S., Radhakrishnan, S., and Tsang, A. (2019), "Corporate social responsibility report narratives and analyst forecast accuracy", *Journal of Business Ethics*, Vol. 154, pp. 1119–1142.

O'Sullivan, M., Percy, M., and Stewart, J. (2008), "Australian evidence on corporate governance attributes and their association with forward-looking information in the annual report", *Journal of Management and Governance*, Vol. 12, pp. 5–35.

Patel, S. A., Balic, A., and Bwakira, L. (2002), "Measuring transparency and disclosure at firm level in emerging markets", *Emerging Markets Review*, Vol. 3, No. 4, pp. 325–337.

Pereira, R., and Peterson, R. K. (2011), "Disclosure and CEO turnover", American Accounting Association Annual Meeting, Denver, CO.

Qu, W., Ee, M., Liu, L., Wise, V., and Carey, P. (2015), "Corporate governance and quality of forward-looking information: Evidence from the Chinese stock market", *Asian Review of Accounting*, Vol. 23, No. 1, pp. 39–67.

Raimo, N., de Nuccio, E., Giakoumelou, A., Petruzzella, F., and Vitolla, F. (2021), "Non-financial information and cost of equity capital: An empirical analysis in the food and beverage industry", *British Food Journal*, Vol. 123, No. 1, pp. 49–65.

Rogers, J., and Van Buskirk, A. (2009), "Shareholder litigation and changes in disclosure behaviour", *Journal of Accounting and Economics*, Vol. 47, pp. 136–156.

Rogers, J. L., and Stocken, P. C. (2005), "Credibility of management forecasts", *The Accounting Review*, Vol. 80, No. 4, pp. 1233–1260.

Scannella, E., and Polizzi, S. (2021), "How to measure bank credit risk disclosure? Testing a new methodological approach based on the content analysis framework", *Journal of Banking Regulation*, Vol. 22, pp. 73–95.

Schleicher, T., and Walker, M. (2010), "Bias in the tone of forward-looking narratives", *Accounting and Business Research*, Vol. 40, No. 4, pp. 371–390.

Tirado-Beltrán, J. M., and Cabedo-Semper, J. D. (2020), "Risk information disclosure and its impact on analyst forecast accuracy", *Estudios Gerenciales*, Vol. 36, No. 156, pp. 314–324.

Wang, M., and Hussainey, K. (2013), "Voluntary forward-looking statements driven by corporate governance and their value relevance", *Journal of Accounting and Public Policy*, Vol. 32, pp. 26–49.

Warren, J. (2020), "Analyst coverage and managers' disclosure of forward-looking information", Available at SSRN: https://ssrn.com/abstract=3702576 (accessed January 3, 2020).

Zalata, A., Ntim, C., Choudhry, T., Hassanein, A., and Elzahar, H. (2019), "Female directors and managerial opportunism: Monitoring versus advisory female directors", *The Leadership Quarterly*, Vol. 30, No. 5, pp. 1048–9843.

# 4 Risk reporting quality

## A review of current practices, trends and future directions for research

*Mahmoud Marzouk, Philip Linsley and Shraddha Verma*

## 4.1 Introduction

Corporate risk disclosure (CRD) has attracted considerable attention, particularly since the US accounting scandals and corporate failures of the early 2000s and the global financial crisis of 2007–2008. These crises served as a wake-up call for companies, investors, policy makers, capital market authorities and other stakeholder groups to pay more attention to risk management (RM) and risk reporting (RR). Consequently, there has been a growing demand for companies to provide more, and better, risk information (RI). Professional bodies have proposed guidelines encouraging companies to provide more information on their risk exposure (RE). Furthermore, there have been regulatory responses with different countries issuing regulations that oblige companies to report RI. Previous studies have focused on examining CRD quantity and its determinants. Although some studies suggest companies have increased their risk disclosures, others highlight that companies are not necessarily reporting more informative RI. Concerns have been raised about CRD quality and usefulness, and yet CRD quality is still an underresearched area.

Many previous CRD studies focus on counting the number of words and/ or sentences disclosing RI in corporate reports regardless of how informative it is for information users (for example, Linsley and Shrives, 2006; Marzouk, 2016; Haddad and Alali, 2021). The primary purpose of corporate reporting is to enhance information users' decision-making by providing useful information (FASB, 2010). Therefore, it is imperative to examine CRD quality and usefulness, and this can be achieved by understanding stakeholders' perspectives on CRD quality and, in particular, the perspectives of information users and information providers.

As noted above, earlier CRD studies did not address CRD quality adequately. A number of previous CRD studies attempted to examine CRD quality by focusing on identifying different RI characteristics of risk sentences, including quantitative/qualitative characteristics, time orientation and good/bad news characteristics (for example, Beretta and Bozzolan, 2004a; Dobler, Lajili and Zéghal, 2011; Linsley and Shrives, 2006; Lajili et al., 2021; Leopizzi et al., 2020). Abraham and Shrives (2014) adopt a different approach and propose a model for assessing

DOI: 10.4324/9781003095385-6

and enhancing CRD quality. However, the study is very limited as they investigate only three criteria: disclosure of company-specific RI, providing up-to-date information and reporting key risks and uncertainties. Campbell and Slack (2008) investigate the usefulness of narrative reporting from an investment analyst's perspective, whereas Slack and Campbell (2016) conduct semi-structured interviews to identify the needs of and use by investment analysts in terms of integrated reporting, and explore its usefulness. Consequently, although their studies include important discussions relating to CRD quality, their research does not have a primary focus on examining CRD or CRD quality. Therefore, there is a research gap in relation to research on the quality of CRD and, we argue that an effective analysis of CRD quality and usefulness can be achieved through investigating information users' perspectives on the subject.

This chapter is structured as follows. Section 4.2 discusses early studies that have a relation to CRD. Section 4.3 discusses the two foundational CRD studies that have influenced subsequent CRD studies. CRD literature published subsequent to these two foundational studies is then reviewed in Section 4.4 while Section 4.5 summarises the reports published by professional bodies. Section 4.6 then discusses CRD quality and Section 4.7 discusses how the few CRD studies that purport to study CRD quality differ, in fact, in respect of how they address the issue of CRD quality. This then leads to identification, and discussion, of the research gap, which is highlighted in Section 4.8. Section 4.9 concludes the chapter.

## 4.2 Early studies related to risk disclosure

It can be argued that the CRD studies undertaken by Beretta and Bozzolan (2004a) and Linsley and Shrives (2006), which will be discussed in Section 4.3, were primarily responsible for initiating research in this area. Furthermore, a large number of subsequent CRD studies have been influenced in how they approach CRD research by the studies of Beretta and Bozzolan (2004a) and Linsley and Shrives (2006). However, it is important to recognise that there have been studies published prior to these two articles that can be described as CRD studies and this section reviews these papers.

Meier, Tomaszewski and Tobing (1995) is the earliest of these studies and analyses the disclosure of political risks resulting from the Gulf War of 1990–1991 in the annual reports of US companies operating in Kuwait. The key finding is that companies provided inadequate disclosures of the impacts of the war on their exposure to political risks. This leads Meier, Tomaszewski and Tobing (1995) to conclude that the existing disclosure regulations did not provide sufficient guidance on the assessment and reporting of political risks.

The other early studies related to CRD are similarly focused on examining the disclosure of very specific categories of risk. Whereas Meier, Tomaszewski and Tobing (1995) have a specific focus on political risks, the other early studies explore the disclosure of financial risks. In particular, they analyse market risk disclosures associated with the use of derivative financial instruments. These studies were largely concerned with investigating the impact of introducing a new disclosure regulation/requirement, Financial Reporting Release (FRR) 48 (Disclosure of Accounting Policies for Derivative Financial Instruments and Derivative Commodity Instruments, and Disclosure of Quantitative and Qualitative Information About Market Risk Inherent in Derivative Financial Instruments, Other Financial Instruments and Derivative Commodity Instruments). This regulation was issued by the Securities Exchange Commission (SEC) in 1997 and the emphasis was placed on examining the relationship between market risk disclosures and the volatility of interest rates, exchange rates, commodity prices, trading volumes and equity prices (Rajgopal, 1999; Roulstone, 1999; Blankley, Lamb and Schroeder, 2002; Linsmeier et al., 2002; Abdelghany, 2005).

These early studies conclude that companies tend to disclose more information on market risks in response to these newly adopted disclosure requirements. However, Roulstone (1999) found that market risk disclosures lack quality and clarity in terms of a lack of information on market risk assessment methods and management actions, and companies do not fully comply with disclosure requirements. Roulstone (1999) examined market RI quality in the narrow sense as discussed below.

In the UK, there has also been a considerable amount of professional body CRD literature published in the late 1990s and early 2000s, particularly by the Institute of Chartered Accountants in England and Wales (ICAEW) which has highlighted the benefits of CRD to investors and companies. These early ICAEW reports (ICAEW, 1997, 1999, 2002) were primarily seeking to encourage companies to provide more useful RI.

In 2000, Linsley and Shrives published an article in the Journal of Risk. This article is not a study of risk disclosures but provides a critical discussion in respect of the ICAEW (1997) proposals. Linsley and Shrives (2000) set out the benefits of reporting on risk, discuss potential problems associated with the ICAEW proposal that listed companies provide a "Statement of Business Risk" in their annual report (AR) and briefly discuss four theories (agency, signalling, political costs and legitimacy theory) that might explain why companies would voluntarily provide such a statement. Although this article does not study specific risk disclosures, it is of note that, by drawing on the ICAEW (1997) report, it reiterates a key argument that has subsequently become a central tenet in CRD research. This argument, which is rarely examined in any depth, is that it is essential that companies provide RI in the AR as it enables the reader to make an assessment of how these risks might impact on the company's future performance.

The two further ICAEW reports (1999, 2002) again highlight the importance of RR and encourage companies to provide more disclosures regarding their principal risks and to explain how the principal risks are being managed and mitigated. In these early reports, the ICAEW emphasises a belief that better RR leads to lower cost of equity capital, which is supported by the findings of Heinle and Smith (2017), and also highlights the importance of CRD to investors in assessing a company's RE and predicting its future cash flows as well as holding managers to account for their RM practices. However, Kothari, Li and Short (2009) demonstrate that positive RI contributes to lower cost of capital whereas negative RI is associated with a higher cost of capital.

## 4.3 The two foundational CRD studies

Beretta and Bozzolan (2004a) and Linsley and Shrives (2006) are the first two academic studies to examine CRD in a comprehensive manner. Both studies examine some attributes and determinants of RR in the annual reports of non-financial companies in Italy and the UK, respectively, using the content analysis method to identify and measure risk disclosures by counting the number of risk sentences. To identify the risk sentences, the two studies also adopt a broad definition of risk either implicitly (Beretta and Bozzolan, 2004a) or explicitly (Linsley and Shrives, 2006) that encompasses both downside risks (threats) and upside risks (opportunities). The majority of the prior studies also adopted the broad definition of risk following the two foundational studies. However, more recently, Ibrahim and Hussainey (2019) strongly argue that risk should be defined solely in terms of its negative impacts.

The two studies investigate the association between CRD and a number of company-specific characteristics including company size, industry type and company level of risk. Beretta and Bozzolan (2004a) find that there is a lack of forward-looking RI in the Management's Discussion and Analysis (MD&A) section of the AR of Italian listed companies which is contradictory to the findings of Linsley and Shrives (2006). Beretta and Bozzolan (2004a) also indicate that company size and industry sector have no impact on the amount of RI disclosed, while Linsley and Shrives (2006) report the result that the quantity of CRD is positively associated with company size. Linsley and Shrives (2006) also find that RR in the UK AR sample is predominantly qualitative, and they conclude that current CRD practices are insufficient to meet information users' needs.

Although Beretta and Bozzolan (2004a) claim to be measuring quality through a proposed model, they are not actually doing so. They only examine certain attributes of RI, including the types of risk disclosed, the tone of CRD (good, bad or neutral information), quantification of CRD (monetary *vs* non-monetary information) and time orientation of RI (past *vs* future) and RM actions in place. They then attempt to measure the quality of risk disclosures based on the quantity of RI and the richness of information content. They refer to the richness of information content as the "semantic properties" of information disclosed and propose a four-dimensional framework that takes into account the risk factors (risk categories); the *economic sign* of the potential impacts (the tone of CRD; positive, negative or neutral), the measurement of potential impacts (monetary or non-monetary), and the *outlook orientation* (the management risk mitigation strategy). Then, they develop a measurement method for each of the four dimensions. However, the authors revert to using the number of CRD sentences to measure each of the above dimensions which contradicts their argument that they are measuring quality rather than quantity of CRD. Shevlin (2004) critiques the proposed model, stating "I could envision nearly every sentence in a company's

MD&A section ... as being concerned with some element of the above three categories and dimensions" (p. 299). Beretta and Bozzolan (2004b) also argue that CRD quality should be examined from information users' perspectives and based on their information needs.

The above two studies are highly cited in the RR literature and have greatly influenced subsequent CRD studies. Their subsequent influence is also evident in that these two studies have informed the research design and approach of the majority of subsequent studies. Thus, whereas these two studies paved the way for the evolution of the subsequent RR literature, they have, in some respects, lead to these later studies being constrained in how they approach researching CRD.

## 4.4 Mainstream CRD studies

Following Beretta and Bozzolan (2004a) and Linsley and Shrives (2006), CRD has grown as a topic of importance in accounting research and there is a burgeoning literature. While it is a distinct area of research, it is also allied to other types of disclosure studies within the accounting domain, including narrative disclosure studies. Existing research investigating RR practices and their potential determinants is more prevalent with respect to developed countries; however, there is also a growing body of research on CRD in emerging economies.

The primary research methodology adopted in the prior studies is content analysis to measure the amount of CRD by counting the number of sentences or words and to explore the characteristics of CRD. The approach to undertaking the content analysis is either manual (see, for example, Linsley and Shrives, 2006; Marzouk, 2016) or computerised/automated (see, for example, Elshandidy, Fraser and Hussainey, 2013, 2015; Elshandidy and Shrives, 2016; Hassanein and Elsayed, 2021). The manual approach is time consuming, but computerised textual analysis is problematic. Computerised textual analysis in CRD studies relies on searching for key words such as "risk", "risky" and "uncertainty" but there is a problem in knowing whether risk discussions have been fully identified. This is particularly so as "risk" is a difficult concept to define. Previous studies have attempted to identify the key characteristics of the RI or to identify any associations between the risk disclosures and a range of company-specific characteristics and corporate governance (CG) mechanisms (Abraham and Cox, 2007; Beretta and Bozzolan, 2004a; Elshandidy and Neri, 2015; Grassa, Moumen and Hussainey, 2021; Linsley and Shrives, 2006; Mokhtar and Mellett, 2013).

Typically, the types of characteristics being identified are whether the risk disclosures are (i) forward-looking or backward-looking, (ii) quantified (or monetary) or not, and (iii) providing good (or positive) news or bad (or negative) news. The rationale for examining these characteristics is that it is more useful if risk disclosures are forward-looking and quantified, and that managers may be inclined to provide more good news RI.

When looking to test for associations between amounts of CRD (often measured by the number of CRD sentences provided in the AR) and CG mechanisms, it is common to use some form of regression analysis. For example, a study might test for an association between the size of the board of directors and the amount of CRD. It can also be observed that studies of non-financial firms are more prevalent than studies of financial firms. This is likely to have arisen because of the difficulties inherent in analysing the risk disclosures of financial firms which are far more extensive and far more complex in such a heavily regulated industry. Therefore, it is understandable that some of these CRD studies of financial firms choose not to examine the entire set of risk disclosures but instead look at only one sub-set of risk disclosures; for example, Barakat and Hussainey (2013) examine operational risk disclosures.

The largest body of CRD research has been conducted in the UK and the USA. In some countries (USA, Germany, Italy and Finland), CRD has received more regulatory attention through the introduction of more detailed and specific CRD regulations. For example, US companies are required to disclose both quantitative and qualitative information on their RE within the form 10-K as Risk Factors under Item 1A. Likewise, the German Accounting Standard (GAS) 5 was introduced in 2001 to address CRD, and was then replaced by GAS 20 that requires companies to provide quantitative RI.

However, there has been an increasing interest in CRD in both developed and emerging countries. There have been an increasing number of studies that examine RR practices and determinants, particularly in Asian countries. Examples include Japan (Kim and Yasuda, 2018; Fukukawa and Kim, 2017; Konishi and Ali, 2007), China (Tan, Zeng and Elshandidy, 2017), Indonesia (Achmad, Faisal and Oktarina, 2017; Aryani and Hussainey, 2017), Malaysia (Amran, Bin and Hassan, 2009; Arshad and Ismail, 2011; Othman and Ameer, 2009; Zadeh and Eskandari, 2012a, 2012b), Hong Kong (Chan and Welford, 2005; Tong, 2013), United Arab Emirates (UAE) (ElKelish and Hassan, 2014; Halbouni and Yasin, 2016; Hassan, 2009, 2011, 2014; Uddin and Hassan, 2011), Saudi Arabia (Al-Maghzom, Hussainey and Aly, 2016a, 2016b; Alzead and Hussainey, 2017; Ibrahim, Habbash and Hussainey, 2019), Qatar (Elgammal, Hussainey and Ahmed, 2018), Kuwait (Al-Shammari, 2014), Bahrain (Mousa and Elamir (2013, 2014) and Jordan (Alshirah, Alshira'h and Lutfi, 2021; Tahat, 2014).

Other studies have been undertaken in other economies, including Australia and countries in Europe and Africa. For example, Australia (Buckby, Gallery and Ma, 2015; Carlon, Loftus and Miller, 2003; Taylor, Tower and Neilson, 2009; Zhang et al., 2013), France (Combes-Thue´lin, Henneron and Touron, 2006), the Netherlands (Deumes, 2008), Sweden (Jankensgård, Hoffmann and Rahmat, 2014), Belgium (Vandemaele, Vergauwen and Michiels, 2009), Switzerland (Hunziker, 2013), Bosnia and Herzegovina (Grbavac, Klepić and Papac, 2015), Poland (Wieczorek-Kosmala, Błach and Gorczyńska, 2014), Egypt (Khalil and Maghraby, 2017; Marzouk, 2016; Mokhtar and Mellett, 2013), Tunisia (Hemrit and Ben Arab, 2011; Salem, Ayadi and Hussainey, 2019, 2020; Salem and Hussainey, 2021), Malawi (Tauringana and Chithambo, 2016) and South Africa (Elshandidy, Elmassri and Elsayed, 2021; Ntim, Lindop and Thomas, 2013).

## 4.5 Professional body reports

It was stated earlier that the ICAEW published a series of CRD reports in the late 1990s and early 2000s. In addition, the ICAEW published another report in 2011, reiterating its demands for better RR, particularly following the 2007–8 financial crisis. The report emphasises a number of challenges of CRD, including the inherent uncertainty and subjectivity of risk assessment, the costs companies may incur as a result of RR and superficial compliance by companies that are not providing informative CRD. The report also suggests seven general principles for companies to enhance their RR, including identifying and meeting users' needs, disclosing more quantitative and forward-looking RI, linking CRD with other corporate disclosures and the business model, disclosing up-to-date RI through other disclosure channels such as corporate websites, focusing on principal risks, highlighting ongoing risks and issues and discussing their risk experience in terms of the difference between the expected risks and their impact and the actual ones.

The ICAEW (2011) report argues that, although it may not be possible for a company's CRD to be perfect, it can be improved, and it underlines the need for research on CRD that takes into account the information needs of users. The report is comprehensive in its discussions of CRD, and it is valuable in providing some detail. The report also implicitly refers to providing timely RI, considering the changing nature of some risks and whether reporting risk-related information on corporate websites might be more appropriate because of the lack of timeliness of annual reports. The report also highlights a number of aspects related to the presentation of RI. First, reporting on risks in the context of other corporate information related to the company's operations, business model and prospects is suggested as this should give a clear picture of the risks a company is exposed to. The report demonstrates that risk is inherent in a company business model and strategy and needs to be understood in this context. Thus, it recommends that understanding the company's business model is essential for assessing its RE. Accordingly, in this report, the ICAEW does not seem to give exactly the same support for a separate statement for RR as previously suggested in 1997. Second, it favours a short list of risks in order to make it easy for investors to understand and focus their attention on key risks, an approach which is consistent with Lee's (2012) suggestion to rank risks and disclose the top five ranked ones. Finally, reporting on the RM process during the past year and discussing the successes and failures during this period is a possible way of improving CRD, a suggestion supported by Ryan (2012).

The Association of Chartered Certified Accountants (ACCA) also issued a number of reports addressing RR either implicitly (Campbell and Slack, 2008; Slack and Campbell, 2016) or explicitly (Souabni, 2011; ACCA, 2014). The report of Campbell and Slack (2008) does not look directly at CRD but focuses instead on voluntary narrative reporting in the AR in general. However, it includes some discussion of RR. Nineteen semi-structured interviews with investment analysts specialising in the banking industry are used to investigate the usefulness of narrative reporting for their decision-making. The report reveals that CRD was perceived by the interviewees to be generic/boilerplate, which hinders its usefulness. In another ACCA report, Souabni (2011) conducted a cross-country study to examine RR practices of companies across seven countries, jurisdictions and industry sectors. The key finding is that CRD practices vary across the different jurisdictions due to disclosure regulations and voluntary guidelines adopted in each country.

More recently and more significantly, ACCA published another report on CRD in 2014. The report addresses a number of aspects of CRD from the perspective of investors, regulators and annual report preparers through a series of interviews to identify users' needs, companies' concerns and challenges to higher CRD quality. The report demonstrates the importance of RR and calls for better CRD as it recognises a key limitation of current CRD relating to the disclosure of generic and boilerplate RI where companies are concerned about the commercial sensitivity of information and the potential loss of competitive advantage. The findings also underline users' RI needs in terms of explaining principal risks in plain English and how they are being assessed and re-assessed.

In addition, the Institute of Chartered Accountants of Scotland (ICAS) published a report which explores some facets of RR, including the relevance of different disclosure channels, the influence of regulations on CRD practices, the RI currently being disclosed in annual reports, the relevance of CRD to investment analysts and managerial discretion over whether to reveal or withhold RI through conducting a number of interviews with investment analysts and AR preparers (Abraham, Marston and Darby, 2012). The interview questions were broad and did not directly investigate CRD quality attributes. The findings reveal that private meetings with management is a significant source of a company's RE, on which investment analysts place more importance than annual reports. The report indicates that managers are constrained by the sensitivity of information that competitors may exploit and show that another disincentive for RR is related to senior managers' personal interests and preferences. The report also examines CRD practices of some UK listed companies in the food and beverage sector, applying the same method used in the mainstream literature, namely content analysis to count the number of risk-related sentences. The report argues that CRD quantity has improved over time, yet it questions its usefulness. The results show that CRD is predominantly boilerplate and companies provide more qualitative and less forward-looking RI.

The Association of Insurance and Risk Managers in Industry and Commerce (Airmic) and the Institute of Chartered Secretaries and Administrators (ICSA) produced a joint report on RR (Airmic, 2013). The report analyses the risk disclosures made by a sample of UK companies across eight industry sectors to highlight examples of higher quality CRD which other companies can follow as a best practice. The report uses five criteria to assess CRD practices: risk agenda, risk assessment, risk response, risk communication and risk governance. The results demonstrate significant variations in CRD practices across companies and sectors. The report also emphasises the benefits that companies can obtain from better RR including, among others, providing assurance to investors and enhancing their confidence, and improving organisational resilience.

The most recent report was jointly commissioned by the Association of Chartered Certified Accountants (ACCA), the International Integrated Reporting Council (IIRC) and the International Association for Accounting Education and Research (IAAER) (Slack and Campbell, 2016). The report addresses RR implicitly as it specifically investigates integrated reporting. The report explores the views of investment analysts and capital providers, such as investment bankers, on the relevance of integrated reporting and its perceived benefit in terms of decision-usefulness. The findings conclude that CRD is generic in nature which confirms the findings of other professional reports. The report also refers to the lack of forward-looking information and the lack of linkage between the different types of narrative disclosure, including RR, business model and strategy.

The above reports are primarily concerned with analysing current RR practices and the perception of information users of its relevance but do not directly address CRD quality. Although, unlike previous CRD studies, some of these reports investigate CRD from the perspective of information users, they predominantly focus on investment analysts as a user group as these are (supposedly) experts in analysing a company's performance and RE. Typically, these reports only provide some general principles and guidelines for improving CRD quality/usefulness. There is also a lack of research investigating the challenges to RR from the perspective of AR preparers.

## 4.6 Research gap and implications for future research

According to the FASB (2010), the ultimate purpose of corporate reporting is to enhance investors' ability to make informed decisions by providing useful information. This is of importance in the context of CRD as it should also be the purpose of RR that it satisfies this criterion of decision-usefulness, which arguably may be the prime indicator of the quality of CRD provided in an AR. Therefore, useful RI should help information users assess a company's risk profile and prospects.

However, defining and assessing CRD quality/usefulness is problematic. This could be one reason why previous studies have focused on counting risk sentences or words. Shrives and Brennan (2015) state that "quality of reporting is difficult to determine but that does not undermine its importance" (p. 98). Likewise, different information users have different interests in the company and hence different information needs. However, Beretta and Bozzolan (2004a) rightly argue that CRD quantity cannot be used as a proxy for quality. Information quality is not solely about how much a company discloses, but also about the informativeness of disclosures to the users of information. This implies that characteristics of information quality, such as relevance, accuracy, completeness, comparability and timeliness, are pertinent to assessing the quality of CRD.

It could be argued that some previous studies which have focused on examining the quantity of CRD have also addressed quality/usefulness but only to a limited extent (for example, Beretta and Bozzolan, 2004a; Dobler, Lajili and Zeghal, 2011; Linsley and Shrives, 2006). These studies examine some specific attributes of CRD, particularly the disclosure of quantitative and forward-looking RI and

CRD tone in terms of disclosing downside risks (bad news) and upside risk (good news) (for example, Elshandidy and Zeng, 2021). Cabedo and Tirado (2004) argue that reporting quantitative RI should enhance usefulness of CRD and help information users assess the company's profitability and RE. These three aspects do not necessarily reflect the quality of RI disclosed. Similarly, the ICAEW (1999) underlines the importance of disclosing forward-looking and quantified RI for improving CRD quality. The ICAEW (1999) also recommends providing information on the types of risks, risk assessment methods and RM actions.

On the contrary, Lee (2012) states that "numbers are simply not enough" (p.325) and highlights the importance of discussing a company's RI in qualitative terms, in addition to providing quantitative RI, to explain the significance of numbers, enhance understandability and boost investors' confidence. Furthermore, Lee (2012) claims that investors greatly appreciate qualitative information.

FASB (2010) emphasises the significance of the concept of "usefulness" in corporate reporting, stating that "usefulness in making decisions is the objective of financial reporting" (p.12). Therefore, CRD should be deemed useful and of good quality if it meets the decision-making needs of information users. Previous studies and professional reports have raised major concerns about the quality/usefulness of CRD as discussed above. For example, Linsley and Lawrence (2007) call for improving clarity and readability of CRD to enhance its informativeness to information users, rather than just increasing the quantity of RI provided.

However, none of the previous studies seem to have investigated in depth the attributes of high-quality RI and neither have they sought to employ the qualitative characteristics set by the FASB including relevance, faithful representation, comparability, verifiability, timeliness and understandability. Previous CRD studies that attempt to address CRD quality and usefulness, including, for example, Mousa and Elamir (2014) and Maffei et al. (2014), apply the same research method. That method is content analysis and the number of CRD sentences or words are counted, which is the method used in the majority of previous CRD studies as discussed above, and the result is that their assessment of CRD quality ultimately rests on the number of sentences or words. Other studies use a CRD index that examines the existence of particular RI, regardless of its quality and usefulness (Hassan, 2009; Uddin and Hassan, 2011).

Although CRD quantity is not a valid and comprehensive proxy for its quality, it can still be regarded as an aspect of quality. Shrives and Brennan (2015) argue that the amount of disclosure is an aspect of quality because it reflects the time and effort spent on producing and providing this information. Therefore, it could be argued that investors may appreciate the quantity of RI disclosed. Moreover, Miihkinen (2012) finds a positive association between CRD quantity and quality. Nevertheless, CRD quantity should not be the only or the key indicator of quality and other qualitative characteristics should be taken into account.

Previous studies have also addressed other aspects of CRD quality and usefulness. For example, Ryan (2012) suggests that companies use a tabular format to present RI and disclose their risk experience and changes in their RE and their RM plans. However, he also argues that information users should not have high expectations for CRD, acknowledging the complexities of risk and risk assessment. Linsley and Shrives (2000) note that companies should give particular attention to risk identification and ranking in terms of their impact on company performance and likelihood of occurrence when providing RI, although Abraham, Marston and Darby (2012) indicate that companies do not rank the risks they are exposed to and support the provision of a separate statement for CRD. Breen, Clearfield and Klimczak (2011) advocate a stand-alone statement for RR and highlight that RM actions and practices, including risk assessment, have developed after the financial crisis, which in turn should be reflected in CRD practices and accompanied by improvements in the quality and informativeness of RI released by companies.

Although the vast majority of previous CRD studies have focused on examining the quantity of risk disclosures, Beretta and Bozzolan (2004a) indicate that more attention has to be paid to the quality of RI. Dobler (2005) also emphasises the lack of research conducted to address the usefulness of risk disclosures. Furthermore, Linsley and Lawrence (2007) argue that increased risk disclosure is not a guarantee of high-quality or useful RI unless it is presented in a clear and readable manner, which is also considered one aspect of understandability (FASB, 2010). Yet, there is little empirical or theoretical work that has addressed RR quality and usefulness. Prior literature has also focused on explaining the lack of CRD instead of suggesting a way forward for improving CRD quality.

One major aspect of CRD quality that previous studies seem not to have considered is the needs of information users and their views on the usefulness of RI disclosed by companies. Botosan (2004) and Beretta and Bozzolan (2004b) argue that CRD quality should be investigated from the perspectives of information users. Greco (2012) also recommends that companies should attempt to identify and meet the information needs of users. It can be argued that RI is of good quality and useful to investors if it enables them to make informed decisions. Likewise, understanding information users' views on CRD practices and quality can provide a better understanding of their information needs and expectations.

Furthermore, Abraham and Shrives (2014) highlight the role of different stakeholders, namely information users, AR preparers, regulators and auditors, in improving CRD quality. Similarly, Breen, Clearfield and Klimczak (2011) and the International Corporate Governance Network (ICGN) (2010) encourage companies to engage stakeholders and investors in particular in CRD and RM. Moreover, Mokhtar and Mellett (2013) underline the critical role external auditors can play in assuring RR quality and find that companies audited by large auditing firms tend to comply with CRD requirements. It is also important to consider managers' perspectives on CRD and their incentives and disincentives to disclose RI. Botosan (2004) also underlines the importance of identifying the information needs of different user groups for measuring disclosure characteristics, particularly understandability and relevance.

One potential argument is that CRD should be primarily intended for investors and, if this argument is accepted, CRD quality should be investigated from their perspectives in terms of its relevance to making informed decisions. Jonas and Blanchet (2000) state that "as the customers of financial reporting, the users should define reporting quality" (p. 358). The ICAEW (2011) also emphasises that companies should identify and meet users' RI needs to help them properly assess a company's RE and profile.

Considering the limitations of current CRD practices discussed above, there is also a need for understanding managers' concerns about disclosing RI and how to mitigate these concerns. Other stakeholders including regulators and auditors can also play a key role in improving CRD quality and hence their views should be considered.

The research gap can be addressed in two main ways. First, the limitations within the research methods used in prior CRD studies need to be acknowledged. The majority of previous studies use CRD quantity as a proxy for quality and this needs to be taken into account when considering the results and conclusions of these types of studies. For example, Elshandidy and Shrives (2016) examine the impact of CRD on stock market liquidity and investors' perceived risk measured by the volatility of market returns to assess the usefulness of RI, using the number of risk sentences and CRD tone based on key words. However, it may be extremely difficult to attribute the volatility of market return or share prices to the disclosure of particular information.

Second, in terms of research methodology, there is a need to move away from the approach of previous CRD studies and to find alternative methodologies besides approaches using content analysis or a disclosure index to examine RR practices. For example, there have been very few studies that have examined stakeholders' perspectives on CRD directly through conducting interviews with relevant stakeholders. Azim and Nahar (2021) is an example of this type of study. They investigate the CRD practices and driving factors of government-owned banks in Bangladesh, engaging in interviews with regulators and with managers in the banks. In an unpublished study, Abraham, Marston and Slack (2014) adopt an interview-based approach to investigate only one aspect of CRD, namely the usefulness of RI from the perspective of one stakeholder group of institutional investors/investment analysts. Another example of an alternative approach is Solomon et al. (2000) who use a survey questionnaire aimed at probing the views of UK investment analysts/institutional investors on existing RR practices in terms of their level and relevance to their decision-making and indicate that RI provided by companies is inadequate. However, they do not directly examine CRD quality and its characteristics. Additionally, a survey questionnaire cannot fully capture the different aspects of CRD quality or enable researchers to investigate it in more depth and detail, and they focus on only one stakeholder group. There are other research methodologies which might usefully be employed to investigate CRD. Focus groups could be utilised as an alternative to individual interviews. Another example of a possible approach is to conduct linguistic analyses which might be used to investigate how risks and risk management strategies are being communicated. As risk is such a complex concept, then understanding how companies can be more effective in CRD communications would be valuable.

Some professional reports discussed above have also used a qualitative approach to explore the views of stakeholders on RR practices through interviews. Despite the limitations of these reports, they have attempted, to some extent, to develop an understanding of current CRD practices and the perceived relevance and benefits of RI, and to provide some suggestions for improving CRD quality, which is missing in the existing CRD literature. However, they also focus on particular stakeholder groups (investment analysts) and do not fully examine CRD quality.

Therefore, it is important to examine CRD quality in a more comprehensive manner. This importance stems from the concerns raised about the quality and usefulness of RI provided by companies, as discussed above. Although some studies find that CRD has improved over time, particularly in terms of the quantity of RI (Deumes, 2008; Haddad and Alali, 2021; Ibrahim and Hussainey, 2019; Konishi and Ali, 2007; Neri, 2010; Leopizzi et al., 2020; Rajab and Handley-Schachler, 2009), others have raised concerns about the quality and informativeness of risk disclosures provided to information users (Beretta and Bozzolan, 2004a; Dobler, 2008; Lajili and Zeghal, 2005). Likewise, some studies have argued that the current CRD is insufficient and vague RI is provided by companies (Linsley and Shrives, 2005; Linsley and Shrives, 2006). Likewise, Linsley and Lawrence (2007) have investigated the readability of CRD and find a low level of CRD readability implying that RI is difficult to read.

In addition, previous studies and professional reports emphasise the benefits of better CRD for companies and investors. Some previous studies also address the problems and costs associated with non-disclosure to encourage companies to voluntarily disclose more RI. Cabedo and Tirado (2004), though they focus on CRD quantity, point out that the lack of CRD hinders investors' ability to make better decisions. Dobler (2008) also argues that managers could use RR, considering the discretion inherent in CRD, as a tool for RM through influencing information users' decisions, behaviours and reactions. Furthermore, Miihkinen (2013) suggests that higher CRD quality leads to lower information asymmetry.

The characteristics of useful information have already been developed by regulatory bodies, such as the FASB and IASB, but these characteristics should be carefully defined and operationalised in the context of CRD to meet users' information needs, considering the nature of risk. Generally, CRD quality depends on a number of factors, including the information needs of users, the nature of risk, company-specific characteristics, the regulatory framework and managerial incentives for CRD.

Previous CRD literature has focused on examining the relationship between CRD quantity and company-specific characteristics, and other studies have examined the impact of CG mechanisms on CRD practices as discussed above (e.g. Elshandidy, Neri and Guo, 2018; Grassa, Moumen and Hussainey, 2021; Hao and Dong, 2022; Hassanein and Elsayed, 2021; Salem, Ayadi and Hussainey, 2019; Saggar, Arora and Singh, 2021; Seebeck and Vetter, 2021). However, these factors may not necessarily reflect CRD practices and behaviours, considering the subjectivity in measuring CRD quantity.

It could be argued that organisational and managerial incentives and disincentives play a key role in determining the level and quality of CRD. This study analyses factors related to managers' CRD decisions that may be difficult to investigate quantitatively. Understanding the factors influencing CRD behaviours could help to explain existing CRD practices and suggest a way forward for improving CRD quality. CRD incentives and disincentives depend largely on managers' perception of risk and RM approach.

CRD incentives and disincentives are related to the perceived benefits and consequences of CRD. Hence, managers will always consider the costs and benefits, organisational and personal, associated with CRD. Interestingly, some of these factors can be both an incentive and a disincentive at the same time, including investor reaction. Investors could react unfavourably and/or irrationally to the disclosure of downside or upside risks. Generally, the role of incentives and disincentives depends on different factors. For example, Abraham, Marston and Darby (2012) address directors' concerns about personal liability for the disclosure of downside risks in particular. Managers may exercise their discretion over the amount, type and timing of RI to report publicly considering the nature of CRD. CRD is a contentious area where disclosure and non-disclosure could have unfavourable consequences.

## 4.7 Conclusion

CRD has gained increasing attention from academics as well as professional and regulatory bodies particularly in developed and highly regulated countries. There has been a particular emphasis on examining CRD practices of non-financial companies. Financial companies are seen to be more complex in terms of the nature of their business activities, the type of risks they face, the regulations they are subject to and the risk disclosures they provide.

Previous studies have predominantly focused on investigating CRD quantity and its determinants. Prior studies generally highlight the lack of RR quality in terms of disclosing vague and generic RI and the lack of quantitative and forward-looking RI. Likewise, prior studies that find an increasing trend in CRD quantity demonstrate that companies provide poor quality RI. Therefore, it is surprising that empirical work has, to date, not fully addressed CRD quality. A major limitation of the prior literature is overlooking the views of information users, annual report preparers and other stakeholders on CRD quality and the incentives and disincentives for RR.

There are a number of motives behind investigating CRD quality. First, there is a dearth of research on CRD quality that has arisen as most previous studies have focused on examining the quantity rather than the quality of risk disclosures. Moreover, CRD quality has not been adequately addressed in the current literature. Second, prior CRD studies have continually raised concerns about the relevance and usefulness of RI to information users and, therefore, it is important to undertake a research project which is wholly focused on CRD quality. Third, the particular importance of providing high-quality RI to stakeholders (e.g., investors), companies, the capital market and the economy has been emphasised in many studies and professional reports. Investigating CRD quality is challenging and complex but having greater understanding of what constitutes quality in the context of CRD can potentially lead to improved CRD practices.

## References

Abdelghany, K. (2005). Disclosure of market risk or accounting measures of risk: An empirical study. *Managerial Auditing Journal*, 20(8), 867–875.

Abraham, S. and Cox, P. (2007). Analysing the determinants of narrative risk information in UK FTSE 100 annual reports. *The British Accounting Review*, 39(3), 227–248.

Abraham, S., Marston, C. and Darby, P. (2012). *Risk reporting: Clarity, relevance and location*. Edinburgh: Institute of Chartered Accountants of Scotland.

Abraham, S., Marston, C. and Slack, R. (2014). Annual report business risk factor statements: Views of UK institutional investors. Unpublished paper presented at 'Multiple perspectives on risk management'. 6th European Risk Conference. 4–5 September 2014. Napoli.

Abraham, S. and Shrives, P. (2014). Improving the relevance of risk factor disclosure in corporate annual reports. *The British Accounting Review*, 46(1), 91–107.

Achmad, T., Faisal, F. and Oktarina, M. (2017). Factors influencing voluntary corporate risk disclosure practices by Indonesian companies. *Corporate Ownership & Control*, 14(3–2), 286–292.

Albitar, K., Al-shaer, H. and Elmarzouky, M. (2021). Do assurance and assurance providers enhance COVID-related disclosures in CSR reports? An examination in the UK context. *International Journal of Accounting & Information Management*, 29(3), 410–428.

Al-Maghzom, A., Hussainey, K. and Aly, D. (2016a). The level of risk disclosure in listed banks: Evidence from Saudi Arabia. *Corporate Ownership & Control*, 14(1–1), 175–194.

Al-Maghzom, A., Hussainey, K. and Aly, D. (2016b). Corporate governance and risk disclosure: Evidence from Saudi Arabia. *Corporate Ownership & Control*, 13(2), 145–166.

Al-Shammari, B. (2014). Kuwait corporate characteristics and level of risk disclosure: A content analysis approach. *Journal of Contemporary Issues in Business Research*, 3(3), 128–153.

Alzead, R. and Hussainey, K. (2017). Risk disclosure practice in Saudi non-financial listed companies. *Corporate Ownership & Control*, 14(4–1), 293–298.

Amran, A., Bin, A. and Hassan, B. (2009). Risk reporting: An exploratory study on risk management disclosure in Malaysian annual reports. *Managerial Auditing Journal*, 24(1), 39–57.

Arshad, R. and Ismail, F. (2011). Discretionary risk disclosure: A management perspective. *Asian Journal of Accounting and Governance*, 2, 67–77.

Aryani, D. and Hussainey, K. (2017). The determinants of risk disclosure in the Indonesian non-listed banks. *International Journal of Trade and Global Markets*, 10(1), 58–66.

Association of Chartered Certified Accountants. (2014). *Reporting risk*. London: Association of Chartered Certified Accountants.

Association of Insurance and Risk Managers in Industry and Commerce. (2013). *Risk reporting review of risk reporting by selected FTSE350 companies and commentary on the relevance and benefits of detailed risk disclosure*. London: Association of Insurance and Risk Managers in Industry and Commerce.

Azim, M. and Nahar, S. (2021). Risk disclosure practices: Does institutional imperative matter? *Public Money & Management*. In press.

Barakat, A. and Hussainey, K. (2013). Bank governance, regulation, supervision, and risk reporting: Evidence from operational risk disclosures in European banks. *International Review of Financial Analysis*, 30, 254–273.

Beretta, S. and Bozzolan, S. (2004a). A framework for the analysis of firm risk communication. *The International Journal of Accounting*, 39(3), 265–288.

Beretta, S. and Bozzolan, S. (2004b). Reply to: Discussion of a framework for the analysis of firm risk communication. *The International Journal of Accounting*, 39(3), 303–305.

Blankley, A., Lamb, R. and Schroeder, R. (2002). The disclosure of information on market risk: Evidence from the Dow 30. *Managerial Auditing Journal*, 17(8), 438–451.

Botosan, C. (2004). Discussion of a framework for the analysis of risk communication. *The International Journal of Accounting*, 39(3), 289–295.

Breen, E., Clearfield, A. and Klimczak, K. (2011). ICGN corporate risk oversight guidelines: The role of the board and institutional shareholders. [Online]. SSRN. Available at: http://ssrn.com/abstract=1963358 [Accessed 10 March 2015].

Buckby, S., Gallery, G. and Ma, J. (2015). An analysis of risk management disclosures: Australian evidence. *Managerial Auditing Journal*, 30(8/9), 812–869.

Cabedo, J. and Tirado, J. (2004). The disclosure of risk in financial statements. *Accounting Forum*, 28(2), 181–200.

Campbell, D. and Slack, R. (2008). *Narrative reporting: Analysts' perceptions of its value and relevance*. London: Association of Chartered Certified Accountants.

Carlon, S., Loftus, J. and Miller, M. (2003). The challenge of risk reporting: Regulatory and corporate reponses. *Australian Accounting Review*, 13(3), 36–51.

Chan, J. and Welford, R. (2005). Assessing corporate environmental risk in China: An evaluation of reporting activities of Hong Kong listed enterprises. *Corporate Social Responsibility and Environmental Management*, 12(2), 88–104.

Combes-Thuélin, E., Henneron, S. and Touron, P. (2006). Risk regulations and financial disclosure: An investigation based on corporate communication in French traded companies. *Corporate Communications: An International Journal*, 11(3), 303–326.

Deumes, R. (2008). Corporate risk reporting: A content analysis of narrative risk disclosures in prospectuses. *Journal of Business Communication*, 45(2), 120–157.

Dobler, M. (2005). How informative is risk reporting? A review of disclosure models. [Online]. SSRN. Available at http://papers.ssrn.com/sol3/papers.cfm?abstract_id =640522&download=yes [Accessed 7 November 2012].

Dobler, M. (2008). Incentives for risk reporting – A discretionary disclosure and cheap talk approach. *The International Journal of Accounting*, 43(2), 184–206.

Dobler, M., Lajili, K. and Zéghal, D. (2011). Attributes of corporate risk disclosure: An international investigation in the manufacturing sector. *Journal of International Accounting Research*, 10(2), 1–22.

Elgammal, M., Hussainey, K. and Ahmed, F. (2018). Corporate governance and voluntary risk and forward-looking disclosures. *Journal of Applied Accounting Research*, 19(4), 592–607.

ElKelish, W. and Hassan, M. (2014). Organizational culture and corporate risk disclosure: An empirical investigation for United Arab Emirates listed companies. *International Journal of Commerce and Management*, 24(4), 279–299.

Elshandidy, T., Elmassri, M. and Elsayed, M. (2021). Integrated reporting, textual risk disclosure, and market value. *Corporate Governance*, 22(1), 173–193.

Elshandidy, T., Fraser, I. and Hussainey, K. (2013). Aggregated, voluntary, and mandatory risk disclosure incentives: Evidence from UK FTSE all-share companies. *International Review of Financial Analysis*, 30, 320–333.

Elshandidy, T., Fraser, I. and Hussainey, K. (2015). What drives mandatory and voluntary risk reporting variations across Germany, UK and US? *The British Accounting Review*, 47(4), 376–394.

Elshandidy, T. and Neri, L. (2015). Corporate governance, risk disclosure practices, and market liquidity: Comparative evidence from the UK and Italy. *Corporate Governance: An International Review*, 23(4), 331–356.

Elshandidy, T., Neri, L., and Guo, Y. (2018). Determinants and impacts of risk disclosure quality: Evidence from China. *Journal of Applied Accounting Research*, 19(4), 518–536.

Elshandidy, T. and Shrives, P. (2016). Environmental incentives for and usefulness of textual risk reporting: Evidence from Germany. *The International Journal of Accounting*, 51(4), 464–486.

Elshandidy, T. and Zeng, C. (2021). The value relevance of risk-related disclosure: Does the tone of disclosure matter? *Borsa Istanbul Review*, 22(3), 498–514.

Financial Accounting Standards Board (FASB). (2010). *Statement of financial accounting concepts no. 8, conceptual framework for financial reporting: Chapter 1, the objective of general purpose financial reporting, and chapter 3, qualitative characteristics of useful financial information (a replacement of FASB concepts statements no. 1 and no. 2).* Norwalk, CT: FASB.

Fukukawa, H. and Kim, H. (2017). Effects of audit partners on clients' business risk disclosure. *Accounting and Business Research*, 47(7), 780–809.

German Accounting Standard (GAS 20). (2012). *Group management report.* Berlin: Accounting Standards Committee of Germany (ASCG).

Grbavac, J., Klepić, Z. and Papac, N. (2015). Corporate risk reporting in Bosnia and Herzegovina. *Journal of International Scientific Publications*, 9(1), 411–421.

Grassa, R., Moumen, N. and Hussainey, K. (2021). What drives risk disclosure in Islamic and conventional banks? An international comparison. *International Journal of Finance and Economics*, 26(4), 6338–6361.

Greco, G. (2012). The management's reaction to new mandatory risk disclosure: A longitudinal study on Italian listed companies. *Corporate Communications: An International Journal*, 17(2), 113–137.

Haddad, A. and Alali, H. (2021). Risk disclosure and financial performance: The case of Islamic and conventional banks in the GCC. *Journal of Islamic Accounting and Business Research*, In press.

Hao, Y. and Dong, B. (2022). Determinants and consequences of risk disclosure: Evidence from Chinese stock markets during the COVID-19 pandemic. *Emerging Markets Finance and Trade*, 58(1), 35–55.

Halbouni, S. and Yasin, A. (2016). Risk disclosure: Empirical investigation of UAE companies' compliance with international accounting standards. *International Journal of Business and Management*, 11(8), 134–144.

Hassan, M. (2009). UAE corporations-specific characteristics and level of risk disclosure. *Managerial Auditing Journal*, 24(7), 668–687.

Hassan, M. (2011). Risk regulations and disclosure in the United Arab Emirates: An institutional theory analysis. *Corporate Ownership & Control*, 8(4), 514–526.

Hassan, M. (2014). Risk narrative disclosure strategies to enhance organizational legitimacy: Evidence from UAE financial institutions. *International Journal of Disclosure and Governance*, 11(1), 1–17.

Hassanein, A. and Elsayed, N. (2021). Voluntary risk disclosure and values of FTSE350 firms: The role of an industry-based litigation risk. *International Journal of Managerial and Financial Accounting*, 13(2), 110–132.

Heinle, M. and Smith, K. (2017). A theory of risk disclosure. *Review of Accounting Studies*, 22(4), 1459–1491.

Hemrit, W. and Ben Arab, M. (2011). The disclosure of operational risk in Tunisian insurance companies. *Journal of Operational Risk*, 6(2), 69–111.

Hunziker, S. (2013). The disclosure of market risk information under IFRS 7 evidence from swiss listed non-financial companies. [Online]. Available at: https://blog.hslu.ch /financialmanagement/files/2013/07/Paper-Internal-Control-Disclosure-and-Agency -Costs.pdf [Accessed 20 May 2014].

Ibrahim, A., Habbash, M. and Hussainey, K. (2019). Corporate governance and risk disclosure: Evidence from Saudi Arabia. *International Journal of Accounting, Auditing and Performance Evaluation (IJAAPE)*, 15(1), 89–111.

Ibrahim, A. and Hussainey, K. (2019). Developing the narrative risk disclosure measurement. *International Review of Financial Analysis*, 64, 126–144.

ICGN. (2010). ICGN corporate risk oversight guidelines. [Online]. ICGN. Available at https://www.icgn.org/sites/default/files/ICGN%20CRO%20Guidance%20%282010 %29_%20March%202013%20print.pdf [Accessed 20 September 2014].

Institute of Chartered Accountants in England and Wales. (1997). *Financial reporting of risk – Proposals for a statement of business risk.* London: Institute of Chartered Accountants in England and Wales.

Institute of Chartered Accountants in England and Wales. (1999). *No surprises – The case for better risk reporting.* London: Institute of Chartered Accountants in England and Wales.

Institute of Chartered Accountants in England and Wales. (2002). *No surprises: Working for better risk reporting.* London: Institute of Chartered Accountants in England and Wales.

Institute of Chartered Accountants in England and Wales. (2011). *Reporting business risks: Meeting expectations.* London: Institute of Chartered Accountants in England and Wales.

Jankensgård, H., Hoffmann, K. and Rahmat, D. (2014). Derivative usage, risk disclosure, and firm value. *Journal of Accounting and Finance*, 14(5), 159–174.

Jonas, G. and Blanchet, J. (2000). Assessing quality of financial reporting. *Accounting Horizons*, 14(3), 353–363.

Khalil, A., and Maghraby, M. (2017). The determinants of internet risk disclosure: empirical study of Egyptian listed companies. *Managerial Auditing Journal*, 32(8), 746–767.

Kim, H. and Yasuda, Y. (2018). Business risk disclosure and firm risk: Evidence from Japan. *Research in International Business and Finance*, 45, 413–426.

Konishi, N. and Ali, M. (2007). Risk reporting of Japanese companies and its association with corporate characteristics. *International Journal of Accounting, Auditing and Performance Evaluation*, 4(3), 263–285.

Kothari, S., Li, X. and Short, J. (2009). The effect of disclosures by management, analysts, and business press on cost of capital, return volatility, and analyst forecasts: A study using content analysis. *The Accounting Review*, 84(5), 1639–1670.

Lajili, K., Dobler, M., Zéghal, D. and Bryan, M. (2021). Risk reporting in financial crises: A tale of two countries. *International Journal of Accounting & Information Management*, 29(2), 181–216.

Lajili, K. and Zeghal, D. (2005). A content analysis of risk management disclosures in Canadian annual reports. *Canadian Journal of Administrative Sciences*, 22(2), 125–142.

Lee, P. (2012). Discussion of 'risk reporting quality: Implications of academic research for financial reporting policy' by Stephen G. Ryan (2012). *Accounting and Business Research*, 42(3), 325–327.

Leopizzi, R., Lazzi, A., Venturelli, A. and Principale, S. (2020). Nonfinancial risk disclosure: The "state of the art" of Italian companies. *Corporate Social Responsibility and Environmental Management*, 27(1), 358–368.

Linsley, P. and Lawrence, M. (2007). Risk reporting by the largest UK companies: Readability and lack of obfuscation. *Accounting, Auditing & Accountability Journal*, 20(4), 620–627.

Linsley, P. and Shrives, P. (2000). Risk management and reporting risk in the UK. *Journal of Risk*, 3(1), 115–129.

Linsley, P. and Shrives, P. (2005a). Examining risk reporting in UK public companies. *Journal of Risk Finance*, 6(4), 292–305.

Linsley, P. and Shrives, P. (2006). Risk reporting: A study of risk disclosures in the annual reports of UK companies. *The British Accounting Review*, 38(4), 387–404.

Linsmeier, T., Thornton, D., Venkatachalam, M. and Welker, M. (2002). The effect of mandated market risk disclosures on trading volume sensitivity to interest rate, exchange rate, and commodity price movements. *The Accounting Review*, 77(2), 343–377.

Maffei, M., Aria, M., Fiondella, C., Spanò, R. and Zagaria, C. (2014). (Un)useful risk disclosure: Explanations from the Italian banks. *Managerial Auditing Journal*, 29(7), 621–648.

Marzouk, M. (2016). Risk reporting during a crisis: Evidence from the Egyptian capital market. *Journal of Applied Accounting Research*, 17(4), 378–396.

Meier, H., Tomaszewski, S. and Tobing, R. (1995). Political risk assessment and disclosure in annual financial reports: The case of the Persian Gulf War. *Journal of International Accounting, Auditing and Taxation*, 4(1), 49–68.

Miihkinen, A. (2012). What drives quality of firm risk disclosure? The impact of a national disclosure standard and reporting incentives under IFRS. *The International Journal of Accounting*, 47(4), 437–468.

Miihkinen, A. (2013). The usefulness of firm risk disclosures under different firm riskiness, investor-interest, and market conditions: New evidence from Finland. *Advances in Accounting, Incorporating Advances in International Accounting*, 29, 312–331.

Mokhtar, E. and Mellett, H. (2013). Competition, corporate governance, ownership structure and risk reporting. *Managerial Auditing Journal*, 28(9), 838–865.

Mousa, G. and Elamir, E. (2013). Content analysis of corporate risk disclosures: The case of Bahraini capital market. *Global Review of Accounting and Finance*, 4(1), 1–27.

Mousa, G. and Elamir, E. (2014). The effect of governance mechanisms on the quality of risk disclosure: Using bootstrap techniques. *American Journal of Finance and Accounting*, 3(2/3/4), 128–151.

Neri, L. (2010). The informative capacity of risk disclosure: Evidence from Italian stock market. [Online]. SSRN. Available at: http://papers.ssrn.com/sol3/papers.cfm?abstract_id=1651504 [Accessed 25 November 2013].

Ntim, C., Lindop, S. and Thomas, D. (2013). Corporate governance and risk reporting in South Africa: A study of corporate risk disclosures in the pre- and post-2007/2008 global financial crisis periods. *International Review of Financial Analysis*, 30, 363–383.

Othman, R. and Ameer, R. (2009). Market risk disclosure: Evidence from Malaysian listed firms. *Journal of Financial Regulation and Compliance*, 17(1), 57–69.

Rajab, B. and Handley-Schachler, M. (2009). Corporate risk disclosure by UK firms: Trends and determinants. *World Review of Entrepreneurship, Management and Sustainable Development*, 5(3), 224–243.

Rajgopal, S. (1999). Early evidence on the informativeness of the SEC's market risk disclosures: The case of commodity price risk exposure of oil and gas producers. *The Accounting Review*, 74(3), 251–280.

Roulstone, D. (1999). Effect of SEC financial reporting release no. 48 on derivative and market risk disclosures. *Accounting Horizons*, 13(4), 343–363.

Ryan, S. (2012). Risk reporting quality: Implications of academic research for financial reporting policy. *Accounting and Business Research*, 42(3), 295–324.

Saggar, R., Arora, N. and Singh, B. (2021). Gender diversity in corporate boardrooms and risk disclosure: Indian evidence. *Gender in Management: An International Journal*, 37(2), 182–201.

Salem, I., Ayadi, S. and Hussainey, K. (2019). Corporate governance and risk disclosure quality: Tunisian evidence. *Journal of Accounting in Emerging Economies*, 9(4), 567–602.

Salem, I., Ayadi, S. and Hussainey, K. (2020). The joint effect of corporate risk disclosure and corporate governance on firm value. *International Journal of Disclosure and Governance*, 17(2), 123–140.

Salem, I. and Hussainey, K. (2021). Risk disclosure and corporate cash holdings. *Journal of Risk and Financial Management*, 14(7), 328.

Seebeck, A. and Vetter, J. (2021). Not just a gender numbers game: How board gender diversity affects corporate risk disclosure. *Journal of Business Ethics*,177, 395–420.

Shevlin, T. (2004). Discussion of "a framework for the analysis of firm risk communication". *The International Journal of Accounting*, 39(3), 297–302.

Shrives, P. and Brennan, N. (2015). A typology for exploring the quality of explanations for non-compliance with UK corporate governance regulations. *The British Accounting Review*, 47(1), 85–99.

Slack, R. and Campbell, D. (2016). *Meeting users' information needs: The use and usefulness of integrated reporting.* London: Association of Chartered Certified Accountants.

Solomon, J., Solomon, A., Norton, S. and Joseph, N. (2000). A conceptual framework for corporate risk disclosure emerging from the agenda for corporate governance reform. *The British Accounting Review*, 32(4), 447–478.

Souabni, S. (2011). *Predicting an uncertain future: Narrative reporting and risk information.* London: Association of Chartered Certified Accountants.

Tahat, Y. (2014). Risk disclosure associated with financial statements reporting of Jordanian public corporations. *International Journal of Business and Emerging Markets*, 6(2), 139–162.

Tan, Y., Zeng, C. and Elshandidy, T. (2017). Risk disclosures, international orientation, and share price informativeness: Evidence from China. *Journal of International Accounting, Auditing, and Taxation*, 29, 81–102.

Tauringana, V. and Chithambo, L. (2016). Determinants of risk disclosure compliance in Malawi: A mixed-method approach. *Journal of Accounting in Emerging Economies*, 6(2), 111–137.

Taylor, G., Tower, G. and Neilson, J. (2009). Corporate communication of financial risk. *Accounting and Finance*, 50(2), 417–446.

Tong, S. (2013). Exploring corporate risk transparency: Corporate risk disclosure and the interplay of corporate reputation, corporate trust and media usage in initial public offerings. *Corporate Reputation Review*, 16(2), 131–149.

Uddin, M. and Hassan, M. (2011). Corporate risk information in annual reports and stock price behavior in the United Arab Emirates. *Academy of Accounting and Financial Studies Journal*, 15(1), 459–476.

Vandemele, S., Vergauwen, P. and Michiels, A. (2009). Management risk reporting practices and their determinants: A study of Belgian listed firms. [Online]. Available at: https://uhdspace.uhasselt.be/dspace/bitstream/1942/9392/2/CorporateriskB.pdf [Accessed 22 December 2013].

Wieczorek-Kosmala, M., Błach, J. and Gorczyńska, M. (2014). Voluntary risk reporting in annual reports – Case study of the practices of polish public companies. *e-Finanse: Financial Internet Quarterly*, 10(4), 46–59.

Zadeh, F. and Eskandari, A. (2012a). Firm size as company's characteristic and level of risk disclosure: Review on theories and literatures. *International Journal of Business and Social Science*, 3(17), 1–9.

Zadeh, F. and Eskandari, A. (2012b). Looking forward to financial risk disclosure practices by Malaysian firms. *Australian Journal of Basic and Applied Sciences*, 6(8), 208–214.

Zhang, J., Taylor, D., Qu, W. and Oliver, J. (2013). Corporate risk disclosures: Influence of institutional shareholders and audit committee. *Corporate Ownership & Control*, 10(4), 341–353.

# 5 Corporate governance and narrative disclosure features

## A literature review

*Marwa Soliman and Walid Ben-Amar*

## 5.1 Introduction

Corporate filings represent the key source of information for investors, financial analysts and other stakeholders. Whether discretionary or non-discretionary, corporate disclosures include significant information about a firm's operations and profitability and have substantial implications for capital allocation decisions and the efficiency of capital markets. Even though narrative disclosure represents more than 80% of the content of corporate filing (Lo et al., 2017), academic research has extensively focused on quantitative disclosure, overlooking the role of narrative disclosure in disseminating corporate information to market participants. However, due to the technological advances in the textual analysis and processing fields, a growing body of recent accounting literature has put more emphasis on the role of narrative disclosure in mitigating problems of information asymmetry in financial markets. It also pushed several regulators around the world to take a series of steps to review incumbent regulations with the intention of improving the transparency and effectiveness of narrative disclosures (Dyer et al., 2017).

Recent research has largely established that linguistic features of narrative disclosure have significant economic implications, including, but not limited to, analysts' forecasting abilities (Lehavy et al., 2011), information asymmetry (Bushee et al., 2018), cost of equity (Rjiba et al., 2021), probability of future crash risk (Ertugrul et al., 2017), stock market volatility (Li, 2010) and corporate valuations (Hwang and Kim, 2017). Given the discretionary nature of textual disclosures, managers tend to strategically manage the content of such disclosures according to their own incentives. Previous literature has shown that managerial motives play a significant role in language choices and the quality of narrative disclosures. For example, Asay et al. (2018) provides empirical evidence on how the management reporting goals and the firm performance affect management's language choices. They find that managers with self-enhancement motives tend to make bad news less readable than good news. The results suggest that disclosure obfuscation is intentional rather than being driven by the complexity of the firm's operations. Li (2008) shows also that annual report complexity is positively associated with lower earnings and less persistent positive earnings. Similarly, Lo

DOI: 10.4324/9781003095385-7

et al. (2017) argue that firms that engage more in earnings management provide complex disclosures to influence investors' understanding of the firm's value.

Consequently, a growing thread of literature has emerged to discuss and evaluate the role of different corporate governance mechanisms in mitigating opportunistic managerial behaviour in narrative disclosure. In this chapter, we intend to provide a summary of recent literature that investigates the relationship between corporate governance attributes and textual features of corporate narrative reporting. We acknowledge that the literature in this area is still in its infancy, but we believe it is important to highlight the current contribution and provide new insights for future research. This review is motivated by the fact that financial communications have become more complex over time, raising concerns about the ability of users to extract and comprehend relevant information (Cazier and Pfeiffer, 2015; Guay et al., 2016; Lehavy et al., 2011; Loughran and Mcdonald, 2011). Previous findings highlight the need for a strong corporate governance structure to strengthen the control and monitoring mechanisms over narrative disclosure.[1]

Our literature survey shows mixed results on the effectiveness of different corporate governance mechanisms on improving a firm's narrative disclosures. We show that the results are not yet conclusive and further research is needed. We also highlight that most of the previous studies' findings may not be generalisable as they do not take into account the dynamic nature of narrative disclosure and the structural differences in corporate governance across different countries and market sectors. The existing literature also overlooks the interactive effects among different corporate governance mechanisms. Moreover, our survey highlights that previous findings vary according to the disclosure medium. The relationship between corporate governance and narrative disclosure attributes in mandatory annual reports differ from what we observe in voluntary sustainability reports or environmental reports. These findings confirm the need for further investigation about the relationship between narrative disclosure features and corporate governance.

The remainder of this chapter is organised as follows. Section 5.2 presents major theoretical frameworks used to explain the narrative disclosure from a preparer's perspective. Section 5.3 summarises the existing literature on the association between different corporate governance mechanisms and textual features of narrative disclosure. Section 5.4 provides some insights on previous studies and suggests directions for future research. Finally, Section 5.5 concludes the chapter.

## 5.2 Narrative disclosure: Preparer perspective

To understand the role of corporate governance in improving the quality and effectiveness of narrative disclosure, it is imperative that we first discuss what the preparer hopes to achieve from such disclosure and to what extent the discrepancies between narrative and quantitative disclosures may provide additional insights into the preparer's motives. In their comprehensive review, Merkl-Davies and Brennan (2007) argues that there are five theoretical frameworks which can help us understand the preparer perspective: agency theory, signalling theory, legitimacy theory, stakeholder theory and institutional theory.

### 5.2.1 Agency theory

Since the seminal paper of Jensen and Meckling (1976), agency theory has been widely used in business research to provide a better understanding of management decision making and incentives. The narrative disclosure literature is no exception. Using agency theory, previous literature provides two competing arguments on the intuition behind a manager's narrative disclosure. On one side, managers may use narrative disclosure as an information channel that helps to reduce information asymmetry between insiders and outsiders, aiming to enhance share price performance and accordingly increase their managerial compensation (Baginski et al., 2000). On the other hand, another strand of the literature suggests that managers opportunistically use narrative disclosure to mitigate the negative consequences of poor performance and prospects. This strand of literature hypothesises that managers are not neutral in presenting accounting information (Sydserff and Weetman, 1999). This argument has attracted researchers' attention to investigate the impact of narrative obfuscation on capital market participants. In a recent study, Bushee et al. (2018) break down narrative disclosure complexity into information *vs.* obfuscation components and document a negative (positive) relationship between the information (obfuscation) component and information asymmetry.

### 5.2.2 Institutional theory

Merkl-Davis and Brennan (2007) argue that the institutional theory suggests that narrative disclosure is used to adhere to institutional norms and expectations. According to this theory, managers are providing information to market participants to reduce the likelihood of internal or external scrutiny. For example, Bansal and Clelland (2004) use the institutional theory to explain firms' environmental disclosure. They argue that firms affect investors' judgements on a firm's environmental legitimacy by providing information about environmental liabilities and their commitment to the environment.

### 5.2.3 Legitimacy and signalling

The legitimacy theory hypothesises that narrative disclosure can be used as a tool to influence stakeholders' perceptions of a firm's legitimacy. Most of the previous literature in this thread focuses on disclosures related to corporate social responsibility (CSR) and environmental compliance. For example, Wang et al. (2018) and Du and Yu (2021) provide empirical evidence of a positive relationship between CSR performance and the readability and optimism tone of CSR reports. They suggest that the results indicate the firm's commitment to better CSR performance.

Previous literature has also offered another perspective on narrative disclosure, suggesting that managers use such disclosure to either signal their superiority in the market (e.g., Rutherford, 2003; Smith and Taffler, 1992) or to frame poor performance as temporary. For example, Hasan (2020) finds that more able managers provide more readable disclosure to signal their superior ability. Also, it is documented that when managers discuss poor performance in their narrative disclosure, they tend to focus on future-oriented information, use the passive voice and provide fewer pronouns, aiming to signal that poor performance is either temporary or not driven by poor management (Asay et al., 2018).

### *5.2.4 Stakeholder theory*

Finally, stakeholder theory (Freeman, 1984) argues that narrative disclosure is dependent on the demands and expectations of the firm's stakeholders. In this theory, managers decide on the narrative disclosure strategy according to stakeholders' demands for information. Consistent with this theory, previous literature has shown that narrative disclosure is not static, and it may change over the firm's life cycle (Bakarich et al., 2019). Also, amid the increasing demand of investors for information, a growing body of literature shows that, during periods of increased political and economic uncertainty, managers tend to issue more voluntary disclosure (Bird et al., 2017; Boone et al., 2020; Nagar et al., 2019), and present longer disclosures to provide additional information on complex situations (Jiang et al., 2019).

## 5.3  Corporate governance and narrative disclosure

The discussion described in Section 5.2 shows that managers may have different motives behind preparing and deciding on the extent of narrative disclosures in mandatory and voluntary reports. However, most of the literature has understandable focused on agency theory. The agency theory suggests that, as managers' and owners' interests are not aligned, corporate governance is essential to keep managers' myopic behaviour intact. Although previous literature has extensively tested the relationship between corporate governance and disclosure quality (e.g., Cohen et al., 2004), a growing number of studies discuss the association between corporate governance and features of narrative disclosure. In this section, we provide a synthesis of the literature on the association between corporate governance mechanisms and corporate narrative reporting. We use the Google Scholar search engine to locate publications/working papers on corporate governance and narrative disclosure through to 2021. We determine their relevance to our research objective and use judgement in selecting papers to be included in this review. Our review includes both relevant published and working papers. We identify four central themes based on the corporate governance mechanism, namely the role of the board of directors' composition, ownership structure, CEO's power and managerial compensation.

### *5.3.1  Board of directors and audit committee*

The board of directors serves as an advisor and gatekeeper to protect shareholders' interests. The board is appointed by the owners to hire the firm's management, oversee their performance and assess the overall strategy of the firm. In addition, it also has a direct role in the disclosure process. The Securities Exchange Commission requires the majority of the board of directors to sign the filings of the firm. Also, the audit committee which is a subset of the board, is heavily involved with the process of directly overseeing the firm's financial reports and filings. Hence, it is important that we understand to what extent the board of directors' structure and composition can affect the output of a firm's narrative disclosure.

### 5.3.1.1 Board of directors: annual filings and voluntary disclosure.

Cerbioni and Parbonetti (2007) were among the first to investigate the relationship between the board of directors and narrative disclosure. Analysing the content of voluntary intellectual capital disclosure of European biotechnology firms, their finding is that the quantity of a firm's voluntary disclosure is negatively related to board size, CEO duality and board structure, but positively related to the proportion of independent directors. They also show that small board size, a majority of independent directors, CEO non-duality and the inclusion of nominating and compensation committees improve the overall quality of corporate voluntary disclosure, proxied by the annual report's overall readability and disclosure of internal structure and forward-looking information. Although Cerbioni and Parbonetti (2007) provide a comprehensive study on the relationship between the board of directors and narrative disclosure, the study suffers from multiple limitations. For example, it focuses solely on biotechnology firms without considering the differences in board composition and disclosure practices in different sectors. It also narrowed the scope of voluntary disclosure to study exclusively voluntary intellectual capital disclosure which may be of specific importance for biotechnology firms, but not to other market sectors, limiting the extent to which the study's findings could be generalised.

Focusing on risk disclosure, Abraham and Cox (2007) provide additional results about the relationship between the composition of the board of directors and textual disclosures. Using a sample of one hundred FTSE UK firms, they show that increasing the number of either executive directors or independent non-executive directors improves the transmission of risk disclosure to market participants. The results suggest that having a balanced board may be beneficial to the quality of narrative disclosure. More recently, new evidence has emerged suggesting that not only does board independence matter to narrative disclosure but that also other factors, including directors' age, gender, education and financial expertise, are associated with the quality of narrative disclosure. For example, Martikainen et al. (2019) show that directors' age is negatively associated with 10-K narrative disclosure tone, whereas directors' uniformity, educational and financial experience are positively associated with disclosure tone. They further find that board turnover is positively (negatively) associated with negative (positive) and total tone. They interpret these findings as evidence of the role of directors' human and social capital on narrative disclosure. Consistent with these findings, Ginesti et al. (2018) provide empirical evidence from Italian firms that the percentage of women directors on the board is positively associated with annual reports' readability in firms with small boardroom connections, whereas the percentages of female board members and female CEOs are negatively associated with annual reports' readability in firms with large boardroom connections. They interpret the findings as evidence that small boardroom connections may value diversity by selecting skilled female directors, whereas large boardrooms mainly use female directors to meet the market pressure for diversity.

### 5.3.1.2 Board of directors: CSR and environmental disclosure.

As discussed in Section 5.2, corporations may use narrative disclosure to signal or add legitimacy to their operations. In this regard, CSR and environmental disclosure may serve this purpose to alter investors' perceptions of the firm's image. Investigating this perspective, Jizi et al. (2014) examine the impact of board of directors' characteristics on the CSR disclosure attributes in annual reports. The study evaluates four CSR categories, namely product and customer service quality, environment, community involvement and employees. The evaluation is based on scores on the presence and comprehensiveness of information included in each category. The results reveal that board independence, board size and CEO duality are positively related to CSR disclosure, suggesting the importance of these characteristics in promoting the interests of the firm's shareholders and other stakeholders. Similar findings were reported by Yekini et al. (2015), who found in a sample of UK firms that effective, independent directors increased the quality of community disclosures in annual reports.

With regard to environmental disclosure, Arena et al. (2015) document that the structure of the board of directors mediates the relationship between optimistic language in environmental disclosures and future environmental performance. They show that both board monitoring, proxied by board size, CEO duality and the number of independent directors, and stakeholder orientation, proxied by directors' connections, board diversity and the presence of a CSR committee and directors who are community influential, play a significant role in this relationship. The results show that the positive relationship between tone of optimism and future environmental performance only exists for firms with low board monitoring or low stakeholder orientation. However, in the firms with high board monitoring or high stakeholder orientation (or both), there is no significant relationship between optimistic language and future environmental performance. These findings suggest that board governance is a substitute for an environmental disclosure with an optimistic tone to signal the firm's superior environmental performance.

### 5.3.1.3 Audit committee

Recently, the audit committee has become an effective mechanism by which to enhance a firm's corporate governance (Chen et al., 2008). The interest in the quality of audit committees to improve their effectiveness in overseeing managers has increased dramatically in recent years. Hence, prior studies examined the effectiveness of different attributes of the audit committee in improving the quality of financial reporting. These attributes include independence, competency and activity.

In highlighting the effective role of the audit committee in improving the quality of narrative disclosure over the period 2001–2012, Lee and Park (2019) report that accounting financial expertise (supervisory expertise) on the audit committee is negatively associated (not associated) with an abnormal tone in the MD&A section of annual reports. The study measures the accounting financial expertise based on whether the audit committee member has experience related directly to accounting, whereas the supervisory expertise is measured based on whether the audit committee members hold positions that require supervision of financial statement preparation. This finding suggests that the accounting knowledge on the audit committees helps to mitigate the behaviour of opportunistic managers. In a cross-sectional analysis, the study finds that this relation is more pronounced when the power of the audit committee exceeds that of the CEO or in the case of higher litigation risks, supporting the importance of the audit committee's ability and incentive in effectively disciplining managers from using the tone of the MD&A section to obfuscate outsiders.

### 5.3.2 Ownership structure: institutional ownership and family firms

#### 5.3.2.1 Institutional ownership

Previous literature shows that institutional ownership affects the quality of corporate disclosure through improving the firm's information environment and by providing effective governance. For example, Velury and Jenkins (2006) find a positive association between institutional ownership and earning quality, although they also show that concentrated ownership may have a detrimental effect on earnings quality. These results suggest that institutional investors may serve as a monitoring mechanism to decrease the information asymmetry between managers and shareholders but that having concentrated ownership may decrease this positive impact amid self-interest motives. Although the relationship between financial reporting quality and institutional ownership is common, there is limited research on the impact of institutional ownership on the features of narrative disclosure.

To fill this gap in the literature, a recent study has incorporated this relationship, suggesting that there is a positive relationship between institutional ownership and the readability of corporate annual filings and risk disclosure. As part of investigating the relationship between institutional ownership and audit quality, Chen et al. (2017) show that there is a positive relationship between institutional ownership and the readability of 10-K textual disclosure of Russell 3000 firms. Specifically, they find that the disclosure complexity measured by the Gunning Fog Index decreases by 8.56% for each 1% increase in institutional ownership.

They also find corroborated results using FleschRead and file size as alternative proxies for disclosure complexity.

The results above suggest that institutional ownership plays an important role in determining the quality of narrative disclosure, but further investigation is needed to understand the channel through which institutional ownership can help improve the information environment and alleviate the information asymmetry in the financial market.

### 5.3.2.2  Family firms

Previous literature shows that family firms' disclosures may be different from those of non-family firms. For example, Chen et al. (2008) find that family firms provide fewer earnings forecasts and conference calls, and more earnings warnings compared with non-family peers. They suggest that family firms may have a longer investment horizon, more effective governance structure and lower information asymmetry, but higher litigation and reputational risk.

To understand the relationship between family ownership and narrative disclosure, Liao et al. (2020) study a sample of US listed firms over the period 2003–2013. They show that family firms provide more readable annual reports than do non-family firms. The readability of 10-Ks is measured by the Bog Index, the modified Fog Index and the proportion of numbers used in the narrative disclosure. They relate this result to the long-term horizon of the insiders and the desire to maintain family reputation and for inter-generational transfer of the firm to family successors. Supporting the positive impact of different corporate governance mechanisms, they find that the results only hold true with stronger board governance and for firms without dual-class share structures.

### 5.3.3  CEO power: tenure and duality

Given the nature of narrative reporting as unstructured and unregulated disclosures, it provides the researcher with a rare opportunity to understand how managers' characteristics may affect their language choices. Previous literature shows that demographic characteristics, such as the CEO's age, confidence, optimism and equity incentives may explain managers' disclosure choices (Ahmed and Duellman, 2013; Hambrick, 2007). In this section, we focus on the relationship between the CEO's power and features of narrative disclosure. More specifically, we discuss prior evidence documenting the role of the CEO's tenure and the CEO's duality on narrative disclosure.

CEO tenure has been used extensively as a proxy of CEO power or entrenchment (e.g., DeBoskey et al., 2019; Lewellyn and Muller-Kahle, 2012). Pan et al. (2016) argue that CEOs who stay in the firm for a long time tend to handle the constraints imposed on them by the board and decide the corporate investment agenda according to their own self-interests. To study the relationship between the tone of narrative disclosure and both the CEO's duality and tenure, DeBoskey et al. (2019) use a sample of US firms between the years 2008–2013. They find that CEO's power, measured by CEO's duality and tenure, is positively associated with the tone of the earnings announcement. However, this positive relationship is weaker when the board monitoring role is more effective or when the reputational cost is high. The results suggest that powerful CEOs tend to use a more optimistic tone, but the effective monitoring role of the board can curb over-optimistic earnings announcements. Consistent with previous findings, Garcia Osma et al. (2018) also find that early-tenured CEOs use a less optimistic tone in firms' 10-K narrative disclosures as the optimistic disclosure tone increases attention and litigation risk. Yet, highly capable CEOs use a more optimistic tone early in their career to signal their ability, suggesting the importance of narrative tone in affecting the market's perception about CEO ability.

Although previous studies report a positive relationship between CEO power and narrative disclosure tone, recent findings are not conclusive. For example, using a large sample of earnings conference calls for the period between 2006 and 2014, Bochkay et al. (2019) argue that uncertainty about early-tenured CEOs' abilities exacerbates their career concerns and hence drives demand for and supply of information. Specifically, they show that CEOs in the early years of their tenure 1) provide more forward-looking disclosures to respond to investors' demand for information and resolve their uncertainty, and 2) use a more optimistic tone to favourably influence outsiders. Over time, due to the greater observability of the CEO's practices and the accumulation of private knowledge by outsiders, along with the CEO's tenure, the uncertainty about his actions, strategies and ability is reduced. Consequently, the optimism and forward-looking disclosures of CEOs decline over their tenure.

### 5.3.4 Managerial compensation

In an attempt to investigate how equity-based incentives affected the tone of the narrative section of earnings press releases for the period between 2004 and 2012, Arslan-Ayaydin et al. (2016) show that managers inflate the tone of earnings press releases when the managerial portfolio value is associated with the firm's stock price (portfolio delta) and deflate the tone of earnings press releases when the change in the managerial portfolio value is more sensitive to firm's stock return volatility (portfolio vega). These findings suggest the opportunistic use of tone in earnings press releases either to maximise a firm's stock price in the case of portfolio delta or to increase uncertainty about the firm's future prospects in the case of portfolio vega. Similarly, using a sample of annual reports over the period 1993–2015, Chakrabarty et al. (2018) find that stock-options-based compensation (greater vega) induces managers to provide less readable disclosures. They argue that managers exploit disclosures to achieve their objectives, either directly through increased return volatility (option value), or indirectly by allowing greater earnings management. The study also shows that this relation is moderated by effective corporate governance, proxied by institutional ownership, the Entrenchment Index (E-Index) and analyst following.

Laksmana et al. (2012) also examine the relationship between the readability of the Compensation Discussion and Analysis section (CD&A) in the 2007 and

2008 proxy statements and the proportion of CEO pay not related to the economic determinants of compensation. They document that firms provide less readable CD&As when CEO pay is higher than the benchmark pay in the 2007 proxy season. However, firms improve the readability of CD&As when CEO pay exceeds the benchmark pay in the 2008 proxy season, suggesting that the readability of compensation disclosure has improved under regulatory oversight and public scrutiny. In addition, using a sample of UK firms over the period 2003–2009, Hooghiemstra et al. (2017) show that, in firms with excessive CEO pay, a lower remuneration report readability decreases the extent of say-on-pay voting dissent, supporting the idea that obfuscation of compensation disclosures is an effective tool in the case of excessive CEO pay. However, the effectiveness of this obfuscation strategy decreases with an increase in institutional ownership. Rather, with the increase in the percentage of institutional investors, a less readable remuneration report even increases say-on-pay voting dissent.

### 5.3.5 Corporate governance: international evidence

Most studies reviewed so far have focused on the US setting, leaving many unanswered questions about this relationship in other jurisdictions. In this section, we present the findings of the few studies that use international data to describe the relationship between corporate governance and narrative disclosure attributes.

Using data for Spanish companies over the period 2010–2016, Melón-Izco et al. (2021) find that readability of management reports, measured with the Fernández Huerta index, is positively related to compliance with a greater number of good governance recommendations as described in the codes of good governance by the National Commission of the Stock Market. Also, Chan et al. (2014) find a positive relationship between corporate governance quality and the voluntary CSR disclosure in the annual report among the top 300 Australian companies in 2004. They use the WHK Horwath (2005) corporate governance report which is an independent ranking of the overall corporate governance quality of Australian listed companies. This report uses firms' performance in six key corporate governance areas to rank Australian companies, namely board of directors, audit committee, remuneration committee, nomination committee, external auditor independence and code of conduct and other policy disclosures. This finding suggests the positive impact of corporate governance on the provision of voluntary CSR disclosures.

Moreover, Kent and Stewart (2008) examine the relationship between the amount of disclosure about the transition to Australian International Financial Reporting Standards (AIFRSs) and different corporate governance mechanisms. The amount of disclosure is measured by 1) the number of sentences that explain the management of the transition to AIFRSs and the major variations in accounting policies that are expected to occur because of the adoption of AIFRSs, and 2) an index of the number of differences in accounting policies that are covered in the note to the accounts regarding the transition to AIFRSs. The corporate governance mechanisms include various attributes of the board of directors (board independence, CEO duality, board size and diligence) and the audit committee (independence and expertise of committee members, audit committee size and diligence), and the choice of auditor (large or small audit firms). The results show a positive relationship between the quantity of disclosure and some aspects of superior corporate governance, such as the number of board and audit committee meetings and the choice of auditor. These findings indicate the substitution effects between various governance attributes and shed light on the important role of board and audit committee diligence and the choice of a high-quality audit firm in increasing the level of disclosure.

Focusing on Chinese companies in heavy-pollution industries over the period 2008–2014, Liu and Zhang (2017) find that different corporate governance mechanisms impact the extent of social responsibility information disclosure. They show that the level of social responsibility information disclosure is positively associated with the proportion of state-owned shareholding, the board size, frequency of board meetings and proportion of managerial staff shareholding but negatively related to the share proportion of the largest shareholder.

Wang and Hussainey (2013) examine the association between corporate governance mechanisms and the levels of forward-looking statements in the narrative sections of UK annual reports. The study finds that the level of forward-looking statements is not related to institutional investors nor to the independence and the financial expertise of the audit committee's members, is positively associated with board size and board independence and negatively associated with executive directors' ownership, CEO duality and audit committee size. The results show that institutional investors as an external corporate governance mechanism do not affect the level of forward-looking information disclosure, suggesting that they might have other ways of communicating with the firm's managers. Also, the study finds that audit committee independence and competency have no impact on the disclosure level, raising doubt on their effectiveness in improving narrative disclosure. However, Al-Najjar and Abed (2014) find that forward-looking disclosure related positively to audit committee independence, negatively to blockholder ownership, and showed no association with board independence and CEO turnover.

Based on a sample of Spanish firms, García Osma and Guillamón-Saorín (2011) analyse the relationship between a broader set of corporate governance mechanisms and both quantitative and qualitative financial information, measured by (1) disclosure tone, (2) emphasis, (3) performance comparisons and (4) selectivity in press releases. The corporate governance mechanisms are proxied by an aggregate governance measure which includes the proportion of independent directors and institutional directors on the board, CEO duality, the board size, existence of a nomination–remuneration committee, the number of board meetings and monitoring activity by audit and nomination–remuneration committees as measured by their annual number of meetings. In general, the results show that strong governance mechanisms constrain managerial incentives to manipulate both qualitative and quantitative impression management.

Using a sample of French companies over the period 2000–2004, Nekhili et al. (2016) examine the relation between R&D narrative disclosure and different corporate governance mechanisms including audit committee independence, board independence and size, CEO duality and equity-based management compensation. The study uses the R&D disclosure index which combines the scores in five categories of information, namely current and future information on spending, inputs, outputs, accounting and budgeting and strategy. The results reveal that only equity-based compensation and audit committee independence are positively related to the extent of R&D narrative disclosure, suggesting the significance of these mechanisms in improving the communication on R&D activities.

Haniffa and Cooke (2005) examine the relationship between the CSR disclosure in annual reports of Malaysian corporations in the years 1996 and 2002, measured by an index score and number of words, and corporate governance characteristics including board composition, number of directorships and type of shareholders. The results show that the CSR disclosure is positively related to the number of executive directors, the number of directorships held by the chair of the board of directors and foreign share ownership. This finding shows the limited role of non-executive directors of Malaysian companies in shaping CSR disclosure policies.

## 5.4 Discussion and future research opportunities

### 5.4.1 Discussion

In this section, we discuss the main findings of the review and comment on the existing literature. First, our review highlights the strong focus on one aspect theory of corporate governance. Most narrative disclosure–corporate governance literature is based on agency theory (Jensen and Meckling, 1976), which assumes that governance mechanisms should monitor and control agents (managers). Therefore, it is argued that stronger monitoring mechanisms are associated with less ambiguous, more readable and shorter narrative disclosures. However, other theories of governance could explain the effect on different features of narrative disclosure – e.g., institutional theory (the purpose of governance mechanisms is to support external legitimacy rather than reflecting actual monitoring). Supporting the idea that different theories might explain the role of a corporate governance mechanism, Beasley et al. (2009) use in-depth interviews to examine whether audit committees support agency theory (they provide oversight of financial reporting), or institutional theory (they are considered to be "ceremonial bodies" to enhance legitimacy). The findings of the study support both the substantive monitoring and the ceremonial role of audit committees.

Second, much of the narrative disclosure–governance research focuses only on a limited subset of governance mechanisms (e.g., independence of the board of directors and the expertise, diligence and size of the audit committee, CEO duality, other directorships). Excluding other characteristics of corporate governance makes it difficult to draw valid inferences. For example, under internal governance theory developed by Acharya et al. (2011), bottom-up (instead of top-down) corporate governance exercised by key subordinate executives could be an alternative governance mechanism to restrain self-interested behaviour on the part of the CEO. Supporting this argument, Cheng et al. (2016) find that bottom-up corporate governance from key subordinate executives negatively affects real earnings management, suggesting the effectiveness of internal governance mechanism by subordinates over independent or competent boards in monitoring day-to-day operations to add much value to a firm (Aggarwal et al., 2017).

Third, the relationship between corporate governance and narrative disclosure is complex. Prior studies provide mixed results on whether the quality of corporate disclosures and corporate governance are substitutes (negative relationship) or complementary (positive relationship). Consistent with the argument that corporate governance and disclosure quality are substitutes, Arena et al. (2015) show that board governance (monitoring and stakeholder orientation) is a substitute mechanism for the optimistic tone of environmental disclosure to signal the firm's superior environmental performance. In other words, greater environmental optimism tone is associated with low board governance to reflect the improved future environmental performance. Supporting the complementary relationship, García Osma and Guillamón-Saorín (2011) find a positive relationship between a set of corporate governance mechanisms and both quantitative and qualitative financial information. We also need to realise that different corporate governance mechanisms may substitute for one another in providing higher quality narrative disclosures. For example, Kent and Stewart (2008) find that only a few corporate governance mechanisms related positively to the amount of disclosure about the transition to AIFRSs, suggesting the substitution effect between various governance attributes.

Fourth, prior corporate governance literature also shows a lack of consistency in measuring governance characteristics. For example, to measure the board independence, some studies use the percentage of the independent members whereas others use a dummy variable equal to one if the board is 100% independent, and zero otherwise. Another example is the variation in defining the audit committee's financial expertise. Some studies define it based on Section 407 of the Sarbanes-Oxley Act, whereas others base the definition on whether the member has an accounting background (e.g., Lee and Park, 2019). In addition, recently, we note the increased use of the indices (e.g., G-index, Gov-Score, E-index) to capture multiple dimensions of corporate governance. However, these indices assign equal weight to each dimension, assuming they are complements, not substitutes. In sum, this variability in measuring corporate governance mechanisms across studies might create inconsistency in defining whether the corporate governance attribute is good or bad, leading to conflicting results.

Fifth, the effectiveness of corporate governance characteristics is unlikely to be "one-size-fits-all" and it is better to describe corporate governance as highly context-specific. The optimum corporate governance can differ among industries and according to the firm stage in its life cycle. Also, various combinations of financial structure (market *vs* bank-based) and legal system (common law *vs* civil law) cause huge differences in the corporate governance structure (Anderson and Gupta,

2009). The agency conflicts in countries with disperse shareholders are between managers and owners, whereas in countries with concentrated shareholders (family firms and most emerging markets), the agency conflicts are between minority and majority shareholders. Hence, the optimum corporate governance mechanisms to ensure transparent and informative disclosure should not be the same in these two different systems. For example, Elshandidy and Neri (2015) examine the impact of a set of corporate governance characteristics on mandatory and voluntary disclosure of corporate risk in the narrative sections of annual reports in the UK and Italy. They show differences in the effectiveness of various corporate governance mechanisms on risk disclosure practices between UK and Italian firms.

### 5.4.2 *Future research*

Given the conflicting results, we believe that the effectiveness of various corporate governance mechanisms in improving different features of narrative disclosure needs further investigation. Future research should take into consideration the specific context of the sample under investigation, use different proxies of narrative disclosure quality and effective corporate governance structure and employ various disclosure channels.

We suggest implementing a holistic approach combining multiple corporate governance mechanisms to assess their interaction and developing governance practices that best influence firms' narrative disclosure practices.[2] In addition to the traditional corporate governance mechanisms examined in prior studies, we also suggest incorporating internal governance exercised by subordinate managers (Acharya et al., 2011) to examine the impact on different features of narrative disclosure. This would further expand our understanding of the effectiveness of different corporate governance mechanisms in improving corporate disclosure.

The uniformity in corporate governance structure makes it more difficult to further explore the relationship between narrative disclosure attributes and traditional corporate governance mechanisms.[3] We urge future research to consider different research methods (such as experiments, field studies, interviews, and surveys) other than archival methods to deepen our understanding of how a board and/or audit committee discharges its responsibilities. Investigating the board/audit committee processes which have been implemented show their effectiveness in distinguishing successful boards from less successful ones in improving disclosure quality.

## 5.5 Conclusion

Prior literature shows that different corporate governance mechanisms are important drivers of financial reporting practices. Yet, the literature discussing the effect of corporate governance on managers' disclosure strategies is still limited, and little is known about the effectiveness of various corporate governance mechanisms in improving the attributes of a firm's narrative disclosure strategies. Contrary to quantitative disclosures, that are subject to specific restrictions and should be prepared in accordance with certain rules, and hence are more easily verified and evaluated, corporate narratives are largely unregulated and subject to a wide, managerial discretion. Thus, narrative disclosures are harder to regulate or to litigate against, providing managers with an opportunity to strategically manage the perceptions of market participants about current and future performances.

As qualitative characteristics of narrative disclosure portray a genuine picture of a firm's performance beyond quantitative information, this chapter provides an overview of the recent literature on the association between corporate governance mechanisms and textual features of narrative disclosures. The review shows mixed results for the association between different corporate governance mechanisms and the quality of narrative disclosures. Our survey shows that this relationship depends on the definitions of corporate governance and narrative disclosure. Most of the previous literature has focused on a single aspect of corporate governance overlooking other governance mechanisms. Earlier studies have implicitly assumed that the relationship between corporate governance and narrative disclosure is static and did not pay enough attention to the dynamic nature of narrative disclosure and whether the effectiveness of corporate governance in shaping narrative disclosure is contingent on the firm's performance, life cycle and sector norms. Furthermore, although most of the previous studies have focused on the narrative features of mandatory annual reports, others consider different reporting media and investigate definitions of narrative disclosure such as CSR, environmental or auditors' reports, which may limit the generalisability of prior findings. Overall, our survey suggests that the literature in this area is still in its infancy and would greatly benefit from further investigation and refinement of the association between corporate governance and narrative disclosure features.

## Notes

1  To evaluate the informativeness of narrative disclosures, Dyer et al. (2017) examine 10-Ks of a sample of US firms over the period 1996–2013. They find that the quality of narrative disclosure sharply decreased (e.g., text length, redundancy, stickiness and boilerplate largely increased whereas readability and specificity largely decreased).
2  Ho and Shun Wong (2001) argue that a very limited number of the earlier studies incorporate different governance mechanisms in one study, whereas most of them depend on a single, corporate governance mechanism.
3  Beasley et al. (2010) show that corporate governance structures of fraud firms are the same as those found in a matched sample of firms.

## References

Abraham, S., Cox, P., 2007. Analysing the Determinants of Narrative Risk Information in UK FTSE 100 Annual Reports. *The British Accounting Review* 39(3), 227–248.

Acharya, V.V., Myers, S.C., Rajan, R.G., 2011. The Internal Governance of Firms. *The Journal of Finance* 66(3), 689–720.

Aggarwal, R.K., Fu, H., Pan, Y., 2017. *An Empirical Investigation of Internal Governance (SSRN Scholarly Paper No. ID 1571740)*. Social Science Research Network, Rochester, NY.

Ahmed, A.S., Duellman, S., 2013. Managerial Overconfidence and Accounting Conservatism. *Journal of Accounting Research* 51(1), 1–30.

Al-Najjar, B., Abed, S., 2014. The Association between Disclosure of Forward-Looking Information and Corporate Governance Mechanisms: Evidence from the UK before the Financial Crisis Period. *Managerial Auditing Journal* 29(7), 578–595.

Anderson, A., Gupta, P.P., 2009. A Cross-Country Comparison of Corporate Governance and Firm Performance: Do Financial Structure and the Legal System Matter? *Journal of Contemporary Accounting and Economics* 5(2), 61–79.

Arena, C., Bozzolan, S., Michelon, G., 2015. Environmental Reporting: Transparency to Stakeholders or Stakeholder Manipulation? An Analysis of Disclosure Tone and the Role of the Board of Directors. *Corporate Social Responsibility and Environmental Management* 22(6), 346–361.

Arslan-Ayaydin, Ö., Boudt, K., Thewissen, J., 2016. Managers Set the Tone: Equity Incentives and the Tone of Earnings Press Releases. *Journal of Banking & Finance* 72, S132–S147.

Asay, H.S., Libby, R., Rennekamp, K., 2018. Firm Performance, Reporting Goals, and Language Choices in Narrative Disclosures. *Journal of Accounting and Economics* 65(2–3), 380–398.

Baginski, S.P., Hassell, J.M., Hillison, W.A., 2000. Voluntary Causal Disclosures: Tendencies and Capital Market Reaction. *Review of Quantitative Finance and Accounting* 15(4), 371–389.

Bakarich, K.M., Hossain, M., Hossain, M., Weintrop, J., 2019. Different Time, Different Tone: Company Life Cycle. *Journal of Contemporary Accounting and Economics* 15(1), 69–86.

Bansal, P., Clelland, I., 2004. Talking Trash: Legitimacy, Impression Management, and Unsystematic Risk in the Context of the Natural Environment. *The Academy of Management Journal* 47, 93–103.

Beasley, M., Hermanson, D., Carcello, J., Neal, T., 2010. *Fraudulent Financial Reporting: 1998–2007: An Analysis of U.S. Public Companies.* Association Sections, Divisions, Boards, Teams.

Beasley, M.S., Carcello, J.V., Hermanson, D.R., Neal, T.L., 2009. The Audit Committee Oversight Process. *Contemporary Accounting Research* 26(1), 65–122.

Bird, A., Karolyi, S.A., Ruchti, T., 2017. Political Uncertainty and Corporate Transparency. SSRN Journal.

Bochkay, K., Chychyla, R., Nanda, D., 2019. Dynamics of CEO Disclosure Style. *The Accounting Review* 94(4), 103–140.

Boone, A.L., Kim, A., White, J.T., 2020. *Local Policy Uncertainty and Firm Disclosure (SSRN Scholarly Paper No. ID 3003157).* Social Science Research Network, Rochester, NY.

Bushee, B.J., Gow, I.D., Taylor, D.J., 2018. Linguistic Complexity in Firm Disclosures: Obfuscation or Information?: Linguistic Complexity in Firm Disclosures. *Journal of Accounting Research* 56(1), 85–121.

Cazier, R.A., Pfeiffer, R.J., 2015. Why are 10-K Filings So Long? *Accounting Horizons* 30(1), 1–21.

Cerbioni, F., Parbonetti, A., 2007. Exploring the Effects of Corporate Governance on Intellectual Capital Disclosure: An Analysis of European Biotechnology Companies. *European Accounting Review* 16(4), 791–826.

Chakrabarty, B., Seetharaman, A., Swanson, Z., Wang, X., 2018. Management Risk Incentives and the Readability of Corporate Disclosures. *Financial Management* 47(3), 583–616.

Chan, M., Watson, J., Woodliff, D., 2014. Corporate Governance Quality and CSR Disclosures. *Journal of Business Ethics* 125(1),59–73.

Chen, J., Duh, R.-R., Shiue, F.N., 2008. The Effect of Audit Committees on Earnings–Return Association: Evidence from Foreign Registrants in the United States. *Corporate Governance: An International Review* 16(1), 32–40.

Chen, T., Dong, H., Lin, C., 2017. *Institutional Ownership and Audit Quality: Evidence from Russell Index Reconstitutions (SSRN Scholarly Paper No. ID 2849685).* Social Science Research Network, Rochester, NY.

Cheng, Q., Lee, J., Shevlin, T., 2016. Internal Governance and Real Earnings Management. *The Accounting Review* 91(4), 1051–1085.

Cohen, J., Krishnamoorthy, G., Wright, A., 2004. The Corporate Governance Mosaic and Financial Reporting Quality. *Journal of Accounting Literature* 23, 87.

DeBoskey, D.G., Luo, Y., Zhou, L., 2019. CEO Power, Board Oversight, and Earnings Announcement Tone. *Review of Quantitative Finance and Accounting* 52(2), 657–680.

Du, S., Yu, K., 2021. Do Corporate Social Responsibility Reports Convey Value Relevant Information? Evidence from Report Readability and Tone. *Journal of Business Ethics* 172(2), 253–274.

Dyer, T., Lang, M., Stice-Lawrence, L., 2017. The Evolution of 10-K Textual Disclosure: Evidence from Latent Dirichlet Allocation. *Journal of Accounting and Economics* 64(2–3), 221–245.

Elshandidy, T., Neri, L., 2015. Corporate Governance, Risk Disclosure Practices, and Market Liquidity: Comparative Evidence from the UK and Italy. *Corporate Governance: An International Review* 23(4), 331–356.

Ertugrul, M., Lei, J., Qiu, J., Wan, C., 2017. Annual Report Readability, Tone Ambiguity, and the Cost of Borrowing. *Journal of Financial and Quantitative Analysis* 52(2), 811–836.

Freeman, R.E., 1984. *Strategic Management: A Stakeholder Aproach.* Pitman, Boston, MA.

Garcia Osma, B., Grande-Herrera, C., Guillamon Saorin, E., 2018. *Optimistic Disclosure Tone and CEO Career Concerns (SSRN Scholarly Paper No. ID 3160100).* Social Science Research Network, Rochester, NY.

García Osma, B., Guillamón-Saorín, E., 2011. Corporate Governance and Impression Management in Annual Results Press Releases. *Accounting, Organizations and Society* 36(4–5), 187–208.

Ginesti, G., Drago, C., Macchioni, R., Sannino, G., 2018. Female Board Participation and Annual Report Readability in Firms with Boardroom Connections. *Gender in Management: An International Review* 33(3), 296–314.

Guay, W., Samuels, D., Taylor, D., 2016. Guiding through the Fog: Financial Statement Complexity and Voluntary Disclosure. *Journal of Accounting and Economics* 62(2–3), 234–269.

Hambrick, D.C., 2007. Upper Echelons Theory: An Update. *Academy of Management Review* 32(2), 334–343.

Haniffa, R.M., Cooke, T.E., 2005. The Impact of Culture and Governance on Corporate Social Reporting. *Journal of Accounting and Public Policy* 24(5), 391–430.

Hasan, M.M., 2020. Readability of Narrative Disclosures in 10-K Reports: Does Managerial Ability Matter? *European Accounting Review* 29(1), 147–168.

Ho, S.S.M., Shun Wong, K., 2001. A Study of the Relationship between Corporate Governance Structures and the Extent of Voluntary disclosure. *Journal of International Accounting, Auditing and Taxation* 10(2), 139–156.

Hooghiemstra, R., Kuang, Y.F., Qin, B., 2017. Does Obfuscating Excessive CEO Pay Work? The Influence of Remuneration Report Readability on Say-On-Pay Votes. *Accounting and Business Research* 47(6), 695–729.

Hwang, B.-H., Kim, H.H., 2017. It Pays to Write Well. *Journal of Financial Economics* 124(2), 373–394.

Jensen, M.C., Meckling, W.H., 1976. Theory of the Firm: Managerial Behavior, Agency Costs and Ownership Structure. *Journal of Financial Economics* 3(4), 305–360.

Jiang, L., Pittman, J., Saffar, W., 2019. *Policy Uncertainty and Textual Disclosure (SSRN Scholarly Paper No. ID 3015420).* Social Science Research Network, Rochester, NY.

Jizi, M.I., Salama, A., Dixon, R., Stratling, R., 2014. Corporate Governance and Corporate Social Responsibility Disclosure: Evidence from the US Banking Sector. *Journal of Business Ethics* 125(4), 601–615.

Kent, P., Stewart, J., 2008. Corporate Governance and Disclosures on the Transition to International Financial Reporting Standards. *Accounting and Finance* 48, 649–671.

Laksmana, I., Tietz, W., Yang, Y., 2012. Compensation Discussion and Analysis (CD&A): Readability and Management Obfuscation. *Journal of Accounting and Public Policy* 31(2), 185–203.

Lee, J., Park, J., 2019. The Impact of Audit Committee Financial Expertise on Management Discussion and Analysis (MD&A) Tone. *European Accounting Review* 28(1), 129–150.

Lehavy, R., Li, F., Merkley, K., 2011. The Effect of Annual Report Readability on Analyst Following and the Properties of Their Earnings Forecasts. *The Accounting Review* 86(3), 1087–1115.

Lewellyn, K.B., Muller-Kahle, M.I., 2012. CEO Power and Risk Taking: Evidence from the Subprime Lending Industry. *Corporate Governance: An International Review* 20(3), 289–307.

Li, F., 2010. Textual Analysis of Corporate Disclosures: A Survey of the Literature. *Journal of Accounting Literature; Gainesville* 29, 143–165.

Li, F., 2008. Annual Report Readability, Current Earnings, and Earnings Persistence. *Journal of Accounting and Economics, Economic Consequences of Alternative Accounting Standards and Regulation* 45(2–3), 221–247.

Liao, Q., Srinidhi, B., Wang, K., 2020. *Do Family Firms Issue More Readable Annual Reports? Evidence from the U.S. (SSRN Scholarly Paper No. ID 2800834).* Social Science Research Network, Rochester, NY.

Liu, X., Zhang, C., 2017. Corporate Governance, Social Responsibility Information Disclosure, and Enterprise Value in China. *Journal of Cleaner Production* 142, 1075–1084.

Lo, K., Ramos, F., Rogo, R., 2017. Earnings Management and Annual Report Readability. *Journal of Accounting and Economics* 63(1), 1–25.

Loughran, T., Mcdonald, B., 2011. When is a Liability Not a Liability? Textual Analysis, Dictionaries, and 10-Ks. *The Journal of Finance* 66(1), 35–65.

Martikainen, M., Miihkinen, A., Watson, L., 2019. *Board Characteristics and Disclosure Tone (SSRN Scholarly Paper No. ID 3410036).* Social Science Research Network, Rochester, NY.

Melón-Izco, Á., Ruiz-Cabestre, F.J., Ruiz-Olalla, C., 2021. Readabilty in Management Reports: Extension and Good Governance Practices. *RC-SAR* 24(1), 19–30.

Merkl-Davies, D.M., Brennan, N., 2007. Discretionary Disclosure Strategies in Corporate Narratives : Incremental Information or Impression Management? *Journal of Accounting Literature* 26, 116–196.

Nagar, V., Schoenfeld, J., Wellman, L., 2019. The Effect of Economic Policy Uncertainty on Investor Information Asymmetry and Management Disclosures. *Journal of Accounting and Economics* 67(1), 36–57.

Nekhili, M., Hussainey, K., Cheffi, W., Chtioui, T., Tchakoute-Tchuigoua, H., 2016. R&D Narrative Disclosure, Corporate Governance and Market Value: Evidence From France. *JABR* 32(1), 111–128.

Pan, Y., Wang, T. Y., Weisbach, M. S., 2016. CEO investment cycles. *Review of Financial Studies* 29(11), 2955–2999.

Rjiba, H., Saadi, S., Boubaker, S., Ding, X.S., 2021. Annual Report Readability and the Cost of Equity Capital. *Journal of Corporate Finance* 67, 101902.

Rutherford, B.A., 2003. Obfuscation, Textual Complexity and the Role of Regulated Narrative Accounting Disclosure in Corporate Governance. *Journal of Management and Governance* 7(2), 187–210.

Smith, M., Taffler, R., 1992. The Chairman's Statement and Corporate Financial Performance. *Accounting and Finance* 32(2), 75–90.

Sydserff, R., Weetman, P., 1999. A Texture Index for Evaluating Accounting Narratives: An Alternative to Readability Formulas. *Accounting, Auditing, and Accountability Journal* 12(4), 459–488.

Velury, U., Jenkins, D.S., 2006. Institutional Ownership and the Quality of Earnings. *Journal of Business Research* 59(9), 1043–1051.

Wang, M., Hussainey, K., 2013. Voluntary Forward-Looking Statements Driven by Corporate Governance and Their Value Relevance. *Journal of Accounting and Public Policy, Special Issue on Accounting and Corporate Governance* 32(3), 26–49.

Wang, Z., Hsieh, T.-S., Sarkis, J., 2018. CSR Performance and the Readability of CSR Reports: Too Good to Be True? *Corporate Social Responsibility and Environmental Management* 25(1), 66–79.

WHK Horwath., 2005. *Corporate governance report*. Horwath (NSW) Pty Limited, Sydney.

Yekini, K.C., Adelopo, I., Andrikopoulos, P., Yekini, S., 2015. Impact of Board Independence on the Quality of Community Disclosures in Annual Reports. *Accounting Forum* 39(4), 249–267.

# 6 Extended auditor reports and key audit matters disclosure as complements to corporate narrative reporting

*Khairul Ayuni Mohd Kharuddin, Ilias G. Basioudis and Omar Al-Farooque*

## 6.1 Introduction

Corporate financial reporting has developed beyond the numbers, and today it includes narrative that underpins the company's broader strategic focus. Corporate narrative reporting comprises important forward-looking and qualitative information beyond the financial statements and notes to the accounts to portray a complete story of a business' well-being. Corporate narrative reports attempt to address aspects and events that are difficult to quantify and monetise, such as the business risks, future outlook, economic uncertainty, business strategy, risk management, corporate social responsibility, governance practices and the company's performance against non-financial operational targets (ACCA, 2010; Yeoh, 2010). Narrative reports are normally presented in the front half of the company's annual report. They include, but are not limited, to the operating and financial review report, strategic report, chairman's statement, directors' report, as well as corporate governance and corporate social responsibility disclosures (ACCA, 2010; Johal, 2018).

This paradigm shift is driven by concern from the capital market, regulators and various stakeholders (such as financial/investment analysts, lenders, tax officers, stockbrokers) that the annual reports lack transparency, hence the need for a more comprehensive, holistic, fair, balanced and understandable assessment of the company's performance and prospects (ICAEW, 2016). Voluntary disclosure of forward-looking information reduces information asymmetry problems and allows investors to better predict future earnings (Hussainey et al., 2003; Schleicher et al., 2007; Hussainey and Walker, 2009). At the same time, lack of narrative reporting on business risks, management's flexibility and discretion in handling and coping with current and future challenges have been claimed to be one of the main causes of the financial markets near-collapse (ACCA, 2010).

In the same spirit as narrative reporting, the auditor reporting regime has also evolved, leading to the emergence of the extended auditor report (EAR), followed by a further regulatory requirement for the disclosure of key audit matters (KAMs). The auditor's report now provides more narratives and contextual information about the approaches they have adopted and the professional

DOI: 10.4324/9781003095385-8

judgements they have made in coming to a view on the truth and fairness of the financial statements (FRC, 2016). The shift is from boilerplate audit reporting with a binary opinion to one that recognises the significance of the exercise of professional judgement and provides unprecedented levels of transparency of the work carried out by the auditor (ACCA, 2018). In the EAR, the auditor reports the risks of material misstatement that have the most significant effect on the audit and how the auditor addresses the assessed risks (FRC, 2013). KAMs are those issues selected by the auditor from matters communicated with those charged with governance, that, based on the auditor's professional judgement, are of greatest importance in the current period audit, and hence require thorough investigation and detailed explanation in the audit report (FRC, 2020b; IAASB, 2015).

The EAR and KAMs disclosures provided by the auditors and the narrative reports prepared by the management tend to complement each other. Higher-quality disclosure narratives by management, particularly on forward-looking information, such as anticipated litigation risk, future financial performance, existing and planned business strategies, changes in industry and macroeconomic environment, help auditors to better assess the risk underlying audit engagements (Hossain et al., 2019; Stanley, 2011; Tee et al., 2017). Auditors would try to obtain client business information from both public and private sources (Hay et al., 2006; DeFond and Zhang, 2013).

Increased narrative disclosures also improve the level of monitoring by the auditors, audit committee and management, as they encourage better dialogue between these parties in resolving accounting and audit issues (Minutti-Meza, 2021). The additional audit information provided in the EAR may promote higher audit quality as management and auditors are now placed under greater scrutiny for their risk disclosures (Christensen et al., 2014). The EAR itself provides incremental information, indirectly forcing companies to offer more explanation in other disclosures (Minutti-Meza, 2021). This is because the auditor's decision to report a matter as a KAM effectively shines a spotlight on an issue that may attract investors' awareness and attention. To minimise the adverse effects of KAM disclosures on the company, management will offer increased disclosures, explaining why the auditor emphasised the matter (Fuller et al., 2021). In addition, management may also choose to be more cooperative and open with their auditors, and the audit committee will be more proactive in their oversight role to resolve audit issues and scrutinise management disclosure decisions (Fuller et al., 2021).

This chapter explores how the EAR and KAMs disclosures complement narrative reporting through their information content. Section 6.2 provides an overview on the developments in auditing and the beginning and growth of changes in the auditor's report. Section 6.3 explores and provides an understanding of KAM disclosures. Section 6.4 explores the benefits and challenges the auditing profession faces in meeting the investors, regulators and public interest demands and expects for more than just a boilerplate explanation. Section 6.5 concludes and provides recommendations for future developments.

## 6.2  Overview and background to the development of the extended audit report

The auditor's report has been the medium of communication between the auditor and various users of the financial statements for more than a century. Historically, the requirement for a basic mandatory audit report/opinion originates from the Companies Act of 1900 in the UK (Stettler, 1994). Subsequent changes in the international standards on auditing (ISAs) enable auditors to issue unqualified, modified but unqualified, qualified, disclaimer and adverse opinions. The written "language" of the auditor's report has been mainly standardised in wordings and format to verify the truth and fairness of the company's financials with reference to a set of financial reporting framework and applicable regulations, except for when modifications are warranted due to disagreement over accounting treatment, insufficient audit evidence or going-concern issues (ICAEW, 2017).

However, the heightened case of financial scandals/crises and corporate failures and increasingly complex financial reporting requirements have led to increased scrutiny over the value of the audit report. In addition, the crisis of confidence surrounding the auditing profession and the expectation gap regarding auditors' role has sparked investors' curiosity and interest to gain an insight into the auditors' work, to determine how their professional judgements are established and how their professional scepticism and expertise are applied to the report prepared for management. Furthermore, given that every company and every audit is unique, then the auditor's report should reflect these dynamics while, at the same time, promoting reliability and transparency. Hence, users of accounts are looking for more than just boilerplate, binary, "pass/fail" audit opinion – they need/want a more transparent, useful and informative report which provides greater insight into the audit and risk-related matters in it. All of these reasons have led to the birth of EAR (Asare and Wright, 2012; IAASB, 2012; Vanstraelen et al., 2012; FRC, 2013; Mock et al., 2013; Bedard et al., 2016).

Improving the auditor's report has been a focus of regulators and standard setters worldwide. The Financial Reporting Council (FRC) in the UK was the first regulator to issue a new standard for audit reports, the International Standard on Auditing (UK) 700, *The Independent Auditor's Report on Financial Statements* (hereafter "ISA 700") in June 2013.[1] The new standard requires auditors to include in the audit report the risks of material misstatement that have the most significant effect on the audit and how auditors address the assessed risks (FRC, 2013). The International Auditing and Assurance Standard Board (IAASB) undertook the regulatory process between 2009 and 2016. The IAASB followed the FRC and issued a collection of new and revised auditor reporting standards.[2] The IAASB expanded report requirements became effective for audits of listed entities with fiscal year-ends on or after December 15, 2016. A post-implementation review carried out by IAASB reported that EAR has been adopted by 67 jurisdictions worldwide as of January 2020 (IAASB, 2020).

The UK was the first country to fully concur with the IAASB's auditing reporting standards in 2016. In addition to increased disclosures related to risks of material misstatement, the UK standard is slightly different from the international one. ISA 700 (UK) requires some additional disclosures about planning materiality and the scoping of the audit. The new style audit report requires auditors to explain how they applied the concept of materiality in planning and performing the audit and what threshold they used as materiality for the financial statements. The new audit report also gives an overview of the scope of the audit, showing how the scope addressed the assessed risk of material misstatements and materiality considerations (FRC, 2015).

The FRC reviewed several EARs implementation by UK companies and found that auditors had been innovative, and every company had adopted different approaches to the EAR (FRC, 2015). Some UK auditors won prizes from The Investment Association, which recognised the most innovative auditor's reports in an annual awards ceremony (ICAEW, 2017). On average, the largest EARs are about three pages in length, with three to four risks disclosed, and the common risks covered are related to accounting for revenue, pensions accounting, impairment of intangibles, legal claims, taxation and loan loss provisions in financial institutions (ICAEW, 2016). The auditing standards ISA 700 (UK) and ISA 701 (UK) were revised again in late 2019 and early 2020 to include amendments relating to accounting estimates and disclosures (FRC, 2020a, 2020b).

In the US, the Public Company Accounting Oversight Board (PCAOB) started the regulatory process in 2011. After a long review process, the new auditor reporting standard (i.e., AS 3101 on *The Audit Report on an Audit of Financial Statements When the Auditor Expresses an Unqualified Opinion*) was issued in May 2016 and then adopted in June 2017 (PCAOB, 2017). In October 2017, the US Securities and Exchange Commission (SEC) approved the 2017 PCAOB standard AS 3101 (SEC, 2017). Some technical distinctions exist between the FRC and IAASB, with such different terms used for key audit matters (i.e., critical audit matters), additional requirement for auditor's tenure disclosure and absence of requirement for discussion of audit scope and materiality (PCAOB, 2017). Although the US PCAOB started its regulatory process as early as other countries, the PCAOB final rules were not approved until 2018.

Among the new auditor reporting standards issued was ISA 701 *Communicating Key Audit Matters in the Independent Auditor's Report*. According to ISA 701, KAMs are those matters that, in the auditor's professional judgement, were of greatest importance in the current period audit, and hence require thorough investigation and explanation. Given that one of the most significant amendments in EAR is the disclosure of KAMs, discussed in the next section, we will explore and provide an understanding of KAM disclosures.

## 6.3  Key audit matters in the extended auditor report

As explained in the previous section, in 2016 the IAASB released *ISA 701 Communicating Key Audit Matters in the Independent Auditor's Report*. The KAMs highlight those issues that, in the auditor's professional judgement, are of most significance in the audit of the financial statements. Auditors therefore are required to determine and disclose issues or areas identified as significant risks (and requiring extra attention in the audit), as significant transactions or events (that have impacted the audit) or significant judgements including the audit of accounting estimates relating to client management decisions and judgements. Key audit matters are selected from matters communicated with those charged with governance. Different terminologies have been used to refer to KAMs in different parts of the world.

KAMs is referred to as critical audit matters (CAMs) in the US. Under the current PCAOB rules, CAMs are defined as "any matter arising from the audit of the financial statements that was communicated or required to be communicated to the audit committee and that (a) relates to accounts or disclosures that are material to the financial statements, and (b) involved especially challenging, subjective or complex auditor judgment" (PCAOB, 2017). The regulatory requirement to disclose CAMs applies to all US issuers starting with financial year end 15 December 2020 (Mintti-Meza, 2021).

Similar to the UK, France and the Netherlands have disclosed KAMs since the 2016 fiscal year end. Although EU Regulation was only effective for financial statements starting on or after June 2016, these three countries were already disclosing KAMs in their audit reports. In France, KAM is referred to as justification of assessments (JOA) and it has been made mandatory since 2003 (Haut Conseil des Commissaires aux Comptes, 2006). The new Australian auditing regulations around KAM reforms were fully adopted in 2017.

Auditors must choose which KAMs to disclose in their report each year and express risks of material misstatement and KAMs in their own words in order to avoid standardised or technical boilerplate language. According to the standard, the description of a KAM should be clear, concise, understandable and entity-specific. In a succinct and balanced way in order to enable intended users to understand, a KAM should explain why the matter was considered to be significant in the audit and how it was addressed during the audit. There should also be a reference to the related disclosure elsewhere in the financial statements (if any).

ISA 701 includes a judgement-based decision-making framework to help auditors determine which matters from the audit that are normally communicated with those charged with governance are KAMs. Out of all the issues on which they communicated with the client company's management and audit committee, auditors need to select KAMs from those issues that required "significant auditor attention".[3] In particular, this decision-making framework is developed to help auditors focus on areas of the financial statements that involve the most significant or complex judgements made by management and areas requiring significant auditor decisions. They should also explicitly consider areas where there might be a higher assessed risk of material misstatement, or significant risks identified in accordance with the risk-based approach in other ISAs.

The description of a KAM should be entity-specific, tailored purposely to the facts and circumstances of the auditor's client company and to the individual audit engagement in order to provide relevant and meaningful information to users. It follows that the level of detail that is included in each description of a KAM is a matter of professional judgement and may vary among clients and auditor characteristics, and furthermore may be related to client-specific audit procedures adopted by auditors. Similarly, the number of KAMs that are communicated in the auditor's report, the selection of topics addressed and the nature in which they may be described can vary as they may be affected by the complexity of the client company, the nature of its business and environment and the facts and circumstances of the audit engagement. The most common KAMs that are disclosed in audit reports relate to the following:

- Impairment of assets (investment, goodwill or of another, intangible asset)
- Valuation (property, plant and equipment (PPE), investment, foreign currencies valuation or inventory)
- Revenue recognition (fraud)
- Investment related (acquisitions and disposals)
- Capitalisation
- Financial instruments
- Provisions (receivables, inventories, claims or restructuring)
- Pension schemes (assets, liabilities or valuations)
- Taxation (current, deferred, litigation or disputes)
- Internal control (management override or IT system implementation)
- Going concern (Brexit, financial covenants concern or COVID-19)
- Legal and regulatory (regulatory compliance, litigation dispute, ongoing investigation or effects of new accounting standards)

All the above examples of KAMs are areas of great subjectivity that require a significant application of judgement from both the company's management and auditors. As expected, some of these KAMs are more prevalent in certain industry sectors than others (for example, revenue recognition in software and telecommunication companies, and asset/licence impairment in mining companies). The common concept is that these are the areas that were reported to be of greatest focus in the audit, but also typically the areas of assessed greatest risk for the audit.

Although the rules and new auditing standards of these regulators/standard setters are somewhat similar, the implementation of EARs resulted in noticeable variations among jurisdictions with respect to the number, types and levels of details in KAMs and CAMs due to different regulatory, legal and market environments (Mazars, 2018; ACCA, 2018) as well as a function of cultural and institutional factors (Nolder and Riley, 2014). In the initial two years of implementation, around 70% of Australian auditees had the same KAMs disclosed in 2017 and 2018, along with differences between large and small audit practitioners (Kend and Nguyen, 2020).

In December 2018, the audit firm Mazars published a report, "*A benchmark of Key Audit Matters by country and by industry sectors; A comparative study highlighting the outcome of ISA 701's application and its influences over the auditor's report*". The report analysed and compared KAM implementation experience in

France, the Netherlands and the UK. In addition, the ACCA also published a report on "*Key audit matters: unlocking the audit secrets of the audit*" in March 2018, which incorporated more countries outside the EU, with audit reports from Brazil, Cyprus, Kenya, Nigeria, Oman, Romania, South Africa, UAE and Zimbabwe. In respect to comparison between the UK, France and the Netherlands, it is observed that the UK is slightly above its peers (FRC, 2016). The average counts of KAMs per audit report is 4.2, 3.7 and 3.3 in the UK, the Netherlands and France, respectively (Mazars, 2018). The typical number of CAMs in the US is between one and two (Gutierrez et al., 2018; Bochkay et al., 2020) and is two in Australia (Kend and Nguyen, 2020). In the US, CAMs are usually discussed within 700 words, with common topics covering business combinations and consolidation, and revenue recognition, accounting for income taxes as well as goodwill valuation and impairment (Bochkay et al., 2020). Building on the understanding of EAR and KAM disclosures, in the next section (Section 6.4), we explore the benefits and challenges relating to these disclosures.

## 6.4 Exploring the benefits and challenges of extended audit report (EAR) and key audit matters (KAMs) disclosures

This section explores the benefits and challenges of EAR and KAM disclosure implementation, drawing upon evidence from selected published studies and reports published by the regulators and professional accountancy bodies.

Four recent reviews of the UK's audit environment carried out by Kingman, BEIS Select Committee, Brydon and the Competitions & Markets Authority (CMA) remarked the new auditor reporting regimes as one of the critical solutions to audit quality issues (Kingman, 2018; BEIS Select Committee, 2019; Brydon, 2019; CMA, 2019). The main benefit of the EAR is that it improved the communicative value of the audit report by making it more insightful. Increased explanation of KAMs and the audit work performed provided users of accounts with greater transparency and a better understanding of the audit process. Despite these claims, there is no conclusive evidence from empirical research to indicate that investors value greatly the additional disclosures provided in EAR and KAMs. For example, studies on expanded reports in the UK by Gutierrez et al. (2018) reported that EAR provides investors with little value as there is no evidence of an incremental short-window market reaction through abnormal returns and abnormal trading volume. Bédard et al. (2019) show that French auditors' disclosure of additional information is somewhat more symbolic than informative in value as JOAs disclosure does not seem to affect the financial market nor the quality or efficiency of the audit. Interestingly, the introduction of KAMs in the audit report has been found to change the users' information search strategies. An experimental study by Sirois et al. (2018) in Canada, using innovative eye-tracking technology, reported that KAMs have an attention-directing impact to help investors effectively navigate financial reports.

From the debt market perspective, improvements to auditor's reports may help banks improve their overall credit risk management in the credit decision process

(Basel Committee on Banking Supervision, 2012). The EAR's broader scope and additional disclosures could help shape loan contracting by reducing borrowers' information asymmetry, as it provides indications of borrower riskiness to mitigate adverse selection problems and reduces lenders' costly screening efforts (Trpeska et al., 2017; Phorumb et al., 2021). For instance, a UK study by Phorumb et al. (2021) documents that adopting the new audit report is associated with more favourable loan contracting terms through changes in loan spread and maturity. On the contrary, Boolaky and Quick (2016) did not find that bank directors' perceptions changed due to KAM disclosures.

The introduction of EAR and KAMs disclosures are expected to have positive implications on audit quality. Auditors are becoming more conscious of the quality of their work and their increased audit risks. Hence, they will exercise more careful judgement and a higher level of professional scepticism. The increased audit effort might lead to higher audit fees being charged by the auditors. A UK study by Reid et al. (2019) reported that the EAR is positively associated with improved financial reporting quality, as evidenced by significant decreases in absolute abnormal accruals and the propensity to just meet or beat analyst forecasts, as well as a substantial increase in earnings response coefficients. However, the study did not detect any significant increase in audit costs, either in audit fees or audit delays. In addition, a UK study by Gutierrez et al. (2018) observed no significant association between audit fees and either the EAR or the number of risks identified by the auditor. However, a significant increase in audit fees was reported following the introduction of EAR in New Zealand (Li et al., 2019). Bédard et al. (2019) reported that audit fees were higher, and audit report lag was longer in France's first year of JOA disclosure but not in the subsequent years. Furthermore, the additional disclosures of KAMs in the EAR could also increase legal liability for auditors when they fail to detect misstatements (Gimbar et al., 2016). Interestingly, on the contrary, some studies have found that disclosing KAMs can reduce auditor liability (Brasel et al., 2016; Kachelmeier et al., 2020), suggesting that the concern over the legal hazards of disclosing KAMs is likely unwarranted.

The disclosed items in the EAR may attract investors, lenders, regulators and public reactions to the company's activities, which leads management to pay more attention to those items. Increased disclosures in the EAR also mean that there will be more conversations and monitoring between the auditor, management and the audit committee, which contributes to better governance over the company's financial reporting process. To reduce the negative implications of KAM disclosures on the company, management may be more cooperative and open with their auditors. In a US study, Fuller et al. (2021) finds that management's related financial disclosures on complex estimates are more informative and forthcoming in the presence of CAM disclosure when the audit committee is effective. Kang (2019) finds that audit committee members tend to scrutinise management more by asking particularly probing and challenging questions about their significant accounting issue in the presence of CAMs disclosure.

Despite the various benefits of the EAR, there are also challenges related to its implementation. There is a concern that the information disclosed may become formulaic and boilerplate over time. There is also a possibility that the auditors might report on only a few matters to reduce the risk of litigation. On the other hand, the auditor might engage in excessive reporting by providing a long list of redundant disclosures with questionable benefits, ambiguous purpose and additional cost. For instance, a study by Bedard et al. (2019) in France reported that 80% of JOAs disclosed and the audit work descriptions were copied from the previous year's audit report. Because KAMs focus on the most complex judgements in the audit process, less sophisticated financial users may find it difficult to understand or interpret the language used to explain the more complex and detailed EAR and KAMs. For instance, the study by Köhler et al. (2020) in Germany reports that non-professional investors have difficulties processing the information conveyed by KAMs compared with professional investors.

Overall, the empirical, academic evidence has provided mixed results and sentiments so far with respect to the effectiveness of the EAR and KAM disclosures. Existing archival and data-driven analysis of EARs provides evidence that EAR and KAM disclosures do not systematically provide incremental firm-specific information to investors or affect the cost or quality of audits.

## 6.5 Conclusion, implications and recommendations for future developments

There have been in the past, and continue to be today, extensive debates on how to create financial reporting information and company annual reports that users find balanced, reliable, understandable, comparable and relevant. The overall aim of narrative reporting is to include information that is both financial and non-financial, historical and forward-looking and which clarifies the main trends and factors underlying the future development, performance and position of the business concerned.

The aims of all auditor reporting standards and, more specifically, ISA 700 – *Forming an Opinion and Reporting on Financial Statements*, and ISA 701 – *Communicating Key Audit Matters in the Independent Auditor's Report*, have been to increase transparency about the audit that was conducted by auditors, to (re)focus the attention of investors and other users on areas in the company annual reports that are subject to significant management judgement and significant auditor consideration, to motivate users to further (re)engage with company management and those charged with governance (e.g., audit committees, boards of directors) about certain matters related to the company, the audited financial statements or the audit itself that was performed. Another aim has been to redirect the auditor's attention to issues to be communicated, which could directly or indirectly result in an improvement in professional scepticism, among other contributors to audit quality.

The EAR and KAM disclosures provided by the auditor, and the narrative reports prepared by the management tend to complement one another. The information disclosed in the narrative reports prepared by management help the auditor to better assess the client's business risk and the audit risk itself. On the other hand, the auditor's detailed explanation in the EARs (including KAMs) provide the client with a better understanding of the risk and issues related to the company's audit, on which might be necessary for management to elaborate further in their narrative reports. This will foster more open and effective communication between management, the auditor and the audit committee.

From the stakeholder's perspective, including KAMs in the EARs may improve audit quality or users' perception of it, which may have added-on benefits with regards to increased users' confidence in the audit and the preparation of the financial statements. On the other hand, doubts are also expressed about the inclusion of KAMs in the EARs in connection with their cost/benefit balance, the objectivity/neutrality of disclosures, potential information overload and usefulness and overall value relevance. It can be said that EARs are becoming repetitive and very lengthy, and this perhaps increases the complexity of those auditor's reports without necessarily providing investors with much additional insight. Their perception as compliance exercises further inhibits the effective communication of an overall picture of the truth and fairness of the financial statements. The way forward should perhaps include avoiding information clutter and "minimum" information reporting to merely comply with the EAR requirements of the standards. Instead, it should consist of more comparable qualitative and incremental information that a wide set of stakeholders would find beneficial.

Standard setters and regulators conduct regular post-implementation reviews of various applicable standards to ensure these standards respond to their intended purpose and users of the financial statements. Similarly, the concept of KAMs is expected to be evolving over time so that investors' needs are continuously addressed. Future refinements in the auditor's reporting standards may include ways for auditors to include more informative audit-specific risks, which in turn can perhaps be more useful to investors. For example, auditors already disclose some high-risk areas in their report, but the impact of KAM disclosure may differ between risk-increasing and risk-decreasing activities and therefore some further development in this area of auditor reporting may be actioned. Conceivably, another area of future consideration may be whether KAM reporting is useful and relevant and can convey new information to investors when potentially different KAMs are reported year on year.

Another possible area of attention required is whether the EARs and the reporting of KAMs can convey actual information about potential company financial reporting issues and/or management misconduct. For example, recent scandals in the UK and Germany have questioned the effectiveness of extended auditor reporting in alerting investors to high-risk areas with low-quality financial reporting and/or fraud. Some have argued that if EARs conveyed useful information, they would have perhaps triggered intense, external scrutiny and meaningfully alerted the shareholders of the shortly-to-be failing companies. Future considerations of regulators and auditors may require changing the tone and language used in reporting KAMs if EARs are supposed to remain relevant and valuable to investors and other users of the financial statements.

Finally, we should make a passing comment on the developing importance of corporate (social) responsibility, which has led to demands for greater transparency in how climate-related risks and opportunities and in general sustainability issues are linked to corporate governance, corporate strategy and risk management and how they affect company earnings and comparative performance. In turn, auditors have already been asked to build capabilities in this area, for example, by the FRC in the UK. This may lead auditors to be required to provide "green" audits to assess the total environmental footprints of client company activities but also to provide more generic corporate (social) responsibility assurance within their EARs and KAM disclosures as related to the expanded narrative reporting sections of the company's annual report.

## Notes

1 The ISA 700 was revised a few times and changed its title to "Forming an Opinion and Reporting on Financial Statements" in June 2016.
2 These standards are: ISA 700 (revised) – Forming an Opinion and Reporting on Financial Statements; ISA 701 – Communicating Key Audit Matters in the Independent Auditor's Report; ISA 705 – Modifications to the Opinion in the Independent Auditor's Report; ISA 706 – Emphasis of Matter Paragraphs and Other Matter Paragraphs in the Independent Auditor's Report; and ISA 720 – The Auditor's Responsibilities Relating to Other Information.
3 ISA 701 provides robust guidance to support the decision-making framework in deciding the relative significance of an issue communicated with management and the audit committee and whether such an issue is a KAM.

## References

Asare, S. K., and Wright, A. M. 2012. Investors', auditors', and lenders' understanding of the message conveyed by the standard audit report on the financial statements. *Accounting Horizons*, 26(2), 193–217.

Association of Chartered Certified Accountants (ACCA). 2010. Hitting the notes, but what's the tune?: An international survey of CFOs' views on narrative reporting. Available at: https://www.accaglobal.com/africa/en/technical-activities/technical-resources-search/2010/september/hitting-the-notes.html.

Association of Chartered Certified Accountants (ACCA). 2018. Key audit matters: Unlocking the secrets of the audit. Available at: https://www.accaglobal.com/content/dam/ACCA_Global/professional-insights/Key-audit-matters/pi-key-audit-matters.pdf.

Basel Committee on Banking Supervision. 2012. Comment on IAASB invitation: Improving the auditor's report. Available at: https://www.ifac.org/system/files/publications/exposure-drafts/comments/BCBS.pdf.

Bédard, J., Coram, P., Espahbodi, R., and Mock, T. J. 2016. Does recent academic research support changes to audit reporting standards? *Accounting Horizons*, 30(2), 255–275.

Bédard, J., Gonthier-Besacier, N., and Schatt, A. 2019. Consequences of expanded audit reports: Evidence from the justifications of assessments in France. *Auditing: A Journal of Practice and Theory*, 38(3), 23–45.

BEIS Select Committee. 2019. Carillion inquiry. London: House of Commons of the United Kingdom. Available at: https://publications.parliament.uk/pa/cm201719/cmselect/cmbeis/1718/1718.pdf.

Boolaky, P. K., and Quick, R. 2016. Bank directors' perceptions of expanded auditor's reports. *International Journal of Auditing*, 20(2), 158–174.

Bochkay, K., Chychyla, R., De George, E. T., Minutti-Meza, M., and Schroeder, J. 2020. SEC comment letter. Available at: https://pcaobus.org/EconomicAndRiskAnalysis/pir/PostImplementationReviewAS3101UnqualifiedOpinion/18_Miguel-Minutti-Meza.pdf.

Brasel, K., Doxey, M., Grenier, J., and Reffett, A. 2016. Risk disclosure preceding negative outcomes: The effects of reporting critical audit matters on judgments of auditor liability. *The Accounting Review*, 91(5), 1345–1362.

Brydon, D. 2019. Report of the independent review into the quality and effectiveness of audit. Available at: https://assets.publishing.service.gov.uk/government/uploads/system/uploads/attachment_data/file/852960/brydon-review-final-report.pdf.

Christensen, B. E., Glover, S. M., and Wolfe, C. J. 2014. Do critical audit matter paragraphs in the audit report change nonprofessional investors' decision to invest? *Auditing: A Journal of Practice and Theory*, 33(4), 71–93.

Competitions & Markets Authority (CMA). 2019. Statutory audit services market study. London. Available at: https://assets.publishing.service.gov.uk/media/5d03667d40f0b609ad3158c3/audit_final_report_02.pdf.

DeFond, M., and Zhang, J. 2013. A review of archival auditing research. *Journal of Accounting and Economics*, 58(2–3), 275–326.

Financial Reporting Council (FRC). 2013. Revision to ISA (UK and Ireland) 700, February 2013. London: The Financial Reporting Council Limited. Available at: https://www.frc.org.uk/getattachment/b567ab62-dfa5-4b61-a052-852c4bf51f0e/;.aspx.

Financial Reporting Council (FRC). 2015. Extended auditor's reports: A review of experience in the first year. Available at: https://www.frc.org.uk/getattachment/561627cc-facb-431b-beda-ead81948604e/Extended-Auditor-Reports-March-2015.pdf.

Financial Reporting Council (FRC). 2016. Extended auditor's reports: A further review of experience. Available at: https://www.frc.org.uk/getattachment/76641d68-c739-45ac-a251-cabbfd2397e0/report-on-the-second-year-experience-of-extended-auditors-reports-jan-2016.pdf.

Financial Reporting Council (FRC). 2020a. Standard. International standard on auditing (UK) 700 (revised November 2019, updated January 2020). London: The Financial Reporting Council Limited. Available at: https://www.frc.org.uk/getattachment/0b1f9783-42a8-44f5-ae4bd4fcd4b538db/ISA-(UK)-700_Revised-November-2019_Updated-January-2020_final-With-Covers.pdf.

Financial Reporting Council (FRC). 2020b. Standard. International standard on auditing (UK) 701(revised November 2019, updated January 2020). London: The Financial Reporting Council Limited. Available at: https://www.frc.org.uk/getattachment/4af1deff-9145-4758-b033-ff637da24117/ISA-(UK)-701_Revised-November-2019_Updated-January-2020_final-With-Covers.pdf.

Fuller, S. H., Joe, J. R., and Luippold, B. L. 2021. The effect of auditor reporting choice and audit committee oversight on management financial disclosures. *The Accounting Review*. Forthcoming.

Gimbar, C., Hansen, B., and Ozlanski, M. 2016. Early evidence on the effects of critical audit matter on auditor liability. *Current Issues in Auditing*, 10(1), A24–A33.

Gutierrez, E., Minutti-Meza, M., Tatum, K. W., and Vulcheva, M. 2018. Consequences of adopting an expanded auditor's report in the United Kingdom. *Review of Accounting Studies*, 23(4), 1543–1587.

Haut Conseil des Commissaires aux Comptes. 2006. *NEP-705 Justification des appréciations. Normes d'Exercice professionnel des Commissaires aux Comptes.* Available at: https://doc.cncc.fr/docs/kk3180.

Hay, D., Knechel, W. R., and Wong, N. 2006. Audit fees: A meta-analysis of the effect of supply and demand attributes. *Contemporary Accounting Research*, 23(1), 141–191.

Hossain, M., Hossain, M., Mitra, S., and Salama, F. 2019. Narrative disclosures, firm life cycle, and audit fees. *International Journal of Auditing*, 23(3), 403–423.

Hussainey, K., Schleicher, T., and Walker, M. 2003. Undertaking large-scale disclosure studies when AIMR-FAF ratings are not available: The case of prices leading earnings. *Accounting and Business Research*, 33(4), 275–294.

Hussainey, K., and Walker, M. 2009. The effects of voluntary disclosure and dividend propensity on prices leading earnings. *Accounting and Business Research*, 39(1), 37–55.

Institute of Chartered Accountants in England and Wales (ICAEW). 2016. Extended audit reports: Exploring challenges and opportunities in implementation. Available at: https://www.icaew.com/-/media/corporate/files/middle-east-hub/icaew-dfsa-briefing-paper.ashx.

Institute of Chartered Accountants in England and Wales (ICAEW). 2017. The start of a conversation: The extended audit report. Available at: https://www.icaew.com/-/media/corporate/files/technical/audit-and-assurance/audit-and-assurance-faculty/publications/extended-audit-report.ashx?la=en.

International Auditing and Assurance Standards Board (IAASB). 2012. Improving the auditor's report. New York: International Federation of Accountants (IFAC). Available at: https://www.iaasb.org/publications/improving-auditor-s-report.

International Auditing and Assurance Standards Board (IAASB). 2015. International standard on auditing (ISA) 701. New York: International Federation of Accountants (IFAC). Available at: https://www.iaasb.org/publications/reporting-audited-financial-statements-new-and-revised-auditorreporting-standards-and-related-11.

International Auditing and Assurance Standards Board (IAASB). 2020. Auditor reporting post implementation review project update. New York: International Federation of Accountants (IFAC). Available at: https://www.iaasb.org/publications/iaasb-auditor-reporting-project-updatejanuary-2020.

Johal, P. 2018. Corporate reporting: From numbers to narrative, in Conway, E., and Byrne, D. (Eds.), *Contemporary issues in accounting* (pp. 105–123). Cham: Palgrave Macmillan.

Kachelmeier, S. J., Rimkus, D., Schmidt, J. J., and Valentine, K. 2020. The forewarning effect of critical audit matter disclosures involving measurement uncertainty. *Contemporary Accounting Research*, 37(4), 2186–2212.

Kang, Y. J. 2019. Are audit committees more challenging given a specific investor base? Does the answer change in the presence of prospective critical audit matter disclosures? *Accounting, Organizations and Society*, 77, 1–14.

Kend, M., and Nguyen, L. A. 2020. Investigating recent audit reform in the Australian context: Analysis of the KAM disclosures in audit reports 2017–2018. *International Journal of Auditing*, 24(3), 412–430.

Kingman, J. 2018. *Independent review of the financial reporting council.* Available at: https://assets.publishing.service.gov.uk/government/uploads/system/uploads/attachment_data/file/767387/frc-independent-review-final-report.pdf.

Köhler, A., Ratzinger-Sakel, N., and Theis, J. 2020. The effects of key audit matters on the auditor's report's communicative value: Experimental evidence from investment professionals and non-professional investors. *Accounting in Europe*, 17(2), 105–128.

Li, H., Hay, D., and Lau, D. 2019. Assessing the impact of the new auditor's report. *Pacific Accounting Review*, 31(1), 110–132.

Mazars. 2018. A benchmark of key audit matters – By country and by industry sectors. Available at: https://www.mazars.com/content/download/950520/49754429/version//file/Mazars-Key-Audit-matters-benchmark-Dec-2018.pdf.

Minutti-Meza, M. 2021. The art of conversation: The expanded audit report. *Accounting and Business Research*, 51(5), 548–581.

Mock, T. J., Bédard, J., Coram, P. J., Davis, S. M., Espahbodi, R., and Warne, R. C. 2013. The audit reporting model: Current research synthesis and implications. *Auditing: A Journal of Practice and Theory*, 32(sp1), 323–351.

Nolder, C., and Riley, T. 2014. Effects of differences in national culture on auditors' judgments and decisions: A literature review of cross-cultural auditing studies from a judgment and decision-making perspective. *Auditing: A Journal of Practice and Theory*, 33(2), 141–164.

Porumb, V.-A., Zengin-Karaibrahimoglu, Y., Lobo, G. J., Hooghiemstra, R., and de Waard, D. 2021. Expanded auditor's report disclosures and loan contracting. *Contemporary Accounting Research*. Forthcoming.

Public Company Accounting Oversight Board (PCAOB). 2017. *The auditor's report on an audit of financial statements when the auditor expresses an unqualified opinion and related amendments to PCAOB standards. PCAOB release no. 2017-001.* Washington, DC. Available at: https://pcaobus.org/Rulemaking/Docket034/2017-001-auditors-report-final-rule.pdf.

Reid, L. C., Carcello, J. V., Li, C., and Neal, T. L. 2019. Impact of auditor report changes on financial reporting quality and audit costs: Evidence from the United Kingdom. *Contemporary Accounting Research*, 31(4), 1501–1539.

Schleicher, T., Hussainey, K., and Walker, M. 2007. Loss firms' annual report narratives and share price anticipation of earnings. *The British Accounting Review*, 39(2), 153–171.

Securities and Exchange Commission (SEC). 2017. Public company accounting oversight board; order granting approval of proposed rules on the auditor's report on an audit of financial statements when the auditor expresses an unqualified opinion, and departures from unqualified opinions and other reporting circumstances, and related amendments to auditing standards. SEC release no. 34-81916; file no. PCAOB-2017-01. Available at: https://www.sec.gov/rules/pcaob/2017/34-81916.pdf.

Sirois, L. P., Bédard, J., and Bera, P. 2018. The informational value of key audit matters in the auditor's report: Evidence from an eye-tracking study. *Accounting Horizons*, 32(2), 141–162.

Stanley, J. D. 2011. Is the audit fee disclosure a leading indicator of clients' business risk? *Auditing: A Journal of Practice and Theory*, 30(3), 157–179.

Stettler, H. 1994. Accounting and auditing history: Major developments in England and the United States from ancient roots through the mid-twentieth century. Auditing Symposium XII, p. 7–44.

Tee, C. M., Gul, F. A., Foo, Y., and Teh, C. G. 2017. Institutional monitoring, political connections and audit fees: Evidence from Malaysian firms. *International Journal of Auditing*, 21(2), 164–176.

Trpeska, M., Atanasovski, A., and Bozinovska, Z. 2017. The relevance of financial information and contents of the new audit report for lending decisions of commercial banks. *Journal of Accounting and Management Information Systems*, 16(4), 455–471.

Yeoh, P. 2010. Narrative reporting: The UK experience. *International Journal of Law and Management*, 52(3), 211–231.

Vanstraelen, A., Schelleman, C., Meuwissen, R., and Hofmann, I. 2012. The audit reporting debate: Seemingly intractable problems and feasible solutions. *European Accounting Review*, 21(2), 193–215.

# Part 2

# Empirical research on narrative reporting

# 7 The readability of narrative disclosures and earnings management

## Empirical evidence from the GCC banking sector

*Mostafa Hassan, Hany Kamel and
Bassam Abu-Abbas*

### 7.1 Introduction

The readability of narrative disclosures (RNDs) has received considerable atten-tion in the accounting literature over the past two decades (Clatworthy and Jones, 2001; Hassan et al., 2019; Jones and Smith, 2014; Loughran and Mcdonald, 2016). RNDs contributes to alleviating information asymmetries between a firm's management and outsiders. However, managers may manipulate their narratives to convey certain messages to the public. Because narrative disclosures (NDs) are not regulated, managers use different linguistic styles when they address their stakeholders about their firm's performance (Brennan et al., 2009; Huang et al., 2014; Li, 2010; Loughran and McDonald, 2011; Smith and Taffler, 2000). Most ND studies have been carried out in European and Western countries (Clatworthy and Jones, 2001; Hrasky and Smith, 2008; Loughran and McDonald, 2016; Pajuste et al., 2021; Smith and Taffler, 2000), and few studies examine the RNDs in emerging economies, such as Qatar (Hassan et al., 2019) and Oman (Dalwai et al., 2021).

The literature on earnings management (EM) documents indicates that the managerial motives to overstate/understate a firm's earnings are a function of the managers' short-term interests (Abbadi et al., 2016). Most EM studies used sam-ples from the non-financial sectors (Atieh and Hussain, 2012; DuCharme et al., 2001; Iatridis and Kadorinis, 2009), with few relying on data obtained from the banking sector (Beatty et al., 1995; Beaver and Engel, 1996; Wahlen, 1994) and very few examined EM in the Middle East and North Africa (MENA) region (e.g., Kamel, 2012; Lassoued et al., 2018).

This chapter, therefore, fills a gap in the literature by investigating the associa-tion between EM and the RND in the Gulf Cooperation Council (GCC) banks. Despite the significant contributions of prior studies which examined the RNDs/ EM association (Ajina et al., 2016; Li, 2008; Lo et al., 2017; Pajuste et al., 2021), our chapter is a pioneer in exploring this association in GCC banks. We choose the GCC banking sector because it represents a major sector in the Gulf region, which mainly relies on oil and gas trading. In an attempt to diversify the GCC

DOI: 10.4324/9781003095385-10

economies and earn non-oil income, GCC banks have crossed local borders and become influential players in the GCC financial systems (Molyneux and Iqbal, 2005). GCC banks are financially strong and mostly family-owned with "a modest state ownership" (Lassoued et al., 2018). GCC banks have similar characteristics regarding levels of governance, regulations and restrictions. They operate in countries that inherited their legislative frameworks from British and French systems before declaring their independence in the mid-1960s (Hassan et al., 2020). Hence, the GCC context provides an appealing opportunity to examine the association between EM and the RNDs reported by GCC banks.

## 7.2  Literature review

Ajina et al. (2016) argue that readability and EM are two different aspects of disclosure by which managers can convey a misleading image of their firm (Ajina et al., 2016). Readability refers to the complexity of narrative reporting (Ajina et al., 2016; Li, 2008; Lo et al., 2017; Pajuste et al., 2021). Merkl-Davies and Brennan (2007) argue that reducing the information asymmetry between managers and investors encourages managers to prepare easy-to-read annual reports. Alternatively, managers may prepare annual reports that rely on obscure language to confuse readers or leave them less well informed (i.e., obfuscation). Obfuscation indicates management's tendency to prepare complex narratives to conceal the firm's negative performance (Caserio et al., 2020; Hassan, 2014; Huang et al., 2014). Several studies examined the association between firms' performance and the RNDs and found that managers obfuscate text in the annual reports when their firms are underperforming (e.g., Courtis, 1998; Dalwai et al., 2021; Hassan et al., 2019; Hrasky et al., 2009; Li, 2008).

Desender et al. (2011) argue that EM is an act of obfuscating annual reports. Healy and Wahlen (1999, p. 368) illustrate that managers make accounting estimates either to "*mislead some stakeholders about the underlying economic performance of the company or to influence contractual outcomes that depend on reported accounting numbers*". EM originates from managers' deliberate use of accounting flexibility to maximise their self-interest at the expense of outsiders such as lenders and shareholders. Li (2008) examines the association between the RNDs and earnings persistence (future performance) and finds that firms with easier-to-read narratives have more persistent positive earnings. In examining the relationship between readability and the current level of earnings, Li (2008) finds that firms with lower earnings have harder-to-read narratives (obfuscation). The latter result has been disputed and criticised because complex narratives do not necessarily set out to cause obfuscation; instead, such complexity may accurately reflect the reporting firm's environment and the topic or the events under review (Bloomfield, 2008; Bushee et al., 2018).

Ajina et al. (2016) examine the association between RNDs and EM in a sample of French firms between 2010 and 2013 and find that managers, who manage earnings to achieve certain targets, prepare complex narratives. Lo et al. (2017) examine the association between EM and the RNDs in the Management

Discussion and Analysis (MD&A) section and find that managers, who manage earnings to achieve certain targets, often prepare difficult-to-read narratives. This result goes against the mainstream belief that positive news is inherently easier to communicate. In examining this association in a sample of Baltic listed firms during the period 2012–2016, Pajuste et al. (2021) find that the EM/narrative complexity relationship exists only with firms that have high levels of liquidity. Pajuste et al. (2021) highlight that firms with greater liquidity are subject to more inspection, examination and reviewing from market participants and hence the managers of these firms tend to obfuscate the content of their narratives. In GCC, Dalwai et al. (2021) investigate the impact of readability on the performance of Omani listed financial firms from 2014 to 2018. They find that better readability is significantly associated with higher performance (asset utilisation and Tobin's Q). Unexpectedly, however, their findings show that difficult-to-read annual reports are positively associated with firms' profitability (return on assets (ROA) ratio).

Although previous studies offer significant insights, they focus mainly on manufacturing sectors in non-Arab economies (Ajina et al., 2016; Lo et al., 2017; Pajuste et al., 2021), with the exception of only one study that addresses readability of disclosures from Oman's financial sector without underscoring its association with EM (Dalwai et al., 2021). Our chapter, therefore, extends the prior literature by examining the association between RNDs and EM in the banks of GCC countries.

## 7.3 Theoretical framework and hypothesis development

Both the impression management and agency theories explain the managerial motives behind obfuscating annual reports, whether through ND or EM (Brennan and Merkl-Davies, 2013; Bushee et al., 2018; Merkl-Davies and Brennan, 2007). Managers manipulate annual reports (through numbers or language) in order to influence the perception of stakeholders. They also decide whether the content of annual reports (accounting estimates and language) should reduce information asymmetries and/or signal good news to stakeholders (e.g., Caserio et al., 2020; Rutherford, 2018). The advocates of agency theory explain managers' motives in terms of the economic consequences of their choices, which are the outcome of the conflict of interests between owners (principals) and managers (agents) (Jensen and Meckling, 1976; Watts and Zimmerman, 1990). To minimise this conflict, managers should reflect the economic condition of their firms and produce information that is quantitatively fair (i.e., free of EM) and qualitatively easy to read (i.e., in the NDs). Impression management theorists posit that managers' honesty is always questionable, and hence they may take advantage of the unregulated nature of NDs and prepare obfuscated narratives to hide their engagement in income-decreasing EM activities or prepare easy-to-read annual reports to signal good news when they engage in income-increasing EM activities. Hence, we hypothesise that:

*H*1: *There is no association between the RNDs and EM in the annual reports of GCC banks*;

*H2: There is an association between the RNDs and EM in the annual reports of GCC banks;*

>   *H2$_a$: There is a positive association between easy-to-read narratives and income-increasing EM in the annual reports of GCC banks (positive impression management)*
>
>   *H2$_b$: There is a negative association between easy-to-read narratives and income-decreasing EM in the annual reports of GCC banks (obfuscation)*

## 7.4 Methodology

### 7.4.1 Sample

We drew up a sample of banks listed on the GCC Stock Exchanges. After excluding foreign banks, merged banks and banks with missing financial reports, the sample size consisted of 61 GCC banks yielding 204 bank-year observations during the period 2014–2017. Table 7.1 shows the sample composition.

### 7.4.2 Research design and measurement of variables

We carried out regression analysis of the RNDs of the banks' annual reports (dependent variable) on the banks' EM activities (main independent variable), banks' governance and characteristics (control variables) (Ajina et al., 2016; Dalwai et al., 2015, 2021; Ginesti et al., 2017; Hassan et al., 2019; Li, 2008; Lo et al., 2017; Velte, 2018). Data were obtained from banks' annual reports, websites and databases, such as COMPUSTAT Global and Arbis Bank Focus. Equation 7.1 presents our regression model as follows:

$$Read_{it} = \alpha_0 + \alpha_1 DLLP_{it} + \alpha_2 BOD\_Size_{it} + \alpha_3 Audit\_CMMeeting_{it}$$
$$+ \alpha_4 Bank\_Size_{it} + \alpha_5 ROA_{it} + \alpha_6 LEV_{it} + \alpha_7 AGE_{it} + Count + Bank\,type + \varepsilon_{it}.$$
$$(7.1)$$

where $Read_{it}$ denotes the RNDs in the annual reports of bank $i$ in year $t$, and $DLLP_{it}$ is the discretionary loan loss provision which presents our proxy for

*Table 7.1* Sample composition

| Country | Number of Banks | Number of Bank-Year Observations |
| --- | --- | --- |
| Bahrain | 9 | 22 |
| Kuwait | 10 | 35 |
| Oman | 11 | 31 |
| Qatar | 10 | 36 |
| Saudi Arabia | 10 | 40 |
| UAE | 11 | 40 |
| Total | 61 | 204 |

EM. Regarding the control variables; $BOD\_Size_{it}$ is the total number of board members; $Audit\_CMMeeting_{it}$ is the total number of audit committee meetings; $Bank\_Size_{it}$ is the natural logarithm of the bank's total assets; $ROA_{it}$ is the return on assets, which equals the income before extraordinary items of bank $i$ in year $t$ divided by the average total assets; $LEV_{it}$ is the financial leverage of bank $i$ in year $t$ measured by the average total debt divided by average total assets; $AGE_{it}$ is the number of years of operation since the bank was incorporated; *Count* is the country effect as embedded in the random-effect or the fixed-effect regressions. *Bank type* is a dummy variable equalling 1 if the bank is a conventional bank and 0 if it is an Islamic one.

### 7.4.2.1 Readability measurement: the dependent variable

We used two formulae to measure the RNDs: the Gunning Fog Index (GFI)[1] in the main regression and the Flesch–Kincaid Grade Level Index (FKGL)[2] in the robustness checks. The GFI "*indicates the number of years of formal education a reader of average intelligence would need to read the text once and understand that piece of writing with its word-sentence workload*" (Li, 2008, p. 225). The relation between GFI and reading ease is as follows: a GFI score of 18 means that the text is unreadable; 14–18, difficult; 12–14, ideal; 10–12, acceptable; and 8–10, childish (ibid., p.225). The FKGL is another formula for measuring readability. It uses the average number of syllables and the average number of sentences. It provides a score that shows the level of schooling or the degree required to understand a document. The higher the score, the more years are required to understand the document, i.e., the more difficult the document is (Ahmed, 2016; Nicolay and de Oliveira, 2019). Following Courtis (1998) and Smith and Taffler (1992), we relied on computer software to generate the GFI and FKGL scores[3]. The use of readability formulae and computer-generated scores improves objectivity. The generated scores were calculated on the basis of certain textual characteristics (the number of words, syllables and sentences) and hence using these scores mitigated any human subjectivity (Li, 2008; Lo et al., 2017; Nicolay and de Oliveira, 2019). The use of formulae and computer-generated scores ensured not only the comparability of our findings with previous studies but also the accuracy of the measurement compared to manual calculations.

### 7.4.2.2 Earning management: main independent variable

In the banking sector, several studies have examined the discretion in "loan loss provisions" (LLP) to assess the engagement in EM practices, because this specific accrual is expected to be very material, requiring substantial judgement in the banking industry (e.g., Beatty et al., 1995; Beaver and Engel, 1996; Moyer, 1990; Scholes et al., 1990; Wahlen, 1994). The distinctive feature of previous studies is their use of generally accepted accounting principles to specify the non-discretionary (ND) component of this specific accrual (NDLLP), which is mainly driven by the normal changes in bank business conditions. The discretionary component of this accrual (DLLP) usually captures managerial opportunism by calculating the difference between actual and non-discretionary "loan loss provisions". Following Lassoued et al. (2018), the non-discretionary component (NDLLP) was estimated in the present study by employing the following regression (Equation 7.2).

$$\frac{LLP_{i,t}}{TA_{i,t-1}} = \alpha_0 + \alpha_1 \frac{LLA_{i,t-1}}{TA_{i,t-1}} + \alpha_2 \frac{NCO_{i,t}}{TA_{i,t-1}} + \alpha_3 \frac{\Delta LOANS_{i,t}}{TA_{i,t-1}}$$

$$+ \alpha_4 \frac{LOANS_{i,t}}{TA_{i,t-1}} + \alpha_5 \frac{NPL_{i,t}}{TA_{i,t-1}} + \alpha_6 \frac{LTB_{i,t}}{TA_{i,t-1}} + \alpha_7 \frac{OL_{i,t}}{TA_{i,t-1}}$$

$$+ \text{Country Controls} + \text{Year Controls} + \varepsilon_{i,t} \qquad (7.2)$$

where

$LLP_{i,t}$ Loan loss provisions for bank $i$ in year $t$;

$LLA_{i,t-1}$ Loan loss allowance for bank $i$ in year $t-1$;

$NCO_{i,t}$ Net loan charge-offs for bank $i$ in year $t$;

$\Delta LOANS_{i,t}$ Change in outstanding total loans for bank $i$ from year $t-1$ to year $t$;

$LOANS_{i,t}$ Outstanding total loans for bank $i$ in year $t$;

$NPL_{i,t}$ Non-performing loans for bank $i$ in year $t$;

$LTB_{i,t}$ Loans to banks provided by bank $i$ in year $t$;

$OL_{i,t}$ Other loans provided by bank $i$ in year $t$;

$TA_{i,t-1}$ Total assets for bank $i$ in year $t-1$;

$\varepsilon_{i,t}$ Error term for bank $i$ in year $t$, which is our estimate of the discretionary component of "loan loss provisions" (DLLP).

We used the absolute value of DLLP as a proxy for the engagement in EM activities, regardless of whether this engagement would result in managing earnings upwards (income-increasing EM strategy through underestimating the provisions for loan losses) or downwards (income-decreasing EM strategy through overestimating the provisions for loan losses).

## 7.5  Results and discussion

### 7.5.1 Descriptive and correlation analysis

Table 7.2 shows that the variables have considerably dispersed statistical scores. The GFI scores range between 10 and 13.90 indicating that the RNDs of GCC banks' annual reports vary between acceptable (10–12) and ideal (12–14). Table 7.2 also shows that the FKGL scores range between 8.70 and 12.40, indicating that the number of years of schooling/education required to understand a given

*Table 7.2* Descriptive statistics

| Variables | No. | Mean | Min. | Max. | Std. Dev. | ANOVA Test-Equality of Mean |
|---|---|---|---|---|---|---|
| GFI score | 204 | 12.205 | 10.00 | 13.90 | 0.8261 | 2.062 |
| FKGL score | 204 | 10.672 | 8.70 | 12.40 | 0.7195 | 0.415 |
| Absolute DLLP | 204 | 0.0036 | 0 | 0.03106 | 0.0046 | 6.111*** |
| Positive DLLP | 97 | 0.0038 | 0 | 0.03106 | 0.0059 | 2.721* |
| Negative DLLP | 107 | −0.0034 | −0.2086 | −0.00003 | 0.0031 | 4.683** |
| BOD_Size | 204 | 9.098 | 6 | 14 | 1.4419 | 4.412** |
| Audit_CMMeeting | 204 | 5.65 | 3 | 12 | 1.8060 | 1.037 |
| ROA | 204 | 0.0142 | −0.0553 | 0.1075 | 0.0146 | 0.255 |
| LEV | 204 | 0.8462 | 0.554 | 0.9159 | 0.0511 | 0.310 |
| AGE | 204 | 32.765 | 3 | 68 | 15.584 | 7.473*** |
| Bank_Size | 204 | 9.8216 | 5.0824 | 13.6061 | 1.9741 | 10.167*** |

*, ** and *** denote the significance levels of 0.10, 0.05 and 0.01, respectively, based on two-tailed tests. Gunning Fog Index (GFI) and the Flesch–Kincaid Grade Level Index (FKGL) measure readability in the annual reports of bank $i$ in year $t$, and $DLLP_{it}$ is the discretionary loan loss provision which presents our proxy for EM. $BOD\_Size_{it}$ is the total number of board members; $Audit\_CMMeeting_{it}$ is the total number of audit committee meetings; $Bank\_Size_{it}$ is the natural logarithm of the bank's total assets; $ROA_{it}$ is the return on assets, which equals the income before extraordinary items of bank $i$ in year $t$ divided by the average total assets; $LEV_{it}$ is the financial leverage of bank $i$ in year $t$ measured by the average total debt divided by average total assets; $AGE_{it}$ is the number of years of operation since the bank was incorporated; *Count* is the country effect as embedded in the random-effect or the fixed-effect regressions. *Bank type* is a dummy variable equalling 1 if the bank is a conventional bank and 0 if it is an Islamic one.

annual report ranges from almost 9 years to almost 13 years. The FKGL score demonstrates that the readers of annual reports should be at higher secondary level or undergraduate university level in order to understand the banks' annual reports. This statistic matches the qualifications of the banks' clients, who may be less educated or even illiterate (Ahmed, 2016; Nicolay and de Oliveira, 2019).

Table 7.2 illustrates that the mean value for the absolute measure of DLLP is 0.0036, but the (un-reported) mean value for the signed measure of DLLP is almost 0, indicating that GCC banks have varied motivations for engaging in EM practices and there is therefore no systematic trend of managing earnings upwards or downwards. Splitting the entire sample (i.e., the 204 observations) into an income-increasing group (through underestimating the provision for loan losses: negative DLLP = 107 observations) and an income-decreasing group (through overestimating the provision for loan losses: positive DLLP = 97 observations) supports the finding that no systematic pattern of EM appears across the sampled banks. Additionally, Table 7.2 shows that the mean size of the boards of directors is almost nine members and the mean number of audit committee meetings is 5.65 per year. The mean of the return on assets is low (1.42%), and the mean of banks' leverage is almost 85%, which is expected in the banking sector. Finally, the mean of bank age and the natural algorithm of bank size are 32.76 and 9.82, respectively.

Table 7.2 also displays the results of an ANOVA test for comparing the differences among the means of all variables between Islamic and conventional banks. The results indicate that there are significant differences in the means of absolute DLLP, positive DLLP, negative DLLP, BOD_Size, AGE and $Bank_{Size}$, implying that the type of bank may affect our regression models. Table 7.3 presents the Pearson's (top) and Spearman's (bottom) correlation coefficients across the variables. The results rule out the multicollinearity problem, since the correlations between the independent variables are below 0.70. Accordingly, we can proceed with confidence to the regression analysis.

### 7.5.2 Multivariate regression analysis results

The $\chi^2$ Hausman statistic suggests that random effects are more appropriate to use for all regression models except Models 12 and 13. Table 7.4 displays three regression models. Model 1 tested the association between the absolute value of our EM proxy (DLLP) and the RNDs in banks' annual reports (measured by GFI), whereas Models 2 and 3 used the positive DLLP (income-decreasing EM) and negative DLLP (income-increasing EM) values, respectively. Following on from Lassoued et al. (2018), we used the absolute value of DLLP in Model 1 as a proxy for the presence of EM (a large absolute value of DLLP indicates more use of loan loss provisions to manage earnings either upwards or downwards). Model 1 explains 28.4% of the variation in the readability of GCC banks' annual reports. It shows a significant positive association between the absolute value of DLLP and the GFI score (coefficient=27.31; $z=2.42$; $p<0.05$), supporting our H2. The higher the absolute value of DLLP, the more complex a bank's annual report. Bank managers prepare complex annual reports when they are involved in EM activities, supporting the theoretical claims of impression management by obfuscation and agency theory. Our results suggest that bank managers, encouraged by the flexibility to choose from a variety of accounting estimates and the unregulated nature of textual discourses, may use their discretion to give a misleading picture of the financial position of their banks. Bank managers either construct easy narratives when they are less involved in EM activities and consequently reduce the information asymmetry (agency theory) or craft complex reports when they are more involved in EM activities in order to conceal this negative news (obfuscating and impression management). Our results are consistent with the findings of Ajina et al. (2016) and Li (2008), which conclude that managers who practice EM tend to prepare complex narratives.

Model 1 also shows a significant positive association between banks' level of risk (LEV) and the readability of reports (coefficient=2.947; $z=2.78$; $p<0.01$). This finding indicates that highly leveraged banks prepare complex narratives. Our finding is consistent with prior studies in non-financial sectors and demonstrates that banks with higher risks have a greater incentive to obfuscate their narratives, resulting in more difficult-to-read annual reports (Bloomfield, 2008; Rutherford, 2003). Bank age is also found to be positively associated with GFI, indicating that the older the bank, the more opaque its annual reports. The latter

*Table 7.3* Pearson's (top) and Spearman's (bottom) correlation coefficients among the variables

| | 1 | 2 | 3 | 4 | 5 | 6 | 7 | 8 | 9 | 10 | 11 |
|---|---|---|---|---|---|---|---|---|---|---|---|
| 1 GFI score | | 0.669 | 0.145 | 0.176 | -0.416 | -0.063 | -0.064 | 0.049 | 0.231 | 0.440 | -0.015 |
| 2 FKGL score | 0.690 | | 0.125 | 0.135 | -0.396 | 0.059 | 0.011 | -0.027 | 0.287 | 0.460 | 0.033 |
| 3 Absolute DLLP | 0.278 | 0.295 | | 1.00 | -1.00 | -0.092 | -0.0056 | -0.011 | -0.143 | -0.001 | -0.017 |
| 4 Positive DLLP | 0.126 | 0.051 | 1.00 | | NA | -0.118 | -0.0139 | 0.081 | -0.103 | -0.176 | -0.011 |
| 5 Negative DLLP | -0.427 | -0.445 | -1.00 | NA | | 0.067 | -0.093 | 0.111 | 0.225 | -0.352 | 0.038 |
| 6 BOD_Size | -0.049 | 0.063 | -0.079 | -0.048 | 0.078 | | 0.178 | -0.081 | -0.030 | 0.173 | 0.202 |
| 7 Audit_CMMeeting | -0.053 | -0.001 | -0.096 | -0.091 | 0.095 | 0.209 | | -0.095 | 0.207 | 0.116 | 0.044 |
| 8 ROA | 0.084 | 0.005 | 0.041 | 0.124 | 0.076 | 0.060 | -0.050 | | -0.022 | 0.084 | 0.194 |
| 9 LEV | 0.431 | 0.532 | 0.099 | -0.027 | 0.001 | 0.071 | 0.177 | -0.179 | | 0.245 | 0.172 |
| 10 AGE | 0.473 | 0.462 | 0.202 | -0.096 | -0.399 | 0.194 | 0.231 | 0.073 | 0.296 | | 0.176 |
| 11 Bank_Size | -0.032 | 0.028 | -0.085 | -0.101 | 0.047 | 0.238 | 0.167 | 0.410 | -0.013 | 0.128 | |

Gunning Fog Index (GFI) and the Flesch–Kincaid Grade Level Index (FKGL) measure readability in the annual reports of bank $i$ in year $t$, and $DLLP_{it}$ is the discretionary loan loss provision which presents our proxy for EM. $BOD\_Size_{it}$ is the total number of board members; $Audit\_CMMeeting_{it}$ is the total number of audit committee meetings; $Bank\_Size_{it}$ is the natural logarithm of the bank's total assets; $ROA_{it}$ is the return on assets, which equals the income before extraordinary items of bank $i$ in year $t$ divided by the average total assets; $LEV_{it}$ is the financial leverage of bank $i$ in year $t$ measured by the average total debt divided by average total assets; $AGE_{it}$ is the number of years of operation since the bank was incorporated; *Count* is the country effect as embedded in the random–effect or the fixed–effect regressions. *Bank type* is a dummy variable equalling 1 if the bank is a conventional bank and 0 if it is an Islamic one.

*Table 7.4* Regression results of readability (Fog score) on independent variables

| Variables | Model 1 Coefficients | Model 1 z-values | Model 2 Coefficients | Model 2 z-values | Model 3 Coefficients | Model 3 z-values |
|---|---|---|---|---|---|---|
| Intercept | 10.03 | 10.41*** | 10.83 | 8.72*** | 11.73 | 9.96*** |
| Absolute DLLP | 27.31 | 2.42** | | | | |
| Positive DLLP | | | 15.39 | 1.40* | | |
| Negative DLLP | | | | | −61.21 | −3.44*** |
| BOD_Size | −0.048 | −1.27 | 0.0008 | 0.16 | −0.029 | −0.80 |
| Audit_CMMeeting | −0.065 | −2.21 | −0.037 | −1.05 | −0.003 | −0.10 |
| ROA | 0.986 | 0.28 | −13.16 | −2.19** | 3.093 | 1.00 |
| LEV | 2.947 | 2.78*** | 0.187 | 0.14 | 0.836 | 0.63 |
| AGE | 0.024 | 6.83*** | 0.002 | 0.31 | 0.010 | 2.41** |
| Bank_Size | −0.041 | −1.46 | 0.075 | 2.08** | −0.007 | −0.27 |
| Bank type | −0.042 | −0.38 | 0.093 | 0.73 | 0.053 | 0.49 |
| Adjusted r$^2$ | 0.284 | | 0.201 | | 0.302 | |
| Wald $\chi^2$ | 76.08*** | | 9.65 | | 31.28*** | |
| Hausman Fixed Effect vs Random Effect test Probability | $\chi^2 = 2.39$ 0.935 | | $\chi^2 = 3.04$ 0.881 | | $\chi^2 = 2.10$ 0.954 | |
| Observations | 204 | | 97 | | 107 | |

*, ** and *** denote the significance levels of 0.10, 0.05 and 0.01, respectively, based on two-tailed tests.

finding may be attributable to the development of complex finance operations over the bank's life. Surprisingly, however, neither of the banks' governance variables (BOD_Size and Audit_CMMeeting) showed a significant association with the readability score. This finding contrasts with that of the Velte (2018) study, which found that audit committee meetings improve the readability of the textual disclosures presented in the firms' integrated reports. In Model 1, bank profitability, size and type also have no significant association with readability.

Model 2 explains 20.1% of the variation in the readability of GCC banks' annual reports. It provides evidence that, when bank managers engage in income-decreasing EM (positive DLLP), they prepare complex and difficult-to-read narratives (obfuscation), consistent with our earlier envisaged relationship in hypothesis H2b. Bank managers prepare difficult-to-read annual reports in order to hide their activities, as well as the bad news of a drop in earnings. This finding is consistent with that of Pajuste et al. (2021), who argue that bank managers are more likely to be under scrutiny, inspection and review from market participants when they engage in income-decreasing strategies; hence, they obfuscate their annual reports. Bank profitability (ROA) is found to be negatively associated with GFI at the $p<0.05$ level, indicating that the higher a bank's profitability, the easier its annual reports are to read. Model 2 also shows that bank size has a significant positive association with GFI at the $p<0.05$ level, implying that larger banks have more complex NDs.

Model 3 examines the association between income-increasing EM activities and readability. The model explains 30.2% of the variation in the readability of GCC banks' annual reports. Model 3 shows that only the negative DLLP and bank age are significantly associated with the readability of banks' annual reports. When bank managers engage in income-increasing activities (negative DLLP), they prepare easy-to-read narratives (coefficient$=-61.21$; $z=-3.44$; $p<0.01$), supporting our hypothesis H2a. In this scenario, bank managers become more transparent and willing to communicate readable annual reports in order to signal to market participants the good news of higher income (impression management) (Ajina et al., 2016; Merkl-Davies and Brennan, 2007). This finding contradicts that of Lo et al. (2017), who have observed that firms which manage their earnings upwards are likely to prepare complex annual reports. One possible explanation of this contradiction is the reliance of Lo et al. (2017) on a sample of non-financial firms, whereas we focus on financial institutions (banks). Both Models 2 and 3 indicate that GCC bank managers adopt reporting strategies of obfuscation and impression management.

### 7.5.3 Robustness checks and further analysis

To ensure the robustness of our results presented in Table 7.4, we performed two checks. First, we used the FKGL scores instead of the GFI scores, with results reported in Table 7.5. The results in this table (for Models 4, 5 and 6) are quite similar to those in Table 7.4 (for Models 1, 2 and 3) except for the bank type (Islamic or conventional) which becomes statistically significant in all regressions. This robustness check, therefore, confirms the results of Table 7.4 but indicates that bank type influences the association between EM and readability.

Second, we used a different EM proxy (DLLP_2), with results reported in Table 7.6. DLLP_2 is the outcome of the EM main proxy (DLLP) multiplied by a dummy variable which indicates whether the bank meets or narrowly exceeds the previous year's earnings performance $ME_{it}$, where $ME_{it}=1$ if the change in earnings per share (EPS) from year $t-1$ to year $t$ is positive but less than 10%,[4] but 0 otherwise. The use of this alternative proxy for EM (DLLP_2) is supported by Burgstahler and Dichev (1997), who find that managers are likely to engage in EM practices if they have an incentive to avoid reporting losses or reduced earnings. Hence, banks managers have a strong incentive to meet or narrowly exceed the previous year's earnings performance, since they are required in the annual reports to compare and contrast performance in the current fiscal year with that of the previous year. Lo et al. (2017, p. 8) also support this view and note that the interaction between these two variables is expected to "*increase the power of detecting firms that have managed earnings, because together the variables capture both the process and outcome of earnings management*".

Table 7.6 shows two regression models where readability (proxied by the GFI or FKGL scores, respectively) is regressed on our alternative proxy for EM (DLLP$_2$). The results using Models 7 and 8 confirmed our findings with Models 3 and 6 and demonstrate that there is a significant negative association between

*Table 7.5* Regression results of readability (Kincaid score) on independent variables

| Variables | Model 4 | | Model 5 | | Model 6 | |
|---|---|---|---|---|---|---|
| | Coefficients | z-values | Coefficients | z-values | Coefficients | z-values |
| Intercept | 7.897 | 9.61*** | 10.29 | 13.47*** | 7.491 | 6.46*** |
| Absolute DLLP | 28.19 | 2.95*** | | | | |
| Positive DLLP | | | 11.14 | 1.66* | | |
| Negative DLLP | | | | | −73.71 | −4.21*** |
| BOD_Size | 0.003 | 0.11 | 0.008 | 0.25 | 0.027 | 0.76 |
| Audit_ CMMeeting | −0.035 | −1.39 | 0.013 | 0.60 | −0.015 | −0.51 |
| ROA | −2.577 | −0.85 | −14.36 | −3.88*** | −0.119 | −0.04 |
| LEV | 3.15 | 3.50*** | −1.260 | −1.53 | 3.621 | 2.74*** |
| AGE | 0.024 | 7.24*** | .0001 | 0.39 | 0.011 | 2.84*** |
| Bank_Size | −0.038 | −1.57 | 0.089 | 3.99*** | −0.020 | −0.77 |
| Bank type | 7.896 | 9.61*** | −0.091 | 13.47*** | −0.190 | −1.79* |
| Adjusted r² | 0.316 | | 0.325 | | 0.294 | |
| Wald χ² | 87.87*** | | 31.84*** | | 43.65*** | |
| Hausman Fixed Effect vs Random Effect test Probability | χ²=10.48 0.163 | | χ²=9.03 0.251 | | χ²=4.00 0.779 | |
| Observations | 204 | | 97 | | 107 | |

*, ** and *** denote the significance levels of 0.10, 0.05 and 0.01 respectively based on two-tailed tests.

*Table 7.6* Regression results of readability on independent variables using alternative proxy for earnings management

| Variables | Model 7 Fog Score | | Model 8 Kincaid Score | |
|---|---|---|---|---|
| | Coefficients | z-values | Coefficients | z-values |
| Intercept | 11.09 | 11.93*** | 8.903 | 11.23*** |
| DLLP_2 | −152.28 | −4.22*** | −142.75 | −4.65*** |
| BOD_Size | −0.043 | −1.18 | 0.009 | 0.31 |
| Audit_CMMeeting | −0.067 | −2.35** | −0.038 | −1.58 |
| ROA | 0.180 | 0.05 | −3.469 | −1.18 |
| LEV | 1.784 | 1.73* | 2.040 | 2.32** |
| AGE | 0.022 | 6.46*** | .0020 | 6.80*** |
| Bank_Size | −0.042 | −1.58 | −0.038 | −1.64* |
| Bank type | 0.059 | 0.57 | −0.155 | −1.72* |
| Adjusted r² | 0.354 | | 0.380 | |
| Wald χ² | 93.54*** | | 106.38*** | |
| Hausman Fixed Effect vs Random Effect test Probability | χ²=1.73 0.943 | | χ²=5.41 0.492 | |
| Observations | 204 | | 204 | |

*, ** and *** denote the significance levels of 0.10, 0.05 and 0.01, respectively, based on two-tailed tests.

DLLP_2 and the readability of banks' annual reports. When bank managers engage in EM practices in order to avoid reporting losses or reduced earnings, they publish less complex annual reports. The results in Table 7.6 also show that bank type has a significant association with readability (see Model 8). Therefore, we decided to split the entire sample into two sub-samples based on bank type (Islamic or conventional), as presented in Table 7.7.

The outcomes of Table 7.7 demonstrate that the results for conventional banks (Models 9, 10 and 11) resemble those of the sample as a whole presented in Table 7.4. Table 7.7 also shows no significant association between RNDs and EM in Islamic banks, as reported in Model 12. However, Models 13 and 14 show that the engagement in income-decreasing (positive *DLLP*) or income-increasing (negative DLLP) EM is statistically associated with the preparation of less complex annual reports at the significance levels of 0.05 and 0.10, respectively. These findings imply that Islamic banks follow narrative reporting strategies – in response to their engagement in EM activities – that differ from the strategies used by conventional banks. The exploration of Islamic bank managers' motivation when they prepare their NDs goes beyond the scope of this particular work, but represent an attractive opportunity for future research.

We also examined the reverse causality between readability (as an independent variable) and EM (as a dependent variable) when controlling for governance mechanisms and bank-specific variables. The un-tabulated results demonstrate that, whereas the RNDs[5] influenced EM, they confirmed our original results as reported in Table 7.4. To address the potential endogeneity and account for any simultaneity, omitted variables or measurement errors in our regressions (Lassoued et al., 2018; Li, 2008; Lo et al., 2017), we relied on two-stage least squares (2SLS) random effects, including the instrumental variables estimator (Table 7.8). We added three instrumental variables: (1) an assets quality measure, calculated by dividing the average total loans and advances by the average total assets,[6] (2) the number of board meetings and (3) the number of audit committee members (Ajina et al., 2016; Elnahass et al., 2014; Lassoued et al., 2018). Although 2SLS regressions show similar outcomes to our results in Models 1 and 3, they revealed that the proxy for EM (absolute DLLP) was not significantly associated with Fog score ($p < 0.16$), whereas it was significantly associated ($p < 0.10$) when using FKGL, as shown in Table 7.8. The 2SLS results, therefore, endorse our main results.

## 7.6 Conclusion

This chapter extends the readability–EM relationship analysis of Ajina et al. (2016), Li (2008), Lo et al. (2017) and Pajuste et al. (2021). It examines the associations between income-decreasing (-increasing) EM activities and readability while linking these associations to bank managers' motivation to prepare easy (difficult) text to signal (conceal) information to/from the market participants (impression management and obfuscation). In general, our findings showed that bank managers prepare complex narratives when they are engaging in EM

*Table 7.7* Regression results of readability (Fog Score) on independent variables in conventional and Islamic banks.

| Variables | Conventional Banks | | | | | | Islamic Banks | | | | | |
|---|---|---|---|---|---|---|---|---|---|---|---|---|
| | Model 9 | | Model 10 | | Model 11 | | Model 12 | | Model 13 | | Model 14 | |
| | Coeff. | z-values | Coeff. | z-values | Coeff. | z-values | Coeff. | t-values | Coeff. | t-values | Coeff. | z-values |
| Intercept | 8.865 | 6.36*** | 8.137 | 3.78*** | 12.78 | 8.97*** | 9.956 | 5.12*** | 4.207 | 2.39** | 9.877 | 3.00*** |
| Absolute DLLP | 35.61 | 2.75*** | | | | | −33.63 | −0.85 | | | | |
| Positive DLLP | | | 23.01 | 1.79* | | | | | −80.39 | −2.46** | | |
| Negative DLLP | | | | | −50.38 | −2.63*** | | | | | −99.60 | −1.79* |
| BOD_Size | −0.024 | −0.50 | 0.083 | 1.14 | −0.027 | −0.60 | −0.256 | −3.19*** | 0.045 | 0.49 | −0.035 | −0.45 |
| Audit_CMMeeting | −0.043 | −1.16 | −0.042 | −0.96 | 0.006 | 0.17 | −0.010 | −0.014 | 0.381 | 3.97*** | −0.050 | −0.84 |
| ROA | 11.62 | 1.46 | 14.50 | 0.93 | −0.779 | −0.12 | −7.434 | −1.32 | −3.291 | −0.38 | 5.467 | 1.22 |
| LEV | 3.494 | 2.37** | 3.158 | 1.45 | −0.313 | −0.19 | 4.844 | 2.09** | 5.969 | 2.86** | 3.391 | 0.92 |
| AGE | 0.024 | 5.20*** | −0.003 | −0.37 | 0.010 | 1.81 | 0.014 | 1.68* | −0.041 | −3.79*** | 0.011 | 1.56 |
| Bank_Size | −0.027 | −0.67 | 0.014 | 0.26 | −0.004 | −0.10 | 0.028 | 0.55 | 0.109 | 2.47** | −0.031 | −0.65 |
| Adjusted r² | 0.309 | | 0.300 | | 0.279 | | 0.351 | | 0.853 | | 0.433 | |
| Wald χ² | 44.26*** | | 7.19 | | 18.36** | | 3.25*** | | 5.79*** | | 13.56* | |
| Hausman Fixed | 4.61 | | 3.33 | | 2.43 | | 17.71 | | 23.68 | | 3.10 | |
| Effect vs Random Effect test Probability | 0.707 | | 0.853 | | 0.933 | | 0.013 | | 0.001 | | 0.876 | |
| Observations | 115 | | 53 | | 62 | | 89 | | 44 | | 45 | |

*, ** and *** denote the significance levels of 0.10, 0.05 and 0.01, respectively, based on two-tailed tests. The results remained qualitatively unchanged when using Kincaid score instead of Fog score.

*Table 7.8* Instrument variable regression: Two-Stage Least Squares (2SLS) Regression Analysis results of readability (Read) on instruments variables

| Variables | Model 15 Fog Score | | Model 16 Kincaid Score | |
|---|---|---|---|---|
| | Coefficients | z-values | Coefficients | z-values |
| Intercept | 8.164 | 4.13*** | 5.770 | 2.97*** |
| Absolute DLLP | 142.8 | 1.40 | 163.9 | 1.64* |
| BOD_Size | −0.012 | −0.23 | 0.041 | 0.78 |
| Audit_CMMeeting | −0.055 | −1.48 | −0.022 | −0.60 |
| ROA | 1.986 | 0.45 | −1.221 | −0.28 |
| LEV | 4.518 | 2.42** | 4.971 | 2.71*** |
| AGE | 0.024 | 5.47*** | 0.021 | 5.01*** |
| Bank_Size | −0.057 | −1.52 | −0.058 | −1.59 |
| Bank type | −0.226 | −1.09 | −0.464 | −2.28** |
| Wald $\chi^2$ | | 49.23*** | | 42.96*** |
| Durbin $\chi^2$ | | 1.95 | | 3.82** |
| Wu-Hausman F | | 1.88 | | 3.70* |
| Observations | | 204 | | 204 |

*, ** and *** denote the significance levels of 0.10, 0.05 and 0.01, respectively, based on two-tailed tests.

activities. However, our further analyses found that, when managers are involved in income-decreasing EM activities, they prepare difficult-to-read narratives (obfuscation). Meanwhile, the managers who engage in income-increasing EM are more willing to communicate readable annual reports in order to signal this good news of higher income to the market participants (impression management).

Our results were robust as indicated by several checks and our main conclusions remained unchanged. However, after splitting the whole sample into two sub-samples – Islamic and conventional banks – the results showed that Islamic banks, in response to their engagement in EM activities, follow narrative reporting strategies that differ from those of conventional banks. Therefore, a fruitful extension of this study would be to investigate the motivations of Islamic bank managers when they prepare the narratives of their banks' annual reports. Furthermore, exploring the moderating effect of the presence of managers who have been on a board for a long time (i.e., entrenched managers, as described by Seifzadeh et al., 2020) on the relationship between EM and the readability of annual reports is another attractive opportunity for future research.

Our results are consistent with Bloomfield's (2008) explanation of the relationships between EM and readability. The management activities related to income decreasing seem to involve more active efforts than the activities related to income increasing. The former includes the use of sophisticated technical language and lengthy annual reports to explain the causes behind reduced income (bad news) and therefore annual reports become difficult to read (Bushee et al., 2018). In contrast, the latter incorporates the use of transparent and easy-to-read narratives that communicate increased income (good news). Our results are also consistent with the incomplete revelation hypothesis, which suggests that managers minimise the effect of bad news by disclosing information which is difficult to read and costly to analyse. Our results show that income-decreasing (-increasing) EM activities are associated with difficult- (easy-) to-read text. In cases of bad news, Bloomfield (2008) adds that managers would naturally be inclined to prepare lengthy annual reports because of their wish to attribute bad news to causes other than poor management or to reduce litigation costs. Theories that link the engagement in income increasing or decreasing activities to the psychological characteristics of bank managers need further investigation.

Our findings have important implications. For academic researchers, our study extends the findings of previous studies and is a pioneer in its field. Hence, we would encourage researchers to refine our conceptual constructs and use different proxies to verify our results. For managers, our study draws attention to the importance of the writing and language style when communicating information in annual reports. Managers need to be careful and diligent in preparing the narrative sections of annual reports and they should always try to improve their writing skills. Likewise, investors need to improve their reading/comprehension skills so that they can distinguish between managers' obfuscation and transparency in banks' annual reports. For policymakers, our study shows the need to set some linguistic standards when preparing annual reports, not only to reduce litigation costs but also to minimise agency costs.

Our study has a number of limitations, which can be viewed as potential avenues for future research. First, our sample addresses GCC banks during the period 2014–2017. Hence, future research can expand this sample by incorporating all MENA banks over a longer timeframe. Second, our study does not address the effect of management entrenchment and managers' characteristics in terms of social psychology on both EM and the writing style. Consequently, future research is strongly recommended to examine these issues. Third, our study does not examine the moderating effect of the cost of capital on the EM–readability association. This is another attractive area for future research in the banking sector.

## Notes

1  GFI = 0.4 × (words per sentence + percentage of complex words)
2  FKGL = 0.39 × (number of words/number of sentences) + 11.8 × (number of syllables/number of words) – 15.59.
3  We used a software programme available at: https://readable.com to calculate both the GFI and FKGL scores.
4  The use of a range between 0% and 10% matches the change in earnings per share (EPS) by 2% to 4%, as suggested by Lo et al. (2017) and Pajuste et al. (2021). However, we opted to use this percentage because our final sample included a number of countries with different currencies.
5  Using both readability scores, for FKGL and GFI.
6  The measurement of assets quality reflects banks' efficiency in managing their assets: the higher the assets quality measure, the better the bank's performance and hence the less complex the annual reports.

# References

Abbadi, A., Hijazi, Q. and Al-Rahahleh, A. (2016) 'Corporate governance quality and earnings management: Evidence from Jordan', *Australasian Accounting, Business and Finance Journal*, 10(2), pp. 54–75.

Ahmed, I. (2016) 'Aspirations of an Islamic bank: An exploration from stakeholders' perspective', *International Journal of Islamic and Middle Eastern Finance and Management*, 9(1), pp. 24–45.

Ajina, A., Laouiti, M. and Msolli, B. (2016) 'Guiding through the fog: Does annual report readability reveal earnings management?', *Research in International Business and Finance*, 38, pp. 509–516.

Atieh, A. and Hussain, S. (2012) 'Do UK firms manage earnings to meet dividend thresholds?', *Accounting and Business Research*, 42(1), pp. 77–94.

Beatty, A., Chamberlain, S. and Magliolo, J. (1995) 'Managing financial reports of commercial banks: The influence of taxes, regulatory capital and earnings', *Journal of Accounting Research*, 33(2), pp. 195–212.

Beaver, W. and Engel, E. (1996) 'Discretionary behaviour with respect to allowances for loan losses and the behaviour of security prices', *Journal of Accounting and Economics*, 22(1/3), pp. 177–206.

Bloomfield, J. (2008) 'Discussion of annual report readability, current earnings, and earnings persistence', *Journal of Accounting and Economics*, 45(2–3), pp. 248–252.

Brennan, N., Guillamon-Saorin, E. and Pierce, A. (2009) 'Impression management: Developing and illustrating a scheme of analysis for narrative disclosures – A methodological note', *Accounting, Auditing and Accountability Journal*, 22(5), pp. 789–832.

Brennan, N. and Merkl-Davies, D. (2013) 'Accounting narratives and impression management', in: Jack, L., Davison, J. and Craig, R. (Eds.), *The Routledge Companion to accounting communication*, Abingdon, Oxon, Routledge, pp. 123–146.

Burgstahler, D. and Dichev, I. (1997) 'Earnings management to avoid earnings decreases and losses', *Journal of Accounting and Economics*, 24(1), pp. 99–126.

Bushee, B.J., Gow, I.D. and Taylor, D.J. (2018) 'Linguistic complexity in firm disclosures: Obfuscation or information?', *Journal of Accounting Research*, 56(1), pp. 85–121.

Caserio, C., Panaro, D. and Trucco, S. (2020) 'Management discussion and analysis: A tone analysis on US financial listed companies', *Management Decision*, 58(3), pp. 510–525.

Clatworthy, M. and Jones, M. (2001) 'The effect of thematic structure on the variability of annual report readability', *Accounting, Auditing and Accountability Journal*, 14(3), pp. 311–326.

Courtis, J. (1998) 'Annual report readability variability: Tests of the obfuscation hypothesis', *Accounting, Auditing and Accountability Journal*, 11(4), pp. 459–471.

Dalwai, T., Basiruddin, R. and Abdul Rasid, S.Z. (2015) 'A critical review of relationship between corporate governance and firm performance: GCC banking sector perspective', *Corporate Governance, The International Journal of Business in Society*, 15(1), pp. 18–30.

Dalwai, T., Chinnasamy, G. and Mohammadi, S. (2021) 'Annual report readability, agency costs, firm performance: An investigation of Oman's financial sector', *Journal of Accounting in Emerging Economies*, 11(2), pp. 247–277.

Desender, K., Castro, C. and De Leon, S. (2011) 'Earning management and culture values', *American Journal of Economics and Sociology*, 70(3), pp. 639–670.

DuCharme, L., Malatesta, P. and Sefcik, S. (2001) 'Earnings management: IPO valuation and subsequent performance', *Journal of Accounting, Auditing, and Finance*, 16(4), pp. 369–396.

Elnahass, M., Izzeldin, M. and Abdelsalam, O. (2014) 'Loan loss provisions, bank valuations and discretion: A comparative study between conventional and Islamic banks', *Journal of Economic Behavior and Organization*, 103, pp. 160–173.

Ginesti, G., Sannino, G. and Drago, C. (2017) 'Board connections and management commentary readability: The role of information sharing in Italy', *Corporate Governance: The International Journal of Business in Society*, 17(1), pp. 30–47.

Hassan, M.K. (2014) 'Risk narrative disclosure strategies to enhance organizational legitimacy: Evidence from UAE financial institutions', *International Journal of Disclosure and Governance*, 11(1), pp. 1–17.

Hassan, M.K., Abu-Abbas, B. and Garas, S. (2019) 'Readability, governance, and performance: A test of the obfuscation hypothesis in Qatari listed firms', *Corporate Governance, The International Journal of Business in Society*, 19(2), pp. 270–298.

Hassan, M.K., Florio, C. and Abbas, B. (2020) 'Corporate governance, transparency, and performance: Empirical evidence from the UAE', *Afro-Asian Journal of Finance and Accounting*, Forthcoming.

Healy, P. and Wahlen, J. (1999) 'A review of the earnings management literature and its implications for standard setting', *Accounting Horizons*, 13(4), pp. 365–383.

Hrasky, M., Manson, C. and Wills, D. (2009) 'The textual complexities of annual reports narratives: A comparison of high and low performance companies', *New Zealand Journal of Applied Business Research*, 7(2), pp. 31–45.

Hrasky, S. and Smith, B. (2008) 'Concise corporate reporting: Communication or symbolism?', *Corporate Communications: An International Journal*, 13(4), pp. 418–432.

Huang, X., Teoh, S. and Zhang, Y. (2014) 'Tone management', *The Accounting Review*, 89(3), pp. 1083–1113.

Iatridis, G. and Kadorinis, G. (2009) 'Earnings management and firm financial motives: A financial investigation of UK listed firms', *International Review of Financial Analysis*, 18(4), pp. 164–173.

Jensen, M. and Meckling, W. (1976) 'Theory of the firm: Managerial behavior, agency costs and ownership structure', *Journal of Financial Economics*, 3(4), pp. 305–360.

Jones, M. and Smith, M. (2014) 'Traditional and alternative methods of measuring understandability of accounting narratives', *Accounting, Auditing and Accountability Journal*, 27(1), pp. 183–208.

Kamel, H. (2012) 'Earnings management and initial public offerings: A new perspective from Egypt', *Journal of Accounting in Emerging Economies*, 2(2), pp. 96–118.

Lassoued, N., Attia, M. and Sassi, H. (2018) 'Earnings management in Islamic and conventional banks: Does ownership structure matter? Evidence from the MENA region', *Journal of International Accounting, Auditing and Taxation*, 30, pp. 85–105.

Li, F. (2008) 'Annual report readability, current earnings, and earnings persistence', *Journal of Accounting and Economics*, 34(2/3), pp. 221–247.

Li, F. (2010) 'Textual analysis of corporate disclosure: A survey of the literature', *Journal of Accounting Literature*, 29(1), pp. 143–165.

Lo, K., Ramos, F. and Rogo, R. (2017) 'Earnings management and annual reports readability', *Journal of Accounting and Economics*, 63(1), pp. 1–25.

Loughran, T. and McDonald, B. (2011) 'When is a liability not a liability? Textual analysis, dictionaries, and 10-Ks', *Journal of Finance*, 66(1), pp. 35–65.

Loughran, T. and McDonald, B. (2016) 'Textual analysis in accounting and finance: A survey', *Journal of Accounting Research*, 54(4), pp. 1187–1230.

Merkl-Davies, D. and Brennan, N. (2007) 'Discretionary disclosure strategies in corporate narratives: Incremental information or impression management?', *Journal of Accounting Literature*, 26, pp. 116–196.

Molyneux, P. and Iqbal, M. (2005) 'Banking and financial systems in Gulf Cooperation Council (GCC) countries', in: Iqbal, M. and Molyneux, P.) (Eds.), *Banking and financial systems in the Arab world*. Palgrave Macmillan Studies in Banking and Financial Institutions, London: Palgrave Macmillan. Pp 113–144.

Moyer, S.E. (1990) 'Capital adequacy ratio regulations and accounting choices in commercial banks', *Journal of Accounting and Economics*, 13(2), pp. 123–154.

Nicolay, R. and de Oliveira, A.J. (2019) 'Inflation volatility, monetary policy signaling and clarity of the central bank communication: Evidence from an inflation targeting emerging economy', *Journal of Economic Studies*, 46(2), pp. 266–283.

Pajuste, A., Poriete, E. and Novickis, R. (2021) 'Management reporting complexity and earnings management: Evidence from the Baltic markets', *Baltic Journal of Management*, 16(1), pp. 47–69.

Rutherford, B. (2003) 'Obfuscation, textual complexity and the role of regulated narrative accounting disclosure in corporate governance', *Journal of Management and Governance*, 7(2), pp. 187–210.

Rutherford, B. (2018) 'Narrating the narrative turn in narrative accounting research: Scholarly knowledge development or flat science?', *Meditari Accountancy Research*, 26(1), pp. 13–43.

Scholes, M., Wilson, G. and Wolfson, M. (1990) 'Tax planning, regulatory capital planning, and financial reporting strategy for commercial banks', *Review of Financial Studies*, 3(4), pp. 625–650.

Seifzadeh, M., Salehi, M., Abedini, B. and Ranjbar, M. (2020) 'The relationship between management characteristics and financial statement readability', *EuroMed Journal of Business*. https://doi.org/10.1108/EMJB-12-2019-0146.

Smith, M. and Taffler, R. (1992) 'Readability and understandability: Different measures of the textual complexity of accounting narrative', *Accounting, Auditing and Accountability Journal*, 5(4), pp. 84–98.

Smith, M. and Taffler, R. (2000) 'The chairman's statement: A content analysis of discretionary narrative disclosures', *Accounting, Auditing, and Accountability Journal*, 13(5), pp. 624–646.

Velte, P. (2018) 'Is audit committee expertise connected with increased readability of integrated reports: Evidence from EU companies', *Problems and Perspectives in Management*, 16(2), pp. 23–41.

Wahlen, J. (1994) 'The nature of information in commercial bank loan loss disclosures', *The Accounting Review*, 69(3), pp. 455–478.

Watts, R. and Zimmerman, J. (1990) 'Positive accounting theory: A ten-year perspective', *The Accounting Review*, 61(1), pp. 131–156.

# 8 The determinants of forward-looking narrative reporting in annual reports of emerging countries

## Evidence from India

*Mohamed Nurullah, Nandita Mishra
and Faozi A. Almaqtari*

### 8.1 Introduction

The importance of forward-looking narrative reporting was highlighted by both the leading accounting researchers (e.g., Hussainey et al., 2003; Beattie et al., 2004; Lehavy et al., 2011) and accounting professional bodies (e.g., ICAEW, IASB). The post-financial crisis demanded further increases in the role of forward-looking narrative reporting because of the dynamic economic and financial conditions. Disclosure of historical financial information, although important, neither fully serves its purpose nor satisfies investors. The fluctuation in economic conditions, financial crisis and fraud have put pressure on companies to emphasise forward-looking disclosures in narrative reporting. Such information helps investors to make informed decisions and to estimate companies' earnings (Hussainey et al., 2003).

Narrative reporting has gained prominence in the past few years by introducing Environmental, Social and Governance (ESG), integrated and sustainability reporting in India. The framing of Sustainable Development Goals (SDGs) has also given it great impetus (Adams, 2013). It is becoming more common in the annual reports of companies. However, one school of thought also thinks that executives can utilise narrative reporting to provide untruthful and misguiding information about the companies' future. Forward-looking statements (FLS) can be more difficult to regulate. Forward-looking statements are speculative by their very nature and hence it is always uncertain as to what extent their inclusion should be encouraged (Gupta, 2013).

There is little research on forward-looking narrative reporting in emerging countries. This chapter focuses on the determinants of forward-looking narrative reporting in India from an emerging country's viewpoint. India has been selected as a sample country because India is one of the fastest-growing economies in the world and is on its way to becoming a major economic power in the world, with a population of nearly 1.4 billion. It is the sixth largest economy by nominal GDP and leads the emerging economies in different world forums. After the reforms in 1991, India is one of the major target markets for global investors. With around

DOI: 10.4324/9781003095385-11

1.2 million registered companies in India, it holds a lot of public funds, providing scope for investment by investors. India's main stock exchange, Mumbai Stock Exchange, is the 9th largest stock exchange in the world in terms of market capitalisation. Research shows that forward-looking disclosures help in reducing the gap between the companies and the investors, improve the decision-making capabilities and reduce the risk with respect to future earnings (Hussainey & Walker, 2009). By carrying out a single-country study, we were able to demonstrate the effect of country-specific variables on firms' performance. India exhibits marked variation with respect to the type of companies, their size and ownership structure. The UK plays a major role in global accounting and corporate rule making. The foundations of accounting and corporate laws, like other political and legal institutions in India, are heavily influenced by the UK system due to historic links in India with the UK. We, therefore, believe that this work will be interesting to a wider audience beyond India.

We have focused on the narrative section of the sampled companies' annual reports, like chairman's statement, vision, mission statement, operating and financial review, ESG report, integrated report, sustainability report and auditor's statement section to evaluate the level of disclosure. In India, the Security & Exchange Board of India (SEBI) has prescribed some disclosure norms, which can be mandatory or voluntary. After introducing guidelines (SEBI, 2017), they have encouraged companies to follow an integrated reporting framework. This leads to increasingly forward-looking disclosures in annual reports of Indian companies (Mishra, 2020a).

This chapter provides three principal contributions. Firstly, it provides empirical evidence from an emerging country, India, where the stock market authority, SEBI, has introduced different requirements, such as the ESG (Environment, Social and Governance), BRR (Business Responsibility Reporting), and the upcoming BRSR (Business Responsibility Sustainability Reporting). Secondly, this chapter provides evidence from the BSE (Bombay Stock Exchange) 100 Index, which includes large companies that carry out the practice of narrative reporting, and the practices of these companies are considered to be a model for other companies. Lastly, this chapter links the results of this study to existing theories and earlier studies in this regard. It utilises recent data with a panel structure to estimate the results. Furthermore, the study uses a content analysis comprised of 30 different items.

The rest of the chapter is organised as follows: Sections 8.2 and 8.3 survey the existing literature and hypothesis development. Section 8.4 deals with the research methodology, sample selection and data collection process, and describes the measurement of variables. The results are discussed in Section 8.5, which is further divided into descriptive, correlations, content analysis and panel data analysis. The last section, Section 8.6, draws the conclusions of this chapter, and describes the scope of future research work.

## 8.2 The background of narrative reporting

In 1993, a UK body called the Accounting Standards Board (ASB[1]) initiated the voluntary "Operating and Financial Review" for the financial reporting of publicly listed firms. In 2013, the Companies Act requirement of companies to produce a Strategic Report and Directors' Report was replaced by narrative reporting regulations. The International Financial Reporting Standards (IFRS) took it as the "Management Commentary" and defines the idea of management commentary as "the information that accompanies financial statements as a part of an entity's financial reporting" (Beattie, et al., 2004).

In India, the accounting standard embraced by companies is called the "Indian Accounting Standards" (Ind-AS). The National Financial Reporting Authority (NFRA), which replaced the Indian Accounting Standards Board (ASB) in 2018, is an autonomous, supervisory body to manage the accounting standards and auditing profession in India. The Ind-AS are named and numbered in a similar manner as the IFRS. NFRA recommend these standards to the Ministry of Corporate Affairs (MCA) of India. The MCA has to determine the accounting standards applicable for companies in India. In 2009, MCA released the "Voluntary Guidelines on Corporate Social Responsibility", which stimulated the introduction of narrative reporting in India. In July 2011, MCA released the "National Voluntary Guidelines on Social, Environmental and Economic Responsibilities of Business, 2011" (NVGs). The introduction of Business Responsibility Reports (SEBI-BRRs/ BRR) by SEBI in 2012 was a remarkable step taken by India in the field of narrative reporting. In 2019, the revised NVGs were issued as the "National Guidelines for Responsible Business Conduct" (NGRBCs). In 2021, the government is all set to implement a revised version of BRR which is named BRSR (Business Responsibility and Sustainability Report) (Mishra et al., 2021). All these developments will give the required boost to narrative reporting in India. The current study is timely and will help us to understand the impact of recent developments on the future annual reports of companies.

## 8.3 Literature review and hypothesis development

In the recent past, forward-looking information reported in the annual report's narrative statement has attracted increased attention (Menicucci & Paolucci, 2017). Previous studies have shown the impact of signalling theory on forward-looking narrative information (Spence, 1978). They also explored the role of agency theory and capital structure on the disclosures (Jensen & Meckling, 1976). These two theories have also been studied together (Elzahar & Hussainey, 2012) to understand their impact on disclosures. Information asymmetry plays an essential role in deciding the effect of agency theory on voluntary disclosures (An et al., 2011). It has been observed by Hassanein and Hussainey (2015) that, with agency costs and reduced information asymmetry, the intensity of forward-looking data improves. This study also links the role of forward-looking narrative data in increasing the value of firms. Signalling theory also plays an essential role in these disclosures. Reduced financing cost and increased corporate value have been identified and linked with signalling theory (Gallego-Álvarez et al., 2011). Signalling theory basically indicates that divulging information in the annual report will send a positive signal to the stakeholders

(Elzahar & Hussainey, 2012). Hence, the disclosure of forward-looking data is always on the agenda of companies who want investors or who want to present a transparent annual report.

In the perspective of companies listed in Australia, Kent and Ung (2003) suggest that big companies disclose more non-financial information than small companies. The reason identified for this is that large companies has less-volatile earnings. In the UK, Tahir et al. (2019) discovered that long-term procedures and non-financial information inspire managers to drive the long-term achievements of the company. Brown and Tucker (2011) used the size of the auditing firm to differentiate between companies. Companies audited by a large auditing firm are categorised under Big-N and companies audited by small firms are categorised under Non-Big-N. The result shows that the firm under Big-N has more clear narrative reporting. Studies have also related forward-looking narrative disclosure and corporate reputation with stock impulsiveness and results show that forward-looking reporting has a positive impact on corporate reputation (Bravo, 2016). Aljifri and Hussainey (2007) have focused on identifying the determinants of forward-looking data with respect to companies and they also took the size of the auditor firm as one of the determinants. Many authors in their papers have stated that the forward-looking information gives benefit to the firm by increasing their creditworthiness, and this is in line with signalling theory (Hussainey et al., 2003; Hussainey & Walker, 2009).

While studying the literature, it was observed that the study of forward-looking narrative reporting in India is very different from that in the United States and elsewhere. In the US, forward-looking disclosures are in the form of quantitative forecasting which is auditable, unlike the forward-looking disclosures in India which are more qualitative in nature, similar to the UK. Also, in India most of the forward-looking disclosures are voluntary. Lawati et al. (2021) have explored the impact of investment efficiency on the voluntary disclosures carried out by the companies and found that the investment efficiency has a positive impact on voluntary disclosure. Studies have found out that corporate investment and governance have positive impacts on corporate disclosure (Elberry & Hussainey, 2020, 2021; Lawati et al., 2021).

Yeoh (2010) indicates that several theoretical frameworks explain corporate disclosures from the perspectives of those undertaking financial reporting. They include agency theory, signalling theory, disclosure theory, stakeholder theory, legitimacy theory and institutional theory. Hussainey and Al-Najjar (2011) used signalling and pecking order theories to explain the relationship between the levels of corporate disclosure and firm size, leverage and the levels of dividends. In the same context, disclosure theory distinguished between voluntary and mandatory approaches. Mandatory reporting, particularly on a more consistent basis, is justified in order to bridge the gap in relevant information for users to employ in comparative analysis. Voluntary disclosure may be less expensive, but looks to suffer from bias due to issues with selective dissemination and the use of creative accounting in earnings reports (Yeoh, 2010). Furthermore, the existence of external "institutional" forces is implied by legitimacy theory. Government directives, the legal environment and the media are examples of institutional elements that influence the design of accountability and control systems (Hoque et al., 2004).

In 2017, the SEBI developed its guidelines for the top 500 companies to voluntarily adopt integrated reporting (SEBI, 2017). There are many other non-financial disclosures that are mandatory in India. Despite all these guidelines, the content of forward-looking narrative reporting is an important area for research as little research have been undertaken in India with respect to these aspects. This chapter is an attempt to fill this research gap and to identify the various determinants of narrative reporting in India.

### 8.3.1 Hypothesis development

Firm size has always been studied as a determinant of the level of corporate disclosures. Many researchers found that big companies have a greater level of forward-looking disclosures than medium- or small-sized companies (Alsaeed, 2006). A higher level of public scrutiny is one of the reasons for this type of result. The findings of several studies have supported the hypothesis that large companies disclose more forward-looking data (Clarkson et al., 1994; O'Sullivan et al., 2008). On the other hand, Aljifri and Hussainey (2007) and Aljifri (2008) found that there is no significant link between the disclosure of forward-looking information and company size. These latter studies are based in countries like Australia and the UAE but very few studies focus on developing economies like India. The first hypothesis framed for testing, therefore, is:

$H_o1$: **There is no significant impact of firm size on the forward-looking disclosure index (FLDI)**

Also, it was found that there were studies on the impact on the level of FLDI of the proportion of independent directors on the board of a company. An independent director is someone who is not an employee of the company and should perform as an unbiased monitor in the company. In India, the term "Independent Director" has been defined in The Companies Act and several requirements relating to the appointment, roles and duties have been defined. The act should be read along with Rules 5 and 4 of the Companies' (Appointment and Qualification of Directors) Rules 2014 to understand the provisions for independent directors in India (Gupta & Mishra, 2019).

Amid these expectations from independent directors, there have been various studies that relate the percentage of independent directors to a firm's performance, corporate fraud and the level of disclosures (Abor & Biekpe, 2007; Cheng & Courtenay, 2006; Kılıç & Kuzey, 2018; Navarro & Urquiza, 2015; Song & Windram, 2004; Uzun et al., 2004). Several studies state that there is a significant connection between board independence and financial reporting quality (e.g, Hashid & Almaqtari, 2020; Almaqtari & Shamim et al., 2020; Almaqtari & Al-Hattami et al., 2020; Farhan et al., 2019; Farhan et al., 2020; Almaqtari & Hashid et al., 2020). A recent study took the ownership pattern a step further and related it to the decision to invest in research and development (Hassanein et al., 2021). On the contrary, many studies demonstrate that there is no substantial relationship between the percentage of independent director and disclosure levels (Haniffa & Cooke, 2005; Ho & Wong, 2003), although in a UK-based study, Wang and Hussainey (2013) determined that there is a definite link between the percentage of non- executive directors and the level of FLDI. To analyse the same relationship with respect to India, the second hypothesis is framed as:

*$H_o2$: There is no significant impact of board independence on FLDI.*

Board size should ideally impact disclosure levels and hence corporate govern-ance. A larger board should be able to have better monitoring of the company's function, although researchers have found mixed evidence to support this. Gandía (2008) supports this notion and found in his study that board size improves the quality of disclosure. Leng and Ding (2011) also supported that the more mem-bers on the board may bring more diversity and expertise and improve the quality of disclosure. The third hypothesis framed for the study is:

*$H_o3$: There is no significant relationship between board size and FLDI.*

Michael, Jensen and Meckling (1976) found that, following the agency theory, a firm with high monitoring costs and high leverage will disclose more informa-tion. Alsaeed (2006) established that a company with higher debt will have higher agency costs, and disclosure of information may be applied as a device to lower agency costs. Furthermore, O'Sullivan et al. (2008) reported that leverage and voluntary disclosures are related to each other but Celik et al. (2006) failed to support this. The fourth hypothesis framed for the study is:

*$H_o4$: There is no significant impact of leverage of a company on FLDI.*

According to signalling theory, a company that is earning more profit will always try to disclose more to its investors (Frias-Aceituno et al., 2014; Watson et al., 2002). Few researchers have reported that the profitability of a firm has a positive relationship with the FLDI (Aljifri & Hussainey, 2007; Alsaeed, 2006), whereas there are a few empirical studies which show no relationship between the two variables (Kent & Ung, 2003). The fifth hypothesis framed for the study is:

*$H_o5$: There is no significant impact of profitability of a company on FLDI.*

Many researchers have argued that a firm's ability to pay short-term debt impacts the level of disclosure (Elzahar & Hussainey, 2012; Watson et al., 2002), but a few studies have highlighted that liquidity is not related to disclosure levels and several established a negative impact on disclosures (Belkaoui & Kahl, 1977; Esa & Ghazali, 2012). The sixth hypothesis is framed as:

*H$_o$6: There is no significant impact of liquidity of a company on FLDI.*

The size of the firm auditing the company has been taken as a dummy variable where the Big Four audit firms are represented by 1 and other audit firms are denoted by 0. It is a general notion that a large audit firm will promote clients to disclose more information, with the narrative reporting being better with large audit firms. A few researchers have found that there is a positive influence of big audit firms on FLDI (Hassanein et al., 2019; Liu, 2015). In a recent study, Al Lawati and Hussainey (2021) studied the relationship between the audit committee and corporate disclosures. It is possible that big audit firms have more experts on board and also support the narrative reporting frameworks and therefore they promote inclusion of more of such information. Olusegun Wallace et al. (1994) emphasises the "theory of association", which suggests that the big audit firms influence and promote the narrative reports. The seventh hypothesis framed for the study is:

*H$_o$7: There is no significant impact of audit firm size on FLDI*

## 8.4  Research methodology and data

Data have been collected from the BSE (Bombay Stock Exchange) 100 Index. For this study, financial companies are ignored because they follow a different set of disclosures which will complicate the analysis. The annual reports of three years from 2016–17 to 2018–19 were analysed. Three years' data have been taken because the annual reports data tend to persist (Graham et al., 2005; Skinner, 2003). The period after 2017 is taken to analyse the impact of the 2017 circular by SEBI where they encouraged all listed companies to adopt integrated reporting (SEBI, 2017). But the circular made the adoption of integrated reporting voluntary for companies and therefore it is interesting to find out the impact of this regulation on the content of companies' annual reports.

Overall, 79 listed companies were observed for the period from 2017 to 2019. Every annual report was scrutinised and coded to calculate the forward-looking disclosure index (FLDI). Content analysis – a prominent research tool – was used to analyse in similar studies (e.g., Jones & Shoemaker, 1994; Smith & Taffler, 1995; Smith & Taffler, 1992; Beattie et al., 2004). For the purpose of framing, an FLDI dummy variable was used. Any information, if disclosed, by the company was given a score of 1, or 0 if the information was not shown in the annual report. The value thus assigned was summated to obtain the overall score of each company's FLDI. The framework used by Ho and Wong (2003) and Liu (2015) was taken as the base for developing FLDI. The equation used for developing the FLDI is as follows:

*FLDI = Total number of forward-looking items disclosed/Maximum number of items disclosed*, where the maximum number of items disclosed is 30.

To achieve reliability of the content analysis, coding was done by all the authors. Milne and Adler (1999) have suggested that, to increase the reliability in content analysis, the coding should be carried out by different authors and any discrepancies should be discussed and resolved. Krippendorff (2010) identified the importance of pilot testing in content analysis and therefore the coding was first performed for five companies and the problems were identified and resolved prior to further analysis and coding.

The present study uses an "inter-rater reliability" method to confirm the reliability and validity of forward-looking disclosure scores. Krippendorff (2010) indicates that the "inter-rater reliability" test can be used to assess the reliability of the ordinal data used, especially in the case of small sample sizes and content analysis. Krippendorff alpha was used to assess the reliability of the present study. The minimum criterion value of the Krippendorff alpha is 0.70. The output value of Krippendorff alpha is 0.84 which is greater than the criterion value, indicating that the forward-looking disclosure score used is reliable and can be used to estimate the research model of the present study. For greater reliability of this research, a split-half reliability method was also used. The forward-looking disclosure score was divided into two sets. An independent sample *t*-test was used to see if there is any significant difference between the two sets. The results show that there is no significant different between the two sets, indicating proper construction of the forward-looking disclosure score.

Based on the literature review, the items were selected to analyse the forward-looking disclosures of the company. Different studies focus on environmental disclosures, risk disclosure, stakeholder engagement disclosures and many others (Acar & Temiz, 2020; Cheng et al., 2014; Gallego-Álvarez et al., 2011; Haniffa & Cooke, 2005; Kent & Ung, 2003; Kılıç & Kuzey, 2018; Almaqtari et al., 2021). Financial information and non-financial information were taken into consideration while selecting individual elements of FLDI. The final list of FLDI consisted of 30 items which are shown in Annexe 1.

The dependent variable in our study is FLDI and the independent variables are stated and defined in Table 8.1.

*Table 8.1* Variable definition

| Variable | Definition |
| --- | --- |
| Firm size (FSIZE) | Total assets |
| Board independence (BIND) | Percentage of independent directors to total number of directors |
| Board size (BSIZE) | Number of members on the board |
| Leverage (LEV) | % of total liabilities relative to total assets |
| Profitability (PROF) | Return on equity |
| Liquidity (LIQ) | Current assets by current liability |
| Audit firm size (AUD) | Dummy variable: 1 for Big Four audit firms, 0 for other audit firms |

The research model of the present study includes two board characteristics (size and independence), and four firm-specific variables: size, profitability, leverage and liquidity. The rationale behind using board characteristics is justified by agency and signalling theories. We advocate that the boards have strong incentives to eliminate agency issues and decrease information asymmetry between management and shareholders by increasing voluntary disclosure. In the same context, firm-specific variables are used by the present study to explore the extent to which firms' size, profitability, leverage and liquidity can affect forward-looking reporting. Furthermore, our model includes external auditing, represented by an audit quality variable that is measured as a dummy variable of 1 for a Big Four audit firm and 0 otherwise. We argue that a firm audited by a Big Four company is to a large extent motivated by management's desire to "signal" better quality of reported information, which is consistent with signalling theory. Alanezi et al. (2012) indicate that prior financial reporting research has employed the capital need theory, agency theory and signalling theory to propose possible incentives for firms to make financial reporting disclosure and to explain variations in the level of financial reporting disclosure between firms.

The model developed for this study is as follows:

$$FLDI_{it} = \beta_0 + \beta_1 FSIZE_{it} + \beta_2 BIND_{it} + \beta_3 BSIZE_{it} + \beta_4 LEV_{it} + \beta_5 PROF_{it}$$
$$+ \beta_6 LIQ_{it} + \beta_7 AUD + \varepsilon_{it} \tag{8.1}$$

where:
   $FLDI_{it}$ = Forward Looking Disclosure Index of a firm i in year t;
   FSIZE = Firm Size of a firm i in year t;
   BIND = Board independence of a firm i in year t;
   BSIZE = Board size of a firm i in year t;
   LEV = Leverage of a firm i in year t;
   PROF = Profitability of a firm i in year t;
   LIQ = Liquidity of a firm i in year t;
   AUD = Audit firm size (dummy variable) of a firm i in year t.
   For measuring FLDI, the following equation has been used:

$$FLDI = \frac{\text{Number of disclosure } i^{\text{th}} \text{ item}}{\text{Total number of disclosure the sample}(N) \text{ i.e., } 30} \times 100$$

Panel data analysis is applied for the study, with FLDI being the dependent variable. For testing whether the fixed effect or random effect model is better, the probability value of chi-squared was analysed using the Hausman test. The null hypothesis of the Hausman test reflects the consistency of the random effect model; if the p-value of the data exceeds 0.05, it is established that the random effect is a better model. The results of the Hausman test are shown in Table 8.4 where the p-value is less than 0.05 so that the fixed effect model is applied for this study.

*Table 8.2* Descriptive analysis

| Variables | Min. | 1st Qu | Median | Mean | 3rd Qu | Max |
|---|---|---|---|---|---|---|
| Firm size (FSIZE) | 10123 | 39772 | 62445 | 69142 | 91816 | 141557 |
| Board independence (BIND) | 17.78 | 50 | 63.39 | 57.59 | 79.64 | 92.85 |
| Board size (BSIZE) | 8 | 9 | 11 | 11.64 | 13.75 | 20 |
| Leverage (LEV) | 0.002 | 0.0925 | 0.31 | 0.4942 | 0.4575 | 2.67 |
| Profitability (PROF) | 6.79 | 13.45 | 18.1 | 25.19 | 25.18 | 128.5 |
| Liquidity (LIQ) | 0.63 | 0.7886 | 1.475 | 1.8487 | 1.955 | 5.16 |
| Audit firm size (AUD) | 0 | 0 | 1 | 0.636 | 1 | 1 |
| FLDI | 21 | 22.25 | 25 | 24.73 | 27 | 29 |

## 8.5 Data analysis and results

### 8.5.1 Descriptive analysis

The selected variables, defined in Section 8.4, are run through the descriptive statistical analysis. The results in Table 8.2 demonstrate that the dependent variable FDLI has a mean of 24.73 with maximum and minimum values of 29 and 21, respectively. This indicates that, on average, the selected companies reveal about 25 items (83%) of the forward-looking disclosure index (FLDI) framed by the present study. This is higher than reported by Uyar and Kiliç (2012). The descriptive analysis also shows that the board size in India is on average around 12, the sampled companies' board size ranging from eight to 20 members. Additionally, board independence ranges from 18% to 92.85%, with an average of 58%. In the same context, audit firm size (AUD) exhibits an average value of 0.636, which signifies that almost 64% of the sampled companies are audited by Big Four audit firms. The results of the descriptive analysis are shown in Table 8.2.

### 8.5.2 Correlation analysis

After proper data cleaning and preparation for analysis, correlation analysis was performed on the data. Before carrying out the panel data analysis, variance inflation factor (VIF) was also calculated to find if there is problem of multicollinearity. According to Thoni et al. (1990), the threshold for VIF is 10 and is 0.9 for correlation. Tables 8.2 and 8.3 show that there was no evidence of multicollinearity in the data. The winsorisation method was used for treating outliers.

The results in Table 8.3 show that FLDI has a positive correlation with all the variables of the study except for liquidity, which has a negative correlation.

### 8.5.3 Panel data analysis

Overall, panel data analysis shows that the adjusted $r^2$ square value is 0.432, which means that 43.2% of the FLDI has been explained by the variables. The model

*Table 8.3* Correlation analysis

|        | FSIZE   | BIND   | BSIZE  | LEV    | PROF   | LIQ    | AUD    | FLDI |
|--------|---------|--------|--------|--------|--------|--------|--------|------|
| FSIZE  | 1       |        |        |        |        |        |        |      |
| BIND   | −0.112  | 1      |        |        |        |        |        |      |
| BSIZE  | −0.07   | 0.254* | 1      |        |        |        |        |      |
| LEV    | 0.377** | 0.071  | 0.147  | 1      |        |        |        |      |
| PROF   | −0.221  | 0.234  | −0.152 | −0.043 | 1      |        |        |      |
| LIQ    | −0.233  | 0.067  | 0.056  | 0.16   | 0.564**| 1      |        |      |
| AUD    | 0.058   | 0.056  | 0.257* | 0.101  | 0.167  | 0.322* | 1      |      |
| FLDI   | 0.056   | 0.319  | 0.457  | 0.177  | 0.167  | −0.156 | 0.387* | 1    |

Note: FLDI:forward-looking disclosure index; FSIZE: firm size; BIND: board independence; BSIZE: board size; LEV: leverage; PROF: profitability; LIQ: liquidity; and AUD: audit firm size (dummy variable).
** and * indicate significance at the level of 1% and 5%, respectively.

fits the data at a probability of $p < 0.01$ Table 8.4 shows the results of panel data analysis and VIF values.

### 8.5.3.1 Firm size

The results show that firm size has a statistically significant effect on FLDI ($p$-value = 0.024). This effect is positive, indicating a positive coefficient ($\beta$ = 0.082). This signifies that there a positive relationship between firm size (as

*Table 8.4* Panel data analysis

|                  | $\beta$ | p-value | VIF   |
|------------------|---------|---------|-------|
| Constant         |         | 0.002   |       |
| FSIZE            | 0.082   | 0.024   | 1.839 |
| BIND             | 0.028   | 0.018   | 1.385 |
| BSIZE            | −0.178  | 0.458   | 1.437 |
| LEV              | −0.418  | 0.128   | 1.567 |
| PROF             | 0.126   | 0.668   | 2.068 |
| LIQ              | −0.287  | 0.278   | 1.481 |
| AUD              | 0.023   | 0.016   | 1.821 |
| $r^2$            |         |         | 0.542 |
| Adjusted $r^2$   |         |         | 0.432 |
| Durbin Watson    |         |         | 1.864 |
| F statistic      |         |         |       |
| Hausman test $\chi^2$ |    | 0.023   | 8.086 |
| Probability of the regression = 0.0245 | | | |

Note: FLDI: forward-looking disclosure index; FSIZE: firm size; BIND: board independence; BSIZE: board size; LEV: leverage; PROF: profitability; LIQ: liquidity; VIF: variance inflation factor; and AUD: audit firm size (dummy variable).

measured by total assets) and FLDI. Hence, $H_0 1$ is rejected, indicating that firm size has a statistically significant positive effect on FLDI, a finding which is in line with Alsaeed (2006), who found that large companies tend to have more narrative disclosures.

### 8.5.3.2 Board independence

The results indicate that independence of board has a statistically significant positive influence on FLDI $p$-value=0.018), with a positive coefficient ($\beta$ =0.028). This means that there the percentage of independent board representatives in the board of directors contribute positively and significantly to FLDI. Accordingly, $H_0 2$ is rejected, with the independence of board members being an important determinant of better functioning and the FLDI. This finding is consistent with that of Wang and Hussainey (2013).

### 8.5.3.3 Board size

Board size exhibits a non-significant effect on FLDI ($p$-value=0.458), with a negative coefficient ($\beta$ =−0.178). This leads to accepting $H_0 3$, indicating that board size has a detrimental though non-significant effect on FLDI. This finding is in line with those from the few, earlier studies (Eng & Mak, 2003; Haniffa & Cooke, 2005).

### 8.5.3.4 Leverage

The results reveal that leverage has a statistically non-significant negative effect on FLDI ($p$-value=0.128) ($\beta$ =−0.418). Hence, hypothesis $H_0 4$ is accepted. Hussainey and Al-Najjar (2009) had a similar finding in their study.

### 8.5.3.5 Profitability

Profitability exhibits a statistically non-significant positive impact on FLDI ($p$-value=0.668) ($\beta$ =0.126). This leads to accepting $H_0 5$ in this regard. Hussainey and Al-Najjar (2009) also had a similar finding in their study.

### 8.5.3.6 Liquidity

The results demonstrate that liquidity has a statistically non-significant negative effect on FLDI ($p$-value=0. 278) ($\beta$ =−0.287). Hence, hypothesis $H_0 6$ is accepted. Espinosa and Trombetta (2007) reported similar results and they argued that decreased liquidity of the firm resulted in an increased level of corporate disclosure.

### 8.5.3.7 Audit firm

The results show a positive relationship between FLDI and the audit firm size (Big Four or not). Audit firm exhibit a statistically significant positive effect on

FLDI *(p*-value=0.016) (β =0.023). This means that firms that are audited by Big Four companies exhibit better forward-looking disclosures than those audited by smaller audit companies. This finding is consistent with that of previous studies (Hassanein et al., 2019; Liu, 2015), who also noted that audit firm size has a significant relationship with FLDI.

## 8.6 Conclusion, limitations and avenues for future research

Working on a sample of BSE-100 listed companies, the authors have examined the determinants of narrative reporting in the period of 2017–19. After the circular of SEBI in Feb 2017, it was very important to analyse the status of voluntary narrative reporting in India. The study shows that Indian firms are likely to divulge more strategic, corporate social responsibility and forward-looking information. The forward-looking disclosure index of the sample companies was fairly high.

Recent years have witnessed the adoption of integrated reporting in India (Mishra, 2020b) and increased emphasis by regulators for companies to disclose more on ESG (Environment, Social and Governance). The requirements imposed in listed companies have led to an increase in forward-looking narrative reporting in India. BRR (Business Responsibility Reporting) is mandatory for listed companies and Ministry of Corporate Affairs is introducing the new BRSR (Business Responsibility Sustainability Reporting), which has further increased the disclosure level.

Using the sample of BSE listed companies, the study shows results consistent with earlier studies where a positive relationship has been found between FLDI and each of firm size, board independence and audit firm size (Hassanein et al., 2019; Kılıç & Kuzey, 2018; O'Sullivan et al., 2008). The findings do not support signalling theory, which suggests that a profitable firm will wish to send signals to their investors and therefore will have a higher disclosure index. Neither liquidity nor leverage were found to be related to the disclosure index.

Our study supports the previous studies conducted by Hassanein et al. (2019) and Liu (2015), which concluded that companies with big audit firms are more active with respect to disclosure and narrative reporting. Furthermore, board independence also impacts the level of narrative reporting carried out by Indian companies (Abor & Biekpe, 2007; Cheng & Courtenay, 2006; Kılıç & Kuzey, 2018; Navarro & Urquiza, 2015; Song & Windram, 2004; Uzun et al., 2004).

The study adds to the existing literature by providing evidence that the size of the firm, audit firm size and independence of the board contribute positively towards high-quality narrative reporting by the companies. There have not been many studies related to narrative reporting in India, and with increasing emphasis of regulators on non-financial disclosures, this study holds a unique relevance and adds markedly to the literature. Furthermore, the findings should be of great relevance to policymakers who are still evaluating the role of independent directors and framing new rules for BRSR.

The research also has a few limitations. The measure of FLDI is not all inclusive. Many attributes relating to narrative reporting may have been ignored in the study. The development of FLDI was done on the assumption that all disclosures are of equal weightage. This assumption, that all attributes are equally important for all the companies, may not be correct for all type of industrial sectors. Another limitation of the study is that, to calculate the disclosure index, only annual reports are analysed, with other sources of disclosures, like websites and press releases, being ignored. Future research should be designed to overcome these limitations, and other source of disclosures should also be analysed for framing the disclosure index. Forward-looking disclosures can be related with "Risk Accounting", which is a combination of risk accounting frameworks and financial reporting (Hassanein et al., 2021). Future studies can also focus on extending this study by including more countries from Asia or other parts of the world to produce more comprehensive results.

## Note

1  The UK ASB of 1990 was replaced by the FRC in 2012 and then the FRC was replaced with the Audit, Reporting and Governance Authority (ARGA) in 2019 and the ARGA is expected to be fully implemented in 2023.

## References

Abor, J., & Biekpe, N. (2007). Corporate governance, ownership structure and performance of SMEs in Ghana: Implications for financing opportunities. *Corporate Governance*, Vol. 7, No. 3, pp. 288–300. https://doi.org/10.1108/14720700710756562.

Acar, M., & Temiz, H. (2020). Empirical analysis on corporate environmental performance and environmental disclosure in an emerging market context: Socio-political theories versus economics disclosure theories. *International Journal of Emerging Markets*, Vol. 15, No. 6, pp. 1061–1082. https://doi.org/10.1108/IJOEM-04-2019-0255.

Adams, C. A. (2013). The sustainable development goals, integrated thinking and the integrated report. IIRC ICAS. Available at: https://apo.org.au/sites/default/files/resource-files/2017-09/apo-nid303601.pdf.

Alanezi, F., Alfaraih, M., Alrashaid, E., & Albolushi, S. (2012). Dual/joint auditors and the level of compliance with international financial reporting standards (IFRS-required disclosure): The case of financial institutions in Kuwait. *Journal of Economic and Administrative Sciences*, 28(8), pp. 109–129.

Al Lawati, H., & Hussainey, K. (2021). Disclosure of forward-looking information: Does audit committee overlapping matter? *International Journal of Accounting and Performance Evaluation*, Forthcoming.

Al Lawati, H., Hussainey, K., & Sagitova, R. (2021). Disclosure quality vis-à-vis disclosure quantity: Does audit committee matter in Omani financial institutions? *Review of Quantitative Finance and Accounting*, Forthcoming.

Aljifri, K. (2008). Annual report disclosure in a developing country: The case of the UAE. *Advances in Accounting*, Vol. 24, No. 1, pp. 93–100.

Aljifri, K., & Hussainey, K. (2007). The determinants of forward-looking information in annual reports of UAE companies. *Managerial Auditing Journal*, Vol. 22, No. 9, pp. 881–894. https://doi.org/10.1108/02686900710829390.

Almaqtari, F. A., Al-Hattami, H. M., Al-Nuzaili, K. M., & Al-Bukhrani, M. A. (2020). Corporate governance in India: A systematic review and synthesis for future research. *Cogent Business & Management*, Vol. 7, No. 1, pp. 1803579. https://doi.org/10.1080/23311975.2020.1803579.

Almaqtari, F. A., Hashed, A. A., & Shamim, M. (2021). Impact of corporate governance mechanism on IFRS adoption: A comparative study of Saudi Arabia, Oman, and the United Arab Emirates. *Heliyon*, Vol. 7, No. 1, pp. e05848. https://doi.org/10.1016/j .heliyon.2020.e05848.

Almaqtari, F. A., Hashed, A. A., Shamim, M., & Al-Ahdal, W. M. (2020). Impact of corporate governance mechanisms on financial reporting quality: A study of Indian GAAP and Indian accounting standards. *Problems and Perspectives in Management*, Vol. 18, No. 4, pp. 1–13. https://doi.org/10.21511/ppm.18(4).2020.01.

Almaqtari, F. A., Shamim, M., Al-Hattami, H. M., & Aqlan, S. A. (2020). Corporate governance in India and some selected Gulf countries. *International Journal of Managerial and Financial Accounting*, Vol. 12, No. 2, pp. 165–185. https://doi.org/10 .1504/IJMFA.2020.109135.

Alsead, K. (2006). The association between firm-specific characteristics and disclosure. *Managerial Auditing Journal*, Vol. 21, No. 5, pp. 476–496. https://doi.org/10.1108 /02686900610667256.

An, Y., Davey, H., & Eggleton, I. R. C. (2011). Towards a comprehensive theoretical framework for voluntary IC disclosure. *Journal of Intellectual Capital*, Vol. 12, No. 4, pp. 571–585. https://doi.org/10.1108/14691931111181733.

Beattie, V., Mcinnes, W., & Fearnley, S. (2004). A methodology for analysing and evaluating narratives in annual reports: A comprehensive descriptive profile and metrics for disclosure quality attributes. *Accounting Forum*, Vol. 28, No. 3, pp. 205–236. https://doi.org/10.1016/j.accfor.2004.07.001.

Belkaoui, A., & Kahl, A. (1977). What Canadian bank financial statements don't tell. *CA Magazine*, Vol. 110, No. 6, pp. 1–32.

Bravo, F. (2016). Forward-looking disclosure and corporate reputation as mechanisms to reduce stock return volatility. *Revista de Contabilidad*, Vol. 19, No. 1, pp. 122–131. https://doi.org/10.1016/j.rcsar.2015.03.001.

Brown, S. V., & Tucker, J. W. (2011). Large-sample evidence on firms' year-over-year MD&A modifications. *Journal of Accounting Research*, Vol. 49, No. 2, pp. 309–346. https://doi.org/10.1111/j.1475-679X.2010.00396.x.

Celik, O., Ecer, A., & Karabacak, H. (2006). Disclosure of forward looking information: Evidence from listed companies on Istanbul stock exchange. *Investment Management and Financial Innovations*, Vol. 3, No. 2, pp. 197–216.

Cheng, E. C., & Courtenay, S. M. (2006). Board composition, regulatory regime and voluntary disclosure. *The International Journal of Accounting*, Vol. 41, No. 3, pp. 262–289. https://doi.org/10.1016/j.intacc.2006.07.001.

Cheng, M., Green, W., Conradie, P., Konishi, N., & Romi, A. (2014). The international integrated reporting framework: Key issues and future research opportunities. *Journal of International Financial Management & Accounting*, Vol. 25, No. 1, pp. 90–119. https://doi.org/10.1111/jifm.12015.

Clarkson, P. M., Kao, J. L., & Richardson, G. D. (1994). The voluntary inclusion of forecasts in the MD&A section of annual reports. *Contemporary Accounting Research*, Vol. 11, No. 1, pp. 423–450. https://doi.org/10.1111/j.1911-3846.1994 .tb00450.x.

Eng, L., & Mak, Y. (2003). Corporate governance and voluntary disclosure. *Journal of Accounting and Public Policy*, 22(4), 325–345.

Elberry, N., & Hussainey, K. (2020). Does corporate investment efficiency affect corporate disclosure practice? *Journal of Applied Accounting Research*, Vol. 21, No. 2, pp. 309–327.

Elberry, N., & Hussainey, K. (2021). Governance vis-à-vis investment efficiency: Substitutes or complementary in their effects on disclosure practice. *Journal of Risk and Financial management*, Forthcoming.

Elzahar, H., & Hussainey, K. (2012). Determinants of narrative risk disclosures in UK interim reports. *Journal of Risk Finance*, Vol. 13, No. 2, pp. 133–147. https://doi.org/10.1108/15265941211203189.

Esa, E., & Anum Mohd Ghazali, N. (2012). Corporate social responsibility and corporate governance in Malaysian government-linked companies. *Corporate Governance*, Vol. 12, No. 3, pp. 292–305. https://doi.org/10.1108/14720701211234564.

Espinosa, M. N., & Trombetta, M. (2007). Disclosure interactions and the cost of equity capital: Evidence from the Spanish continuous market. *Journal of Business Finance & Accounting*, Vol. 34, pp. 1371–1392.

Farhan, N. H., Alhomidi, E., Almaqtari, F. A., & Tabash, M. I. (2019). Does corporate governance moderate the relationship between liquidity ratios and financial performance? Evidence from Indian pharmaceutical companies. *Academic Journal of Interdisciplinary Studies*, Vol. 8, No. 3, pp. 144.

Farhan, N. H., Tabash, M., Almaqtari, F., & Yahya, A. (2020). Board composition and firms' profitability: Empirical evidence from pharmaceutical industry in India. *Journal of International Studies*, Vol. 13, No. 3, pp. 180–194. https://doi.org/10.14254/2071-8330.2020/13-3/12.

Frias-Aceituno, J. V., Rodríguez-Ariza, L., & Garcia-Sánchez, I. M. (2014). Explanatory factors of integrated sustainability and financial reporting. *Business strategy and the environment*, Vol. 23, No. 1, pp. 56–72. https://doi.org/10.1002/bse.1765.

Gallego-Álvarez, I., Rodríguez-Domínguez, L., & García-Sánchez, I. (2011). Information disclosed online by Spanish universities: Content and explanatory factors. *Online Information Review*, Vol. 35, No. 3, pp. 360–385. https://doi.org/10.1108/14684521111151423.

Gandía, J. L. (2008). Determinants of internet-based corporate governance disclosure by Spanish listed companies. *Online Information Review*, Vol. 32, No. 6, pp. 791–817. https://doi.org/10.1108/14684520810923944.

Graham, J., Harvey, C., & Rajgopal, S. (2005). The economic implications of corporate financial reporting. *Journal of Accounting and Economics*, Vol. 40, No. 1–3, pp. 3–73. https://doi.org/10.1016/j.jacceco.2005.01.002.

Gupta, M. (2013). Liability for forward looking statements-discussion of Indian law. *Journal of the Indian Law Institute*. Vol. 55, No. 2, pp. 228–240. https://www.jstor.org/stable/43953643.

Gupta, S., & Mishra, N. (2019). *Independent directors: Position, role and duties - A primer* [WWW Document]. Available at: https://www.icsi.edu/media/filer_public/60/85/6085b2e5-eea2-419c-984f-7b27e6e6656c/niro_nov_19-9.pdf (accessed 12.21.20).

Haniffa, R. M., & Cooke, T. E. (2005). The impact of culture and governance on corporate social reporting. *Journal of Accounting and Public Policy*, Vol. 24, No. 5, pp. 391–430. https://doi.org/10.1016/j.jaccpubpol.2005.06.001.

Hashed, A., & Almaqtari, F. (2020). The impact of corporate governance mechanisms and IFRS on earning management in Saudi Arabia. *Accounting*, Vol. 7, No. 1, pp. 207–224.

Hassanein, A., & Hussainey, K. (2015). Is forward-looking financial disclosure really informative? Evidence from UK narrative statements. *International Review of Financial Analysis*, Vol. 41, No. October, pp. 52–61. https://doi.org/10.1016/j.irfa.2015.05.025.

Hassanein, A., Marzouk, M., & Azzam, M. (2021). How does ownership by corporate managers affect R&D in the UK? The moderating impact of institutional investors.

*International Journal of Productivity and Performance Management*. https://doi.org/10.1108/IJPPM-03-2020-0121.

Hassanein, A., Zalata, A., & Hussainey, K. (2019). Do forward-looking narratives affect investors' valuation of UK FTSE all-shares firms? *Review of Quantitative Finance and Accounting*, Vol. 52, No. 2, pp. 493–519. https://doi.org/10.1007/s11156-018-0717-6.

Hussainey, K., & Al-Najjar, B. (2011). Future-oriented narrative reporting: Determinants and use. *Journal of Applied Accounting Research*, Vol. 12, pp. 123–138.

Ho, S. S., & Wong, K. S. (2003). Preparers' perceptions of corporate reporting and disclosures. *International Journal of Disclosure and Governance*, Vol. 1, No. 1, pp. 71–81.

Hoque, Z., Arends, S., & Alexander, R. (2004). Policing the police service: A case study of the rise of 'new public management' within an Australian police service. *Accounting, Auditing & Accountability Journal*, Vol. 17, No. 1, pp. 59–84.

Hussainey, K., & Al-Najjar, B. (2011). Future-oriented narrative reporting: Determinants and use. *Journal of Applied Accounting Research*, Vol. 12, No. 2, pp. 123–138. https://doi.org/10.1108/09675421111160691.

Hussainey, K., Schleicher, T., & Walker, M. (2003). Undertaking large-scale disclosure studies when AIMR-FAF ratings are not available: The case of prices leading earnings. *Accounting and Business Research*, Vol. 33, No. 4, pp. 275–294. https://doi.org/10.1080/00014788.2003.9729654.

Hussainey, K., & Walker, M. (2009). The effects of voluntary disclosure and dividend propensity on prices leading earnings. *Accounting and Business Research*, Vol. 39, No. 1, pp. 37–55. https://doi.org/10.1080/00014788.2009.9663348.

Jensen, M. C., & Meckling, W. H. (1976). Theory of the firm: Managerial behavior, agency costs and ownership structure. *Journal of Financial Economics*, Vol. 3, No. 4, pp. 305–360. https://doi.org/10.1016/0304-405X(76)90026-X.

Jones, M., & Shoemaker, P. (1994). Accounting narratives: A review of empirical studies of content and readability. *Journal of Accounting Literature*, Vol. 13, No. 1, pp. 142–184.

Kent, P., & Ung, K. (2003). Voluntary disclosure of forward-looking earnings information in Australia. *Australian Journal of Management*, Vol. 28, No. 3, pp. 273–285. https://doi.org/10.1177/031289620302800303.

Kılıç, M., & Kuzey, C. (2018). Determinants of forward-looking disclosures in integrated reporting. *Managerial Auditing Journal*, Vol. 33, No. 1, pp. 115–144. https://doi.org/10.1108/MAJ-12-2016-1498.

Krippendorff, K. (2010). *Content analysis: An introduction to its methodology* (2nd ed.). Organ. Res. Methods. London: Sage Publication.

Lehavy, R., Li, F., & Merkley, K. (2011). The effect of annual report readability on analyst following and the properties of their earnings forecasts. *The Accounting Review*, Vol. 86, No. 3, pp. 1087–1115.

Leng, J., & Ding, Y. (2011). Internal control disclosure and corporate governance: Empirical research from Chinese listed companies. *Technology and Investment*, Vol. 2, No. 4, pp. 1–9. https://doi.org/10.4236/ti.2011.24029.

Liu, S. (2015). Corporate governance and forward-looking disclosure: Evidence from China. *Journal of International Accounting, Auditing and Taxation*, Vol. 25, No. 2015, pp. 16–30. https://doi.org/10.1016/j.intaccaudtax.2015.10.002.

Menicucci, E., & Paolucci, G. (2017). Fair value accounting within a financial crisis: An examination of implications and perspectives. *International Journal of Business and Social Science*, Vol. 8, No. 2, pp. 41 56.

Milne, M. J., & Adler, R. W. (1999). Exploring the reliability of social and environmental disclosures content analysis. *Accounting, Auditing & Accountability Journal*, Vol. 12, No. 2, pp. 237–256. https://doi.org/10.1108/09513579910270138.

Mishra, N. (2020a). International view: Integrated reporting – A trouble-shooter for Indian reporting. *Integr: Integrated Reporting Committee of South Africa*. Available at: https:// integratedreportingsa.org/international-view-integrated-reporting-a-trouble-shooter -for-indian-reporting/ (accessed 11.26.20).

Mishra, N., (2020b). Integrated Reporting: A Structured Analysis of Application and Gaps in India. *TEXILA Int. J. Manag*. Special Edition Dec 2019, pp. 24–30. https://doi.org/10 .21522/tijmg.2015.se.19.02.art004.

Mishra, N., Nurullah, M., & Sarea, A. (2021). An empirical study on company's perception of integrated reporting in India. *Journal of Financial Reporting and Accounting*. https:// doi.org/10.1108/JFRA-03-2020-0081.

Navarro, M. C. A., & Urquiza, F. B. (2015). Board of directors' characteristics and forwardlooking information disclosure strategies. Paper presented at the EAA Annual Congress, Glasgow, 28–30 April. downloaded 9th June 2015. Available at: www .eaacongress.org/userfiles/GGMDLFL_FELHHL_MK3GL7UV.pdf.

O'Sullivan, M., Percy, M., & Stewart, J. (2008). Australian evidence on corporate governance attributes and their association with forward-looking information in the annual report. *Journal of Management & Governance*, Vol. 12, No. 1, pp. 5–35.

Securities and Exchange Board of India (SEBI). (2017). Integrated reporting by listed entities. *CIRCULARSEBI/HO/CFD/CMD/CIR/P/2017/10*. Available at: https://www.sebi.gov.in/ legal/circulars/feb-2017/integrated-reporting-by-listed-entities_34136.html.

Skinner, D. J. (2003). Should firms disclose everything to everybody? A discussion of "Open vs. closed conference calls: The determinants and effects of broadening access to disclosure". *Journal of Accounting and Economics*, Vol. 34, No. 1–3, pp. 181–187. https://doi.org/10.1016/S0165-4101(02)00074-5.

Smith, M., & Taffler, R. (1992). Readability and understandability: Different measures of the textual complexity of accounting narrative. *Accounting, Auditing, and Accountability Journal*, Vol. 5, No. 4, pp. 84–98. https://doi.org/10.1108 /09513579210019549.

Smith, M., & Taffler, R. (1995). The incremental effect of narrative accounting information in corporate annual reports. *Journal of Business Finance and Accounting*, Vol. 22, No. 8, pp. 1195–1210. https://doi.org/10.1111/j.1468-5957.1995.tb00901.x.

Song, J., & Windram, B. (2004). Benchmarking audit committee effectiveness in financial reporting. *International Journal of Auditing*, Vol. 8, No. 3, pp. 195–205.

Spence, M. (1978). Job market signaling. In *Uncertainty in economics* (pp. 281–306). Academic Press. https://doi.org/10.1016/B978-0-12-214850-7.50025-5.

Tahir, M., Ibrahim, S., & Nurullah, M. (2019). Getting compensation right: The choice of performance measures in CEO bonus contracts and earnings management. *The British Accounting Review*, Vol. 51, No. 2, pp. 148–169.

Thoni, H., Neter, J., Wasserman, W., & Kutner, M. H. (1990). *Applied linear regression models*. Biometrics. New York: Taylor & Francis.

Uyar, A., & Kılıç, M. (2012). The influence of firm characteristics on disclosure of financial ratios in annual reports of Turkish firms listed in the Istanbul stock exchange. *International Journal of Accounting, Auditing and Performance Evaluation*, Vol. 8, No. 2, pp. 137–156. https://doi.org/10.1504/IJAAPE.2012.046603.

Uzun, H., Szewczyk, S. H., & Varma, R. (2004). Board composition and corporate fraud. *Financial Analysts Journal*, Vol. 60, No. 3, pp. 33–43.

Wallace, R. O., Naser, K., & Mora, A. (1994). The relationship between the comprehensiveness of corporate annual reports and firm characteristics in Spain. *Accounting and Business Research*, Vol. 25, No. 97, pp. 41–53. https://doi.org/10.1080 /00014788.1994.9729927.

Wang, M., & Hussainey, K. (2013). Voluntary forward-looking statements driven by corporate governance and their value relevance. *Journal of Accounting and Public Policy*, Vol. 32, No. 3, pp. 26–49. https://doi.org/10.1016/j.jaccpubpol.2013.02.009.

Watson, A., Shrives, P., & Marston, C. (2002). Voluntary disclosure of accounting ratios in the UK. *The British Accounting Review*, Vol. 34, No. 4, pp. 289–313.

Yeoh, P. (2010). Narrative reporting: The UK experience. *International Journal of Law and Management*, Vol. 52, No. 3, pp. 211–231. https://doi.org/10.1108/17542431011044652.

## Annexe 1 Forward-Looking Disclosure Index (FLDI)

1. A statement of company's goals
2. Vision and mission statement
3. Actions taken during the year to achieve the company's goal
4. Brief history of the company
5. Significant events calendar
6. Growth opportunities
7. Risk disclosures
8. Discussion of past industry trends
9. Discussion about major regional economic development
10. Stakeholder description and engagement matrix
11. Products share and market share
12. Description of activities and production process
13. Products and innovation
14. Discussion of product safety
15. Company market analysis and competitors' analysis
16. Quality controls and commercial policies
17. Discussion about corporate strategy
18. Impact of strategy on current and/or future results
19. Investment in R&D, human resources and other intangibles
20. Environmental actions affecting companies' activity
21. Advertising and publicity plan(s) (qualitative)
22. Capital expenditure plan(s) (qualitative)
23. Expected cash flows (qualitative)
24. Earning target (qualitative)
25. Statement of corporate social responsibility
26. Six capitals
27. Details about directors (age, academic and professional qualifications, etc.)
28. Details of community programmes implemented
29. Discussion of employees' welfare and employee policy
30. Statement of company environmental policies

# 9 A comparison of integrated reporting practices in Japan and the UK[1]

*Taslima Akhter, Mohammad Badrul Haider and Toshihiko Ishihara*

## 9.1 Introduction

The past few years have witnessed a gradual increase in integrated reporting (IR) around the world (KPMG, 2020). This new reporting framework has emerged to overcome the limitations of traditional corporate reporting, including its narrow focus on historical financial performance, lengthy and complex annual reports and disconnected communication (IIRC, 2011). To address this, an integrated report incorporates both financial and non-financial information (NFI) to provide a holistic picture of organisational performance and the value-creation process (IIRC, 2013). Recent developments in IR practice are influenced by the International Integrated Reporting Council (IIRC), which has itself received widespread support from regulators, investors, accounting professionals and other stakeholders, with the IIRC publishing the International Integrated Reporting Framework in 2013 (IIRC, 2013). However, although IR is a new practice, both public policy and organisational practice in the area have developed rapidly. In 2011, South Africa became the first country to mandate IR on a "comply-or-explain" basis for companies listed on the Johannesburg Stock Exchange (Dumay *et al.*, 2016). At present, some 2,500 companies across 70 countries are practising IR, with the practice rapidly increasing in Japan, France, Malaysia and India (IIRC, no date; KPMG, 2020).

Academic researchers have also shown an interest in IR, with most of the early studies being largely normative in nature as they examine some of the concepts, benefits and challenges of IR ((Eccles and Saltzman, 2011; de Villiers, Rinaldi and Unerman, 2014; Dumay *et al.*, 2016; Rinaldi, Unerman and de Villiers, 2018). Empirical research in the field has also grown significantly (Soriya and Rastogi, 2021). Several of these studies show that there is wide variation in IR practice and several company- and country-level factors explain the adoption of this emerging reporting practice (Velte and Stawinoga, 2016). For the most part, these early IR studies use the context of a single country, a feature that regrettably does not allow country-to-country comparisons of the extent and quality of IR (but also see Eccles, Krzus and Solano, 2019; Ahmed *et al.*, 2021). More recent studies (Velte and Stawinoga, 2016; Rinaldi, Unerman and de Villiers, 2018) call for more comparative research to better understand the influence of various institutional environments on IR practice.

DOI: 10.4324/9781003095385-12

This chapter responds to this call by comparing the extent and quality of integrated reports in both Japan and the UK by conducting content analysis of the annual reports of 20 companies in each. We focus on IR among Japanese and UK companies for several reasons: (a) in terms of the number of companies publishing sustainability reports, both countries have been world leaders for more than a decade (KPMG, 2008, 2020); (b) IR is rapidly increasing in Japan (KPMG AZSA, 2021) and recent regulatory initiatives undertaken in the UK are conducive to integrating financial and NFI (Deloitte, 2015); and (c) the countries have very different systems of corporate governance. Whereas Japanese corporate governance is well known for its stakeholder orientation, UK Anglo-American corporate governance is characterised by the protection of shareholders' interests (Buchanan, 2007). As discussed in Section 9.2, whereas existing studies focus on a single country, this chapter provides a comparative analysis of IR content across two countries in a major contribution to the growing body of IR literature. This contribution is important in that the IIRC aims to attain a uniform understanding of IR worldwide. The present analysis is also one of the first studies known to empirically investigate the content of IR in Japan as the country with the highest growth in voluntary reporting practice (KPMG, 2017).

## 9.2   Literature review

Prior empirical studies cover the following key areas of IR (Soriya and Rastogi, 2021): (a) extent and quality of integrated reports, (b) determinants of adoption of IR, (c) consequences of IR adoption on a firm's value and (d) implementation of IR. This chapter examines the extent and quality of integrated reports and relevant studies are reviewed in this section.

Several studies have examined the early development of IR in South Africa (Solomon and Maroun, 2012; Setia *et al.*, 2015; Ahmed Haji and Anifowose, 2016, 2017; Du Toit, Van Zyl and Schütte, 2017). Using content analysis, these studies investigated the extent and quality of disclosure in integrated reports. Although the adoption of IR has increased social, environmental and other types of disclosures, these studies point to several limitations regarding the current IR practice in South Africa, including the generic nature of disclosures, the poor integration between content elements and the interdependencies of various forms of capital and the lack of quantitative and forward-looking disclosures. These studies concluded that IR in South Africa is largely ceremonial in nature and is mainly used to ensure regulatory compliance and organisational legitimacy.

Other studies extended the literature by analysing the integrated reports of companies worldwide (Melloni, Caglio and Perego, 2017). Pistoni, Songini and Bavagnoli (2018) investigated the quality of 116 integrated reports available on the IIRC database and showed that companies perform better in disclosing the business overview and external environment, risks and opportunities, performance and corporate governance. However, disclosures on the business model and value-creation process, outlook and basis of presentation are found to be scarce in these reports. Although a few studies focused on the IR scenario of other countries, similar inconsistencies and limitations were observed in the integrated reports of the companies in these countries. For example, in a study on 22 FTSE 100 companies, Robertson and Samy (2015) concluded that companies in the UK currently provide "medium to low" levels of linkage between annual reports and sustainability reports. In another study, Zinsou (2018) documented that companies in France are still striving to integrate financial and non-financial disclosures.

In two recent studies, Eccles, Krzus and Solano (2019) and Ahmed *et al.* (2021) provided international comparison regarding IR practice. Eccles, Krzus and Solano (2019) analysed the influence of IR framework in preparing the integrated reports of ten countries. Based on the quality of the relevant integrated reports, the study classified the countries into three categories: high (Germany, the Netherlands and South Africa), medium (France, Italy, South Korea and the UK), and low (Brazil, Japan and the United States). Additionally, Ahmed *et al.* (2021) emphasised the voluntary nature of IR and the lack of a universally accepted IR framework to explain the wide variation in IR practice among the sample companies listed in the following four Gulf countries: Saudi Arabia, Kuwait, the UAE and Qatar.

Overall, the extant literature showed that the quality of integrated reports still remains low and that there is a wide variation in current IR practice worldwide. However, there is limited research on country-to-country comparison on IR practice. The present chapter contributes to the literature by comparing the extent and quality of IR in Japan and the UK.

## 9.3 Institutional context

The institutional environment within which organisations operate plays a significant role in shaping organisational structures, activities and behaviour (Meyer and Rowan, 1977). Given the importance of institutional context in understanding corporate reporting practice, the following sections explain in detail the reporting contexts of Japan and the UK.

### 9.3.1 IR in Japan

Western-style corporate social responsibility (CSR) was introduced to Japan at the beginning of the 21st century (Kawamura, 2003). Following several decades of economic prosperity, Japan experienced a prolonged economic recession during the 1990s, with the country's insider-oriented business system, with its limited emphasis on outside monitoring, proving ineffective. Around this time, Japanese firms started to adopt globalised business and ownership structures. Gradually, the cross-shareholding among Japanese business corporations and financial intermediaries declined and foreign investors became key stakeholders in Japanese firms (Suto and Takehara, 2018). These changing dynamics led Japanese firms to revise and adjust their understanding of the business–society relationship.

The Japanese government also played a significant role in institutionalising CSR practice. Two voluntary guidelines that shaped the early development of environment accounting include the *Environmental Reporting Guidelines* in 2000 and the *Environmental Management Accounting Workbook* in 2002 (Kokubu *et al.*, 2003). The Tokyo Stock Exchange (TSE) also undertook several initiatives aimed at enhancing the effectiveness of corporate governance and related reporting practices. In 2004, the TSE published *Principles of Corporate Governance for Listed Companies* and, in response to increasing expectations, the TSE has required all listed companies to prepare reports on corporate governance since 2006 (TSE, 2007).

In July 2013, the Japanese Ministry of Economy, Trade and Industry (METI) launched a project entitled *Competitiveness and Incentives for Sustainable Growth: Building Favourable Relationships between Companies and Investors*. The project, widely known as the "Ito Review", provides significant implications for IR practice in Japan. Like IIRC (2013), the Ito Review also defines capital from a broader perspective, including financial, human, intellectual, social/relationship and natural capital. The project also recommends the adoption of IR by the companies. To further improve the practice of corporate governance, in 2015 the Financial Services Agency and the TSE jointly published *Japan's Corporate Governance Code*. In terms of information disclosure and transparency, the Code requires that companies go beyond the applicable laws and regulations and appropriately disclose both financial information and NFI, including business plans and strategies, risks and corporate governance (TSE, 2015).

To further promote IR practice, in May 2017, METI published its *Guidance for Collaborative Value Creation*. According to METI (2017), this will ensure that investors receive comprehensive communication about key business information, including management philosophy, business models, strategies and governance systems. Under this extensive but still voluntary regulatory environment, the adoption of IR among Japanese companies has significantly increased in recent years. In evidence, although only 26 companies had published self-declared IR in 2010, this had increased to 579 companies by 2020 (KPMG AZSA, 2021).

### *9.3.2 IR in the UK*

In response to strong criticism of traditional financial reporting, UK companies have been using narrative reporting since the 1990s (Yeoh, 2010). In 1993, the Accounting Standards Board published a voluntary guidance for narrative disclosure in the form of its *Operating and Financial Review* (OFR), and by 2000, the OFR had become an integral part of corporate reporting practice in the UK. In 1998, the International Organization of Securities Commissions in its *International Equity Disclosure Standards* also recommended the provision of narrative disclosure in company reports. The European Union (EU) Accounts Modernisation Directive of 2003 also required that companies publish enhanced business reviews, including both financial and non-financial performance in their director's reports. The 2006 Companies Act also incorporated several provisions that enhanced the scope of the business review in the directors' report. The extended directors' business review must contain a comprehensive review of a company's business and its principal risks and opportunities, as well as its prospects and information on its social and environmental impacts (Davies, 2007).

In 2013, the UK government further revised the Companies Act to require larger companies to prepare a "strategic report" as part of their annual reports. Accordingly, the Financial Reporting Council (FRC) published its *Guidance on the Strategic Report* in June 2014. According to the FRC (2014b), a strategic report "provides shareholders with a holistic and meaningful picture of an entity's business model, strategy, development, performance, position and future prospects" (p. 3). Based on the UK's implementation of the EU directive on the disclosure of NFI and diversity information, public interest entities with more than 500 employees are also required to include a NFI statement in their strategic reports. In July 2018, the FRC published an updated version of the *Guidance on the Strategic Report*, incorporating these recent changes in corporate reporting regulations (FRC, 2018). Among others, it explains the principles and content elements of strategic reports. In their survey on annual reports of FTSE companies, Deloitte (2015) concludes that there is much similarity between the *Guidance on the Strategic Report* and the IIRC Framework. The above discussion clearly shows that, although IR is not mandatory in either Japan or the UK, each country's regulatory environment motivates companies to adopt this innovative reporting practice.

## 9.4 Research methodology

We chose the sample companies from the top 100 companies (based on market capitalisation) listed on each of the TSE and the London Stock Exchange. From these, 20 companies from each country, making a total of 40 companies, were selected on a random basis (see Appendix 1). Considering the existing literature (Robertson and Samy, 2015; Stent and Dowler, 2015), we believe this sample size to be sufficient to understand in detail the reporting practices in both countries. We obtained the 2016 annual reports of the selected companies from each company's website.

We employed content analysis, which is the most common method used for studying corporate social and environmental reporting (Guthrie and Abeysekera, 2006). In relation to this study, content analysis involves codifying the contents of annual reports based on selected criteria to analyse the extent and quality of the IR. In this analysis, we have undertaken several measures to ensure the validity and reliability of the research method. The validity of the research instrument depends on a well-specified classification scheme for content coding and well-specified decision-making rules about what and how to code the data (Milne and Adler, 1999).

This chapter has adapted the disclosure checklist developed by Akhter and Ishihara (2018). Their checklist was chosen for several reasons. Firstly, it is based on the IIRC framework (2013), which is the only international framework for preparing integrated reports. In addition, the checklist also considered the extant literature to make it a comprehensive one. Finally, Akhter and Ishihara (2018) tested this checklist on a small sample of UK companies. This chapter extends their work by increasing the sample size and comparing the IR practice of Japan and UK. The final disclosure checklist contains 43 items under eight content elements of the IIRC framework (Table 9.1).

156  T. Akhter, M. B. Haider and T. Ishihara

Table 9.1 Content analysis

| Disclosure item no | Disclosure items | Maximum possible score | Column A % of companies disclosing each item | | Column B Mean disclosure of each item | | Column C Disclosure quality of each item (in %) | |
|---|---|---|---|---|---|---|---|---|
| | | | Japan | UK | Japan | UK | Japan | UK |
| | **Content element 1: Organisational overview and external environment** | | | | | | | |
| 1 | Organisation's mission, vision, values and culture (no disclosure=0, disclosure=1) | 1 | 100 | 100 | 1 | 1 | 100 | 100 |
| 2 | Principal activities and markets (no disclosure=0, disclosure=1) | 1 | 100 | 100 | 1 | 1 | 100 | 100 |
| 3 | Ownership and operating structure (no disclosure=0, disclosure=1) | 1 | 100 | 100 | 1 | 1 | 100 | 100 |
| 4 | Competitive landscape and market positioning (no disclosure=0, disclosure=1) | 1 | 65 | 85 | 0.65 | 0.85 | 65 | 85 |
| 5 | Key quantitative information (no disclosure=0, only financial KPIs=1, both financial and non-financial KPIs=2, KPIs linked with objectives and/or capital=3) | 3 | 100 | 100 | 2 | 2.65 | 66.67 | 88.33 |
| 6 | Factors affecting external environment and organization's response (no disclosure=0, general disclosure=1, company-specific limited disclosure=2, company-specific adequate disclosure=3) | 3 | 100 | 100 | 1.95 | 2.05 | 65 | 68.33 |
| | **Organisational overview and external environment: total** | 10 | | | 7.6 (76%) | 8.55 (85.5%) | | |
| | **Content element 2: Governance** | | | | | | | |
| 7 | Organisation's leadership structure (no disclosure=0, members of the BOD/Committees are listed=1, names, experience and skills are also listed=2) | 2 | 100 | 100 | 1.85 | 2 | 92.5 | 100 |

| | | | | | | | |
|---|---|---|---|---|---|---|---|
| 8 | Role of highest governance body in setting purpose, values and strategy (no disclosure=0, disclosure=1) | 1 | 100 | 100 | 1 | 1 | 100 | 100 |
| 9 | Role of highest governance body in risk management (no disclosure=0, disclosure=1) | 1 | 100 | 100 | 1 | 1 | 100 | 100 |
| 10 | Specific processes to make strategic decisions and risk management (no disclosure=0, limited disclosure=1, adequate disclosure=2) | 2 | 100 | 100 | 1.6 | 1.8 | 80 | 90 |
| 11 | How remuneration and incentives are linked to value creation (no disclosure=0, general disclosure=1, specific disclosure=2) | 2 | 75 | 100 | 0.75 | 2 | 37.5 | 100 |
| 12 | Actions taken to influence and monitor cultural environment and ethical values of organisation (no disclosure=0, disclosure=1) | 1 | 100 | 100 | 1 | 1 | 100 | 100 |
| | **Governance: Total** | 9 | | | 7.2 (80%) | 8.8 (97.78%) | | |
| | **Content element 3: Business model** | | | | | | | |
| 13 | Explicit identification of key elements of business model (no disclosure=0, disclosure=1) | 1 | 85 | 90 | 0.85 | 0.9 | 85 | 90 |
| 14 | Diagram highlighting key elements of business model, supported by a clear explanation of the relevance of those elements to the organisation (no disclosure=0, disclosure with diagram or narrative=1, disclosure with both diagram and narratives=2) | 2 | 95 | 100 | 1.4 | 1.65 | 70 | 82.5 |

*(Continued)*

*Table 9.1* (Continued)

| Disclosure item no. | Disclosure items | Maximum possible score | Column A — % of companies disclosing each item | | Column B — Mean disclosure of each item | | Column C — Disclosure quality of each item (in %) | |
|---|---|---|---|---|---|---|---|---|
| | | | Japan | UK | Japan | UK | Japan | UK |
| 15 | Relating and disclosing capitals with business model (no disclosure=0, narrative disclosure only=1, narrative with limited quantitative disclosure=2, adequate disclosure=3) | 3 | 80 | 80 | 1 | 1.4 | 33.33 | 46.67 |
| 16 | Interdependencies and trade-offs between the capitals (no disclosure=0, disclosure=1) | 1 | 15 | 35 | 0.15 | 0.35 | 15 | 35 |
| 17 | Connection to information covered by other content elements (no disclosure=0, limited disclosure=1, adequate disclosure=2) | 2 | 65 | 90 | 0.7 | 1.1 | 35 | 55 |
| 18 | Aligning business model with changes in organisation's external environment (no disclosure=0, limited disclosure=1, adequate disclosure=2) | 2 | 95 | 100 | 1.2 | 1.1 | 60 | 55 |
| | **Business model: Total** | 11 | | | 5.3 (48.18%) | 6.5 (59.09%) | | |
| | **Content element 4: Risks and opportunities** | | | | | | | |
| 19 | Specific sources of risks and/or opportunities (no disclosure=0, disclosing only risks=1, disclosing both risk and opportunity=2) | 2 | 100 | 100 | 1.7 | 1.85 | 85 | 92.5 |
| 20 | Possible impacts of risk and opportunity (no disclosure=0, disclosing impacts of only risks=1, disclosing impacts of both risk and opportunity=2) | 2 | 85 | 100 | 1.3 | 1.75 | 65 | 87.5 |

| No. | | | | | | | |
|---|---|---|---|---|---|---|---|
| 21 | Specific steps taken to manage risks or to create value from opportunities (no disclosure=0, disclosure only on risk mitigation=1, disclosure mainly on risk mitigation with limited disclosure on opportunity=2, adequate disclosure both on risks and opportunity=3) | 3 | 90 | 100 | 1.5 | 2.25 | 50 | 75 |
| | **Risks and opportunities: Total** | 7 | | | 4.5 (64.29%) | 5.85 (83.57%) | | |
| | **Content element 5: Strategy and resource allocation** | | | | | | | |
| 22 | Organisation's short-, medium-, and long-term strategic objectives (no disclosure=0,limited disclosure=1, adequate disclosure=2) | 2 | 100 | 100 | 1.8 | 1.45 | 90 | 72.5 |
| 23 | Organisational strategies to achieve strategic objectives (no disclosure=0, disclosure=1) | 1 | 100 | 100 | 1 | 1 | 100 | 100 |
| 24 | Resource allocation plans to implement organisational strategies (no disclosure=0, limited disclosure=1, adequate disclosure=2) | 2 | 95 | 95 | 1.3 | 1.1 | 65 | 55 |
| 25 | Linkage between organisational strategies and resource allocation plans with its business model (no disclosure=0, partial disclosure=1, adequate disclosure=2) | 2 | 60 | 70 | 0.7 | 0.9 | 35 | 45 |
| 26 | Environmental and social considerations embedded into the organisation's strategy (no disclosure=0, disclosure=1) | 1 | 100 | 100 | 1 | 1 | 100 | 100 |
| 27 | Stakeholder engagement in formulating strategies and resource plans (no disclosure=0, identification of related stakeholders=1, specific details on stakeholders=1, specific details on stakeholder engagement=2) | 2 | 90 | 100 | 1.4 | 1.35 | 70 | 67.5 |

*(Continued)*

*Table 9.1* (Continued)

| Disclosure item no. | Disclosure items | Maximum possible score | Column A % of companies disclosing each item | | Column B Mean disclosure of each item | | Column C Disclosure quality of each item (in %) | |
|---|---|---|---|---|---|---|---|---|
| | | | Japan | UK | Japan | UK | Japan | UK |
| | **Strategy and resource allocation: Total** | 10 | | | 7.2 (72%) | 6.8 (68%) | | |
| | **Content element 6: Performance** | | | | | | | |
| 28 | Quantitative indicators with respect to targets, risks and opportunities (no disclosure=0, limited disclosure=1, limited disclosure with trends=2, adequate disclosure=3) | 3 | 100 | 100 | 1.95 | 2.3 | 65 | 76.67 |
| 29 | Organisation's effects, both positive and negative, on the capitals (no disclosure=0, mainly positive disclosure=1, adequate disclosure=2) | 2 | 100 | 100 | 1.05 | 1.05 | 52.5 | 52.5 |
| 30 | Description of key stakeholder relationships (no disclosure=0, limited disclosure=1, adequate disclosure=2) | 2 | 100 | 100 | 1.35 | 1.5 | 67.5 | 75 |
| 31 | Linkages between past and present performance, and outlook (no disclosure=0, limited disclosure=1, adequate disclosure=2) | 2 | 100 | 100 | 1.55 | 1.5 | 77.5 | 75 |
| 32 | KPIs that combine financial measures with other components or monetising certain effects on the capitals (no disclosure=0, limited disclosure=1, company-specific and innovative disclosure=2) | 2 | 35 | 30 | 0.35 | 0.3 | 17.5 | 15 |
| | **Performance: Total** | 11 | | | 6.25 (56.82%) | 6.65 (60.45%) | | |
| | **Content element 7: Outlook** | | | | | | | |

| No. | Item | Max | | | | | | |
|---|---|---|---|---|---|---|---|---|
| 33 | Expectations about external environment (no disclosure=0, general disclosure=1, organisation-specific disclosure=2) | 2 | 100 | 100 | 1.7 | 1.5 | 85 | 75 |
| 34 | Preparedness for future uncertainties (no disclosure=0, disclosure=1) | 1 | 85 | 100 | 0.85 | 1 | 85 | 100 |
| 35 | Potential implications of future uncertainties on capitals (no disclosure=0, limited disclosure=1, adequate disclosure=2) | 2 | 90 | 100 | 0.9 | 1.2 | 45 | 60 |
| 36 | Ways for measuring outlook (no disclosure=0, general disclosure=1, organisation-specific disclosure=2) | 2 | 100 | 100 | 1.65 | 1.9 | 82.5 | 95 |
| 37 | Comparison between performance and targets (no disclosure=0, disclosure=1) | 1 | 95 | 100 | 0.95 | 1 | 95 | 100 |
| | **Outlook: Total** | 8 | | | 6.05 (75.63%) | 6.6 (82.5%) | | |
| | **Content element 8: Basis of preparation and presentation** | | | | | | | |
| 38 | Description of reporting boundary (no disclosure=0, disclosure=1) | 1 | 100 | 100 | 1 | 1 | 100 | 100 |
| 39 | Framework/method to determine material matters (no disclosure=0, disclosure=1) | 1 | 60 | 40 | 0.6 | 0.4 | 60 | 40 |
| 40 | Description of process to determine material matters (no disclosure=0, limited disclosure=1, adequate disclosure=2) | 2 | 55 | 30 | 0.8 | 0.35 | 40 | 17.5 |
| 41 | Role of key personnel in materiality determination process (no disclosure=0, disclosure=1) | 1 | 55 | 40 | 0.55 | 0.4 | 55 | 40 |
| 42 | Impact of material matters on organisation's value-creation process (no disclosure=0, limited disclosure=1, adequate disclosure=2) | 2 | 45 | 40 | 0.5 | 0.5 | 25 | 25 |
| 43 | Stakeholder engagement in materiality determination process (no disclosure=0, disclosure=1) | 1 | 35 | 15 | 0.35 | 0.15 | 35 | 15 |
| | **Basis of preparation and presentation: Total** | 8 | | | 3.8 (47.5%) | 2.8 (35%) | | |
| | **Total IR disclosure score by companies (all content elements)** | 74 | | | 47.9 (64.73%) | 52.55 (71.01%) | | |

Past studies employ both unweighted and weighted coding methods to measure the extent and quality of corporate reporting (Stent and Dowler, 2015; Ahmed Haji and Anifowose, 2016). Consistent with these studies, we followed multiple coding rules, depending on the nature of the disclosure items. We used three types of scoring systems, 0–1, 0–2 and 0–3. For example, items such as "principal activities and markets" and "ownership and operating structure" are coded using a dichotomous variable where 0 represents nondisclosure and 1 represents disclosure of that particular item. For some disclosure items, we used scoring systems of either 0–2 or 0–3. For example, "key quantitative information" is coded using 0–3, where 0 represents nondisclosure, 1 represents only financial KPIs (key performance indicators), 2 represents both financial and non-financial KPIs, and 3 represents KPIs linked with objectives and/or capital. Table 9.1 details necessary assumptions for scoring each item alongside the items.

In this chapter, the extent and quality of IR is calculated for each item and for each country. The extent of IR (column A in Table 9.1) as a percentage is computed as the number of companies disclosing an item multiplied by 100 and divided by the total number of companies in each country. Column B in Table 9.1 shows the mean value of each disclosure item by the companies. Column C in Table 9.1 shows the disclosure quality of each item on the checklist as a percentage which is calculated by multiplying the mean value of each item by 100 and dividing by the maximum possible score for that item.

The first-named author of this chapter coded under the supervision of the second-named author, given the latter's expertise in content analysis and application in previous studies. The first-named author also underwent extensive training in content analysis as part of her doctoral dissertation. To begin, both authors familiarised themselves with a sample of two randomly selected annual reports (one from Japan and one from the UK), the checklist and the decision rules. Both researchers then independently coded these reports. We compared individual scores, discussed any differences and reconciled these before proceeding to the final coding. In manual content analysis, coder fatigue is an important threat to reliability. To overcome the problem of coder fatigue, breaks were taken at regular intervals during the data coding process, following Wagiciengo and Belal (2012). Moreover, repeated coding was also undertaken where applicable to ensure the accuracy of results.

## 9.5 Findings and analysis

### 9.5.1 Overview of IR in Japan and the UK

In this section, we evaluate and compare the extent and quality of IR in Japan and the UK. Table 9.1 presents the findings of the content analysis, which reveals that the quality of the sample reports varies significantly in both countries. For example, the total IR disclosure score of these companies ranges from 36.49% to 75.68% for Japan and from 54.05% to 87.84% for the UK (not reported in Table 9.1). As shown in Table 9.1, the average IR disclosure score is 64.73% for the Japanese companies and 71.01% for the UK companies included in the study. The results also show that "governance" is the most-disclosed content element in both countries (with disclosure scores of 80% and 97.78% in Japan and the UK, respectively), a feature we can attribute to several regulatory initiatives undertaken in these countries in recent years, and as discussed in Sections 9.3.1 and 9.3.2. In both countries, the second-highest disclosed content element is "organisational overview and the external environment" (with disclosure scores of 76% and 85.5% in Japan and the UK, respectively).We also found that the two least-disclosed content elements in both countries are "business model" and the "basis of preparation and presentation". The disclosure quality score of "basis of preparation and presentation" is 47.5% in Japan and 35% in the UK and the quality score of "business model" is 48.18% in Japan and 59.09% in the UK.

In other words, although most of the sample companies (85% and 90% of the companies in Japan and the UK, respectively) explicitly identified key elements in their business models, they failed to demonstrate the "interdependencies and trade-offs between the capitals" (15% and 35% of the companies in Japan and the UK, respectively) under the content element "business model" (Table 9.1). The key issue under the content element "basis of preparation and presentation" is materiality. In both countries, however, disclosure on this content element is minimal. Whereas 40% of UK companies and 60% of Japanese companies mention the "frameworks/methods to determine material matters" (Table 9.1), the share of companies disclosing "stakeholder engagement in materiality determination" is only 35% for Japanese companies and 15% for UK companies. These findings are consistent with the extant literature. Several previous studies also show that disclosure of business models, materiality and connectivity are either missing or generic in nature (Ahmed Haji and Anifowose, 2016, 2017; Pistoni, Songini and Bavagnoli, 2018; Zinsou, 2018). In this regard, several studies point out some reasons for this poor disclosure, noting that IR is in an evolving stage and that the definitions of IR and related concepts, such as business model, integrated thinking, multiple capital framework and materiality, remain unclear (Dumay *et al.*, 2017). The lack of clear guidance to measure non-financial performance is another obstacle to the implementation of IR (Robertson and Samy, 2020).

### 9.5.2 Statistical analysis of IR in Japan and the UK

We conducted *t*-tests of the two samples of companies to compare the differences in the content elements of IR between Japan and the UK. Table 9.2 details the results. As shown, there is no significant difference in the total IR disclosure scores of companies in the two countries. However, there are significant differences in the disclosure scores of three content elements, namely "organisational overview and the external environment", "governance" and "risks and opportunities", for which all scores are statistically significant at $p < 0.01$. Table 9.1 shows that, within the content element of "organizational overview and the external environment", the disclosure quality of "key quantitative information" in Japan

*Table 9.2* Two sample *t*-tests for difference in IR disclosure scores between Japan and the UK

| Content elements | Mean disclosure: Japan | Mean disclosure: UK | Mean difference | t-value | Degrees of freedom | p-value |
|---|---|---|---|---|---|---|
| Total IR disclosure score | 47.9 | 52.550 | −4.650 | −1.959 | 38 | 0.058 |
| Organisational overview and external environment | 7.600 | 8.550 | −0.950 | −2.937*** | 38 | 0.006 |
| Governance | 7.200 | 8.800 | −1.600 | −8.219*** | 38 | 0.000 |
| Business model | 5.300 | 6.500 | −1.200 | −1.798 | 38 | 0.080 |
| Risks and opportunities | 4.500 | 5.850 | −1.350 | −2.702*** | 38 | 0.005 |
| Strategy and resource allocation | 7.200 | 6.800 | 0.400 | 0.859 | 38 | 0.396 |
| Performance | 6.250 | 6.650 | −0.400 | −1.039 | 38 | 0.305 |
| Outlook | 6.050 | 6.600 | −0.550 | −1.621 | 38 | 0.113 |
| Basis of preparation and presentation | 3.800 | 2.800 | 1.000 | 1.279 | 38 | 0.209 |

Note: *** denotes significance at the $p<0.01$ level.

(average disclosure quality of 66.67%) is poor compared to the UK (88.33%). Although all companies in Japan and the UK disclose their financial and non-financial KPIs, the level of linkage creation between the KPIs and other elements, such as strategic objectives, materiality or the value-creation process, differs. We found that whereas only 20% of Japanese companies disclose the linkage between KPIs and strategic objectives/capitals, some 65% of the UK companies attempt to do likewise (not reported in Table 9.1).

This discrepancy could be because of a misunderstanding about CSR, corporate sustainability or IR in the Japanese context. From the beginning, Western-style CSR has been considered "an extra activity of corporate management and … separate from the core business of a company" (Kuroda and Ishida, 2017, p. 67). Whereas European companies have long incorporated the concept of the triple bottom line or corporate sustainability in their reports, until recently in Japan, CSR focused on compliance, environmental preservation and corporate philanthropy (Tanimoto and Suzuki, 2005; Jackson and Bartosch, 2017). In addition, Japanese companies prefer to publish stand-alone CSR/sustainability reports rather than including their non-financial performances in mandatory annual reports (Kawahara, 2017).

Disclosure on the content element "governance" is also statistically different between Japan and the UK ($p < 0.01$). Although "governance" is the highest-disclosed content element in both countries, companies in Japan still lag behind the UK in terms of their disclosure of governance. This finding is consistent with prior studies on corporate governance in Japan. For example, in their analysis of the banking industry, Boolaky and Thomas (2010) also found that disclosure on corporate governance in Japan is still very low when compared to the US or the UK. Several studies have duly criticised traditional corporate governance in Japan for its lack of effectiveness (Hoshi and Kashyap, 2001; Fukao, 2003). In contrast to the Anglo-American governance model, where the emphasis is on external surveillance, Japanese corporate governance is based on the principle of "internalism" (Buchanan, 2007). Traditional features of Japanese businesses, including relationship banking, cross-shareholdings and long-term employment, exert a considerable influence on their governance mechanisms (Jackson and Miyajima, 2008). In this corporate governance system, the demand for external reporting is also low. This is because major investors, such as banks and affiliated companies, usually have direct access to the private accounting information of the investee companies (Gordon, 1999).

The third content element where a significant difference in the quality of IR is observed between Japan and the UK is "risks and opportunities" ($p < 0.01$). This implies that disclosure of the risks and opportunities of Japanese companies are poor compared with similar disclosures by UK companies. This finding is consistent with the existing literature on risk reporting in Japan. Konishi and Ali (2007) show that Japanese companies prefer to provide generic and positive risk information rather than quantitative and specific information. Compared with other developed countries, corporate risk reporting is also a new practice in Japan. Although the practice has traditionally been voluntary, since 2004 listed companies in Japan must disclose information on their business risk in their annual reports (Fukukawa and Kim, 2017). However, there is no clear guidance about how to measure and report risks in annual reports (Konishi and Ali, 2007).

In contrast, since the 1990s, UK companies have been showing increasing interest in risk reporting and this has been influenced by several voluntary regulatory initiatives (Solomon *et al.*, 2000). The Corporate Governance Committee of 1992 (The Cadbury Report) and its successors have emphasised risk disclosure as part of companies' reforming their governance practice. In 1997, the Institute of Chartered Accountants in England and Wales (ICAEW) highlighted the importance of risk reporting in a discussion paper entitled, *Financial Reporting of Risk: Proposals for A Statement of Business Risk.* The 2006 Companies Act also requires that companies' strategic reports include explanations of the principal risks and uncertainties they face. In 2014, the FRC further issued *Guidance on Risk Management, Internal Control and Related Financial and Business Reporting* (FRC, 2014a).

## 9.6 Conclusion

This chapter compares the extent and quality of IR in Japan and the UK. We have used a disclosure checklist containing 43 items based on the content elements of the IIRC framework and analysed annual reports of 20 of the largest listed companies in each country. In doing so, we have generated one of the first studies to provide a country-to-country comparison of emerging IR practice.

We identify several similarities in IR practices between Japan and the UK. For example, "governance" and "organisational overview and the external environment" are the two most-disclosed content elements found in the company reports of both countries. In addition, reporting on the "basis of preparation and presentation" and on companies' "business models" are the least-reported content elements in both countries. The analysis also documents that Japanese companies lag behind UK companies in their disclosure of three content elements, namely "governance", "organisational overview and the external environment" and "risks and opportunities". We explain these statistical differences as being dependent on the historical socio-cultural and regulatory environments for corporate reporting in both countries.

The findings of this analysis have implications for several groups. First, we identify the strengths and weaknesses of contemporary IR practices within voluntary regulatory environments. Given that IR is still at an emerging stage, other countries wishing to improve their corporate reporting practices may find our results useful when introducing this type of reporting in their regulatory regimes. For companies, regulatory authorities and standard-setting bodies, our findings also inform specific areas of IR practices that require further improvement. For example, we argue that the lack of specific guidelines/standards could explain the relatively poor disclosure regarding "business models" and "materiality". Authorities should thus provide specific reporting guidelines on these issues. In addition, the findings on "governance" would be of special interest to Japanese stakeholders. Although recent initiatives have influenced the disclosure on "governance", we argue that there is still much room for improvement.

Of course, there are several limitations with our analysis, all of which suggest future directions for research. First, given that we selected the sample in this analysis from among the largest publicly listed companies in Japan and the UK, any generalisations of the findings should proceed with some caution. Future research could extend the sample size and the comprehensive checklist used here would be useful for this purpose. Second, by analysing the integrated reports of companies for a single year, we can provide only a snapshot of IR practices. Given that this type of reporting is still emerging, it is important to understand the evolution of this practice. We suggest future researchers could focus on longitudinal studies to provide evidence on the historical development of the content of integrated reports. Finally, given the significance of the concepts of "business model" and "materiality" in IR, future in-depth studies could better understand the dynamics of both the internal organisational environment and the external environment for the adoption of IR.

### Note

1  This chapter is based on the PhD dissertation of the first author.

# References

Ahmed, A. H., Elmaghrabi, M. E., Dunne, T. and Hussainey, K. (2021) 'Gaining momentum: Towards integrated reporting practices in Gulf Cooperation Council countries', *Business Strategy and Development*, 4(2), pp. 78–93.

Ahmed Haji, A. and Anifowose, M. (2016) 'The trend of integrated reporting practice in South Africa: Ceremonial or substantive?', *Sustainability Accounting, Management and Policy Journal*, 7(2), pp. 190–224.

Ahmed Haji, A. and Anifowose, M. (2017) 'Initial trends in corporate disclosures following the introduction of integrated reporting practice in South Africa', *Journal of Intellectual Capital*, 18(2), pp. 373–399.

Akhter, T. and Ishihara, T. (2018) 'Assessing the gap between integrated reporting and current corporate reporting : A study in the UK', *International Review of Business*, 18, pp. 137–157.

Boolaky, P. K. and Thomas, K. (2010) 'Corporate governance compliance and disclosure in the banking sector: Using data from Japan', Paper presented at Finance and Corporate Governance Conference, April 7-9, La Trobe University.

Buchanan, J. (2007) 'Japanese corporate governance and the principle of "internalism"', *Corporate Governance: An International Review*, 15(1), pp. 27–35.

Davies, J. (2007) *A guide to directors' responsibilities under the companies act 2006.* ACCA, London.

Deloitte. (2015) *Annual report insights 2015 building a better report.* Deloitte, London.

Dumay, J., Bernardi, C., Guthrie, J. and Demartini, P. (2016) 'Integrated reporting: A structured literature review', *Accounting Forum*, 40(3), pp. 166–185.

Dumay, J., Bernardi, C., Guthrie, J. and La Torre, M. (2017) 'Barriers to implementing the international integrated reporting framework: A contemporary academic perspective', *Meditari Accountancy Research*, 25(4), pp. 461–480.

Eccles, R. G., Krzus, M. P. and Solano, C. (2019) 'A comparative analysis of integrated reporting in ten countries', http://doi.org/10.2139/ssrn.3345590.

Eccles, R. G. and Saltzman, D. (2011) 'Achieving sustainability through integrated reporting', *Stanford Social Innovation Review*, 9(2) Summer, pp. 56–61.

FRC. (2014a) *Guidance on risk management, internal control and related financial and business reporting financial reporting.* FRC, London.

FRC. (2014b) *Guidance on the strategic report.* FRC, London.

FRC. (2018) *Guidance on the strategic report.* FRC, London.

Fukao, M. (2003) 'Japan's lost decade and its financial system', *World Economy*, 26(3), pp. 365–384.

Fukukawa, H. and Kim, H. (2017) 'Effects of audit partners on clients' business risk disclosure', *Accounting and Business Research*, 47(7), pp. 780–809.

Gordon, B. (1999) *A critical evaluation of Japanese accounting changes since 1997.* Master's dissertation, University of Sheffield, UK.

Guthrie, J. and Abeysekera, I. (2006) 'Content analysis of social, environmental reporting: What is new?', *Journal of Human Resource Costing & Accounting*, 10(2), pp. 114–126.

Hoshi, T. and Kashyap, A. K. (2001) *Corporate financing and governance in Japan: The road to the future.* MIT Press, Cambridge, MA.

IIRC. (2011) *Towards integrated reporting- Communicating value in the 21st century.* IIRC. https://www.integratedreporting.org/wp-content/uploads/2011/09/IR-Discussion -Paper-2011_spreads.pdf.

IIRC. (2013) 'The international *<IR> framework*', *IIRC*. https://www.integratedreporting
.org/wp-content/uploads/2013/12/13-12-08-THE-INTERNATIONAL-IR
-FRAMEWORK-2-1.pdf.

IIRC. (n.d.) '10 years of the IIRC', Available at: https://integratedreporting.org/10-years
/10-years-summary (Accessed: 4 August 2021).

Jackson, G. and Bartosch, J. (2017) 'Understanding corporate responsibility in Japanese
capitalism: Some comparative observations', Available at: https://incas.hypotheses.org
/files/2017/05/INCAS-DP-SERIES_2017_04.pdf.

Jackson, G. and Miyajima, H. (2008) 'Introduction: The diversity and change of corporate
governance in Japan', in Aoki, M., Jackson, G., and Miyajima, H. (eds) *Corporate
governance in Japan: Institutional change and organizational diversity*. Oxford
University Press, Oxford, pp. 1–47.

Kawahara, N. (2017) 'Current trends and challenges in sustainability reporting practices
in Japan - Literature review', *Shokei-gakuso: Journal of Business Studies*, 64(2), pp.
113–142.

Kawamura, M. (2003) 'Japanese companies launch new era of CSR management in 2003',
Social Development Research Group, NLI Research Institute.

Kokubu, K., Nashioka, E., Saio, K. and Imai, S. (2003) 'Two governmental initiatives
on environmental management accounting and corporate practices in Japan', in
Bennett, M., Rikhardsson, P. M., and Schaltegger, S. (eds) *Environmental management
accounting — Purpose and progress*. Kluwer Academic Publishers, Dordrecht, pp.
89–113.

Konishi, N. and Ali, M. M. (2007) 'Risk reporting of Japanese companies and its association
with corporate characteristics', *International Journal of Accounting, Auditing and
Performance Evaluation*, 4(3), pp. 263–285.

KPMG. (2008) *KPMG international survey of corporate responsibility reporting 2008*.
KPMG International, Amstelveen, The Netherlands.

KPMG. (2017) *The KPMG survey of corporate responsibility reporting 2017*. KPMG
International.    https://assets.kpmg/content/dam/kpmg/be/pdf/2017/kpmg-survey-of
-corporate-responsibility-reporting-2017.pdf.

KPMG. (2020) *The KPMG survey of sustainability reporting 2020*. KPMG International.
https://assets.kpmg/content/dam/kpmg/xx/pdf/2020/11/the-time-has-come.pdf.

KPMG AZSA. (2021) *Survey of integrated reporting in Japan 2020*. KPMG AZSA.
https://assets.kpmg/content/dam/kpmg/jp/pdf/2021/jp-integrated-reporting2020
.pdf.

Kuroda, K. and Ishida, Y. (2017) 'CSR in Japan: Toward integration and corporate–CSO
partnership', in Hasan, S. (ed.) *Corporate social responsibility and the three sectors in
Asia*. Springer, New York, pp. 45–71.

Melloni, G., Caglio, A. and Perego, P. (2017) 'Saying more with less? Disclosure
conciseness, completeness and balance in integrated reports', *Journal of Accounting
and Public Policy*, 36(3), pp. 220–238.

METI. (2017) *Guidance for collaborative value creation*. METI, Tokyo.

Meyer, J. W. and Rowan, B. (1977) 'Institutionalized organizations: Formal structure as
myth and ceremony', *American Journal of Sociology*, 83(2), pp. 340–363.

Milne, M. J. and Adler, R. W. (1999) 'Exploring the reliability of social and environmental
disclosures content analysis', *Accounting, Auditing & Accountability Journal*, 12(2),
pp. 237–256.

Pistoni, A., Songini, L. and Bavagnoli, F. (2018) 'Integrated reporting quality: An empirical analysis', *Corporate Social Responsibility and Environmental Management*, 25(4), pp. 489–507.

Rinaldi, L., Unerman, J. and de Villiers, C. (2018) 'Evaluating the integrated reporting journey: Insights, gaps and agendas for future research', *Accounting, Auditing & Accountability Journal*, 31(5), pp. 1294–1318.

Robertson, F. A. and Samy, M. (2015) 'Factors affecting the diffusion of integrated reporting – A UK FTSE 100 perspective', *Sustainability Accounting, Management and Policy Journal*, 6(2), pp. 190–223.

Robertson, F. A. and Samy, M. (2020) 'Rationales for integrated reporting adoption and factors impacting on the extent of adoption: A UK perspective', *Sustainability Accounting, Management and Policy Journal*, 11(2), pp. 351–382.

Setia, N., Abhayawansa, S., Joshi, M. and Huynh, A.V. (2015) 'Integrated reporting in South Africa: Some initial evidence', *Sustainability Accounting, Management and Policy Journal*, 6(3), pp. 397–424.

Solomon, J. and Maroun, W. (2012) *Integrated reporting: The influence of King III on social, ethical and environmental reporting*, ACCA, London.

Solomon, J. F., Solomon, A., Norton, S. D. and Joseph, N. L. (2000) 'A conceptual framework for corporate risk disclosure emerging from the agenda for corporate governance reform', *British Accounting Review*, 32(4), pp. 447–478.

Soriya, S. and Rastogi, P. (2021) 'A systematic literature review on integrated reporting from 2011 to 2020', *Journal of Financial Reporting and Accounting*. https://doi.org/10.1108/JFRA-09-2020-0266.

Stent, W. and Dowler, T. (2015) 'Early assessments of the gap between integrated reporting and current corporate reporting', *Meditari Accountancy Research*, 23(1), pp. 92–117.

Suto, M. and Takehara, H. (2018) *Corporate social responsibility and corporate finance in Japan*. Springer, Singapore.

Tanimoto, K. and Suzuki, K. (2005) 'Corporate social responsibility in Japan: Analyzing the participating companies in global reporting initiative', *Stockholm School of Economics*, Working Paper, 208.

Du Toit, E., Van Zyl, R. and Schütte, G. (2017) 'Integrated reporting by South African companies: A case study', *Meditari Accountancy Research*, 25(4), pp. 654–674.

TSE. (2007) *TSE-listed companies White paper of corporate governance 2007*. TSE, Tokyo.

TSE. (2015) *Japan's corporate governance code*. TSE, Tokyo.

Velte, P. and Stawinoga, M. (2016) 'Integrated reporting: The current state of empirical research, limitations and future research implications', *Journal of Management Control*, 28(3), pp. 275–320.

de Villiers, C., Rinaldi, L. and Unerman, J. (2014) 'Integrated reporting: Insights, gaps and an agenda for future research', *Accounting, Auditing and Accountability Journal*, 27(7), pp. 1042–1067.

Wagiciengo, M. M. and Belal, A. R. (2012) 'Intellectual capital disclosures by South African companies: A longitudinal investigation', *Advances in Accounting*, 28(1), pp. 111–119.

Yeoh, P. (2010) 'Narrative reporting: The UK experience', *International Journal of Law and Management*, 52(3), pp. 211–231.

Zinsou, K. M. C. (2018) 'Integrated or non-integrated reports: French listed companies at a crossroads?', *Sustainability Accounting, Management and Policy Journal*, 9(3), pp. 253–288.

## Appendix 1

List of companies

| Japan | The UK |
|---|---|
| 1. NSK Ltd | 1. Ashtead Group |
| 2. MS&AD Insurance Group | 2. AstraZeneca |
| 3. Itochu Corporation | 3. Associated British Foods |
| 4. Omron Corporation | 4. BT Group |
| 5. Hitachi Chemical Company | 5. Easy Jet |
| 6. Mitsubishi UFJ Financial Group | 6. Marks and Spencer Group |
| 7. KDDI Corporation | 7. Coca-Cola HBC |
| 8. Seven & I Holdings | 8. Diageo |
| 9. Asahi Group | 9. United Utilities Group |
| 10. Chugai Pharmaceutical | 10. Rentokil Initial |
| 11. Bridgestone Corporation | 11. BAE Systems |
| 12. Recruit Holdings | 12. Rightmove |
| 13. Sumitomo Corporation | 13. British Land |
| 14. Denso Corporation | 14. Bunzl |
| 15. Nippon Telegraph and Telephone Corporation | 15. Just Eat |
| 16. Mitsubishi Heavy Industries | 16. Smith & Nephew |
| 17. Dentsu Group | 17. Intertek Group |
| 18. Chubu Electric Power | 18. Severn Trent |
| 19. Panasonic Corporation | 19. Melrose Industries |
| 20. Daiichi Sankyo Company | 20. SAGE Group |

# 10 Disclosure trends in intellectual capital disclosure

## A focus on the Asian markets

*Chiara Demartini, Sara Trucco and*
*Valentina Beretta*

### 10.1 Introduction

Traditional financial reporting has been widely criticised (Marzouk, 2016), especially because of the lack of clarity and the short-term orientation (Hoque et al.,
2016). Thus, a complementary disclosure is needed to provide a broader overview
of how value is created in a company, which goes beyond financial information
(Arvidsson, 2011; Kristandl and Bontis, 2007; Bontis et al., 2007; Diamond and
Verrecchia, 1991; Hoque et al., 2016; Watts and Zimmerman, 1983). For this
purpose, disclosure practices of firms have evolved over the past few years (De
Villiers et al., 2014) to provide stakeholders with relevant information concerning
the environmental and societal impact of business activities (Hoque et al., 2016).

Non-financial information has tended to be captured by the disclosure of
intellectual capital (IC) information. Thus, intellectual capital disclosure (ICD)
is adopted by firms to provide additional information related to the value-creation process (Dumay, 2016). The literature on IC reporting is growing and it
analyses the determinants and consequences of IC reporting and disclosure on
several continents, such as the Americas (Bontis, 2003), Europe (Bozzolan et al.,
2003; Brennan, 2001; Dobre et al., 2015; Ramírez-Córcoles and Manzaneque-
Lizano, 2015; Vergauwen and Alem, 2005), Oceania (Clarke et al., 2011), Asia
(Yi and Davey, 2010; Khan, 2010; Abeysekera and Guthrie, 2005; Petty and
Cuganesan, 2005) and Africa (Wagiciengo and Belal, 2012). Disclosing IC
information could provide a variety of benefits which have been discussed in
previous studies (Brüggen et al., 2009; Healy and Palepu, 2001; Mangena et al.,
2010). However, on the other hand, some scholars warn that IC reporting can
also have negative effects (Murthy and Mouritsen, 2011), as it may lead to a
competitive disadvantage since the firm is "giving away company's secrets"
(Armitage and Marston, 2007).

To overcome the limitations that have been widely associated with traditional
reporting (Matuszyk and Rymkiewicz, 2018), more and more companies are disclosing additional information concerning non-financial information. This could
be performed in different, separate reports (e.g., a sustainability report), or by
including both financial and non-financial information in the same report. For this
purpose, the integrated report (IR) emerged as "one report" that firms can adopt to

DOI: 10.4324/9781003095385-13

jointly disclose financial and non-financial information (Dumay, 2016; Eccles and Saltzman, 2011; Krzus, 2011). Over the years, IR has increasingly been adopted as the reporting model in both developed and developing countries (Eccles et al., 2015; Eccles and Krzus, 2014). In particular, emerging markets include regions of historical and ecological significance. Indeed, they are considered one of the most important sources of growth in the 21st century, and they are becoming increasingly important in the worldwide economy. For this reason, ensuring a sustainable future is of utmost importance, especially in emerging markets, as highlighted by the South Asian Federation of Accountants (SAFA), which gave prominence to IR in its agenda for 2016.

Although IR has been widely studied in Europe (e.g.,Beretta, Demartini and Trucco, 2019a, 2019b; Jensen and Berg, 2012), little is known about its diffusion in Asia (Gunarathne and Senaratne, 2018; Petcharat and Zaman, 2019; Rezaee et al., 2019). More specifically, some inter-country analyses of the disclosure trends have been conducted in the Asian context (Chapple and Moon, 2005; Gill et al., 2008; Ho and Taylor, 2007; Singh et al., 2017), but they are only paving the way to drawing the big picture of the non-financial disclosure trends in Asia (Laskar and Maji, 2018) and they are not focusing on the ICD trends in IR in Asia.

This study is aimed at examining the content and semantic properties of ICD in Asian IRs. Accordingly, this study aims to answer the following research question: How does ICD in IR vary across Asian areas?

The remainder of the chapter is structured as follows: first, in Section 10.2, the authors review the literature, whereas a set of hypotheses is developed in Section 10.3; in Section 10.4, the methodological approach to test the research hypotheses is presented, whereas Section 10.5 is dedicated to the presentation of the results; finally, discussion and conclusions are outlined in Section 10.6.

## 10.2  Literature review

### *10.2.1 Integrated reporting and intellectual capital disclosure*

A lot of progress has been made in the way companies report their financial and non-financial performance over the past few years (De Villiers et al., 2014). Hoque and colleagues put forward that stakeholders are interested in the impacts of business activities on society (Hoque et al., 2016). Moreover, traditional financial reporting has been criticised mainly because of its lack of clarity and short-termism (Hoque et al., 2016).

Nowadays, researchers agree on the fact that traditional financial disclosure is not able to describe the value of intangible resources, and this leads to an increase in information asymmetry (Arvidsson, 2011; Kristandl and Bontis, 2007; Diamond and Verrecchia, 1991; Watts and Zimmerman, 1983). For this reason, scholars have started to study the function of external reporting and its encouraging effects (Botosan, 1997; Bozzolan et al., 2003; Sengupta, 1998).

To reduce the fragilities of traditional reporting (Matuszyk and Rymkiewicz, 2018), IR emerged as a single company main document able to present financial and non-financial performance relationships (Krzus, 2011).

Although IC reporting has been replaced by Global Reporting Initiative (GRI)-type, the IR frameworks explicitly consider the three IC components in its set of capitals (Dumay, 2016). ICD is adopted in different reporting frameworks: financial, GRI-type and IR (De Villiers and Sharma, 2017). As argued in previous studies, IC is adopted to disclose what was previously "secret or unknown" (Dumay, 2016, p. 169) and, thus, it fosters value-creating actions inside the organisation (Dumay, 2016), taking into consideration the different components of intellectual capital (human, structural and relational) and other forms of capital (natural, financial and manufactured) (IIRC, 2013).

Given the increased relevance of non-financial disclosure, researchers have started investigating the content of these reports (Beattie et al., 2004; Li, 2010). This is particularly important since stakeholders could take decisions based on the information that is provided in the non-financial reports (Arena et al., 2015; Druz et al., 2017; Hummel et al., 2019; IIRC, 2013). This implies that the importance of the reliability and verifiability of the information contained herein is growing (Hussainey and Walker, 2009).

However, in addition to the quantity of information disclosed, the quality of the disclosure can also have an impact on stakeholders' decisions (Arena et al., 2015; Druz et al., 2017; Hummel et al., 2019; Li, 2010; Merkley, 2014). Therefore, understanding the theoretical approaches that are adopted by managers when disclosing non-financial information is of utmost importance (Beretta et al., 2019b, 2020).

### 10.2.2 Intellectual capital disclosure trends in Asian areas

The relevance of IR has grown worldwide over time, despite it being considered to be a fairly new phenomenon (Elkington and Rowlands, 1999). This topic has gained momentum also in South Asia, where the South Asian Federation of Accountants (SAFA) gave prominence to IR in its agenda for 2016.

According to the statistics of the International Monetary Fund, the share of world GDP based on purchasing-power-parity is growing for emerging economies, moving from 37% in 1980 to 59% in 2018. Thus, emerging markets, also called emerging economies, are considered to be one of the most important sources of growth in the 21st century. In recent years, emerging markets have become more important in the worldwide economy, where they represent more than 74% of worldwide growth.

## 10.3 Hypothesis development

### 10.3.1 ICD components

In accordance with the legitimacy theory, IC "can promote a multiplier effect and more competitive advantages for organizations" (Gallardo-Vázquez et al., 2019, p. 2). Indeed, according to this theory, a company is encouraged to voluntarily disclose non-financial information if it perceives that is relevant for the community in which it operates (Guthrie et al., 2004).

Previous studies had reported that the reporting of IC varies by IC component: human capital (HC), structural capital (SC) and relational capital (RC; Abeysekera, 2008; Abeysekera and Guthrie, 2005; Steenkamp, 2018). Results from studies from Asian areas are mixed. Previous research found that external – relational – capital is the best-represented IC component in Sri Lanka (Abeysekera, 2008; Abeysekera and Guthrie, 2005), Malaysia (Ahmed Haji and Mohd Ghazali, 2012) and India (Singh and Kansal, 2011). On the other hand, internal – structural – capital has the highest level of ICD in Chinese firms (Yi and Davey, 2010). In addition, HC is represented at a higher level than other IC components in Bangladesh (Khan and Ali, 2010; Nurunnabi and Hossain, 2011). According to these results, different Asian countries assign different levels of importance to different ICD components. Previous studies have been conducted separately in different Asian countries in order to be able to capture differences in the contexts of analysis. However, there has been a lack of studies analysing the trends across all Asian IRs. Thus, the following hypothesis will be tested.

***H1: ICD components are not equally disclosed in Asian IRs.***

### 10.3.2 Geographic region

Legitimacy theory implies that a social contract exists between a company and the society in which it operates, in which expectations and desired actions are expressed (Deegan, 2014). Thus, "This requires the company to be responsive to the environment in which it operates" (Guthrie et al., 2004, p. 284). Previous studies found differences in ICD across Asian countries. In particular, a low ICD level has been detected in Bangladesh (Nurunnabi and Hossain, 2011), a lower ICD has been observed in Singapore than in Sri Lanka (Abeysekera, 2008) and poorer ICD quality in China compared with India (Wang, Sharma and Davey, 2016).

Previous studies focusing on Asia found important differences in the non-financial information disclosure trends between countries (Laskar and Maji, 2018). Differences in disclosure trends among Asian countries have been detected primarily as a result of the institutional differences among countries (Campbell, 2007; Hahn and Kühnen, 2013; Tran and Beddewela, 2020). Hence, this study aims at testing the following hypothesis.

***H2: ICD features across Asian countries are not similar.***

### 10.3.3 Environmentally sensitive industry

As argued in previous studies, some companies are encouraged to disclose more non-financial information because of the nature of their operations (Guthrie et al., 2004). Indeed, following the legitimacy theory, companies in environmentally sensitive industries report this type of information in order to communicate their concerns and attention to specific environmental and societal aspects (Berrone et al., 2017; Lindblom, 1994).

Firms in environmentally sensitive industries are supposed to provide deeper and more positive ICD to redeem themselves from operating in stigmatised industries (Cho et al., 2010). However, more recent studies found no association between ICD tone and operating in an environmentally sensitive industry (Beretta et al., 2019b; Melloni, 2015), suggesting that there are no explicit incentives to vary the tone of ICD among different industries. The economic development and industrialisation in Asia have produced large effects on the environment and the sector of environmentally sensitive industries has grown (Mohanty and Chaturvedi, 2006; Shafii et al., 2006). To have a better understanding of the trends of ICD in both environmentally sensitive and other industries, the following hypothesis will be tested.

**H3: *ICD features are similar in both environmentally sensitive and other industries.***

## 10.4 Methodology

To test the research hypotheses, all the IRs of the Asian listed companies presented in the IIRC's integrated reporting emerging practice example database were downloaded for the period between 2014 and 2018, since, to the best of our knowledge, no studies have been conducted over this time-period in the Asian setting. All 112 IRs available were screened. This resulted in 16 reports being excluded for referring to unlisted firms, leaving a total of 96 IRs, related to 21 Asian listed firms, to constitute the study sample. The sample is composed of all Asian listed firms since previous studies focused the analysis on different individual countries in Asia, but little is known on the general trends of firms across Asia.

Data analysis proceeded in two stages. In the first stage, content analysis has been used to assess the content and the semantic properties of ICDs. Consistent with previous studies, the content analysis has been performed to capture information related to both the quantity and the quality of the disclosure (e.g., Beretta et al., 2019b; Melloni, Caglio and Perego, 2017). Table 10.1 provides information related to the description of the quantity and quality measures coded.

In the second stage, a statistical analysis has been performed to test the research hypotheses. More specifically, descriptive statistics were carried out for all the collected variables; to determine whether the means of any two populations are significantly different, the *t* test has been employed. This method is considered appropriate on the basis of its reliability in testing differences among research variables (Ruxton, 2006). To perform the *t* test, the observations have been grouped into different categories according to their geographic area and industry. Details about the categorisation are provided in Table 10.2.

## 10.5 Results

### *10.5.1 Sample description*

Table 10.3 provides information related to the sample composition. The most highly represented countries are Hong Kong, South Korea and India, while the

*Table 10.1* Definitions of quantity and quality parameters

| | | | *Number of text units* |
|---|---|---|---|
| **Quantity parameters** | | | |
| Type of capital (Abhayawansa and Guthrie, 2016) | Human capital | A text unit referring to the know-how, education, vocational qualification, work-related knowledge and competencies and entrepreneurial spirit of the firm's employees. | 37 |
| | Structural capital | A text unit referring to the intangible infrastructure and the intellectual property of the firm. | 146 |
| | Relational capital | A text unit referring to the value of the relationships with external stakeholders and of the firm's reputation. | 121 |
| **Quality parameters** | | | |
| Type of evidence (Beattie et al., 2004) | Discursive | A text unit disclosed in narrative/written form with a non-numerical meaning in relation to an IC subcategory. | 220 |
| | Numerical | A text unit disclosed in numerical form in relation to an IC subcategory. | 84 |
| ICD tone (Loughran and McDonald, 2011) | Positive | A text unit in an IC subcategory, including good news for the company. | 295 |
| | Negative | A text unit in an IC subcategory, including bad news for the company. | 189 |
| Time orientation (Abed, Al-Najjar, & Roberts, 2016; Aromí, 2018; Hussainey, 2004; Loughran & McDonald, 2011; Matsumoto, Pronk, & Roelofsen, 2011) | Forward-looking | A text unit in an IC subcategory referring to the firm's future prospects, strategy and expectations. | 232 |
| | Backward-looking | A text unit in an IC subcategory referring to the past or present. | 94 |

*Table 10.2* Definitions of group variables

| | Geographic region |
|---|---|
| South Asia | Dummy variable equal to 1 if country equals Sri Lanka or India, otherwise 0. |
| Western Asia | Dummy variable equal to 1 if country equals United Arab Emirates or Qatar, otherwise 0. |
| Far East | Dummy variable equal to 1 if country equals China, Hong Kong or South Korea, otherwise 0. |
| South East Asia | Dummy variable equal to 1 if country equals Malaysia, the Philippines, Singapore or Thailand, otherwise 0. |
| | Industry |
| ENV_SENS_IND | Dummy variable equal to 1 if the industry is a member of oil and gas, basic materials, industrials or utilities sector, otherwise 0. |

*Table 10.3* Number of integrated reports by year, country and industry

| Year | | Country | | Industry | |
|---|---|---|---|---|---|
| *Variable* | *No. of IRs* | *Variable* | *No. of IRs* | *Variable* | *No. of IRs* |
| 2014 | 16 | Hong Kong | 20 | Basic materials | 4 |
| 2015 | 17 | India | 19 | Consumer services | 5 |
| 2016 | 21 | Malaysia | 6 | Financial services | 21 |
| 2017 | 21 | The Philippines | 3 | Industrials | 24 |
| 2018 | 21 | Qatar | 5 | Oil and gas | 10 |
| | | Singapore | 9 | Real estate | 9 |
| | | South Korea | 19 | Telecommunications | 13 |
| | | Sri Lanka | 5 | Utilities | 10 |
| | | Thailand | 5 | | |
| | | United Arab Emirates | 5 | | |
| Total | 96 | Total | 96 | Total | 96 |

least represented country is the Philippines. Concerning the industry, 24 IRs are related to companies in the industrial sector, while only 4 IRs are related to companies in the basic material sector.

Empirical findings from this study show that awareness of IR in Asian emerging companies increased especially between 2016 and 2018, with the highest number of IRs disclosed in 2018. Furthermore, findings demonstrate that Hong Kong is the country where companies release most IRs and that the financial services sector provides more IRs than the other sectors examined. Results also show that ICD components are not equally disclosed among Asian IRs and features of disclosure across Asian countries are not the same.

### 10.5.2 Statistical analysis

Results of the statistical analysis are provided in this subsection.

Results presented in Table 10.4 show that, on average, there are 305 text units dedicated to IC, which represents 8% of the entire IRs. Half of them are, on average, dedicated to the disclosure of information related to SC, 37% are dedicated to the disclosure of RC whereas only 13% of the total number of IC text units are dedicated to the disclosure of HC information. Results of the Analysis of Variance test confirm a statistically significant difference in the disclosure of the three different IC components. Thus, the hypothesis "H1: ICD components are not equally disclosed in Asian IRs" is supported.

Results presented in Table 10.5 show that, on average, companies in the Far East – China, Hong Kong or South Korea compared to other geographic regions dedicate more space to IR disclosure (10% of the IR), and, on average, SC is the IC component most frequently disclosed.

*Table 10.4* ICD components analysis

| Variable | Mean |
|---|---|
| IC | 305 |
| IC_Coverage | 8% |
| RC % | 50% |
| SC % | 13% |
| HC % | 37% |
| *p*-value of the *t* test | |
| HC vs SC | <0.001 |
| RC vs SC | 0.061 |
| RC vs HC | <0.001 |

In terms of IC disclosure quantity, therefore, there is a significantly lower IC disclosure in South Asia – Sri Lanka or India than in either the Far East or South East Asia. On the other hand, companies in South Asia disclose a significantly higher amount of information related to RC in their IRs than companies in the Far East.

In terms of the quality of IC disclosure, Table 10.5 shows that almost all of IC disclosure is forward-looking, positive and discursive. In particular, companies disclosing IRs in South Asia adopt a more time-oriented approach (forward- or backward-looking) compared with companies in South East Asia. Companies in the Far East adopt a more positive tone in their IRs than those in South Asia and

*Table 10.5* ICD components analysis by region

| Variable | Region | | | | 1 vs 3 | 1 vs 4 | 3 vs 4 | 1 vs 2 | 2 vs 4 |
|---|---|---|---|---|---|---|---|---|---|
| | South Asia | Western Asia | Far East | South East Asia | | | | | |
| | -1 | -2 | -3 | (4) | | | | | |
| | | | | Quantity | | | | | |
| IC_Coverage | 6% | 7% | 10% | 8% | 0.0027 | 0.049 | | | |
| SC % | 46% | 49% | 52% | 53% | 0.037 | 0.04 | | | |
| HC % | 13% | 13% | 12% | 13% | | | | | |
| RC % | 41% | 38% | 36% | 34% | 0.0832 | | | | |
| | | | | Quality | | | | | |
| Forward | 84% | 78% | 78% | 70% | | 0.0561 | | | |
| Backward | 34% | 33% | 31% | 29% | | 0.0448 | | | |
| Positive | 83% | 89% | 113% | 89% | 0.0219 | | 0.0651 | | |
| Negative | 67% | 71% | 68% | 54% | | 0.0139 | 0.0273 | | 0.015 |
| Numerical | 28% | 20% | 28% | 29% | | | | 0.0265 | |
| Discursive | 72% | 80% | 72% | 71% | | | | 0.0265 | |

South Asia: Dummy variable equal to 1 if country equals Sri Lanka or India, otherwise 0.
Western Asia: Dummy variable equal to 1 if country equals United Arab Emirates or Qatar, otherwise 0.
Far East: Dummy variable equal to 1 if country equals China, Hong Kong or South Korea, otherwise 0.
South East Asia: Dummy variable equal to 1 if country equals Malaysia, the Philippines, Singapore or Thailand, otherwise 0.

*Table 10.6* ICD components analysis by industry

| Variable | ENV_SENS_IND | | p-value of the t test |
|---|---|---|---|
| | 1 | 0 | |
| Quantity | | | |
| IC_Coverage | 8% | 8% | |
| SC % | 54% | 47% | 0.022 |
| HC % | 13% | 12% | |
| RC % | 33% | 41% | 0.0090 |
| Quality | | | |
| Forward | 84% | 71% | 0.0140 |
| Backward | 34% | 29% | 0.0211 |
| Positive | 106% | 89% | 0.0558 |
| Negative | 72% | 58% | 0.0035 |
| Numerical | 26% | 29% | |
| Discursive | 74% | 71% | |

South East Asia. A less negative approach is adopted by companies in South East Asia than the rest of the firms. Finally, firms issuing IRs in South Asia adopt a more numerical approach than companies in Western Asia, which, in turn, adopt a more discursive approach in their IRs.

Thus, the hypothesis "H2: ICD features across Asian areas are not similar" is supported.

Results presented in Table 10.6 show that there are statistically significant differences in the disclosure of SC and RC between environmentally sensitive and environmentally non-sensitive industries, with the former disclosing more information related to SC, and the latter disclosing more information related to RC.

In terms of the quality of the disclosure, firms in environmentally sensitive industries tend to use more time-oriented and less neutral (in terms of tone) disclosures compared with companies in environmentally non-sensitive industries.

Thus, the hypothesis "H3: ICD features are similar in both environmentally sensitive and other industries" is only partially supported by the data. Indeed, ICD features are similar in both environmentally sensitive and other industries for the amount of ICD. However, qualitative ICD features are not similar in environmentally sensitive and environmentally non-sensitive industries.

Overall, the empirical study on the characteristics of ICD in IRs in the Asian context (partially) supported the hypotheses theoretically developed above (Table 10.7). More specifically, the first two hypotheses (H1: ICD components are not equally disclosed in Asian IRs, and H2: ICD features across Asian areas are not similar) are confirmed by the results of this study. With respect to the third hypothesis, investigating the role of environmentally sensitive industries in the disclosure of IC by Asian companies adopting the IR framework, empirical findings support evidence of the different reporting strategies concerning the qualitative features of ICD, but not of the amount of IC information disclosed.

*Table 10.7* Summary of results

| Research Hypothesis | Summary Results |
| --- | --- |
| H1: ICD components are not equally disclosed in Asian IRs. | Supported. |
| H2: ICD features across Asian areas are not similar. | Supported. |
| H3: ICD features are similar in both environmentally sensitive and non-sensitive industries. | Partially supported.<br>ICD features are similar in both environmentally sensitive and non-sensitive industries for IC in general with respect to quantity. However, ICD features are not similar in both environmentally sensitive and non-sensitive industries with respect to quality. |

## 10.6 Discussion and conclusion

The aim of this study, which is based on the legitimacy theory, is to analyse the content and semantic properties of ICD in Asian IRs, thereby answering the following research question – how does ICD in IR vary across Asian areas? Previous studies on this topic focused the analysis on different individual Asian countries to be able to capture differences in the contexts of analysis, so this chapter attempts to study the trends in all Asian countries and provides a sub-analysis in terms of South Asia, Western Asia, the Far East and South East Asia.

To answer the aforementioned research question, this study examines ICD content and semantic properties in IRs in Asia. The study is based on secondary data collected from the IRs available on the IIRC's integrated reporting emerging practice example database of listed Asian companies for the period 2014–2018.

Results are in line with those from earlier studies which demonstrate that components of ICD are not equally disclosed in Asian IRs (Abeysekera and Guthrie, 2005; Steenkamp, 2018); indeed, in line with prior literature, this study found that SC is the most represented component in the emerging markets (more specifically, in Asia) compared with other IC components (Abeysekera, 2006, 2008; Yi and Davey, 2010). Furthermore, also in line with earlier literature, RC is well represented in Asian IRs, especially in Sri Lanka, Malaysia and India (Ahmed Haji and Mohd Ghazali, 2012; Singh and Kansal, 2011). In contrast with some of the earlier studies (Khan and Ali, 2010; Nurunnabi and Hossain, 2011), however, the results of the current study found that HC is the least frequently represented IC component in Asian firms. However, these studies are either focused on IC disclosed in traditional financial reporting (Khan and Ali, 2010; Nurunnabi and Hossain, 2011), or on a specific and highly regulated sector, i.e., banking (Khan and Ali, 2010).

With respect to the geographic region, this study confirms findings from earlier studies of significant differences in the non-financial information disclosure (such as ICD) across Asian countries (Laskar and Maji, 2018); indeed, ICD components in South Asia firms are different from ICD components in the Far East and South East Asia (Abeysekera, 2008). ICD components in Western Asia firms are similar to the mean of the ICD components in the sample in the current study. This study highlights in particular that Western Asia firms show different behaviour than South East Asia firms in terms of the quality of ICD (Wang, Hsieh and Sarkis, 2018). Consistent with the findings from earlier studies, this chapter confirms that differences across disclosure trends among Asian countries may be found as a result of the institutional differences among countries (Campbell, 2007; Hahn and Kühnen, 2013; Tran and Beddewela, 2020).

Finally, this chapter confirms some differences among industries (Berrone et al., 2017; Lindblom, 1994), since, in line with previous studies, some firms are more encouraged to disclose non-financial information because of the nature of their business and activities (Guthrie et al., 2004). Although ICD features are similar in both environmentally sensitive and environmentally non-sensitive industries for the amount of ICD, this study found that SC is higher in environmentally sensitive industries than other industries (Berrone et al., 2017; Lindblom, 1994), whereas RC is higher in environmentally non-sensitive industries than environmentally sensitive industries. ICD quality differed between environmentally sensitive and non-sensitive industries, except for numerical and discursive features (Cho et al., 2010). In line with the previous studies, we argue that the economic development in Asia has had large impacts on the environment and on environmentally sensitive industries (Mohanty and Chaturvedi, 2006; Shafii et al., 2006).

### 10.6.1 Contributions

This chapter contributes to the prior literature in several ways. First, this chapter contributes to the literature on the legitimacy theory, since it contributes to that part of studies which demonstrated that a firm is encouraged to voluntarily disclose non-financial information in terms of ICD if it perceives that this kind of information is pivotal for the community in which it operates (Guthrie et al., 2004). Second, this chapter contributes to the current literature on the diffusion of non-financial information, since scholars are aware that the traditional financial disclosure is not able to describe the value of intangible resources (Arvidsson, 2011; Kristandl and Bontis, 2007; Diamond and Verrecchia, 1991; Watts and Zimmerman, 1983) and contributes to the literature on ICDs by introducing new evidence on firms' motivations for non-financial disclosures in integrated reports in emerging markets (Nurunnabi and Hossain, 2011). In addition, this current study advances some of the understanding related to the quantity and the quality of the information provided in the IR of companies in Asian countries (Petcharat and Zaman, 2019; Rezaee et al., 2019), by highlighting the general trend of all Asian ICDs and providing some evidence on the differences in ICDs among South Asia, Western Asia, the Far East and South East Asia. Third, it contributes to voluntary disclosure theory (Beattie et al., 2004; Verrecchia, 2001) by providing further evidence related to the voluntary disclosure strategies that companies may adopt in practice (Merkl-Davies and Brennan, 2007). Fourth, the study extends the literature on integrated thinking and integrated report preparation (Flower, 2015; IIRC, 2013) and its beneficial use in practice in the Asian market (an emerging market).

Finally, the study extends the literature on IC disclosure in IR in emerging markets (Dumay, 2016). From a practical standpoint, practitioners and firms can benefit from this study by being aware of the diffusion of the ICD in the Asian setting. Furthermore, the findings of this study are also relevant for policymakers, who can decide to introduce new rules, regulations and frameworks to develop best practices guidelines for ICD and IR, to facilitate the disclosure of non-financial information among Asian firms and to encourage compliance with the rules and guidelines in improving the level of quality of the non-financial information.

### *10.6.2 Future research directions*

In line with previous research, this study is not without its limitations that open up avenues for future research. First, future studies could be conducted to analyse the relationship between the tone of IR to the (non-)financial performance of firms, taking into consideration its trends in the different sections of non-financial disclosures. Second, given the heterogeneity of the non-financial information disclosed, additional studies could be conducted for the development of customised measures to capture IC properties. Third, further research could analyse the impact of the introduction of the IIRC framework on the tone of ICDs as well as on the relationship between tone and firms' performance. Fourth, comparing Asian with European firms could provide insightful results to identify similarities, differences and best practices in different social, economic and reporting contexts.

## 10.7 References

Abed, S., Al-Najjar, B. and Roberts, C. (2016), "Measuring annual report narratives disclosure: Empirical evidence from forward-looking information in the UK prior the financial crisis", *Managerial Auditing Journal*, Vol. 31, No. 4/5, pp. 338–361.

Abeysekera, I. (2006), "The project of intellectual capital disclosure: Researching the research", *Journal of Intellectual Capital*, Vol. 7, No. 1, pp. 61–77.

Abeysekera, I. (2008), "Intellectual capital disclosure trends: Singapore and Sri Lanka", *Journal of Intellectual Capital*, Vol. 9, No. 4, pp. 723–737.

Abeysekera, I. and Guthrie, J. (2005), "An empirical investigation of annual reporting trends of intellectual capital in Sri Lanka", *Critical Perspectives on Accounting*, Vol. 16, No. 3, pp. 151–163.

Abhayawansa, S. and Guthrie, J. (2016), "Does intellectual capital disclosure in analysts' reports vary by firm characteristics?", *Advances in Accounting*, Vol. 35, pp. 26–38.

Ahmed Haji, A. and Mohd Ghazali, N.A. (2012), "Intellectual capital disclosure trends: Some Malaysian evidence", *Journal of Intellectual Capital*, Vol. 13, No. 3, pp. 377–397.

Arena, C., Bozzolan, S. and Michelon, G. (2015), "Environmental reporting: Transparency to stakeholders or stakeholder manipulation? An analysis of disclosure tone and the role of the board of directors", *Corporate Social Responsibility and Environmental Management*, Vol. 22, No. 6, pp. 346–361.

Armitage, S. and Marston, C. (2007), *Corporate disclosure and the cost of capital: The views of finance directors*, ICAEW Centre for Business Performance, London.

Aromí, J.D. (2018), "GDP growth forecasts and information flows: Is there evidence of overreactions?", *International Finance*, Vol. 21, No. 2, pp. 122–139.

Arvidsson, S. (2011), "Disclosure of non-financial information in the annual report: A management-team perspective", *Journal of Intellectual Capital*, Vol. 12, No. 2, pp. 277–300. https://doi.org/10.1108/14691931111123421.

Beattie, V., McInnes, B. and Fearnley, S. (2004), "A methodology for analysing and evaluating narratives in annual reports: A comprehensive descriptive profile and metrics for disclosure quality attributes, accounting forum", *Accounting Forum*, Vol. 28, pp. 205–236.

Beretta, V., Demartini, C. and Trucco, S. (2019a), "State of the art of IR disclosure in Europe. A research agenda", *Economia Aziendale Online*, Vol. 10, No. 2, pp. 203–217.

Beretta, V., Demartini, M.C. and Trucco, S. (2019b), "Does environmental, social and governance performance influence intellectual capital disclosure tone in integrated reporting?", *Journal of Intellectual Capital*, Vol. 20, No. 1. Available at: https://doi.org /10.1108/JIC-02-2018-0049.

Beretta, V., Demartini, M.C. and Trucco, S. (2020), "Tone at top in integrated reporting: The role of non-financial performance", *Non-Financial Disclosure and Integrated Reporting: Practices and Critical Issues*, Vol. 34, pp. 147–174.

Berrone, P., Fosfuri, A. and Gelabert, L. (2017), "Does greenwashing pay off? Understanding the relationship between environmental actions and environmental legitimacy", *Journal of Business Ethics*, Vol. 144, No. 2, pp. 363–379.

Bontis, N. (2003), "Intellectual capital disclosure in Canadian corporations", *Journal of Human Resource Costing & Accounting*, Vol. 7, No. 1/2, pp. 9–20.

Bontis, N., Bart, C., Wakefield, P. and Kristandl, G. (2007), "Constructing a definition for intangibles using the resource based view of the firm", *Management Decision*, Vol. 45, No. 9, pp. 1510–1524.

Botosan, C.A. (1997), "Disclosure level and the cost of equity capital", *Accounting Review, JSTOR*, Vol. 72, No. 3, pp. 323–349.

Bozzolan, S., Favotto, F. and Ricceri, F. (2003), "Italian annual intellectual capital disclosure: An empirical analysis", *Journal of Intellectual Capital*, Vol. 4, No. 4, pp. 543–558.

Brennan, N. (2001), "Reporting intellectual capital in annual reports: Evidence from Ireland", *Accounting, Auditing and Accountability Journal*, Vol. 14, No. 4, pp. 423–436.

Brüggen, A., Vergauwen, P. and Dao, M. (2009), "Determinants of intellectual capital disclosure: Evidence from Australia", *Management Decision*, Vol. 47, No. 2, pp. 233–245.

Campbell, J.L. (2007), "Why would corporations behave in socially responsible ways? An institutional theory of corporate social responsibility", *Academy of Management Review*, Vol. 32, No. 3, pp. 946–967.

Chapple, W. and Moon, J. (2005), "Corporate social responsibility (CSR) in Asia: A seven-country study of CSR web site reporting", *Business & Society*, Vol. 44, No. 4, pp. 415–441.

Cho, C.H., Roberts, R.W. and Patten, D.M. (2010), "The language of US corporate environmental disclosure", *Accounting, Organizations and Society*, Vol. 35, No. 4, pp. 431–443.

Clarke, M., Seng, D. and Whiting, R.H. (2011), "Intellectual capital and firm performance in Australia", *Journal of Intellectual Capital*, Vol. 12, No. 4, pp. 505–530. https://doi .org/10.1108/14691931111181706.

Deegan, C. (2014), *Financial accounting theory*. Australia: McGraw-Hill Education.

Diamond, D.W. and Verrecchia, R.E. (1991), "Disclosure, liquidity, and the cost of capital", *The Journal of Finance*, Vol. 46, No. 4, pp. 1325–1359.

Dobre, E., Stanila, G.O. and Brad, L. (2015), "The influence of environmental and social performance on financial performance: Evidence from Romania's listed entities", *Sustainability, Multidisciplinary Digital Publishing Institute*, Vol. 7, No. 3, pp. 2513–2553.

Druz, M., Petzev, I., Wagner, A.F. and Zeckhauser, R.J. (2017), *When managers change their tone, analysts and investors change their tune*, SSRN Scholarly Paper No. ID 2559157, Social Science Research Network, Rochester, NY.

Dumay, J. (2016), "A critical reflection on the future of intellectual capital: From reporting to disclosure", *Journal of Intellectual Capital*, Vol. 17, No. 1, pp. 168–184. https://doi.org/10.1108/JIC-08-2015-0072.

Eccles, R.G. and Krzus, M.P. (2014), *The integrated reporting movement: Meaning, momentum*, John Wiley & Sons, Hoboken, NJ.

Eccles, R.G., Krzus, M.P. and Ribot, S. (2015), "Meaning and momentum in the integrated reporting movement", *Journal of Applied Corporate Finance*, Vol. 27, No. 2, pp. 8–17.

Eccles, R.G. and Saltzman, D. (2011), "Achieving sustainability through integrated reporting", *Stanford Social Innovation Review*, Vol. 9, No. 3, pp. 56–61.

Elkington, J. and Rowlands, I.H. (1999), "Cannibals with forks: The triple bottom line of 21st century business", *Alternatives Journal*, Vol. 25, No. 4, p. 42.

Flower, J. (2015), "The international integrated reporting council: A story of failure", *Critical Perspectives on Accounting*, Vol. 27, pp. 1–17.

Gallardo-Vázquez, D., Valdez-Juárez, L.E. and Lizcano-Álvarez, J.L. (2019), "Corporate social responsibility and intellectual capital: Sources of competitiveness and legitimacy in organizations' management practices", *Sustainability*, Vol. 11, No. 20. Available at: https://doi.org/10.3390/su11205843.

Gill, D.L., Dickinson, S.J. and Scharl, A. (2008), "Communicating sustainability: A web content analysis of North American, Asian and European firms", *Journal of Communication Management*, Vol. 12, No. 3, pp. 243–262. https://doi.org/10.1108/13632540810899425.

Gunarathne, A.D.N. and Senaratne, S. (2018), "Country readiness in adopting integrated reporting: A diamond theory approach from an asian pacific economy. In: Lee, K.H. and Schaltegger, S. (eds), *Accounting for sustainability: Asia Pacific perspectives. Eco-efficiency in industry and science*, Vol. 33. Springer, Cham. https://doi.org/10.1007/978-3-319-70899-7_3.

Guthrie, J., Petty, R., Yongvanich, K. and Ricceri, F. (2004), "Using content analysis as a research method to inquire into intellectual capital reporting", *Journal of Intellectual Capital*, Vol. 5, No. 2, pp. 282–293. https://doi.org/10.1108/14691930410533704.

Hahn, R. and Kühnen, M. (2013), "Determinants of sustainability reporting: A review of results, trends, theory, and opportunities in an expanding field of research", *Journal of Cleaner Production*, Vol. 59, pp. 5–21.

Healy, P.M. and Palepu, K.G. (2001), "Information asymmetry, corporate disclosure, and the capital markets: A review of the empirical disclosure literature", *Journal of Accounting and Economics*, Vol. 31, No. 1, pp. 405–440.

Ho, L.-C.J. and Taylor, M.E. (2007), "An empirical analysis of triple bottom-line reporting and its determinants: Evidence from the United States and Japan", *Journal of International Financial Management & Accounting*, Vol. 18, No. 2, pp. 123–150.

Hoque, I., Chatterjee, A., Bhattacharya, S., Biswas, R., Auddy, S. and Mondal, K. (2016), "A review on different types of the non steroidal anti-inflammatory drugs (NSAIDs)", *International Journal of Advanced Multidisciplinary Research*, Vol. 3, No. 3, pp. 41–51.

Hummel, K., Mittelbach-Hörmanseder, S., Cho, C.H., Matten, D., Mittelbach-Hoermanseder, S., Cho, C.H. and Matten, D. (2019), "Explicit corporate social responsibility disclosure: A textual analysis", SSRN, SSRN Scholarly Paper, University of Zurich, Rochester, NY, No. 3090976.

Hussainey, K. and Walker, M. (2009), "The effects of voluntary disclosure and dividend propensity on prices leading earnings", *Accounting and Business Research*, Vol. 39, No. 1, pp. 37–55.

Hussainey, K.S.M. (2004), *Study of the ability of (partially) automated disclosure scores to explain the information content of annual report narratives for future earnings*, University of Manchester, Manchester.

IIRC. (2013), "*International <IR> Framework*".

Jensen, J.C. and Berg, N. (2012), "Determinants of traditional sustainability reporting versus integrated reporting: An institutionalist approach", *Business Strategy and the Environment*, Vol. 21, No. 5, pp. 299–316.

Khan, M. and Ali, M. (2010), "An empirical investigation and users' perceptions on intellectual capital reporting in banks: Evidence from Bangladesh", *Journal of Human Resource Costing & Accounting*, Vol. 14, No. 1, pp. 48–69.

Khan, R. (2010), "Human capital disclosure practices of top Bangladeshi companies", *Journal of Human Resource Costing & Accounting*, Vol. 14, pp. 329–349.

Kristandl, G. and Bontis, N. (2007), "The impact of voluntary disclosure on cost of equity capital estimates in a temporal setting", *Journal of Intellectual Capital*, Vol. 8, No. 4, pp. 577–594. https://doi.org/10.1108/14691930710830765.

Krzus, M.P. (2011), "Integrated reporting: If not now, when", *Zeitschrift Für Internationale Rechnungslegung*, Vol. 6, No. 6, pp. 271–276.

Laskar, N. and Maji, S.G. (2018), "Disclosure of corporate sustainability performance and firm performance in Asia", *Asian Review of Accounting*, Vol. 26, No. 4, pp. 414–443. https://doi.org/10.1108/ARA-02-2017-0029.

Li, F. (2010), "The information content of forward-looking statements in corporate filings—A naïve bayesian machine learning approach", *Journal of Accounting Research*, Vol. 48, No. 5, pp. 1049–1102.

Lindblom, C.K. (1994), "The implications of organizational legitimacy for corporate social performance and disclosure", Critical Perspectives on Accounting Conference, New York, 1994.

Loughran, T. and McDonald, B. (2011), "When is a liability not a liability? Textual analysis, dictionaries, and 10-Ks", *The Journal of Finance*, Vol. 66, No. 1, pp. 35–65.

Mangena, M., Pike, R. and Li, J. (2010), *Intellectual capital disclosure practices and effects on the cost of equity capital: UK evidence*, Institute of Chartered Accountants of Scotland, Edinburgh.

Marzouk, M. (2016), "Risk reporting during a crisis: Evidence from the Egyptian capital market", *Journal of Applied Accounting Research*, Vol. 17, No. 4, pp. 378–396. https://doi.org/10.1108/JAAR-02-2015-0012.

Matsumoto, D., Pronk, M. and Roelofsen, E. (2011), "What makes conference calls useful? The information content of managers' presentations and analysts' discussion sessions", *The Accounting Review*, Vol. 86, No. 4, pp. 1383–1414.

Matuszyk, I. and Rymkiewicz, B. (2018), "Integrated reporting as a tool for communicating with stakeholders–Advantages and disadvantages", *E3S Web of Conferences*, Vol. 35, p. 6004. EDP Sciences.

Melloni, G. (2015), "Intellectual capital disclosure in integrated reporting: An impression management analysis", *Journal of Intellectual Capital*, Vol. 16, No. 3, pp. 661–680.

Melloni, G., Caglio, A. and Perego, P. (2017), "Saying more with less? Disclosure conciseness, completeness and balance in integrated reports", *Journal of Accounting and Public Policy*, Vol. 36, No. 3, pp. 220–238.

Merkl-Davies, D.M. and Brennan, N.N. (2007), "Discretionary disclosure strategies in corporate narratives: Incremental information or impression management?", *Journal of Accounting Literature*, Vol. 26, pp. 116–196.

Merkley, K.J. (2014), "Narrative disclosure and earnings performance: Evidence from R&D disclosures", *Accounting Review*, Vol. 89, No. 2, pp. 725–757.

Mohanty, S.K. and Chaturvedi, S. (2006), "Impact of SAFTA on trade in environmentally sensitive goods in South Asia: Emerging challenges and policy options", *Asia-Pacific Trade and Investment Review*, Vol. 2, No. 2, pp. 3–25.

Murthy, V. and Mouritsen, J. (2011), "The performance of intellectual capital: Mobilising relationships between intellectual and financial capital in a bank", *Accounting, Auditing & Accountability Journal*, Vol. 24, No. 5, pp. 622–646.

Nurunnabi, M., Hossain, M. and Hossain (2011), "Intellectual capital reporting in a South Asian country: Evidence from Bangladesh", *Journal of Human Resource Costing & Accounting*, Vol. 15, No. 3, pp. 196–233. https://doi.org/10.1108/14013381111178587.

Petcharat, N. and Zaman, M. (2019), "Sustainability reporting and integrated reporting perspectives of Thai-listed companies", *Journal of Financial Reporting and Accounting*, Vol. 17, No. 4, pp. 671–694. https://doi.org/10.1108/JFRA-09-2018-0073.

Petty, R. and Cuganesan, S. (2005), "Voluntary disclosure of intellectual capital by Hong Kong companies: Examining size, industry and growth effects over time", *Australian Accounting Review*, Vol. 15, No. 36, pp. 40–50.

Ramírez-Córcoles, Y. and Manzaneque-Lizano, M. (2015), "The relevance of intellectual capital disclosure: Empirical evidence from Spanish universities", *Knowledge Management Research & Practice*, Vol. 13, No. 1, pp. 31–44.

Rezaee, Z., Tsui, J., Cheng, P. and Zhou, G. (2019), *Business sustainability in Asia: Compliance, performance, and integrated reporting and assurance*, John Wiley & Sons, Hoboken, NJ.

Ruxton, G.D. (2006), "The unequal variance t-test is an underused alternative to Student's t-test and the Mann–Whitney U test", *Behavioral Ecology*, Vol. 17, No. 4, pp. 688–690.

Sengupta, P. (1998), "Corporate disclosure quality and the cost of debt", *Accounting Review, JSTOR*, Vol. 73, No. 4, pp. 459–474.

Shafii, F., Arman Ali, Z. and Othman, M.Z. (2006), *Achieving sustainable construction in the developing countries of Southeast Asia*, Citeseer. Proceedings of the 6th Asia-Pacific Structural Engineering and Construction Conference (APSEC 2006), 5 – 6 September 2006, Kuala Lumpur, Malaysia.

Singh, P.J., Sethuraman, K. and Lam, J.Y. (2017), "Impact of corporate social responsibility dimensions on firm value: Some evidence from Hong Kong and China", *Sustainability, Multidisciplinary Digital Publishing Institute*, Vol. 9, No. 9, p. 1532.

Singh, S. and Kansal, M. (2011), "Voluntary disclosures of intellectual capital: An empirical analysis", *Journal of Intellectual Capital*, Vol. 12, No. 2, pp. 301–318. https://doi.org/10.1108/14691931111123430.

Steenkamp, N. (2018), "Top ten South African companies ' disclosure of materiality determination process and material issues in integrated reports", Available at: https://doi.org/10.1108/JIC-01-2017-0002.

Tran, M. and Beddewela, E. (2020), "Does context matter for sustainability disclosure? Institutional factors in Southeast Asia", *Business Ethics: A European Review*, Vol. 29, No. 2, pp. 282–302.

Vergauwen, P.G.M.C. and van Alem, F.J.C. (2005), "Annual report IC disclosures in the Netherlands, France and Germany", *Journal of Intellectual Capital*, Vol. 6, No. 1, pp. 89–104.

Verrecchia, R.E. (2001), "Essays on disclosure", *Journal of Accounting and Economics*, Vol. 32, No. 1–3, pp. 97–180.

De Villiers, C. and Sharma, U. (2017), "A critical reflection on the future of financial, intellectual capital, sustainability and integrated reporting", *Critical Perspectives on Accounting*, Vol. 70, p. 101999.

De Villiers, C., Unerman, J., Rinaldi, L. and Unerman, J. (2014), "Integrated Reporting: Insights, gaps and an agenda for future research", *Accounting, Auditing & Accountability Journal*, Vol. 27, No. 7, pp. 1042–1067.

Wagiciengo, M.M. and Belal, A.R. (2012), "Intellectual capital disclosures by South African companies: A longitudinal investigation", *Advances in Accounting*, Vol. 28, No. 1, pp. 111–119.

Wang, Q., Sharma, U. and Davey, H. (2016), "Intellectual capital disclosure by Chinese and Indian information technology companies: A comparative analysis", *Journal of Intellectual Capital*, Vol. 17, No. 3, pp. 507–529. https://doi.org/10.1108/JIC-02-2016 -0026.

Wang, Z., Hsieh, T.-S. and Sarkis, J. (2018), "CSR performance and the readability of CSR reports: Too good to be true?", *Corporate Social Responsibility and Environmental Management*, Vol. 25, No. 1, pp. 66–79.

Watts, R.L. and Zimmerman, J.L. (1983), "Agency problems, auditing, and the theory of the firm: Some evidence", *The Journal of Law and Economics*, Vol. 26, No. 3, pp. 613–633.

Yi, A. and Davey, H. (2010), "Intellectual capital disclosure in Chinese (mainland) companies", *Journal of Intellectual Capital*, Vol. 11, No. 3, pp. 326–347. https://doi.org/10.1108/14691931011064572

# 11 Do integrated financial and extra-financial narrative disclosures in the management commentary affect firm valuation? International evidence

*Muhammad Jahangir Ali, Sudipta Bose and Muhammad Shahin Miah*

## 11.1 Introduction

The corporate world has witnessed a proliferation of different types of disclosures in the past two decades, including narrative disclosures in corporate financial reports, attracting significant attention from regulators, researchers, investors and financial analysts worldwide. Narrative disclosures are an integral part of corporate financial reports, reflecting the view of a firm's operations through the eyes of its management (Aerts 2015; Muslu et al. 2015). The management commentary section is an important component of the corporate annual report as it provides managerial commentary about a firm's current position and future prospects (Muslu et al. 2015; International Accounting Standards Board (IASB) 2020).[1] This section of the annual report provides an opportunity for managers to communicate a holistic picture of the firm's performance including their future expectations and strategic plans directly to the public (Muslu et al. 2015). However, due to its voluntary nature, management has discretion about the content of the management commentary, raising concerns about the quantity and quality of the information provided.

Although companies traditionally provide both quantitative and qualitative information regarding their future outlook and prospects, strategies and intentions (IASB 2020), debate is growing regarding the inclusion of extra-financial information in the management commentary. Extra-financial information is defined as information that has a short-term, medium-term or long-term effect on how well a business performs (Global Reporting Initiative (GRI) et al. 2012). Extra-financial information includes non-financial information, such as corporate governance, occupational health and safety, climate change and natural resource management, biodiversity and community impacts, human rights, intellectual capital management, customer satisfaction, consumer and public health, reputation risk, human capital practices, innovation and research and development (R&D) (Global Reporting Initiative et al. 2012). Although previous studies examined the impact of narrative disclosures in the management commentary on various capital market

DOI: 10.4324/9781003095385-14

outcomes (Wang & Hussainey 2013; Muslu et al. 2015), studies are lacking on the integration of financial and extra-financial information in the management commentary. Our study is motivated by such concerns.

In this study, we examine the association of integrated financial and extra-financial narrative disclosures in the management commentary with a firm's valuation, as well as the moderating role of internal and external governance mechanisms in this association. Narrative disclosures in the management commentary provide incremental information to relevant stakeholders, reducing information asymmetry between managers and stakeholders (Leung, Parker & Courtis 2015). The inclusion of extra-financial information in the management commentary helps investors to consider the impact of non-financial information as well as information that has a short-term, medium-term, or long-term effect on a firm's performance (Global Reporting Initiative et al. 2012). Given the voluntary nature of integrating financial and extra-financial information in the management commentary, it can be argued that companies providing this type of information will have less information asymmetry. We argue that reduced information asymmetry *via* the integration of financial and extra-financial information in the management commentary may help financial analysts and investors to more precisely estimate future earnings, leading, in turn, to higher firm valuations. Furthermore, prior studies argue that better corporate governance enhances the levels of corporate disclosure by reducing information asymmetry between managers and shareholders (Kanagaretnam, Lobo & Whalen 2007; Wang & Hussainey 2013). For this reason, we examine the moderating role of both internal and external governance in the association between the integration of financial and extra-financial narrative disclosures in the management commentary and firm valuation.

Using 31,327 firm-year observations across 63 countries over the period 2003–2019, we find a positive association between integrated financial and extra-financial narrative disclosures in the management commentary section and a firm's valuation. This finding is interpreted to mean that firms with a strategy of integrating both financial and extra-financial information in the management commentary have higher market valuation. We also find that the positive association between this strategy and firm valuation is more pronounced for firms with stronger mechanisms of internal governance (corporate governance) and external governance (institutional investors' ownership and analysts' coverage). Our findings prove to be robust to a battery of sensitivity analyses including unobservable self-selection bias using the Heckman (1979) two-stage analysis.

Our study contributes in several ways to the growing literature on narrative disclosures. Firstly, our study is one of the first to use cross-country evidence to examine the firm value effect of integrating both financial and extra-financial narrative disclosures in the management commentary. Secondly, our study provides insights into the importance of integrating both financial and extra-financial information in the management commentary, showing that these types of information create value for shareholders. Thirdly, our study contributes to the internal and external corporate governance literature, showing that firm-level corporate governance performance, institutional investors' ownership and financial analysts' coverage accentuate the firm-value effect of narrative disclosures in the management commentary. Finally, our findings contribute to the debate on the relative costs and benefits of providing integrated financial and non-financial narrative disclosures in the management commentary and have important implications for regulators, policy makers, investors, financial analysts and company management throughout the world.

The rest of this chapter is organised as follows. Section 11.2 presents the literature review and hypothesis development. Section 11.3 outlines the research design, including sample selection, measurement of variables and empirical models. Section 11.4 discusses the findings of the study, while Section 11.5 presents the results of additional analyses. The final section (Section 11.6) concludes the chapter.

## 11.2 Theoretical background, literature review and hypothesis development

Jensen and Meckling (1976) argue that an agency problem exists between managers and shareholders due to the separation of management and control in publicly listed companies. The reason is that managers have access to internal information to which investors have limited access, a situation leading to information asymmetry between managers and investors. Corporate disclosure plays a vital role in diminishing information asymmetry and mitigating agency problems occurring between company managers and users of financial statements (Davis & Tama-Sweet 2012). Consistent with this view, previous studies report that a greater level of both financial and non-financial disclosures leads to reduced cost of equity capital (Botosan 1997; Dhaliwal et al. 2014), reduced cost of debts (Sengupta 1998; Goss & Roberts 2011) and improved stock market liquidity (Leuz & Verrecchia 2000; Chang et al. 2018). Furthermore, corporate disclosures enhance a firm's market valuation by improving a firm's cost of capital and cash flows, both of which benefit shareholders (Lang, Lins & Miller 2002).

Narrative disclosures in the management commentary are regarded as a component of general-purpose financial reporting (IASB 2020). The purpose of the management commentary is to provide effective information to stakeholders so that they can evaluate the firm's future cash inflows and the management of a company's resource stewardship role (IASB 2020). Moreover, narrative disclosures in the management commentary provide incremental information to stakeholders through in-depth discussion of accounting methods and disclosures, thus reducing information asymmetry between managers and stakeholders (Leung et al. 2015). Prior studies find that narrative disclosures in the management commentary make it easier to predict future earnings (Barron, Kile & O'Keefe 1999; Wang & Hussainey 2013); estimate future cash flows (Brown & Tucker 2011); predict whether a firm will cease as a going concern (Mayew, Sethuraman & Venkatachalam 2015); improve bond market intermediaries' opinions and reduce cost of debt (Bonsall & Miller 2017); and improve investment efficiency (Durnev & Mangen 2020). Existing research also finds that narrative disclosures in the management commentary improve a firm's performance (Merkley 2014) and improve stock prices (Muslu et al. 2015). After surveying investors and analysts, the Global Reporting Initiative et al. (2012) report that over 80% of surveyed participants believe that extra-financial information is very relevant for their investment decisions. Therefore, we predict that the integration of financial and extra-financial narrative disclosures in the management commentary will create shareholder value through reducing information asymmetry. We formally state this prediction in the following hypothesis:

**H1: The integration of financial and extra-financial narrative disclosures in the management commentary is positively associated with market valuation.**

Good corporate governance can act as an essential monitoring mechanism to improve information quality and reduce agency costs and information asymmetry problems (Attig et al. 2012). Effective corporate governance mechanisms protect the firm's capital providers from value destruction and management's expropria-tion activities. La Porta et al. (1998) argue that effective corporate governance mechanisms are likely to provide efficient oversight of managers' activities in line with stakeholders' interests. Wang and Hussainey (2013) report that better corporate governance enhances voluntary forward-looking disclosures. Cohen, Krishnamoorthy and Wright (2004) contend that a firm's good corporate gov-ernance practices improve the information environment and discourage manag-ers' opportunism, leading to improved firm value. We therefore argue that strong internal corporate governance mechanisms will ensure the integration of financial and extra-financial narrative disclosures in the management commentary section which, in turn, enhances the firm's market valuation. We hypothesise this predic-tion as follows:

**H2: The positive association between the integration of financial and extra-financial narrative disclosures in the management commentary and market valuation is stronger for firms with better internal corporate governance mechanisms.**

In the capital market, institutional investors are the main suppliers of capital to the firm. These investors play an active role in monitoring management performance (Jensen & Meckling 1976). Prior studies argue that companies with more insti-tutional investors provide more voluntary disclosures to ensure investors' confi-dence (Wang & Hussainey 2013; Hassanein, Marzouk & Azzam 2021), which enhances the firm's performance (Bose, Podder & Biswas 2017a; Bose, Khan & Monem 2021a). Furthermore, financial analysts play a vital role in the capital market as a monitoring agent in reducing agency costs and motivating managers (Chung & Jo 1996). Merton (1987) argues that investors' awareness is one of the determinants of improving firm performance and that financial analysts' coverage helps to increase this awareness. Chung and Jo (1996) find that financial analysts' coverage increases firm value. Therefore, it can be argued that effective external corporate governance mechanisms will ensure a firm's access to external financing, lowering the cost of capital and enhancing the market value of the firm. Based on the above discussion, we expect that monitoring by institutional investors and financial analysts will enhance the integration of financial and extra-financial narrative disclosures in the management commentary section, enhancing the value of the firm by reducing information asymmetry and discouraging managerial self-dealings. Hence, we formally develop the following hypothesis:

**H3:** *The positive association between the integration of financial and extra-financial narrative disclosures in the management commentary and market valuation is stronger for firms with better external corporate governance mechanisms.*

## 11.3  Research methodology

### 11.3.1  Sample selection and data collection

Our initial sample comprises all firms covered by the Refinitiv ESG database (previously, Thomson Reuters ASSET4) in the period 2002–2019. Financial data and stock market data are collected from the Refinitiv Worldscope and DataStream databases, corporate governance and non-financial data from the Refinitiv ESG database, institutional investors' ownership data from the FactSet LionShares database and financial analysts' data from the Refinitiv Institutional Brokers' Enterprise Systems (I/B/E/S) database. Country-level variables are collected from the World Bank database. Our sampling period is restricted by the limitations of the Refinitiv ESG database which started data collection in 2002, with 2019 being the final year of data collection. We drop one year of data due to the lead–lag analysis approach of this study. After excluding incomplete data, the final sample size is 6,205 unique firms with 31,327 firm-year observations across 63 countries covering the period 2003–2019. Table 11.1, Panel A describes the sample selection procedure for our analysis.

Table 11.1, Panel B provides the industry-wise distribution of firms in our sample. In our sample, the financial industry has the largest proportion of companies (13.79%), followed by the computer industry (7.95%), whereas companies from "other industries" (not covered by major industries) have the lowest proportion. Regarding the year-wise distribution, 2019 accounts for the greatest proportion of observations (14.09%), followed by 2018 (12.42%), whereas 2003 accounts for the lowest proportion (0.12%).

### 11.3.2  Measures of narrative disclosures

We measure narrative disclosures (NDISC) as the integrated strategy of both financial and non-financial information in the management commentary section of the corporate annual report. We collect these data from the Refinitiv ESG database. Specifically, Refinitiv reports a datapoint titled "Does the company

*Table 11.1* Sample selection and distribution

**Panel A: Sample selection**

| | |
|---|---|
| Refinitiv data coverage from 2002 to 2019 | 68,544 |
| Less: Firm-year observations without management commentary data | (28,762) |
| Less: Firm-year observations dropped due to lead–lag approach | (5,681) |
| Less: Firm-year observations dropped due to insufficient control variables | (2,774) |
| **Final test sample from 2002 to 2019** | **31,327** |

**Panel B: Industry-wise distribution of firms in sample**

| Name of Industry | Number of firms | % of sample |
|---|---|---|
| Mining/Construction | 2,388 | 7.62 |
| Food | 1,167 | 3.73 |
| Textiles/Printing/Publishing | 981 | 3.13 |
| Chemicals | 1,085 | 3.46 |
| Pharmaceuticals | 1,140 | 3.64 |
| Extractive | 1,780 | 5.68 |
| Manufacturing: Rubber/glass/etc. | 531 | 1.70 |
| Manufacturing: Metal | 765 | 2.44 |
| Manufacturing: Machinery | 947 | 3.02 |
| Manufacturing: Electrical Equipment | 605 | 1.93 |
| Manufacturing: Transport Equipment | 1,139 | 3.64 |
| Manufacturing: Instruments | 862 | 2.75 |
| Manufacturing: Miscellaneous | 156 | 0.50 |
| Computers | 2,490 | 7.95 |
| Transportation | 2,428 | 7.75 |
| Utilities | 1,517 | 4.84 |
| Retail: Wholesale | 833 | 2.66 |
| Retail: Miscellaneous | 1,582 | 5.05 |
| Retail: Restaurant | 269 | 0.86 |
| Financial | 4,319 | 13.79 |
| Insurance/Real Estate | 1,829 | 5.84 |
| Services | 2,353 | 7.51 |
| Others | 161 | 0.51 |
| **Total Sample** | **31,327** | **100** |

**Panel C: Year-wise distribution of sample firms**

| Year | Number of firms | % of sample |
|---|---|---|
| 2003 | 37 | 0.12 |
| 2004 | 42 | 0.13 |
| 2005 | 124 | 0.40 |
| 2006 | 223 | 0.71 |
| 2007 | 221 | 0.71 |
| 2008 | 540 | 1.72 |
| 2009 | 1,410 | 4.50 |
| 2010 | 1,780 | 5.68 |
| 2011 | 2,126 | 6.79 |
| 2012 | 2,262 | 7.22 |
| 2013 | 2,258 | 7.21 |
| 2014 | 2,258 | 7.21 |
| 2015 | 2,401 | 7.21 |
| 2016 | 3,162 | 7.67 |
| 2017 | 3,891 | 10.09 |
| 2018 | 4,414 | 12.42 |
| 2019 | 4,178 | 14.09 |
| **Total** | **31,327** | **13.34** |

explicitly integrate financial and extra-financial factors in its management discussion and analysis (MD&A) section in the annual report?" We utilise this datapoint as a proxy for narrative disclosures. Firms operating in the US provide non-financial information under the MD&A section of Form 10-K while firms based in the UK and in other countries provide information in the strategic report and business review section within the annual report, respectively. NDISC is measured as an indicator variable taking a value of 1 if the firm integrates both financial and extra-financial narrative disclosures in the management commentary, and 0 otherwise.

### *11.3.3 Empirical models*

We adopt a lead–lag approach in all our regression models to address potential endogeneity issues arising from reverse causality related to NDISC and TOBINQ. We estimate the following baseline model to test Hypothesis 1 (H1):

$$TOBINQ_{i,t+1} = \beta_0 + \beta_1 NDISC_{i,t} + \beta_2 SIZE_{i,t} + \beta_3 LEV_{i,t} + \beta_4 ROA_{i,t} + \beta_5 CAPIN_{i,t}$$

$$+ \beta_6 DIVIDEND_{i,t} + \beta_7 LIQUIDITY_{i,t} + \beta_8 GROWTH_{i,t} + \beta_9 CSR_{i,t}$$

$$+ \beta_{10} LNGDP_{i,t} + \beta_{11} COMMON\_LAW_{i,t} + \beta_{12} LEGAL_{i,t} + \Sigma YEAR_{i,t}$$

$$+ \Sigma INDUSTRY_{i,t} + \varepsilon_{i,t}$$

(11.1)

where *TOBINQ* is Tobin's Q, measured as the sum of the book value of total assets plus the market value of equity minus the book value of equity divided by total assets. *NDISC* is narrative disclosures, measured as an indicator variable of 1 if the firm integrates both financial and extra-financial narrative disclosures in the management commentary section, and 0 otherwise. We separately include the interaction terms *NDISC × CGOV*, *NDISC × INSTOWN*, and *NDISC × ANACOV* in Equation (11.1) to test Hypothesis 2 (H2) and Hypothesis 3 (H3). *CGOV* refers to corporate governance; *INSTOWN* is the percentage of ownership held by institutional owners; and *ANACOV* is the 12-month average of the number of analysts who issued annual earnings forecasts. Table 11.2 provides the definition of all variables.

Following the earlier literature (Roll, Schwartz & Subrahmanyam 2009; Bose et al. 2017a; Bose et al. 2017b; Bose et al. 2021a; Bose et al. 2021b), we control for firm size (SIZE); leverage (LEV); profitability (ROA); capital intensity (CAPIN); dividend payout (DIVIDEND); liquidity (LIQUIDITY); revenue growth (GROWTH); corporate social responsibility performance (CSR); country-level gross domestic product (LNGDP); common law (COMMON_LAW); and the legal environment *(LEGAL)*. For reasons of brevity, we do not provide a justification here for selecting each control variable.

*Table 11.2* Definitions of variables

| Variable(s) | | Explanation |
|---|---|---|
| TOBINQ | Tobin's Q | The sum of the book value of total assets plus the market value of equity minus the book value of equity divided by total assets. |
| NDISC | Narrative disclosures | An indicator variable that takes a value of 1 if the firm explicitly integrates financial and extra-financial information in its management commentary section in the annual report, and 0 otherwise. |
| CGOV | Corporate governance | The corporate governance performance score from the Refinitiv database. This score is a combination of management score, shareholder score and CSR strategy score. |
| INSTOWN | Institutional investors' ownership | The percentage of ownership held by institutional investors. |
| ANACOV | Analysts' coverage | The 12-month average of the number of analysts who issued annual earnings forecasts in I/B/E/S for the firm of interest. |
| SIZE | Firm size | The natural logarithm of the market value of equity. |
| LEV | Leverage | The ratio of total debts divided by total assets at the end of the fiscal year. |
| ROA | Profitability | The ratio of net income scaled by total assets. |
| CAPIN | Capital intensity | The ratio of capital expenditure to total sales. |
| DIVIDEND | Dividend | An indicator variable that takes a value of 1 if the firm pays a dividend, and 0 otherwise. |
| LIQUIDITY | Liquidity | Ratio of the number of shares traded to total shares outstanding at the end of the year. |
| GROWTH | Growth | The percentage change in annual sales. |
| CSR | CSR performance | The corporate social responsibility (CSR) performance score from the Refinitiv database which is the average of the environmental pillar and social pillar scores. |
| LNGDP | Gross domestic product | The natural logarithm of country-level gross domestic product (GDP) per capita. |
| COMMON_ LAW | Common law | An indicator variable that takes a value of 1 if the firm is domiciled in a common-law country, and 0 otherwise. |
| LEGAL | Legal environment | The rule of law score from the World Bank. |
| PROPDISC | Industry pressure | The proportion of firms in an industry that integrate financial and non-financial information in their narrative disclosures in the management commentary section in the annual report. |

## 11.4  Results

### 11.4.1  Descriptive statistics and correlations

Table 11.3 displays descriptive statistics for all the variables used in this study. The mean (median) value of TOBINQ is 1.819 (1.337). Approximately, 22.30% of firms in our sample integrate both financial and extra-financial narrative disclosures in their management commentary section of the annual report. The mean value of corporate governance performance (CGOV) is 0.499. The average institutional ownership is 0.442, suggesting that, on average, about 44.20% of ownership is held by institutional investors. Furthermore, firms in our sample are followed, on average, by 11.978 financial analysts. The average firm size (SIZE), measured as the natural log of the market value of equity, is 8.296, suggesting that the average market capitalisation of firms in our sample is US$12,274.66 million. The average profitability or return on assets (ROA) of firms in our sample is 3.60%. About 75.60% of firms in our sample pay dividends.

Table 11.4 presents country-wise descriptive statistics of the key variables. These statistics show that our sample is dominated by firms from the US (44.60%), followed by firms from the UK (7.84%) and Japan (7.41%), whereas the country with the lowest proportion of firms is Uganda (0.001%). Approximately 74.77% of the UK firms provide integrated financial and extra-financial narrative disclosures in the management commentary section, followed by Austria (73.97%).

Table 11.5 presents a Pearson's correlation matrix between the dependent and independent variables. The correlation matrix shows that no coefficient value exceeds 0.80, with Gujarati and Porter (2009) stating that correlations less than 0.80 do not create any multicollinearity problems. The mean variance inflation factor (VIF) value of the variables is 1.92, with the lowest VIF value being 1.05

*Table 11.3* Descriptive statistics

|  | N | Mean | Std. Dev. | Median | p25 | p75 |
| --- | --- | --- | --- | --- | --- | --- |
| TOBINQ | 31,327 | 1.819 | 1.369 | 1.337 | 1.038 | 2.025 |
| NDISC | 31,327 | 0.223 | 0.416 | 0.000 | 0.000 | 0.000 |
| CGOV | 31,327 | 0.499 | 0.221 | 0.504 | 0.323 | 0.674 |
| INSTOWN | 31,327 | 0.442 | 0.376 | 0.417 | 0.000 | 0.815 |
| ANACOV | 31,327 | 11.978 | 8.006 | 10.750 | 5.667 | 16.833 |
| SIZE | 31,327 | 8.296 | 1.435 | 8.261 | 7.375 | 9.205 |
| LEV | 31,327 | 0.260 | 0.195 | 0.239 | 0.104 | 0.379 |
| ROA | 31,327 | 0.036 | 0.101 | 0.037 | 0.010 | 0.076 |
| CAPIN | 31,327 | 0.139 | 0.299 | 0.043 | 0.020 | 0.112 |
| DIVIDEND | 31,327 | 0.756 | 0.429 | 1.000 | 1.000 | 1.000 |
| LIQUIDITY | 31,327 | 1.684 | 1.699 | 1.172 | 0.555 | 2.183 |
| GROWTH | 31,327 | 0.105 | 0.324 | 0.060 | −0.026 | 0.164 |
| CSR | 31,327 | 33.150 | 34.331 | 22.53 | 0.000 | 64.100 |
| LNGDP | 31,327 | 10.512 | 0.834 | 10.789 | 10.606 | 10.961 |
| COMMON_LAW | 31,327 | 0.748 | 0.434 | 1.000 | 0.000 | 1.000 |
| LEGAL | 31,327 | 1.352 | 0.662 | 1.610 | 1.453 | 1.651 |

*Table 11.4* Country-wise descriptive statistics

| Country | N | % | NDISC (%) | CGOV | INSTOWN (%) | ANACOV | COMMON_ LAW | LEGAL |
|---|---|---|---|---|---|---|---|---|
| Argentina | 30 | 0.1 | 23.33 | 59.97 | 59.71 | 2.50 | 0 | −0.285 |
| Australia | 1,094 | 3.49 | 34.10 | 51.70 | 52.02 | 7.97 | 1 | 1.762 |
| Austria | 73 | 0.23 | 73.97 | 49.78 | 45.45 | 12.29 | 0 | 1.847 |
| Belgium | 90 | 0.29 | 35.56 | 55.40 | 38.96 | 13.03 | 0 | 1.401 |
| Bahrain | 8 | 0.03 | 50.00 | 63.70 | 33.48 | 0.38 | 1 | 0.435 |
| Bermuda | 92 | 0.29 | 4.35 | 56.53 | 85.71 | 12.08 | 1 | 1.039 |
| Brazil | 220 | 0.70 | 30.45 | 54.31 | 57.99 | 8.60 | 0 | −0.129 |
| Canada | 2,600 | 8.30 | 27.27 | 50.05 | 56.58 | 8.17 | 1 | 1.802 |
| Cayman Islands | 32 | 0.10 | 0.00 | 71.27 | 79.37 | 3.78 | 1 | 0.805 |
| Chile | 47 | 0.15 | 42.55 | 52.40 | 35.10 | 4.45 | 0 | 1.258 |
| China | 1,522 | 4.86 | 24.84 | 50.57 | 37.30 | 13.86 | 0 | −0.341 |
| Colombia | 24 | 0.08 | 62.50 | 44.14 | 55.07 | 2.47 | 0 | −0.333 |
| Cyprus | 12 | 0.04 | 75.00 | 73.55 | 32.23 | 12.10 | 1 | 0.916 |
| Czech Republic | 18 | 0.06 | 22.22 | 57.38 | 54.98 | 6.99 | 0 | 1.043 |
| Denmark | 108 | 0.34 | 59.26 | 56.27 | 45.69 | 15.27 | 0 | 1.912 |
| Egypt | 21 | 0.07 | 19.05 | 43.94 | 29.89 | 5.85 | 0 | −0.416 |
| Finland | 44 | 0.14 | 59.09 | 57.28 | 61.20 | 17.65 | 0 | 1.983 |
| France | 364 | 1.16 | 36.26 | 51.82 | 56.91 | 17.14 | 0 | 1.450 |
| Germany | 492 | 1.57 | 64.63 | 54.25 | 56.35 | 21.04 | 0 | 1.672 |
| Greece | 21 | 0.07 | 23.81 | 66.76 | 24.04 | 12.85 | 0 | 0.491 |
| Hong Kong | 923 | 2.95 | 26.00 | 45.22 | 42.59 | 12.15 | 1 | 1.676 |
| Hungary | 30 | 0.10 | 70.00 | 41.18 | 58.00 | 13.36 | 0 | 0.604 |
| Indonesia | 267 | 0.85 | 15.73 | 51.07 | 36.82 | 14.58 | 0 | −0.442 |
| India | 826 | 2.64 | 57.99 | 49.50 | 55.39 | 19.23 | 1 | −0.031 |
| Ireland | 249 | 0.79 | 24.10 | 51.95 | 75.45 | 12.85 | 1 | 1.636 |
| Israel | 47 | 0.15 | 4.26 | 54.25 | 47.93 | 5.33 | 1 | 1.035 |
| Italy | 138 | 0.44 | 53.62 | 52.86 | 41.60 | 15.71 | 0 | 0.374 |
| Japan | 2,322 | 7.41 | 12.75 | 52.68 | 35.12 | 10.76 | 0 | 1.428 |
| Kenya | 3 | 0.01 | 100.00 | 50.00 | 29.55 | 8.19 | 1 | −0.447 |
| Kuwait | 16 | 0.05 | 0.00 | 55.52 | 11.92 | 3.51 | 0 | 0.247 |
| Luxembourg | 59 | 0.19 | 28.81 | 47.85 | 66.29 | 11.05 | 0 | 1.803 |
| Macao | 24 | 0.08 | 0.00 | 66.67 | 49.45 | 20.22 | 0 | 0.829 |
| Malta | 3 | 0.01 | 100.00 | 58.89 | 88.69 | 6.33 | 0 | 1.084 |
| Malaysia | 308 | 0.98 | 53.57 | 49.98 | 58.01 | 15.82 | 1 | 0.501 |
| Mexico | 190 | 0.61 | 1.58 | 53.06 | 52.17 | 9.15 | 0 | −0.550 |
| New Zealand | 47 | 0.15 | 21.28 | 47.56 | 40.85 | 5.08 | 1 | 1.912 |
| Netherlands | 245 | 0.78 | 49.39 | 54.27 | 69.44 | 17.04 | 0 | 1.855 |
| Norway | 47 | 0.15 | 61.70 | 57.84 | 50.55 | 18.24 | 0 | 1.954 |
| Oman | 40 | 0.13 | 52.50 | 45.48 | 29.92 | 2.66 | 0 | 0.436 |
| Panama | 8 | 0.03 | 0.00 | 25.87 | 100.00 | 12.42 | 0 | −0.077 |
| Peru | 9 | 0.03 | 22.22 | 57.04 | 70.03 | 1.30 | 0 | −0.559 |
| Philippines | 163 | 0.52 | 2.45 | 51.44 | 38.79 | 8.81 | 0 | −0.435 |
| Poland | 38 | 0.12 | 21.05 | 50.94 | 64.37 | 11.40 | 0 | 0.637 |

(*Continued*)

*Table 11.4* (Continued)

| Country | N | % | NDISC (%) | CGOV | INSTOWN (%) | ANACOV | COMMON_ LAW | LEGAL |
|---|---|---|---|---|---|---|---|---|
| Portugal | 20 | 0.06 | 20.00 | 51.79 | 48.07 | 9.91 | 0 | 1.080 |
| Puerto Rico | 21 | 0.07 | 0.00 | 43.33 | 81.96 | 4.86 | 0 | 0.660 |
| Qatar | 23 | 0.07 | 30.43 | 60.04 | 14.94 | 5.31 | 0 | 0.774 |
| Russia | 184 | 0.59 | 22.28 | 52.03 | 44.81 | 5.12 | 0 | −0.787 |
| Saudi Arabia | 20 | 0.06 | 55.00 | 62.60 | 7.38 | 8.50 | 0 | 0.136 |
| Singapore | 278 | 0.89 | 12.59 | 48.78 | 42.72 | 13.31 | 1 | 1.747 |
| South Africa | 340 | 1.09 | 57.94 | 52.41 | 1.92 | 6.52 | 1 | 0.071 |
| South Korea | 311 | 0.99 | 12.54 | 57.56 | 45.80 | 17.62 | 0 | 1.045 |
| Spain | 102 | 0.33 | 51.96 | 52.11 | 43.89 | 20.08 | 0 | 1.074 |
| Sri Lanka | 7 | 0.02 | 100.00 | 50.00 | 61.72 | 1.96 | 1 | −0.049 |
| Sweden | 109 | 0.35 | 54.13 | 52.78 | 56.41 | 14.20 | 0 | 1.954 |
| Switzerland | 340 | 1.09 | 23.24 | 56.37 | 49.52 | 15.11 | 0 | 1.876 |
| Thailand | 151 | 0.48 | 8.61 | 48.30 | 40.15 | 12.48 | 1 | −0.086 |
| Turkey | 25 | 0.08 | 52.00 | 55.26 | 50.95 | 13.46 | 0 | −0.032 |
| Uganda | 1 | 0.00 | 100.00 | 75.00 | 17.91 | 1.00 | 1 | −0.295 |
| Uruguay | 3 | 0.01 | 100.00 | 13.03 | 0.00 | 3.97 | 0 | 0.605 |
| United Arab Emirates | 46 | 0.15 | 58.70 | 52.48 | 51.15 | 7.27 | 0 | 0.645 |
| United Kingdom (UK) | 2,457 | 7.84 | 74.77 | 53.54 | 86.95 | 12.95 | 1 | 1.721 |
| United States (US) | 13,973 | 44.6 | 5.29 | 47.55 | 33.70 | 11.86 | 1 | 1.589 |
| Virgin Islands | 2 | 0.01 | 0.00 | 27.55 | 0.00 | 5.21 | 0 | 0.627 |
| **Total/ Average** | **31,327** | **100** | **22.31** | **49.86** | **0.44** | **11.98** | | **1.352** |

and the highest VIF value being 5.66, indicating that multicollinearity problems are unlikely in our regression models.

### 11.4.2 Regression results

Table 11.6 presents the regression results of our hypotheses. Model (1) reports the regression results of the association of the integration of financial and non-financial narrative disclosures (NDISC) in the management commentary with the firm value (TOBINQ). Model (2) shows the regression results of the moderating role of internal governance (CGOV), whereas Models (3) and (4) show the regression results of the moderating role of external governance [measured by institutional investors' ownership (INSTOWN) and financial analysts' coverage

Table 11.5 Correlation matrix

| | [1] | [2] | [3] | [4] | [5] | [6] | [7] | [8] | [9] | [10] | [11] | [12] | [13] | [14] | [15] |
|---|---|---|---|---|---|---|---|---|---|---|---|---|---|---|---|
| TOBINQ [1] | 1 | | | | | | | | | | | | | | |
| NDISC [2] | **0.056** | 1 | | | | | | | | | | | | | |
| CGOV [3] | **-0.081** | **0.158** | 1 | | | | | | | | | | | | |
| INSTOWN [4] | -0.016 | **0.173** | 0.040 | 1 | | | | | | | | | | | |
| ANACOV [5] | **0.117** | **0.093** | **0.228** | 0.071 | 1 | | | | | | | | | | |
| SIZE [6] | **0.10** | 0.033 | **0.266** | -0.020 | **0.607** | 1 | | | | | | | | | |
| LEV [7] | **-0.118** | -0.014 | -0.001 | -0.036 | -0.060 | -0.006 | 1 | | | | | | | | |
| ROA [8] | **0.198** | 0.038 | **0.086** | 0.025 | **0.167** | **0.307** | **-0.118** | 1 | | | | | | | |
| CAPIN [9] | -0.069 | 0.005 | -0.064 | 0.039 | **-0.101** | **-0.122** | **0.112** | **-0.175** | 1 | | | | | | |
| DIVIDEND [10] | **-0.151** | **0.137** | **0.192** | 0.016 | **0.108** | **0.290** | 0.01 | **0.261** | -0.099 | 1 | | | | | |
| LIQUIDITY [11] | **0.066** | **-0.226** | -0.044 | **-0.118** | **0.127** | -0.028 | 0.087 | -0.098 | -0.009 | **-0.260** | 1 | | | | |
| GROWTH [12] | **0.104** | -0.052 | **-0.106** | -0.009 | -0.063 | -0.031 | -0.033 | 0.000 | 0.111 | **-0.141** | 0.01 | 1 | | | |
| CSR_STRATEGY [13] | **-0.120** | **0.456** | **0.440** | 0.078 | **0.329** | **0.402** | 0.018 | 0.081 | -0.039 | **0.25** | **-0.186** | **-0.116** | 1 | | |
| LNGDP [14] | 0.007 | **-0.165** | -0.023 | -0.018 | **-0.117** | **-0.108** | 0.010 | **-0.106** | 0.032 | **-0.172** | **0.236** | -0.007 | **-0.149** | 1 | |
| COMMON_LAW [15] | **0.131** | -0.061 | -0.075 | 0.014 | -0.074 | **-0.152** | 0.032 | -0.042 | 0.097 | **-0.198** | **0.221** | 0.036 | **-0.193** | **0.327** | 1 |
| LEGAL [16] | **0.016** | -0.052 | -0.022 | 0.058 | -0.055 | **-0.118** | -0.005 | -0.088 | 0.058 | **-0.139** | **0.179** | -0.024 | -0.089 | **0.880** | **0.466** |

Notes: A correlation coefficient in bold indicates that the correlation is statistically significant at least at the 10% level. Variable definitions are provided in Table 11.2.

*Table 11.6* Regression results between narrative disclosures and firm valuation

| | Dependent variable=$TOBINQ_{i,t+1}$ | | | |
|---|---|---|---|---|
| | Model (1) | Model (2) | Model (3) | Model (4) |
| NDISC | 0.093*** | −0.008 | −0.041 | −0.019 |
| | (3.495) | (−0.124) | (−0.586) | (−0.318) |
| NDISC × CGOV | | 0.178* | | |
| | | (1.869) | | |
| CGOV | | −0.295*** | | |
| | | (−3.039) | | |
| NDISC × INSTOWN | | | 0.265*** | |
| | | | (2.678) | |
| INSTOWN | | | −0.109*** | |
| | | | (−3.073) | |
| NDISC × ANACOV | | | | 0.008** |
| | | | | (2.051) |
| ANACOV | | | | 0.005* |
| | | | | (1.995) |
| SIZE | 0.156*** | 0.159*** | 0.157*** | 0.133*** |
| | (5.297) | (5.203) | (5.394) | (4.370) |
| LEV | −0.571*** | −0.574*** | −0.571*** | −0.564*** |
| | (−4.364) | (−4.455) | (−4.389) | (−4.460) |
| ROA | 2.252*** | 2.267*** | 2.244*** | 2.269*** |
| | (2.771) | (2.822) | (2.791) | (2.789) |
| CAPIN | 0.105** | 0.101** | 0.110** | 0.106** |
| | (2.218) | (2.115) | (2.374) | (2.249) |
| DIVIDEND | −0.311*** | −0.301*** | −0.314*** | −0.309*** |
| | (−5.165) | (−4.671) | (−5.199) | (−5.127) |
| LIQUIDITY | −0.010 | −0.009 | −0.011 | −0.015 |
| | (−0.759) | (−0.675) | (−0.781) | (−1.042) |
| GROWTH | 0.259*** | 0.250*** | 0.260*** | 0.266*** |
| | (3.724) | (3.854) | (3.798) | (3.990) |
| CSR | −0.006*** | −0.005*** | −0.006*** | −0.006*** |
| | (−7.182) | (−7.426) | (−7.180) | (−7.316) |
| LNGDP | −0.135* | −0.129 | −0.137* | −0.106 |
| | (−1.677) | (−1.567) | (−1.685) | (−1.442) |
| COMMON_LAW | 0.391*** | 0.393*** | 0.386*** | 0.399*** |
| | (3.925) | (3.915) | (3.846) | (4.292) |
| LEGAL | 0.039 | 0.033 | 0.036 | 0.005 |
| | (0.332) | (0.275) | (0.304) | (0.044) |
| Intercept | 2.678** | 2.601** | 2.707** | 2.546** |
| | (2.424) | (2.326) | (2.472) | (2.331) |
| Year Fixed Effects | Yes | Yes | Yes | Yes |
| Industry Fixed Effects | Yes | Yes | Yes | Yes |
| Observations | 31,327 | 31,327 | 31,327 | 31,327 |
| R-squared | 0.272 | 0.274 | 0.273 | 0.273 |

Notes: This table shows the regression results for the association between narrative disclosures and firm valuation. Model (1) shows the regression results between narrative disclosures and firm valuation; Model (2) shows the moderating role of corporate governance performance in the association between narrative disclosures and firm valuation; Model (3) presents the moderating role of institutional investors' ownership in the association between narrative disclosures and firm valuation; and Model (4) shows the moderating role of analysts' coverage in the association between narrative disclosures and firm valuation. Coefficient values (robust *t*-statistics) are indicated with standard errors clustered at the country level. Superscript ***, ** and * represent statistical significance at the 1%, 5% and 10% levels, respectively. Definitions of variables are provided in Table 11.2.

(ANACOV)] mechanisms. The $R$-squared ($R^2$) values range between 27.20% and 27.40% across the three models, as presented in Table 11.6, suggesting that our independent variables comfortably explain the dependent variable. The coefficient of NDISC in Model (1) is positive and statistically significant ($\beta$ = 0.093, $p$ < 0.01), suggesting that companies integrating both financial and non-financial narrative disclosures in the management commentary have higher firm valuations. With regard to economic significance, the coefficient estimates from Model (1) indicate that firms with narrative disclosures that integrate both financial and non-financial information have 9.30% higher firm valuations than their counterparts without these disclosures.

In Model (2), we examine the role of corporate governance performance in the relationship of the integration of financial and non-financial narrative disclosures in the management commentary with the valuation of the firm. In Model (2), the key variable of interest is the interaction term between NDISC and CGOV (NDISC × CGOV). The coefficient of NDISC × CGOV is positive and statistically significant ($\beta$ = 0.178, $p$ < 0.10), suggesting that strong internal corporate governance accentuates the positive association between NDISC and the firm's value. Thus, Hypothesis 2 (H2) is supported.

In Models (3) and (4), we examine the role of external governance mechanisms, measured by institutional investors' ownership (INSTOWN) and analysts' coverage (ANACOV), on the relationship between narrative disclosures and firm value. As shown in Models (3) and (4), the key variables of interest are the interaction terms between NDISC and INSTOWN (NDISC × INSTOWN) and NDISC and ANACOV (NDISC × ANACOV). The coefficients of NDISC × INSTOWN in Model (3) and NDISC × ANACOV in Model (4) are positive and statistically significant ($\beta$ = 0.265, $p$ < 0.01 in Model (3) and $\beta$ = 0.008, $p$ < 0.05 in Model (4)). These results suggest that strong external corporate governance accentuates the positive association between NDISC and the firm's value. Thus, Hypothesis 3 (H3) is supported.

Regarding the control variables, as shown in Table 11.6, we find that the coefficients of SIZE, ROA and GROWTH are positive and statistically significant, suggesting that firms of larger size that are highly profitable, and have greater capital intensity and sales growth enjoy improved firm value. On the other hand, we find that the coefficients of LEV, DIVIDEND and *CSR* are negative and statistically significant, suggesting that firms with high leverage that pay dividends and have better CSR performance have a lower market value. Regarding country-level variables, we find that firms in countries with higher gross domestic product (GDP) have lower firm values, and that firms domiciled in stakeholder-oriented countries have higher firm values. The signs of the coefficients of all control variables are consistent with our expectation, except for CSR performance.

Overall, our findings provide evidence that companies with narrative disclosures integrating both financial and extra-financial information in the management commentary have higher firm values. Furthermore, better internal and external corporate governance mechanisms accentuate this relationship.

## 11.5  Sensitivity analyses

### *11.5.1  Heckman's (1979) two-stage analysis*

As narrative disclosures with integrated financial and extra-financial information in the management commentary are largely voluntary, this may create self-selection bias in our findings, so we employ Heckman's (1979) two-stage analysis method to address any self-selection bias. In the first stage, we model companies' propensity to integrate both financial and extra-financial information in the management commentary and estimate the model with probit regression. To be specific, we estimate the following model:

$$NDISC_{i,t} = \beta_0 + \beta_1 PROPDISC_{i,t} + \beta_2 SIZE_{i,t} + \beta_3 LEV_{i,t} + \beta_4 ROA_{i,t} + \beta_5 CAPIN_{i,t}$$

$$+ \beta_6 DIVIDEND_{i,t} + \beta_7 LIQUIDITY_{i,t} + \beta_8 GROWTH_{i,t} + \beta_9 CSR_{i,t}$$

$$+ \beta_{10} LNGDP_{i,t} + \beta_{11} COMMON\_LAW_{i,t} + \beta_{12} LEGAL_{i,t} + \Sigma YEAR_{i,t}$$

$$+ \Sigma INDUSTRY_{i,t} + \varepsilon_{i,t}$$

$$(11.2)$$

In Equation (11.2), NDISC is the dependent variable which is measured as an indicator variable that takes a value of 1 if the company explicitly integrates both financial and extra-financial narrative disclosures in its management commentary; otherwise, the value is 0. We include several variables in Equation (11.2) based on prior studies. Furthermore, as shown in Equation (11.2), we include PROPDISC to satisfy the exclusion restriction criteria in the first-stage model. The rationale behind including PROPDISC is that it captures industry pressure. If more firms in a given industry integrate both financial and extra-financial information in their narrative disclosures, then firms in that industry will be under greater pressure to do the same in order to minimise the negative perceptions of external capital providers. We measure PROPDISC as the proportion of firms in an industry that integrate financial and extra-financial information in their narrative disclosures in the management commentary section. We expect a positive sign on PROPDISC (see Table 11.2 for definitions of other variables).

Table 11.7, Panel A presents the first-stage regression results. Consistent with our expectation, the coefficient of PROPDISC is positive and statistically significant ($\beta = 3.631$, $p < 0.01$). The model has a pseudo-$R^2$ value of 54.10% and a partial $R^2$ value for PROPDISC of 35.10%, which is statistically significant ($p < 0.01$), suggesting that PROPDISC is a reasonable exogenous variable to satisfy the exclusion restriction criteria. Table 11.7, Panel B reports the second-stage regression results. These show that the coefficient of NDISC is positive and statistically significant in Model (1), and that the coefficients of NDISC × CGOV in Model (2), NDISC × INSTOWN in Model (3) and NDISC × ANACOV in Model (4) are positive and statistically significant. Moreover, the coefficient of the

*Table 11.7* Heckman's (1979) two-stage regression results between narrative disclosures and firm valuation

*Panel A: Heckman's (1979) first-stage logistic regression results*

| | Coefficient | z-statistic | p-value |
|---|---|---|---|
| PROPDISC | 3.631 | 77.820 | 0.000*** |
| SIZE | −0.097 | −9.590 | 0.000*** |
| LEV | −0.166 | −2.330 | 0.020** |
| ROA | 0.007 | 0.050 | 0.959 |
| CAPIN | −0.108 | −2.530 | 0.011** |
| DIVIDEND | 0.179 | 4.990 | 0.000 |
| LIQUIDITY | −0.011 | −1.200 | 0.230 |
| GROWTH | 0.115 | 2.970 | 0.003*** |
| CSR | 0.020 | 49.000 | 0.000*** |
| LNGDP | 0.057 | 1.800 | 0.071* |
| COMMON_LAW | 0.117 | 3.950 | 0.000*** |
| LEGAL | −0.107 | −2.590 | 0.009*** |
| Intercept | −2.028 | −4.500 | 0.000*** |
| Year Fixed Effects | | Yes | |
| Industry Fixed Effects | | Yes | |
| Observations | | 31,327 | |
| Pseudo-*R*-squared | | 0.541 | |
| Wald Chi² | | 9665.49 | |
| Log pseudolikelihood | | −7637.605 | |
| Partial $R^2$–PROPDISC | | 0.351*** | |

*Panel B: Heckman's (1979) second-stage regression results between narrative disclosures and firm valuation*

| | Dependent variable=$TOBINQ_{i,t+1}$ | | | |
|---|---|---|---|---|
| | Model (1) | Model (2) | Model (3) | Model (4) |
| NDISC | 0.127*** | 0.034 | −0.015 | 0.023 |
| | (6.436) | (0.718) | (−0.540) | (0.738) |
| NDISC × CGOV | | 0.161** | | |
| | | (2.346) | | |
| CGOV | | −0.292*** | | |
| | | (−7.759) | | |
| NDISC × INSTOWN | | | 0.286*** | |
| | | | (6.394) | |
| INSTOWN | | | −0.103*** | |
| | | | (−4.864) | |
| NDISC × ANACOV | | | | 0.008*** |
| | | | | (4.002) |
| ANACOV | | | | 0.005*** |
| | | | | (4.115) |
| SIZE | 0.151*** | 0.154*** | 0.152*** | 0.126*** |
| | (23.609) | (23.893) | (23.695) | (16.636) |
| LEV | −0.577*** | −0.580*** | −0.577*** | −0.570*** |

(*Continued*)

*Table 11.7* (Continued)

Panel B: Heckman's (1979) second-stage regression results between narrative
disclosures and firm valuation

| | Dependent variable=TOBINQ$_{i,t+1}$ | | | |
|---|---|---|---|---|
| | Model (1) | Model (2) | Model (3) | Model (4) |
| | (−11.477) | (−11.549) | (−11.499) | (−11.322) |
| ROA | 2.258*** | 2.273*** | 2.250*** | 2.277*** |
| | (14.712) | (14.840) | (14.666) | (14.829) |
| CAPIN | 0.104*** | 0.100*** | 0.109*** | 0.105*** |
| | (3.224) | (3.097) | (3.373) | (3.253) |
| DIVIDEND | −0.304*** | −0.294*** | −0.306*** | −0.301*** |
| | (−15.902) | (−15.427) | (−15.977) | (−15.703) |
| LIQUIDITY | −0.012** | −0.011** | −0.013** | −0.018*** |
| | (−2.337) | (−2.050) | (−2.452) | (−3.267) |
| GROWTH | 0.263*** | 0.253*** | 0.264*** | 0.271*** |
| | (8.383) | (8.097) | (8.440) | (8.652) |
| CSR | −0.005*** | −0.004*** | −0.005*** | −0.005*** |
| | (−14.866) | (−12.639) | (−14.555) | (−14.963) |
| LNGDP | −0.150*** | −0.143*** | −0.152*** | −0.122*** |
| | (−6.934) | (−6.556) | (−7.019) | (−5.726) |
| COMMON_LAW | 0.389*** | 0.391*** | 0.384*** | 0.397*** |
| | (21.932) | (22.062) | (21.658) | (22.237) |
| LEGAL | 0.056** | 0.048** | 0.052** | 0.023 |
| | (2.275) | (1.961) | (2.124) | (0.924) |
| IMR | 0.042*** | 0.039*** | 0.046*** | 0.047*** |
| | (2.869) | (2.700) | (3.124) | (3.202) |
| Intercept | 3.337*** | 3.304*** | 3.397*** | 3.214*** |
| | (2.854) | (2.808) | (2.986) | (2.765) |
| Year Fixed Effects | Yes | Yes | Yes | Yes |
| Industry Fixed Effects | Yes | Yes | Yes | Yes |
| Observations | 31,327 | 31,327 | 31,327 | 31,327 |
| R-squared | 0.272 | 0.274 | 0.273 | 0.274 |

Notes: This table shows Heckman's (1979) two-stage regression results for the association between narrative disclosures and firm valuation. Panel A shows the logistics regression results. Panel B shows the second-stage regression results. Coefficient values (robust *t*-statistics) are shown with standard errors clustered at the country level. Superscript ***, ** and * represent statistical significance at the 1%, 5% and 10% levels, respectively. Definitions of variables are provided in Table 11.2.

inverse Mills ratio, IMR, is positive and statistically significant across all models from Models (1) to (4). This suggests that our findings are robust after addressing the self-selection bias, corroborating our main findings.

### 11.5.2  *Country analysis*

Our sample is dominated by firms in the US (44.60%), followed by Canada (8.30%) and the UK (7.84%). To check the robustness of our findings, we re-ran all our regression analyses, separating US firms from non-US firms. We do not report the regression results here for reasons of brevity. Nevertheless, the unreported results show that the findings are qualitatively similar. Furthermore, for the country-sensitivity tests, we re-ran our regression models after excluding each of the following groups, one at a time: (1) Canadian firms; (2) UK firms; and (3) countries with less than 10, 20, 30, 50, or 100 observations. We find that each analysis (untabulated) produces qualitatively similar outcomes.

## 11.6 Conclusion

In this study, we examine the association between the integration of financial and extra-financial narrative disclosures in the management commentary and firm valuation, as well as the moderating roles of internal and external corporate governance mechanisms in this association. We measure the internal governance mechanism using the corporate governance score rated by the Refinitiv ESG database, and the external governance mechanisms using the percentage of institutional investors' ownership and financial analysts' coverage. Using 31,327 firm-year observations across 63 countries over the period 2003–2019, we find that firms integrating financial and extra-financial narrative disclosures in the management commentary have higher firm valuations, with this relationship positively moderated by both internal and external corporate governance mechanisms. The study findings have important implications for regulators, policy makers, investors, financial analysts and company managers throughout the world, given that extra-financial narrative disclosures are gaining momentum. One of the limitations of this study is that we operationalise the binary variable as a proxy for the integration of financial and extra-financial narrative disclosures in the management commentary. Future research could examine the capital market impact of the textual analysis of the management commentary of firms that integrate both financial and extra-financial narrative disclosures.

## Note

1 Companies operating in the United States provide narrative disclosures through the management discussion and analysis (MD&A) section of Form 10-K, while companies based in the United Kingdom and other countries provide information in the strategic report and business review section, the chairman's statement, or the CEO's letter to shareholders within the annual report. Therefore, we use the term "management commentary" to cover all companies operating in any country.

## References

Aerts, W. (2015). Narrative accounting disclosures, in C. Clubb and S. Imam eds, *Wiley Encyclopedia of Management* (John Wiley & Sons Ltd), 1–7. https://onlinelibrary .wiley.com/doi/abs/10.1002/9781118785317.weom010055.

Attig, N., Cleary, S., El Ghoul, S. and Guedhami, O. (2012). Institutional investment horizon and investment–cash flow sensitivity. *Journal of Banking and Finance*, 36(4), pp. 1164–1180.

Barron, O. E., Kile, C. O. and O'keefe, T. B. (1999). MD&A quality as measured by the SEC and analysts' earnings forecasts. *Contemporary Accounting Research*, 16(1), pp. 75–109.

Bonsall, S. B. and Miller, B. P. (2017). The impact of narrative disclosure readability on bond ratings and the cost of debt. *Review of Accounting Studies*, 22(2), pp. 608–643.

Bose, S., Khan, H. Z. and Monem, R. M. (2021a). Does green banking performance pay off? Evidence from a unique regulatory setting in Bangladesh. *Corporate Governance: An International Review*, 29(2), pp. 162–187.

Bose, S., Shams, S., Ali, M. J. and Mihret, D. (2021b). COVID-19 impact, sustainability performance and firm value: International evidence. https://doi.org/10.1111/acfi .12801.

Bose, S., Podder, J. and Biswas, K. K. (2017a). Philanthropic giving, market-based performance and institutional ownership: Evidence from an emerging economy. *The British Accounting Review*, 49(4), pp. 429–444.

Bose, S., Saha, A., Khan, H. Z. and Islam, S. (2017b). Non-financial disclosure and market-based firm performance: The initiation of financial inclusion. *Journal of Contemporary Accounting and Economics*, 13(3), pp. 263–281.

Botosan, C. A. (1997). Disclosure level and the cost of equity capital. *The Accounting Review*, 72(3), pp. 323–349.

Brown, S. V. and Tucker, J. W. (2011). Large-sample evidence on firms' year-over-year MD&A modifications. *Journal of Accounting Research*, 49(2), pp. 309–346.

Chang, X. S., Tan, W., Yang, E. and Zhang, W. (2018). Stock liquidity and corporate social responsibility. http://doi.org/10.2139/ssrn.3130572.

Chung, K. H. and Jo, H. (1996). The impact of security analysts' monitoring and marketing functions on the market value of firms. *Journal of Financial and Quantitative Analysis*, 31(4), pp. 493–512.

Cohen, J. R., Krishnamoorthy, G. and Wright, A. (2004). The corporate governance mosaic and financial reporting quality. *Journal of Accounting Literature*, 23, pp. 87–152.

Davis, A. K. and Tama-Sweet, I. (2012). Managers' use of language across alternative disclosure outlets: Earnings press releases versus MD&A. *Contemporary Accounting Research*, 29(3), pp. 804–837.

Dhaliwal, D. S., Li, O. Z., Tsang, A. and Yang, Y. G. (2014). Corporate social responsibility disclosure and the cost of equity capital: The roles of stakeholder orientation and financial transparency. *Journal of Accounting and Public Policy*, 33(4), pp. 328–355.

Durnev, A. and Mangen, C. (2020). The spillover effects of MD&A disclosures for real investment: The role of industry competition. *Journal of Accounting and Economics*, 70(1), pp. 1–19.

Global Reporting Initiative (GRI), Accounting for Sustainability (A4s) and Radley Yeldar. (2012). *The value of extra-financial disclosure: What investors and analysts said.* Available at: https://www.globalreporting.org/resourcelibrary/The-value-of-extra -financial-disclosure.pdf (accessed on 21 July 2021).

Goss, A. and Roberts, G. S. (2011). The impact of corporate social responsibility on the cost of bank loans. *Journal of Banking and Finance*, 35(7), pp. 1794–1810.

Gujarati, D. N. and Porter, D. C. (2009). *Basic econometrics*. McGraw-Hill Irwin, New York.

Hassanein, A., Marzouk, M. and Azzam, M. E. A. (2021). How does ownership by corporate managers affect R&D in the UK? The moderating impact of institutional investors. *International Journal of Productivity and Performance Management*. https://doi.org/10.1108/IJPPM-03-2020-0121.

Heckman, J. J. (1979). Sample selection bias as a specification error. *Econometrica*, 47(1), pp. 153–161.

International Accounting Standards Board (IASB). (2020). Management commentary. Available at: https://www.ifrs.org/projects/work-plan/management-commentary/#about (accessed on 20 July 2021).

Jensen, M. C. and Meckling, W. H. (1976). Theory of the firm: Managerial behavior, agency costs and ownership structure. *Journal of Financial Economics*, 3(4), pp. 305–360.

Kanagaretnam, K., Lobo, G. J. and Whalen, D. J. (2007). Does good corporate governance reduce information asymmetry around quarterly earnings announcements? *Journal of Accounting and Public Policy*, 26(4), pp. 497–522.

La Porta, R., Lopez-De-Silanes, F., Shleifer, A. and Vishny, R. W. (1998). Law and finance. *Journal of Political Economy*, 106(6), pp. 1113–1155.

Lang, M. H., Lins, K. V. and Miller, D. (2002). ADRs, analysts, and accuracy: Does cross listing in the United States improve a firm's information environment and increase marke value? *Journal of Accounting Research*, 41(2), pp. 317–345.

Leung, S., Parker, L. and Courtis, J. (2015). Impression management through minimal narrative disclosure in annual reports. *The British Accounting Review*, 47(3), pp. 275–289.

Leuz, C. and Verrecchia, R. E. (2000). The economic consequences of increased disclosure. *Journal of Accounting Research*, 38, pp. 91–124.

Mayew, W. J., Sethuraman, M. and Venkatachalam, M. (2015). MD&A disclosure and the firm's ability to continue as a going concern. *The Accounting Review*, 90(4), pp. 1621–1651.

Merkley, K. J. (2014). Narrative disclosure and earnings performance: Evidence from R&D disclosures. *The Accounting Review*, 89(2), pp. 725–757.

Merton, R. C. (1987). A simple model of capital market equilibrium with incomplete information. *The Journal of Finance*, 42(3), pp. 483–510.

Muslu, V., Radhakrishnan, S., Subramanyam, K. and Lim, D. (2015). Forward-looking MD&A disclosures and the information environment. *Management Science*, 61(5), pp. 931–948.

Roll, R., Schwartz, E. and Subrahmanyam, A. (2009). Options trading activity and firm valuation. *Journal of Financial Economics*, 94(3), pp. 345–360.

Sengupta, P. (1998). Corporate disclosure quality and the cost of debt. *The Accounting Review*, 73(4), pp. 459–474.

Wang, M. and Hussainey, K. (2013). Voluntary forward-looking statements driven by corporate governance and their value relevance. *Journal of Accounting and Public Policy*, 32(3), pp. 26–49.

# Part 3

# Narrative sustainability reporting

# 12 An exploratory study on climate-related financial disclosures

## International evidence

*Sudipta Bose and Amir Hossain*

## 12.1 Introduction

Climate change has been recognised as an imminent risk that needs to be addressed for the global economy's financial stability and resilience (Intergovernmental Panel on Climate Change (IPCC) 2014; Task Force on Climate-related Financial Disclosures (TCFD) 2017). Although climate changes constitute a natural phenomenon traceable to human actions in our planet's history (IPCC 2014),[1] the corporate sectors, as one of the major emitters of greenhouse gases (GHGs), have been identified as a critical climate change contributor (Kolk, Levy & Pinkse 2008; IPCC 2014). Globally, organisations emit around 70% of global aggregate greenhouse gas (GHG) emissions (The Guardian 2017).[2] The rapid increase in these emissions increases the concentrations of GHGs such as carbon dioxide and methane, which could bring social and financial disasters to the world economy by causing a further 2°C warming compared to the pre-industrial period (IPCC 2014). To mitigate the risk and impacts of climate change, 195 nations formed an agreement in 2015, known as the Paris Agreement, to hold the "increase in the global average temperature to well below 2°C above pre-industrial levels and to pursue efforts to limit the temperature increase to 1.5°C above pre-industrial levels" (United Nations 2015, p. 3).

Climate change causes extreme weather events, such as floods, cyclones, storms and droughts that can directly affect the value of assets as well as indirectly drive lower growth and returns on assets (Economist Intelligence Unit (EIU) 2015; Bernstein, Gustafson & Lewis 2019; Bolton & Kacperczyk 2020; Huynh, Nguyen & Truong 2020; Huynh & Xia 2020). These factors ultimately have substantial consequences for businesses, society and the economy at large. Moreover, the magnitude and long-term nature of climate change issues make them particularly difficult to address, especially with regard to financial decision making (TCFD 2017). Investors, lenders and other stakeholders therefore are demanding comprehensive climate-related financial information for efficient resource allocation and transition to the lower-carbon economy (Krueger, Sautner & Starks 2020; Painter 2020). In response, the Task Force on Climate-related Financial Disclosures (TCFD) was formed by the Financial Stability Board (FSB) in 2015, with the objective of addressing climate-related financial risks and opportunities

DOI: 10.4324/9781003095385-16

faced by companies worldwide. Companies across the world are supporting the TCFD, disseminating information on their climate change-related financial risks and opportunities through disclosures that include both costs and benefits.[3] However, to date, firm-level compliance with the TCFD framework at the global level is not known. The current study fills this gap in the literature.

In this study, we examine the extent of firm-level disclosure of climate-related financial information based on the TCFD framework. The framework covers four groups of the recommended disclosures: governance, strategy, risk management and metrics and targets. Our analysis is based on the companies' responses to the CDP (previously, Carbon Disclosure Project) climate change questionnaire because CDP has aligned its climate change questionnaire with the TCFD framework since the release of the framework in 2017. We adopt the content analysis technique to analyse the CDP climate change-related discretionary narrative disclosures to address our research question. Using 3,887 firm-year observations that responded to the CDP climate change questionnaire from CDP2019 to CDP2020 across 57 countries, we find that the level of climate-related financial disclosures has gradually increased after the issuance of the TCFD framework, indicating companies' commitment to recognising and integrating climate change risks and opportunities into their operations, with the objective of reducing their climate change footprint.

Our study contributes to the literature in several ways. To the best of our knowledge, this study is one of the first to examine the level of climate change-related disclosure based on the TCFD framework, using the cross-country context. Our study shows the current status of the extent of firm-level climate-related financial disclosures in line with this framework. The findings of the study help corporate management to integrate climate-related financial risks and opportunities in their governance, business strategy and business models to achieve economic efficiency and resilience in addressing potential climate change effects and the transition to the lower-carbon economy. Our findings also offer practical insights into companies' climate-related financial disclosure practices which may help investors, lenders, insurance underwriters, credit rating agencies, equity analysts and fund managers in assessing their investment risk and making informed economic decisions. Finally, the results of this study offer an insight into companies' climate-related financial disclosure practices for regulators, stock exchanges, governments, standard-setters and policymakers that may provide the grounds for a comprehensive disclosure policy to shape companies' climate change-related financial disclosure practices. This will aim to achieve financial stability and transition to the lower-carbon economy at national and supra-national levels.

## 12.2 Literature review

### 12.2.1 Background of the Task Force on Climate-related Financial Disclosures (TCFD)

A growing policy concern at governmental and regulatory levels worldwide is how companies are to manage the risks and opportunities resulting from climate change that may disrupt financial stability. Generally, a lack of information can prompt the mispricing of assets and misallocation of capital which may further increase concerns about financial stability. Therefore, the demand from investors for climate change-related financial risk information is growing in their attempts to make informed economic decisions (Christophers 2017; Eccles & Krzus 2017). Currently, several frameworks (e.g., CDP, Global Reporting Initiatives [GRI], United Nations Global Compact) are available on the market that incorporate environmental issues in corporate reporting, although no unique standard exists for measuring and disclosing climate-related financial information. However, investors need comprehensive information to assess and price climate change-related risks and opportunities when making their investment decisions (TCFD 2017). Perceiving these concerns, the Financial Stability Board (FSB), with the support of the G20 Finance Ministers and Central Bank Governors, established the TCFD with the objective of enhancing the transparency of climate change-related financial disclosures. The TCFD emphasises the importance of clear, comparable and consistent information on risks and opportunities arising from climate change, with this information not only assisting the efficient allocation of resources but also smoothing the path for transitioning to a lower-carbon economy (TCFD 2017).

The TCFD has issued four noteworthy recommendations on climate-related risks and opportunities that are applicable to any type of organisation, irrespective of its industry or jurisdiction, with these built on four thematic core elements of how organisations operate: strategy, governance, risk management and metrics and targets. Moreover, these four core recommendations are supported by 11 recommended disclosures that provide a more precise understanding to investors and other users with which to assess risks and opportunities arising from climate change under each core element. Figure 12.1 illustrates the core recommendations and supporting recommended disclosures for reporting climate-related risks and opportunities in accordance with the TCFD framework.

The TCFD highlighted that organisations should apply the principle of materiality in incorporating climate-related disclosures in their annual financial filings, as well as weighing the balance of the costs and benefits of generating these disclosures (TCFD 2017). The TCFD pointed out that its recommendations on climate-related disclosures aimed to leverage rather than replace existing disclosure frameworks (e.g., CDP, International Integrated Reporting Council [IIRC], GRI, and Sustainability Accounting Standards Board [SASB]). It also stated that its framework should not be treated as an additive disclosure framework over existing reporting frameworks, as it drew from them (TCFD 2017). The TCFD releases guidance to support all types of organisation to implement these recommendations, as well as issuing sector-specific supplemental guidelines (TCFD 2017).[4]

### 12.2.2 *Climate change-related risk and opportunities*

Climate change poses a significant financial risk to investors in the present and foreseeable future. The International Energy Agency (IEA) (2016) reported that the normal transition to a lower-carbon economy is estimated to require around

| Governance | Strategy | Risk Management | Metrics and Targets |
|---|---|---|---|
| Disclose the organization's governance around climate-related risks and opportunities | Disclose the actual and potential impacts of climate-related risks and opportunities on the organization's businesses, strategy, and financial planning where such information is material. | Disclose how the organization identifies, assesses, and manages climate-related risks. | Disclose the metrics and targets used to assess and manage relevant climate-related risks and opportunities where such information is material. |
| **Recommended Disclosures** | **Recommended Disclosures** | **Recommended Disclosures** | **Recommended Disclosures** |
| a) Describe the board's oversight of climate-related risks and opportunities. | a) Describe the climate-related risks and opportunities the organization has identified over the short, medium, and long term. | a) Describe the organization's processes for identifying and assessing climate-related risks. | a) Disclose the metrics used by the organization to assess climate-related risks and opportunities in line with its strategy and risk management process. |
| b) Describe management's role in assessing and managing climate-related risks and opportunities. | b) Describe the impact of climate-related risks and opportunities on the organization's businesses, strategy, and financial planning. | b) Describe the organization's processes for managing climate-related risks. | b) Disclose Scope 1, Scope 2, and, if appropriate, Scope 3 greenhouse gas (GHG) emissions, and the related risks. |
| | c) Describe the resilience of the organization's strategy, taking into consideration different climate-related scenarios, including a 2°C or lower scenario. | c) Describe how processes for identifying, assessing, and managing climate-related risks are integrated into the organization's overall risk management. | c) Describe the targets used by the organization to manage climate-related risks and opportunities and performance against targets. |

*Figure 12.1* TCFD (2017) recommendations and supporting recommended disclosures. Source: Task Force on Climate-related Financial Disclosures (TCFD). (2017). Recommendations of the Task Force on Climate-related Financial Disclosures. Available at: https://www.fsb-tcfd.org/wp-content/uploads/2017/06/FINAL-2017-TCFD-Report-11052018.pdf (accessed on 12 July 2021).

US$1 trillion of annual investments for a long time, creating new venture openings. The number of climate-related loss events has increased three-fold since the 1980s, for which insurance losses (about US$50 billion) have increased fivefold over the past decade (Carney 2015). According to the EIU (2015), the value of risks to the total global stock of manageable assets will range between US$4.2 trillion to US$43 trillion between now and the end of this century. The EIU (2015) also states that the impact on future resources comes not only through the causes of direct physical harm but also more broadly through weaker development and lower resource returns across the board. The nature of these problems is interconnected, indicating that, even if resources are not directly impacted by physical causes, climate change is likely to reduce return on assets (EIU 2015). Additionally, future returns are difficult to estimate at this moment due to the uncertain nature of climate change and a lack of data. However, to make informed economic decisions, investors, lenders and other stakeholders require comprehensive information on climate change-related financial disclosures to make their economic decisions (Bolton & Kacperczyk 2020; Huynh et al. 2020; Huynh & Xia 2020; Painter 2020).

The two main types of climate change risk identified by the TCFD are physical and transition risks that can substantially damage organisations' physical assets as well as their financial value. The TCFD breaks physical risks down into acute and chronic risks. Physical risks caused by climate change can arise from tropical tornados, droughts, wildfires, severe heatwaves, storms, floods and cyclones. All of these events have the potential to result in asset damage and destruction, operational interruptions, forced relocations, resource scarcity and, ultimately, increased costs and insurance liabilities, capital and labour losses and revenue and growth declines (Halkos & Skouloudis 2016; Christophers 2017; Hong, Li & Xu 2019). On the other hand, the transition risks of climate change are associated with transitioning to a lower-carbon economy. Transition risks may arise due to extensive changes in policy, legal, technology and market patterns that address mitigation and adaptation requirements related to climate change (Chava 2014; TCFD 2017; Fard, Javadi & Kim 2020). The TCFD divides transition risks into policy and legal, technology, market and reputation risks. Transition risks affect not only organisations' financial performance and/or position but also their reputational capital, which varies with the nature and magnitude of these risks.

The TCFD identified several areas of opportunities from climate change, such as increased resource efficiency through the innovation of technologies, low-emission energy sources (e.g., wind, solar, wave, tidal, hydro, geothermal, nuclear, biofuels and carbon capture and storage), and low-emission products and services. New market opportunities also arise through green bonds and infrastructure, including low-emission energy production, energy efficiency, grid connectivity and transport networks, as well as the enhancement of corporate resilience to cope with climate change. Figure 12.2 illustrates how climate-related risks and opportunities are likely to impact on an organisation's future financial position.

### 12.2.3 Previous studies

As found in the current literature, although a growing number of organisations has started to take a proactive stance on climate change and to incorporate climate change-related data more than at any time in the recent past, "numerous organisations generally remain latent, embracing a 'wait-and-see' attitude" (Elijido-Ten 2017, p. 958). Talbot and Boiral (2018) find that most companies disclosed opaque information, concealing their GHG emissions measurement method, and manipulating direct and indirect emissions data. Liesen et al. (2015) and Comyns (2016) also report that companies' climate change disclosures are insufficient for stakeholders to make economic decisions due to the low quality of information, despite the fact that companies disclosed significant amount of quantitative information. In a similar line of study, Comyns and Figge (2015) did not find any improvement in the quality of disclosures from 1998 to 2010. However, they find that larger companies disclose more quantitative information about GHG emissions than qualitative information. Momin, Northcott and Hossain (2017) found that carbon-intensive firms (power companies) do not disclose substantive climate risk-related information. They also found that organisations are occupied with a

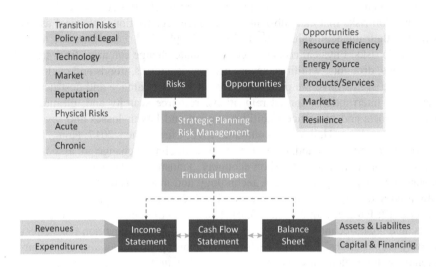

*Figure 12.2* Climate-related risks, opportunities and financial impact. Source: Task Force on Climate-related Financial Disclosures (TCFD). (2017). Recommendations of the Task Force on Climate-related Financial Disclosures. Available at: https://www.fsb-tcfd.org/wp-content/uploads/2017/06/FINAL-2017-TCFD -Report-11052018.pdf (accessed on 12 July 2021).

symbolic legitimacy attitude through uncovering their acknowledgement of risk identified with GHG emission discharges instead of revealing their endeavours to oversee such risks. Haque, Deegan and Inglis (2016) also showed that companies disclosed a low level of climate change-related exposures. Similarly, Talbot and Boiral (2015) provide evidence that companies have a tendency to disclose unreliable information, to minimise the impact of their activities and to blame others. Stakeholders are increasingly concerned about how companies manage their environmental responsibilities and the consistency of the data that they discover when evaluating an organisation's climate change performance (Liesen et al. 2015; Talbot & Boiral 2018). Furthermore, the existing climate change and sustainability reporting frameworks (e.g., CDP, GRI) failed to incorporate the financial implications of climate-related risk aspects of an organisation due to inconsistent, lack of context for information, use of boilerplate and non-comparable disclosures (TCFD 2017). Consequently, markets may fail to accurately assess and price the risks and opportunities arising from climate change due to the lack of appropriate and/or adequate information. This may result in a misallocation of resources that further increases concerns about organisations' financial stability as markets may not be readily able to adjust or correct the potential impacts of climate change (Carney 2015).

Therefore, investors, lenders and other stakeholders demand comprehensive climate-related financial information for efficient allocation of resources and transition to the lower-carbon economy. De Bernardi, Venuti and Bertello (2019) argue that companies and their board should not view disclosures in accordance with the TCFD recommendations as merely a "compliance" activity. Rather, it should be considered to be an effective response to the growing market demand for climate risk disclosure. Hence, we investigate the extent to which companies disclose climate-related financial information based on the four core recommendations of the TCFD framework, namely, governance, strategy, risk management and metrics and targets.

## 12.3  Research methodology

### *12.3.1  Samples and data*

The initial sample of this study comprises all the companies that responded to the CDP climate change questionnaire from CDP2019 to CDP2020. We select CDP2019 as this is the first period after the release of the TCFD framework, while CDP2020 is the most recent year with available data. We use the CDP climate change questionnaire as CDP has aligned its climate change questionnaire with the TCFD framework since the release of the framework in 2017.[5] We merge CDP data with Refinitiv (previously, Thomson Reuters) ESG database and the Worldscope database to identify publicly listed companies available on the CDP database. After merging these three databases and excluding missing market capitalisation and total assets data, the final sample size is 3,887 firm-year observations covering 1,860 firms in CDP2019 and 2,027 firms in CDP2020 across 57 countries.

Table 12.1 shows the industry distribution of companies in our study's sample. It shows that our sample is dominated by companies operating in the financial industry in both CDP2019 and CDP2020 (12.42% and 13.12%, respectively). This is not surprising given the TCFD's recognition of the financial sector's significant role in assessing climate-related issues and improving the pricing of climate risks and opportunities, thus leading to more informed business and capital allocation decisions (CDP 2020). Furthermore, we find that 36.74% of firms in our sample operate in carbon-sensitive industries, with 63.26% operating in carbon non-sensitive industries (unreported here).

Table 12.2 provides the country distribution of sample companies. It shows that our sample is dominated by companies from the United States (21.51% in CDP2019 and 19.73% in CDP2020), followed by Japan (13.17% in CDP2019 and 14.50% in CDP2020) and the United Kingdom (10.32% in CDP2019 and 9.47% in CDP2020), whereas several countries (such as Cyprus, Egypt, Guernsey, Indonesia, Kuwait, Malta, Panama, Papua New Guinea, Qatar and Uruguay) in our sample had the lowest number of observations (0.05%). Furthermore, the CDP ranks each company every year based on that company's responses to the climate change questionnaire. Table 12.3 shows the CDP climate change disclosure ranks for CDP2019 and CDP2020. Approximately 8.76% of sample companies received an A-rank for their climate change disclosures in CDP2019, whereas the figure rose to 11.84% in CDP2020. Moreover, about 32.53% of the companies

*Table 12.1* Industry distribution of sample companies

| Industry | CDP2019 | | CDP2020 | |
|---|---|---|---|---|
| | N | % | N | % |
| Mining/Construction | 115 | 6.18 | 125 | 6.17 |
| Food | 99 | 5.32 | 108 | 5.13 |
| Textiles/Print/Publishing | 70 | 3.76 | 73 | 3.60 |
| Chemicals | 97 | 5.22 | 111 | 5.48 |
| Pharmaceuticals | 55 | 2.96 | 58 | 2.86 |
| Extractive | 72 | 3.87 | 77 | 3.80 |
| Manufacturing: Rubber/glass/etc. | 45 | 2.42 | 49 | 2.42 |
| Manufacturing: Metal | 56 | 3.01 | 60 | 2.96 |
| Manufacturing: Machinery | 70 | 3.76 | 77 | 3.80 |
| Manufacturing: Electrical Equipment | 46 | 2.47 | 50 | 2.47 |
| Manufacturing: Transport Equipment | 78 | 4.19 | 88 | 4.34 |
| Manufacturing: Instruments | 50 | 2.68 | 56 | 2.76 |
| Manufacturing: Miscellaneous | 13 | 0.70 | 13 | 0.64 |
| Computers | 136 | 7.35 | 152 | 7.50 |
| Transportation | 165 | 8.87 | 177 | 8.73 |
| Utilities | 113 | 6.08 | 120 | 5.92 |
| Retail: Wholesale | 40 | 2.15 | 45 | 2.22 |
| Retail: Miscellaneous | 91 | 4.89 | 95 | 4.69 |
| Retail: Restaurant | 10 | 0.54 | 12 | 0.59 |
| Financial | 237 | 12.42 | 266 | 13.12 |
| Insurance/Real Estate | 74 | 3.98 | 84 | 4.14 |
| Services | 115 | 6.18 | 121 | 5.97 |
| Others | 13 | 0.70 | 14 | 0.69 |
| **Total** | **1,860** | **100** | **2,027** | **100** |

achieved a B-rank for their climate change disclosures, whereas the figure was 28.12% in CDP2020.

## 12.4 Discussion of findings

For our analyses, we apply the content analysis technique (Bose et al. 2017; Bose, Khan & Monem 2021; Khan et al. 2021) and employ two years of data, namely CDP2019 and CDP2020. In the following sub-sections, the extent of company-level disclosure of climate-related financial information is discussed, based on the four recommendations of the TCFD framework, namely, governance, strategy, risk management and metrics and targets.

### 12.4.1 Climate change-related governance disclosures

The first recommendation of the TCFD framework addresses governance. Under this recommendation, companies need to "disclose the organisation's governance around climate-related risk and opportunities". More specifically, the governance

*Table 12.2* Country distribution of sample companies

| Country | CDP2019 | | CDP2020 | | Country | CDP2019 | | CDP2020 | |
|---|---|---|---|---|---|---|---|---|---|
| | N | % | N | % | | N | % | N | % |
| Australia | 58 | 3.12 | 59 | 2.91 | Luxembourg | 3 | 0.16 | 4 | 0.20 |
| Austria | 14 | 0.75 | 17 | 0.84 | Malta | 1 | 0.05 | 1 | 0.05 |
| Belgium | 13 | 0.70 | 16 | 0.79 | Malaysia | 4 | 0.22 | 5 | 0.25 |
| Bermuda | 5 | 0.27 | 4 | 0.20 | Mexico | 14 | 0.75 | 19 | 0.94 |
| Brazil | 34 | 1.83 | 40 | 1.97 | Netherlands | 34 | 1.83 | 35 | 1.73 |
| Canada | 80 | 4.30 | 89 | 4.39 | New Zealand | 14 | 0.75 | 18 | 0.89 |
| Chile | 5 | 0.27 | 5 | 0.25 | Norway | 29 | 1.56 | 34 | 1.68 |
| China | 13 | 0.70 | 29 | 1.43 | Panama | 1 | 0.05 | 1 | 0.05 |
| Colombia | 7 | 0.38 | 6 | 0.30 | Papua New Guinea | 1 | 0.05 | – | – |
| Cyprus | 1 | 0.05 | 1 | 0.05 | Philippines | 8 | 0.43 | 7 | 0.35 |
| Czech Republic | 2 | 0.11 | 2 | 0.10 | Poland | 3 | 0.16 | 4 | 0.20 |
| Denmark | 16 | 0.86 | 22 | 1.09 | Portugal | 8 | 0.43 | 9 | 0.44 |
| Egypt | 1 | 0.05 | 1 | 0.05 | Qatar | 1 | 0.05 | 1 | 0.05 |
| Finland | 29 | 1.56 | 25 | 1.23 | Russia | 12 | 0.65 | 15 | 0.74 |
| France | 85 | 4.57 | 91 | 4.49 | Saudi Arabia | – | – | 2 | 0.10 |
| Germany | 72 | 3.87 | 75 | 3.70 | Singapore | 16 | 0.86 | 17 | 0.84 |
| Greece | 4 | 0.22 | 4 | 0.20 | South Africa | 56 | 3.01 | 50 | 2.47 |
| Guernsey | 1 | 0.05 | 1 | 0.05 | South Korea | 37 | 1.99 | 46 | 2.27 |
| Hong Kong | 18 | 0.97 | 24 | 1.18 | Spain | 40 | 2.15 | 43 | 2.12 |
| Hungry | 2 | 0.11 | 3 | 0.15 | Sweden | 43 | 2.31 | 47 | 2.32 |
| India | 35 | 1.88 | 37 | 1.83 | Switzerland | 51 | 2.74 | 52 | 2.57 |
| Indonesia | 1 | 0.05 | 1 | 0.05 | Taiwan | 53 | 2.85 | 58 | 2.86 |
| Ireland | 20 | 1.08 | 26 | 1.28 | Thailand | 13 | 0.70 | 15 | 0.74 |
| Isle of Man | – | – | 2 | 0.10 | Turkey | 21 | 1.13 | 26 | 1.28 |
| Israel | 2 | 0.11 | 3 | 0.15 | United Arab Emirates | 3 | 0.16 | 3 | 0.15 |
| Italy | 37 | 1.99 | 42 | 2.07 | United Kingdom | 192 | 10.32 | 192 | 9.47 |
| Japan | 245 | 13.17 | 294 | 14.50 | United States | 400 | 21.51 | 400 | 19.73 |
| Jersey | 2 | 0.11 | 2 | 0.10 | Uruguay | = | = | 1 | 0.05 |
| Kuwait | – | – | 1 | 0.05 | **Total** | **1,860** | **100** | **2,027** | **100** |

dimension of the TCFD framework seeks information as to whether the company has established a board-level oversight of climate-related issues, the position(s) of the individual(s) responsible on the board for dealing with these issues and the highest management-level position(s) or committee(s) with responsibility for such issues. Table 12.4 provides details of the number of companies with established board-level oversight of climate-related issues. We find that approximately 80.05% of companies responding to CDP2019 had established board-level oversight of climate-related issues, whereas this figure was 82.29% in CDP2020, indicating an upward trend over time of companies establishing board-level oversight of climate-related issues.

Table 12.5 shows the position(s) of the individual(s) on the board with the responsibility for climate-related issues. About 30.27% of companies had

*Table 12.3* CDP climate change disclosure rank of sample companies

| Rank | CDP2019 | | CDP2020 | |
|---|---|---|---|---|
| | N | % | N | % |
| A | 163 | 8.76 | 240 | 11.84 |
| A– | 267 | 14.35 | 422 | 20.82 |
| B | 605 | 32.53 | 570 | 28.12 |
| B– | 97 | 5.22 | 140 | 6.91 |
| C | 462 | 24.84 | 420 | 20.72 |
| C– | 2 | 0.11 | 5 | 0.25 |
| D | 234 | 12.58 | 202 | 9.97 |
| D– | 30 | 1.61 | 28 | 1.38 |
| **Total** | **1,860** | **100** | **2,027** | **100** |

*Table 12.4* Board-level oversight of climate-related issues

| | CDP2019 | | | CDP2020 | | |
|---|---|---|---|---|---|---|
| | N | Disclosed | % | N | Disclosed | % |
| Yes | 1,860 | 1,489 | 80.05 | 2,027 | 1,668 | 82.29 |
| No | 1,860 | 66 | 3.55 | 2,027 | 49 | 2.4217 |
| **Total** | | **1,555** | **83.6** | | **1,717** | **84.71** |

*Table 12.5* Position(s) of individual(s) on board with responsibility for climate-related issues

| | CDP2019 | | | CDP2020 | | |
|---|---|---|---|---|---|---|
| | N | Disclosed | % | N | Disclosed | % |
| Board Chair | 1,860 | 220 | 11.83 | 2,027 | 278 | 13.71 |
| Board-level Committee | 1,860 | 563 | 30.27 | 2,027 | 769 | 37.94 |
| Chief Executive Officer (CEO) | 1,860 | 561 | 30.16 | 2,027 | 687 | 33.89 |
| Chief Financial Officer (CFO) | 1,860 | 127 | 6.83 | 2,027 | 155 | 7.65 |
| Chief Operating Officer (COO) | 1,860 | 84 | 4.52 | 2,027 | 78 | 3.85 |
| Chief Procurement Officer (CPO) | 1,860 | 12 | 0.65 | 2,027 | 20 | 0.99 |
| Chief Risk Officer (CRO) | 1,860 | 46 | 2.47 | 2,027 | 49 | 2.42 |
| Chief Sustainability Officer (CSO) | 1,860 | 80 | 4.30 | 2,027 | 105 | 5.18 |
| Director on Board | 1,860 | 282 | 15.16 | 2,027 | 325 | 16.03 |
| President | 1,860 | 70 | 3.76 | 2,027 | 73 | 3.60 |
| Other C-suite Officer | 1,860 | 130 | 6.99 | 2,027 | 142 | 7.01 |
| Others | 1,860 | 328 | 17.63 | 2,027 | 281 | 13.86 |
| Questions not applicable | 1,860 | 68 | 3.66 | 2,027 | 53 | 2.61 |

board-level committees with this responsibility, followed by the Chief Executive Officer (CEO) (30.16%) in CDP2019, while these figures were 37.94% (board-level committee) and 33.89% (CEO) in CDP2020. The positions of various individuals on the board with the responsibility for climate-related issues included the board chair, Chief Financial Officer (CFO), Chief Operating Officer (COO), Chief Procurement Officer (CPO), Chief Risk Officer (CRO), Chief Sustainability Officer (CSO), board director and President, among others.

Furthermore, Table 12.6 provides the list of the highest management-level position(s) or committee(s) with responsibility for climate-related issues.

*Table 12.6* Highest management-level position(s) or committee(s) with responsibility for climate-related issues

| | CDP2019 | | | CDP2020 | | |
|---|---|---|---|---|---|---|
| | *N* | *Disclosed* | *%* | *N* | *Disclosed* | *%* |
| Business Unit Manager | 1,860 | 84 | 4.52 | 2,027 | 80 | 3.95 |
| Chief Executive Officer (CEO) | 1,860 | 487 | 26.18 | 2,027 | 681 | 33.60 |
| Chief Financial Officer (CFO) | 1,860 | 165 | 8.87 | 2,027 | 221 | 10.90 |
| Chief Investment Officer (CIO) | – | – | – | 2,027 | 14 | 0.69 |
| Chief Operating Officer (COO) | 1,860 | 160 | 8.60 | 2,027 | 162 | 7.99 |
| Chief Procurement Officer (CPO) | 1,860 | 29 | 1.56 | 2,027 | 30 | 1.48 |
| Chief Risk Officer (CRO) | 1,860 | 126 | 6.77 | 2,027 | 170 | 8.39 |
| Chief Sustainability Officer (CSO) | 1,860 | 270 | 14.52 | 2,027 | 319 | 15.74 |
| CSR/Sustainability Committee | 1,860 | 415 | 22.31 | 2,027 | 487 | 24.03 |
| Energy Manager | 1,860 | 44 | 2.37 | 2,027 | 41 | 2.02 |
| Environment/ Sustainability Manager | 1,860 | 194 | 10.43 | 2,027 | 195 | 9.62 |
| Environment, Health and Safety Manager | 1,860 | 176 | 9.46 | 2,027 | 172 | 8.49 |
| Facility Manager | – | – | – | 2,027 | 42 | 2.07 |
| Other C-suite Officer | – | – | – | 2,027 | 542 | 26.74 |
| Other Committee | – | – | – | 2,027 | 258 | 12.73 |
| Others | 1,860 | 1,384 | 74.41 | 2,027 | 799 | 39.42 |
| President | 1,860 | 78 | 4.19 | 2,027 | 95 | 4.69 |
| Process Operation Manager | 1,860 | 12 | 0.65 | 2,027 | 11 | 0.54 |
| Procurement Manager | 1,860 | 13 | 0.70 | 2,027 | 17 | 0.84 |
| Risk Committee | 1,860 | 158 | 8.49 | 2,027 | 164 | 8.09 |
| Risk Manager | 1,860 | 38 | 2.04 | 2,027 | 34 | 1.68 |
| No Committee | 1,860 | 3 | 0.16 | 2,027 | 3 | 0.15 |

Approximately 26.18% of companies in our sample had the CEO being responsible for climate-related issues, followed by the corporate social responsibility (CSR)/ sustainability committee (22.31%) in CDP2019. The corresponding figures were 33.60% (CEO) and 24.03% (CSR/sustainability committee) in CDP2020, suggesting that a similar upward trend was observed over the sample period. Overall, the findings show an upward trend of board-level oversight of climate-related issues over the sample period.

### 12.4.2 *Climate change-related strategy disclosures*

The second recommendation of the TCFD framework addresses strategy. Under this dimension, companies need to "disclose the actual and potential impacts of climate-related risks and opportunities on the organisation's businesses, strategy and financial planning where such information is material". More specifically, the strategy dimension of the TCFD framework seeks information on whether the company has strategies relating to the identification of climate-related risks and opportunities. In addition, the framework seeks responses on whether the company has strategies on how to deal with these risks and opportunities over the short, medium and long terms, with the potential to have a substantive financial or strategic impact on the business. The TCFD also recommends and strongly encourages companies to incorporate climate-related scenario analysis in this dimension to demonstrate possible future financial impacts of climate-related issues. As shown in Table 12.7, approximately 84.03% of companies had defined climate change risks and opportunities as having short-, medium- or long-term horizons in CDP2019, while the corresponding figure was 84.71% in CDP2020. Of interest is the fact that all disclosing companies identified and recognised the importance of climate change risks and opportunities over those periods in which they incorporated them into their business strategy, which is promising when seeking to transition to an economy that is lower carbon and sustainable.

Furthermore, Table 12.8, Panel A shows that about 72.42% and 76.61% of companies in our sample in CDP2019 have identified climate-related risks and opportunities, respectively, over the short-, medium- and long-term periods with the potential to have a substantive financial or strategic impact on the business, whereas the figures (as shown in Table 12.8, Panel B) were 74.30% (climate-related risks) and 78.59% (climate-related opportunities) in CDP2020. Table 12.8,

*Table 12.7* Short-, medium- and long-term horizons

|  | CDP2019 | | | CDP2020 | | |
|---|---|---|---|---|---|---|
|  | N | Disclosed | % | N | | % |
| Short-term horizon | 1,860 | 1563 | 84.03 | 2,027 | 1,717 | 84.71 |
| Medium-term horizon | 1,860 | 1563 | 84.03 | 2,027 | 1,717 | 84.71 |
| Long-term horizon | 1,860 | 1563 | 84.03 | 2,027 | 1,717 | 84.71 |

*Table 12.8* Identification of climate-related risks and opportunities

**Panel A: Climate-related risks and opportunities: disclosure related to CDP2019**

| | CDP2019 | | | | | |
| | Climate-related risks | | | Climate-related opportunities | | |
| | N | Disclosed | % | N | Disclosed | % |
|---|---|---|---|---|---|---|
| Yes | 1,860 | 1,347 | 72.42 | 1,860 | 1,425 | 76.61 |
| No | 1,860 | 207 | 11.13 | 1,860 | 128 | 6.88 |
| **Total** | | **1,554** | **83.55** | | **1,556** | 83.66 |

**Panel B: Climate-related risks and opportunities: disclosure related to CDP2020**

| | CDP2020 | | | | | |
| | Climate-related risks | | | Climate-related opportunities | | |
| | N | Disclosed | % | N | Disclosed | % |
|---|---|---|---|---|---|---|
| Yes | 2,027 | 1,506 | 74.30 | 2,027 | 1,593 | 78.59 |
| No | 2,027 | 209 | 10.31 | 2,027 | 120 | 5.92 |
| **Total** | | **1,715** | **84.61** | | **1,737** | **85.69** |

**Panel C: Integration of climate-related issues with business strategy**

| | CDP2019 | | | CDP2020 | | |
| | N | Disclosed | % | N | Disclosed | % |
|---|---|---|---|---|---|---|
| Yes | 1,860 | 1,482 | 79.68 | 2,027 | 1,661 | 81.94 |
| No | 1,860 | 73 | 3.92 | 2,027 | 54 | 2.66 |
| **Total** | | **1,555** | **83.60** | | **1,715** | **84.61** |

Panel C shows that, in CDP2019, approximately 79.68% of companies integrated climate-related issues with their business strategy, although the figure was 81.94% in CDP2020. Overall, this upward trend shows that companies in the sample had identified climate-related risks and opportunities over the sample period and had integrated climate-related issues with their business strategy.

Table 12.9 shows that about 32.22% of the companies in CDP2019 employed both qualitative and quantitative climate-related scenario analyses, whereas the figure was 32.46% in CDP2020. Furthermore, 6.12% and 13.66% of companies employed only quantitative or qualitative climate-related scenario analyses, respectively, in their business strategy in CDP2019, while the corresponding figures were 5.23% and 12.25%, respectively, in CDP2020. A significant proportion of companies in CDP2019 (32.09%) and CDP2020 (27.25%) reported that they had not employed any climate-related scenario analyses in their business strategy, but they expected to do so within the following two years. Moreover, 11.15% and 5.77% of companies had not used any climate-related scenario analyses in their

*Table 12.9* Climate-related scenario analysis

| | CDP2019 (N=1,860) | | CDP2020 (N=2,027) | |
|---|---|---|---|---|
| | Disclosed | % | Disclosed | % |
| Yes – qualitative and quantitative | 500 | 32.22 | 658 | 32.46 |
| Yes – quantitative | 95 | 6.12 | 106 | 5.23 |
| Yes – qualitative | 212 | 13.66 | 210 | 12.25 |
| No, but anticipate doing so in the next two years | 498 | 32.09 | 467 | 27.25 |
| No, and do not anticipate doing so in the next two years | 173 | 11.15 | 117 | 5.77 |
| Questions not applicable | 74 | 4.77 | 56 | 2.76 |
| **Total** | **1,552** | **83.44** | **1,714** | **84.56** |

business strategy in CDP2019 and CDP2020, and they mentioned that they did not expect to do so in the following two years. These results further supported the findings of Elijido-Ten (2017, p. 958) that "numerous organisations generally remain latent, embracing a 'wait-and-see' attitude".

Table 12.10, Panel A shows that, in CDP2019, 95.48% and 66.45% of companies had identified that climate-related risks would increase their indirect (operating) and direct costs, respectively, over the short-, medium- and long-term periods, with the potential to have a substantive financial or strategic impact on the business, whereas the corresponding figures were 68.92% and 59.30%, respectively, in CDP2020. The other types of financial impact from climate-related risks comprised increased capital expenditures, credit risks, insurance claims liability, decreased revenues, access to capital and assets value.

Furthermore, Table 12.10, Panel B shows that, in CDP2019, 78.82% of companies had identified increased revenue resulting from increased demand for products and services as a financial impact of climate-related opportunities, whereas the figure was 99.26% in CDP2020. Moreover, a significant percentage of companies in CDP2019 and CDP2020 also identified reduced direct costs (32.90% and 24.96%, respectively) and reduced indirect costs (53.71% and 47.21%, respectively), as a financial impact of climate-related opportunities. The other types of financial impact from climate-related opportunities consisted of increased revenue through access to new and emerging markets and increased production capacity, increased access to capital, greater value of fixed assets and diversification of financial assets, increased portfolio value and increased returns on investment (ROI) in low-emission technologies.

### 12.4.3 Climate change-related risk management disclosures

The third recommendation of the TCFD framework addresses risk management. Under this dimension, companies need to "disclose how the organization identifies,

*Table 12.10* Different types of financial impact of identified climate-related risks and opportunities

**Panel A: Different types of financial impact of identified climate-related risks**

| | CDP2019 (N=1,860) | | CDP2020 (N=2,027) | |
|---|---|---|---|---|
| | Disclosed | % | Disclosed | % |
| Increased direct costs | 1,236 | 66.45 | 1,202 | 59.30 |
| Increased indirect (operating) costs | 1,776 | 95.48 | 1,397 | 68.92 |
| Increased capital expenditure | 292 | 15.70 | 405 | 19.98 |
| Increased credit risk | 115 | 6.18 | 143 | 7.05 |
| Increased insurance claims liability | 89 | 4.78 | 139 | 6.86 |
| Decreased revenue due to reduced demand for products and services | 464 | 24.95 | 1,087 | 53.63 |
| Decreased revenue due to reduced production capacity | 641 | 34.46 | 768 | 37.89 |
| Decreased access to capital | 99 | 5.32 | 127 | 6.27 |
| Decreased asset value or asset useful life leading to write-offs, asset impairment or early retirement of existing assets | 115 | 6.18 | 148 | 7.30 |
| Reduced profitability of investment portfolios | – | – | 29 | 1.43 |
| Other | 841 | 45.22 | 355 | 17.51 |
| Questions not applicable | – | | 282 | 13.91 |

**Panel B: Different types of financial impact of identified climate-related opportunities**

| | CDP2019 (N=1,860) | | CDP2020 (N=2,027) | |
|---|---|---|---|---|
| | Disclosed | % | Disclosed | % |
| Reduced direct costs | 612 | 32.90 | 506 | 24.96 |
| Reduced indirect (operating) costs | 999 | 53.71 | 957 | 47.21 |
| Increased revenue resulting from increased demand for products and services | 1466 | 78.82 | 2,012 | 99.26 |
| Increased revenue through access to new and emerging markets | 248 | 13.33 | 606 | 29.90 |
| Increased revenue resulting from increased production capacity | 56 | 3.01 | 104 | 5.13 |
| Increased access to capital | 19 | 1.02 | 112 | 5.53 |
| Increased value of fixed assets | 29 | 1.56 | 37 | 1.83 |
| Increased diversification of financial assets | 91 | 4.89 | 73 | 3.60 |
| Increased portfolio value due to upward revaluation of assets | – | – | 20 | 0.99 |
| Returns on investment in low-emission technology | 144 | 7.74 | 246 | 12.14 |
| Questions not applicable | 179 | 9.62 | 201 | 9.92 |
| Others | 1,162 | 62.47 | 445 | 21.95 |

*Table 12.11* Processes for integrating climate-related risks into organisation's overall risk
management

|  | CDP2019 (N=1,860) | | CDP2020 (N=2,027) | |
|---|---|---|---|---|
|  | Disclosed | % | Disclosed | % |
| Integrated into multidisciplinary company-wide risk identification, assessment and management processes | 1,391 | 74.79 | 1,965 | 96.94 |
| A specific climate change risk identification, assessment and management process | 97 | 5.22 | 356 | 17.56 |
| No documented processes for identifying, assessing and managing climate-related issues | 61 | 3.28 | 62 | 3.06 |

assesses and manages climate-related risks." More specifically, the risk management dimension of the TCFD framework seeks information on the organisation's
integration of processes for identifying, assessing and managing climate-related
risks into the organisation's overall risk management, the frequency and time
horizon for identifying and assessing climate-related risks, and the types of risks
in their assessment of climate-related risks. Table 12.11 shows that, in CDP2019,
74.79% of companies disclosed that they integrated climate-related risk into multidisciplinary company-wide risk identification, assessment and management
processes, whereas the figure was 96.94% in CDP2020. Furthermore, 5.22% and
17.56% of companies in CDP2019 and CDP2020, respectively, mentioned only a
specific climate change risk identification, assessment and management process.[6]

Table 12.12, Panel A shows that approximately 21.18% and 36.75% of companies in CDP2019 and CDP2020, respectively, identified and assessed climate-related
risks annually, whereas 57.42% of companies in CDP2019 identified and assessed
climate-related issues every six months or more frequently, and 70.25% of companies in CDP2020 identified and assessed climate-related issues more than once
a year. Moreover, 58.98% of companies had a time horizon of more than six years
for identifying and assessing climate-related risks in CDP2019, as shown in Table
12.12, Panel B. In CDP2020, 79.87% of companies mentioned that they used short-,
medium- and long-term horizons for identifying and assessing climate-related risks.[7]

Table 12.13 shows that 84.03% and 84.71% of companies in CDP2019 and
CDP2020, respectively, identified various types of risks in their climate-related
risk assessments. These types of risks comprised acute physical, chronic physical,
current regulation, emerging regulation, legal, market, reputation, technology and
downstream and upstream risks.

### 12.4.4 Climate change-related metric and target disclosures

The final recommendation of the TCFD framework addresses metrics and
targets. Under this dimension, companies need to "disclose the metrics and

*Table 12.12* Frequency and time horizon for identifying and assessing climate-related risks

*Panel A: Frequency for identifying and assessing climate-related risks*

| | CDP2019 | | | CDP2020 | | |
|---|---|---|---|---|---|---|
| | N | Disclosed | % | N | Disclosed | % |
| Annually | 1,860 | 394 | 21.18 | 2,027 | 745 | 36.75 |
| Every two years | 1,860 | 11 | 0.59 | 2,027 | 27 | 1.33 |
| Every three years or more | – | – | – | 2,027 | 41 | 2.02 |
| More than once a year | – | – | – | 2,027 | 1,424 | 70.25 |
| Never | 1,860 | 1 | 0.05 | 2,027 | – | – |
| Not defined | 1,860 | 12 | 0.65 | 2,027 | 71 | 3.50 |
| Questions not applicable | 1,860 | 68 | 3.66 | 2,027 | 62 | 3.06 |
| Six months or more frequently | 1,860 | 1,068 | 57.42 | 2,027 | – | – |

*Panel B: Time horizon for identifying and assessing climate-related risk*

| | CDP2019 (N=1,860) | | | CDP2020 (N=2,027) | |
|---|---|---|---|---|---|
| | Disclosed | % | | Disclosed | % |
| 1–3 years | 148 | 9.52 | Short-term | 115 | 5.67 |
| 3–6 years | 209 | 11.24 | Medium-term | 87 | 4.29 |
| More than 6 years | 1,097 | 58.98 | Long-term | 104 | 5.13 |
| Not applicable | 68 | 3.66 | Not applicable | 62 | 3.06 |
| Unknown | 14 | 0.75 | All three terms | 1,619 | 79.87 |
| Up to 1 year | 18 | 0.97 | Combination of terms[8] | 395 | 19.49 |

targets used to assess and manage relevant climate-related risks and opportunities where such information is material". More specifically, the metric and target disclosure dimension of the TCFD framework seeks information on the targets and metrics used by companies for managing climate-related risks and opportunities and their performance against targets. As shown in Table 12.14, Panel A, in CDP2019, 26.24% of companies reported an absolute GHG emissions target followed by 26.24% of companies reporting an emissions intensity target, whereas these figures were 29.90% (absolute GHG emissions target) and 22.40% (emissions intensity target) in CDP2020. Moreover, in CDP2019 and CDP2020, 19.36% and 20.62% of companies, respectively, reported both absolute GHG emissions and emissions intensity targets. Table 12.14, Panel B shows that about 83.17% of companies disclosed Scope 1 GHG emissions data

*Table 12.13* Types of risk considered in climate-related risk assessments

|  | CDP2019 | | | CDP2020 | | |
|---|---|---|---|---|---|---|
|  | N | Disclosed | % | N | Disclosed | % |
| Acute physical | 1,860 | 1,563 | 84.03 | 2,027 | 1,717 | 84.71 |
| Chronic physical | 1,860 | 1,563 | 84.03 | 2,027 | 1,717 | 84.71 |
| Current regulation | 1,860 | 1,563 | 84.03 | 2,027 | 1,717 | 84.71 |
| Downstream | 1,860 | 1,563 | 84.03 | – | – | – |
| Emerging regulation | 1,860 | 1,563 | 84.03 | 2,027 | 1,717 | 84.71 |
| Legal | 1,860 | 1,563 | 84.03 | 2,027 | 1,717 | 84.71 |
| Market | 1,860 | 1,563 | 84.03 | 2,027 | 1,717 | 84.71 |
| Reputation | 1,860 | 1,563 | 84.03 | 2,027 | 1,717 | 84.71 |
| Technology | 1,860 | 1,563 | 84.03 | 2,027 | 1,717 | 84.71 |
| Upstream | 1,860 | 1,563 | 84.03 | – | – | – |

*Table 12.14* Active carbon emissions target and disclosure of global GHG emissions

*Panel A: Disclosure of gross global Scope 1 and 2 emissions in metric tons $CO_2e$*

|  | CDP2019 | | | CDP2020 | | |
|---|---|---|---|---|---|---|
|  | N | Disclosed | % | N | Disclosed | % |
| Absolute target | 1,860 | 488 | 26.24 | 2,027 | 606 | 29.90 |
| Intensity target | 1,860 | 488 | 26.24 | 2,027 | 454 | 22.40 |
| Both absolute and intensity targets | 1,860 | 360 | 19.36 | 2,027 | 418 | 20.62 |
| No target | 1,860 | 219 | 11.77 | 2,027 | 239 | 11.79 |
| **Total** |  | **1,555** | **83.60** |  | **1,717** | **84.71** |

*Panel B: Disclosure of gross global Scope 1 and 2 emissions in metric tons CO2e*

|  | CDP2019 | | | CDP2020 | | |
|---|---|---|---|---|---|---|
|  | N | Disclosed | % | N | Disclosed | % |
| Scope 1 | 1,860 | 1,547 | 83.17 | 2,027 | 1,704 | 84.07 |
| Scope 2 | 1,860 | 1,472 | 79.14 | 2,027 | 1,627 | 80.27 |

Note: $CO_2e$ = carbon dioxide-equivalents

in CDP2019, whereas the figure was 84.07% in CDP2020. Furthermore, 79.14% of companies disclosed Scope 2 GHG emissions data in CDP2019, compared with 80.27% in CDP2020.

Furthermore, Table 12.15 reports the disclosure of global Scope 3 GHG emissions data. Scope 3 GHG emissions cover a variety of sources of emissions, with relevant sources listed in Table 12.15. Among the more prominent sources of

*Table 12.15* Disclosure of gross global Scope 3 emissions in metric tons $CO_2e$

| | CDP2019 (N=1,860) | CDP2020 (N=2,027) | CDP2019 (N=1,860) | CDP2020 (N=2,027) | CDP2019 (N=1,860) | CDP2020 (N=2,027) |
|---|---|---|---|---|---|---|
| | *Relevant and calculated* | | *Not relevant, calculated* | | *Relevant, not yet calculated* | |
| | % | % | % | % | % | % |
| Business travel | 58.83 | 61.83 | 7.19 | 8.02 | 7.03 | 7.08 |
| Capital goods | 24.91 | 31.73 | 2.25 | 2.92 | 18.46 | 15.89 |
| Downstream leased assets | 8.86 | 10.69 | 1.99 | 2.08 | 5.15 | 4.90 |
| Downstream transportation and distribution | 25.34 | 27.18 | 1.99 | 2.43 | 12.99 | 13.56 |
| Employee commuting | 36.61 | 42.82 | 6.28 | 7.03 | 16.16 | 14.60 |
| End-of-life treatment of sold products | 16.26 | 20.64 | 2.25 | 2.48 | 11.59 | 11.44 |
| Franchises | 3.60 | 4.01 | 1.72 | 1.93 | 2.36 | 1.98 |
| Fuel- and energy-related activities | 43.26 | 48.76 | 3.54 | 3.96 | 9.29 | 8.61 |
| Investments | 9.23 | 7.87 | 1.93 | 2.18 | 11.38 | 6.19 |
| Other (downstream) | 1.99 | 1.39 | 0.91 | 0.79 | 2.36 | 1.68 |
| Other (upstream) | 2.20 | 2.33 | 1.07 | 0.94 | 2.09 | 1.44 |
| Processing of sold products | 5.58 | 6.83 | 1.40 | 1.49 | 8.59 | 8.81 |
| Purchased goods and services | 47.77 | 53.42 | 1.83 | 1.58 | 18.30 | 16.63 |
| Upstream leased assets | 8.75 | 10.69 | 3.06 | 3.37 | 6.07 | 5.45 |
| Upstream transportation and distribution | 33.60 | 10.69 | 2.95 | 3.37 | 16.37 | 5.45 |
| Use of sold products | 22.60 | 26.04 | 0.91 | 0.84 | 12.29 | 12.77 |
| Waste generated in operations | 39.56 | 45.84 | 7.30 | 7.62 | 13.85 | 11.93 |

Note: $CO_2e$ = carbon dioxide-equivalents

Scope 3 GHG emissions are business travel, employee commuting, fuel and energy-related activities, purchases of goods and services, upstream transportation and distribution, use of sold products and waste generated in operations. Some 58.83% (61.83%) and 36.61% (42.82%) of companies disclosed their business travel and employee commuting emissions, respectively in CDP2019 (CDP2020)

*Table 12.16* Other types of climate-related metrics

| | CDP2019 | | | CDP2020 | | |
|---|---|---|---|---|---|---|
| | N | Disclosed | % | N | Disclosed | % |
| Energy usage | 1,860 | 310 | 16.67 | 2,027 | 390 | 19.24 |
| Land use | 1,860 | 19 | 1.02 | 2,027 | 37 | 1.83 |
| Other | 1,860 | 443 | 23.82 | 2,027 | 475 | 23.43 |
| Waste | 1,860 | 489 | 26.29 | 2,027 | 580 | 28.61 |
| Water | 1,860 | 115 | 6.18 | 2,027 | 167 | 8.24 |

whereas 43.26% (48.76%) of companies disclosed their fuel and energy-related emissions in CDP2019 (CDP2020). The other types of Scope 3 emissions data are provided in Table 12.15.

Table 12.16 shows that 26.29% (23.82%) of companies reported waste ('Other' type) in CDP2019, whereas the figures were 28.61% (23.43%) in CDP2020. Furthermore, 16.67% of companies disclosed energy usage as an 'Other' type of climate-related metrics, whereas the corresponding figure was 19.24% in CDP2020.

## 12.5 Conclusion

In this study, we examine the extent of firm-level disclosure of climate-related financial information, based on the TCFD recommendations. We find that the level of climate-related financial disclosures has gradually increased after the issuance of the TCFD framework in 2017, through our study of companies that responded to the CDP climate change questionnaire from CDP2019 to CDP2020 across 57 countries. The study's findings offer an insight into companies' climate-related financial disclosure practices to regulators, policymakers and standard-setters that will facilitate the creation of a comprehensive disclosure policy to shape organisations' climate-related financial disclosure practices for long-term financial stability.

For reasons of brevity, we cannot cover all the items available in the CDP climate change disclosure questionnaire in our study of compliance with the TCFD framework. This is one of our study's limitations. Future studies could develop a composite climate-related financial disclosures score, following the TCFD framework, for each company, based on its responses to the CDP climate change questionnaire. Future studies could also examine the firm-level and country-level determinants for the company's adoption of the TCFD framework and the extent of its disclosures in line with the framework. Notwithstanding these limitations, our study contributes to the literature by examining the extent of firm-level disclosures of climate-related financial information.

## Notes

1  Carney (2015, p.2) states that "evidence is mounting of man's role in climate change. Human drivers are judged extremely likely to have been the dominant cause of global

warming since the mid-20th century. While natural fluctuations may mask it temporarily, the underlying human-induced warming trend of two-tenths of a degree per decade has continued unabated since the 1970s".

2 However, a solution for dealing with climate change-related risks cannot be found without the involvement of these organisations. Gray (2010, p.57) argues that "any solution to the exigencies of sustainability must involve corporations as no other solutions are feasible".

3 For details, see https://www.fsb-tcfd.org/tcfd-supporters/ (accessed on 20 July 2021).

4 Two supplemental guidelines are issued for dealing with the financial sector (e.g., banks, insurance companies, asset owners, asset managers) and non-financial sectors (e.g., energy, transportation, materials and buildings and agriculture, food and forest products), with the non-financial sectors being those most severely affected by climate change.

5 CDP2019 corresponds to the fiscal year 2018, while CDP2020 corresponds to the fiscal year 2019.

6 Processes for integrating climate-related risks into the organisation's overall risk management are based on value-chain stages that include direct operations, downstream and upstream.

7 The frequency and time horizon for identifying and assessing climate-related risks are based on value-chain stages that include direct operations, downstream and upstream.

8 Combination of terms means: long term and medium term; medium term and short term; or long term and short term.

# References

Bernstein, A., Gustafson, M. T. and Lewis, R. (2019). Disaster on the horizon: The price effect of sea level rise. *Journal of Financial Economics*, 134(2), pp. 253–272.

Bolton, P. and Kacperczyk, M. (2020). Do investors care about carbon risk? *Journal of Financial Economics*. https://doi.org/10.1016/j.jfineco.2021.05.008.

Bose, S., Khan, H. Z. and Monem, R. M. (2021). Does green banking performance pay off? Evidence from a unique regulatory setting in Bangladesh. *Corporate Governance: An International Review*, 29(2), pp. 162–187.

Bose, S., Saha, A., Khan, H. Z. and Islam, S. (2017). Non-financial disclosure and market-based firm performance: The initiation of financial inclusion. *Journal of Contemporary Accounting & Economics*, 13(3), pp. 263–281.

Carney, M. (2015). Breaking the tragedy of the horizon—Climate change and financial stability. Available at: https://www.climatealliance.org.au/blog/2015/breaking-the -tragedy-of-the-horizon-climate-change-and-financial-stability-speech-by-mark -carney (accessed on 10 July 2021).

CDP. (2020). Disclosing in line with the TCFD's recommendations in 2020. Available at: https://www.tcfdhub.org/resource/cdp-technical-note-on-the-tcfd/ (accessed on 16 July 2021).

Chava, S. (2014). Environmental externalities and cost of capital. *Management Science*, 60(9), pp. 2223–2247.

Christophers, B. (2017). Climate change and financial instability: Risk disclosure and the problematics of neoliberal governance. *Annals of the American Association of Geographers*, 107(5), pp. 1108–1127.

Comyns, B. (2016). Determinants of GHG reporting: An analysis of global oil and gas companies. *Journal of Business Ethics*, 136(2), pp. 349–369.

Comyns, B. and Figge, F. (2015). Greenhouse gas reporting quality in the oil and gas industry. *Accounting, Auditing & Accountability Journal*, 28(3), pp. 403–433.

De Bernardi, P., Venuti, F. and Bertello, A. (2019). The relevance of climate change related risks on corporate financial and non-financial disclosure in Italian listed companies. *In:* Vincentiis, P. D., Culasso, F. and Cerrato, S. A. (eds.) *The future of risk management, volume I: Perspectives on law, healthcare, and the environment.* Cham, Switzerland: Palgrave Macmillan, pp. 77–107.

Eccles, R. G. and Krzus, M. P. (2017). An analysis of oil & gas company disclosures from the perspective of the task force on climate-related financial disclosures. http://doi.org /10.2139/ssrn.3091232.

Economist Intelligence Unit (EIU). (2015). The cost of inaction: Recognising the value at risk from climate change. Available at: https://eiuperspectives.economist.com/ sustainability/cost-inaction (accessed on 17 July 2021).

Elijido-Ten, E. O. (2017). Does recognition of climate change related risks and opportunities determine sustainability performance? *Journal of Cleaner Production*, 141, pp. 956–966.

Fard, A., Javadi, S. and Kim, I. (2020). Environmental regulation and the cost of bank loans: International evidence. *Journal of Financial Stability*, 51, p. 100797.

Gray, R. (2010). Is accounting for sustainability actually accounting for sustainability… and how would we know? An exploration of narratives of organisations and the planet. *Accounting, Organizations & Society*, 35(1), pp. 47–62.

Halkos, G. and Skouloudis, A. (2016). Exploring the current status and key determinants of corporate disclosure on climate change: Evidence from the Greek business sector. *Environmental Science & Policy*, 56, pp. 22–31.

Haque, S., Deegan, C. and Inglis, R. (2016). Demand for, and impediments to, the disclosure of information about climate change-related corporate governance practices. *Accounting & Business Research*, 46(6), pp. 620–664.

Hong, H., Li, F. W. and Xu, J. (2019). Climate risks and market efficiency. *Journal of Econometrics*, 208(1), pp. 265–281.

Huynh, T. D., Nguyen, T. H. and Truong, C. (2020). Climate risk: The price of drought. *Journal of Corporate Finance*, 65, pp. 1–26.

Huynh, T. D. and Xia, Y. (2020). Climate change news risk and corporate bond returns. *Journal of Financial & Quantitative Analysis*, pp. 1–25, https://doi.org/10.1017/ S0022109020000757.

Intergovernmental Panel on Climate Change (IPCC). (2014). Synthesis report. Available at: https://www.ipcc.ch/report/ar5/syr/ (accessed on 12 June 2021).

International Energy Agency (IEA). (2016). Global energy investment down 8% in 2015 with flows signaling move towards cleaner energy. Available at: https://www.iea.org /news/global-energy-investment-down-8-in-2015-with-flows-signalling-move-towards -cleaner-energy (accesed on 15 June 2021).

Khan, H. Z., Bose, S., Mollik, A. T. and Harun, H. (2021). "Green washing" or "authentic effort"? An empirical investigation of the quality of sustainability reporting by banks. *Accounting, Auditing & Accountability Journal*, 34(2), pp. 338–369.

Kolk, A., Levy, D. and Pinkse, J. (2008). Corporate responses in an emerging climate regime: The institutionalization and commensuration of carbon disclosure. *European Accounting Review*, 17(4), pp. 719–745.

Krueger, P., Sautner, Z. and Starks, L. T. (2020). The importance of climate risks for institutional investors. *Review of Financial Studies*, 33(3), pp. 1067–1111.

Liesen, A., Hoepner, A. G., Patten, D. M. and Figge, F. (2015). Does stakeholder pressure influence corporate GHG emissions reporting? Empirical evidence from Europe. *Accounting, Auditing & Accountability Journal*, 28(7), pp. 1047–1074.

Momin, M. A., Northcott, D. and Hossain, M. (2017). Greenhouse gas disclosures by Chinese power companies: Trends, content and strategies. *Journal of Accounting & Organizational Change*, 13(3), pp. 331–358.

Painter, M. (2020). An inconvenient cost: The effects of climate change on municipal bonds. *Journal of Financial Economics*, 135(2), pp. 468–482.

Talbot, D. and Boiral, O. (2015). Strategies for climate change and impression management: A case study among Canada's large industrial emitters. *Journal of Business Ethics*, 132(2), pp. 329–346.

Talbot, D. and Boiral, O. (2018). GHG reporting and impression management: An assessment of sustainability reports from the energy sector. *Journal of Business Ethics*, 147(2), pp. 367–383.

Task Force on Climate-Related Financial Disclosures (TCFD). (2017). Recommendations of the task force on climate-related financial disclosures. Available at: https://www .fsb-tcfd.org/wp-content/uploads/2017/06/FINAL-2017-TCFD-Report-11052018.pdf (accessed on 12 July 2021).

The Guardian. (2017). Just 100 companies responsible for 71% of global emissions. Available at: https://www.theguardian.com/sustainable-business/2017/jul/10/100 -fossil-fuel-companies-investors-responsible-71-global-emissions-cdp-study-climate -change (accessed on 17 July 2021).

United Nations. (2015). Paris agreement. Available at: http://unfccc.int/files/essential _background/convention/application/pdf/english_paris_agreement.pdf (accessed on 15 July 2021).

# 13 Corporate social and environmental responsibility disclosure

## A literature review with a particular emphasis on China and social media disclosure

*Jiaxu Du, Mahmoud Marzouk and Fatima Yusuf*

### 13.1 The concept of corporate social and environmental responsibility (CSER)

The origins of the social component in enterprise operations can be dated back to ancient Roman Law (Chaffee, 2017), while the origins of modern corporate social responsibility (CSR) can be traced back to as early as the 1930s (Barnard, 1938). However, the modern concept of CSR was first presented by Bowen (1953) where he defined CSR as "obligations of business to pursue those policies, to make those decisions or to follow those lines of action which are desirable in terms of the objectives and values of our society" (p. 6). Since then, there has been growing research on the relationship between business operations and their social and environmental practices. McGuire (1964) claimed that the original definition lacked clarity and defined CSR as a function focusing on political concerns, community welfare, education and the happiness of employees and the wider social world, because CSR is an obligation that goes beyond legal and economic obligations. Friedman (1970) argued that social responsibility should arise under market rather than political motivations and warned that CSR was a threat to capitalism. Furthermore, Friedman illustrated that companies had one social responsibility which is utilising their resources to increase corporate profits and maximise shareholder wealth. Business managers have no responsibility in matters of public policy (Friedman, 1962).

The earlier definition of CSR did not include economic obligations. Carroll (1979) proposed that CSR included economic, legal, ethical and philanthropic obligations. In *A Three-Dimensional Conceptual Model of Corporate Performance*, Carroll (1979) provided a practical model to evaluate corporate social performance based on discretionary moral, legal and economic responsibility. The model was first proposed *via* a systematic analysis method of CSR. Later, Carroll (1991) explained CSR through a four-pyramid model including economic, legal, ethical and philanthropic requirements, as shown in Table 13.1.

The development of the CSER concept informs the development of closely related concepts and principles, such as environmental, social and governance (ESG) (Bendell, Miller and Wortmann, 2011), and triple bottom-line (TBL) (Aguinis and Glavas, 2012). This chapter focuses on the CSER concept.

DOI: 10.4324/9781003095385-17

*Table 13.1* Carroll's (1991) CSER model

| Principles | Definition |
|---|---|
| Philanthropic responsibility | Being a good corporate citizen, contributing resources to society and improving quality of life |
| Ethical responsibility | Being ethical, having an obligation to do what is right, just and fair |
| Legal responsibility | Obey the law, play by the rules of the game |
| Economic responsibilities | Produce high-quality products and provide excellent service to consumers |

Source: Carroll (1991) 'The pyramid of corporate social responsibility: Toward the moral management of organizational stakeholders', *Business Horizons*, 34(4), pp. 39–48.

The remainder of this chapter is structured as follows. Section 2 addresses CSER communication strategies. Section 3 explores the determinants of CSER disclosure practices, whereas Section 4 focuses on CSER disclosure practices in China. Section 5 explores CSER practices on social media outlets, and Section 6 concludes.

## 13.2 CSER communication strategies

This section discusses the various communication strategies used by managers in disclosing CSER information. Grunig and Hunt (1984) proposed four models for communicating information between firms and stakeholders: (i) press agentry/publicity, (ii) public information, (iii) two-way asymmetrical and (iv) two-way symmetrical.

The press agentry/publicity model focuses on publicity and agenda, whereas organisations seek attention by any possible means and may publish distorted, incomplete or manipulated information. The public information model suggests the use of journalists in-house for dissemination of objective information through mass media such as newsletters, brochures and direct mail. The two-way asymmetric model characterises the use of two-way communication where the client attempts to change the beliefs and behaviours of the target audience without introducing any change in its own belief system. Finally, the two-way symmetric model, in contrast, enables two-way communication where the organisation (client) as well as the audience (public) are willing to change their behaviours and beliefs to accommodate one another.

Morsing and Schultz (2006) adapted three of Grunig and Hunt's public relations models and developed the following three communication strategies.

### 13.2.1 Stakeholder information strategy

The stakeholder information strategy refers to a firm adopting a one-way communication method similar to the press agentry/publicity model in Grunig & Hunt's public relations model. This communication strategy is only telling, not listening. Morsing and Schultz (2006) described the stakeholder information strategy as ensuring that stakeholders only receive information beneficial to the business. Nevertheless, they highlight that good intentions are fundamental to the stakeholder information strategy as it lacks stakeholder monitoring. Thus, the reliability and accuracy of the information are greatly dependent on the purpose and motives of managers and decision makers.

### 13.2.2 Stakeholder response strategy

The stakeholder response strategy was developed from the two-way asymmetric communication model. This communication strategy is an optimisation and improvement of the traditional CSER communication/disclosure methods/channels such as annual reports and paper reports. Moreover, companies increase the efficiency of disclosure by communicating with stakeholders when reporting CSER information (Morsing and Schultz, 2006). This is a common strategy of CSER information communication *via* social media where stakeholders can respond to and engage in CSER communication by sending messages and comments.

### 13.2.3 Stakeholder involvement strategy

This strategy emphasises that businesses and stakeholders are interconnected and may communicate with each other about the process or outcome of CSER communication. Ideally, CSER communications are symmetric. This strategy also indicates that the company should respond to stakeholders' needs. This strategy may be detrimental to the company's image as it may be difficult for the company to control stakeholders' comments and response. However, recent studies have found that a growing number of companies are actively adopting this strategy.

## 13.3  Determinants of CSER practices

Existing research attempts to examine companies' behaviour and attitudes towards CSER and to primarily analyse the level of CSER disclosure (e.g., Jenkins, 2006; Gallego-Álvarez and Quina-Custodio, 2016; Garcia-Sanchez, Cuadrado-Ballesteros and Frias-Aceituno, 2016). Another research domain focuses on voluntary disclosure and the reasons for withholding or disclosing more-or-less relevant information. These studies focus on analysing the determinants of CSER disclosure (e.g., Li and Belal, 2018; Shnayder, Rijnsoever and Hekkert, 2016).

With the change of business models and the development of CSER research disclosure, determinants are becoming more complex, and different researchers have developed different CSER determinant categories for CSER practices. Maignan and Ralston (2002) classify CSER communication into the following groups: value driven, performance driven and stakeholder driven. However, the motivation for CSER disclosure is not the same as the motivation for CSER

*Table 13.2* Determinants of CSER disclosure

| Determinants | Examples |
| --- | --- |
| Corporate characteristics | Size, industry, financial performance, share price |
| External characteristics | Country, media pressure, political, social, time, economic |
| Internal characteristics | Company chair, corporate ethic, board, corporate structure, governance procedures |

Source: Adapted from Adams (2002) 'Internal organisational factors influencing corporate social and ethical reporting: Beyond current theorising', *Accounting, Auditing & Accountability Journal*, 15(2), pp. 223–250.

behaviours. To perform an in-depth analysis of the motivations for CSER disclosure, Adams (2002) examined the prior literature on the determinants of CSER disclosure and developed the three categories presented in Table 13.2 for the determinants of CSER disclosure practices.

Table 13.2 shows that Adams (2002) also accounted for internal factors and emphasised the influence of corporate governance and organisational structure on CSER information disclosure. Adam's classification is useful to inform CSER disclosure research and does include all of the principal determinants of CSER (Ali, Frynas and Mahmood, 2017).

### 13.3.1 Corporate characteristics

Among company characteristics, the most significant influencing factors on CSER disclosure are firm size and industry (Patten, 1991; Hackston and Milne, 1996; Cormier and Magnan, 1999). Firm size has a positive relationship with CSER disclosure, showing that large companies are more likely to disclose more CSER (Cormier and Magnan, 2003; Alsaeed, 2006; Chu, Chatterjee and Brown, 2013; Wang, Song and Yao, 2013). The research in developed countries mainly focuses on listed and large companies and indicates that company size affects its CSER disclosure behaviour (Sethi, 1979; Idowu and Towler, 2004; Brammer and Pavelin, 2008). For example, Thorne et al. (2014) examined 221 Canadian listed companies that had reported CSER scores in 2008 concluding that large companies are more willing to disclose CSER reports than small firms. Bhattacharyya (2014) examined 47 Australian companies' social and environmental reporting and found that large companies provided higher-value disclosure. Brammer and Pavelin (2008) examined the determinants of voluntary environmental disclosures using a sample of 450 large UK companies, revealing that firm size had a positive effect on disclosure.

This strand of literature shows that large companies are more likely to disclose high-quality CSER information. However, the review of this literature also reveals that CSER information disclosure is inadequate in more developed countries and the existing research predominantly focuses on locally listed companies in developed countries (Kotonen, 2009; Thorne, Mahoney and Manetti, 2014;

Dobbs and Staden, 2016) or large, local companies (Brammer and Pavelin, 2008; Duff, 2016). This emphasis on large, local companies indicates that a large number of non-listed companies are excluded by the existing research. This issue is recognised and repeatedly emphasised in the commentary on the research limitations and gaps in research. For example, Ramón-Llorens et al. (2019) recommend that researchers in the field of CSER should also examine non-listed and small- and medium-sized companies. Perry and Towers (2009) are among the few researchers who have paid attention to CSER practices of small enterprises and revealed that small- and medium-sized UK firms lacked the resources required to implement adequate CSER disclosure. They also urged researchers to pay more attention to examining the driving factors influencing CSER disclosure by small- and medium-sized businesses. Furthermore, existing studies do not explore the reasons for the differences in disclosure practices between large and small enterprises.

A few studies qualitatively examine the motivations for disclosing CSER information in the context of developing countries (e.g., Belal and Owen, 2007; Mitchell and Hill, 2009). These studies indicate that the motivations of disclosure in these contexts are different and need to be considered in relation to external factors. Mitchell and Hill (2009) found that the main reason for South African companies not voluntarily disclosing CSER-related information is the lack of legal requirements, with companies being unwilling to release information beyond the legal requirements. Belal and Owen (2007) found that the CSR disclosure practices in Bangladesh were driven by a concern to improve corporate image and manage economically powerful stakeholders (international buyers and investors). Thus, it can be argued that that the motivations of CSER disclosure in developing countries vary from one country to another. We will explain later in the chapter how the Chinese government plays a decisive role in CSER disclosure by Chinese companies.

Another limitation of the existing research in the field of CSER is the particular focus on a handful of industries. Previous studies have predominantly examined financial companies, and banks in particular (Menassa, 2010; Matuszak, Różańska and Macuda, 2019; Khan, Bose and Johns, 2020). There is also more attention paid to CSER practices of manufacturing companies, whereas other industries are under-researched, which highlights the need for more CSER research on all sectors/industries.

### 13.3.2 External factors

There is a large body of literature that has examined how external factors influence CSER disclosure in developed countries. The existing research shows that the external pressure on CSER disclosure practices varies across different developed countries. For example, some studies carried out on UK-based companies found that the pressure for CSER disclosure comes mainly from government regulations (Idowu and Towler, 2004; Day and Woodward, 2009). Some of the studies in Oceania countries, such as Australia and New Zealand, however, have shown that the primary external pressure for a local company is exerted by local communities (Bhattacharyya, 2014; Dobbs and Staden, 2016).

It is important to note that the relevant research lacks a deeper analysis, such as from the perspective of national culture and institutionalisation. Thorne et al. (2014) found, *via* a questionnaire survey, that local Canadian enterprises voluntarily disclose CSER information due to public pressure, particularly the pressure of stakeholders. However, Thorne's (2014) research did not explain the motivation (i.e., culture, philosophy) for enterprises to agree to disclose relevant information. The same problem was noticed in other similar studies. Day and Woodward (2009) analysed content, including annual reports and stand-alone CSER reports in the British financial services sector, that indicated that social and environmental disclosure by the UK financial services industry was "lamentably low", and the local financial services industry mainly offered disclosure in order to deal with the morals of stakeholders. However, the study contained no in-depth discussion about what the moral issues of these stakeholders entailed. Nevertheless, there are some studies on the external motivations for CSER information disclosure from the perspective of culture and philosophy. For example, Lynes and Andrachuk (2008) found that the CSER disclosures of local Scandinavian enterprises was mainly due to the impact of the community, according to both content analysis and interviews.

More specifically, Lynes and Andrachuk (2008) discussed the reason why enterprises choose to respond to the needs of stakeholders, stating that this was because the local Scandinavian spirit was respectful of the environment. However, there are still few studies featuring any in-depth understanding and analysis of CSER information disclosure by enterprises and organisations.

In line with developed countries, previous research in developing countries primarily concentrates on external factors affecting CSER disclosure. However, there is little sociological analysis on the reasons for this motivation, such as relevant philosophy, culture or ethnology. Furthermore, the CSER studies and analyses of most annual reports or stand-alone reports are based on longitudinal analysis. The only interest of these studies is to investigate the external determinants, rather than to discuss in-depth why these corporations had the motivation to meet the external determinants. For instance, Ratanajongkol et al. (2006) assessed CSER disclosure in the 40 largest Thai companies. The survey indicated that media pressure was one of the dominant external pressures. However, the research did not reveal how human resources affected these target corporations. The study could have provided a more in-depth examination of human resources and tried to discuss whether there was an institutional or social reason behind the thinking which drove the behaviour.

The external pressure for information disclosure in developing countries primarily comes as a response to government regulation (Amran and Susela Devi, 2008; Menassa, 2010; Aggarwal and Singh, 2019), and to satisfy the requirements of accounting standards or CSER standard (Amran and Susela Devi, 2008; Coffie, Aboagye-Otchere and Musah, 2018). Due to the different national conditions of different countries, the impact of external pressure on enterprises also differs.

However, there is a lack of research investigating how various external and institutional factors affect CSER disclosures in the context of developing countries. Amran and Susela Devi (2008) posited that researchers could investigate the influence of factors such as government, activist groups and local communities on CSER disclosures. Kiliç et al. (2015) noted that the scope of disclosures was extensive, and these disclosures meet the requirements of both creditors and shareholders, including customers, suppliers, staff and the government, as well as the stakeholders. However, these factors remain largely unexamined, showing that the existing studies of the stakeholders' effects on CSER disclosure are limited and inadequate.

### 13.3.3 Internal organisational factors and CSER disclosure

Compared with the external pressures and motivations faced by individual enterprises, research in the context of developed countries pays less attention to the internal factors of enterprise information disclosure. Most of the studies pay attention to the analysis of corporate governance (Haniffa and Cooke, 2005; Jo and Harjoto, 2012; Ramón-Llorens, García-Meca and Pucheta-Martínez, 2019).

In this classification, corporate governance is the main internal factor. To be more specific, relevant research analyses the impact of corporate governance on CSER disclosure. Specifically, these studies were interested in investigating effects such as board diversity (Kiliç et al., 2015), board size (Haji, 2013), board attitude (Adams, 2002; Belal and Owen, 2007), board leadership (Matuszak et al., 2019) and governance structure (Haniffa and Cooke, 2005; Jo and Harjoto, 2012).

Although initial studies in the field focused on the impact of corporate governance on CSER disclosure, more researchers are now focusing on the impact of specific board members as an essential factor in CSER disclosure. For example, a few studies examining the banking industry found that the presence of female directors on the board was beneficial to CSR, encouraging corporations to disclose social responsibility information (Kiliç, Kuzey and Uyar, 2015; Matuszak, Różańska and Macuda, 2019) and demonstrating that governance structure plays a positive role in CSER disclosure (Haniffa and Cooke, 2005). More studies are presented in Table 13.3.

## 13.4  CSER disclosure practices in China

Similar to previous research in other countries, Chinese studies also focus on company size. Almost all of the relevant studies emphasise that firm size is one of the most important factors affecting CSER disclosure, and ascertain that small- and medium-sized listed enterprises are far behind larger, listed companies in terms of social and environmental responsibility disclosure (Liu and Anbumozhi, 2009; Zeng et al., 2010; Chu, Chatterjee and Brown, 2013). Some studies have further found that CSER disclosure from government-controlled subsidiaries was better than that of many private companies (Zeng et al., 2012; Chu, Chatterjee and Brown, 2013; Lee, Walker and Zeng, 2017). However, there is no research

*Table 13.3* An overview of the literature on the determinants/motivations of CSER disclosure

| Authors | Sample size | Country | Period | Method | Theory | Key findings |
|---|---|---|---|---|---|---|
| Wiseman (1982) | 26 largest companies | US | 1972–1976 | Content analysis | NA | Corporate environmental disclosures are incomplete and are not related to firm's actual environmental performance. |
| Belkaoui and Karpik (1989) | 23 companies | US | 1973 | Content analysis | Agency theory | A positive relationship between social information disclosure and firm's financial performance and political visibility. |
| Patten (1991) | 128 companies | US | 1985 | Content analysis | Legitimacy theory | Company size and industry are significantly positively related to social disclosure. |
| Roberts (1992) | 130 large companies | US | 1984–1986 | Content analysis | Stakeholder theory | Stakeholder power, strategic posture and economic performance are significantly related to the level of CSR disclosure. |
| Hackston and Milne (1996) | 50 listed companies | New Zealand | 1992 | Content analysis | NA | Both size and industry are significantly associated with the amount of disclosure. |
| Adams et al. (1998) | Largest 25 companies | Six European countries | 1992 | Content analysis | Legitimacy theory | There are significant differences in terms of both the type and amount of information disclosed by companies from different countries. |
| Neu et al. (1998) | 33 companies | Canada | 1982–1991 | Content analysis | Legitimacy theory | There is an association between environmental disclosures and actual performance. |
| Cormier and Magnan (1999) | 33 companies | Canada | 1986–1993 | Content analysis | Cost and benefit framework | Information costs and a firm's financial condition are key determinants of environmental disclosure. |
| Wilmshurst and Frost (2000) | 500 listed companies | Australia | 1994–1995 | Content analysis | Legitimacy theory | The analysis provides limited support for legitimacy theory as an explanatory link between identified influential factors in management's decision process and actual environmental disclosure. |

*(Continued)*

*Table 13.3* (Continued)

| Authors | Sample size | Country | Period | Method | Theory | Key findings |
| --- | --- | --- | --- | --- | --- | --- |
| Buhr and Freedman (2001) | 68 companies | Canada, US | 1988 and 1994 | Content analysis | NA | Canadian companies provided greater environmental disclosure than their US counterparts. |
| Patten (2002) | 131 companies | US | 1990 | Content analysis | Legitimacy theory | There is a significant negative relation between performance and disclosure. |
| Cormier and Magnan (2003) | 57 companies | France | 1992–1997 | Content analysis | Cost and benefit framework | Firm size, proprietary costs, information costs and media visibility determine corporate environmental reporting. |
| Adams (2004) | One company (Alpha) | UK | 1993 and 1999 | Case study | NA | The report does not demonstrate a high level of accountability to key stakeholder groups on ethical, social and environmental issues. |
| Hammond and Miles (2004) | 31 companies and 60 interviewees | UK | 2000–2001 | Interviews | NA | Benchmarking and award schemes are important drivers of CSR. |
| Idowu and Towler (2004) | 17 companies | UK | NA | Comparative study | NA | Some companies issue separate reports for their CSR activities while others devote a section in their annual reports for providing information on these activities. |
| Haniffa and Cooke (2005) | 139 companies | Malaysia | 2002 | Content analysis | Legitimacy theory | A significant relationship between corporate social disclosure and boards dominated by Malay directors, and boards dominated by executive directors. |
| Alsaeed (2006) | 40 companies | Singapore | 2003 | Content analysis | Legitimacy theory | Firm size was significantly positively associated with the level of disclosure. |
| de Villiers and van Staden (2006) | Top 100 companies in mining industry | South Africa | 1994–2002 | Content analysis | Legitimacy theory | Companies in industries known for their negative environmental impacts prefer to disclose less specific and more general environmental information. |

| | | | | | | |
|---|---|---|---|---|---|---|
| Ratanajongkol et al. (2006) | 40 largest Thai companies | Thailand | 1997, 1999 and 2001 | Content analysis | Legitimacy theory, stakeholder theory and political economy theory | The theme of human resources dominated Thai company disclosure compared to earlier cross cultural studies. More declarative and good news information is disclosed. |
| Belal and Owen (2007) | 23 companies | Bangladesh | NA | Interview | NA | The main motivation behind current reporting practice lies in a desire on the part of corporate management to manage powerful stakeholder groups. |
| van Staden and Hooks (2007) | 54 companies | New Zealand | 2002 | Content analysis | Legitimacy theory | A significant positive correlation between the independent ranking and our rankings based on the quality and extent of disclosure. |
| Brammer and Pavelin (2008) | 450 large companies | UK | 2000 | Content analysis | NA | A high-quality disclosure is primarily associated with large firms and those in sectors most closely related to environmental concerns. |
| Amran and Devi (2008) | 133 listed companies | Malaysia | 2002–2003 | Content analysis | Institutional theory | The study provides evidence on the impact of government influence. |
| Lynes and Andrachuk (2008) | Scandinavian Airlines | Sweden | NA | Case study | NA | Culture is a determining social and environmental factor at SAS. |
| Mitchell and Hill (2009) | 792 business | South Africa | NA | Interview | NA | Legislations can promote greater CSR disclosure. |
| Day and Woodward (2009) | 27 companies in financial services sector | UK | 2005 | Content analysis | NA | The level of disclosure is lamentably low across the financial services sector with an observable tendency for compliance to be related to size. |

(*Continued*)

*Table 13.3* (Continued)

| Authors | Sample size | Country | Period | Method | Theory | Key findings |
| --- | --- | --- | --- | --- | --- | --- |
| Kotonen (2009) | 31 large Finnish companies | Finland | 2006 | Content analysis | NA | Corporate characteristics such as industry type and internationalisation stage as well as general contextual factors such as social and cultural contexts affect voluntary CSR reporting. |
| Reverte (2009) | All listed firms in Spanish stock exchange | Spain | 2005–2006 | Content analysis | Accounting theory, legitimacy theory and stakeholder theory | The most influential variables explaining variation in CSR ratings are media exposure followed by firm size and industry. |
| Menassa (2010) | 24 Lebanese commercial banks | Lebanon | NA | Content analysis | Legitimacy theory | Banks attribute a greater importance to human resources, product and customers disclosures. |
| Jo and Harjoto (2012) | 2,952 companies | US | 1993–2004 | Content analysis | Agency theory and stakeholder theory | CSR engagement positively influences corporate financial performance. |
| Haji (2013) | 85 listed companies | Malaysia | 2006 and 2009 | Content analysis | Legitimacy theory | A significant overall increase in both the extent and quality of CSR disclosures between the two years covered in the study. |
| Khan et al. (2013) | 135 manufacturing companies | Bangladesh | 2005–2009 | Content analysis | Legitimacy theory | Public ownership, foreign ownership, board independence and the existence of an audit committee have significant positive impact on CSR disclosures. |
| Bhattacharyya (2014) | 47 companies | Australia | 2006–2007 | Content analysis | Legitimacy and reputation | The extent of total disclosure was unrelated to firm age and external auditor's size. |

| Study | Sample | Country | Year | Method | Theory | Findings |
|---|---|---|---|---|---|---|
| Cho et al. (2014) | 216 companies in Fortune 500 | USA | 2010 | Content analysis | NA | Industry membership and disclosure extensiveness both appear to influence the choice to attain third-party assurance on CSR reports in the USA, and assurance is not associated with higher market value for report-issuing companies. |
| Thorne et al. (2014) | 57 companies | Canada | NA | Questionnaire | Assurance prospective | Large firms have more political visibility and are subject to greater external scrutiny than smaller firms. |
| Kiliç et al. (2015) | 26 banks | Turkey | 2008–2012 | Content analysis | NA | A significant positive effect of size, ownership diffusion, board composition and board diversity on CSR disclosure. |
| Dobbs and Staden (2016) | Five companies | New Zealand | NA | Survey and Content analysis | NA | Community concerns and shareholder rights were the most important factors that influenced companies' decision to report. |
| Duff (2016) | 20 largest professional accounting firms | UK | 2009 | Content analysis | Legitimacy theory | The public interest role firms play is an important driver of publicising CSR activity. |
| Coffie et al. (2018) | 33 listed companies | Global | 2008–2013 | Content analysis | Legitimacy theory | Multinational activities have a positive association with both the quantity and quality of CSR disclosure. |

NA: Not applied

to discuss why the CSER disclosure of small- and medium-sized listed enterprises in China is less comprehensive than that of large enterprises. In addition, the research on Chinese information disclosure adopts mostly listed companies as the research object, which is very different from the relevant research of other countries. At present, the Chinese stock exchange has formulated a series of provisions on CSER disclosure of listed companies, although these laws and regulations are not mandatory.

On the one hand, previous research indicates that including large, listed Chinese companies would improve the quality of information disclosure in order to meet compliance requirements. However, the information disclosure of small- and medium-sized enterprises, or growth enterprises, in China is relatively inconsistent. Academic research cannot ignore the disclosure of information by these enterprises because it is voluntary and flexible. At the same time, the existing research concerns itself disproportionately with the information disclosure of China's manufacturing industry. China has recently issued a large number of laws and regulations in the manufacturing industry, especially in the clothing manufacturing industry (such as CSC9000T Management System – China Social Compliance for Textile & Apparel Industry, an organisation affiliated with China National Textile and Apparel Council (CNTAC)), which promotes relevant research focusing on the manufacturing industry (Zeng et al., 2012; Lee et al., 2017; Li and Belal, 2018). However, with studies now overly concerned with manufacturing, other industries are neglected, especially the service sector. China's tertiary industry ("service sector") accounted for over 60% of Gross Domestic Product (GDP) in 2019, according to the information disclosed by the National Bureau of Statistics (2020). However, the relevant research only focuses on the manufacturing industry in China. Furthermore, almost all the research samples are from A-share companies. Nevertheless, the manufacturing, information technology and financial industries account for more than half of the Chinese top 500 A-share enterprises, which are companies based in mainland China that are listed on either the Shanghai or Shenzhen stock exchanges, according to official information disclosure. Therefore, as existing studies are concentrated on the manufacturing industry, there is a lack of diversity in industries examined in the existing research.

Unlike Western countries, most of the studies in China emphasise that the government plays a significant role in corporate information disclosure (Liu and Anbumozhi, 2009; Zeng et al., 2010). However, there is little research that analyses why enterprises choose to disclose relevant information under the influence of the government. It is worth noting that Li and Belal (2018) tried to answer this question through case analysis and interviews with a Chinese holding enterprise and found that, since state-owned enterprises need to perform various government functions, such as promoting environmental awareness to peer firms, the state-owned enterprises need to have better environmental information disclosure. However, there are a few researchers curious enough to examine the motives or reasons behind the information disclosure. In recent years, researchers have begun to analyse the problem from multiple perspectives, such as Hu, Tucker, and Hu (2018), who found that the information disclosures of non-state-owned enterprises is of low quality and posited that this problem might be caused by defects of corporate governance in China. Yu and Zheng (2020) found that foreign investors can encourage Chinese enterprises to disclose relevant information of a higher quality. Both of these studies emphasise the role of auditors in information disclosure and they conjecture that the quality of information disclosure is low because a relevant audit procedure is lacking. International investors employ professional auditors to evaluate the information disclosure of enterprises, which, in turn, promotes the disclosure of more information. These two studies demonstrate that there is an extensive research gap regarding the stakeholders of Chinese enterprises, such as corporate auditors, external auditors and corporate boards of directors.

## 13.5  CSER practices on social media

### *13.5.1  CSER communication practices*

Existing research has found that companies can enhance their stakeholder relationships by disclosing CSER using traditional forms of communication, such as annual reports, meetings and third-party reports. However, CSER on social media can also strengthen stakeholder relationships and encourage their engagement. Because social media is open and inclusive (Etter, 2014), it is a versatile tool for corporate and stakeholder communication, unlike the traditional disclosure channels which are one-way communication. Therefore, in response to the interactive nature of social media, Morsing and Schultz (2006) developed a public relations theory and proposed three CSER communication strategies: *broadcasting, reactive* and *engagement*. Existing research on corporate social media communication strategies has evolved from the three previous strategies to analyse and demonstrate how companies engage in, or reply to, their stakeholders after posting CSER-related information on their social media outlets.

Through a qualitative content analysis of Twitter accounts of the 30 most active companies, Etter (2014) found that companies prefer to use the broadcasting strategy (one-way communication) in communicating CSER information in order to maintain the asymmetry of corporate-related information. Moreover, companies are selective about what they post, which means that, unlike companies that post extensive and detailed CSER information in their annual reports, companies are more willing to post information about environment and climate change on social media than disclosing information about corporate governance and customer relations. Etter (2014) discusses companies' preferences for social media communication but does not explore companies' motivations for choosing one-way and selective communication. Likewise, Kollat and Farache (2017) found that many consumers attempt to communicate with companies about the CSER information they post, but only a few companies respond with relevant information, with most companies using a stakeholder information strategy to refuse to respond to relevant comments from consumers. They raise questions about the impact of institutional and cultural motivations on companies' choice of one-way communication.

Kucukusta et al. (2019) analyse the CSER content of four- to five-star hotels on Facebook and find that, although these hotels post both market- and CSER-related information on Facebook, they choose the *reactive* strategy (two-way communication) on market information but have very little engagement in CSER communication. They also find that CSER-related information posted by companies on social media is very limited, representing 5% of the total disclosure. However, it is worth noting that the number of retweets and views for CSER information is not significantly lower than those for market-related information. This suggests that companies are underestimating the importance of CSER communication in social media.

Existing research on corporate communication strategies is also concerned with the communication strategies of firms after social media messages are released. There is a lack of research analysing why firms choose different communication strategies and why firms are more likely to post market information when CSER is popular on social media. Etter (2014) argues that understanding firms' motivations can help to explain the differences in terms of CSER communication strategies.

Another strand of research on the use of social media for CSER communication focuses on consumer and corporate profile analysis. Adi and Grigore (2015) find that Pfizer does not have a uniform social media communication practice in terms of CSER information. They also demonstrate that the content, frequency and interaction of Pfizer's six European offices are different in terms of their CSER practices on social media, but these CSER messages are intended to improve the public image of the company. Lunenberg et al. (2016) analysed the content of CSER on corporate social media and found that companies adopt a positive tone to enhance their brand image. They also claim that companies may be under pressure from shareholders to publish CSER news on social media. Okazaki et al. (2020) examine eight global brands posting CSER messages on Twitter and find that most of the content posted by companies is not related to CSER, with one-way communication being used to reveal CSER-related information. They attribute the lack of disclosure to companies' concerns about negative reviews/comments and how to monitor and respond to them. Current research mainly focuses on the content of CSER information on social media and its impact on corporate image, yet there is lack of research investigating the motivation behind CSER practices on social media.

### 13.5.2  CSER practices in China

China has its own social media platforms such as Weibo, Douyin (Tik-Tok) and WeChat, which have been developed by Chinese corporations. Chinese social media is vastly different from Western social media and hence requires its own, more relevant research. Chang, Shim and Yi (2019) finds that companies are more willing to post CSER information in countries with free and less-regulated media, which suggests that institutional pressures can discourage companies from voluntarily disclosing CSER information. China has a strict social media censorship system (Hu and Zheng, 2019), meaning it is possible that Chinese companies may be influenced by institutional pressures to disclose their CSER information on social media. Opinion leaders also play an important role on Chinese social media (Wang et al., 2020), so it is worth investigating whether CSER communication is influenced by opinion leaders. It has also been found that Chinese social media users are sensitive to environmental information and may react adversely to negative environmental information on social media (Shan, Peng and Wei, 2021). Therefore, the communication of CSER information in Chinese social media may have implications and could be perceived differently by stakeholders.

Previous research shows that CSER practices on Chinese social media are different from those on Western social media in that they are influenced by factors such as stricter social media regulations. However, there is a lack of research on CSER communication in Chinese social media and their determinants. This is a clear research gap that should be investigated. There is a growing body of international research on the communication of CSER information by companies on social media, but most of it focuses on the process and outcome of communication. There is a lack of analysis of the reasons and motives for companies choosing social media to disseminate CSER information, and existing research is focused on the content released. Moreover, more research is needed on companies' communication behaviour.

Accordingly, Chinese social media, such as Tik-Tok, Weibo and WeChat, are gaining popularity, and a large number of companies are disclosing information on these Chinese social media platforms. However, few studies have focused on corporate CSER communication on Chinese social media platforms.

## 13.6 Conclusion

This chapter discusses the concept of CSER and provides a review of the existing literature. The chapter discusses how the CSER concept has evolved over time, including the conflicting views on whether companies should be held accountable for their CSR initiatives and practices or whether financial performance should be used to measure their success. This chapter also addresses the various CSER communication strategies that organisations use, yet there is a need for more research to examine how companies implement their communication strategies. However, with the rising popularity of social media disclosure, corporate disclosure is no longer a one-way flow of information between companies and their stakeholders.

This chapter discusses CSER disclosure practices and their determinants. The review in this chapter reveals that the existing research focuses on specific industries and companies, which highlights a gap in the literature, in the Chinese context in particular. Future research could focus on non-manufacturing industries/companies and CSER disclosure by Chinese companies of different sizes. This chapter also finds that the Chinese government plays a significant role in influencing CSER disclosure by Chinese firms, and that there is a large number of studies focusing on the impact of the Chinese government on firms' disclosure behaviour.

*Table 13.4* An overview of the literature on the determinants/motivations of CSER disclosure by Chinese companies

| Author(s) | Sample | Period | Method | Theory | Key findings |
|---|---|---|---|---|---|
| Liu and Anbumozhi (2009) | 175 Large Listed companies | 2006 | Content analysis | Stakeholder theory | Corporate environmental disclosure is significantly related to firm environmental sensitivity and size. |
| Zeng et al. (2010) | 871 listed manufacturing companies | 2005–2008 | Content analysis | NA | Significant differences in terms of selective disclosure of environmental information by listed companies. |
| Zeng et al. (2012) | 784 manufacturing companies | 2006–2008 | Content analysis | Institutional theory | Firms that are state owned, operate in environmentally sensitive industries and/or have good reputations are more likely to disclose environmental information. |
| Chu et al. (2013) | Top 100 A-share companies listed on Shanghai Stock Exchange | 2011 | Content analysis | Legitimacy theory | The results indicate that large companies operating in an industry which has higher level of carbon dioxide emissions tend to have higher levels of greenhouse gas disclosures, which is consistent with the proposition of the legitimacy theory. |
| Dong et al. (2014) | All mining and minerals companies listed on the Shanghai and Shenzhen Stock Exchanges | 2007–210 | Content analysis | Stakeholder theory | The central government, salient stakeholders with a significant impact include international consumers, while unexpectedly mining industry associations, local communities and employees are not considered as salient as they do not have a significant impact on CSR reporting practices. |

| | | | | | |
|---|---|---|---|---|---|
| Lee et al. (2017) | All manufacturing listed companies | 2008–2012 | Content analysis | NA | The state subsidies have a material influence on CSR disclosure choices beyond the variables commonly examined and reported in the Western contexts. |
| Luo et al. (2017) | All listed companies on Shenzhen or Shanghai Stock Exchanges | 2008–2011 | Regression analysis | Institutional theory | Firms with attributes that increase scrutiny from institutional constituencies experienced heightened tension and responded by providing low-quality disclosure. |
| Hu et al. (2018) | 1,839 Chinese listed firms | 2010 | Content analysis | Stakeholder salience theory | Chinese stock exchanges exert a positive influence on the likelihood of a firm producing a CSR report. |
| Li and Belal (2018) | State-owned company | 2014 | Case study | Multi-level institutional theory | There are multiple levels of motivation for information disclosure by Chinese state-owned enterprises. |
| Yu and Zheng (2020) | 335 companies | 2004–2013 | Content analysis | Institutional theory | Local institutional investors' ownership and investment weight relative to the market portfolio also increased following the mandate for firms to provide CSR reporting. |

NA: Not applied

*Table 13.5* An overview of the literature on CSER disclosure on social media

| Authors | Platform | Sample size | Period | Method | Key findings |
|---------|----------|-------------|--------|--------|--------------|
| Fieseler et al. (2010) | CSR blog | McDonald | 1.5 year | Case study | McDonald disclosed CSR information on the blog which could enable a dialogue-based relationship between the company and its stakeholders. |
| Castelló et al. (2013) | No | No | No | Theoretical research | Further research is needed to understand how communicative legitimacy is constituted in CSR communication. |
| Lee et al. (2013) | Twitter | Fortune 500 companies | 18 days | Statistics | Firm discloses socially responsible can harvest proactive stakeholders' participation (user-driven communication) without investing in more resources (firm-driven communication). |
| Eberle et al. (2013) | Twitter | A fictitious company | 1 year | Experiment | The company disclosed CSR information CSR messages were perceived as more interact. |
| Zhang (2015) | Twitter, YouTube, Facebook | Randomly selected 120 companies | 1 fiscal year | Content analysis | Company engagement in information disclosure on new media increases a company's influence and reach. |
| Castelló et al. (2016) | Twitter | A multinational pharmaceutical corporation | 41 months | Case study | A new communication environment could change in stakeholders' engagement. |
| Manetti and Bellucci (2016) | Twitter, Facebook, YouTube | 332 companies | 1 year | Content analysis | The authors found that social media for one-way communication to users (especially customers) and for legitimising the presence of the organisation within society is a consolidated and robust tendency. |

| Author (Year) | Platform | Sample | Duration | Method | Findings |
|---|---|---|---|---|---|
| Gomez-Carrasco and Michelon (2017) | Twitter | Eight banks | 187 days | Statistics | Information published *via* Twitter could impact stakeholders' decisions. |
| Tsai and Men (2018) | WeChat | A random company | 1 year | Statistics | Users are high levels of engagement with the companies disclosed social information they followed on WeChat. |
| Neu et al. (2019) | Twitter | 113,882 original Tweets | 14 days | Content analysis | Social media disseminates, aggregates and democratises social accountability, and hence encourages organisations to promote actively and champion such initiatives. |
| She and Michelon (2019) | Facebook | S&P 100 firms' Facebook posts | 1 year | Content analysis | Companies use organised hypocrisy CSER disclosure strategies in social media which help them manage stakeholders' perceptions and maintain legitimacy. |
| Saxton et al. (2019) | Twitter, Facebook | Fortune 500 companies | 1 year | Content analysis | Companies disclosed positive information on CSER topics. |
| Kucukusta et al. (2019) | Facebook | A total of 13 hotels in Hong Kong | 1 year | Content analysis | Although the number of CSER-related posts is significantly lower than marketing-oriented posts, they achieve a comparable level of popularity and engagement. |
| Okazaki et al. (2020) | Twitter | Two pharmaceutical brands, two food brands, Two banking brands | 1 year | Machine learning | Brands are creating online CSER dialogue among consumers, yet they fail to interact with them. |

However, these studies ignore the role and influence of other stakeholder groups, which is a particular avenue for future research.

Finally, there are a growing number of studies examining CSER disclosures on social media. However, current research on CSER disclosure on social media remains limited to exploring and explaining the social phenomenon in its entirety and lacks a deeper investigation into the phenomenon. Furthermore, current research confines its selection of social media to a few outlets such as Twitter and Facebook, omitting more diverse and regional social media platforms. Future research could address CSER disclosure practices on different social media platforms and in different cultural contexts.

## References

Adams, C.A. (2002) 'Internal organisational factors influencing corporate social and ethical reporting: Beyond current theorising', *Accounting, Auditing and Accountability Journal*, 15(2), pp. 223–250.

Adams, C.A. (2004) 'The ethical, social and environmental reporting-performance portrayal gap', *Accounting, Auditing and Accountability Journal*, 17(5), pp. 731–757.

Adams, C.A., Hill, W.-Y. and Roberts, C.B. (1998) 'Corporate social reporting practices in Western Europe: Legitimating corporate behaviour?', *The British Accounting Review*, 30(1), pp. 1–21.

Adi, A. and Grigore, G. (2015) 'Communicating CSR on social media: The case of Pfizer's social media Communications in Europe', in: Adi, A., Grigore, G. and Crowther, D. (eds.) *Developments in corporate governance and responsibility*. Emerald Group Publishing Limited, Bingley, pp. 143–163.

Aggarwal, P. and Singh, A.K. (2019) 'CSR and sustainability reporting practices in India: An in-depth content analysis of top-listed companies', *Social Responsibility Journal*, 15(8), pp. 1033–1053.

Aguinis, H. and Glavas, A. (2012) 'What we know and don't know about corporate social responsibility: A review and research agenda', *Journal of Management*, 38(4), pp. 932–968.

Ali, W., Frynas, J.G. and Mahmood, Z. (2017) 'Determinants of corporate social responsibility (CSR) disclosure in developed and developing countries: A literature review: Determinants CSR of disclosure', *Corporate Social Responsibility and Environmental Management*, 24(4), pp. 273–294.

Alsaeed, K. (2006) 'The association between firm-specific characteristics and disclosure: The case of Saudi Arabia', *Managerial Auditing Journal*, 21(5), pp. 476–496.

Amran, A. and Susela Devi, S. (2008) 'The impact of government and foreign affiliate influence on corporate social reporting: The case of Malaysia', *Managerial Auditing Journal*, 23(4), pp. 386–404.

Barnard, C.I. (1938) *The functions of the executive*. Cambridge, MA: Harvard University Press. Available at: http://books.google.com/books?id=K4xEAAAAIAAJ (Accessed: 17 November 2021).

Belal, A. and Owen, D. (2007) 'The views of corporate managers on the current state of, and future prospects for, social reporting in Bangladesh: An engagement-based study', *Accounting, Auditing & Accountability Journal*, 20(3), pp. 472–494.

Belkaoui, A. and Karpik, P.G. (1989) 'Determinants of the corporate decision to disclose social Information', *Accounting, Auditing and Accountability Journal*, 2(1), pp. 36–51.

Bendell, J., Miller, A. and Wortmann, K. (2011) 'Public policies for scaling corporate responsibility standards: Expanding collaborative governance for sustainable development', *Sustainability Accounting, Management and Policy Journal*, 2(2), pp. 263–293.

Bhattacharyya, A. (2014) 'Factors associated with the social and environmental reporting of Australian companies', *Australasian Accounting, Business and Finance Journal*, 8(1), pp. 25–50.

Bowen, H.R. (1953) *Social responsibilities of the businessman*. New York: Harper & Brothers.

Brammer, S. and Pavelin, S. (2008) 'Factors influencing the quality of corporate environmental disclosure', *Business Strategy and the Environment*, 17(2), pp. 120–136.

Buhr, N. and Freedman, M. (2001) 'Culture, institutional factors and differences in environmental disclosure between Canada and the United States', *Critical Perspectives on Accounting*, 12(3), pp. 293–322.

Carroll, A.B. (1979) 'A three-dimensional conceptual model of corporate performance', *Academy of Management Review*, 4(4), pp. 497–505.

Carroll, A.B. (1991) 'The pyramid of corporate social responsibility: Toward the moral management of organizational stakeholders', *Business Horizons*, 34(4), pp. 39–48.

Castelló, I., Etter, M. and Årup, F.N. (2016) 'Strategies of legitimacy through social media: The networked strategy: Strategies of legitimacy through social media', *Journal of Management Studies*, 53(3), pp. 402–432.

Castelló, I., Morsing, M. and Schultz, F. (2013) 'Communicative dynamics and the polyphony of corporate social responsibility in the network society', *Journal of Business Ethics*, 118(4), pp. 683–694.

Chaffee, E.C. (2017) 'The origins of corporate social responsibility', *University of Cincinnati Law Review*, 85, pp. 353–379.

Chang, K., Shim, H. and Yi, T. (2019) 'Corporate social responsibility, media freedom, and firm value', *Finance Research Letters*, 30, pp. 1–7.

Cho, C., Michelon, G., Patten, D. and Roberts, R.(2014) 'CSR report assurance in the USA: An empirical investigation of determinants and effects', *Sustainability Accounting, Management and Policy Journal*, 5(2), pp. 130–148.

Chu, C.L., Chatterjee, B. and Brown, A. (2013) 'The current status of greenhouse gas reporting by Chinese companies: A test of legitimacy theory', *Managerial Auditing Journal*, 28(2), pp. 114–139.

Coffie, W., Aboagye-Otchere, F. and Musah, A. (2018) 'Corporate social responsibility disclosures (CSRD), corporate governance and the degree of multinational activities: Evidence from a developing economy', *Journal of Accounting in Emerging Economies*, 8(1), pp. 106–123.

Cormier, D. and Magnan, M. (1999) 'Corporate environmental disclosure strategies: Determinants, costs and benefits', *Journal of Accounting, Auditing and Finance*, 14(4), pp. 429–451.

Cormier, D. and Magnan, M. (2003) 'Environmental reporting management: A continental European perspective', *Journal of Accounting and Public Policy*, 22(1), pp. 43–62.

Day, R. and Woodward, T. (2009) 'CSR reporting and the UK financial services sector', *Journal of Applied Accounting Research*, 10(3), pp. 159–175.

Dobbs, S. and van Staden, C. (2016) 'Motivations for corporate social and environmental reporting: New Zealand evidence', *Sustainability Accounting, Management and Policy Journal*, 7(3), pp. 449–472.

Dong, S., Burritt, R. and Qian, W. (2014) 'Salient stakeholders in corporate social responsibility reporting by Chinese mining and minerals companies', *Journal of Cleaner Production*, 84, pp. 59–69.

Duff, A. (2016) 'Corporate social responsibility reporting in professional accounting firms', *The British Accounting Review*, 48(1), pp. 74–86.

Eberle, D., Berens, G. and Li, T. (2013) 'The impact of interactive corporate social responsibility communication on corporate reputation', *Journal of Business Ethics*, 118(4), pp. 731–746.

Etter, M. (2014) 'Broadcasting, reacting, engaging – Three strategies for CSR communication in Twitter', *Journal of Communication Management*, 18(4), pp. 322–342.

Fieseler, C., Fleck, M. and Meckel, M. (2010) 'Corporate social responsibility in the blogosphere', *Journal of Business Ethics*, 91(4), pp. 599–614. https://doi.org/10.1007/s10551-009-0135-8.

Friedman, M. (1962) *Capitalism and freedom*. Chicago, IL: University of Chicago Press. Available at: https://press.uchicago.edu/ucp/books/book/chicago/C/bo68666099.html (Accessed: 21 February 2021).

Friedman, M. (1970) 'A Friedman doctrine – The social responsibility of business is to increase its profits', *The New York Times*. Available at: https://www.nytimes.com/1970/09/13/archives/a-friedman-doctrine-the-social-responsibility-of-business-is-to.html (Accessed: 21 February 2021).

Gallego-Álvarez, I. and Quina-Custodio, I.A. (2016) 'Disclosure of corporate social responsibility information and explanatory factors', *Online Information Review*, 40(2), pp. 218–238.

Garcia-Sanchez, I.-M., Cuadrado-Ballesteros, B. and Frias-Aceituno, J.-V. (2016) 'Impact of the institutional macro context on the voluntary disclosure of CSR information', *Long Range Planning*, 49(1), pp. 15–35.

Gomez-Carrasco, P. and Michelon, G. (2017) 'The power of stakeholders' voice: The effects of social media activism on stock markets', *Business Strategy and the Environment*, 26(6), pp. 885–872.

Grunig, J.E. and Hunt, T. (1984) *Managing public relations*. Holt: Rinehart and Winston.

Hackston, D. and Milne, M.J. (1996) 'Some determinants of social and environmental disclosures in New Zealand companies', *Accounting, Auditing and Accountability Journal*, 9(1), pp. 77–108.

Haji, A.A. (2013) 'Corporate social responsibility disclosures over time: Evidence from Malaysia', *Managerial Auditing Journal*, 28(7), pp. 647–676. https://doi.org/10.1108/MAJ-07-2012-0729.

Hammond, K. and Miles, S. (2004) 'Assessing quality assessment of corporate social reporting: UK perspectives', *Accounting Forum*, 28(1), pp. 61–79.

Haniffa, R.M. and Cooke, T.E. (2005) 'The impact of culture and governance on corporate social reporting', *Journal of Accounting and Public Policy*, 24(5), pp. 391–430.

Hu, J. and Zheng, Y. (2019) 'Social media, state control and religious freedom in china', *Political Theology*, 5(20), p. 11.

Hu, Y., Tucker, Y. and Hu, Y.(2018) 'Ownership influence and CSR disclosure in China', *Accounting Research Journal*, 31(1), pp. 8–21.

Idowu, S.O. and Towler, B.A. (2004) 'A comparative study of the contents of corporate social responsibility reports of UK companies', *Management of Environmental Quality: an International Journal*, 15(4), pp. 420–437.

Jenkins, H. (2006) 'Small business champions for corporate social responsibility', *Journal of Business Ethics*, 67(3), pp. 241–256.

Jo, H. and Harjoto, M.A. (2012) 'The causal effect of corporate governance on corporate social responsibility', *Journal of Business Ethics*, 106(1), pp. 53–72.

Khan, A., Muttakin, M.B. and Siddiqui, J. (2013) 'Corporate governance and corporate social responsibility disclosures: Evidence from an emerging economy', *Journal of Business Ethics*, 114(2), pp. 207–223.

Khan, H.Z., Bose, S. and Johns, R. (2020) 'Regulatory influences on CSR practices within banks in an emerging economy: Do banks merely comply?', *Critical Perspectives on Accounting*, 71, p. 102096.

Kiliç, M., Kuzey, C. and Uyar, A. (2015) 'The impact of ownership and board structure on corporate social responsibility (CSR) reporting in the Turkish banking industry', *Corporate Governance: The International Journal of Business in Society*, 15(3), pp. 357–374.

Kollat, J. and Farache, F. (2017) 'Achieving consumer trust on Twitter via CSR communication', *Journal of Consumer Marketing*, 34(6), pp. 505–514.

Kotonen, U. (2009) 'Formal corporate social responsibility reporting in Finnish listed companies', *Journal of Applied Accounting Research*, 10(3), pp. 176–207.

Kucukusta, D., Perelygina, M. and Lam, W.S. (2019) 'CSR communication strategies and stakeholder engagement of upscale hotels in social media', *International Journal of Contemporary Hospitality Management*, 31(5), pp. 2129–2148.

Lee, E., Walker, M. and Zeng, C. (2017) 'Do Chinese state subsidies affect voluntary corporate social responsibility disclosure?', *Journal of Accounting and Public Policy*, 36(3), pp. 179–200.

Lee, K., Oh, W.-Y. and Kim, N. (2013) 'Social media for socially responsible firms: Analysis of fortune 500's Twitter profiles and their CSR/CSIR ratings', *Journal of Business Ethics*, 118(4), pp. 791–806.

Li, T. and Belal, A. (2018) 'Authoritarian state, global expansion and corporate social responsibility reporting: The narrative of a Chinese state-owned enterprise', *Accounting Forum*, 42(2), pp. 199–217.

Liu, X. and Anbumozhi, V. (2009) 'Determinant factors of corporate environmental information disclosure: An empirical study of Chinese listed companies', *Journal of Cleaner Production*, 17(6), pp. 593–600.

Lunenberg, K., Gosselt, J.F. and De Jong, M.D.T. (2016) 'Framing CSR fit: How corporate social responsibility activities are covered by news media', *Public Relations Review*, 42(5), pp. 943–951.

Luo, X.R., Wang, D. and Zhang, J. (2017) 'Whose call to answer: Institutional complexity and firms' CSR reporting', *Academy of Management Journal*, 60(1), pp. 321–344.

Lynes, J.K. and Andrachuk, M. (2008) 'Motivations for corporate social and environmental responsibility: A case study of Scandinavian airlines', *Journal of International Management*, 14(4), pp. 377–390.

Maignan, I. and Ralston, D.A. (2002) 'Responsibiliity U.S.: Insights from businesses' self-presentations', *Journal of International Business Studies*, 33(3), pp. 497–514.

Manetti, G. and Bellucci, M. (2016) 'The use of social media for engaging stakeholders in sustainability reporting', *Accounting, Auditing and Accountability Journal*, 29(6), pp. 985–1011.

Matuszak, Ł., Różańska, E. and Macuda, M. (2019) 'The impact of corporate governance characteristics on banks' corporate social responsibility disclosure: Evidence from Poland', *Journal of Accounting in Emerging Economies*, 9(1), pp. 75–102.

McGuire, J. (1964) *Business and society.* New York: McGraww-Hill. Available at: https://www.jstor.org/stable/3101288.

Menassa, E. (2010) 'Corporate social responsibility: An exploratory study of the quality and extent of social disclosures by Lebanese commercial banks', *Journal of Applied Accounting Research*, 11(1), pp. 4–23.

Mitchell, C.G. and Hill, T. (2009) 'Corporate social and environmental reporting and the impact of internal environmental policy in South Africa', *Corporate Social Responsibility and Environmental Management*, 16(1), pp. 48–60.

Morsing, M. and Schultz, M. (2006) 'Corporate social responsibility communication: Stakeholder information, response and involvement strategies', *Business Ethics: A European Review*, 15(4), pp. 323–338.

National Bureau of Statistics. (2020) *Scale expansion and structure optimization of China's tertiary industry, Scale expansion and structure optimization of China's tertiary industry.* Available at: http://www.stats.gov.cn/tjsj/zxfb/201912/t20191204 _1715262.html.

Neu, D., Saxton, G., Rahman, A. and Everett, J.(2019) 'Twitter and social accountability: Reactions to the Panama papers', *Critical Perspectives on Accounting*, 61, pp. 38–53.

Neu, D., Warsame, H. and Pedwell, K. (1998) 'Managing public impressions: Environmental disclosures in annual reports', *Accounting, Organizations and Society*, 23(3), pp. 265–282.

Okazaki, S., Plangger, K., West, D. and Menéndez, H.(2020) 'Exploring digital corporate social responsibility communications on Twitter', *Journal of Business Research*, 117, pp. 675–682.

Patten, D.M. (1991) 'Exposure, legitimacy, and social disclosure', *Journal of Accounting and Public Policy*, 10(4), pp. 297–308.

Patten, D.M. (2002) 'The relation between environmental performance and environmental disclosure: A research note', *Accounting, Organizations and Society*, 27(8), pp. 763–773.

Perry, P. and Towers, N. (2009) 'Determining the antecedents for a strategy of corporate social responsibility by small- and medium-sized enterprises in the UK fashion apparel industry', *Journal of Retailing and Consumer Services*, 16(5), pp. 377–385.

Ramón-Llorens, M.C., García-Meca, E. and Pucheta-Martínez, M.C. (2019) 'The role of human and social board capital in driving CSR reporting', *Long Range Planning*, 52(6), pp. 101846–101856.

Ratanajongkol, S., Davey, H. and Low, M. (2006) 'Corporate social reporting in Thailand: The news is all good and increasing', *Qualitative Research in Accounting and Management*, 3(1), pp. 67–83.

Reverte, C. (2009) 'Determinants of corporate social responsibility disclosure ratings by Spanish listed firms', *Journal of Business Ethics*, 88(2), pp. 351–366.

Roberts, R.W. (1992) 'Determinants of corporate social responsibility disclosure: An application of stakeholder theory', *Accounting, Organizations and Society*, 17(6), pp. 595–612.

Saxton, G.D. *et al.* (2019) 'Do CSR messages resonate? Examining public reactions to firms' CSR efforts on social media', *Journal of Business Ethics*, 155(2), pp. 359–377.

Sethi, S. (1979) 'A conceptual framework for environmental analysis of social issues and evaluation of business response patterns', *Academy of Management Review*, 4(1), pp. 63–74.

Shan, S., Peng, J. and Wei,Y. (2021) 'Environmental Sustainability assessment 2.0: The value of social media data for determining the emotional responses of people to river pollution—A case study of Weibo (Chinese Twitter)', *Socio-Economic Planning Sciences*, 75,p. 100868.

She, C.and Michelon, G. (2019) 'Managing stakeholder perceptions: Organized hypocrisy in CSR disclosures on Facebook', *Critical Perspectives on Accounting*,61, pp. 54–76.

Shnayder, L., Rijnsoever, F. and Hekkert, M. (2016). 'Motivations for Corporate Social Responsibility in the packaged food industry: An institutional and stakeholder management perspective', *Journal of Cleaner Production*, 122, 212–227.

van Staden, C.J. and Hooks, J. (2007) 'A comprehensive comparison of corporate environmental reporting and responsiveness', *The British Accounting Review*, 39(3), pp. 197–210.

Thorne, L., Mahoney, L.S. and Manetti, G. (2014) 'Motivations for issuing standalone CSR reports: A survey of Canadian firms', *Accounting, Auditing and Accountability Journal*, 27(4), pp. 686–714.

Tsai, W.-H.S. and Men, R.L. (2018) 'Social messengers as the new frontier of organization-public engagement: A WeChat study', *Public Relations Review*, 44(3), pp. 419–429.

de Villiers, C. and van Staden, C.J. (2006) 'Can less environmental disclosure have a legitimising effect? Evidence from Africa', *Accounting, Organizations and Society*, 31(8), pp. 763–781.

Wang, J., Song, L. and Yao, S. (2013) 'The determinants of corporate social responsibility disclosure: Evidence From China', *Journal of Applied Business Research (JABR)*, 29(6), pp. 1833–1848.

Wang, Z., Liu, H., Liu, W. and Wang, S. (2020) 'Understanding the power of opinion leaders' influence on the diffusion process of popular mobile games: Travel Frog on Sina Weibo', *Computers in Human Behavior*, 109, pp. p. 106354.

Wilmshurst, T.D. and Frost, G.R. (2000) 'Corporate environmental reporting: A test of legitimacy theory', *Accounting, Auditing and Accountability Journal*, 13(1), pp. 10–26.

Wiseman, J. (1982) 'An evaluation of environmental disclosures made in corporate annual reports', *Accounting, Organizations and Society*, 7(1), pp. 53–63.

Yu, W. and Zheng, Y. (2020) 'Does CSR reporting matter to foreign institutional investors in China?', *Journal of International Accounting, Auditing and Taxation*, 40, p. 100322.

Zeng, S.X., Xu, X. D., Dong, Z. Y. and Tam, V. (2010) 'Towards corporate environmental information disclosure: An empirical study in China', *Journal of Cleaner Production*, 18(12), pp. 1142–1148.

Zeng, S. X.,Xu, X. D.,Yin, H. T. and Tam, C. M. (2012) 'Factors that drive Chinese listed companies in voluntary disclosure of environmental information', *Journal of Business Ethics*, 109(3), pp. 309–321.

Zhang, J. (2015) 'Voluntary information disclosure on social media', *Decision Support Systems*, 73, pp. 28–36.

# 14 Accounting for sustainable development (ASD) practices

## Theoretical emergence and development

*Mohamed Saeudy*

## 14.1 Introduction

The main objective of this chapter is to explore how accounting tools and practices could be used to develop accounting for sustainable development (ASD) data recording and reporting practices to address social and environmental considerations. This chapter uses a systematic review to identify the main theoretical framework and approaches that have been used to understand and explain the ontological framework of ASD practices. This framework involves stakeholder theory, legitimacy theory and the triple bottom line (TBL) approach. These theoretical approaches are used to understand and interpret the development of ASD data recording and reporting practices in business organisations (Mansell, 2013).

ASD is one of the main extensions and developments of social and environmental accounting (SEA) research (Bebbington, 2001). It involves sets of practices and theories that could be used to understand the organisational behaviour towards society and the environment. There are many conceptual contexts (e.g., stakeholder and legitimacy theories) that have been used to study the ASD framework and practices, such as sustainability reporting. However, there are many challenges to using these theoretical lenses to understand and envisage the main imperatives of sustainable development (SD) as core business activities. These challenges involve the complications of using some themes of SD in business organisations, such as social justice, income equality, social inclusion, ecological biodiversity and democracy. For example, the concepts of fair and efficient distribution of resources and opportunities between the present and future generations (World Commission on Environment and Development, 1987; Gray & Milne, 2002) seem to involve some theoretical contests to identifying the characteristics and expectations of the present and future generations. This example illustrates just one side of the difficulties of developing ASD as a coherent accounting discipline. Therefore, this chapter contributes to the ongoing debate on the theoretical background of ASD practices. This chapter categorises (and clarifies) the main theories and theoretical approaches that have been used in the literature to understand and develop organisational ASD practices.

Recently, the concepts of sustainability, SD, ASD and positive social and environmental impact have been described and have emerged in the accounting

DOI: 10.4324/9781003095385-18

literature, business organisations and public institutions. However, there is no single explanation of the concept of SD. This concept has been defined in the Brundtland report to support the environmental policy agenda (World Commission on Environment and Development, 1987). This report described SD as "development that meets the needs of the present without compromising the ability of future generations to meet their own needs". It seems that this definition does not provide a clear explanation for the fundamental meaning of sustainability in terms of organisational practices or activities (Bartelmus, 1994). Furthermore, it does not explain the main imperatives of SD to manage human activities and fulfil the needs of future and current generations (Lélé, 1991). It was argued that, based on the current context of some of the main imperatives of SD issues, e.g., climate change; carbon emissions; human rights issues; global water shortages and gender equality, the determination of the needs of future generations involves some measurement challenges and difficulties to predict these future needs and expectations (McElroy & Engelen, 2012).

Sustainability and SD[1] have been developed and used for many years as mutually inclusive, but not identical, concepts to develop business practices to explain the relationships between ecological issues and corporate behaviour (Bebbington & Gray, 2001; Gray, 2006; Spence & Gray, 2007). SD has been used as a framework by which to address the organisational social, environmental and economic impacts (Milne & Gray, 2013).

The main purpose of this chapter is to explore the main tools, theoretical lenses, criticisms and challenges of developing ASD practices in the literature. Therefore, the structure of this chapter will be organised as follows. Section 14.2 reviews the motivation for identifying ASD as contemporary accounting practice. Section 14.3 discusses the emergence and the context of ASD practices. Section 14.4 discusses the ASD framework and Section 14.5 discusses the ASD theories. Section 14.6 presents the narrative forms of ASD practices, whereas Section 14.7 provides concluding thoughts of ASD practices.

## 14.2 The motivation for identifying ASD as contemporary accounting practices

The term "organisational practices" was used to refer to the analysis of patterns of organisational behaviour and routine work in organisations (Costello, 2000). This lens involves some analytical insights to explain how organisations manage the relationships between organisational strategies and actual performance (Wahab, 2021). Hence, the establishment of organisational practices might be used to describe the processes of organisational planning to convert and implement organisational strategies into socially accomplished activities (Jarzabkowski & Balogun, 2009). Using this lens, the analysis of organisational practices involves some pragmatic insights to illustrate how strategy actually works to manage the differences between actual and expected performance (Cunningham & Harney, 2012).[2] In addition, the definition of organisational practices entails sub-managerial activities that should be followed to develop the concepts of practitioner and praxis (Jarzabkowski & Spee, 2009). These concepts shape the various aspects of organisational changes that were followed to develop ASD data recording and reporting practices to increase the effectiveness of organisational performance (Wahab, 2021). For example, this argument entails the identification of any new activities and ethics, such as sustainable values, that should be created to increase the overall level of organisational effectiveness (Jarzabkowski et al., 2012).

Organisational practices involve two main roles. The first role describes how to specify the actual organisational performance according to the experience and power of the key players. The second role clarifies the developmental aspects of organisational practices to change the organisational strategies in the future to commercialise social and environmental business opportunities. However, accounting practices have been used to create some theoretically informed understanding of accounting insights for practitioners and business institutions (Scapens, 2006). These insights involve a descriptive explanation of the developmental role of accounting to clarify the linkage between the rules and routines and the day-to-day actions.

Other literature used the notion of accounting practices to refer to a practical set of institutional rules and routines that could be followed to achieve a particular set of outcomes or goals (Burns & Scapens, 2000). These rules involve some accounting tools and technologies such as financial and non-financial analysis, recording, reporting and measurement. However, accounting practices are also considered to be a radical activity to explain the sense or legitimacy of using a certain accounting technique in a specific field, such as using environmental data recording in order to manage the implications of environmental issues in business organisations (Jones, 2014).

Generally, a review of key management and accounting literature distinguished four components or levels of accounting practices: (i) pragmatic components (Changwony & Paterson, 2019), (ii) strategy-based components, (iii) integrational components and (iv) the developmental level components (see Roberts & Scapens, 1985; Burns & Scapens, 2000; Jarzabkowski & Balogun, 2009; Cunningham & Harney, 2012). The pragmatic component focuses on the actual and daily accounting activities, e.g., data recording of business transactions (Roberts & Scapens, 1985).

The main point here is that accounting practices were described as a set of institutional assurance rules and activities to be followed to achieve a particular set of objectives or outcomes (Channuntapipat et al., 2020). These rules were used to institutionalise the theoretical themes of stakeholder theory (social contract) and institutional theory (institutional change). It was used as well to describe the organisational processes to commercialise social and environmental projects.

## 14.3  The emergence and context of ASD practices

In order to clarify the context and meaning of ASD practices, this chapter reviews three main groups of accounting literature. The first group aims to describe sustainability reporting and process as ASD practice. The second group is focused on studying the re-organisation of ASD practices within SEA literature. The third group is focused on exploring the concept of unsustainable practices and the sustainability impediments.

### 14.3.1 Group one: The social and environmental reporting process

Reporting corporate information represents a fundamental process of accounting and auditing activities, including ASD, in order to produce information by managers for stakeholders for the purposes of accountability and control (Gray, 2006). From this perspective, sustainability reporting represents a conception of legitimacy strategy that was used, in sustainability policies, to influence the users of information and to manage a firm's internal risk (O'Dwyer et al., 2011). Sustainability reporting practices have been used to provide some knowledge of the corporate commitment to responsible business practices (O'Dwyer et al., 2005). The definition of corporate social disclosure has been used to highlight the social and environmental impact of business activities as indicated in the following quote:

> Corporate social disclosure (CSD) can be defined as the process by which organisations, particularly business organisations, communicate the social and environmental impacts of their activities, products and services to particular interest groups within society and to society at large.
>
> (O'Dwyer et al., 2005; p. 783)

The above quote indicates that corporate social disclosure was focused on the reporting process of the social and environmental impact of business activities. O'Dwyer et al. (2005) assert that corporate sustainability requires a collective and cumulative assessment of economic activity relative to the resources base.

Some literature has developed some organisational lenses[3] to assess corporate disclosure about environmental and social performance in the banking institutions as they are one of the major players in the international markets (Deegan, 2004). Some banks in the UK and USA have used social and environmental performance extensively to assess the credit-worthiness of their customers' environmental risk (Bhimani & Soonawalla, 2010). Earnings management and corporate social responsibility (CSR) activities have been used to assess the quality of financial reporting (Grougiou et al., 2014).[4] For example, financial reporting practices are considered to provide the instrumental power to develop a socially responsible organisational profile.

The demand for social and environmental information is increasing over time in order to manage the environmental liabilities that could become the responsibility of banks (Deegan, 2004). Bhimani and Soonawalla (2010) described sustainability reporting as a connected reporting framework (CRF). This framework has developed voluntary sustainability reporting guidance such as The Equator Principles[5] in order to link banks' sustainability activities, both operational and strategic.

It seems vital to identify how we produce such an account thorough sustainability reporting, as an ASD practice, in order to discharge corporate responsibility. The word "account" was used in the accounting literature to demonstrate two different meanings in French and Latin (McKernan & McPhail, 2012). McKernan & McPhail (2012) explained the roots of the word "account" in both the French "*a conter*", meaning "to tell a story", and in the Latin "*accomputare*", meaning "to compute". The French meaning of account will be used in this chapter to refer to the different stories and dimensions of ASD practices. In the meantime, the French meaning of the term "account" seems to be consistent with the context of soft accounting information that emerged from subjective interviews and surveys of accounting information (Rowe et al., 2012).[6] The storytelling dimension and context of soft accounting information seem to add key dimensions to explore the unconventional meaning of the term "account" in business organisations. This meaning has been indicated in the ASD literature (Bebbington et al., 2007) as clarified in the following quote:

> There needs to be more empirically driven investigations that focus upon exploring attempts at accounting for SD. Presently (and as evident from Ian Thomson's Chapter 1), research is narrowly focused on a subset of issues that are connected to accounting for SD, but not directly focused on it. As a result, the evidential background that could be used to understand and further develop accounting for SD does not exist. In particular, exploring the themes of how to link spatial and inter-/intra-generational imperatives in SD to entity-level accounts would be a crucial task of such investigation. Such a task is likely to involve the use of a number of different, but complementary in-depth research methods.
>
> (Bebbington et al., 2007; p. 348)

This quote suggests another dimension of the term "account" as an organisational response that should be developed to manage the main themes of SD. Furthermore, it highlights the need to develop empirical investigations to explore the characteristics of organisational actions and activities to manage the main requirements of SD in actual business activities.

It has been noted that corporate accountability involves a clear organisational account to identify a set of stakeholder expectations from different interest groups (Unerman & Bennett, 2004).[7] This kind of engagement represents a corporate licence that could be managed (maintained) to operate and exist in society.

In looking at how business institutions shape and manage ASD practices, some literature has clarified how organisations build a sustainability strategy into the rhythm of their core business activities (White, 2009). This strategy includes designing sustainable innovations to improve the environmental profile of internal operations and developing transparent stakeholder partnerships. Furthermore, the impediments of sustainability reporting have been investigated to explore how organisations develop sustainability reporting practices to improve overall sustainability performance and accountability (Adams & McNicholas, 2007). Adams

& McNicholas (2007) argued that stakeholder engagement represents one of the most important components of a sustainability reporting framework. In addition, ASD practices were used, as developmental themes, to explore lessons of best practices and introduce standards and guidelines for social accounting practices including critiques of this kind of accounting (Gray et al., 1997). Therefore, social accounting was used to record data and responses from stakeholders to suggest different levels of action to construct a social image of the organisation. The actual reform of social accounting has been critically evaluated to develop organisational reform to empower stakeholders and improve corporate sustainability (Cooper & Owen, 2007). For example, corporate social reporting is not enough to increase stakeholders' accountability. It was argued that corporate social and sustainability reporting represent the very initial attempt to understand and manage corporate sustainability issues.

To sum up, there are many theoretical and ideological challenges facing business institutions in developing ASD data reporting practices.[8] Some of these challenges of ASD reporting were summarised in the need to understand the broader ecological systems and environmental changes in order to set up appropriate business decision-making arrangements and institutions (Gray & Milne, 2002).

The main argument here is that the regulatory process of social and environmental reporting requires more institutional changes to create higher levels of accountability. These levels of accountability involve the introduction of integrated reporting to create more value-added to stakeholders. This process was used to increase the organisational involvement and commitment to maintaining the main imperatives of SD.

### 14.3.2  Group two: ASD and sustainability accounting

Initially, the parameters of SEA can be framed by reference to conventional accounting (Gray, 2007). Conventional accounting can be defined by reference to the current accounting framework, standards and practices and/or by reference to describing what accountants do in business institutions. This definition seems to be imprecise for ASD as there are no compulsory standards or guidelines to describe it. So, ASD is what we have in practice when the restrictions on conventional accounting are removed (Gray et al., 2010).

The current human, social and organisational practices are not financially sustainable in the long term (Bebbington & Unerman, 2011). So, ASD is used as a control tool to achieve the objectives of financial feasibility and social and environmental equity. The growing awareness of sustainability issues is the result of successive changes in the economy, technology and climate (McElroy & Engelen, 2012). These changes represent a challenging demand to develop some ASD practices to deal with these changes in organisations (Hopwood, 2007). Socially sustainable organisations add value to the communities within which they operate by increasing the human capital of individual partners as well as by furthering the development of these communities (Spence & Gray, 2007).

Furthermore, corporate accountability has been used to illustrate corporate social, environmental, economic and ethical governance in order to understand stakeholders' expectations through opening interactive dialogues (Unerman & Bennett, 2004). In addition to such conceptual claims, the academic debate surrounding corporate accountability has been used to explore the actual dimension of corporate transparency, anti-corruption measures and corporate citizenship (Waddock, 2004). These dimensions represent the foundation values of economic, governmental, civil society and ecological spheres. The term "corporate citizenship" has also been used, as a normative extension of corporate accountability, to explain the social control of companies and the internal management mechanisms, e.g., policies, strategies, activities and decision-making systems (Valor, 2005).

The main issue here is the re-organisation of sustainability accounting, and ASD involves many challenges and opportunities that could be identified to gain the required levels of corporate legitimacy. These levels of legitimacy are used to gain the social acceptance of the desirable objectives of profit growth and wealth accumulation.

### 14.3.3  Group three: literature on unsustainable practices

Some of the accounting literature has focused on explaining the meaning of SD for the business world and the accounting profession in order to illustrate the unfavourable (unsustainable) social and environmental effects of the economic activities of business operations (Bebbington & Gray, 2001). The unsustainable practices have been used to assess social and environmental issues in terms of the cost calculation necessary to measure the additional costs that should be incurred to save the planet from any harmful organisational activities (Gray, 1992). This lens was used to create organisational accounts to highlight the costs incurred to rebuild or renew the governmental regulations (Mombeuil, 2020) regarding the consumed resources, such as the cost of helping to protect the environment by minimising carbon emissions or planting more trees, for example (see Jones, 2014).

However, some accounting literature has offered increased concern for sustainability issues and the new role of accounting tools to consider the impact of organisational activities on the environment (Milne, 1996). This lens offered the possibility of studying the ability of current generations to damage or harm the ecosystem. The role of accounting has been identified in some areas of organisational development in order to manage the relationship between accounting and sustainability (Bebbington & Gray, 2001). These areas focused on explaining the role of contingent liabilities, asset impairment and provisions to maintain the relationships between accounting and environmental issues. Some other critical accounting theorists argued that accounting was used to support sustainability through developing analytical accounting lenses to deconstruct the source of accounting effects on society and the environment (Owen et al., 1997). These efforts were used to construct some accounting mechanisms to maintain the planet by developing sustainability reporting as a reflection of how we could change the organisational management strategies and practices to achieve this kind of sustainability (Buhr, 2007).

The main point here is that the identification of the unsustainable organisational practices were used as an institutional approach to managing some of the main imperatives of SD, e.g., income inequality, ecological biodiversity and social exclusion. This process was managed as a part of the social contract between the organisation and society.

Hence, the following section provides a review of the development and emergence of ASD practices in the accounting literature in order to understand how and why these practices have been managed in organisations.

## 14.4 The ASD framework

The term ASD first emerged within the SEA literature (Bebbington, 1999). It has been used to explain how accounting could be used to create calculative, written and spoken accounts of organisational sustainability. These accounts illustrate the modern forms of accounting. In addition, ASD refers broadly to a set of accounting tools used in environmental accounting, such as environmental cost accounting, life cycle assessment and environmental liabilities (Birkin, 2000). Some alternative concepts for ASD have been used such as "greening of accountancy" to refer to the assessment process of the corporate behaviour towards achieving the objectives of SD in order to represent and assess the organisational ecology.

However, SEA is described as a universe of all possible non-conventional accounting tools that are used to create additional values and benefits to stakeholders (Gray et al., 2010). Therefore, in the absence of a compulsory and complete structure for SEA, some contemporary accounting concepts have emerged to offer a coherent framework for SEA, such as accounting for carbon emissions (Lovell et al., 2010), accounting for biodiversity (Jones, 1996; Jones, 2003), accounting for climate change (Andrew & Cortese, 2011), integrated social and environmental reporting (O'Dwyer, 2000) and ASD (Lamberton, 2000). Bebbington and Unerman (2011) argued that current human, social and organisational practices are not financially sustainable in the long term. So, ASD was used as a control tool to achieve the objectives of this kind of sustainability. However, there are some organisational challenges to identify the precise definition of the sustainability objectives (Gray et al., 2010).

It seems appropriate to develop an analytical review to identify the main theoretical perspectives associated with ASD in the literature. Therefore, the purpose of the following section is to address the main tools, purposes, criticisms and research methods of developing ASD practices. The structure of this review will be organised as follows: (i) stakeholder theory, (ii) legitimacy theory and (iii) the TBL approach.

## 14.5 The ASD theories and approaches

ASD represents a complex and important area of research because it develops unique theoretical accounting insights aimed at understanding the meaning and challenges of SD (Unerman & Chapman, 2014). Hence, ASD practices were used to explore ways of linking organisational activities and outputs to SD (Lawrence et al., 2006).[9] These ways illustrate the possibility of business enterprises having social and environmental accountability for their business activities. In addition, ASD practices were used to examine the sustainability drivers and the management of environmental issues, such as water utilisation, chemicals and waste management (Gabzdylova et al., 2009).[10] However, there are different ways of using accounting tools and techniques to manage social and environmental issues in business institutions (Bebbington & Larrinaga, 2014). In this sense, McElroy and Englen (2012) used the context-based sustainability (CBS) approach to assess the financial returns of maintaining social and environmental issues, as ASD practices, in business institutions.

Similarly, the ambition of studying ASD data recording and reporting practices involves the explanation of how they have been shaped in business organisations. This perspective seems to involve some practical roles of the accounting function to manage non-financial issues such as gender equality, human resilience, green energy consumption and social equity (Bebbington & Thomson, 2013). Such non-financial issues have been used in the corporate reporting literature to introduce a new form of integrated corporate reporting (Humphrey et al., 2014).[11]

Accordingly, the following subsections (14.5.1–14.5.3) provide an analytical review of three possible analytical lenses (stakeholder theory, legitimacy theory and institutional theory) that have been used extensively to understand the emergence and development of ASD practices in organisations. These lenses have been selected to understand the nature of ASD practices from an academic point of view. Therefore, this chapter uses stakeholder and legitimacy theories as theoretical frameworks to interpret and explore ASD practices.

### *14.5.1 Stakeholder theory*

There are at least two variants/perspectives of stakeholder theory: (i) managerial perspective and (ii) non-managerial perspective[12] (Hörisch et al., 2020). The managerial perspective prioritises the managers' expectations in the corporate management processes (Mansell, 2013). This perspective represents some kind of managerial unaccountability (ethical failure) to have a single direction or objective to guide the organisational activities (Phillips, 2003). Phillips (2003) argued that this perspective entails a form of managerial opportunism to allow corporate managers to act in their own self-interest by claiming a specific direction from a selected group of stakeholders.

Furthermore, it seems significant to identify the main characteristics of these expectations in order to develop suitable business plans and actions to gain the organisational legitimacy in society (Friedman & Miles, 2006). Hence, some of the shareholder ideologists (Hörisch et al., 2020) developed theoretical claims regarding the tension between the concepts of stakeholder theory and the economic freedom of business enterprises because they believe that this freedom has been threatened by adding extra managerial responsibilities necessary to maintain the stakeholder interests (Freeman et al., 2004). These additional responsibilities inform institutional challenges and impediments. These challenges have been managed, in some of the SEA literature, to explain the rationales for considering the needs of certain group(s) of stakeholders (see, for example, Hörisch et al., 2020; Friedman & Miles, 2006; Mansell, 2013). This includes an apparent conceptual overlap with stakeholder theory and the profit maximisation business model (Friedman & Miles, 2006).

In addition, the most influential stakeholders may be able to help business organisations in commercialising the social and environmental projects as an institutional approach to introduce this new sustainable business model. Understanding this new sustainable business model will represents one of the main challenges of business organisations over the next few years (Bocken & Short, 2021). For example, business organisations may need to answer some of the following critical questions regarding SD:

- Who will value the nature and society? (see Jones, 2014a)
- How could business organisations ensure fair and equal allocations of chances and opportunities between current and future generations? (see Gray & Milne, 2002)
- How much of the net profit should be sacrificed, by business organisations, to help the environment (nature) to re-develop (create) the consumed organisational resources to be used by the future generations? (Milne & Gray, 2013)
- What do we know about the requirements and needs of future generations?
- Who will have the proxy to identify the needs of future generations?
- How do business organisations obtain the organisational legitimacy from stakeholders (society) to accept their desires for profit growth and wealth accumulation?

### 14.5.2 Legitimacy theory

A key emphasis of legitimacy theory asserts that organisations continually work to ensure that they do their business within the limits and expectations of their respective stakeholders in society (Brown & Deegan, 1998). These expectations were addressed to develop the required organisational techniques to manage the corporate reputational risk and open communication channels with prospective stakeholders (Bebbington et al., 2008).[13] Brown and Deegan (1998) argued that organisations should develop reasonable and timely responses to stakeholders, in order to manage organisational legitimacy, because they could have different needs and expectations over time. Therefore, legitimacy theory seems to be used to explain how organisations obtain the licence to grow and operate in society (Hummel & Schlick, 2016). This licence imposes an implicit social contract between the organisation and its stakeholders to develop CSR reporting practices (Unerman, 2008). This contract represents a strategic approach to develop some of the ASD practices such as developing CSR practices to manage a corporate's reputational risk. In addition, the potential economic damage or business losses that could occur as a result of a bad or less favourable reputation seems to add long-term implications that could not be managed by traditional business solutions (Fombrun et al., 2000).

It seems important to identify and manage the reputational risk and increase the value of reputational capital for organisations. The discursive expansion of reputational risk was used to develop effective communications with targeted stakeholders through building a business case for integrated corporate environmental reporting (Kuruppu & Milne, 2010). However, the emphasis on distinguishing the difference between reputational risk and the management of corporate legitimacy represents a key component of organisational business policies and strategies. It is important for organisations to develop social activities, based on direct interactions with stakeholders, to explore and assess their social level of legitimacy without pre-social expectations (Chen & Roberts, 2010).[14] These activities involve developing organisational channels to communicate with targeted audiences with a specific business plan or objectives (Silva, 2021). This view, which is derived from improved environmental corporate disclosure, suggests that organisational legitimacy was managed in compliance with the terms and conditions of a social contract that should be managed by organisations or industries (Deegan & Blomquist, 2006). This contract was empirically dominated by the analysis of social and environmental impact in order to understand and explain the different themes of corporate legitimacy (Thomson, 2007). This insight involves another dimension of legitimacy theory to be used to understand the social aspects of business organisations.

To sum up, legitimacy theory is used as a theoretical perspective to understand how organisations manage and maintain the licence to operate in society. This licence involves some organisational practices to explore and/or translate societal expectations into the core activities and decision-making processes. This insight was used as well to create an organisational account to manage the organisational image and to assess the social responsiveness strategies of business organisations.

### *14.5.3 TBL approach*

This subsection aims to address the main analytical structure of the TBL approach in order to employ it in understanding collected and empirical data in this chapter. The growing awareness of sustainability is argued to be the result of successive changes in the global economy, technology, climate change and some other environmental pressures, such as global water shortages (McElroy & Engelen, 2012). These changes are increasingly resulting in the emergence of exciting new innovations that have made ASD better informed and in higher demand than before (Hopwood, 2007). The TBL approach was arguably seen as an early pillar of ASD practices and corporate responsibility (Walker et al., 2020).

The TBL approach was introduced by Elkington (1997) and formally adopted by Novo Nordisk in 2001 (Hopwood et al., 2010). Some measures have been suggested to detail the progress of economic, social and environmental commitments, primarily by means of organisational targets imposed on strategic areas and core activities, such as reducing the carbon footprint in order to maintain some environmental protection (Nordisk, 2008). The TBL approach involves non-compulsory activities, such as voluntary sustainability reporting, assessment of health and safety issues and elimination of unsustainable performance (Milne and Gray, 2013). In addition, the role of social entrepreneurs (Dainienė & Dagilienė, 2015) in developing a TBL approach has been suggested to identify the unserved needs of the world's underprivileged communities (Elkington, 1997). But the characteristics of these communities seem to be unclear and require a precise framework to identify them. However, the World Business Council for Sustainable Development (WBCSD, 2012) participated in an international partnership to achieve the millennium development goals.[15] This partnership used some components of the TBL approach to implementing the SD initiative to overcome poverty and inequality issues in different countries.

Hence, the TBL approach has been used as a descriptive characteristic of corporate responsibility (Walker et al., 2020) to communicate effectively with stakeholders on progress towards economic prosperity, environmental quality and social justice (Elkington, 1997). It seems that the TBL approach has been used as a metaphor for SD (Pedroso et al., 2021), rather than as a practical tool to develop organisational practices (Milne & Gray, 2013). For example, the TBL approach does not explain how business institutions could manage sustainability issues.

## 14.6  Narrative forms of ASD practices

This section aims to present some narrative forms of ASD practices, such as social contract, legitimacy accounts and stakeholders' engagement. The emphasis on a social contract as organisational practice goes back to the need to manage societal expectations and assess the impact of organisations on society and the environment (Clarkson, 1995). This impact involves an assessment process of corporate responsibility for developing favourable social values to maintain community balance and consistency (Friedman & Miles, 2002). Clarkson (1995) suggested two reasons for the need to manage the organisational social contract. First, this contract enables organisations to identify the influence of each stakeholder group. Second, the idea of a social contract was used to explore overall societal expectations. Therefore, the idea of a social contract represents a tool to identify or describe the role of sustainable organisations. It was used as well to study the level of social acceptance of sustainable organisations and manage any expected conflict in the future. Therefore, the idea of a social contract, within the framework of legitimacy and stakeholder theories, was used mainly to understand and explore the relationships between sustainability reporting, for example, as ASD practices, and corporate behaviour in business organisations (Gray, 2006a; Bebbington & Unerman, 2011). Hence, ASD practices were used to explore the sustainability processes to manage the societal level of legitimacy (see Kuruppu & Milne, 2010). In the meantime, the level of corporate legitimacy was assessed by investigating the social and environmental impact of the economic activities of business organisations.

Some critical theorists advocate for and support the idea of identifying the legitimacy level (accounts), as ASD practice, to understand the new roles of accounting tools in supporting the environment and social reporting (Lee & Cassell, 2008).[16] But some of those critical theorists view legitimacy levels (accounts) as a potential distraction that could not be readily assimilated into conventional accounting practices (Tinker, 2005).[17] Lee and Cassell (2008) argued that it is important for accounting practitioners to facilitate alliances between all who want to achieve progressive, social and environmental change for the conventional accounting practices. However, the legitimacy accounts represent social boundaries to improve the overall organisational accountability. On the other hand, some other critical theorists have argued that social (legitimacy) accounts were informed by conventional accounting tools in order to promote more effective principles of equitable society (Cooper et al., 2005). But this new role for conventional accounting involves some practical difficulties in assessing and evaluating the organisational success of promoting these principles, especially within the current (traditional) accounting framework. For example, the contextual sense of conventional accounting focuses on growth and capitalism (see Jones, 2014a). This orientation of conventional accounting seems to ignore the considerations of the social dimensions of economic business activities.

Ultimately, the framework of green human resource management (GHRM) has been used as an organisational account to transform the human resource policies (from recruitment to exit) into sustainable practices and to reveal the new role of HRM (Renwick et al., 2013). But the effectiveness and viability of GHRM seem to add new roles and levels of corporate sustainability (Anwar et al., 2020). Accounting practices could be used in this process to develop data recording, reporting and evaluating mechanisms for GHRM activities (as ASD practices). These mechanisms establish other forms of ASD practices for different activities, such as fair trade supply activities, recyclables management, the management of the carbon footprint and renewable energy consumption. This process represents an ASD tool to promote transparency, ensure high levels of corporate accountability and improve social, ethical and sustainable performance (Wahab, 2021).

## 14.7   Concluding thoughts on ASD practices

This chapter provides some critical analysis of SEIs as a voluntary framework to help business organisations in developing narrative ASD data recording and reporting practices to manage social and environmental considerations. In addition, it provides some future suggestions to develop the operational frameworks of these SEIs to help business organisations to commercialise social and environmental business opportunities. These suggestions describe the operational framework for building sustainable business models. Furthermore, this chapter provides some theoretical analysis of stakeholder and legitimacy theories as supportive lenses for developing ASD data recording, and reporting practices.

In addition, this chapter provides some theoretical aspects of ASD data recording and reporting practices, such as social contract, legitimacy accounts and stakeholders engagement. The emphasis on a social contract as organisational practice goes back to the need to manage societal expectations and assess the impact of organisations on society and the environment (Clarkson, 1995). This impact involves an assessment process of corporate responsibility for developing favourable social values to maintain the community balance and consistency (Friedman & Miles, 2002). Clarkson (1995) suggested two reasons for the need to manage the organisational social contract. First, this contract enables organisations to identify the influence of each stakeholder group. Second, the idea of a social contract was used to explore overall societal expectations. Therefore, the idea of a social contract, within the framework of legitimacy and stakeholder theories, was used mainly to understand and study the relationships between sustainability reporting, for example, as ASD practices, and corporate behaviour in business organisations (Gray, 2006; Bebbington & Unerman, 2011). Hence, ASD practices explore the sustainability processes and activities to manage the societal level of legitimacy (Kuruppu & Milne, 2010). In the meantime, the level of corporate legitimacy could be assessed by investigating the social and environmental impact of the economic activities of business organisations.

## Notes

1　It seems relevant to distinguish between SD and sustainability from an accounting perspective. Gray (2006) described sustainability as a state and SD as a process to reach this state. It could be argued that the existence of some of the SD activities does not lead to, in some cases, the creation of a whole sustainable society. So, it could be important to manage the challenges between sustainable and unsustainable activities to create a more sustainable society.

2　The main emphasis of this reference is focused on exploring the key challenges and opportunities that that strategy may face in organisations. It also highlights the theoretical debates and critical reflection on some issues that have shaped strategic management research and practice.

3　Some of these lenses involve several attempts to develop integrated reporting for social and environmental issues (Bhimani & Soonawalla, 2010). These attempts of integrated reporting could entail the study of the expected added value to stakeholders (Unerman & O'Dwyer, 2007).

4　The main context of this paper focused on investigating the relationships between CSR activities and earnings management in selected US banks. This paper discussed the role of financial reporting as an accounting practice in managing corporate profitability. It highlighted the role of CSR activities in developing a socially responsible organisational profile. It used the themes of legitimacy theory to interpret the rationale behind financial reporting practices.

5　The Equator Principles could be described as a risk management framework.

6　The main purpose of this paper was focused on exploring how people harden soft accounting information and identifying factors that affect how and how well that information is created to make it persuasive for planning organisational change.

7　The main context of this paper focused on addressing some of the practical challenges (problems) of stakeholder engagement. Some of these challenges represent the need to identify and reach a wide range of stakeholders and develop a set of stakeholder expectations from different stakeholder groups.

8 ASD data reporting practices have been called on in some of the accounting literature sustainability reporting practices (see, for example, Gray and Milne, 2002, and
O'Dwyer et al., 2005).
9 This paper explored how small economic business entities could develop sustainability
practices in New Zealand. It examined how these entities adopted the conventional
model of business ethics and new forms of corporate accountability and reporting practices to address their social and environmental impact. It looked at actual practices
that were developed to link economic business activities and the main imperatives of
SD. Environmental and social business activities represented the two main sustainability business practices. Environmental activities included the protection of the natural environment, recycling programmes, waste reduction and environmental reporting
practices. Socially responsible activities involved a communitarian approach that was
used to support local communities and employees' engagement. These sustainability
practices were used to develop new powerful relationships (accountability) between
accountee and accountor.
10 This paper explored how to develop sustainable practices in the New Zealand wine
industry. It focused on the influential role of stakeholders in the decision-making
systems. These practices involved water utilisation, chemical and waste management. The main drivers for developing sustainable practices were focused on three
main factors. These factors are ethical personal values, work enjoyment and product
quality.
11 This paper examined the developmental processes for institutionalising an integrated corporate reporting framework. It focused on examining the attempts of
IIRC to institutionalise reporting practices to create value and manage the longer-
term sustainability of businesses. It called for the development of an integrated
reporting profession besides integrated reporting practices in order to institutionalise the field.
12 This chapter focuses on the main aspects of the managerial perspective of stakeholder
theory in order to understand ASD practices in banking institutions. These aspects
involve some elements of the societal and environmental components of business strategies and policies, such as how managers want to do their business, and specifically
what kinds of accounts they want and need to create within the society and environment.
13 This paper provided an analytical review and discussion on commentary papers on
corporate social responsibility reporting in the light of legitimacy theory. It highlighted
the complexities of CSR reporting practices. These complexities involved the need to
consider main themes of reputation risk management in these practices.
14 This paper addressed some conceptual relationships between legitimacy, stakeholders,
institutional and resource dependence theories in order to develop social and environmental accounting research. It suggested two main theoretical themes which should
be considered to achieve this development. The **first theoretical theme** was focused
on exploring the legitimacy and motivation for developing social activities. The **second theoretical theme** was focused on identifying the role of these four theories in
interpreting business social phenomena. This paper provided some ideas by which to
describe the relationships between an organisation and society. These thoughts were
uncontested in order to minimise the complexity of these four theories.
15 This partnership was published in June 2012 by a network of multilateral UN agencies
and international NGOs to address critical poverty, environment and climate change
issues within the framework of international efforts to achieve the objectives of Green
Economy International Campaign. For more details, see the following link http://www
.unep.org/pdf/PEP_Paper-Final_2.pdf (accessed on 21 August 2020).
16 The main context of this paper was focused on exploring reconciliation of critical
(Marxist) views with those of supporters of social and environmental accounting and
reporting (SEAR). It investigated some information about learning issues in the annual

and social reports to assess the progression of social justice concept at work that could be used to enhance accountability and strengthen trade unions.

17 The main purpose of this paper was focused on exploring the progression of accounting research in the field of critical reflection. It examined four streams of progressive accounting research: (i) professional analysis, (ii) culturalist studies, (iii) ethnographic studies and (iv) epistemic contributions.

## References

Adams, C. A. & McNicholas, P., 2007. Making a Difference Sustainability Reporting, Accountability and Organisational Change. *Accounting, Auditing and Accountability Journal*, 20(3), pp. 382–402.

Andrew, J. & Cortese, C., 2011. Accounting for Climate Change and the Self-Regulation of Carbon Disclosures. *Accounting Forum*, 35(3), pp. 130–138.

Anwar, N. et al., 2020. Green Human Resource Management for Organisational Citizenship Behaviour towards the Environment and Environmental Performance on a University Campus. *Journal of Cleaner Production*, 256.

Bartelmus, P., 1994. *Environment, Growth and Development: Concepts and Strategies of Sustainability*. 2nd ed. London: Routledge.

Bebbington, J., 1999. *Accounts of and Accounting for Sustainable Development*. Unpublished Ph.D. dissertation, University of Dundee, Dundee.

Bebbington, J., 2001. Sustainability Development: A Review of the International Development, Business and Accounting Literature. *Accounting Forum*, June, 25(2), pp. 128–157.

Bebbington, J. & Gray, R., 2001. An Account of Sustainability: Failure, Success and A Reconceptualization. *Critical Perspectives on Accounting*, 12(5), pp. 557–587.

Bebbington, J. & Larrinaga, C., 2014. Accounting and Sustainable Development: An Exploration. *Accounting, Organizations and Society*, 39(6), pp. 395–413.

Bebbington, J., Larrinaga-Gonzalez, C. & Moneva-Abadıa, J. M., 2008. Legitimating Reputation/the Reputation of Legitimacy Theory. *Accounting, Auditing and Accountability Journal*, 21(3), pp. 371–374.

Bebbington, J., O'Dwyer, B. & Unerman, J., 2007. Postscript and Conclusions. In: J. Unerman, J. Bebbington & B. O'Dwyer, eds. *Sustainability Accounting and Accountability*. Oxon: Routledge, pp. 345–351.

Bebbington, J. & Thomson, I., 2013. Sustainable Development, Management and Accounting: Boundary Crossing. *Management Accounting Research*, 24(4), pp. 277–283.

Bebbington, J. & Unerman, J., 2011. The Importance of Peer-Reviewed Social and Environmental Accountability Research in Advancing Sustainability. *Social and Environmental Accountability Journal*, 31(1), pp. 1–6.

Bhimani, A. & Soonawalla, K., 2010. Sustainability and Organizational Connectivity at HSBC. In: A. Hopwood, J. Unerman & J. Fries, eds. *Accounting for Sustainability: Practical Insights*. London: Earthscan, pp. 173–190.

Birkin, F., 2000. The Art of Accounting for Science: Aprerequisite for Sustainable Development. *Critical Perspectives on Accounting*, 11(3), pp. 289–309.

Bocken, N. M. & Short, S. W., 2021. Unsustainable Business Models – Recognising and Resolving Institutionalised Social and Environmental Harm. *Journal of Cleaner Production*, 312(20).

Brown, N. & Deegan, C., 1998. The Public Disclosure of Environmental Performance Information—A Dual Test of Media Agenda Setting Theory and Legitimacy Theory. *Accounting and Business Research*, Winter, 29(1), pp. 21–41.

Buhr, N., 2007. Histories of and Rationales for Sustainability Reporting. In: J. Unerman, J. Bebbington & B. O'Dwyer, eds. *Sustainability Accounting and Accountability*. New York: Routledge, pp. 57–69.

Burns, J. & Scapens, R. W., 2000. Conceptualizing Management Accounting Change: An Institutional Framework. *Management Accounting Research*, 11(1), pp. 3–25.

Changwony, F. K. & Paterson, A. S., 2019. Accounting Practice, Fiscal Decentralization and Corruption. *The British Accounting Review*, 51(5).

Channuntapipat, C., Samsonova-Taddei, A. & Turley, S., 2020. Variation in Sustainability Assurance Practice: An Analysis of Accounting versus Non-Accounting Providers. *The British Accounting Review*, 52(2).

Chen, J. C. & Roberts, R. W., 2010. Toward a More Coherent Understanding of the Organization–Society Relationship: A Theoretical Consideration for Social and Environmental Accounting Research. *Journal of Business Ethics*, 97(4), pp. 651–665.

Clarkson, M. E., 1995. A Stakeholder Framework for Analyzing and Evaluation of Corporate Social Performance. *Academy of Management Review*, 20(1), pp. 92–117.

Cooper, C., Taylor, P., Smith, N. & Catchpowel, L., 2005. A Discussion of the Political Potential of Social Accounting. *Critical Perspectives on Accounting*, 16(7), pp. 951–974.

Cooper, S. M. & Owen, D. L., 2007. Corporate Social Reporting and Stakeholder Accountability: The Missing Link. *Accounting, Organizations and Society*, 32(7–8), pp. 649–667.

Costello, N., 2000. *Stability and Change in High-Tech Enterprises: Organisational Practices and Routines*. London: Routledge.

Cunningham, J. & Harney, B., 2012. *Strategy & Strategists*. Oxford: Oxford University Press.

Dainienė, R. & Dagilienė, L., 2015. A TBL Approach Based Theoretical Framework for Measuring Social Innovations. *Procedia - Social and Behavioral Sciences*, 213(1), pp. 275–280.

Deegan, C., 2004. Environmental Disclosures and Share Prices- A Discussion About Efforts to Study this Relationship. *Accounting Forum*, 28(1), pp. 87–97.

Deegan, C. & Blomquist, C., 2006. Stakeholder Infuence on Corporate Reporting: An Exploration of the Interaction between WWF-Australia and the Australian Minerals Industry. *Accounting, Organizations and Society*, 31(4–5), pp. 343–372.

Elkington, J., 1997. *Cannibals with Fork- The Triple Bottom Line of 21st Century Business*. Oxford: Capstone.

Fombrun, C. J., Gardberg, N. A. & Barnett, M. L., 2000. Opportunity Platforms and Safety Nets: Corporate Citizenship and Reputational Risk. *Business and Society Review*, 105(1), pp. 85–106.

Freeman, E., Wicks, A. C. & Parmar, B., 2004. Stakeholder Theory and "the Corporate Objective Revisited". *Organization Science*, 15(3), pp. 364–369.

Friedman, A. L. & Miles, S., 2002. Developing Stakeholder Theory. *Journal of Management Studies*, 39(1), pp. 1–21.

Friedman, A. L. & Miles, S., 2006. *Stakeholders: Theory and Practice*. New York: Oxford University Press.

Gabzdylova, B., Raffensperger, J. F. & Castka, P., 2009. Sustainability in the New Zealand Wine Industry: Drivers, Stakeholders and Practices. *Journal of Cleaner Production*, 17(11), pp. 992–998.

Gray, R., 1992. Accounting and Environmentalism: An Exploration of the Challenge of Gently Accounting for Accountability, Transparency and Sustainability. *Accounting, Organizations and Society*, 17(5), pp. 399–425.

Gray, R., 2006. Does Sustainability Reporting Improve Corporate Behaviour?: Wrong Question? Right Time? *Accounting and Business Research*, 36(Sup1), pp. 65–88.

Gray, R., 2007. A Few Thoughts on Theory, Methodology and Research Design in Social Accounting: (or Why is Social Accounting So Difficult? Part II). *Socail and Environmental Accounting Journal*, April, 27(1), pp. 17–22.

Gray, R., Bebbington, J. & Gray, S., 2010. *Social and Environmental Accounting*. 1st ed. London: SAGE Publications Ltd.

Gray, R., Dey, C., Owen, D., Evans, R. & Zadek, S., 1997. Struggling with the Praxis of Social Accounting: Stakeholders, Accountability, Audits and Procedures. *Accounting, Auditing and Accountability Journal*, 10(3), pp. 325–364.

Gray, R. & Milne, M., 2002. Sustainability Reporting: Who's Kidding Whom. *Chartered Accountants Journal of New Zealand*, 81(6), pp. 66–70.

Grougiou, V., Leventis, S., Dedoulis, E. & Owusu-Ansah, S., 2014. Corporate Social Responsibility and Earnings Management in US Banks. *Accounting Forum*, 38(2), pp. 92–106.

Hopwood, A. G., 2007. Whither Accounting Research? *The Accounting Review*, October, 82(5), pp. 1365–1374.

Hopwood, A., Unerman, J. & Fries, J., 2010. *Accounting for Sustainability; Practical Insights*. 1st ed. London: Earthscan.

Hörisch, J., Schaltegger, S. & Freeman, R. E., 2020. Integrating Stakeholder Theory and Sustainability Accounting: A Conceptual Synthesis. *Journal of Cleaner Production*, 275(1).

Hummel, K. & Schlick, C., 2016. The Relationship between Sustainability Performance and Sustainability Disclosure – Reconciling Voluntary Disclosure Theory and Legitimacy Theory. *Journal of Accounting and Public Policy*, 35(5).

Humphrey, C., O'Dwyer, B. & Unerman, J., 2014. *The Rise of Integrated Reporting Understanding Attempts to Institutionalize a New Reporting Framework*. St Andrews: Centre for Social & Environmental Accounting Research (CSEAR).

Jarzabkowski, P. & Balogun, J., 2009. The Practice and Process of Delivering Integration through Strategic Planning. *Journal of Management Studies*, December, 46(8), pp. 1255–1288.

Jarzabkowski, P. & Spee, A. P., 2009. Strategy-as-Practice: A Review and Future Directions for the Field. *International Journal of Management Reviews*, 11(1), pp. 69–95.

Jarzabkowski, P. A., Lê, J. K. & Feldman, M. S., 2012. Toward a Theory of Coordinating: Creating Coordinating Mechanisms in Practice. *Journal of Organization Science*, July–August, 23(4), pp. 907–927.

Jones, M., 2014. Creating a Theoretical Framework for Biodiversity Accounting. In: M. Jones, ed. *Accounting for Biodiversity*. New York: Routledge, pp. 23–45.

Jones, M. J., 1996. Accounting for Biodiversity: A Pilot Study. *The British Accounting Review*, 28(4), pp. 281–303.

Jones, M. J., 2003. Accounting for Biodiversity: Operationalising Environmental Accounting. *Accounting, Auditing and Accountability Journal*, 16(5), pp. 762–789.

Kuruppu, S. & Milne, M., 2010. Dolphin Deaths, Organizational Legitimacy and Potential Employees' Reactions to Assured Environmental Disclosures. *Accounting Forum*, 34(1), pp. 1–19.

Lamberton, G., 2000. Accounting for Sustainable Development—A Case Study of City Farm. *Critical Perspectives on Accounting*, 11(5), pp. 583–605.

Lawrence, S., Collins, E., Pavlovich, K. & Arunachalam, M., 2006. Sustainability Practices of SMEs: The Case of New Zealand. *Journal of Business Strategy and the Environment*, 15(4), pp. 242–257.

Lee, B. & Cassell, C., 2008. Employee and Social Reporting as a War of Position and the Union Learning Representative Initiative in the UK. *Accounting Forum*, 32(4), pp. 276–287.

Lélé, S. M., 1991. Sustainable Development: A Critical Review. *Journal of World Development, June*, 19(6), pp. 607–621.

Lovell, H., Aguiar, T. S. D., Bebbington, J. & Larrinaga-Gonzalez, C., 2010. *Accounting for Carbon*. London: International Emissions Trading Association.

Mansell, S. F., 2013. *Capitalizm, Corporations and the Social Contarct*. 1st ed. Cambridge: Cambridge University Press.

McElroy, M. & Engelen, J. V., 2012. *Corporate Sustainability Management*. 1st ed. New York: Earthscan.

McKernan, J. F. & McPhail, K., 2012. Accountability and Accounterability. *Critical Perspectives on Accounting*, 23(3), pp. 177–182.

Milne, M., 1996. On Sustainability; the Environment and Management Accounting. *Management Accounting Research*, 7(1), pp. 135–161.

Milne, M. J. & Gray, R., 2013. W(h)lther Ecology? The Triple Bottom Line, the Global Reporting Initiative, and Corporate Sustainability Reporting. *Journal of Business Ethics*, November, 118(1), pp. 13–29.

Mombeuil, C., 2020. Institutional Conditions, Sustainable Energy, and the UN Sustainable Development Discourse: A Focus on Haiti. *Journal of Cleaner Production*, 254.

Nordisk, N., 2008. *Annual Report*. Bagsvaerd: Novo Nordisk.

O'Dwyer, B., 2000. Evidence and the Public Interest versus Expediency: Critical Commentary on "Could Corporate Environmental Reporting Shadow Financial Reporting?" by Aris Solomon. *Accounting Forum*, 24(2), pp. 223–230.

O'Dwyer, B., Owen, D. & Unerman, J., 2011. Seeking Legitimacy for New Assurance Forms: The Case of Assurance on Sustainability Reporting. *Accounting, Organizations and Society*, 36(1), pp. 31–52.

O'Dwyer, B., Unerman, J. & Hession, E., 2005. User Needs in Sustainability Reporting: Perspectives of Stakeholders in Ireland. *European Accounting Review*, 14(4), pp. 759–787.

Owen, D., Bebbington, J. & Gray, R., 1997. Green Accounting: Cosmetic Irrelevance or Radical Agenda for Change? *Asian Pacific Review of Accounting*, 4(2), pp. 175–198.

Pedroso, C. B., Tate, W. L., Silva, A. L. D. & Carpinetti, L. C. R., 2021. Supplier Development Adoption: A Conceptual Model for Triple Bottom Line (TBL) Outcomes. *Journal of Cleaner Production*, 314(10).

Phillips, R., 2003. *Stakeholder Theory and Organizational Ethics*. 1st ed. Oakland, CA: Berrett-Koehler Pulisher, Inc.

Renwick, D. W., Redman, T. & Maguire, S., 2013. Green Human Resource Management: A Review and Research Agenda. *International Journal of Management Reviews*, 15(1), pp. 1–14.

Roberts, J. & Scapens, R., 1985. Accounting Systems and Systems of Accountability: Understanding Accounting Practices in Their Organisational Contexts. *Accounting, Organizations and Society*, 10(4), pp. 443–456.

Rowe, C., Shields, M. D. & Birnberg, J. G., 2012. Hardening Soft Accounting Information: Games for Planning Organizational Change. *Accounting, Organizations and Society*, 37(4), pp. 260–279.

Scapens, R. W., 2006. Understanding Management Accounting Practices: A Personal Journey. *The British Accounting Review*, 38(1), pp. 1–30.

Silva, S., 2021. Corporate Contributions to the Sustainable Development Goals: An Empirical Analysis Informed by Legitimacy Theory. *Journal of Cleaner Production*, 292(10).

Spence, C. & Gray, R., 2007. *Social and Environmental Reporting and the Business Case.* London: Certified Accountants Educational Trust.

Thomson, I., 2007. Managing the Terrain of Sustainability Accounting. In: J. Unerman, J. Bebbington & B. O'Dwyer, eds. *Sustainability Accounting and Accountability.* 1st ed. New York: Routledge, pp. 19–36.

Tinker, T., 2005. The Withering of Criticism A Review of Professional, Foucauldian, Ethnographic, and Epistemic Studies in Accounting. *Accounting, Auditing and Accountability Journal*, 18(1), pp. 100–135.

Unerman, J., 2008. Strategic Reputational Risk Management and Corporate Social Responsibility Reporting. *Accounting, Auditing and Accountability Journal*, 21(3), pp. 362–364.

Unerman, J. & Bennett, M., 2004. Increased Stakeholder Dialogue and the Internet: Towards Greater Corporate Accountability or Reinforcing Capitalist Hegemony? *Accounting, Organizations and Society*, 29(7), pp. 685–707.

Unerman, J. & Chapman, C., 2014. Academic Contributions to Enhancing Accounting for Sustainable Development. *Accounting, Organizations and Society*, 39(6), pp. 385–394.

Unerman, J. & O'Dwyer, B., 2007. The Business Case for Regulation of Corporate Social Responsibility and Accountability. *Accounting Forum*, 31(4), pp. 332–353.

Valor, C., 2005. Corporate Social Responsibility and Corporate Citizenship: Towards Corporate Accountability. *Business and Society Review*, June, 110(2), pp. 191–212.

Waddock, S., 2004. Creating Corporate Accountability: Foundational Principles to Make Corporate Citizenship Real. *Journal of Business Ethics*, 50(4), pp. 313–327.

Wahab, M. A., 2021. Is an Unsustainability Environmentally Unethical? Ethics Orientation, Environmental Sustainability Engagement and Performance. *Journal of Cleaner Production*, 294(20).

Walker, K., Yu, X. & Zhang, Z., 2020. All for One or All for Three: Empirical Evidence of Paradox Theory in the Triple-Bottom-Line. *Journal of Cleaner Production*, 275.

WBCSD, 2012. *Building an Inclusive Green Economy for All: Opportunities and Challenges for Overcoming Poverty and Inequality.* Geneva: World Business Council for Sustainable Development.

White, P., 2009. "Building a Sustainability Strategy Into the Business" Corporate Governance. *The International Journal of Business in Society*, 9(4), pp. 386–394.

World Commission on Environment and Development, 1987. *Our Common Future.* Oxford: Oxford University Press.

# 15 The relationships between corporate narrative reporting practices and sustainable business models

*Mohamed Saeudy*

## 15.1 Introduction

One of the biggest challenges facing the world today is to understand the implications of sustainability for people's everyday lives. This is true especially in the world of business, where the sustainability agenda is increasingly coming to bear on the decision making of customers, managers, shareholders, lenders, suppliers and employees. A growing range of issues has a bearing on this agenda, including regulatory challenges, global biodiversity loss, climate change (Bevan et al., 2020) and increased expectations on companies with regard to product responsibility, human rights and providing a decent work environment for employees. In order to address this agenda, companies are increasingly turning to the sustainable business model (SBM). This model focuses on commercialising social and environmental activities as core business transactions. It requires a new corporate strategy, new sustainable accounting tools and processes by which business organisations can identify and manage these opportunities. The actual conceptual framework of this SBM is quite unclear in the literature. Therefore, this chapter aims to clarify the role of narrative reporting in managing SBM in business organisations.

This chapter argues that the relationships between corporate narrative reporting practices and SBMs are not fully covered in the accounting literature. Therefore, the current chapter explores these relationships as well as investigating how accounting tools and practices have been used to develop SBM. These practices aim to manage the social and environmental considerations of the main operations of business activities. Narrative reporting was linked to financial reporting in the accounting literature (Roslender & Nielsen, 2017). This link was made to create integrated business reporting models and to put financial information into a meaningful context. Narrative reporting represents a crucial component of any financial report according to the 2001 International Accounting Standards Board (IASB) framework for the preparation and presentation of financial statements (Beattie & Smith, 2013).

The motivational features of developing this chapter are to study the main factors of developing corporate narrative reporting practices and managing the SBM, which are mostly related to institutional factors such as top management and

DOI: 10.4324/9781003095385-19

stakeholder engagement (Adams & Abhayawansa, 2021). In addition, the main theoretical challenges to devolving and managing these practices were related to operational and pragmatic considerations such as sustainability culture and attitudes. The identification of these empirical challenges could represent initial outlines that could be considered in developing the future role of corporate narrative reporting.

This chapter contributes to the literature by studying the role of narrative reporting managing and developing SBMs. These models could be used to achieve sustainable development goals such as, for example, reducing carbon emissions, supporting human rights, empowering the low-income people in society, addressing climate change and supporting economic democracy. These imperatives require coherent sets of organisational narrative reporting practices to manage the social and environmental activities of the economic operations of the SBM (Adams & Abhayawansa, 2021). Therefore, the structure of this chapter will be as follows. Section 15.2 will clarify the concept of narrative reporting practices. Section 15.3 presents the development of the SBM, while Section 15.4 illustrates the role of sustainability initiatives in developing narrative corporate reporting. Section 15.5 explains the role of sustainability initiatives in managing the SBM and Section 15.6 explores the alternative ways in which narrative reporting are reflected in the accounting and finance literature. Section 15.7 presents the relationships between the SBM and corporate narrative reporting practices, while, finally, Section 15.8 provides some concluding thoughts on narrative reporting.

A number of studies have attempted to document the use of accounting as a measurement system to articulate visible corporate social reporting mechanisms in large UK institutions (Coupland, 2006). These studies have focused on examining the levels of organisational involvement in the social and environmental issues within the banking industry. So, it seems more relevant for this chapter to consider social and environmental issues (including narrative reporting practices) as a core component in attempts by the banking institutions to create a coherent SBM. The theoretical framing of this chapter focuses on the identification of the theoretical components of stakeholder theory (e.g., social contract), legitimacy theory (e.g., institutional image and social acceptance of profit and wealth accumulation) and institutional theory (e.g., institutional sustainability entrepreneurs).

This chapter investigates the existence of a new business model which aims to develop organisational accounts of accounting for non-sustainability (Spence & Gray, 2007). The model was used to commercialise social and environmental projects as core business activities within organisations. It provides new interpretations of the relationships between the main components of capitalism, e.g., consumers, producers, market regulations and government (Long & Sievers, 2012). It has been argued that this new business model shows how business organisations can make reasonable economic returns (profits) without harming or damaging the environment and society. The level of corporate accountability and stakeholder engagement in this business model can then be investigated.

## 15.2  The development of SBM

Recently, the concepts of sustainability, sustainable development (SD) and positive social and environmental impact have been identified and have emerged in business research, business organisations and public institutions. However, there is no single explanation of the concept of SD. This concept has been defined in the Brundtland report to support the environmental policy agenda (World Commission on Environment and Development, 1987). This report described SD as "development that meets the needs of the present without compromising the ability of future generations to meet their own needs". It seems that this definition does not provide a clear explanation for the fundamental meaning of sustainability in terms of organisational practices or activities (Bartelmus, 1994). Furthermore, it does not identify the main imperatives of SD to manage human activities and to fulfil the needs of future and current generations (Lélé, 1991).

Sustainability and SD have been developed and used for many years as mutually inclusive, but not identical, concepts by which to develop business practices to explain the relationships between ecological issues and corporate behaviour (Bebbington & Gray, 2001; Gray, 2006; Spence & Gray, 2007). SD was used as a framework with which to address the organisational, social, environmental and economic impacts (Milne & Gray, 2013).

In response to the growing recognition that companies must respond to the sustainability agenda, a number of international efforts have been introduced over the past ten years to guide and manage sustainability policies at the corporate level. These include the Global Reporting Initiative (GRI, 2013), the United Nations Environmental Programme Finance Initiative (UNEPFI)[1] and the Financial Institutions Resources, Solutions and Tools (FIRST[2]) initiative that was developed by the International Finance Corporation (IFC). These initiatives were used to provide a conceptual framework to help business organisations to manage the main imperatives of SD. At its most basic, sustainability reporting initiatives such as those noted above are intended to facilitate disclosure of the organisation's impact (be it positive or negative) on the environment, society and economy.

A good start to understanding what this means for business is to distinguish between the terms "sustainability" and "sustainable development". "Sustainability" refers to the degree to which a company has made progress in its aim to achieve economic, ecological and social viability. It involves a radical agenda for change in both organisational life and organisational accountability. This involves maintaining the relationship the company has with the ecosystem and society in which it operates, subject to the need to make and grow profits. These concerns present fundamental challenges for decision making on the part of managers of such organisations. As such, sustainability was considered to be the desired state and "sustainable development" as the process to reach this state. Sustainability seeks ways to address the increasingly pressing exigencies of SD in companies. However, there are some other complicated issues involved in introducing the themes of SD into corporate activities, such as the efficient and fair distribution of resources and opportunities between present and future

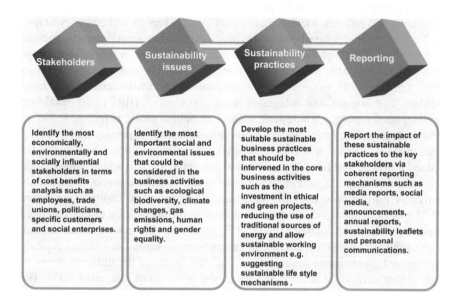

*Figure 15.1* Sustainability management process in business organisations and the role of narrative reporting.

generations (Hopwood et al., 2010). The practical management of these challenges in daily activities implies the identification of four basic phases as indicated in Figure 15.1.

Figure 15.1 illustrates the four sustainability management phases; these are all facilitated by the adoption of narrative reporting practices within the company. The first phase is to identify the company's stakeholder groups, defined as those who have an impact on or are impacted by the company's activities (Gray, 2006). The second phase then attempts to record these impacts in economic, social and environmental terms (Cunningham & Harney, 2012).[3] The third stage is to manage these impacts, which will inevitably generate challenges as tensions arise between those activities that are considered sustainable and those that are currently practised (Andrew & Cortese, 2011). There will also inevitably be impediments to making the changes required for the company to become more sustainable. As such, it is helpful at this stage to identify the desired sustainable position (or status) of each business unit across the whole organisation. Much of this work can be done by modifying existing sustainable business practices. This final phase involves producing and reporting information, and this is one of the core business activities.

To this end, international business sustainability frameworks (such as GRI and UNEPFI) have been adopted by many accountancy professionals, universities (Filho et al., 2019), institutional investors and corporate practitioners. As such, reporting the impact of SBM has now become a common component of published, organisational documents and reports, including publications such as sustainability reports and policies, social impact reports, media reports and ethical policies.

Various rationales have been used to encourage business institutions to embrace and produce SBM voluntarily. For example, the Equator Principles encourage financial institutions to develop a voluntary framework to assess the sustainability impact of a project's business transactions and report it to the company's stakeholders. The International Integrated Reporting Council (IIRC) also developed an integrated reporting framework in 2013 to help organise corporate reporting practices, including financial, social, and environmental reporting (IIRC, 2013). This framework promotes SBM as a main organisational approach to create added value for present and future generations of stakeholders. This added value reflects the commercial, social and environmental context of the company's core daily activities. Furthermore, the IIRC has identified six forms of "capital" (see Figure 15.2) that were managed and developed through the application of the integrated reporting framework. These comprise financial capital, manufactured capital, human capital, intellectual capital, social relationship capital and natural capital.

Figure 15.2 indicates the interconnectedness between the different forms of capital that need to be developed through the adoption of integrated SBM. The management and development processes of these forms of capital involve a number of organisational challenges, such as gaining top management commitment and support, measuring long-term outcomes and adapting measurement practices. The successful management and development of these challenges could manage the financial values of these capitals.

In summary, SBM aims to develop organisational reports of accounting for non-sustainability (Spence & Gray, 2007). It was used to commercialise social and environmental projects as core business activities within organisations. It provides new interpretations of the relationships between the main components of

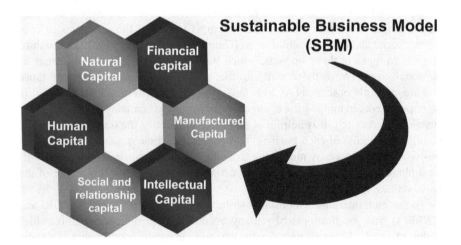

*Figure 15.2* IIRC's six forms of capital.

capitalism, e.g., consumers, producers, market regulators and government (Long & Sievers, 2012).

## 15.3 The role of sustainability initiatives in developing corporate narrative reporting

Some of the sustainability entrepreneur initiatives (e.g., GRI and The Equator Principles) have been used to clarify the main characteristics of SBM (Macve & Chen, 2010)[4] and Milne & Gray, 2013). This chapter explains the meaning of the entrepreneurship concept in the literature in order to be used as a flagship concept of institutional entrepreneurs. Basically, the definition of entrepreneurship involves varying themes for different contexts (Gartner, 1990). For example, Gartner (1990) suggested two main groups of thoughts to clarify the meaning of entrepreneurship. The first group focused on characteristics of entrepreneurship, such as high risk, uniqueness and innovation, to describe the actual features of the term (Shakeel et al., 2020). The second group focused on describing the definition of entrepreneurship by explaining the main research objects, such as new venture creation, growth opportunity and entrepreneurial cognition (Leitch et al., 2010). In addition, the entrepreneur concept has been used to demonstrate the conversion of opportunities and new proposals into marketable ideas to add value through time (Kuratko, 2014). It involves the risk of exposing concepts to the competitive market to accept and implement these ideas. It seems significant to identify the main challenges and impediments that have been faced to achieve an added value. This view involves some kind of ambiguity to identify the characteristics of the unique personality and the sources of these opportunities in order to explore the contextual meaning of the term. Therefore, the notion of institutional sustainability entrepreneurs was used in this chapter to refer to the national and international organising and guiding bodies (UNEP FI, FORGE, GRI and The Equator Principles) that are providing practical frameworks and guidelines on managing social and environmental sustainability.

The absence of compulsory sustainability reporting guidelines represents a key challenge for managing the main imperatives of SD in business organisations (Gray & Milne, 2002). However, there are some international and national attempts that have been introduced to manage the main imperatives of SD in the economic activities of business institutions (e.g., The Equator Principles, UNEP FI, GRI and FORGE). This section aims to address the institutional sustainability entrepreneurs' initiatives and efforts that have been made to guide and manage the social and environmental activities of business organisations, especially in the business sector. These institutional sustainability entrepreneurs are involved in developing the social and environmental (sustainability) reporting, and assessment practices. The institutions and bodies which have made some effort to generate guidelines to manage these practices include UNEP FI, GRI and The Equator Principles.

## 15.4 The role of sustainability initiatives in managing SBM

The United Nation Environmental Programme Finance Initiative (UNEP FI) introduced a specialised initiative to develop and promote linkages between sustainability and financial performance for business institutions (UNEP FI, 2011). This initiative[5] aims to identify, promote and encourage the adoption of best environmental and sustainability practices at all levels of banking institution operations. But the accounting sense of these practices seems to be important in this context. In other words, the explanation of how we use accounting tools and practices to understand the main imperatives of SD represents a key stream or pillar because this initiative offers some broad principles of SD as a conceptual framework for sustainability efforts. In addition, the contents of this guide involve attempts to manage some of the main imperatives of SD in the business activities such as environmental and social screening, employees' engagement and disclosure engagement. The best sustainability practices were shared by international organisations from all over the world. Moreover, this guide was constructed based on the Bruntland Report's definition of SD to incorporate or accommodate the social and environmental issues in the main core of business operations. Therefore, it defines what sustainability means to different roles and departments within an institution, and how these can each take action to make business institutions more sustainable. So, this initiative incorporates a more detailed framework for sustainable practices in business institutions to develop the overall sustainable performance in order to assess the social and environmental impact of the economic activities of business operations.

Furthermore, GRI was developed initially to manage social, environmental and economic reporting practices (GRI, 2013).[6] The latest version of GRI (G4) has introduced a set of tools and indicators that have been developed through international open (and sometimes public) discussions and engagement in order to enhance corporate sustainability reporting. These indicators provide material information on the social, environmental and economic performance or the impact of an organisation on these three aspects. Milne and Gray (2013) criticised the disconnect between corporate sustainability reporting practices and the sustainability process to support ecological systems and humanity. In addition, this disconnect has led to greater levels of non-sustainability in some cases. These claims were consistent with the failure of GRI reporting guidelines (Moneva et al., 2006) to enhance corporate sustainability performance and accountability because of the inability of some organisations to consider the main sustainability imperatives such as greenhouse gas emissions, social justice and human rights issues.

Moreover, FORGE was developed as one of the global sustainability initiatives by the FORGE group[7] to provide institutional guidelines on environmental management and reporting for the financial sector (FORGE, 2000). It contains a detailed practical toolkit to institutionalise environmental management and reporting systems. Environmental management systems (EMS) were established to assess environmental risks and to develop internal coherent arrangements to manage these risks (Jeucken, 2004). The FORGE group represents an example of cooperative trends to institutionalise environmental systems and practices. It focuses on providing collaborative expertise in two main activities (FORGE, 2000). The first group of activities involves the core business practices such as risk control, portfolio management, commercial lending and retail banking. The second group of activities involves operational practices such as waste management, property and facilities management, energy management (Goggins et al., 2019) and supply chain. The integration between these two groups of activities and the internal accounting systems existed as indicated in the quote below:

> It is important that the environmental management structure is clear, logical and appropriate for the business. The structure should reflect, and make use of, existing group management systems and structures. In particular, data management systems should be embedded into, or aligned with, existing management and financial (accounting) systems.
>
> (FORGE, 2000, p. 24)

The abovementioned statement indicates that there is a need to integrate and incorporate EMS in the traditional management and financial accounting systems. This process includes the involvement of EMS and reporting systems in the corporate governance practices, accounting and audit standards. It seems significant to maintain additional organisational considerations to create a positive environmental impact. This impact involves the management of the cultural landscape, reducing greenhouse gas emissions and maintaining ecological biodiversity by looking after the rare fauna and flora (Jones, 2014). These considerations involve some ideological and practical challenges to be included in the core capitalist strategies (agenda) of some financial institutions. However, these considerations represent one of the main components of the social contract between organisations and society.

## 15.5 Ways in which narrative reporting is reflected in accounting and finance literature

This chapter argues that, although some business institutions have developed narrative reporting practices, the sustainability motivations and challenges for these practices are not well known. Therefore, this chapter explores these challenges as well as investigating how accounting tools and practices can be used to develop narrative reporting practices to manage the social and environmental issues of the main operations of organisational activities.

Financial and accounting tools were used to evaluate and assess the management of this new sustainable business model (SBM) and the imperatives that it promotes, e.g., by reducing carbon emissions, supporting human rights, empowering low-income people in society, addressing climate change and supporting economic democracy (Milne and Gray, 2013). These imperatives require coherent sets of corporate narrative reporting practices to manage the social and environmental activities of the economic operations of business organisations. It is significant to compare the costs of maintaining this SBM against the conventional one. This process was managed in terms of cost-benefits analysis. If the cost of maintaining an SBM is greater than the benefits of the conventional model, it will be relevant to think about some public policies to pay for this extra cost.

The theoretical links between accounting and the main imperatives of SD open up empirical research avenues to explore how narrative reporting practices were developed to manage social and environmental aspects of business activities. The management process associated with the social and environmental issues of business activities has been developed in different forms and for different purposes. The legitimacy of narrative reporting practices involves the need to obtain societal acceptance of profit and capital accumulation. The role of governmental policies and plans was used to create collectivist ownership as a new form of capitalism (Kaletsky, 2010). This form requires the basic human activities to operate more ethically and humanistically within society. This initiative does not stipulate the need to develop natural resources and other environmental factors. But it stands for more responsible considerations for the social and environmental impacts that arise from the activities of the organisation.

Narrative reporting practices are continuing to legitimise organisational activities within some industrial sectors, e.g. health and public service; manufacturing; energy efficiency (Schulz et al., 2019); retail and commercial enterprise; banking and financial services; and universities and higher education institutions (Jeucken, 2004; McElroy & Engelen, 2012). However, there is a significant degree of convergence between TBL components and organisational practices (Milne and Gray, 2013). Climate change, global financial crises, reformed legal frameworks and economic pressures on business enterprises have added new dimensions to the role played by the accounting profession (Hopwood, et al., 2010).

Therefore, there is a significant motivation to promote and explore narrative reporting practices in an organisational context in order to reinforce the institutional legitimacy and create a positive impact from the organisational activities (see Coupland, 2006; Spence & Gray, 2007; McElroy & Engelen, 2012). These motivations have been supported by a dramatic increase in sustainability initiatives proposed by international organisations, such as the United Nations (UN), GRI and the Sustainability Context Group in the USA[8].

The main argument here is that there are some social and cultural issues that affect the organisational decision-making process (Sherer et al., 2016). This theoretical argument aims to provide conceptual guidance to understand the legitimacy of narrative reporting practices (Roslender & Nielsen, 2017). This emphasis has been used to explore why and how narrative reporting practices have emerged in business institutions, e.g., how business institutions manage the social and environmental accounts of their organisational activities.

## 15.6  The relationships between SBM and corporate narrative reporting practices

Corporate narrative reporting has been developed and presented in business organisations by using accounting technologies to address social and environmental practices as well as to examine the issues that arise from the impact of organisational activities (Gray, 2006). This process was analysed by using the themes of management theories to understand how narrative reporting was used in a broader context, e.g., with regard to global sustainability issues (Bebbington, 2009). Furthermore, there are two main lenses through which to develop the maturation of SBM (including narrative reporting) in the accounting literature (Unerman & Chapman, 2014). The first lens is focused on the need to prepare empirical investigations to explore attempts made in this new field as well as to explore the themes to link the principles of SD to the entity level accounts as SBM. The second lens is concentrated on the need to introduce useful and sophisticated theoretical lenses to explore the organisational practices of SD in business institutions. Nevertheless, SBM has been used deliberately to address some issues of environmental and social reporting and accountability (Gray, 2006). These accounts were developed by focusing on how an organisation might provide actual contribution to SD in terms of the well-being of the planet. So, the failures of organisational accounts to discharge accountability or to sufficiently embrace this context may lead to unsustainable performance (Milne & Gray, 2007). The identification of corporate narrative reporting was used to improve the overall corporate sustainability by developing the relevant sustainable reporting practices that should be used to achieve social and environmental improvements (Adams & Abhayawansa, 2021).

In addition, various forms of narrative reporting practices have been investigated through different contexts in the accounting literature. For example, Unerman and Chapman (2014) highlight the need to examine how narrative reporting practices can and have been used to embed the considerations of SD into the decision-making systems at different levels within organisations. This effort suggests a wide range of organisational frameworks to understand these practices (Bebbington & Thomson, 2013). Accounting theories provide analytical insights from a combination of novel theorisations, constructivism and empirical observations to develop and understand narrative reporting practices. The meaningful application of this suggestion would require a clear investigation of the main critique made for SBM. This critique involves the clarification of the merits of narrative reporting practices. In other words, business organisations should decide why they need these narrative reporting practices and what are the main failures in the conventional business models that could be improved by incorporating narrative reporting (Thomson, 2011). In order to explain the conceptual framework of narrative reporting practices, the interpretive-hermeneutic circle has been used to identify the characteristics of these practices. The hermeneutic circle represents one of the main traditions of the interpretive approach (Yanow, 2014). The idea of the hermeneutics circle focuses on how to make sense of complex notions by developing and refining distinctions between two realities. Hence, the hermeneutic circle has been used to identify the main realities of narrative reporting practices in terms of the actual realities of conventional accounting as indicated in Table 15.1. It illustrates the distinction between narrative reporting and conventional financial reporting frameworks. This distinction involves some conceptual and pragmatic differentiation between the two frameworks. The conceptual aspects of this distinction involve the ontological approaches, materiality of the key topics and the description of each framework. The pragmatic aspects of

*Table 15.1* Comparison between narrative reporting and conventional financial reporting

| Criteria | Narrative reporting | Conventional financial reporting |
| --- | --- | --- |
| Description | The provision of environmental, social, and economic information on organisational activities | The process of producing qualitative and quantitative information about financial transactions |
| Organising and controlling framework | • UNEP FI<br>• FORGE<br>• GRI<br>• The Equator Principles | • Regulators<br>• Supervisory authorities<br>• Professional accounting bodies |
| Regulatory framework | Non-compulsory protocols | • Accounting standards<br>• Accounting principles |
| Data recording mechanism | Quantified and unquantified methods to register social and environmental data, e.g., natural inventory system (see Jones, 2014a). | Double-entry recording system for financial business transactions (see King and Crowther, 2004) |
| Reporting mechanism | Voluntary reporting framework | Regulated financial reporting framework |
| Evaluation mechanisms | Social and environmental data assessment (impact) | • Financial and ratio analysis<br>• Investment appraisal |
| Final outputs | Comprehensive accounts and best organisational practices | Financial statements, accounts and reports |
| Materiality and power | The benefits of saving the organisational and natural resources | How to report the important information such as the units of consumed natural resources |
| Outreach | Create healthy relationships with society and the environment. | Communicating financial and non-financial information to users |
| Boundaries | How SD practices are evidenced in the organisational activities | Financial matters with limited emphases on social and environmental issues |
| Approaches | Managing the value of the replenishment process of the consumed organisational and natural resources | Managing the values of consumed organisational resources |
| Challenges/limitations | The absence of the regulatory and the compulsory framework of narrative reporting practices. | The intellectual spaces between qualitative and quantitative data for financial transactions. |

these two frameworks involve the practical outlines of each framework, such as organising bodies, practices, mechanisms, communication, final outputs and the challenges of each framework.

Table 15.1 summarises the main differences between conventional and narrative reporting practices. It shows some of the main theoretical and practical frameworks of narrative reporting practices. It was argued that narrative reporting practices could be developed by using conventional accounting practices to manage social and environmental aspects of business and organisational activities. These activities involve carbon footprint, fair trade supply chains, green energy consumption, social contract and ecological biodiversity (Mansell, 2013; Jones, 2014). These frameworks offer analytical lenses through which to use accounting techniques and tools to understand the organisational management process of narrative reporting practices. The main emphasis of this chapter focuses only on the financial and non-financial data (narrative) reporting in order to gain deeper insights into various aspects of the management processes of narrative reporting practices. The main reason for choosing the narrative reporting mechanisms is that these practices represent a new field of accounting, in terms of academic scrutiny and professional business experience, compared with the heritage of conventional accounting. So, this field of accounting started to be developed recently in terms of research (as publications) and professional development.

In addition, it could be quite challenging to assess the impact of the narrative reporting practices without a detailed and proper narrative reporting mechanism for these practices in order for comparison from one year to another to evaluate the organisational progress towards SD (Jones, 2014). In addition, the narrative reporting practices mechanisms represent the major components of any accounting system. Narrative reporting practices identify the difference between the current organisational position and a sustainable future (Bebbington & Gray, 2001; Gray, 2010).

The role of narrative reporting practices to manage the relationships between organisations and the planet involve some attractive benefits. One of these benefits represents the ability to develop multiple and coherent accounts of organisational (un)sustainability in order to identify the organisational progression toward maintaining social and environmental enhancement (Bebbington & Thomson, 2013; Unerman & Chapman, 2014).

Conventional accounting uses financial reporting to provide information about business organisations to people outside the management function (Alexander et al., 2011). It was argued that the management can obtain whatever information it needs from within the organisation but external users rely on some sort of negotiation or regulations to obtain what they want to know about the organisation. The tension may represent a key challenge that should be managed by management and regulators in order to obtain the societal licence to operate.

Most of the narrative reporting mechanisms are organised by voluntary reporting frameworks. There are at least two possible ways to understand the purposes of narrative reporting. The first possibility came from the need to develop them as business practices and the second possibility came from the need to engage and communicate with the most influential stakeholders (Unerman, 2008). The second possibility, in some cases, involves unidirectional efforts because they are not mutually exclusive. One of the main purposes of narrative reporting is to create actual behavioural development to change management strategies and information systems (Buhr, 2007). In addition, reporting corporate social practices represents additional accounts of the social contract (Moneva, et al., 2006) to manage some of the organisational externalities and to ameliorate the consequences of economic activities. The information flow of this contract (between the organisation and its stakeholders) involves some legal, ethical and societal considerations to understand the notion of corporate accountability. Accordingly, the core business of accounting for social and environmental factors involves the communication of information (e.g., social and environmental reporting) concerning the organisational impact on society (Gray, 2006a; Moneva, et al., 2006). The social and environmental reporting in the financial industry was guided by a set of voluntary guidelines, e.g., UNEP FI and FORGE. These guidelines have been developed to respond to a wide range of stakeholders' interest to obtain more information about organisations. For example, the FORGE guidelines were developed in 2000 to progress the understanding of CSR for the financial services sector to obtain the licence to operate in the society (Association of British Insurers, 2002).

In summary, there are some significant opportunities and challenges, in conventional accounting, to integrated narrative reporting. These opportunities explore the combined forms of integration between financial and non-financial reporting practices (Humphrey et al., 2014).[9] The intellectual spaces between financial and non-financial reporting seem to be less organised or regulated by the regulatory and professional bodies. In addition, there is some sort of unwillingness on the part of business organisations to adequately understand and manage sustainability issues within the organisational contexts such as profit maximisation and associated beliefs (Gray, 2006). In addition, the absence of the regulatory and compulsory framework of narrative reporting practices represents a major criticism for the academic credibility of narrative reporting practices and their organisational merits.

Therefore, the practical and theoretical structure of narrative reporting practices was identified based on the structure of conventional accounting. For example, narrative reporting practices represent a process of conventional accounting to manage the main imperatives of SD, such as economic welfare, social exclusion, income inequality, ecological biodiversity and climate changes. This process involves some fundamental challenges and impediment, e.g., the quantification of these imperatives and the lack of institutional expertise to manage these imperatives in business organisations.

## 15.7 Concluding thoughts

This chapter investigates the existence of a new business model. This new business model aims to develop organisational narrative reporting practices of accounting for unsustainability (see Spence and Gray, 2007). It was used to commercialise social and environmental projects as core business activities within business organisations. It provides new interpretations of the relationships between the main components of capitalism, e.g., consumers, producers, market regulations and government (Long & Sievers, 2012). It was argued that this new business model reports how business organisations can make reasonable economic returns (profits) without damaging the environment or society. The level of corporate accountability and stakeholder engagement requires unique narrative reporting mechanisms to produce the SBM.

This chapter looked for narrative financial and accounting tools to evaluate and assess the management of this new SBM and the imperatives that it promotes, e.g., reducing carbon emissions, supporting human rights, empowering low-income people in society, addressing climate change and supporting economic democracy. These imperatives require coherent sets of organisational narrative reporting practices to manage the social and environmental activities of the economic operations of the SBM. It is significant to compare the costs of maintaining this SBM against the conventional one. This process could be managed in terms of cost-benefit analysis. If the cost of maintaining an SBM is greater than the benefits of the conventional model, it will be relevant to think about some governmental policies to pay for this extra cost. These policies could involve a new tax regime, investment incentives or operational guidelines.

The theoretical contribution of this chapter could benefit two groups of stakeholders. The first group of implications includes managerial implications that benefit academics and business managers (accountants). The second group of implications involves the non-managerial implications that could benefit other stakeholders, e.g., SD researchers and activists, investors, customers, supervisory authorities, government, professional bodies, customers and shareholders. The managerial implications involve the possibility of developing integrated narrative reporting practices to organise and manage the SBMs. These practices represent an internal organisational guide to manage the main challenges of SD and develop more coherent organisational policies such as zero carbon emissions, green investments and sustainable finance policies. In addition, the managerial implications involve the possibility of creating organisational accounts to identify the targeted or the most influential stakeholders that should be considered in the business planning and decision-making processes. In addition, it could be relevant to develop other organisational policies to manage the organisational contribution to environmental improvement. This account could involve the organisational impact on the less influential stakeholders who are negatively affected by environmental damage.

The non-managerial implications involve some of the practical benefits that could be delivered to external or other stakeholders. For example, this thesis provides empirical evidence to support any future development of coherent narrative reporting practices. This support involves the practical considerations that should be raised and maintained in these practices such as the sustainability culture and engagement by top management and stakeholders.

## Notes

1 United Nations Environmental Programme Finance Initiative (UNEP FI) was established in 1992 as a platform associating the United Nations and the financial sector globally. It aims to provide guidance on managing the relationships between finance

and the environment, social and governance challenges, and the role of financial institutions in creating a more sustainable world. For more information, see http://www .unepfi.org/about/ (accessed on 25 August 2020).

2 This initiative has been developed by the International Finance Corporation (IFC). This initiative was developed mainly in the emerging markets to manage environmental and social risks for IFC's portfolio. The researcher decided to disregard the analysis of this initiative because it was tailored only for IFC's investment portfolio with some specifications for emerging markets only. For more information, see the following link: http://firstforsustainability.org/sustainability/development-finance-institutions/ifc -approach-to-sustainability/ (accessed on 27 August 2020).

3 The main emphasis of this reference is focused on exploring the key challenges and opportunities that the strategy may face in organisations. It also highlights the theoretical debates and critical reflections on some issues that have shaped strategic management research and practice.

4 The purpose of this paper is to investigate both the nature of the success and the shortcomings of The Equator Principles reporting framework. It discussed the role or the positive impact of The Equator Principles reporting framework on the environment. This paper was based on a review of various publications by NGOs and professional accounting organisations. It investigated the disclosure made by Barclays and HSBC in 2008 because these two banks were the largest UK participants in The Equator Principles Financial Institutions.

5 This initiative was published in October 2011 as a general guide for banks. It aims to help understand and implement sustainability based on the UNEP statement of commitment by financial institutions on SD. It provides explicit guidance to the banking community regarding the meaning and implementation of sustainability for different groups of 200 banks and practitioners across banking operations, especially for institutions and/or employees new to the topic. For more information see the following link: http://www.unepfi.org/fileadmin/documents/guide_banking_statements.pdf (accessed in 25 August 2020).

6 G4 represents the latest sustainability reporting guidelines framework that has been developed by the GRI. These guidelines offer reporting principles, standard disclosures and an implementation manual for preparing a sustainability report. It also offers international reference for all those interested in the disclosure of governance approach and social, environmental and economic performance. For more information, see https://www.globalreporting.org/reporting/g4/Pages/default.aspx (accessed on 30 August 2020).

7 It is a consortium of some of the UK's financial service organisations. The consortium consists of representatives from The Abbey National Bank, Barclays, Lloyds TSB Bank, The Royal Bank of Scotland and Royal & Sun Alliance. For more information, see https://www.greenbiz.com/sites/default/files/document/O16F20407.pdf (accessed on 31 July 2020).

8 The Sustainability Context Group (SCG) is an international association of sustainability academics and practitioners. The main objective of this group is focused on finalising language to be used in a submission to the GRI urging it to take concrete steps to strengthen the guidance on how to operationalise the sustainability context principles in the fourth generation of *Sustainability Reporting Guidelines.* For more information, see the following link: http://www.st-andrews.ac.uk/~csearweb/conferencesnews/2012 -Half-Day-Leaflet-3.pdf (accessed on 16 August 2020).

9 This paper examined the developmental processes for institutionalising an integrated, corporate reporting framework. It focused on examining the attempts of IIRC to institutionalise reporting practices to create value and manage the longer-term sustainability of businesses. It called for the development of an integrated reporting profession in addition to integrated reporting practices in order to institutionalise the field.

# References

Adams, C., & Abhayawansa, S., 2021. Connecting the COVID-19 Pandemic, Environmental, Social and Governance (ESG) Investing and Calls for 'Harmonisation' of Sustainability Reporting. *Critical Perspectives on Accounting*. Vol 82.

Alexander, D., Britton, A., & Jorissen, A., 2011. *International Financial Reporting and Analysis*. 5th Éd. Hampshire, UK: Cengage Learning EMEA, pp. 55–65.

Andrew, J., & Cortese, C., 2011. Accounting for Climate Change and the Self-Regulation of Carbon Disclosures. *Accounting Forum*, 35(3), pp. 130–138.

Association of British Insurers, 2002. *Guidance on Corporate Social Responsibility Management and Reporting for the Financial Services Sector (FORGE)*. London, UK: Association of British Insurers.

Bartelmus, P., 1994. *Environment, Growth and Development: Concepts and Strategies of Sustainability*. 2nd Éd. London: Routledge.

Beattie, V., & Smith, S. J., 2013. Value Creation and Business Models: Refocusing the Intellectual Capital Debate. *The British Accounting Review*, 45(4), pp. 243–254.

Bebbington, J., 2009. Measuring Sustainable Development Performance: Possibilities and Issues. *Accounting Forum*, 23(3), pp. 189–193.

Bebbington, J., & Gray, R., 2001. An Account of Sustainability: Failure, Success and A Reconceptualization. *Critical Perspectives on Accounting*, 12(5), pp. 557–587.

Bebbington, J., & Thomson, I., 2013. Sustainable Development, Management and Accounting: Boundary Crossing. *Management Accounting Research*, 24(4), pp. 277–283.

Bevan, L. D., Colley, T., & Workman, M., 2020. Climate Change Strategic Narratives in the United Kingdom: Emergency, Extinction, Effectiveness. *Energy Research and Social Science*, 69.

Buhr, N., 2007. Histories of and Rationales for Sustainability Reporting. In J. Unerman, J. Bebbington, & B. O'Dwyer, éds. *Sustainability Accounting and Accountability*. New York: Routledge, pp. 57–69.

Coupland, C., 2006. Corporate Social and Environmental Responsibility in Web-Based Reports: Currency in the Banking Sector? *Critical Perspectives on Accounting*, 17(7), pp. 865–881.

Cunningham, J., & Harney, B., 2012. *Strategy & Strategists*. Oxford: Oxford University Press.

Filho, W. L. et al., 2019. The Role of Higher Education Institutions in Sustainability Initiatives at the Local Level. *Journal of Cleaner Production*, 233, pp. 1004–1015.

FORGE, 2000. *Guidelines on Environmental Management and Reporting for the Financial Services Sector: A Practical Toolkit*. London: FORGE.

Gartner, W. B., 1990. What Are We Talking About When We Talk About Entrepreneurship? *Journal of Business Venturing*, 5(1), pp. 15–28.

Goggins, G., Fahy, F., & Jensen, C. L., 2019. Sustainable Transitions in Residential Energy Use: Characteristics and Governance of Urban-Based Initiatives across Europe. *Journal of Cleaner Production*, 237.

Gray, R., 2006. Does Sustainability Reporting Improve Corporate Behaviour?: Wrong Question? Right Time? *Accounting and Business Research*, 36(Sup1), pp. 65–88.

Gray, R., & Milne, M., 2002. Sustainability Reporting: Who's Kidding Whom. *Chartered Accountants Journal of New Zealand*, 81(6), pp. 66–70.

Gray, R., 2010. Is accounting for sustainability actually accounting for sustainability… and how would we know? An exploration of narratives of organisations and the planet *Accounting, Organizations and Society*, 35(1), pp. 47–62.

GRI, 2013. *G4 Sustainability Reporting Guidelines: Reporting Principles and Standard Disclosures*. Amsterdam, The Netherlands: Global Reporting Initiative.

Hopwood, A., Unerman, J., & Fries, J., 2010. *Accounting for Sustainability; Practical Insights*. 1st Éd. London: Earthscan.

Humphrey, C., O'Dwyer, B., & Unerman, J., 2014. *The Rise of Integrated Reporting Understanding Attempts to Institutionalize a New Reporting Framework*. St Andrews: Centre for Social & Environmental Accounting Research (CSEAR).

IIRC, 2013. *Capitals Background Paper for Integrated Reporting*. London, UK: International Integrated Reporting Council.

Jeucken, M., 2004. *Sustainability in Finance- Banking on the Planet*. Amsterdam: Eburon Academic Publishers.

Jones, M., 2014. Ecosystem and Natural Inventory Biodiversity Frameworks. In M. Jones, éd. *Accounting for Biodiversity*. New York: Routledge, pp. 39–61.

Kaletsky, A., 2010. *Capitalism 4.0: The Birth of a New Economy in the Aftermath of Crisis*. London: Bloomsbury.

King, J. E. & Crowther, M. R., 2004. The Measurement of Religiosity and Spirituality Examples and Issues from Psychology. *Journal of Organizational Change Management*, 17(1), pp. 83–101.

Kuratko, D. F., 2014. *Entrepreneurship: Theory, Process and Practice*. 9th Éd. Mason: South-Western Cengage Learning.

Leitch, C. M., Hill, F. M., & Harrison, R. T., 2010. The Philosophy and Practice of Interpretivist Research in Entrepreneurship: Quality, Validation, and Trust. *Organizational Research Methods*, January, 13(1), pp. 67–84.

Lélé, S. M., 1991. Sustainable Development: A Critical Review. *Journal of World Development, June*, 19(6), pp. 607–621.

Long, S., & Sievers, B., 2012. Money, Finance and Capitalism: Issues in Organisational Life for Now and the Future. In S. Long & B. Sievers, éds. *Toward a Socioanalysis of Money, Finance and Capitalizm: Beneath the Surface of the Financial Industry*. Oxon: Routledge, pp. 250–272.

Macve, R., & Chen, X., 2010. The "Equator Principles": A Success for Voluntary Codes? *Accounting, Auditing and Accountability Journal*, 23(7), pp. 890–919.

Mansell, S. F., 2013. *Capitalizm, Corporations and the Social Contarct*. 1st Éd. Cambridge: Cambridge University Press.

McElroy, M., & Engelen, J. V., 2012. *Corporate Sustainability Management*. 1st Éd. New York: Earthscan.

Milne, M., & Gray, R., (eds.), 2007. Future Prospects for Corporate Sustainability Reporting. In *Sustainability Accounting and Accountability*. New York: Routledge, pp. 184–207.

Milne, M. J., & Gray, R., 2013. W(h)ither Ecology? The Triple Bottom Line, the Global Reporting Initiative, and Corporate Sustainability Reporting. *Journal of Business Ethics*, November, 118(1), pp. 13–29.

Moneva, J. M., Archel, P., & Correa, C., 2006. GRI and the Camouflaging of Corporate Unsustainability. *Accounting Forum*, 30(2), pp. 121–137.

Roslender, R., & Nielsen, C., 2017. Lessons for Progressing Narrative Reporting: Learning from the Experience of Disseminating the Danish Intellectual Capital Statement Approach. *Accounting Forum*, 41(3), pp. 161–171.

Schulz, K. A., Gstrein, O. J., & Zwitter, A. J., 2019. Exploring the Governance and Implementation of Sustainable Development Initiatives through Blockchain Technology. *Futures*, 122.

Shakeel, J., Mardani, A., Chofreh, A. G., Goni, F. A., & Klemeš, J. J., 2020. Anatomy of Sustainable Business Model Innovation. *Journal of Cleaner Production*, 261.

Sherer, S. A., Meyerhoefer, C. D., & Peng, L., 2016. Applying Institutional Theory to the Adoption of Electronic Health Records in the U.S. *Information & Management*, 53(5), pp. 570–580.

Spence, C., & Gray, R., 2007. *Social and Environmental Reporting and the Business Case*. London: Certified Accountants Educational Trust.

Thomson, I., 2011. Is Accounting for Sustainability Actually Accounting for Sustainability… and How Would We Know? An Exploration of Narratives of Organisations and the Planet (article review). *Social and Environmental Accountability Journal*, 31(1), pp. 99–100.

UNEP FI, 2011. United Nations Environmental Programme Finance Initiative. [En: ligne] Available at: http://www.unepfi.org/about/ [Accès le 28 August 2020].

Unerman, J., 2008. Strategic Reputational Risk Management and Corporate Social Responsibility Reporting. *Accounting, Auditing and Accountability Journal*, 21(3), pp. 362–364.

Unerman, J., & Chapman, C., 2014. Academic Contributions to Enhancing Accounting for Sustainable Development. *Accounting, Organizations and Society*, 39(6), p. 385394.

World Commission on Environment and Development, 1987. *Our Common Future*. Oxford: Oxford University Press.

Yanow, D., 2014. Interpretive Analysis and Comparative Research. In: Engeli, I., Allison, C.R. (eds) *Comparative Policy Studies*. Research Methods Series. Palgrave Macmillan, London. pp. 131–159.

# Part 4

# Narrative reporting in times of crisis

# 16 Changes in governance of corporate risks

Evidence from British Petroleum's response to the Deepwater Horizon Incident through narrative reporting

*Nader Elsayed*

## 16.1 Introduction

> 2010 was a profoundly painful and testing year. In April, a tragic accident on the Deepwater Horizon Rig claimed the lives of 11 men and injured others. [...] We are shocked and saddened that it did. The spill that resulted caused widespread pollution. Our response has been unprecedented in scale, and we are determined to live up to our commitments in the Gulf. We will also do everything necessary to ensure BP is a company that can be trusted by shareholders and communities around the world. [...] As a board, we have much to do.
>
> (Annual Report (AR), 2010, pp. 6–7)

The quotation above expressed British Petroleum's (BP) Chairman Carl-Henric Svanberg accounted for mitigating the risks that had arisen from the Deepwater Horizon (DWH) incident. It caused a huge oil spill into the Gulf of Mexico, put BP at the forefront of the global media and political attention, claimed the lives of 11 men and injured others and led to the establishment of a $20-billion fund to demonstrate its preparedness to cover all legitimate claims (Elsayed and Ammar, 2020).

This disaster, which marked the largest oil spill in history, had massive environmental and social implications and raised questions regarding BP's risk disclosures, corporate governance (CG) structuration and mechanisms of operationalisation that have threatened BP's continuation as one of the largest multinational companies in the oil and gas industry. Incidents, therefore, offer a good opportunity to understand the corporate response to material risks and the complexity of organisational change after such an incident.

To articulate how BP actors changed how corporate risks are governed, this chapter explores how BP responded to the DWH incident through narrative reporting. It relies on an illustrative longitudinal case study of BP's ARs over the period 2008–2017 through the lens of Institutional Logics Perspective (ILP). This chapter, therefore, proceeds as follows. Section 16.2 explores the prior literature.

DOI: 10.4324/9781003095385-21

Section 16.3 outlines the structuring concepts of ILP. Section 16.4 presents the research methodology. Section 16.5 discusses BP's risk governance case, while Section 16.6 provides the conclusions, implications and suggestions for future research.

## 16.2  Literature review

Existing risk management (RM) literature (e.g., Falkner and Hiebl, 2015; Giovannoni et al., 2016; Carlsson-Wall et al., 2018) has addressed a set of open research questions relating to risk identification, risk perception, risk control, risk analysis and managerial attitude towards risk, but with little focus on the formality and structuration of a corporate RM system. Consequently, Stein and Wiedemann (2016) called for an investigation of the interaction between CG and RM, highlighting the conceptualisation of risk governance (RG) as a relatively new practice through which corporate risks are managed, and discussing how the dynamic business environment is affected when it is not adopted. They further raised the questions of how corporate RG is structured or restructured and which methods are applicable to identify, prioritise and aggregate the preserved risks. Recently, the proponents of RG have moved further towards the institutional processes that integrate collective activities of handling risks (Klinke and Renn, 2021) since an institution with improved RG can avoid or mitigate incident loss (Zuo et al., 2017). Therefore, there is a need to articulate how organisational actors contribute to changing how corporate risks are governed for corporate strategic success, consistent with (Stein et al., 2019). The current study, therefore, aims at exploring BP's response to the DWH incident since the implications of such an incident on managerial changes have not yet been addressed.

With relatively few exceptions (cf. Meidell and Kaarbøe, 2017; Carlsson-Wall et al., 2018), there has been little focus on case study research in RM literature within a specific organisation. The vast majority of existing studies (e.g., Lundqvist, 2015; Florio and Leoni, 2017; Gontarek and Belghitar, 2018; Sheedy and Griffin, 2018, etc.) focus merely on the empirical examination of the association between RG and the implementation of RM jointly with or separate from company performance. Although they generally found positive relationships that reflect the importance of enhancing the existing RM system to improve corporate progress, others reported negative findings (e.g., Aljughaiman and Salama, 2019). Despite the insights obtained from these empirical studies, they do not articulate how organisational actors changed how corporate risks are governed. The current study, therefore, addresses this shortcoming and deepens our understanding of how risk implications are governed by corporate actors through an in-depth longitudinal case study.

While the available literature underlines the importance of corporate strategy in managing material risks (e.g., Falkner and Hiebl, 2015; Aljughaiman and Salama, 2019, etc.), this strategy is sequentially influenced not only by the stakeholders' perceptions and participations (Hardy and Maguire, 2016) but most importantly by the actors' beliefs and ideations (i.e., logics), consistent with Thornton et al.

(2012). The empirical study of Lundqvist (2015), for example, found that the level of RG is positively associated with the CEO's influence. This finding suggests that the motives and dynamics of corporate actors play a significant role in the subsequent actions of a corporation. Since the mainstream of prior literature had emphasised the role of organisational actors in oversight and running the business, it is still far from clear how they use their knowledge, expertise and values to manage material risks and implement a risk practice. The current researcher, therefore, has opted to use ILP, which is a significant development within the institutional theory, to inform the current case study research. Furthermore, this study adds to the very few studies that utilise ILP since a recent review study by Damayanthi and Gooneratne (2017) finds that ILP has received limited attention in previous management control research.

## 16.3 Institutional logics perspective

Over the years, researchers (e.g., Lounsbury, 2007; Carlsson-Wall et al., 2016; Mutch, 2018) have adopted the ILP to conceptualise and understand accounting practices through the identification of structured and coherent logics of individual and collective actors and the subsequent examination of their connections. Thornton et al. (2012, p. 2) defined ILP as *the socially constructed, historical patterns of cultural symbols and material practices, including assumptions, values, and beliefs, by which individuals and organisations provide meaning to their daily activity, organise time and space and reproduce their lives and experiences.* Organisational actors, therefore, attempt through their interactions to conceptualise their values and expectations (Järvinen, 2016) for shaping any heterogeneity or change (Thornton et al., 2012), although their reactions may substantially vary (Lounsbury, 2007).

Logics are considered to be the beliefs and rules that shape the cognitions, behaviours and actions of organisational actors that eventually provide taken-for-granted practices to achieve organisational targets (Carlsson-Wall et al., 2016). Thornton et al. (2012) developed an integrated model of ILP arguing that these taken-for-granted practices are subject to change during an environmental or societal issue. This framework documented the benefits of a dynamic ILP in terms of availability, accessibility, communication and activation, ultimately leading to logically consistent decisions. It comprises a set of toolkits that start by focusing the attention of organisational actors on the issue at hand and end by providing improvements to organisational practice(s) as a reaction to that issue. This creates a window of opportunity for the individual agency through which the actors are allowed to view the organisation's practice(s) and provide insights for changes to occur (Corbett et al., 2018). ILP, therefore, ultimately shape the material aspects represented by organisational practice(s) since they affect organisational actions through the actors' cognitions, behaviours and conceptions that reflect the symbolic aspects of their ideations and meanings in their interactions.

Organisational actors would utilise their knowledge and expertise, which is available from their backgrounds and the surrounding environment (Mutch,

2018), in their cognitive processes through their interactions and communications. The accessibility and applicability of the available knowledge would lead to focusing the actors' attention on current and/or subsequent matters. The availability, accessibility and applicability of that knowledge would therefore evolve as embedded organisational practice even in situations of multiple logics since a change in actors' logics in the presence of an environmental or societal issue would diffuse throughout the corporate management control system to enhance its effectiveness. Consequently, the activation of actors' attention depends considerably on the applicability of the accessible knowledge driving the top-down knowledge perspective to the salient aspects of that environmental issue, as well as the environment driving a bottom-up environmental stimulus perspective to the actors' attention and cognitions (Modell, 2015).

This activation of actors' attention is, therefore, shaped in two active directions, namely top-down and bottom-up trends (Thornton et al., 2012), enabling them to achieve their ends. The first involves the top-down knowledge perspective, in which actors generate top-down knowledge both vertically (i.e., multi-level) and horizontally (i.e., cross-level) through their participation in multiple organisational orders for enabling information to be shared and processed. The second could be driven by bottom-up environmental stimuli, in which organisational actors face situations where the existing practice is not congruent with the observed behaviours and outcomes in the environment. As a result, the embedded organisational practice requires actors from different organisational orders to provide appropriate judgements by using their knowledge, expertise and values through their interactions and communications (Corbett et al., 2018). Such interactions between the actors in different organisational orders, multilevel and/or cross-level, and their effective decision-making, sense-making and collective mobilisation processes, eventually provide support in mediating the conflicts between actors' logics and handling the embedded organisational practice.

## 16.4 Research methodology

### 16.4.1 Research approach and strategy

This study adopts a qualitative approach to articulate the way in which BP actors changed how corporate risks are governed by exploring how BP responded to the DWH incident. This approach is a standard research methodology that is frequently utilised in the management accounting discipline (Parker, 2012). Although this approach provides support in exploring the risk that arises from the organisational control context (Elsayed and Ammar, 2020), it also enables RG to be analysed over time, retrospectively (Zuo et al., 2017; Gontarek and Belghitar, 2018; Sheedy and Griffin, 2018).

This chapter relies on an illustrative, longitudinal case study (Parker, 2012; Scapens, 2004) to enrich our understanding of how BP responded to the DWH incident. Case studies have been widely acknowledged in the literature and are preferred when contemporary phenomena are under examination, as they aim to illustrate and explain accounting *in practice* within a specific organisation (Giovannoni et al., 2016; Meidell and Kaarbøe, 2017; Carlsson-Wall et al., 2018). Case studies are, therefore, adequate to answer the how and why questions that require a deep understanding of organisational processes (Yin, 2009).

BP following the DWH incident has been selected as an illustrative, longitudinal case study (Scapens, 2004) for two reasons. The first reason is the international nature of BP's operations as one of the largest multinational companies specialising in the oil and gas sector and maintaining investments geographically distributed throughout over 70 countries.[1] This diversity in its investments offers an opportunity to understand the complexity of organisational change when a disaster occurs. The second reason is the DWH incident in April 2010 that represents one of its most significant investments and pulled BP to the forefront of global media and political attention. During that time, BP experienced turbulence relating to its safety and environmental profile, its relationships with its shareholders and overall corporate reputation. Consequently, BP, as a multinational company, has needed to act in a more socially desirable manner.

### 16.4.2 Data collection method and analysis

Drawing on the ILP, this case study utilises BP's ARs[2] over ten years (2008–2017). These reports are considered the key means by which BP communicates with relevant stakeholders concerning its risk trends and indicators since the incident pushed BP's managerial team to respond through reporting disclosures. They also provide complementary data on (a) the committees' structuration, (b) the demographics of each committee chair and member, such as their background, relevant work experience and skills information, and (c) the meetings and interactions between the board members and executive management. BP's RG practice is primarily investigated during the period 2010–2017. However, the two years before the incident, 2008 and 2009, are also examined to signal the change in BP's practices at the time of the DWH incident and to report the consequences of this incident on risk reporting patterns before and after the incident.

Archival thematic analysis was conducted by uploading, managing and examining the outcomes of hand-collected data with NVivo software. This analysis offers flexibility and accessibility because it does not use a specific theoretical framework, and it provides clarity about how the qualitative data were examined (Braun et al., 2016). The analysis involved coding terms and creating themes. The coding process began with browsing all the targeted ARs, careful line-by-line reading and then coding the relevant texts. This identified the epidemic terms (i.e., codes) that convey the same meaning for data consistency. This mechanism then enables the creation of consistent patterns (i.e., themes) based on the theoretical lens of ILP to articulate their appearance and frequency to form generalisations about the outcomes and detect whether the epidemic codes have changed throughout the investigation.

After the codes were identified and analysed, two key themes were outlined, namely (a) *attention process*, and (b) *activation process*. The first theme concerns

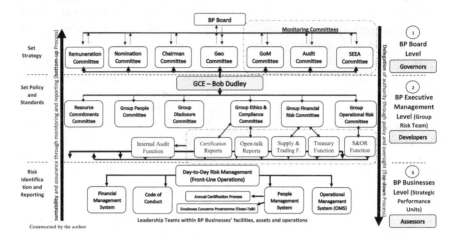

*Figure 16.1* BP risk structuration.

BP's focus of attention regarding its RM system to articulate the evolution of the constructed material risk practices, whereas the second theme concerns the mechanisms of interactions between different BP organisational orders, which explicitly evolved after the DWH incident. This latter theme revealed the presence of three sub-themes representing the three detected organisational orders of the BP's RM system, namely (1) *risk governance* (led by the BP board and its monitoring committees), (2) *risk mobilisation* (led by the BP executive management committees) and (3) *risk assessment* (led by the BP businesses), as shown in Figure 16.1. This figure articulates the interplay between these three organisational orders, which is discussed in the following section.

## 16.5 BP's risk governance case

### 16.5.1 Attention process

BP's RM system already existed before the DWH incident, as highlighted in the AR (2008, p.18): "*Our system of risk management provides the response to risks of group significance through the establishment of standards and other controls*". It aims to understand the risk environment and obtain assurance that the system is appropriately active in identifying, assessing, reporting and mitigating material risks; and to examine the potential consequences of its failure.

However, after the DWH incident, the BP board's attention to risk shifted to ensure that the company is efficiently operating through an integrated RM system, leading to the construction of logic-consistent decisions (Thornton and Ocasio, 2008). This came under the responsibility of Bob Dudley the newly-appointed Group Chief Executive (GCE) (AR, 2010, p.92):

*One of the tasks of the BP board is to ensure that the company is run effec-tively and that the material risks are identified, understood and that the sys-tems of risk management and internal control are in place to manage these risks.*

Bob Dudley, who spent his entire career in the oil and gas industry, had suc-ceeded to the GCE position, replacing Tony Hayward in October 2010, after the DWH incident. Before becoming BP's GCE, he took the responsibility for man-aging BP's response to the tragic oil spill by leading the Gulf Coast Restoration Organization (GCRO), which was established as a quick organisational treatment for the crisis. His deep and substantial global experience in strategic management indicated he possessed the necessary knowledge to lead the BP executive man-agement. The focus of attention and awareness perceived by Bob Dudley in his understanding of the situation can be seen in his statement in the AR (2010, p. 10):

*I grew up in Mississippi and spent summers with my family swimming and fishing in the Gulf. I know those beaches and waters well. When I heard about the accident, I could immediately picture how it might affect the people who live and work along that coast.*

The BP board's attention is not only restricted by the appointment of a new GCE, but also by the presence of two new board committees: the Gulf of Mexico Committee and the Geopolitical Committee. The Gulf of Mexico Committee was directly established after the incident in 2010, upon the establishment of GCRO, and it was terminated in 2015. For six years, this committee took the responsibil-ity of supervising the implications of the DWH incident, as reported by the BP Chairperson. The Geopolitical Committee was formed in 2015 after the conse-quences of the DWH incident were resolved, resulting in the dissolution of the Gulf of Mexico Committee. Moreover, BP's attention was turning to the potential implications of geopolitics on their investments around the world, as initially out-lined in the AR (2015, p. 52): "*Geopolitical risk is inherent to many regions in which we operate, and heightened political or social tensions or changes in key relationships could adversely affect the group*".

BP's attention could also be outlined by the formation of an investigation team under the leadership of Mark Bly. He was charged by the GCE to analyse the facts surrounding the incident and provide recommendations that would enable BP to avoid similar incidents in the future. This team concluded that no spe-cific factor caused the incident; however, it might arise from "*a complex and interlinked series of mechanical failures, human judgements, engineering design, operational implementation and team interfaces*" (AR, 2010, p. 37). One of the team's recommendations was reviewing and assessing the consistency, accuracy and effectiveness of BP's RM system to monitor how BP was running its business and managing its material risks.

These different aspects of BP's attention have resulted in the reconsideration of the existing RM system to address the risk implications of the DWH incident.

This reconsideration reflects a change in the actors' logics shaping their cognitions, behaviours and actions as they evolved this system for achieving BP's new targets (Thornton et al., 2012). Risk, therefore, became a dominating dimension for BP actors, to review the embedded risk practice and provide insights for changes to implement (Corbett et al., 2018). The activation process of BP's attention, through which the evolution of the RM system is outlined, is described in the following section.

### 16.5.2 Activation process

#### 16.5.2.1 Risk governance

> *The board and its monitoring committees (Audit, SEEAC and Gulf of Mexico) monitored the group risks, which had been allocated following the board's review of the annual plan at the end of 2010. The annual plan, group risk reviews and the strategy are central to our risk management programme as they provide a framework for the board to consider significant risks and manage the group's overall risk exposure.*

(AR, 2011, p. 124)

As specified, the three BP monitoring committees are Audit; Safety, Ethics and Environmental Assurance (SEEA); and the Gulf of Mexico. They maintain a forward-looking approach to risk exposure. The BP CG framework is also comprised of another four board committees: the Chairman, Remuneration, Nomination and Geopolitical Committees. The first three are not related directly to BP's RM structure, whereas the latter was established in 2015 to monitor BP's management of geopolitical risks after the closure of the Gulf of Mexico Committee (AR, 2015), as presented in Table 16.1, which outlines the structuration of BP boardroom risk committees during the 2008–2017 period.

The Audit Committee aims to review how effective and active BP's internal financial controls and its RM system are (AR, 2010). It monitors and assures the *financial risks*, under the leadership of three directors: Sir Ian Prosser before the incident, Douglas Flint in 2010 and Brendan Nelson from 2011 until 2017. Nelson played a vital role in the evolution of the profession's approach to UK bank audits, with a particular focus on the establishment of auditing standards (AR, 2011). The SEEA committee's role is to review BP's environmental, safety and ethical performance and to identify and mitigate material *non-financial risks* (AR, 2010). Throughout the period, it was under the leadership of Sir William Castell (2008–2011), Paul Anderson (2012–2015) and Alan Boeckmann (2016–2017). Anderson brought the valuable experience of driving safety-related cultural change (AR, 2011), while Boeckmann brought experience in the energy industry and advanced technology (AR, 2015). The Gulf of Mexico Committee emerged in July 2010 to review the environmental work of mitigating the oil spill's impacts on the Gulf's waters and on the affected shorelines. It provides non-executive oversight over the GCRO to support the efforts of rebuilding BP's trust and reputation (AR, 2010).

*Table 16.1* Structural analysis of BP's monitoring committees

| BP Board Members | Gender | Nationality | Position | (1) Audit Committee | | | | | | | | | | (2) Safety, Ethics & Environmental Assurance (SEEA) Committee | | | | | | | | | | (3) Gulf of Mexico (GoM) Committee | | | | | | | | | | (4) Geopolitical (Geo) Committee | | | | | | | | | |
|---|---|---|---|---|---|---|---|---|---|---|---|---|---|---|---|---|---|---|---|---|---|---|---|---|---|---|---|---|---|---|---|---|---|---|---|---|---|---|---|---|---|---|---|
| | | | | 2008 | 2009 | 2010 | 2011 | 2012 | 2013 | 2014 | 2015 | 2016 | 2017 | 2008 | 2009 | 2010 | 2011 | 2012 | 2013 | 2014 | 2015 | 2016 | 2017 | 2008 | 2009 | 2010 | 2011 | 2012 | 2013 | 2014 | 2015 | 2016 | 2017 | 2008 | 2009 | 2010 | 2011 | 2012 | 2013 | 2014 | 2015 | 2016 | 2017 |
| Alan Boeckmann | Male | US | Non-executive director | | | | | | | - | - | M | M | | | | | | | M | M | C | C | | | | | | | M | M | | | | | | | | | | - | - |
| Bob Dudley | Male | British-US | **Group Chief Executive** | | | | | | | | | | | | M | M | M | M | M | M | M | M | M | | | M | M | M | M | M | M | M | | | | | M | M | M |
| Brendan Nelson | Male | British | Non-executive director | | | M | C | C | C | C | C | C | C | | | | | | | - | - | - | - | | | | C | C | C | C | C | - | | | | | | | - | - |
| Ian Davis | Male | British | Non-executive director | | M | M | | | | | M | M | | | M | | | | | | | | | | M | | | | | | | | | | | | M | M |
| Nils Anderson | Male | Danish | Non-executive director | | | | | | | | | M | M | | | | | | | | M | | | | | | | | | | | | | | | | | |
| Paul Anderson | Male | US | Non-executive director | | | | | | - | - | M | M | M | | M | C | C | C | C | C | C | M | M | | M | M | M | M | M | | | | | | | | | |
| Sir John Sawers | Male | British | Non-executive director | | | | | | - | - | M | M | M | | | | | | | M | M | M | M | | | | | | | | | | | | | C | C | C |
| Antony Burgmans | Male | Dutch | Non-executive director | | | | | | | | | | | M | M | M | M | M | M | M | M | M | M | | | | | | | | | | | | | | | |
| Iain Conn | Male | British | **Executive** | | M | M | M | M | M | | | | | M | M | M | M | M | M | M | | | | M | M | M | M | M | M | | | | | | | | | |
| Dr Byron Grote | Male | - | **Executive Vice President (CFO)** | M | M | M | M | M | M | | | | | M | M | M | M | M | M | | | | | M | M | M | M | M | | | | | | | | | | |
| Sir William Castell | Male | - | Non-executive director | M | - | - | | | | | | | | C | C | C | C | | | | | | | | | | | | | | | | | | | | | |
| Douglas Flint | Male | - | Non-executive director | M | M | C | M | | | | | | | | | | | | | | | | | | | | | | | | | | | | | | | |
| Sir Ian Prosser | Male | - | Non-executive director | C | C | M | | | | | | | | - | - | | | | | | | | | | | | | | | | | | | | | | | |
| Tony Hayward | Male | British | **Chief Executive** | M | M | M | | | | | | | | M | M | M | | | | | | | | | M | | | | | | | | | | | | | |

Abbreviations: C = Chair; M = Member

The committee was led by Ian Davis until it was disbanded in 2015. His experience in global financial and strategic matters and, most importantly, government affairs, gave him the ability to provide invaluable judgment relating to geopolitical and reputational risks (AR, 2012). The DWH incident pushed BP Company to equip its board with members who can enhance corporate actions by sharing knowledge and expertise through their interactions (Thornton and Ocasio, 2008).

These changes in the structuration and memberships of BP board-level monitoring committees highlight its direction in conceptualising its risk practice as a logical supplement to BP's governance (Stein and Wiedemann, 2016). They reflect the evolution of RG as a crucial organisational practice through the cognitive beliefs and ideations of qualified BP board members with the necessary knowledge and expertise to enhance the existing RM system (Thornton et al., 2012). For activation purposes, BP's RM system requires material risks to be identified through several mechanisms. These mechanisms articulate the ways by which BP risks are governed through different interactions of multiple actors within all organisational levels for enhancing its RM system (Corbett et al., 2018), for example:

(1) The Audit and SEEA committees are found holding an annual joint meeting to assess the effectiveness of BP's RM system. This interaction "*enables the board and its committees to consider the systems of risk management and internal control being operated for managing significant risks*" (AR, 2010, p. 104) by reviewing the reports received from executive management at their regular meetings.
(2) The board committees are interlinked through joint meetings and cross-memberships to enrich the discussions of risk review and oversight. For instance, "*the Gulf of Mexico Committee has cross-membership with both the SEEAC and the audit committee*" (AR, 2012, p. 124). This ensures the effectiveness of their respective risk schema that neither duplicates nor omits any material risk.
(3) The Audit committee established two key initiatives to review directly the work relating to the ethics and compliance functions for its 2013 programme, namely the Annual Certification Report and Open-Talk to review regularly the risk elements reported by its businesses. The former provides great support in indicating the individuals' level of understanding of the governance principles, whereas the latter determines any concerns that might be raised regarding infractions of compliance, ethics or the code of conduct, including safety issues, as highlighted in the AR (2012, p. 122).
(4) The BP board showed interest in understanding the feedback of its shareholders regarding the information needed to assess the company's performance, business model and strategy "*either directly following meetings with the chairman or other board members or indirectly through an annual investor audit undertaken by a third party*" (AR, 2011, p. 124).

Activating these mechanisms reflects the delegation of BP board members' authority to the executive management to set risk policy through multiple interactions.

They enabled the BP boardroom to prioritise and aggregate the perceived risks targeted by RG (Stein and Wiedemann, 2016) to understand not only corporate reality in terms of risk threats but also whether BP employees perceived the BP policy and standards positively or negatively, as a sense-giving tactic (Will and Pies, 2018) for monitoring BP's overall performance. This is consistent with the finding of Aljughaiman and Salama (2019) that the adoption of RG mechanisms is significantly associated with greater risk exposure.

Since the risks that have arisen from either the internal or external environment are changeable from one period to another, this ongoing organisational practice is liable to change over time. These changes require the inclusion of specific organisational actors with specific backgrounds and experiences to share their ideations and cognitions through their discussions and interactions (Thornton et al., 2012) to make sense of risk oversight and control (Will and Pies, 2018). The deployment approach through which the BP board are actively delegating their risk strategy and authority to executive management is described in the following subsection.

### 16.5.2.2 Risk mobilisation

Bob Dudley takes the responsibility for establishing and structuring the executive management committees, which represent the middle level of BP's RM system, to implement the risk policy developed by the system's upper level and oversee the management of risks throughout the year. This requires the GCE to select executives with the appropriate background and expertise for reaching appropriate logic-consistent decisions. This organisational order has evolved to pursue the provision of independent assurance regarding the design and functionality of BP's RM system. It comprises six committees:

(1) The Group Operations Risk Committee (GORC), chaired by Bob Dudley himself, for safety and environmental risks;
(2) The Group Financial Risk Committee (GFRC), led by the CFO, for financial and trading risks;
(3) The Group Ethics and Compliance Committee (GECC), which was established in 2012, under the lead of the Group General Counsel, for legal and regulatory compliance risks;
(4) The Group Disclosure Committee (GDC) for risks related to financial reporting;
(5) The Group People Committee (GPC) for personnel risks;
(6) The Resource Commitments Committee (RCM) for risks regarding investment decisions.

These committees take the responsibility for developing new risk metrics, which are aligned with the risks that need particular upper-level oversight and cascade down to BP businesses for identification and reporting purposes through executive-associated functions. These functions have also evolved to monitor BP's strategic performance *via* the provision of guidance on the efficacy of the business's systematic application of standards. One of these functions as outlined in the AR (2012, p. 46): "*Our new safety and operational risk (S&OR) function supports the business line in delivering safe, reliable and compliant operations across the group's operated business*", under the supervision of the GORC. Another two function as articulated in the AR (2017, p. 170), "*[...] trading activities are managed within the integrated supply and trading function. Treasury function holds foreign exchange and interest-rate products in the financial markets*", under the direction of the GFRC.

These changes in the structuration and memberships of BP executive management committees emphasise the need to have executive members with the necessary knowledge and expertise (Thornton et al., 2012) to report the identified material risks based on the risk policy and standards. This practice of risk mobilisation, therefore, provides great support and enrichment to the RG practice as a reaction to the DWH incident. As part of the executive team's activities leading to risk practice evolution, they all provide frequent updates to the board and its monitoring committees through several mechanisms for overseeing and managing significant risks that are identified, assessed and reported by the BP businesses (i.e., the BP frontline operations worldwide). Some examples:

(1) The GCE put assurance that group operational risks are identified and managed effectively through the monitoring of safety and compliance in BP's operations, which is conducted by the S&OR function.
(2) The GORC sent regular reports independently to SEEAC to monitor non-financial risk incidents, relationships with outside parties and performance across the group.
(3) The GECC made quarterly reports to SEEAC to review compliance with BP's code of conduct to enforce a standard of acceptable behaviour on a global basis. The same applies to BP's general auditor, who reported directly on the audit work regarding RM activities to the chairs of the Audit Committee and SEEAC.
(4) The CFO provides advice on financial risks and the appropriate financial RG framework for the GFRC, which, in turn, assures the GCE that the financial risk-taking activity is governed by appropriate policies and procedures.

These mechanisms reflect the risk mobilisation practice's efficacy in setting risk policy and standards for BP's businesses based on the risk strategy developed by BP's boardroom and providing BP's upper management with BP businesses' outcomes of the detected risks (Stein and Wiedemann, 2016; Will and Pies, 2018). Therefore, regular updates of material risks are subjected to a high level of interactions between the executive management and its associated functions with BP's businesses and their segmental functions, which operate across the globe and are chaired by each business head, as articulated in the following subsection.

### 16.5.2.3 Risk assessment

BP is geographically distributed across more than 70 countries where the frontline businesses are operated and its associated segmental functions are located, representing the lower level of BP's RM system. These business-segmental functions (cf. the Code of Conduct and the Management Systems for Operations, Finance, and People [AR, 2012, p. 117]) aim to integrate into the executive-associated functions to provide assurance of the understanding and implementation of BP's standards at the operational level and identify, assess and report material risks.

These functions represent the strategic performance units, where the management and their staff take responsibility to address and report risks since

> [t]he nature of our business operations is long term, resulting in many of our identified risks being enduring in nature. Nonetheless, risks can develop and evolve over time and their potential impact or likelihood may vary in response to internal and external events.
>
> (AR, 2013, p. 49)

The approach that BP's RM system has adopted to facilitate the daily risk identification, assessment and reporting of the outcomes of environmental stimuli in the BP frontline operations and their associated segmental functions indicates bottom-up directional communication (Thornton et al., 2012).

After the incident, an evolved form of risk reporting, called the Risk Management Report (RMR), is utilised to address all corporate risks that BP is expected to face. "*During 2011, functions, strategic performance units, divisions and segments within BP were requested to prepare the risk management reports (RMRs) using the new, common approach*" (AR, 2011, p. 44). These risks are categorised into three common groups (i.e., strategic and commercial risks, compliance and controls risks and safety and operational risks) to identify, assess and report them *via* RMRs as a sense-giving tactic (Will and Pies, 2018), as presented in Table 16.2, which summarises the BP's reported risks during the 2008–2017 period.

Over the period under investigation, there were multiple changes in all risk categories after the DWH incident in terms of risk identification, assessment, reclassification and reporting. These changes show the increasing level of risk disclosure and transparency as an indication of the continued efforts of BP's actors to manage and improve risk outcomes (Carlsson-Wall et al., 2018), and a reflection of the values and expectations of BP's stakeholders (Hardy and Maguire, 2016). "*Assessing risk management activities, making further improvements and planning new activities*" (AR, 2014, p. 46) are the BP's targets for providing ongoing assurance of a well-constructed alignment between the existing risk schema and the identified risks from the environment. Through the utilisation of the RMR approach, the identified risks for the current year require particular executive committee oversight and monitoring during the coming year for management consideration, challenge, resource allocation and intervention, if necessary (AR, 2015, p. 51).

The structuration and functionality of risk assessment practice highlight the technical view of BP's RM system through identifying, assessing and reporting

*Table 16.2* Structural analysis of BP Group's risk reporting

| Risk Categories | Risk Indicators | 2008 | 2009 | 2010 | 2011 | 2012 | 2013 | 2014 | 2015 | 2016 | 2017 |
|---|---|---|---|---|---|---|---|---|---|---|---|
| **Strategic and Commercial Risks** | Access and renewal | ✓ | ✓ | ✓ | ✓ | ✓ | ✓ | ✓ | ✓ | ✓ | ✓ |
| | Reserves replacement | ✓ | ✓ | ✓ | ✓ | ✓ | ✓ | ✓ | ✓ | ✓ | ✓ |
| | Prices and markets | ✓ | ✓ | ✓ | ✓ | ✓ | ✓ | ✓ | ✓ | ✓ | ✓ |
| | Climate change and carbon pricing | ✓ | ✓ | | | ✓ | ✓ | ✓ | | | ✓ |
| | Socio-political | ✓ | ✓ | ✓ | ✓ | ✓ | ✓ | ✓ | ✓ | ✓ | ✓ |
| | Competition | ✓ | ✓ | ✓ | ✓ | ✓ | ✓ | ✓ | ✓ | ✓ | ✓ |
| | Investment efficiency | ✓ | ✓ | ✓ | ✓ | ✓ | ✓ | █ | █ | █ | █ |
| | Liquidity, financial capacity and financial exposure | ✓ | | | | ✓ | ✓ | ✓ | | | |
| | Insurance | | ✓ | ✓ | ✓ | ✓ | ✓ | ✓ | | | |
| | Rosneft transaction | | | █ | █ | █ | █ | █ | █ | █ | █ |
| | Gulf of Mexico oil spill | | ✓ | █ | █ | ✓ | ✓ | ✓ | | | ✓ |
| | Macroeconomic outlook | | ✓ | ✓ | ✓ | ✓ | ✓ | ✓ | | | ✓ |
| **Compliance and Control Risks** | Regulatory | ✓ | ✓ | ✓ | ✓ | ✓ | ✓ | ✓ | ✓ | ✓ | ✓ |
| | Ethical misconduct and non-compliance | ✓ | ✓ | ✓ | ✓ | ✓ | ✓ | ✓ | ✓ | ✓ | ✓ |
| | Liabilities and provisions | | ✓ | ✓ | ✓ | ✓ | ✓ | | | | |
| | Reporting | | | ✓ | ✓ | ✓ | ✓ | | | | |
| | Changes in external factors | █ | █ | █ | █ | █ | ✓ | █ | █ | █ | █ |
| | Our settlement with the US Department of Justice and the SEC | | | | | █ | █ | █ | █ | █ | █ |

**Safety and Operational Risks**

Process safety
Personal safety
Environmental
Security
Product quality
Drilling and production
Transportation
Major project delivery
Digital infrastructure
Business continuity and disaster recovery
Crisis management
People and capability
Treasury and trading activities
Joint ventures and other contractual arrangements

risk indicators. These newly re-classified and eliminated indicators diffuse the sense of risk identification and assessment for BP executive management (Will and Pies, 2018), and will reverberate in the cognitive processes for providing taken-for-granted structures to manage material risks (Carlsson-Wall et al., 2016).

The DWH incident was the main stimulus behind not only constituting the BP's RM system but also detecting the changes in how BP risks are governed. Consequently, the annual changes in all risk categories and indicators reflect the changes in BP's RG practice as the BP's board and risk-monitoring committees serve to filter the abundant information that the executive management committees receive, and therefore influence how they make judgements intended to mitigate material risks.

## 16.6  Conclusions and implications

This chapter aimed to explore how BP responded to the DWH incident through narrative reporting. This case study relied on ILP to articulate how BP actors changed how corporate risks are governed. It offers subsequent findings with contributions to the literature, policymakers and organisations alike.

The interdisciplinary RG literature has embraced concerns relating to the interaction between CG and RM within an organisation (Lundqvist, 2015; Stein and Wiedemann, 2016; Sheedy and Griffin, 2018). However, findings suggest that RG goes beyond the corporate evolution of the strategic, compliance and operational risk dimensions by taking environmental, safety and geopolitical matters into consideration, especially in complex organisations, for identifying, evaluating and controlling corporate risks.

The structuration of BP's RM system is sophisticated, constituting of three organisational orders that are shaped and constrained by the interplay among major actors who render their knowledge and expertise to manage corporate risks effectively. These orders are represented by *Governors* (who set the BP's strategy and oversight), *Developers* (who set the BP's policy and standards and who develop dynamic risk metrics under the lead of the GCE) and *Assessors* (who address and report the financial and non-financial risks daily). They are interlinked through two-directional mechanisms. The first is a top-down mechanism for the delegation of authority through strategy, policy and oversight, whereas the second is a bottom-up mechanism for accountability with assurance through monitoring and reporting.

Findings show that the structural and directional interdependences are upheld, which emphasise the tightness of inter-controls at the boardroom level. Structural interdependence involves actors' functionality in terms of their memberships, as well as their relevant past experiences and roles. Findings, for example, reveal that boardroom committees are assigned different but interdependent tasks. Additionally, BP directors participate in more than one of these committees and are equipped with adequate knowledge and background. These provide a window of opportunity for each committee and actor to view the RG practice and share insights for changes to enhance the corporate RM system. Directional interdependence underlines two dynamic means of accountability: multilevel and cross-level. Whereas committees of RG are vertically accountable to Bob Dudley, they are also horizontally accountable to each other, interconnected through key members in addition to the GCE. Such sophisticated interactions between the BP's significant actors in different organisational orders has resulted in effective RG practice in dealing with material risks.

The BP governance of risk significations fluctuated before (prospectively), during (in real-time) and after (retrospectively) the DWH incident (Hardy and Maguire, 2016). The prospective mode was shaped to identify hazards before they occurred to avoid or minimise them through the RM system. After the incident, BP implemented a protocol to control corporate risks and contain their consequences. This orientation, however, has revealed several managerial consequences, such as the forming of the Gulf of Mexico Committee, through which BP's response to the legal, environmental and safety implications of the DWH incident has been tightly governed. Having five years of accumulated experience enabled BP to extend its organisational focus to political instability through the formation of the Geopolitical Committee. This position went beyond mitigating existing concerns to focus on the prospective identification and assessment of risks arising from geopolitics for investments.

These outcomes have practical implications for the literature, policymakers and organisations alike. First, they begin to resolve the academic debate on how risk explains CG change by highlighting the evolution of how BP risks are governed through the lens of ILP. Second, the outcomes also provide insights to policymakers to reconsider the existing guidelines that regulate CG and assess RM to enhance the quality of risk disclosure. Third, they may also be useful for organisations in clarifying that RG is not limited to internal concerns but also extends to include geopolitical threats: Since business risk is changing, RG should be able to absorb these changes. These implications support the integration of multiple logics to change how corporate risks are governed and suggest opportunities for further research to explore in more depth the interactions between RG and corporate strategy; the role of political connections and their implications for such corporations; and corporate performance, both with and without the adoption of RG.

## Notes

1 See the BP website: https://www.bp.com/en/global/corporate/what-we-do/bp-at-a -glance.html, and the Reuters website: https://www.reuters.com/finance/stocks/companyProfile/BP
2 BP's annual reports are available at: https://www.bp.com/en/global/corporate/investors .html

## References

Aljughaiman, A. and Salama, A. (2019) 'Do banks effectively manage their risks? The role of risk governance in the MENA region', *Journal of Accounting and Public Policy*, 38(5), pp. 1066–1080.

BP-plc, 2017 BP Annual Report and Form 20-F.
BP-plc, 2016 BP Annual Report and Form 20-F.
BP-plc, 2015 BP Annual Report and Form 20-F.
BP-plc, 2014 BP Annual Report and Form 20-F.
BP-plc, 2013 BP Annual Report and Form 20-F.
BP-plc, 2012 BP Annual Report and Form 20-F.
BP-plc, 2011 BP Annual Report and Form 20-F.
BP-plc, 2010 BP Annual Report and Form 20-F.
BP-plc, 2009 Annual Report and Accounts.
BP-plc, 2008 Annual Report and Accounts.
Braun, V., Clarke, V. and Weate, P. (2016) 'Using thematic analysis in sport and exercise research', in Smith, B. and Sparkes, A. (eds.) *Routledge handbook of qualitative research in sport and exercise* (pp. 191–205). London: Routledge.
Carlsson-Wall, M., Kraus, K., Meidell, A. and Tran, P. (2018) 'Managing risk in the public sector – The interaction between vernacular and formal risk management systems', *Financial Accountability and Management*, 35(1), pp. 1–17.
Carlsson-Wall, M., Kraus, K. and Messner, M. (2016) 'Performance measurement systems and the enactment of different institutional logics: Insights from a football organization', *Management Accounting Research*, 32, pp. 45–61.
Corbett, J., Webster, J. and Jenkin, T. (2018) 'Unmasking corporate sustainability at the project level: Exploring the influence of institutional logics and individual agency', *Journal of Business Ethics*, 147(2), pp. 261–286.
Damayanthi, S. and Gooneratne, T. (2017) 'Institutional logics perspective in management control research: A review of extant literature and directions for future research', *Journal of Accounting and Organizational Change*, 13(4), pp. 520–547.
Elsayed, N. and Ammar, S. (2020) 'Sustainability governance and legitimisation processes: Gulf of Mexico oil spill', *Sustainability Accounting, Management and Policy Journal*, 11(1), pp. 253–278.
Falkner, E. and Hiebl, M. (2015) 'Risk management in SMEs: A systematic review of available evidence', *The Journal of Risk Finance*, 16(2), pp. 122–144.
Florio, C. and Leoni, G. (2017) 'Enterprise risk management and firm performance: The Italian case', *The British Accounting Review*, 49(1), pp. 56–74.
Giovannoni, E., Quarchioni, S. and Riccaboni, A. (2016) 'The role of roles in risk management change: The case of an Italian bank', *European Accounting Review*, 25(1), pp. 109–129.
Gontarek, W. and Belghitar, Y. (2018) 'Risk governance: Examining its impact upon bank performance and risk-taking', *Financial Markets, Institutions and Instruments*, 27(5), pp. 1–38.
Hardy, C. and Maguire, S. (2016) 'Organizing risk: Disclosure, power, and 'Riskification'', *Academy of Management Review*, 40(1), pp. 80–108.
Järvinen, J. (2016) 'Role of management accounting in applying new institutional logics: A comparative case study in the non-profit sector', *Accounting, Auditing and Accountability Journal*, 29(5), pp. 861–886.
Klinke, A. and Renn, O. (2021) 'The coming of age of risk governance', *Risk Analysis*, 41(3), pp. 544–557.
Lounsbury, M. (2007) 'A tale of two cities: Competing logics and practice variation in the professionalizing of mutual funds', *Academy of Management Journal*, 50(2), pp. 289–307.
Lundqvist, S.A. (2015) 'Why firms implement risk governance – Stepping beyond traditional risk management to enterprise risk management', *Journal of Accounting and Public Policy*, 34(5), pp. 441–466.

Meidell, A. and Kaarbøe, K. (2017) 'How the enterprise risk management function influences decision-making in the organization - A field study of a large, global oil and gas company', *The British Accounting Review*, 49(1), pp. 39–55.

Modell, S. (2015) 'Making institutional accounting research critical: Dead end or new beginning?', *Accounting, Auditing and Accountability Journal*, 28(5), pp. 773–808.

Mutch, A. (2018) 'Practice, substance, and history: Reframing institutional logics', *Academy of Management Review*, 43(2), pp. 242–258.

Parker, L. (2012) 'Qualitative management accounting research: Assessing deliverables and relevance', *Critical Perspectives on Accounting*, 23(1), pp. 54–70.

Scapens, R. (2004) 'Doing case study research', in Humphrey, C. and Lee, B. (eds.) *The real life guide to accounting research: A behind-the-scenes view of using qualitative research methods* (pp. 257–279). Oxford: Elsevier Ltd.

Sheedy, E. and Griffin, B. (2018) 'Risk governance, structures, culture, and behavior: A view from the inside', *Corporate Governance: International Review*, 26(1), pp. 4–22.

Stein, V. and Wiedemann, A. (2016) 'Risk governance: Conceptualization, tasks, and research agenda', *Journal of Business Economics*, 86(8), pp. 813–836.

Stein, V., Wiedemann, A. and Bouten, C. (2019) 'Framing risk governance', *Management Research Review*, 42(11), pp. 1224–1242.

Thornton, P.H. and Ocasio, W. (2008) 'Institutional logics', in Greenwood, R., Oliver, C., Sahlin, K. and Suddaby, R. (eds.) *The Sage handbook of organizational institutionalism* (pp. 99–129). Thousand Oaks, CA: Sage.

Thornton, P.H., Ocasio, W. and Lounsbury, M. (2012) *The institutional logics perspective: A new approach to culture, structure and process*. New York: Oxford University Press.

Will, M. and Pies, I. (2018) 'Sensemaking and sensegiving: A concept for successful change management that brings together moral foundations theory and the ordonomic approach', *Journal of Accounting and Organizational Change*, 14(3), pp. 291–313.

Yin, R. (2009) *Case study research: Design and methods (applied social research methods)*. Thousand Oaks, CA: Sage.

Zuo, W., Zhu, W., Wang, F., Wei, J. and Bondar, A. (2017) 'Exploring the institutional determinants of risk governance: A comparative approach across nations', *International Journal of Disaster Risk Reduction*, 24, pp. 135–143.

# 17 Examining the directors' remuneration reports

## The case of Thomas Cook

*Nader Elsayed*

## 17.1 Introduction

One area of great interest for the academic arenas and the public has been how executive remuneration (ER) is determined to achieve the alignment of interests in the good practice of corporate governance (CG) for modern UK corporations. This has led to questioning the suitability of company constitutions in determining ER where aggressive pay schemes are commonplace, especially after the failures of several well-known companies (for instance, Polly Peck and BCCI) in 1991, again after the financial crisis of 2007–2009, and more recently Carillion and Thomas Cook in 2018 and 2019, respectively.

These waves of scandal increased the concerns of both stockholders and policymakers regarding the quality of judgements provided by corporate top management and the links between these judgements and the extent of disclosure relating to ER (Carpenter et al., 2004; Clarkson et al., 2011; Menz, 2012; Ntim et al., 2015; Elsayed and Elbardan, 2018, etc.). Consequently, there has been great focus on greater disclosure and better transparency of information as a key principle of CG, in general, and ER, particularly, in the UK economy to ensure its stability and accountability, consistent with the 1992 Cadbury Report, the 1995 Greenbury Report, the 2006 Companies Act, and the UK Corporate Governance Code.

To explore the governance role of the Remuneration Committee (RC) of a recent UK-FTSE corporation (i.e., Thomas Cook Group, TCG), which faced serious problems from 2015 until its collapse in 2019, in sustaining the pay–performance alignment, this chapter provides a case study research through examining the narrative section of its Directors' Remuneration Reports (DRRs) for the period 2009–2018. This study contributes to the existing literature in three important ways. First, it aims to examine the governance role of TCG's RC in determining the level and composition of ER, an objective that the existing literature in remuneration governance does not address. Such examination may perhaps outline several behavioural and institutional factors that influence the association between ER and company performance. Second, the researcher adopts a number of theoretical perspectives (i.e., agency, managerial power, tournament, and upper echelons), which are utilised as a means either to establish the appropriate mechanisms for determining the level and structure of ER or to act as explicators for

DOI: 10.4324/9781003095385-22

setting ER. Third, this study is pioneering in using case study analyses of how the ER is governed within a specific corporation since the vast majority of the present research are empirical-based studies that reported mixed relationships between ER and company performance.

This chapter is organised as follows. Section 17.2 explores the background of pay-performance alignment in the UK. Section 17.3 reviews the underlying theoretical perspectives. Section 17.4 describes the research methodology. Section 17.5 examines the DRRs of TCG, whereas the final section (Section 17.6) provides a general overview of what it is possible to learn from such a study and discusses areas that seem to justify further research.

## 17.2 Background of pay–performance alignment

In the 1970s, in terms of structuration and roles, compensation committees in the US (remuneration committees in the UK) were generally a child in the evolution of CG. Due to globalisation and the development of symmetric CG approaches, UK corporations broadly followed the US pattern quickly, probably under the leadership of the multinational functions and/or dual listing in both the US and the UK stock markets (Main and Johnston, 1993).

The presence of a RC represents a significant ingredient in almost all initiatives since the issuance of the Cadbury Report (1992) for improving the governance quality relating to the topic of ER (Main and Johnston, 1993). Presently, RCs are widely established in the UK corporate culture. However, how successful the RCs are in fulfilling their roles has been questioned by academics, regulators and the public. In addition, have the UK corporations contributed to tightening the gap between the ER packages and the average corporate pay over the period? What are the proportions of corporate executive's base salary and performance-related remunerations? What is the level of remuneration paid to executives for extraordinary performance? How should company performance and executive performance be examined and how should these levels of performance be identified?

In 1995, the Greenbury Report was published with a particular focus on public and stakeholder concerns regarding ER. This report sanctioned the role of a RC within the structuration of CG as a powerful party in determining the mechanisms and structures that set the volume and extent of ER. This committee permits only non-executive directors to set a remuneration agenda for executives. This agenda includes the structuration of ER packages, which should be adequate to attract, retain and motivate highly qualified and talented executives. These packages should be based mainly on the components of performance-related remuneration, such as bonuses, share options, and/or long-term incentive plans (LTIPs), which should be set in a manner to align the interests of executives with those of stockholders (Greenbury, 1995). These propositions were carried forward into the Combined Code, which was issued initially in 1998 and has been restated in its consequent revisions from 2000 to 2020, consistent with Roberts et al. (2020).

According to the UK regulatory initiatives and literature, ER packages comprise a number of separate, but interrelated, pay components. These components will typically include a base salary along with several performance-related remunerations. These remunerations, therefore, are associated with both short- and long-term reflections of company performance, consistent with the agency theory (Jensen and Murphy, 1990). El-Sayed's (2013) study articulated that the UK performance-related remunerations include bonuses, LTIPs and stock options; however, stock options are not as widespread in the UK as they are in the US. Additionally, executive directors may be supplementarily benefited by a set of reimbursements (such as monetary allowances for accommodation, transportation, pensions based on the base salary, performance stocks or stock appreciation rights, in addition to one-off payments, for instance, retention plans and/or camouflage payments (e.g., executive loans, golden hello, golden goodbye, etc.)).

This ER package is typically categorised into two separate strands between which the UK corporations need to provide a clear distinction (Frydman and Saks, 2005). The first strand is based on behavioural-based contracts that are largely based on organisational hierarchies and is characterised as constant in its structure and amounts (comprising basic salaries, allowances and pensions). The second strand is focused on outcome-related contracts that are associated with actual and/or perceived performance, and contains pay components that show far more variation than the first strand in its structure and amounts (consisting of annual bonuses, share options and LTIPs). The underlying concern for both types of contracts is how to design an ER package that will be optimum to align the executive desires with the stockholders' interests to mitigate the agency costs (Jensen and Murphy, 1990; Elsayed and Elbardan, 2018). In contrast, payments of bonuses, for instance, are part of good management practices, indicating that executives have accomplished their duties and responsibilities with adequate care and diligence, consistent with Section 174 of the Companies Act (2006). Gregg et al. (2012) outlined that executive bonuses should be provided for extraordinary performance and must be related to the long-term business success. However, they (Gregg et al. 2012) do not indicate how extraordinary performance can be identified and measured. Such an association between ER and company performance opens up the arguments on the role of RCs in designing an appropriate remuneration package to ensure the ability of boardroom executives to take effective strategic decisions for enhancing company performance.

Preparing DDRs lies directly on the corporate board of directors as consistent with Section 420(1) of the Companies Act (2006), which must be presented to the entire interested parties, most importantly the stockholders, at the AGMs, according to Section 423(1), to seek their approval, consistent with Section 439(4). However, it does not articulate what are the strategies for taking an action by the corporate stockholders to change a remuneration component in terms of increasing, decreasing or freezing it. Such actions arguably need to be clarified to notify corporate stockholders about how that would affect the company's plans through aligning its achievements with its remuneration policy. Although the stockholders' votes on these DRRs are still advisory, their oppositions to these reports are considered a signal of their dissatisfactions to the actual or prospective ER packages. This is consistent with the study of Chu et al. (2021), who found little evidence of the effect of the UK law and regulations that require periodic binding stockholders' approval on the large listed UK companies' pay levels and pay–performance sensitivity, although it is inconsistent with the studies of Magee (2021) and Liang et al. (2020) in the Australian context.

## 17.3 Underlying theoretical perspectives based on the literature

In parallel with the development of several regulatory initiatives (e.g., Cadbury Report, 1992; Greenbury Report, 1995; the Code, 1998–2020), there is a rapidly expanding literature with the goal of exploring different aspects of ER that has led to a significant contribution of academic research in this discipline starting from the 1990s at the earliest. This literature emphasised CG mechanisms (Main and Johnston, 1993; Ozkan, 2011; Khurshed et al., 2011), in addition to the corporate-and/or personnel-dependent effects (Beiner et al., 2006; Devers et al., 2007; Dia et al., 2014) on matters relating to ER.

The ER matters consist of, but are not limited to, the ER level and composition, the extent of remuneration policies' disclosure and the practices of determining ER packages and evaluating company performance to sustain the pay–performance alignment. This alignment was under question from prior empirical research (e.g., Conyon et al., 1995, 2009; Clarkson et al., 2011; Ozkan, 2011; El-Sayed, 2013; Shiyyab et al., 2013; Dia et al., 2014; Ntim et al., 2015; Elsayed and Elbardan, 2018, etc.) that reported positive, negative or even no relationships between ER and company performance. These mixed outcomes are more likely to be aligned with different theoretical perspectives (such as agency (Jensen and Meckling, 1976), managerial power (Gomez-Mejia and Wiseman, 1997), tournament (Lazear, 1998), and upper echelons (Hambrick and Mason, 1984)).

Initial academic work in the ER field broadly emphasised agency theory (Jensen and Meckling, 1976). The application of this perspective to the corporation suggests the most direct association between ER and company performance and focuses on the contradictory motivations between corporate stockholders (the principals) and executive directors (the agents). Whereas the former are seeking to maximise their profits within adequate risk categories, the ambitions of the latter are to obtain high remuneration packages within appropriate levels of effort (Hendry and Kiel, 2004; Elsayed and Elbardan, 2018). The RC is viewed as a potentially useful mechanism of CG in seeking to minimise the agency problems and information asymmetry between both stockholders and executives through increasing the level of disclosure and transparency.

Alternatively, the managerial hegemony perspective has been theoretically supported by previous research (e.g., Gomez-Mejia and Wiseman, 1997; Bebchuk et al., 2002; Sapp, 2008). These studies proposed that executive directors might utilise their powers to structure their remuneration packages, even when their company performances were influenced. This perspective, therefore, requires the RC to disclose further details regarding ER to articulate that they do not misappropriate the corporate assets.

Another, contrasting but interlinked, perspective (namely tournament theory) has been introduced to motivate junior executive directors by highlighting the incentives which they will receive after senior executives leave. Its specific application emphasises the relatively high payments provided to those at the top of the ladder, which is considered motivational especially for the lower-level executives within the corporation, whose ambition is to win the senior executives' high package of remuneration by replacing them when they leave (Lazear, 1998). This perspective therefore suggests that the RC has a significant role in providing useful information regarding how the actual performance of executives are monitored as a signal to enhance the future progress of the corporation (Shiyyab et al., 2013; Elsayed and Elbardan, 2018).

In recent years, the perspective of the upper echelons (Hambrick and Mason, 1984), with its focus on the cognitive thinking of upper-level directors, has attracted extensive attention in the literature (for example, Carpenter et al., 2004; Menz, 2012), which is considered to be an underpinning perspective of research into, and explanation of, organisational actions and outcomes. Such a relationship between observable managerial characteristics (e.g., knowledge and expertise) and the strategic outcomes within a corporation reflects ultimately the cognitive thinking of its boardroom directors (i.e., the upper echelons), who have the authority to make judgements about the organisational strategy and therefore shape the form and the fate of a corporation.

## 17.4 Research methodology

This study adopts a qualitative approach to exploring the governance role of TCG's RC in sustaining the pay–performance alignment through examining the narrative section of its DRRs. It is supplemented by an illustrative, longitudinal case study (Parker, 2012; Scapens, 2004) to examine the actual role of TCG's RC in determining the level and composition of ER, especially before it fails to continue in operation. This strategy is widely acknowledged by the literature and is preferred when contemporary phenomena are under examination (Yin, 2009).

As a longitudinal case study, TCG has been chosen for two reasons. The first reason is the international nature of TCG's operations as a British global holiday-making corporation, which was listed on both the London and Frankfurt Stock Exchanges. It was formed in 2007 after the successful merger between Thomas Cook AG's owners and MyTravel Group.[1] The second reason is the TCG's collapse in 2019 after facing serious problems since 2015. For example, an inquest held in 2015 regarding a death case of two tourists in 2006, concluded that the travel group had "breached its duty of care".[2] Furthermore, TCG had to sell its Belgian airline operations in 2017 to Lufthansa.[3] In 2019, TCG announced the closure of many of its travel offices and the redundancy of numerous staff because the majority of travel bookings were being made online, and reported for the first half of its fiscal year a loss of £1.5 billion. These reasons make TCG a particularly interesting case in which to study its RC role in sustaining the pay–performance alignment.

Drawing on multiple theoretical perspectives, this case study utilises TCG DRRs[4] over ten years (2009–2018). These reports are deemed to be the main source by which TCG provides relevant information regarding the ER levels and composition. Additionally, they include data on the demographics of its board and RC. The main reason behind the selection of the ten-year period is that it enables an investigation period of ER after its formation in 2007 and the influence of the financial crisis in 2007–2008 is revealed until its closure in 2019, especially before the effects of Brexit and the COVID-19 pandemic are disclosed.

NVivo[5] is used to perform automated content analysis for measuring the trend of focus on utilising the three targeted references (i.e., remuneration, performance and governance), which is disclosed in the narrative section of the TCG's DRRs. This form-oriented content analysis is associated with "*routine counting of words or concrete references*" (Smith and Taffler, 2000, p.627). Following previous literature (Hussainey and Walker, 2009; Krippendorff, 2004; Hussainey et al., 2003), word as a unit of analysis is used, rather than a sentence, to offer further information towards the disclosure behaviour trend of TCG's RC team in preparing the DRRs in the light of aligning the ER with the actual and/or perceived performance within the principles of CG.

## 17.5 TCG's remuneration governance case

### *17.5.1 Structuration of the TCG's board and remuneration committee*

The TCG's board structuration was comprised of six committees during 2009–2018. Three committees, namely, the Audit, Management Development & Remuneration, and Nominations committees, were led only by independent non-executives, consistent with the Greenbury Report in 1995. Two committees (i.e., Health, Safety & Environment and Finance & Administrative committees) were monitored by the executive and non-executive directors, whereas the Disclosure committee was only controlled by executives. As presented in Table 17.1, the board had increased in size, starting with seven members in 2009 and ending with 11 members in 2018. It is worth noting that the 2009 boardroom members were all males; however, the representation of female directors increased, reaching around 45% in 2014 and then drawing back to 36% in 2018. This is aligned with recent research that supports their presence in boardrooms since they generally have a positive impact on corporate disclosure readability (Ginesti et al., 2018), and their representations do not influence equity risk (Sila et al., 2016).

The Management Development & Remuneration committee, the name of which was changed to "Remuneration Committee" in 2011, was set up to advise the board on ER and to set a remuneration policy for the TCG's employees. Table 17.1 demonstrates that there were three RC members in 2009, constituting 43% of the total board members. This representation had increased to five members in 2014 and 2016, representing 56% of the TCG's members. This growth indicates the vital role the RC played to ensure that the remuneration policy designed was aligned with the TCG's strategy, and directly linked the

Table 17.1 Demographics of the TCG Board and Remuneration Committee (RC)

| | 2009 | 2010 | 2011 | 2012 | 2013 | 2014 | 2015 | 2016 | 2017 | 2018 |
|---|---|---|---|---|---|---|---|---|---|---|
| Chairman | 1 | 1 | 1 | 1 | 1 | 1 | 1 | 1 | 1 | 1 |
| Independent non-executive directors | 4 | 5 | 6 | 4 | 6 | 6 | 5 | 6 | 8 | 8 |
| Non-executive directors | – | – | 1 | 1 | 1 | – | – | – | – | – |
| Executive directors | 2 | 3 | 2 | 2 | 2 | 2 | 2 | 2 | 2 | 2 |
| Board size | 7 | 8 | 9 | 8 | 10 | 9 | 8 | 9 | 11 | 11 |
| Gender diversity | 7 Male 0 Female | 7 Male 1 Female | 7 Male 2 Female | 5 Male 3 Female | 6 Male 4 Female | 5 Male 4 Female | 5 Male 3 Female | 5 Male 4 Female | 7 Male 4 Female | 7 Male 4 Female |
| Remuneration Committee size (weight: [RC × 100]/Board) | 3 (43%) | 3 (38%) | 3 (33%) | 3 (38%) | 4 (40%) | 5 (56%) | 4 (50%) | 5 (56%) | 5 (45%) | 5 (45%) |

ER to the delivery of good performance, consistent with the Greenbury Report (1995). However, there was a huge fluctuation in members' appointments and memberships not only within the RC but also within the TCG boardroom, as presented in Table 17.2.

Table 17.2 outlines the structuration of the TCG board in general, and its remuneration committee in particular, during the 2009–2018 period. During this period, the board had 2 chairmen, 4 CEOs, 4 CFOs, 14 independent non-executives and 1 non-executive director, with extensive backgrounds and expertise in the travel, finance, technology and media industries. Additionally, it has been also noticed that four of the seven board members in 2009 came from their positions held in MyTravel Group, although its share was only 48% of the TCG after the merger. Although the upper echelons' perspective emphasises utilising the directors' knowledge and expertise to improve the organisational outcomes (Carpenter et al., 2004), these multiple changes in the TCG management structuration reflect the poor company performance, consistent with Crutchley et al. (2002), as an attempt to protect stockholders' investments. Furthermore, this board instability was aligned with the media news covering the main reasons behind the collapse of TCG's share price in 2019.[6]

This long-term mismanagement is also reflected in the RC structuration, where five different directors took the committee leadership, starting with Michael Beckett in 2009, then Nigel Northridge 2009–2010, Peter Middleton 2010–2012, Roger Burnell 2012–2014 and ending with Warren Tucker 2014–2018. Most importantly, it has been found that the majority of those directors did not serve as RC members before chairing the committee, which contradicts the Code (2018) as stated (p.13) that *"Before appointment as chair of the remuneration committee, the appointee should have served on a remuneration committee for at least 12 months"*. In addition to the increase in the size of the committee, it has been noted that the number of meetings and attendees also increased over the period and, most importantly, all independent non-executives, along with the directors of HR and Reward, as well as the external auditor, were present in 2017 and 2018, reflecting the prominence of remuneration agenda topics under discussion.

### 17.5.2 Types of the TCG's directors' remuneration packages

The TCG's ER package during the period consisted of the base salary, annual bonus, pensions, LTIPs, taking the forms of Performance Share Plan (PSP) and/ or Co-Investment Plan (COIP), as well as other benefits, including private health insurance, disability cover, personal accident cover, death-in-service benefit and car allowance. The RC determined this ER package. On the other hand, the remuneration of TCG's chairman was set by a Committee of Independent Non-Executive Directors, whereas fees for other non-executives were determined by the board in alignment with the Code (DRR, 2009, p. 57). These fees for non-executives were reviewed for the first time in 2009 since the merger and were benchmarked against other FTSE 350 companies. From 2010 onwards, the RC took the responsibility of determining the chairman's remuneration (DRR, 2010, p. 65).

*Table 17.2* Structural analysis of the TCG Board and Remuneration Committee

| Names | Sex | Age in 2009 | Position | Appointment | Main Skills & Experience | Remuneration Committee (Number of meetings attended / Total number of meetings) | | | | | | | | | |
|---|---|---|---|---|---|---|---|---|---|---|---|---|---|---|---|
| | | | | | | 2009 | 2010 | 2011 | 2012 | 2013 | 2014 | 2015 | 2016 | 2017 | 2018 |
| **Board** | | | | | | | | | | | | | | | |
| **Michael Beckett** | Male | 73 | Non-executive Chairman | March 2007 | He was the Chairman of **MyTravel Group plc**, as well as London Clubs International plc, Ashanti Goldfields Company Limited and Clarkson plc. | C 8/8 | A | Left in 11-2011 | | | | | | | |
| **Frank Meysman** | Male | 57 | Non-executive Chairman | October 2011 | He was the executive chairman of Procter & Gamble, Douwe Egberts and the Sara Lee Corporation. | | | Left in 12-2011 | | | | | | | |
| **Manny Fontenla-Novoa** | Male | 55 | Group Chief Executive Officer | July 2007 | He was the director of Sunworld and has over 30 years of experience in the travel industry. | A | A | Left in 8-2011 | | | | | | | |
| **Sam Weihagen** | Male | 59 | Chief Executive, Northern Europe | November 2009 | He was an Executive Director of **MyTravel Group plc**. He has 34 years of experience in the travel industry. | | | Took control in 8-2011 | Left in 7-2012 | | | | | | |
| **Harriet Green** | Female | 47 | Group Chief Executive Officer | July 2012 | She was CEO of Premier Farnell plc. She has extensive experience in the worldwide technology and industrial markets. | | | | Join in 7-2012 | A | A | A | | | |
| **Dr Peter Fankhauser** | Male | 49 | Chief Executive Officer | November 2014 | He held senior roles in the Thomas Cook Group. He was CEO for UK & Continental Europe. He has over 25 years of experience in the travel market. | | | | | | | A | A | A | A |

| Name | Gender | Age | Position | Date appointed | Background | | | | | | | | | |
|---|---|---|---|---|---|---|---|---|---|---|---|---|---|---|
| **David Allvey** | Male | 64 | Non-executive Director | March 2007 | He was a Non-executive Director of **MyTravel Group plc**. He was Group Finance Director of Barclays Bank plc, B.A.T Industries plc and was Group Chief Operating Officer for Zurich Financial Services AG. | A | A | | | | | | | |
| **Roger Burnell** | Male | 59 | Senior Independent Director | March 2007 | He was a Non-executive Director of **MyTravel Group plc**. He was Chief Operating Officer and a Director of Thomson Travel Group plc. | M 8/8 | M 7/7 | M 6/6 | C 4/4 | C 5/5 | C 2/2 | | | |
| **Bo Lerenius** | Male | 62 | Non-executive Director | July 2007 | He was Group Chief Executive of Associated British Ports Holdings Plc. | M 7/7 | M 6/6 | M 2/2 | | | | | | |
| **Nigel Northbridge** | Male | 53 | Non-executive Director | August 2008 | Over his 30-year career with the Gallaher Group, he held senior positions in general management and sales & marketing roles. | M 8/8 | C 4/4 | | | | | | | |
| **Peter Middleton** | Male | 69 | Non-executive Director | November 2009 | He was CEO of Thomas Cook, CEO of Lloyds of London and CEO of Salomon Brothers International Ltd. | C 3/3 | C 6/6 | C 2/2 | | | | | | |
| **Dawn Airey** | Female | 49 | Non-executive Director | January 2010 | She has over 25 years of experience within the media industry. She is currently President of CLT-UFA UK Television Ltd within the RTL Group. | | | M 1/2 | M 4/5 | M 4/5 | M 4/4 | A | A | M 6/6 |
| **Martine Verluyten** | Female | 58 | Non-executive Director | May 2011 | She has held senior finance positions across the telecommunications, electronics and materials sectors, and has significant financial and IT expertise. | | | M 2/2 | M 5/5 | A | A | A | A | M 6/6 |

*(Continued)*

*Table 17.2* (Continued)

| Names | Sex | Age in 2009 | Position | Appointment | Main Skills & Experience | Remuneration Committee (Number of meetings attended / Total number of meetings) | | | | | | | | | |
|---|---|---|---|---|---|---|---|---|---|---|---|---|---|---|---|
| | | | | | | 2009 | 2010 | 2011 | 2012 | 2013 | 2014 | 2015 | 2016 | 2017 | 2018 |
| **Peter Marks** | Male | 60 | Non-executive Director | October 2011 | He has over 44 years of experience in the retail industry and has managed a broad range of businesses and functions. | | | | A | A | A | | | | |
| **Emre Berkin** | Male | 48 | Non-executive Director | November 2012 | He has experience across the technology sector and international markets. | | | | | M 3/3 | M 5/5 | M 4/4 | M 5/5 | M 6/6 | A |
| **Carl Symon** | Male | 63 | Non-executive Director | October 2013 | He has extensive global business operations and management experience from IBM, as he was the Chairman and CEO of IBM UK. | | | | | | M 3/3 | | | | |
| **Warren Tucker** | Male | 47 | Non-executive Director | October 2013 | He has experience in international business and strategic transformations. He was CFO of Cobham plc. | | | | | | C 3/3 | C 4/4 | C 5/5 | C 6/6 | C 6/6 |
| **Annet Aris** | Female | 51 | Non-executive Director | July 2014 | She is an Adjunct Professor of Strategy at INSEAD, France, and before that was a partner of McKinsey & Company in Germany. | | | | | | M 1/1 | M 4/4 | M 5/5 | M 6/6 | M 6/6 |
| **Lesley Knox** | Female | | Non-executive Director | March 2016 | She has over 17 years of financial services experience. She is an experienced Non-executive Director with a strong record in **remuneration.** | | | | | | | | M 3/3 | M 5/6 | M 6/6 |

| | | | | | | | M 1/1 | | M 6/6 |
|---|---|---|---|---|---|---|---|---|---|

| | | | | | | | | |
|---|---|---|---|---|---|---|---|---|
| **Paul Edgecliffe-Johnson** | Male | Non-executive Director | July 2017 | He has in-depth knowledge of the global hotel industry. He is a Chartered Accountant with extensive experience in debt and equity markets. | | | M 1/1 | M 6/6 |
| **Jürgen Schreiber** | Male | Non-executive Director | July 2017 | He has broad experience serving at the board level of large multinational consumer-facing businesses. He has in-depth knowledge of international markets. | | | A | A |
| **Group Executive Board** | | | | | | | | |
| **Ludger Heuberg** | Male | 50 | Group Chief Financial Officer | 2004 | He was CFO of Lufthansa Cargo AG, CFO of Kolbenschmidt-Pierburg AG and director of Mauser Waldeck AG. | | | |
| **Paul Hollings-worth** | Male | 39 | Group Chief Financial Officer | January 2010 | He was the CFO of Mondi Group. He was previously Group Finance Director of BPB plc, De La Rue plc and Ransomes plc. | Left in 6-2012 | | |
| **Michael Healy** | Male | 49 | Group Chief Financial Officer | July 2012 | He was Group Finance Director of Kwik-Fit Group. He has international experience across a broad range of industries. | | | |
| **Bill Scott** | Male | | Chief Financial Officer | January 2018 | He has experience in strategic financial planning and reporting. He is a Chartered Accountant with expertise in leading large corporate transactions. | | | |

*(Continued)*

*Table 17.2* (Continued)

| Names | Sex | Age in 2009 | Position | Appointment | Main Skills & Experience | Remuneration Committee (Number of meetings attended / Total number of meetings) | | | | | | | | | |
|---|---|---|---|---|---|---|---|---|---|---|---|---|---|---|---|
| | | | | | | 2009 | 2010 | 2011 | 2012 | 2013 | 2014 | 2015 | 2016 | 2017 | 2018 |
| **Paul Wood** | Male | 39 | Group Director, HR | 2006 | He joined **MyTravel Group plc** in 2006. He held senior reward and human resources roles at Clifford Chance, Atos Origin, Geest plc, Vodafone plc and De La Rue plc. | A | A | (A) Left in 3-2011 | | | | | | | |
| **Anne Billson-Ross** | Female | 41 | Group Director, HR | April 2011 | She held senior HR roles within the UK HR department, including HR Director, UK & Ireland. | | | A | | | | | | | |
| **Group General Counsel and Group Company Secretary** | | | | | | | | | | | | | | | |
| **Derek Woodward** | Male | 51 | Group Company Secretary | 2008 | He spent six years as Head of Secretariat at Centrica plc. From 1998, he was Company Secretary of Allied Zurich plc. | A | A | A | A | A | A | | | | |
| **Judith Mackenzie** | Female | | Group Head of Reward | | They provided their expertise in making sure that corporate People Agenda is going forward | | | A | A | A | A | Attend as required. | Attend as required. | Attend as required. | Attend as required. |
| **Sandra Campopiano** | Female | | Chief People Officer | September 2013 | | | | | | A | A | | | | |
| **Craig Stoehr** | Male | 42 | Group General Counsel | April 2013 | He served as General Counsel and a member of the Executive Management Committee of Eastgate Capital Group. | | | A | A | A | A | | | | |
| **Alice Marsden** | Female | | Group General Counsel & Company Secretary | September 2015 | She joined the Company in 2014 as Group Senior Legal Counsel and has since taken on the roles of Group Company Secretary (from September 2015) and Head of Legal for the UK&I and Group. | | | | | | | A | A | A | A |

C (chair), M (member), and A (attend)

Table 17.3 demonstrates the fixed and variable remuneration amounts of TCG's board executive and non-executive directors from 2009 to 2018. The fixed remuneration for executives consisted of base salary, pension payments and benefits, while their variable remunerations included bonuses and/or LTIPs. Non-executive directors received only fees and additional benefits for additional services, such as chairing committees. During the first three years until the first CEO, Manny Fontenla-Novoa, resigned in 2011, his fixed remuneration was increased from £0.94m in 2009 to £1.19m in 2011, while his bonuses were decreased from £1.43m in 2009 to zero in 2011. The same trend was followed for Paul Hollingsworth, the CFO, and Sam Weihagen, the CEO of the Northern Europe sector before taking the lead after Manny Fontenla-Novoa left the corporation. Although the decline in bonuses might probably be aligned with the poor TCG's performance during that time, it is clear that more emphasis had been placed on providing behavioural-based payments compared with outcome-related payments. The reason behind this might be that the executive directors were risk averse, and they exercised the power to have incremental base salaries rather than raises in variable components, consistent with the managerial hegemony perspective (Bebchuk et al., 2002; Gomez-Mejia and Wiseman, 1997). On the other hand, this could be interpreted as the management team intending to create motivational impact for lower-level executives at all TCG's branches through the incremental salaries and benefits provided to senior executives, consistent with tournament theory (Elsayed and Elbardan, 2018; Lazear, 1998).

Before Sam Weihagen left the TCG in 2012 and was replaced by Harriet Green in 2013, Sam received £1.01m as a fixed remuneration package and £0.3m as bonuses, whereas Harriet received £1.07m and £1.79m, respectively. Additionally, Michael Healy, the new CFO, received £0.62m for fixed pay and £0.72m for variable pay. These high levels of bonuses may reflect the executive management power or influence exerted over their pay packages, consistent with the managerial hegemony perspective (Hendry and Kiel, 2004; Bebchuk et al., 2002). It may also be related to the good performance that the management team achieved during that time; however, the amounts of fixed remuneration are still questionable. Most interestingly, £11,000 had been provided as salary to Richard Pennycook, an independent non-executive director, who was appointed in April 2013 and resigned directly in June 2013. This is aligned more with the management instability (Crutchley et al., 2002), and probably with the poor TCG performance since no variable remuneration payments were provided to the executive team in 2014. The year 2015 was the only year that LTIPs in the form of PSP and/or COIP were provided. This had been reflected in the rise of the variable ER package. After £0 variable payments in 2014, Dr Peter Fankhauser, the new CEO, and Michael Healy were awarded £3.47m and £2.97m as bonuses and LTIPs, respectively. For the remaining period, the CEO and CFO received an incrementally fixed remuneration, while their variable remuneration fluctuated, reaching £0 payments in 2018, reflecting the continuous unsteadiness of the TCG's progress over the period.

*Table 17.3* Total directors' remuneration

Total Directors' Remuneration (Audited) for the financial years ending 30 September (£'000)

| Names | 2009 F | 2009 V | 2010 F | 2010 V | 2011 F | 2011 V | 2012 F | 2012 V | 2013 F | 2013 V | 2014 F | 2014 V | 2015 F | 2015 V | 2016 F | 2016 V | 2017 F | 2017 V | 2018 F | 2018 V |
|---|---|---|---|---|---|---|---|---|---|---|---|---|---|---|---|---|---|---|---|---|
| **Michael Beckett** | 250 | – | 250 | – | 250 | – | | | | | | | | | | | | | | |
| **Frank Meysman** | | | | | 0 | – | 329 | – | 313 | – | 316 | – | 333 | – | 316 | – | 305 | – | 307 | – |
| **Manny Fontenla-Novoa** | 937 | 1428 | 1082 | 1190 | 1193 | 0 | | | | | | | | | | | | | | |
| **Sam Weihagen** | 500 | – | 481 | 636 | 453 | 0 | 1012 | 300 | | | | | | | | | | | | |
| **Harriet Green** | | | | | | | 181 | 0 | 1070 | 1785 | 1046 | 0 | | | | | | | | |
| **Dr Peter Fankhauser** | | | | | | | | | | | | | 790 | 3472 | 973 | 236 | 1000 | 837 | 1024 | 0 |
| **David Allvey** | 80 | – | 80 | – | 80 | – | | | | | | | | | | | | | | |
| **Roger Burnell** | 60 | – | 70 | – | 70 | – | 76 | – | 80 | – | 31 | – | | | | | | | | |
| **Bo Lerenius** | 60 | – | 60 | – | 60 | – | 43 | – | | | | | | | | | | | | |
| **Nigel Northridge** | 60 | – | 40 | – | | | | | | | | | | | | | | | | |
| **Peter Middleton** | | | 60 | – | 80 | – | 58 | – | 60 | – | 60 | – | | | | | | | | |
| **Dawn Airey** | | | 28 | – | 60 | – | 60 | – | 60 | – | 60 | – | 63 | – | 72 | – | 73 | – | 106 | – |
| **Martine Verluyten** | | | | | 24 | – | 73 | – | 80 | – | 80 | – | 84 | – | 84 | – | 89 | – | 89 | – |
| **Peter Marks** | | | | | 0 | – | 66 | – | 70 | – | 66 | – | 76 | – | | | | | | |
| **Emre Berkin** | | | | | | | 0 | – | 55 | – | 66 | – | | | | | | | | |
| **Carl Symon** | | | | | | | | | 0 | – | 72 | – | 85 | – | 76 | – | 87 | – | 84 | – |
| **Warren Tucker** | | | | | | | | | | | 15 | – | 63 | – | 88 | – | 83 | – | 84 | – |
| **Annet Aris** | | | | | | | | | | | | | | | 66 | – | 67 | – | 65 | – |
| **Lesley Knox** | | | | | | | | | | | | | | | 36 | – | 61 | – | 61 | – |

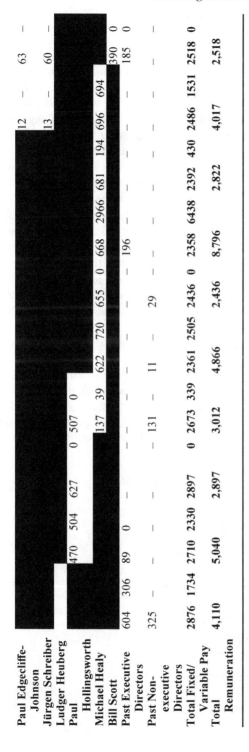

| | | | | | | | | | | | | | | | | | | | |
|---|---|---|---|---|---|---|---|---|---|---|---|---|---|---|---|---|---|---|---|
| **Paul Edgecliffe-Johnson** | 12 | – | | | | | | | | | | | | | | – | 63 | – | |
| **Jürgen Schreiber** | 13 | – | | | | | | | | | | | | | – | – | 60 | | |
| **Ludger Heuberg** | | | | | | | | | | | | | | | | | | | |
| **Paul Hollingsworth** | 470 | 504 | 627 | 0 | 507 | 0 | 622 | 720 | 655 | 0 | 668 | 2966 | 681 | 194 | 696 | 694 | | | |
| **Michael Healy** | | | | 137 | 39 | | | | | | | | | | | | | | |
| **Bill Scott** | 0 | – | – | – | – | – | – | – | – | – | – | – | – | 390 | 0 | | | | |
| **Past Executive Directors** | 604 | 89 | – | – | – | – | – | – | 196 | – | – | – | – | 185 | 0 | | | | |
| **Past Non-executive Directors** | 325 | – | – | 131 | – | 11 | 29 | – | – | – | – | – | – | – | | | | | |
| **Total Fixed/Variable Pay** | 2876 | 1734 | 2710 | 2330 | 2897 | 0 | 2673 | 339 | 2361 | 2505 | 2436 | 0 | 2358 | 6438 | 2392 | 430 | 2486 | 1531 | 2518 | 0 |
| **Total Remuneration** | **4,110** | **5,040** | **2,897** | **3,012** | **4,866** | **2,436** | **8,796** | **2,822** | **4,017** | **2,518** | | | | | | | | | |

F (fixed) and V (variable)

### 17.5.3 Analysis of remuneration, performance and governance references

To quantify the level of remuneration, performance and governance references in DRRs, several steps are followed, as described by Hussainey et al. (2003). First, NVivo is used to run an analysis for all words within the 2009–2018 DRRs. Second, similar words are combined that, in most cases, are associated with the three targeted references. Third, several DRRs are read to take notes of any other words that are associated with the three targeted references before creating a list of these related words. Fourth, *Thesaurus* is utilised to search for any synonyms. A list of 89, 58 and 16 words are initially created for the references of remuneration, performance and governance, respectively. Fifth, 50 randomly selected DRRs of FTSE 350 companies between 2009 and 2018 are read to determine how often the reported words are associated with the three targeted references to ensure that they expressed the intended meanings. Finally, a list of key similar words is assembled, which includes 31, 9 and 4 keywords for the references of remuneration, performance and governance, respectively, as follows: for "remuneration": *compensate, compensation, earn, earned, pay, paying, pays, payment, payments, remunerated, remuneration, award, awards, awarding, awarded, salaries, salary, bonus, bonuses, bonusable, incentive, incentives, pension, pensions, pensionable, benefit, benefits, gain, gains, allowance* and *allowances*; for "performance": *perform, performance, performance, performed, performing, achievable, achievement, achievements* and *achieving*; and for "governance": *governance, governed, code* and *regulations*. The weighted count for each reference is utilised by measuring the ratio of the total number of the targeted word divided by the total words of a specific corporate narrative document, as described by Lang and Lundholm (2000). Figure 17.1 demonstrates the weighted percentage of these three targeted references within the TCG's DRRs during the 2009–2018 period.

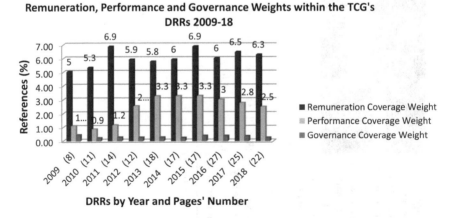

*Figure 17.1* Remuneration, performance and governance weights within the TCG's DRRs 2009–2018

As expected, the outcomes showed that the trend of utilising the reference "*remuneration*" was the highest among the other references in the documents focusing on the directors' remuneration. However, it reached a peak in 2011 and 2015. The reason for the peak in 2011 was that, on many occasions in the 2011 DRR, no bonuses were provided because of the poor TGC's performance, as stated, for instance, in the DRR (2011, p. 61): "*For the year, the Group financial targets were not met and the Committee determined that no bonus would be payable to any of the Executive Directors*". This is consistent with the agency theory (Jensen and Meckling, 1976) since variable remuneration is associated with both short- and/or long-term company performance to minimise agency problems and information asymmetry between stockholders and executives.

The high number of mentions of "remuneration" in 2015 DRR was for the need to articulate several times in the 2015 DRR that the highest remuneration payments awarded to the top-level executives were in the form not only of bonuses but also LTIPs; however, no proper explanations or justifications were provided regarding how these payments were related to the company or the actual executive performance. As an example for bonuses: "*For the year, the maximum Group Bonus Plan award opportunity for both the CEO and CFO was 150% of salary, one-third of which would be deferred as shares for two years*" (DRR, 2015, p. 97). Another example for LTIPS: "*The performance condition applying to the June 2012 PSP and COIP awards, which was based on absolute share price, was met in full and 100% of the awarded shares [were] vested in July 2015*" (DRR, 2015, p. 89). This is more likely aligned with the managerial hegemony perspective (Gomez-Mejia and Wiseman, 1997), which may reflect the exercise by TCG's executives of their power to obtain high pay packages.

On the other hand, the reference "*performance*" increased in use over time but not to the same extent as the "remuneration" reference. This may indicate the intention of TCG's boardroom to align what the executives gained with what they actually achieved and/or would perceivably achieve in the narrative reporting of DRRs. It was gradually increased during the period of examination until reaching the peak in the years 2013, 2014 and 2015 before falling to the end of the period, where no outcome-related remunerations were provided. As outlined, for example, in the DRR (2018, p. 89):

> *Following challenging trading conditions in the summer, we did not achieve our financial targets nor our performance hurdles and following the FY18 Bonus Plan rules no bonus is payable. [...] As performance against the targets have not been achieved, awards held by Executive Directors will lapse on the third anniversary of the grant date in December 2018.*

Finally, the reference "*governance*" was consistently used in the narrative reporting of DRRs; however, the peak was in 2009 due to the termination of the Relationship Agreement between TCG and Arcandor, and the shift in compliance with the Code. As stated in the DRR (2009, p. 3), *The Board is committed to high standards of corporate governance and, following the termination of the*

*Relationship Agreement with Arcandor on 10 September 2009, we made several changes to our governance arrangements in line with the Combined Code.*

However, this shift was not completely in line17 with the Code since the majority of RC chairpersons, for instance, did not serve as RC members before chairing the committee.

## 17.6 Conclusion and implications

The main purpose of this chapter has been to examine the DRRs of TCG for the past 10 years of performing its operational activities. This case study relied on multiple theoretical perspectives to shed some light on the governance role of its RC in sustaining the pay–performance alignment, and its implications in understanding its remuneration governance as an organisational practice. It offers the subsequent findings which could be of value to academics, policymakers and corporations alike.

Worldwide concerns regarding the provision of excessive ER packages have been the underlying motivation behind this case study. Previous literature (e.g., El-Sayed, 2013; Frydman and Saks, 2005) highlighted the historical evolution of ER in the UK from a situation where it was largely an internal matter for the corporation, its boardroom and its stockholders to the current, existing situation where there are extensive influences from both guidance and statute. Guidance has been emphasised through the recommendations of several reporting bodies, starting from the Greenbury Committee in 1995, then carried forward in various iterations of the Combined Code. ER has been also contained in a statute, most notably the 2002 UK Directors' Remuneration Report Regulations, and subsequenty into the Companies Act (2006) to facilitate reducing the information asymmetry. However, these UK regulatory evolvements and provisions are still incomplete and piecemeal in their effect in strengthening the pay–performance alignment, in line with Chu et al. (2021).

Although the TCG boardroom, in general, and its RC in particular, were gradually enlarged in size and their compositions, such as the representation by female directors during the period under examination, there were enormous changes towards directors' appointments and memberships of both the TCG boardroom and its RC. This substantial fluctuation in appointments and memberships reflects the board's instability, which might reflect not only the presence of poor company performance but also the likelihood of influencing its subsequent performance (Crutchley et al., 2002). Additionally, this fluctuation in TCG directorship reflects the board not acting consistently in line with the principles of good CG for listed companies (Code, 2018) through choosing directors to be the RC's chairpersons, although they had not served before as committee members without explaining why they did not comply.

By comparing the fixed and variable ER packages, the fixed ER package noticeably increased over time compared with the variable ER package. This might be explained by the top-level executives being risk averse and exercising their influence over their pay packages (Bebchuk et al., 2002). It might be also interpreted that the TCG boardroom created such incremental behavioural-based payments intentionally to motivate lower-level executives to be replaced by those senior executives in the future (Elsayed and Elbardan, 2018), as illustrated by the case of appointing Sam Weihagen in the year 2011. In contrast, the variable ER package was periodically provided in the form of bonuses and LTIPs, which should only be granted for extraordinary performance reflecting long-term business success (Gregg et al., 2012). However, this contradicts the TCG board instability over time, which reflects the proposition of power exercise by senior executives over their pay packages (Hendry and Kiel, 2004). By performing an automated content analysis to measure the TCG's disclosure behaviour trend of focusing on using the references remuneration, performance and governance, the outcomes revealed that the remuneration trend focused on awarding variable ER payments (or not) without providing proper disclosures regarding the justifications behind such actions, and their alignments with actual executive performance.

The aforementioned examination has significant implications for academics, policymakers and corporations alike. Remuneration governance is an organisational practice constituted under the accountability of a RC, whose members are independently involved in setting ER packages. Those members have to consider the necessity of associating the determination of the amount and structuring of ER not only with the overall company performance but also with the individual executive performance, consistent with agency theory (Jensen and Meckling, 1976). The reason behind this is that their propositions are subject to approval by the full boardroom members and eventually by the stockholder body who put great store by observing the link between what they (stockholders) are obtaining as returns with what executive directors are receiving as remuneration packages. Additionally, those members have also to consider not only the prior-period performance in determining the amount and structuration of ER but also a reasonable estimated payment for prospective achievements in the future as consistent with tournament theory (Lazear, 1998). The reason behind this is to keep the executive directors enthusiastic about enhancing the performance of their corporation over time. These insights lead sequentially to the consideration of linking both fixed and variable components of ER to the performances of executive directors and the overall corporation at different levels to sustain the pay–performance alignment.

As a result, the members of a RC should be knowledgeable and have relevant expertise (Menz, 2012; Carpenter et al., 2004) not only in how ER is set in alignment with prior and future targets but also in linking what executive members receive in terms of remunerations with respect to their actual achievements alongside the overall company performance. Policymakers who put an interest in remuneration governance as an organisational practice may require rethinking and reconsidering the present Code to evolve the existing guidelines of setting ER packages. Such guidelines could be examined through further academic projects within the CG discipline and/or by surveying the interested regulators as to the effectiveness of remuneration governance within corporations in providing a satisfactory level of disclosures for corporate stakeholders.

## Notes

1  The Independent report: MyTravel and Thomas Cook merge | The Independent | The Independent
2  The BBC News report: Christi and Bobby Shepherd Corfu deaths bungalow to be demolished - BBC News
3  The Reuters report: Thomas Cook's Belgian unit to extend ties with Brussels Airlines | Reuters
4  TCG Annual Reports for the period 2009–2018 are available at: Thomas Cook Group plc - AnnualReports.com
5  A qualitative analysis software that provides the opportunity to classify and organise the data collected. This analysis offers flexibility and accessibility through its freedom from adopting a specific theoretical framework, as well as providing clarity about how the qualitative data were examined (Braun et al., 2016).
6  The Motley Fool report: The Thomas Cook share price is down another 20%. Is this the end? - The Motley Fool UK

## References

Bebchuk, L., Fried, J. and Walker, D. (2002) 'Managerial power and rent extraction in the design of executive compensation', *The University of Chicago Law Review*, 69(3), pp. 751–846.

Beiner, S., Drobetz, W., Schmid, F. and Zimmermann, H. (2006) "An integrated framework of corporate governance and firm valuation', *European Financial Management*, 12(2), pp. 249–283.

Braun, V., Clarke, V. and Weate, P. (2016) 'Using thematic analysis in sport and exercise research', in Smith, B. and Sparkes, A. (eds.) *Routledge handbook of qualitative research in sport and exercise* (pp. 191–205). London: Routledge.

Cadbury, A. (1992) *Report on the committee on the financial aspects of corporate governance.* London: Gee Publishing Ltd.

Carpenter, M.A., Geletkanycz, M.A. and Sanders, W.G. (2004) 'Upper echelons research revisited: Antecedents, elements, and consequences of top management team composition', *Journal of Management*, 30(6), pp. 749–778.

Chu, J., Gupta, A. and Livne, G. (2021) 'Pay regulation – Is more better?', *Accounting and Business Research*, 51(1), pp. 1–35.

Clarkson, P., Walker, J. and Nicholls, S. (2011) 'Disclosure, shareholder oversight and the pay-performance link', *Journal of Contemporary Accounting and Economics*, 7, pp. 47–64.

Conyon, M., Gregg, P. and Machin, S. (1995) 'Taking care of business: Executive compensation in the United Kingdom', *The Economic Journal*, 105(430), pp. 704–714.

Conyon, M., Peck, S.I. and Sadler, G.V. (2009) 'Compensation consultants and executive pay: Evidence from the United States and the United Kingdom', *Academy of Management Perspectives*, 23(1), pp. 43–55.

Crutchley, C., Garner, J. and Marshall, B. (2002) 'An examination of board stability and the long-term performance of initial public offerings', *Financial Management*, 31(3), pp. 63–90.

Devers, C., Cannella, A., Reilly, G. and Yoder, M. (2007) 'Executive compensation: A multidisciplinary review of recent developments', *Journal of Management*, 33(6), pp. 1016–1072.

Dia, Z., Jin, L. and Zhang, W. (2014) 'Executive pay-performance sensitivity and litigation', *Contemporary Accounting Research*, 31(1), pp. 152–177.

El-Sayed, N. (2013) 'An examination of executive directors' remuneration in FTSE 350 companies', University of Exeter. Available at: https://ore.exeter.ac.uk/repository/ bitstream/handle/10871/14025/El-SayedN.pdf?sequence=1&isAllowed=y.

Elsayed, N. and Elbardan, H. (2018) 'Investigating the associations between executive compensation and firm performance: Agency theory or tournament theory', *Journal of Applied Accounting Research*, 19(2), pp. 245–270.

Financial Reporting Council. (2018). *The UK corporate governance code* (pp. 1–20). London: Financial Reporting Council.

Financial Reporting Council. (2020) *The annual review of the UK corporate governance code* (pp. 1–20). London: Financial Reporting Council.

Frydman, C. and Saks, R. (2005) 'Historical trends in executive compensation 1936–2003', Harvard University Working Paper. Available at: https://web.stanford.edu/group/scspi /media/_media/pdf/Reference%20Media/Frydman%20and%20Saks_2005_Elites.pdf.

Ginesti, G., Drago, C., Macchioni, R. and Sannino, G. (2018) 'Female board participation and annual report readability in firms with boardroom connections', *Gender in Management: An International Journal*, 33(4), pp. 296–314.

Gomez-Mejia, L. and Wiseman, R. (1997) 'Reframing executive compensations: An assessment and outlook', *Journal of Management*, 23(3), pp. 291–374.

Greenbury, R. (1995) *Directors' remuneration: Report of a study group chaired by Sir Richard Greenbury*. London: Gee Publishing Ltd.

Gregg, P., Jewell, S. and Tonks, I. (2012) 'Executive pay and performance: Did bankers' bonuses cause the crisis?', *International Review of Finance*, 12(1), pp. 89–122.

Hambrick, D.C. and Mason, P. (1984) 'Upper echelons: The organization as a reflection of its top managers', *Academy of Management Review*, 9(2), pp. 193–206.

Hendry, K. and Kiel, G. (2004) 'The role of the board in firm strategy: Integrating agency and organizational control perspectives', *Corporate Governance*, 12(4), pp. 500–520.

Hussainey, K., Schleicher, T. and Walker, M. (2003) 'Undertaking large-scale disclosure studies when AIMR-FAF ratings are not available: The case of prices leading earnings', *Accounting and Business Research*, 33(4), pp. 275–294.

Hussainey, K. and Walker, M. (2009) 'The effects of voluntary disclosure and dividend propensity on prices leading earnings', *Accounting and Business Research*, 39(1), pp. 37–55.

Jensen, M. and Meckling, W. (1976) 'Theory of a firm: Managerial behavior, agency costs and ownership structure', *Journal of Financial Economics*, 3(4), pp. 305–360.

Jensen, M. and Murphy, K. (1990) 'Performance pay and top-management incentives', *Journal of Political Economy*, 98(2), pp. 225–264.

Khurshed, A., Lin, S. and Wang, M. (2011) 'Institutional block-holdings of UK firms: Do corporate governance mechanisms matter?', *European Journal of Finance*, 17(2), pp. 133–152.

Krippendorff, K. (2004) *Content analysis: An introduction to its methodology*. 2nd ed. Los Angeles, CA: Sage.

Lang, M. and Lundholm, R. (2000) 'Voluntary disclosure and equity offerings: Reducing information asymmetry or hyping the stock?', *Contemporary Accounting Research*, 17(4), pp. 623–662.

Lazear, E. (1998) *Personnel economics for managers*. New York: John Wiley & Sons, Ltd.

Liang, Y., Moroney, R. and Rankin, M. (2020) 'Say-on-pay judgements: The two-strikes rule and the pay-performance link', *Accounting and Finance*, 60, pp. 943–970.

Magee, S., Ng, C.M. and Wright, S. (2021) 'How executive remuneration responds to guidance: Evidence from the Australian banking industry', *Accounting and Finance*, Forthcoming.

Main, B. and Johnston, J. (1993) 'The remuneration committees and corporate governance', *Accounting and Business Research*, 23, pp. 351–362.

Menz, M. (2012) 'Functional top management team members', *Journal of Management*, 38(1), pp. 45–80.

Ntim, C., Lindop, S., Osei, K. and Thomas, D. (2015) 'Executive compensation, corporate governance and corporate performance: A simultaneous equation approach', *Managerial and Decision Economics*, 36(2), pp. 67–96.

Ozkan, N. (2011) 'CEO compensation and firm performance: An empirical investigation of UK panel data', *European Financial Management*, 17(2), pp. 260–285.

Parker, L. (2012) 'Qualitative management accounting research: Assessing deliverables and relevance', *Critical Perspectives on Accounting*, 23(1), pp. 54–70.

Roberts, J., Sanderson, P., Seidl, D. and Krivokapic, A. (2020) 'The UK corporate governance code principle of 'comply or explain': Understanding code compliance as 'subjection'', *ABACUS*, 56(4), pp. 602–626.

Sapp, S. (2008) 'The impact of corporate governance on executive compensation', *European Financial Management*, 14(4), pp. 710–746.

Scapens, R. (2004) 'Doing case study research', in Humphrey, C. and Lee, B. (eds.) *The real life guide to accounting research: A behind-the-scenes view of using qualitative research methods* (pp. 257–279). Oxford: Elsevier Ltd.

Shiyyab, F., Girardone, C. and Zakaria, I. (2013) 'Pay for no performance? Executive pay and performance in EU banks', *Unpublished working paper*, *Essex business school* (pp. 1–48). University of Essex.

Sila, V., Gonzalez, A. and Hagendorff, J. (2016) 'Women on board: Does boardroom gender diversity affect firm risk?', *Journal of Corporate Finance*, 36, pp. 26–53.

Smith, M. and Taffler, R.J. (2000) 'The chairman's statement: A content analysis of discretionary narrative disclosures', *Accounting, Auditing and Accountability Journal*, 13(5), pp. 624–646.

TCG-plc, 2018 Directors' Remuneration Report.

TCG-plc, 2017 Directors' Remuneration Report.

TCG-plc, 2016 Directors' Remuneration Report.

TCG-plc, 2015 Directors' Remuneration Report.

TCG-plc, 2014 Directors' Remuneration Report.

TCG-plc, 2013 Directors' Remuneration Report.

TCG-plc, 2012 Directors' Remuneration Report.

TCG-plc, 2011 Directors' Remuneration Report.

TCG-plc, 2010 Directors' Remuneration Report.

TCG-plc, 2009 Directors' Remuneration Report.

The Stationery Office Limited. (2002). *The United Kingdom directors' remuneration report regulations* (pp. 1–16). London: The Stationery Office Limited.

The Stationery Office Limited. (2006) *Companies Act: Chapter 46* (pp. 1–761). London: The Stationery Office Limited.

The Combined Code. (2000) *Principles of good governance and code of best practice*. London: The Committee of Corporate Governance.

Yin, R. (2009) *Case study research: Design and methods (applied social research methods)*. Thousand Oaks, CA: Sage.

# 18 Digital narrative reporting and legitimation tactics in Dieselgate time(s)

*Cristina Florio, Giulia Leoni and Alice Francesca Sproviero*

## 18.1 Introduction

Narrative reporting is fully integrated into corporate external reporting, as it helps to portray a comprehensive view of the company's performance to stakeholders. Narratives provide non-financial information on several important aspects of a company's conduct that financial numbers alone are unable to fully depict (Beattie 2014), such as its market position, strategy, future plans, corporate social responsibility (CSR), environmental sustainability and governance.

Thanks to the development of digital technologies, companies can now use digital channels as "*an additional medium that is quick and cheap*" (ICAEW 2004: p.14) to deliver their narrative disclosures (Merkl-Davies et al. 2011) and improve their ability to reach stakeholders and appear more transparent (ICAEW 2004). As a result, narratives on a company's financials and non-financials are now scattered around different outlets, such as press releases, results presentation recordings, social and environmental reports on websites, as well as posts and tweets on social media profiles. Furthermore, the digitalisation of corporate disclosure allows corporations to communicate information on their corporate events in (almost) real time as well as to render available at any moment their corporate reports, thereby enhancing a continuous dialogue with their stakeholders (Vasarhelyi et al. 2015; Arnaboldi et al. 2017; Lodhia 2018).

While the means to provide narrative disclosure have multiplied, the motivations to provide such reports are usually linked to the need for companies to mould corporate legitimacy (Gray et al. 1995; Suchman 1995; Deegan 2002; Merkl-Davies et al. 2011; Lodhia 2018; Kuruppu et al. 2019), thereby justifying their right to exist and conveying that "*they operate within the bounds and norms of their respective societies*" (Guthrie et al. 2004: p.284). Whenever companies break such norms with socially unacceptable behaviours, such as human rights violations, pollution or corruption, their legitimacy is questioned. To regain such legitimacy, companies may engage in legitimation tactics (Hahn and Lülfs 2014; Rudkin et al. 2019), including them in the construction of their narrative reporting, which grants flexibility in terms of contents, and a wide reach thanks to digital outlets (Suddaby et al. 2017; Kuruppu et al. 2019).

DOI: 10.4324/9781003095385-23

Although past scandals that have threatened corporate legitimacy have been largely investigated to reveal companies' legitimation strategies as displayed in CSR reports (e.g., Cho 2009; Hrasky 2012; Hahn and Lülfs 2014; Rudkin et al. 2019), little is still known regarding the legitimising tactics employed in response to more recent scandals, when the affected companies can count on more extensive narrative reporting and various means of communication, especially digital ones. To such an end, this chapter aims at exploring the legitimising tactics employed in the corporate narratives delivered through digital reporting means that were produced by three carmakers in response to the so-called Dieselgate, a recent environmental scandal related to manipulation of nitrogen dioxide emissions in the automotive sector. The scandal erupted in September 2015, when Volkswagen (VW) was accused of manipulating emissions from diesel engines installed in its cars. The scandal caused an increase in VW's negative media coverage followed by several investigations, class actions and maxi-sanctions (Clemente and Gabbioneta 2017). As VW legitimacy was challenged, its operations were perceived as breaking the social bounds and norms. However, this conduct was not limited to VW alone. It was soon uncovered that emissions manipulation was implicating other leading automotive Groups, namely Daimler and BMW. In response to this fallout, it is reasonable to expect that the automotive industry, and especially the Groups directly blamed for manipulations, tried to recover from this loss of legitimacy and regain the trust of their stakeholders by using both actions and disclosure (as shown by Kuruppu et al. 2019 with regards to the VW case).

To achieve its aim, we rely on the close reading technique informed on the eight legitimising tactics proposed by Hahn and Lülfs (2014). Close reading particularly allows undertaking of a fine-grained descriptive analysis (Smith 2016; Brummett 2018) of the various narratives included in annual reports, sustainability reports, press releases and social media communications of the carmakers accused of engine manipulations, namely VW, Daimler and BMW.

The rest of the chapter proceeds as follows. The next section (Section 18.2) provides a brief review on the literature on corporate scandals and their effects on companies' legitimacy. Section 18.3 provides a chronicle of the Dieselgate scandal. Section 18.4 presents the research method and the analytical framework that informed the data analysis, the findings of which are presented in Section 18.5. Finally, the chapter concludes with Section 18.6, with a brief discussion and concluding remarks, where contributions and future research are provided.

## 18.2  Prior literature

Whether and how companies leverage narrative reporting to repair legitimacy in the aftermath of corporate scandals is an extensive topic of debate. Research demonstrates that narrative reporting is leveraged for legitimation purposes in annual reports (Blanc et al. 2019; Cho 2009; O'Donovan 2002; Rudkin et al. 2019; Vourvachis et al. 2016) as well as CSR reports (Blanc et al. 2019; Corazza et al. 2020; Siano et al. 2017), press releases (Painter and Martins 2017) and other forms of public statements (Painter and Martins 2017; Peng et al. 2021). Disclosure strategies are adopted to manage organisational legitimacy notwithstanding the nature of the scandal (e.g., Blanc et al. 2019 on public corruption; Vourvachis et al. 2016 on airline accidents). However, companies tend to adopt a broader mix of strategies in disclosing environmental rather than accounting and social scandals, thus suggesting that they perceive a greater risk of losing legitimacy in the former case than in the latter (Rudkin et al. 2019). Especially when environmental scandals are highly visible (Kuruppu et al. 2019), managers use disclosure in response to legitimacy-threatening events in an attempt to be accountable, to reassure stakeholders, and highlight past achievements (O'Donovan 2002).

Empirical evidence on the specific legitimation strategies adopted in narrative reporting following environmental scandals is mixed. Referring to two major environmental disasters caused by the petroleum company Total SA, it is found that the company increased the extent of environmental disclosure in its annual reports and doubled its press releases after the second incident compared with the first one (Cho 2009). Conversely, the cruise line company Costa Crociere froze corporate communication and sustainability reporting in the year after the Costa Concordia disaster (Corazza et al. 2020). Observing multiple cases, evidence is obtained that, once involved in an environmental incident, companies tend to simply acknowledge the facts and quickly move forward to explain the corrective actions implemented to resolve the situation and/or prevent the occurrence of similar events in the future; among the latter, collaboration with authorities or other respected third parties are leveraged to endorse the steps taken by the company (Rudkin et al. 2019).

With reference to the Dieselgate scandal, few studies have investigated the aftermath of the scandal. Siano et al. (2017: p.32) show that VW CSR reports before the Dieselgate scandal underlined a strong environmental commitment of the company, although VW managers admitted they had only a "general awareness" of such environmental projects. Valentini and Kruckeberg (2018) also confirm the contradictory behaviour of the company, whereas Painter and Martins (2017) reveal that VW attempted to mitigate the negative effects of Dieselgate mainly by downplaying the entire case in press releases, reports and communications with stakeholders. Also, reporting differences were noticed over time: statements that express mortification (e.g., apologies) prevailed at the beginning, but were then replaced by statements aimed at boosting a positive image. Only the study by Florio and Sproviero (2021) has investigated VW disclosure in the aftermath of Dieselgate under the lens of legitimacy, by showing that the company chose specific discourses on the event, a few actors and processes and well-recognized corporate qualities to repair its threatened legitimacy. Such discourses were shaped by blending the use of grammatical, lexical and semantic features of discourses to restore pragmatic, moral and cognitive legitimacy.

## 18.3 Research setting: the Dieselgate cases

The Dieselgate scandal erupted publicly on 18 September 2015, with the issuance of a notice of violation of the Clean Air Act by the United States (US) Environmental Protection Agency (EPA) against VW. The vehicles were manufactured over a six-year period, from 2009 to 2015. Following the allegations in the US, Europe started to question the car manufacturers' conduct around vehicles' emissions. As shown in the Netflix documentary Hard NOx (Netflix 2018), Hans Koberstein's experiments to measure emissions of a BMW car, a Mercedes car and a VW car brought the discovery that they were all generating 40–50 times more pollutants than those detected during laboratory tests.

In March 2017, after the weekly *Die Zeit* published a testimony by an employee, Stuttgart prosecutors investigated Daimler AG employees for manipulating diesel emissions to circumvent testing. BMW AG was instead cited by the German non-governmental organization (NGO) Deutsche Umwelthilfe (DHU) which discovered incorrect emission values on a BMW 320d Euro 6. The Group was accused of altering car performance during the homologation tests.

The scandal produced far from negligible impacts on the performance and reputation of the three leading Groups of the automotive industry (i.e., VW, BMW and Daimler), according to the financial, market and reputational data reported in Table 18.1. Overall, the emission scandal impacted Europe heavily, due to the European Union financial incentives to induce European car drivers to choose diesel over gasoline vehicles. Among European countries, Germany had the most cars equipped with the "defeat device" (about 2.8 million cars) (Jung and Park 2017).

## 18.4 Research method

Multiple data sources provided the material for this study. We downloaded annual reports and sustainability reports issued by VW, Daimler and BMW in the year of Dieselgate (2015 for VW, 2017 for Daimler and BMW) from their corporate websites. We also searched for the press releases issued in the six months after each scandal broke, using the keywords "EPA", "diesel issue", "diesel engines" and/or "investigation". For the same timeframe, we identified the Twitter posts published in the official profiles of the three German Groups. Overall, the empirical material analysed includes 3 annual reports, 2 sustainability reports, 15 press releases (10 by VW, 4 by Daimler and 1 by BMW), and around seventy Twitter posts (around 50 by VW, 10 by Daimler and 10 by BMW).

The analysis of the companies' narratives has entailed a close reading, i.e., "*the mindful, disciplined reading of an objec*t [a text] *with a view to a deeper understanding of its meanings*" (Brummett 2018: p.2). Close reading focuses on literary aspects of a text and requires the provision of a descriptive analysis which highlights its qualitative characteristics. By looking for patterns of meaning and rhetoric features, such analysis extends the reading of a text to its interpretation (Schur 1998; Smith 2016; Brummett 2018). Close reading is particularly useful to gather a comprehensive view of the qualitative characteristics of the companies' disclosure and examine its literary aspects. Widely adopted by prior accounting studies to analyse speeches of chief executive officers and historical writings (Armenic and Craig 2017; Leoni 2021; Twyford 2021), the results obtained by close reading do support the interpretation of the textual meanings. The analytical framework adopted to analyse and interpret digital

*Table 18.1* Data on financial, market and reputational impacts

| Data | Volkswagen AG | Daimler AG | BMW AG |
|---|---|---|---|
| Sales and revenues | 2017: −18% and −24.3%, respectively | 2017: no changes | 2018: no changes |
| Share prices | March 2015: €250 September 2015: €161.17 October 2015: €102.50 | March 2015: €94.8 July 2016: €52.25 January 2019: €40.67 | March 2015: €122.60 September 2018: €58.70 |
| RepRisk Index* | October 2014: 71 November 2015: 76 August 2019: ~60 | 2007–2016: 39 on average 2017: 65 2018: ~60 | 2007–2017: 39 on average Spring 2018: 65 Late 2018: ~60 |
| Vehicles involved | ~11 million worldwide | >700,000 in Europe ~250,000 in the US | ~11,400 in Europe |
| Fines and settlements | $10,000 to each client overall ~$30 billion in the US €750 million to settle a 240,000 car owners' class-action €29,000 to each German car-owner Class actions still ongoing in European countries (e.g., the UK and Italy) | €870 million fine in Germany $1.5 billion agreement with the US Justice Department and EPA, (including $875 million fines) Other legal claims in Canada and Germany | ~€10 million fine |
| Arrests and searches | January 2017: an executive arrested for fraud in Florida August 2017: an engineer arrested for conspiracy to defraud the US government | May 2017: fraud inquiry of German offices September 2019: notice from German public prosecutor of negligent violation of supervisory duties since 2008 | March 2018: authorities raided Munich headquarters and a site in Austria No intentional deception finally confirmed by authorities |

*RepRisk Index denotes the level of media and stakeholder attention of a company related to environmental, social and governance (ESG) issues. It ranges from 0 to 100: 0–25 = low risk exposure; 26–49 = medium risk exposure; 50–59 = high risk exposure; 60–74 = very high-risk exposure; 75–100 = extremely high-risk exposure. Source: RepRisk.

narratives on the Dieselgate scandals is one of legitimation tactics, i.e., communication techniques which companies employ for disclosing negative events to their stakeholders. In detail, we make reference to the eight legitimation tactics that were derived by Hahn and Lülfs (2014) following their analyses of how negative events were disclosed in sustainability reports. These tactics are briefly described in Table 18.2, together with textual characteristics that are commonly used to enable each tactic.

Drawing on the above legitimation tactics, the following section highlights the tactics adopted by each carmaker in chronological order according to the findings of the close reading performed on the narratives issued by VW, Daimler and BMW during the Dieselgate timeframe.

## 18.5  Findings

### 18.5.1  Volkswagen AG

Since the first press release after the scandal erupted, VW implicitly acknowledges its illegal conduct and tries to downplay the effect of the defeat device installed in its diesel engines. An approximate number of vehicles involved in the emissions manipulation was also provided, however without any explanation or additional information, thus leaving any possible judgement to the reader. This suggests the adoption of both the *marginalization* and the *indicating facts* tactics:

> *For the majority of these engines the software does not have any effect.*
> (Press release 22 September 2015)

> *The internal evaluation revealed that approximately five million Volkswagen Passenger Cars brand vehicles are affected worldwide.*
> (Press release 25 September 2015)

Furthermore, in this second press release, VW communicates a commitment to taking measures to remedy the scandal by carrying out a full collaboration with authorities. However, both when it mentions the internal evaluation and when it underlies its support for the authorities, VW provides vague information about the actions taken to rectify the event, thus combining two other legitimation tactics, namely *corrective action type 1* and *authorisation*:

> *[...] We are working intensively on remedial measures in close coordination with the certification authorities.*
> (Press release 25 September 2015)

At the beginning of October 2015, VW decided to postpone the shareholders annual meeting. In disclosing such a decision, VW recalls the "theoretical" need to meet stakeholders' expectations and explains that the postponement was necessary to fulfil such a duty and prioritise shareholders' expectations. These are signs of a *theoretical rationalisation* tactic:

> *[...] in view of the time available and the matters to be considered, it would not be realistic to provide well-founded answers which would fulfil the shareholder's justified expectations.*
> (Press release 1 October 2015)

*Table 18.2* Legitimation tactics: description and characteristics of the text

| Tactics | | Description | Characteristics of text |
|---|---|---|---|
| Marginalisation | | Downplaying the event and/or rendering its negative consequences irrelevant, unimportant or negligible | Judgemental phrases and adjectives |
| Abstraction | | Generalising the negative event as being common throughout the whole industry | Vague and ambiguous expressions |
| Indicating facts | | Mentioning accurate figures relating to the negative event without providing explanations or justifications | Quantification of negative aspect |
| Rationalisation | Instrumental | Emphasising the positive outcomes of the negative event | Explanation of factual reasons |
| | Theoretical | Emphasising the event as a normal or natural development of the occurrences | Explanation of the inevitability |
| Authorisation | | Underlining the involvement, validation and/or judgement of the negative event by authorities (e.g., belonging to the legal, academic and/or business field) | Mentioning of legitimising authority |
| Corrective action | Type 1 | Acknowledging the negative event through the imprecise provision of measures, ideas or intent to rectify the event | Inexact, imprecise adjectives and phrases |
| | Type 2 | Acknowledging the negative event through the concrete provision of measures, ideas or intent to tackle the event or avoid it in the future | Concrete provision of measures, numbers, specific descriptions of processes |

Source: Author's elaboration based on R. Hahn and R. Lülfs, 'Legitimizing negative aspects in GRI-oriented sustainability reporting: A qualitative analysis of corporate disclosure strategies', *Journal of Business Ethics* 123(3), 2014, 401–20.

Approaching the year's end, an attempt to justify the scandal is made in another press release where VW explains that the manipulation of diesel emissions was the consequence of a strategic decision to perform a massive launch of diesel cars in the US market. This indicates an *instrumental rationalisation* tactic, whereby the prioritisation of market strategies is used to provide a rational explanation for the deception:

> *The starting point was a strategic decision to launch a large-scale promotion of diesel vehicles in the United States in 2005.*
>
> (Press release 10 December 2015)

In the same press release, VW announced the suspension of nine managers suspected to be involved in the scandal, again without providing further details (e.g., on the content and length of the suspension, the exact working position of said managers). Such disclosure is in line with an *indicating facts* tactic, combined with a *corrective action type 1* tactic:

> *As a first step, nine managers who may have been involved in the manipulations were suspended.*
>
> (Press release 10 December 2015)

A *corrective action type 1* tactic is also found in Twitter posts published that same week, where VW provides vague information about the measures taken to remedy the scandal:

> *NOx issue: customers are being informed, implementation is starting.*
>
> (Tweet 16 December 2015)

When recalling the emissions issue within the 2015 annual report, VW leverages an *instrumental rationalisation* tactic to underline how it will turn the negative event into a positive outcome:

> *I have believed it is important we use this crisis as an opportunity: an opportunity to realign the Group in an automotive world that is facing epoch-making change.*
>
> (2015 Annual Report: p.9)

The *corrective action type 1* and *type 2* tactics are also implemented in the annual report. On the one hand, in the letter to shareholders, VW uses a generic "*everything*" to underline what it is doing "*to overcome this crisis*" (2015 Annual Report: p.7), thus adopting a soothing, yet evasive, language. On the other hand, in the section specifically dedicated to the emissions issue, it analytically informs about concrete measures and "*a five-point plan*" designed "*to realign the Group*" (2015 Annual Report: p.54).

### 18.5.2 Daimler AG

To start dealing with narratives on the Dieselgate issue, Daimler compares the scandal to a natural consequence of a greater turbulence. It implicitly admits a possible involvement in the scandal and attempts to justify it as an inevitable fact. Such a *theoretical rationalisation* tactic is clearly visible in its first tweet:

> *Unexpected turbulence may occur on the journey to the future of mobility.*
>
> (Tweet 9 March 2017)

In an attempt to make itself accountable in the preliminary investigations, Daimler neglects any direct involvement until proven by the competent public institution. In doing so, *indicating facts, marginalisation* and *authorisation* tactics are all employed together:

> *In connection with its preliminary investigations of known and unknown employees of Daimler AG due to suspicion of fraud and criminal advertising relating to the possible manipulation of exhaust-gas aftertreatment in passenger cars with diesel engines, the Stuttgart public prosecutor's office is about to search premises of Daimler AG at several locations in Germany. The company is fully cooperating with the authorities.*
>
> (Press release 23 May 2017)

A few weeks later, Daimler associates Dieselgate with a matter of public dispute, an issue that affects the entire automotive industry. It thus employs an *abstraction* tactic once more. Daimler also blames the public debate for the uncertainty generated in its customers but presents itself as ready to act to protect its customers and provide "service actions". *Corrective action type 1* and *marginalisation* tactics are employed together, in that Daimler only refers to the measures it has promoted to diminish the scandal and restore customers' confidence. It avoids describing such measures, yet it emphasises that they will be cost-free for its customers:

> *The public debate about diesel engines is creating uncertainty – especially for our customers. We have therefore decided on additional measures to reassure drivers of diesel cars and to strengthen confidence in diesel technology. [...] The service actions involve no costs for the customers.*
>
> (Press release 18 July 2017)

In another press release, the specific measures carried out to tackle the scandal are described (*corrective action type 2*), they are placed temporally and their effects on emissions and diesel vehicles are reported through quantitative data. Besides such an *indicating facts* tactic, the company also adopts an *instrumental rationalisation* tactic by explaining how such measures will have a positive impact on the emission performance of diesel vehicles:

> *In order to effectively improve the emission performance of EU5 and EU6 vehicles in Europe, two weeks ago the company had already decided to expand its ongoing service measures. As a result, the NOx emissions of more than three-million Mercedes-Benz vehicles will drop by an average of 25 to 30 percent under normal driving conditions.*
>
> (Press release 2 August 2017)

In several press releases, Daimler depicts itself as one of the carmakers working to solve the problem with diesel engines and the overall automotive industry. Accordingly, it uses the *corrective action type 2* tactic to provide detailed information on the remedies undertaken. Such a tactic emerges when explaining that owners of affected vehicles would have been offered a fair compensation to replace their car and when the company underlines other specific initiatives to provide an increased level of customer service as well as the launch of a new line of diesel engine vehicles:

> *The plan comprises a massive expansion of the current service action for vehicles in customers' hands as well as a rapid market launch of a completely new Diesel engine family.*
>
> (Press release 18 July 2017)

> *In order to effectively rejuvenate the vehicle fleet on the road, the company is offering owners of Euronorm 4 vehicles, depending on the model, a four-digit environmental bonus if they choose to buy a new Mercedes-Benz later this year.*
>
> (Press release 2 August 2017)

In the 2017 annual and sustainability reports, the tone changes and Daimler cares more about the consequences of Dieselgate and how it has spread throughout the industry. The tactic here is of *abstraction*, as attention is moved from the company to the entire industry in an attempt to undermine the association of Daimler with Dieselgate:

> *Discussions regarding the future of diesel engines now spread to many other countries with a negative impact on the entire sector.*
>
> (2017 Annual Report: p.8)

> *As a result of the diesel controversy, public criticism has been levelled against the automotive industry, including Daimler.*
>
> (2017 Sustainability Report: p.34)

### 18.5.3  BMW AG

In its first press release, BMW replaces the word "investigation" with "criticism", thereby making a word choice that eliminates any negative meaning, in line with a *marginalisation* tactic:

*The tests were carried out following criticism of the car's emissions' performance in December 2017 by the environmental lobby group "Deutsche Umwelthilfe" (Environmental Action Germany).*

(Press release 15 February 2018)

A *marginalisation* tactic is also found in the same press release, as well as in tweets, where minimal – if any – information is provided about Dieselgate. This is used to firmly exclude any involvement in the scandal, as well as to ask stakeholders to rely on BMW diesel vehicles:

*There is no intervention ("manipulation") of any kind that could influence vehicle emissions.*

(Press release 15 February 2018)

*As a matter of principle, BMW Group vehicles are not manipulated and comply with all respective legal requirements. Our diesel engines are clean. The public and policymakers can rely on that – and, most of all, so can our customers and employees.*

(Press release and tweet 15 February 2018)

Still in the first press release, BMW underlines how the German authority in charge of motor vehicle regulation validates its diesel vehicles as compliant with the law, thereby implementing an *authorisation* tactic. The same tactic is used to question the professionalism and reliability of the German NGO that cited the BMW vehicles:

*The German Federal Motor Transport Authority (KBA) [...] confirmed that the vehicle examined fully complies with all legal requirements. [...] The KBA test findings show quite clearly that the vehicle examined was not manipulated. We therefore find the procedure adopted by 'Deutsche Umwelthilfe' to be unprofessional and its results meaningless.*

(Press release 15 February 2018)

BMW communication techniques employed in the narratives in the 2017 annual and sustainability reports differ significantly from the those of the press release and tweets. First, the Group downplays the scandal by stating how the social and political debate on vehicles emissions has shifted its focus from carbon to nitrogen dioxide and has indiscriminately involved all German carmakers. This indicates an *abstraction* tactic, which was not used before by BMW:

*[T]he diesel discussion in Germany. This discussion was very prominent of course. A few years ago, there was a strong international focus on $CO_2$ emissions. Then, in 2017, NOx emissions were often at the forefront – especially in our home market here in Germany. There were a number of discussions about potentially banning diesel vehicles in cities.*

(2017 Sustainability Report: p.6)

*Table 18.3* Legitimation tactics: evidence from VW, Daimler and BMW digital narrative disclosure

| Tactics | | VW | Daimler | BMW |
|---|---|---|---|---|
| Marginalisation | | √ | √ | √ |
| Abstraction | | | √ | √ |
| Indicating facts | | √ | √ | |
| Rationalisation | Instrumental | √ | √ | |
| | Theoretical | √ | √ | |
| Authorisation | | √ | √ | √ |
| Corrective action | Type 1 | √ | √ | √ |
| | Type 2 | √ | √ | |

*The debate about diesel engines had a further negative impact on the German automobile sector.*

(2017 Annual Report: p.25)

*In some European countries, in particular Germany and the UK, diesel engines were often the subject of political discussions in 2017.*

(2017 Annual Report: p.25)

Remedial actions are displayed in the annual and sustainability reports even though *via* general terms and vague measures only. This suggests that BMW uses the *corrective action type 1* tactic. Indeed, it announces attempts at engagement with political leaders and representatives of the working class and NGOs to gain ideas and opinions on how to tackle the challenge of diesel vehicles emissions:

*By engaging in active and open dialogue with political decision-makers, union representatives, associations and NGOs, we play a constructive and transparent role in helping to shape the general political framework for our business activities. [...] In the period under report, the main topics in this regard were favourable conditions for electromobility, antitrust complaints, exhaust gas purification for diesel vehicles.*

(2017 Sustainability Report: p.27)

To summarise the findings, Table 18.3 offers an overview of the tactics used by each carmaker.

## 18.6  Discussion and conclusions

This chapter has explored the legitimation tactics employed in digital narrative disclosure by three carmakers that were involved in the scandal of diesel emission manipulations – namely VW, Daimler and BMW. The analysis focuses primarily on the digital disclosure that was discharged by the companies in the aftermath of authorities' allegations regarding emission manipulations, which questioned their right to operate in line with societal norms (Gray et al. 1995; Suchman 1995; Guthrie et al. 2004).

From the close reading, it emerges that all the companies downplayed the event, underlined the engagement with authorities and provided general information about the measures undertaken to cope with the scandal. More precisely, VW employed all legitimation tactics in disclosing Dieselgate (Hahn and Lülfs 2014; Kuruppu et al. 2019; Rudkin et al. 2019), with only one exception. The company could not move the attention to the entire industry, as, at that time, the accusations did not involve Daimler and BMW. It is no surprise that the latter Groups exploited such a possibility, even though in two different ways. Whereas Daimler took full responsibility for the occurrence and presented itself as a solution to Dieselgate, BMW undermined its responsibility and depicted itself as the victim of an industry scandal perpetrated by others. Moreover, Daimler adopted the full spectrum of tactics and soon described concrete measures to tackle the issue. Conversely, BMW halved the legitimation tactics employed and displayed remedial actions exclusively *via* general terms and vague measures.

With its results, this study provides insights into the different approaches to the scandal by VW, Daimler and BMW. A reactive approach is adopted by VW, which delivered the first digital narratives *via* its corporate website and tried to make the scandal appear less important compared with the description offered by newspapers (Clemente and Gabbioneta 2017; Siano et al. 2017; Valentini and Kruckenberg 2018). VW disclosed without clear rigour or a pre-defined strategy, as demonstrated by the choice to withdraw the sustainability report in the year after Dieselgate, following an approach like the one adopted by Costa Crociere after the Costa Concordia sinking (Corazza et al. 2020). Being the first Group involved in the scandal, VW was forced to cope with an unprecedented situation with a great deal of uncertainty. The uncertainty navigated by VW is confirmed by the numerous narratives published in the six months after the scandal broke and by the minimal and vague disclosures provided in the early phase of the scandal. Such finding reinforces previous evidence on VW disclosure behaviour after Dieselgate (Painter and Martins 2017) and demonstrates how disclosure choices were pursuing a legitimation tactic, rather than simply downplaying the case.

The uncertainty in coping with Dieselgate is less pronounced in Daimler and BMW, who show that they have learned from VW how to regain legitimacy, though *via* diverse approaches. Daimler follows a proactive approach in leveraging the legitimation tactics. Such proactivity stems from the means used to communicate detailed interventions to stakeholders in almost real time (i.e., both Twitter and press releases). Moreover, Daimler disclosure is usually characterised by a combination of two or more legitimation tactics within a single sentence, which suggests that the Group has sophisticated its tactics. This provides new insights into legitimation strategies of companies, especially those hit by scandals that originated from a competitor. Indeed, the learning process regarding legitimation tactics is evident and contributes to the literature by highlighting the importance of investigating multiple case studies (O'Donovan 2002; Rudkin et al. 2019) to reveal the disclosure patterns that are generated in time.

As opposed to VW and Daimler, BMW prefers a defensive approach. It limited the number of both the narratives disclosed and the tactics employed. This finding complements previous literature that supports an increase in the extent of disclosure when the same scandal re-involves a company (Cho 2009). It particularly shows that, when the same scandal spreads over diverse companies, disclosure tends to decrease, and tactics become more sophisticated. In BMW narratives, such sophistication of tactics stems from the clever word choice made in the digital narratives (e.g., "investigation" becomes "criticism" and "manipulation" changes into "intervention"), thereby turning negative meanings into positives. Such an accurate choice of words confirms the role of semantic features in using legitimisation tactics while disclosing Dieselgate, thus adding to previous evidence on how textual features are leveraged in the aftermath of corporate scandals (Florio and Sproviero 2021).

The study also unveils the different legitimation power assigned to different categories of stakeholders by the carmakers. VW is concerned mainly with shareholders as deemed the most displeased of the fall in VW share price in the aftermath of the Dieselgate outbreak. Only later did VW also pay attention to the customers. Conversely, customers are at the core of Daimler's digital disclosure, as they are identified as the key stakeholders whose expectations have been disappointed. Instead, BMW only referred to its stakeholders in the annual report, without any mention of them in digital narratives preceding this document. These findings enrich prior research on Dieselgate (Painter and Martins 2017; Siano et al. 2017), suggesting that companies develop more sophisticated legitimation tactics over time to regain legitimacy and may show different considerations about their stakeholders.

The chapter contributes to the existing literature and has impacts on narrative reporting research and practice in various ways. First, it advances our knowledge of the role of digital narrative disclosure as a legitimation tool in times of scandal. It particularly highlights the relevant role that social media posts can have in enabling ongoing, quick and cheap communication (ICAEW 2004; Lodhia 2018) between an organisation and its stakeholders, instead of relying only on official press releases or corporate reports. In this vein, it offers evidence on the use of different outlets for narrative reporting (e.g., unconventional posts on Twitter *versus* traditional annual reports) but the same common aim of legitimising a company's conduct. Secondly, it adds to prior research on Dieselgate (Siano et al. 2017; Florio and Sproviero 2021) by enlarging the research focus to carmakers other than VW – namely, Daimler and BMW – and to other forms of reporting, such as digital narratives, thereby underlining the importance of multiple case studies in such contexts. Thirdly, the chapter confirms the usefulness of legitimation tactic analysis in revealing how companies involved in the same scandal may respond differently. In so doing, it produces implications for research by extending the application of legitimation tactics proposed by Hahn and Lülfs (2014) to a greater extent of narratives, including social media posts and press releases. It also extends the use of close reading as a methodology to deeply analyse a company's digital narratives and detect the legitimation strategies therein adopted.

Finally, the chapter also has practical implications. On one hand, it suggests companies leverage digital communication and social media posts as part of their corporate narrative reporting, especially in times of scandal. Indeed, digital outlets may convey timely reports and disclosure to stakeholders and, in so doing, may preserve the company's legitimacy and foster a continuous dialogue with constituents. On the other hand, the chapter advises stakeholders about the tactics that can be implemented by organisations when disclosing a scandal, knowing that legitimation tactics may help stakeholders be aware of the company's legitimation strategy and, if necessary, demand a greater deal of accountability. Although our analysis is limited to three organisations and a relatively short timeframe, it opens up future avenues in narrative reporting research. Further research may explore the effects of digital narratives by corporations on specific users by using interviews and experiments, thereby revealing the stakeholders' perceptions of such narratives.

## References

J. Amernic and R. Craig, 'CEO speeches and safety culture: British Petroleum before the Deepwater Horizon disaster', *Critical Perspectives on Accounting* 47, 2017, 61–80.

M. Arnaboldi, C. Busco and S. Cuganesan, 'Accounting, accountability, social media and Big Data: Revolution or hype?', *Accounting, Auditing & Accountability Journal* 30(4), 2017, 762–76.

V. Beattie, 'Accounting narratives and the narrative turn in accounting research: Issues, theory, methodology, methods and a research framework', *The British Accounting Review* 46(2), 2014, 111–34.

R. Blanc, C.H. Cho, J. Sopt and M.C. Branco, 'Disclosure responses to a corruption scandal: The case of Siemens AG', *Journal of Business Ethics* 156(2), 2019, 545–61.

B. Brummett, *Techniques of close reading*. Thousand Oaks, CA: Sage Publications, 2018.

C.H. Cho, 'Legitimation strategies used in response to environmental disaster: A French case study of total SA's Erika and AZF incidents', *European Accounting Review* 18(1), 2009, 33–62.

M. Clemente and C. Gabbioneta, 'How does the media frame corporate scandals? The case of German newspapers and the Volkswagen diesel scandal', *Journal of Management Inquiry* 26(3), 2017, 287–302.

L. Corazza, E. Truant, S.D. Scagnelli and C. Mio, 'Sustainability reporting after the Costa Concordia disaster: A multi-theory study on legitimacy, impression management and image restoration', *Accounting, Auditing & Accountability Journal* 33(8), 2020, 1909–41.

C. Deegan, 'Introduction: The legitimising effect of social and environmental disclosures – A theoretical foundation', *Accounting, Auditing & Accountability Journal* 15(3), 2002, 282–311.

C. Florio and A.F. Sproviero, 'Repairing legitimacy through discourses: Insights from the Volkswagen's 2015 diesel scandal', *Meditari Accountancy Research* 23(9), 2021, 524–42.

R. Gray, R. Kouhy and S. Lavers, 'Corporate social and environmental reporting: A review of the literature and a longitudinal study of UK disclosure', *Accounting, Auditing & Accountability Journal* 8(2), 1995, 47–77.

J. Guthrie, R. Petty, K. Yongvanich and F. Ricceri, 'Using content analysis as a research method to inquire into intellectual capital reporting', *Journal of Intellectual Capital* 5(2), 2004, 282–93.

R. Hahn and R. Lülfs, 'Legitimizing negative aspects in GRI-oriented sustainability reporting: A qualitative analysis of corporate disclosure strategies', *Journal of Business Ethics* 123(3), 2014, 401–20.

S. Hrasky, 'Carbon footprints and legitimation strategies: Symbolism or action?', *Accounting, Auditing & Accountability Journal* 25(1), 2012, 174–98.

ICAEW (Institute of Chartered Accountants in England & Wales), *Digital reporting: A progress report*, 2004. Available at: https://www.icaew.com/-/media/corporate/files /technical/financial-reporting/information-for-better-markets/ifbm-reports/digital -reporting-a-progress-report.ashx.

J.C. Jung and S.B. "Alison" Park, 'Case study: Volkswagen's diesel emissions scandal', *Thunderbird International Business Review* 59(1), 2017, 127–37.

S.C. Kuruppu, M.J. Milne and C.A. Tilt, 'Gaining, maintaining and repairing organisational legitimacy', *Accounting, Auditing & Accountability Journal* 32(7), 2019, 2062–87.

G. Leoni, 'Rudimentary capital budgeting for a Utopian Italian colony in Australia: Accounting as an advocating device', *Accounting History*, 2021. https://doi.org/10 .1177/1032373220981422.

S. Lodhia, 'Is the medium the message?', *Meditari Accountancy Research* 26(1), 2018, 2–12.

D. Merkl-Davies, N. Brennan and P. Vourvachis, 'Text analysis methodologies in corporate narrative reporting research', In: *23rd CSEAR International Colloquium*, September 2011, St Andrews, 1–45.

Netflix, 'Dirty Money TV series – Episode 1: Hard $NO_x$', 2018. Retrieved 8 February 2018. Available at: https://www.netflix.com/it-en/title/80118100.

G. O'Donovan, 'Environmental disclosures in the annual report: Extending the applicability and predictive power of legitimacy theory', *Accounting, Auditing & Accountability Journal* 15(3), 2002, 344–71.

C. Painter and J.T. Martins, 'Organisational communication management during the Volkswagen diesel emissions scandal: A hermeneutic study in attribution, crisis management, and information orientation', *Knowledge & Process Management* 24(3), 2017, 204–18.

C. Peng, S. Liu and Y. Lu, 'The discursive strategy of legitimacy management: A comparative case study of Google and Apple's crisis communication statements', *Asia Pacific Journal of Management* 38, 2021, 519–45.

RepRisk AG, *ESG risk database*, 2020. Available at: https://www.reprisk.com/.

B. Rudkin, D. Kimani, S. Ullah, R. Ahmed and S.U. Farooq, 'Hide-and-seek in corporate disclosure: Evidence from negative corporate incidents', *Corporate Governance, The International Journal of Business & Society* 19(1), 2019, 158–75.

D. Schur, *An introduction to close reading*. Cambridge, MA: Harvard University Press, 1998.

A. Siano, A. Vollero, F. Conte and S. Amabile, '"More than words": Expanding the taxonomy of greenwashing after the Volkswagen scandal', *Journal of Business Research* 71, 2017, 27–37.

B.H. Smith, 'What was 'close reading'? A century of method in literary studies', *Minnesota Review* 87, 2016, 57–75.

M.C. Suchman, 'Managing legitimacy: Strategic and institutional approaches', *Academy of Management Review* 20(3), 1995, 571–10.

R. Suddaby, A. Bitektine and P. Haack, 'Legitimacy', *Academy of Management Annals* 11(1), 2017, 451–78.

E. Twyford, 'A thanatopolitical visualisation of accounting history: Giorgio Agamben and Nazi Germany', *Accounting History* 26(3), 2021, 352–74.

C. Valentini and D. Kruckeberg, '"Walking the environmental responsibility talk" in the automobile industry', *Corporate Communications: An International Journal* 23(4), 2018, 524–43.

M.A. Vasarhelyi, A. Kogan and B.M. Tuttle, 'Big Data in accounting: An overview', *Accounting Horizons* 29(2), 2015, 381–96.

P. Vourvachis, T. Woodward, D.G. Woodward and D.M. Patten, 'CSR disclosure in response to major airline accidents: A legitimacy-based exploration', *Sustainability Accounting, Management & Policy Journal* 7(1), 2016, 26–43.

# 19 A content analysis of narrative COVID-19 disclosure in Omani Islamic banks

*Issal Haj-Salem and Khaled Hussainey*

## 19.1 Introduction

Transparency remains a major tool for any commercial institution since it ensures both short- and long-term profit progression and survival (Haj-Salem, 2020). Transparency can be achieved particularly through disclosure. The disclosure of relevant information becomes crucial in times of crisis. A large number of researchers (e.g., Elshandidy et al., 2018) highlighted the role of the disclosure of different types of information to reassure stakeholders and legitimate the institution's reputation.

The past two years have seen the spread of the COVID-19 pandemic, which has resulted in a disastrous social and economic situation on a global scale. This pandemic caused a severe recession which was considered by the World Bank to be the deepest global recession since World War II. According to the World Bank, the GDP in several countries has experienced a sharp decline in 2020, and even if there will be a modest improvement in 2021, the global GDP will remain 4.4% lower than earlier projections prior to the pandemic.

This recession was also even deeper in emerging countries than in developed ones. For this reason, special attention should be paid to save the world economy. Along the same lines, David Malpass, the president of the World Bank, on 13 March 2021, asserted that "To counter the investment headwind, there needs to be a major push to improve business environments, increase labour and product market flexibility and strengthen transparency and governance". It is important to point out the role of transparency in the context of a crisis in several economic and financial entities. Among these entities, the banks have not been immune to this health crisis. However, banks have successfully managed this crisis, since they have experienced a strengthening of financial soundness through several regulations introduced since the subprime crisis to be able to cope in a crisis. Moreover, banks have also played a crucial role in supporting the economy. Indeed, they were asked by public authorities to help countries' finances, for example by granting loans to damaged companies, making loan adjustments and reviewing policies for loan repayments to citizens.

Disclosure in Islamic banks has attracted the attention of many researchers all over the world, who have contributed to studying the methods and consequences

DOI: 10.4324/9781003095385-24

of disclosure (Elgattani and Hussainey, 2021; Grassa et al., 2018; Grassa et al., 2020, 2021a, 2021b; Saidani et al., 2021). Islamic banks are encouraged to disclose COVID-19 information in their annual reports. In May 2020, the Accounting and Auditing Organisation for Islamic Financial Institutions (AAOIFI) published a statement that addresses relevant issues following the COVID-19 pandemic. AAOIFI encourages Islamic banks to voluntarily disclose information to enable the readers of the annual reports to better understand and assess bank performance during the pandemic. This move motivated us to investigate narrative COVID-19 disclosure in Omani Islamic banks.

Oman offers an interesting context to investigate narrative COVID-19 disclosure in the annual reports of Islamic banks. We choose the Islamic banking sector since, even if it is in its infancy compared to conventional banks, it is growing rapidly in the global financial sector. Furthermore, Islamic finance attracts attention from Muslims in particular, who care about the compliance of their transactions with Sharia principles and expect that these institutions are honest and fair with all stakeholders (Elgattani and Hussainey, 2020). Indeed, accountability and adequate transparency are among the main ingredients of Islamic banking principles (Elgattani and Hussainey, 2020), which enable them to improve their ethical behaviour (Haniffa and Hudaib, 2007), to reflect their identity and to meet accountability towards both stakeholders and society (Harun et al., 2020). Consequently, the unique principles of Islamic institutions, in addition to the encouragement by the AAOIFI, lead to expectations of greater transparency and a voluntary narrative disclosure of COVID-19 information.

To this end, this chapter aims to investigate narrative COVID-19 disclosure in the two Islamic banks in Oman: Alizz Islamic Bank and Nizwa Bank. We use the content analysis method to measure the number of narrative COVID-19 statements in annual reports of 2020. We find that Omani Islamic banks disclose more strategic information related to the pandemic than conventional banks. However, they disclose less performance information than conventional banks related to the pandemic. We also find that bank profitability has not been significantly affected by the pandemic, although both liquidity and risk have been negatively affected.

The remainder of the chapter is organised as follows. Section 19.2 discusses the concepts of Islamic banks and disclosure. Section 19.3 reviews the literature, while Section 19.4 discusses the research method and Section 19.5 reports the findings. Section 19.6 concludes the discussion of this chapter and suggests future research avenues.

## 19.2 Theoretical background

### 19.2.1 The concept of Islamic banks

A bank is a financial institution that plays a crucial role in the contribution of wealth creation in a country thanks to the various activities that it carries out between the financial market and the economic agents. It helps to ensure financial and economic stability (Musa et al., 2020). Islamic banking has emerged in the recent four decades (since 1975). Compared with conventional banks, Islamic banks must seek to meet profitability targets as required by financial markets around the world and comply with Islamic principles, two goals which may lead to contradictions. Many researchers related the emergence of Islamic banks to the global financial crisis and consider them as an alternative to conventional banks (Khan, 2010). Moreover, some researchers believe that the resilience of Islamic banks is greater than for conventional banks during the global financial crisis (Hasan and Dridi, 2011). However, the findings of many researchers who tried to compare the performance between Islamic and conventional banks (e.g., Beck et al., 2013; Johnes et al., 2014; Kabir et al., 2015; Bader et al., 2008) and the behaviour of depositors (e.g Aysan et al., 2017) lead to mixed results. Moreover, Doumpos et al. (2017) found that the financial strength of the two banking models differs among countries.

The Gulf Cooperation Council (GCC) operates among the countries that have introduced Islamic banking activities. Oman was considered to be the last member of the GCC to introduce Islamic banking activities. The legal framework of Islamic banking in Oman took place by the Decree 69/2012, dated 6 December 2012, following which the Central Bank of Oman (CBO) published the Islamic Banking Regulatory Framework (IBRF) on 18 December 2012. The latter provides the necessary regulations to be respected within the framework of Islamic banking activities. For example, it deals with licensing requirements, general obligations and governance, accounting standards and auditor reports, power of supervision and control, capital adequacy and the different risks. Currently, there are two Islamic banks[1] in Oman and six Islamic windows[2] of conventional banks, which are regulated and controlled by the Central Bank of Oman (CBO) with Sharia governance framework to ensure Sharia compliance in Islamic banking activities (CBO, 2021).

Moreover, Islamic financial institutions (IFIs) in Oman are following the Islamic financial standards, comprising approximately 100 standards, that have been established by AAOIFI. AAOIFI is the leading international not-for-profit Islamic financial organisation, created in 1991 and based in Bahrain. Its standards involve Shari'ah, accounting, auditing, ethics and governance and are used by the leading IFIs across the world. Several institutional members from over 45 countries support the AAOIFI, such as central banks, financial institutions, accounting and auditing firms, etc. Its standards are currently followed by all the leading IFIs across the world and are adopted, either fully or partially, as mandatory regulatory requirements in many countries and jurisdictions (AAOIFI, 2021).[3]

### 19.2.2 The concept of disclosure

Disclosure could be defined as the dissemination of any information about the commercial entity. This provides sufficient information about its performance to different stakeholders and to better assess the compliance with the interests of investors (Healy and Palepu, 2001). However, disclosure could be mandatory or voluntary. Mandatory disclosure involves any information required by regulations, whereas, in contrast, voluntary disclosure involves the dissemination of any information which is not required by law or regulations. This practice enhances the transparency and accountability of any entity.

Researchers believe in the importance of disclosure, particularly in times of crisis (Elmarzouky et al., 2021). Companies may disclose performance information and how they manage any potential risks related to the crisis. This reassures shareholders and keeps them satisfied since they will be made aware of the possible ways to overcome or avoid negative circumstances (Hassan, 2014; Salem et al., 2019). Accordingly, in the context of the COVID-19 pandemic, we expect more disclosure on COVID-19 in the narrative sections of the annual reports. Indeed, in light of the legitimacy theory, managers have to legitimate the company's situation and save its reputation when there are dangers by disclosing how the latter could be resolved (Haj-Salem and Hussainey, 2021b). Moreover, this enables alleviation of information asymmetry that arises between the internal and external stakeholders (Haj-Salem and Hussainey, 2021b). Moreover, from an Islamic point of view, corporate disclosure allows compliance with Islamic law (Baydoun and Willett, 2000) and ensures fairness to all stakeholders (Elgattani and Hussainey, 2020).

As the context of the COVID-19 pandemic resulted in an unstable economic and regulatory environment, this led the AAOIFI on 22 May 2020, to publish a statement to the IFIs regarding the application of the financial accounting standards (FASs) and the AAOIFI's Conceptual Framework in the context of the health crisis. According to this statement, even though the AAOIFI emphasises the efficiency of FASs to fit this context, it highlights the crucial role of voluntary disclosure to help annual report users to have a better view of the institution's performance and to help them in their decision-making.[3] This statement asserts that the uncertainty is more challenging for IFIs compared to conventional financial institutions since the IFIs are characterised by multiple stakeholders that are expected to share profit and loss. For that, IFIs are encouraged to voluntarily provide any relevant information. For instance, the AAOIFI Accounting Board (AAB) encourages IFIs to disclose additional information to allow stakeholders to assess the economic impact of payment moratoriums and other adjustments due to the COVID-19 pandemic (e.g., general terms and conditions and the effect of moratoriums on the effective rate return).[4]

## 19.3 Literature review

A growing amount of accounting and finance research has been undertaken on the COVID-19 pandemic in 2020 and 2021. Researchers tried to investigate the impact of the COVID-19 pandemic on stock market volatility (Al-Awadhi et al., 2020, Uddin et al., 2021; Xiong et al., 2020). Other researchers investigated the effectiveness of accounting standards (Barnoussi et al., 2020; Neisen and Schulte-Mattler, 2021), auditing quality (Albitar et al., 2021; Appelbaum et al., 2020) and corporate governance (Al Sawalqa, 2020; Elmarzouky et al., 2021; Ltifi and Hichri, 2021; Jebran and Chen, 2021; Kells, 2020; Sivaprasad and Mathew, 2021) in the context of the health crisis. Another research stream focuses on disclosure practices during the COVID-19 pandemic, such as risk disclosure (Al Sawalqa, 2020), performance disclosure (Elmarzouky et al., 2021), Corporate Social Responsibility (Bae et al., 2021; García-Sánchez and García-Sánchez, 2020; Qiu et al., 2021) and Environmental, Social and Governance (ESG) (Adams and Abhayawansa, 2021).

Few studies, however, have been undertaken on banks, and even fewer on Islamic banks. The studies on Islamic banks during the COVID-19 pandemic are focused mainly on the impact of the COVID19 on performance (Akkas and Al Samman, 2021; Ichsan et al., 2021), regulatory policies (Mansour et al., 2021) and digital financial inclusion and innovation (Banna et al., 2021; Raza Rabbani et al., 2021). Therefore, to the best of our knowledge, this is the first study on COVID-19-related disclosure by Islamic banks. We believe that it is crucial to investigate the disclosure practices of Islamic banks and to analyse their performance during this health crisis.

Three theories could be used to understand disclosure practice. According to agency theory (Jensen and Meckling, 1976), disclosure helps to mitigate information asymmetry and agency costs between insiders and outsiders, which is likely to have a positive impact on performance. Furthermore, the signalling theory (Spence, 1973) considers the relevant information disclosed to the different market participants to be signals that mitigate the information asymmetry due to the market imperfections. In addition, IFIs have to disclose more relevant information since it benefits stakeholders in making their decisions (Elgattani and Hussainey, 2020). Thus, COVID-19 disclosure by IFIs could be considered as signals that assist stakeholders in their assessment of the IFI situation.

Moreover, following the legitimacy theory, when institutions are facing bad circumstances, they have to legitimate such a situation to avoid reputation endangerment. For instance, it would be better to disclose the related issues and the ways to overcome them in order to reassure stakeholders and strengthen their trust (Salem et al., 2019). The Islamic banks are likely to be more active and accountable towards stakeholders compared to other institutions since they react with compliance to Islamic principles (Harun et al., 2020). Besides, Azmi et al. (2021) used the moral legitimacy framework to explain the Sharīʿah non-compliant income (SNCI) reporting practices in Islamic banks. They found that Islamic banks are likely to use procedure-enabling themes to gain moral legitimacy among the different stakeholders. However, this does not guarantee better SNCI disclosures. Islamic banks may be considered to be more conservative than non-Islamic ones when the information reflects any risk (Abdallah et al., 2015).

## 19.4 Methodology and data

We follow prior research (Beattie & Thomson, 2007) and use the case study method to explore the COVID-19 narrative disclosure. This method aims to explore a phenomenon in a specific context (Kotb Abdelrahman Radwan et al., 2021). We explore COVID-19 disclosure in annual reports of the Omani Islamic banks, Alizz Islamic Bank and Nizwa Bank. We focused on the annual reports of 2020. We focus on annual reports as these reports are mandatory and the time differences are minimised as most banks release their annual reports within a short period (3–4 months) after the financial year-end. In addition, because of their formalised structure, these reports are more easily comparable. Finally, previous research shows that annual reports are ranked highly as a useful source of information used by stakeholders for the decision-making process (Mousa et al., 2022).

We use the manual content analysis method to analyse the narrative sections of banks' annual reports. Content analysis is defined as "*a research technique for the objective, systematic and quantitative description of the manifest content of communication*" (Berelson, 1952: p.18) and "*a research technique for making inferences by objectively and systematically identifying specified characteristics of messages*" (Carney, 1972: p.21). The content analysis classifies textual material, reducing it to more relevant, manageable pieces of data (Weber, 1990) to make replicable and valid inferences from data to their context (Krippendorff, 1980: p.21). The content analysis method has been used in the accounting literature since 1976. It is defined as "*a research method, which draws inferences from data by systematically identifying characteristics within the data*" (Jones and Shoemaker, 1994: p.142).

The use of content analysis to investigate narrative disclosure involves deciding the basis of coding (e.g., the unit of analysis). Al Lawati et al. (2021) suggest that sentences are the most commonly used unit of analysis in accounting literature. Therefore, we analyse each sentence in the narrative section of each bank's annual report to determine whether it provides COVID-19 information (or not).

## 19.5  The case study of Alizz Islamic Bank and Nizwa Bank

### 19.5.1  Bank overview

Alizz Islamic Bank (SAOC) was founded in November 2012 in accordance with Royal Decree No. 69/2012. It is headquartered in the Central Business District Area in Ruwi, Oman. 40% Of the total paid-up capital of Alizz Islamic Bank, 40% was raised by public investors and 60% was contributed by the bank's promoters.

Nizwa Bank is considered to be the first Islamic bank in Oman that provides products and services with fully Shari'a compliance in accordance with the licence issued by the Central Bank of Oman (CBO) and the Banking Law promulgated by the Royal Decree No. 114/2000 (Nizwa Bank website). Currently, it has 13 branches and it intends to expand its branch network over the next five years.

### 19.5.2  Narrative COVID-19 disclosure

#### 19.5.2.1  The measure of narrative COVID-19 disclosure

To measure narrative COVID-19 disclosure in annual reports of Omani Islamic banks, we relied on the Disclosure and Transparency Framework of the International Finance Corporation (IFC). In response to the health crisis outbreak and the growing environmental uncertainty, the IFC has published guidance entitled "Increasing Resilience and Building Trust during and after the Pandemic". It

*Table 19.1* COVID-19 disclosure index

---

**Strategy**
Operating Environment
Business Model
Strategic Objectives
Risk Analysis and Response
Stakeholder Engagement
Materiality Assessment
Sustainability Risks and Opportunities
**Governance**
Commitment to Environmental, Social and Governance
Structure and Functioning of the Board of Directors
Control Environment
Treatment of Minority Shareholders
Governance of Stakeholder Engagement
**Performance**
Management Report
Financial Resources
Financial Performance
Sustainability Performance
Key Performance Indicators

---

aims to guide both listed and privately-owned companies on their disclosure of corporate reports and data to the different stakeholders. The IFC has highlighted the importance of communicating sufficient information about the economic, environmental and social impacts of the health crisis and how institutions manage them. The IFC classified COVID-19 related information into three categories: strategy, governance and performance (Table 19.1).

### 19.5.3 Analysis of narrative COVID-19 disclosure

#### 19.5.3.1 Strategy-related COVID-19 disclosure

Table 19.2 shows that COVID-19 information disclosed in annual reports is mainly strategic, represented by 55 sentences for Alizz Islamic Bank and 35 sentences for Nizwa Bank. This is expected since the COVID-19 pandemic has raised several challenges, forcing Islamic banks to adapt their strategies to the

*Table 19.2* Descriptive statistics of number of COVID-19 statements

|  | *Alizz Islamic Bank* | *Nizwa Bank* |
| --- | --- | --- |
| Strategy | 55 | 35 |
| Governance | 5 | 1 |
| Performance | 11 | 18 |
| TOTAL | **71** | **54** |

new circumstances and to find solutions to the different disruptions caused by the pandemic (Mihajat, 2021). This finding is consistent with Ghazali and Weetman (2006) who showed that Malaysian companies voluntarily disclosed more strategic information in their reports following the economic crisis. Our analysis shows that both banks highlighted the constraints related to the operating environment and its impact on their strategic objectives. Moreover, they analysed the risks (market risk, credit risk, etc.) and compared them with the previous year. In addition, both banks were engaged to support the growth and prosperity of Oman. For instance, the Board of Directors of Alizz Islamic Bank asserts that:

> In 2020, with the pandemic on the rise, our efforts were directed towards supporting the government in dealing with the pandemic, with direct donations to the Endowment Fund for the Ministry of Health's COVID-19 Efforts as well as redirecting partial income generated through our debit and credit cards to further support the COVID-19 Fund. In addition to the direct support, the bank also worked on accommodating and supporting our customers with a deferment program[me] which was aimed at supporting local businesses as well as those who were affected financially by the pandemic.
>
> (Alizz Islamic Bank, Annual Report 2020, p.50)

In addition, both banks continued to adapt their strategies while taking into account the protection of employees and customers. The following examples illustrate these cases :

> The Bank, in collaboration with other stakeholders, too here onwards as Blockk all necessary measures to ensure the safety of its employees while providing the needed support to its customers affected by these unprecedented circumstances through deferring their instalments and waiving profit, wherever [it] is applicable.
>
> (Alizz Islamic Bank, Annual Report 2020, p.9)

> Besides the very successful implementation of Work from Home solution and the successful merger of Al Yusr, the bank has also introduced some solutions that are aimed at enhancing the customer experience, enhancing operations efficiency and growing the revenue stream of the bank.
>
> (Alizz Islamic Bank, Annual Report 2020, p.49)

> As part of the Business Continuity Management (BCM) Policy Framework, the Bank's Operational Risk working in close coordination with our IT group has completed the testing of BCM along with the Disaster Recovery Center (DRC).
>
> (Alizz Islamic Bank, Annual Report 2020, p.52)

Despite the challenges resulting from COVID-19, Oman is set to embark upon a development programme to shift the economy to a more private sector footing by developing small- and medium-sized enterprises, public-private partnerships (PPPs) and improving the investment climate as part of Oman Vision 2040.

(Bank Nizwa, Annual Report 2020, p.10)

The Central Bank of Oman is enabling the adoption of new modes of service delivery and technologies to serve the market more effectively, especially during the pandemic- related challenging times.

(Bank Nizwa, Annual Report 2020, p.26)

During 2020, the focus had been to stand by the customer during difficult times by offering financial and non-financial relief.

(Bank Nizwa, Annual Report 2020, p.26)

Bank Nizwa offered instalment deferral for Ijara / Diminishing Musharaka Home Finance to low-income customers, as monthly instalments for home finance is a significant household expense.

(Bank Nizwa, Annual Report 2020, p.26)

The division also provided instalment deferral to customers impacted directly by the pandemic or salary reduction.

(Bank Nizwa, Annual Report 2020, p.26)

As the restrictions ended, Bank Nizwa ran an exclusive promotion for front-line 'COVID Warriors' to honour and thank all those who worked hard and selflessly to serve the country and its people.

(Bank Nizwa, Annual Report 2020, pp.26–27)

### 19.5.3.2 Performance-related COVID-19 disclosure

In line with Ghazali and Weetman (2006), Table 19.2 shows that information related to performance takes second place with 18 sentences for Nizwa Bank and 11 sentences for Alizz Islamic bank. The banks' financial performances were presented through several ratios (e.g. Return on Assets (ROA), Return on Equity (ROE) and Liquidity coverage ratio (LCR)). The IFC's Disclosure and Transparency Framework suggested the disclosure of financial/operational/health and safety KPIs for COVID-19, such as operational cash-flow, liquidity, solvency, productivity per employee and percentage of employees with sick-pay leave. Nevertheless, we found that several of the suggested Key Performance Indicators (KPIs) were not disclosed in the annual reports of the sampled banks. The following examples, however, show evidence that both banks disclosed financial and non-financial performance-related COVID-19 information and this is in line with prior research (Elmarzouky et al., 2021) :

The Coronavirus (COVID-19) Pandemic had severe health, social and economic ramifications that have negatively affected Oman's economic growth, impacting various business sectors, including banks.

(Alizz Islamic Bank, Annual Report 2020, p.9)

While there has been a significant uptake in banking services provided remotely, minimising direct customer contact, the linkage of the sector with the real-estate sector as the provider of payment, savings, credit and risk management services extends the negative effect of the COVID-19 crisis to banks and other financial institutions.

(Alizz Islamic Bank, Annual Report 2020, p.47)

Net profit after tax was, however, lesser than the planned growth due to the OMR 6.7 Million (2019: OMR 2.6 Million) provisions taken for expected impact losses, including the impact of COVID-19 on our customers and the economy and consequent credit losses.

(Bank Nizwa, Annual Report 2020, p.9)

"Bank Nizwa recorded the highest growth in net profits in Oman's banking sector, with a growth of 9% despite COVID-19- related challenges."

(Bank Nizwa, Annual Report 2020, p.25)

Wholesale banking recorded remarkable growth during the year, despite a multitude of challenges that were made more pronounced due to the COVID-19 pandemic, and is now poised to address 2021 growth ambitions and client requirements in all business segments.

(Bank Nizwa, Annual Report 2020, p.27)

### 19.5.3.3 Governance-related COVID-19 disclosure

Table 19.2 shows that governance-related COVID-19 disclosure is lower than strategy and performance-related COVID-19 disclosure. It shows that five governance-related COVID-19 statements have been disclosed in the annual report of Alizz Islamic Bank, while one statement has been disclosed in Nizwa Bank's annual report. This finding is in line with Darmadi (2013), who shows that governance disclosure in Islamic banks is relatively low. The following examples illustrate these cases:

The total hotel and travel expense related to the Shari'a Supervisory Board during 2020 is nil because all the meetings during the year have been conducted through a virtual platform as the result of travel restrictions due to COVID-19.

(Alizz Islamic Bank, Annual Report 2020, p.28)

During 2020, despite the restrictions imposed by the pandemic, all main areas of the Bank's operations were reviewed with the team producing over 40 final reports to enable us to give an informed view of the state of the Bank's risk management framework and internal control environment. »

(Alizz Islamic Bank, Annual Report 2020, p.48)

To respond to this situation, the prompt intervention of the Ministries and Government authorities helped the economy to sustain the shock and was successfully able to contain the spread of the virus which is a reflection of the strength and resilience of the system, and the positive impact that new government transformation initiatives is having on the country's development. »

(Bank Nizwa, Annual Report 2020, p.9)

According to the IFC's Disclosure and Transparency Framework, institutions must communicate the changes on governance mechanisms and how it has been adapted to ensure an effective response to the current situation.

### *19.5.4 The performance of Alizz and Nizwa banks*

Table 19.3 presents liquidity, risk and performance indicators collected from the banks' annual reports. Following Basel III guidelines of June 2011, the CBO requires banks to communicate their liquidity coverage ratio (LCR) and Net-Stable Funding Ratio (NSFR). In line with Karim et al. (2021), there is evidence of deterioration of liquidity position and financial health of Islamic banks at the time of the COVID-19 pandemic. Regarding Nizwa Bank, the 2020 LCR ratio sharply decreased to 133.83% (from 237.84% in 2019). Thus, during the COVID-19 crisis, Nizwa Bank is less able to meet short-term obligations. We can also note that the 2020 LCR ratio of Nizwa Bank is higher than that of Alizz Islamic bank in 2020 (122.37%). Regarding NSFR, in 2020 there was a decrease of around −3.88% compared to 2019 for Nizwa Bank. This means that the amount of available stable funding compared to the liabilities is weaker after the health crisis. However, if we compare the two banks, Nizwa Bank presents a higher ratio during the COVID-19 pandemic compared to Alizz Islamic Bank (103.90%). In addition, both banks face higher credit and operational risks compared to the year 2019 which is expected due to the disruptions during the crisis. This supports the findings of Miah et al. (2021), who provided evidence that Islamic banks face more risks than before the COVID-19 pandemic.

Regarding profitability, as measured by return on assets (ROA), Alizz Islamic Bank realised a decrease of around −0.14% compared with 2019. Nizwa Bank also realised a decrease, of −0.04%. Concerning financial performance measured through return on equity (ROE), Alizz Islamic Bank realised a decrease of −1.57%, whereas Nizwa Bank, despite the pandemic, achieved a higher performance in 2020 than in 2019 (around+2.34%). This may explain the better disclosure of performance-related COVID-19 information by Nizwa Bank and this is in line with Elmarzouky et al. (2021). Overall, we can conclude that the financial performance of the sampled Islamic banks has not been affected by the pandemic despite the environment uncertainty and constraints. This also is in line with Elmarzouky et al. (2021) who observe that the impact of the COVID-19 pandemic on financial performance is not the same for all companies. They noted

*Table 19.3* Indicators of Islamic Omani banks' performance (in Riyal Omani (RO))

| | Alizz Islamic Bank | | Nizwa Bank | |
|---|---|---|---|---|
| | December 2020 | December 2019 | December 2020 | December 2019 |
| Total assets | 865,674,692 | 718,833,345 | 1,206,259 | 1,034,364 |
| Total liabilities | 577,895,335 | 493,042,090 | 1,046,571 | 886,457 |
| Liquidity coverage ratio (LCR) | 122.37% | – | 133.83% | 237.84% |
| Net-Stable Funding Ratio (NSFR) | 103.90% | – | 118.98% | 122.86% |
| Ratio of equity to risk* | – | – | 13.68% | 14.46% |
| Credit Risk* | 603,013,718 | 484,964,428 | 1,145,255 | 986,443 |
| Market Risk* | 5,125,000 | | 5,105 | 11,991 |
| Operational Risk* | 36,633,261 | 31,502,299 | 62,106 | 51,566 |
| Return on Assets (ROA) | 5.34% | 5.48% | 4.54% | 4.58% |
| Return on Equity (ROE) | 24.11% | 25.68% | 19.65% | 17.31% |
| Liquid Asset to Short-term Liabilities | – | – | 25.22% | 40.35% |
| Liquid Asset to Total Liabilities | – | – | 12.78% | 18.11% |

* Weighted assets

that, at the time of the COVID-19 pandemic, there are four different scenarios: (i) a significant increase in performance; (ii) a slight increase in performance; (iii) a decrease in performance; or (iv) companies make losses.

## 19.6 Conclusion

In the light of the economic, environmental and social impacts of the COVID-19 pandemic, we believe that is crucial to understand the different changes that took place in institutions to adapt to the new constraints and ensure their continued growth. Our chapter examined narrative COVID-19 disclosure and performance in two Omani Islamic banks, namely, Alizz Islamic Bank and Nizwa Bank. A content manual analysis was conducted to measure narrative COVID-19 disclosure in narrative sections of the annual reports for the year 2020. We relied on the IFC's Disclosure and Transparency Framework to construct our index. We found Islamic Omani banks disclose more strategic information related to the pandemic compared with performance and governance ones. In addition, they disclose weak governance COVID-19 information. Moreover, there was a slight decline in the performance of the two banks, although there was an increase in the financial performance of Nizwa Bank.

Our chapter contributes to the existing literature. In fact, to the best of our knowledge, there is no other study, to date, that examines narrative COVID-19 disclosure on Islamic banks. Accordingly, our study has theoretical and practical implications. It adds to the existing and growing literature on Islamic banks. Moreover, we suggest that regulatory authorities implement guidelines for Islamic banks regarding COVID-19 narrative disclosure, particularly regarding governance and performance information.

## Notes

1 Nizwa Bank and Alizz Islamic Bank
2 Al Yusr Islamic Banking of Oman Arab Bank; Meethaq Islamic Banking of Bank Muscat; Muzn Islamic Banking of National Bank of Oman; Sohar Islamic Bank; Maisarah Islamic Banking of Bank Dhofar; and Al Hilal Islamic Bank of Bank Al Ahli.
3 https://www.iasplus.com/en-gb/news/2020-en-gb/05/aaoifi-COVID-19
4 AAOIFI statement *"Accounting Implications of the Impact of the COVID-19 Pandemic"* p.8.

## References

AAOIFI. (2021) 'The accounting and auditing organization for Islamic financial institutions (AAOIFI)', Available at https://aaoifi.com/?lang=en (accessed on November 2021).

Abdallah, A. A. N., Hassan, M. K. and McClelland, P. L. (2015) 'Islamic financial institutions, corporate governance, and corporate risk disclosure in Gulf Cooperation Council countries', *Journal of Multinational Financial Management*, 31, 63–82.

Adams, C. A. and Abhayawansa, S. (2021) 'Connecting the COVID-19 pandemic, environmental, social and governance (ESG) investing and calls for 'harmonisation' of sustainability reporting', *Critical Perspectives on Accounting*, 82, 102309.

Akkas, E. and Al Samman, H. (2021) 'Are Islamic financial institutions more resilient against the COVID-19 pandemic in the GCC countries?', *International Journal of Islamic and Middle Eastern Finance and Management*, Forthcoming.

Al-Awadhi, A. M., Alsaifi, K., Al-Awadhi, A. and Alhammadi, S. (2020) 'Death and contagious infectious diseases: Impact of the COVID-19 virus on stock market returns', *Journal of Behavioral and Experimental Fnance*, 27, 100326.

Al Lawati, H., Hussainey, K. and Sagitova, R. (2021) 'Disclosure quality vis-à-vis disclosure quantity: Does audit committee matter in Omani financial institutions?', *Review of Quantitative Finance and Accounting*, 57, 557–594.

Al Sawalqa, F. A. (2020) 'Risk disclosure patterns among Jordanian companies: An exploratory study during the COVID-19 pandemic', *Accounting and Finance Research*, 9(3), 69–84.

Albitar, K., Gerged, A., Kikhia, H. and Hussainey, K. (2021) 'Auditing in times of social distancing: The effect of COVID-19 on auditing quality', *International Journal of Accounting and Information Management*, 29(1), 169–178.

Appelbaum, D., Budnik, S. and Vasarhelyi, M. (2020) 'Auditing and accounting during and after the COVID-19 crisis', *The CPA Journal*, 90(6), 14–19.

Aysan, A. F., Disli, M., Duygun, M. and Ozturk, H. (2017) 'Islamic banks, deposit insurance reform, and market discipline: Evidence from a natural framework', *Journal of Financial Services Research*, 51(2), 257–282.

Azmi, A. C., Rosman, R. and Omar, N. (2021) 'Sharīʿah non-compliant income disclosures and the moral legitimacy strategies of Islamic banks', *Journal of Islamic Accounting and Business Research*, Forthcoming.

Bader, M. K. I., Mohamad, S., Ariff, M. and Shah, T. H. (2008) 'Cost, revenue, and profit efficiency of Islamic versus conventional banks: International evidence using data envelopment analysis', *Islamic Economic Studies*, 15(2), 23–75.

Bae, K. H., El Ghoul, S., Gong, Z. J. and Guedhami, O. (2021) 'Does CSR matter in times of crisis? Evidence from the COVID-19 pandemic', *Journal of Corporate Finance*, 67, 101876.

Banna, H., Hassan, M. K., Ahmad, R. and Alam, M. R. (2021) 'Islamic banking stability amidst the COVID-19 pandemic: The role of digital financial inclusion', *International Journal of Islamic and Middle Eastern Finance and Management*, Forthcoming.

Barnoussi, A. E., Howieson, B. and van Beest, F. (2020) 'Prudential application of IFRS 9: (Un)Fair reporting in COVID-19 crisis for banks worldwide?!', *Australian Accounting Review*, 30(3), 178–192.

Baydoun, N. and Willett, R. (2000) 'Islamic corporate reports', *Abacus*, 36(1), 71–90.

Beattie, V. and Thomson, S. J. (2007) 'Lifting the lid on the use of content analysis to investigate intellectual capital disclosures', *Accounting Forum*, 31(2), 129–163.

Beck, T., Demirgüç-Kunt, A. and Merrouche, O. (2013) 'Islamic vs. conventional banking: Business model, efficiency and stability', *Journal of Banking and Finance*, 37(2), 433–447.

Berelson, B. (1952) *Content analysis in communication research*. Glencoe, IL: Free Press.

Carner, T. (1972) *Content analysis: A technique for systematic inference for communications*. London: B T Batsford.

Central Bank of Oman. (2021) 'Monthly Statistical Bulletin', Available at https://cbo.gov.om/report/MonthlyBulletins/107 (accessed on July 2021).

Darmadi, S. (2013) 'Corporate governance disclosure in the annual report: An exploratory study on Indonesian Islamic banks', *Humanomics*, 29(1), 4–23.

Doumpos, M., Hasan, I. and Pasiouras, F. (2017) 'Bank overall financial strength: Islamic versus conventional banks', *Economic Modelling*, 64, 513–523.

Elgattani, T. and Hussainey, K. (2020) 'The determinants of AAOIFI governance disclosure in Islamic banks', *Journal of Financial Reporting and Accounting*, 18(1), 1–18.

Elgattani, T. and Hussainey, K. (2021) 'The impact of AAOIFI governance disclosure on Islamic banks performance', *Journal of Financial Reporting and Accounting*, 19(3), 434–454.

Elmarzouky, M., Albitar, K. and Hussainey, K. (2021) 'Covid-19 and performance disclosure: Does governance matter?', *International Journal of Accounting and Information Management*, Forthcoming.

Elshandidy, T., Shrives, P. J., Bamber, M. and Abraham, S. (2018) 'Risk reporting: A review of the literature and implications for future research☆', *Journal of Accounting Literature*, 40(1), 54–82.

García-Sánchez, I. M. and García-Sánchez, A. (2020) 'Corporate social responsibility during COVID-19 pandemic', *Journal of Open Innovation: Technology, Market, and Complexity*, 6(4), 126.

Ghazali, N. A. M. and Weetman, P. (2006) 'Perpetuating traditional influences: Voluntary disclosure in Malaysia following the economic crisis', *Journal of International Accounting, Auditing and Taxation*, 15(2), 226–248.

Grassa, R., Chakroun, R. and Hussainey, K. (2018) 'Corporate governance and Islamic banks' products and services disclosure', *Accounting Research Journal*, 31(1), 75–98.

Grassa, R., Moumen, N. and Hussainey, K. (2020) 'Is bank creditworthiness associated with risk disclosure behavior? Evidence from Islamic and conventional banks in emerging countries', *Pacific-Basin Finance Journal*, 61, 101327.

Grassa, R., Moumen, N. and Hussainey, K. (2021a) 'What drives risk disclosure in Islamic and conventional banks? An international comparison', *International Journal of Finance and Economics*, 26(4), 6338–6361.

Grassa, R., Moumen, N. and Hussainey, K. (2021b) 'Do ownership structures affect risk disclosure in Islamic banks? International evidence', *Journal of Financial Reporting and Accounting*, 19(3), 369–391.

Haj-Salem, I. (2020) 'Board structure and voluntary disclosure: Tunisian evidence', In: A. Alqatan, K. Hussainey, H. Khlif (eds), *Corporate governance and its implications on accounting and finance*, 280–304. Hershey, Pennsylvania: IGI Global.

Haj-Salem, I. and Hussainey, K. (2021a) 'Does risk disclosure matter for trade credit?', *Journal of Risk and Financial Management*, 14(3), 133.

Haj-Salem, I. and Hussainey, K. (2021b) 'Risk disclosure and corporate cash holdings', *Journal of Risk and Financial Management*, 14(7), 328.

Haniffa, R. and Hudaib, M. (2007) 'Exploring the ethical identity of Islamic banks via communication in annual reports', *Journal of Business Ethics*, 76(1), 97–116.

Harun, M. S., Hussainey, K., Mohd Kharuddin, K. A. and Farooque, O. A. (2020) 'CSR disclosure, corporate governance and firm value: A study on GCC Islamic banks', *International Journal of Accounting and Information Management*, 28(4), 607–638.

Hasan, M. and Dridi, J. (2011) 'The effects of the global crisis on Islamic and conventional banks: A comparative study', *Journal of International Commerce, Economics and Policy*, 2(2), 163–200.

Hassan, M. K. (2014) 'Risk narrative disclosure strategies to enhance organizational legitimacy: Evidence from UAE financial institutions', *International Journal of Disclosure and Governance*, 11(1), 1–17.

Healy, P. M. and Palepu, K. G. (2001) 'Information asymmetry, corporate disclosure, and the capital markets: A review of the empirical disclosure literature', *Journal of Accounting and Economics*, 31(1–3), 405–440.

Ichsan, R. N., Suparmin, S., Yusuf, M., Ismal, R. and Sitompul, S. (2021) 'Determinant of Sharia bank's financial performance during the COVID-19 pandemic', *Budapest International Research and Critics Institute (BIRCI-Journal): Humanities and Social Sciences*, 4(1), 298–309.

Jebran, K. and Chen, S. (2021) 'Can we learn lessons from the past? COVID-19 crisis and corporate governance responses', *International Journal of Finance and Economics*, in press. https://doi.org/10.1002/ijfe.2428.

Jensen, M. C. and Meckling, W. H. (1976) 'Theory of the firm: Managerial behavior, agency costs and ownership structure', *Journal of Financial Economics*, 3(4), 305–360.

Johnes, J., Izzeldin, M. and Pappas, V. (2014) 'A comparison of performance of Islamic and conventional banks 2004–2009', *Journal of Economic Behavior and Organization*, 103, S93–S107.

Jones, M. J. and Shoemaker, P. A. (1994) '"Accounting narrative: A review of empirical studies of content and readability"', *Journal of Accounting Literature*, 13, 142–184.

Kabir, M. N., Worthington, A. and Gupta, R. (2015) 'Comparative credit risk in Islamic and conventional bank', *Pacific-Basin Finance Journal*, 34, 327–353.

Karim, M. R., Shetu, S. A. and Razia, S. (2021) 'COVID-19, liquidity and financial health: Empirical evidence from South Asian economy', *Asian Journal of Economics and Banking*, 5(3), 307–323.

Kells, S. (2020) 'Impacts of COVID-19 on corporate governance and assurance, international finance and economics, and non-fiction book publishing: Some personal reflections', *Journal of Accounting and Organizational Change*, 16(4), 69–635.

Khan, F. (2010) 'How "Islamic" is Islamic banking?', *Journal of Economic Behavior and Organization*, 76(3), 805–820.

Kotb Abdelrahman Radwan, E., Omar, N. and Hussainey, K. (2021) 'Social responsibility of Islamic banks in developing countries: Empirical evidence from Egypt', *Journal of Sustainable Finance and Investment*, in press. https://doi.org/10.1080/20430795.2021 .1949890.

Krippendorff, K. (1980) *Content analysis: An introduction to its methodology*. Newbury Park, CA: Sage.

Ltifi, M. and Hichri, A. (2021) 'The effects of corporate governance on the customer's recommendations: A study of the banking sector at the time of COVID-19', *Journal of Knowledge Management*, Forthcoming.

Mansour, W., Ajmi, H. and Saci, K. (2021) 'Regulatory policies in the global Islamic banking sector in the outbreak of COVID-19 pandemic', *Journal of Banking Regulation*, in press. https://link.springer.com/article/10.1057/s41261-021-00147-3.

Miah, M. D., Suzuki, Y. and Uddin, S. M. S. (2021) 'The impact of COVID-19 on Islamic banks in Bangladesh: A perspective of Marxian 'circuit of merchant's capital'', *Journal of Islamic Accounting and Business Research*, 12(7), 1036–1054.

Mihajat, M. I. S. (2021) 'Oman's Islamic banking performance amidst COVID-19 outbreak: Prospects and challenges', *Shirkah: Journal of Economics and Business*, 6(1), 38–51.

Mousa, G. A., Elamir, E. A. and Hussainey, K. (2022) 'Using machine learning methods to predict financial performance: Does disclosure tone matter?', *International Journal of Disclosure and Governance*, 19, 93–112.

Musa, M. A., Sukor, M. E. A., Ismail, M. N. and Elias, M. R. F. (2020) 'Islamic business ethics and practices of Islamic banks: Perceptions of Islamic bank employees in Gulf cooperation countries and Malaysia', *Journal of Islamic Accounting and Business Research*, 11(5), 1009–1031.

Neisen, M. and Schulte-Mattler, H. (2021) 'The effectiveness of IFRS 9 transitional provisions in limiting the potential impact of COVID-19 on banks', *Journal of Banking Regulation*, 22(4), 342–351.

Qiu, S. C., Jiang, J., Liu, X., Chen, M. H. and Yuan, X. (2021) 'Can corporate social responsibility protect firm value during the COVID-19 pandemic?', *International Journal of Hospitality Management*, 93, 102759.

Raza Rabbani, M., Rahiman, H. U., Atif, M., Zulfikar, Z. and Naseem, Y. (2021) 'The response of Islamic financial service to the COVID-19 pandemic: The open social innovation of the financial system', *Journal of Open Innovation: Technology, Market, and Complexity*, 7(1), 85.

Saidani, R., Boulila, N. and Hussainey, K. (2021) 'The investment account holders disclosure level in the annual reports of Islamic banks: Construction of IAHs disclosure index', *The Singapore Economic Review*, Forthcoming.

Salem, I. H., Ayadi, S. D. and Hussainey, K. (2019) 'Corporate governance and risk disclosure quality: Tunisian evidence', *Journal of Accounting in Emerging Economies*, 9(4), 567–602.

Sivaprasad, S. and Mathew, S. (2021) 'Corporate governance practices and the pandemic crisis: UK evidence', *Corporate Governance, The International Journal of Business in Society*, Forthcoming.

Spence, M. (1973) 'Job market signaling', *The Quarterly Journal of Economics*, 355–374.

Uddin, M., Chowdhury, A., Anderson, K. and Chaudhuri, K. (2021) 'The effect of COVID–19 pandemic on global stock market volatility: Can economic strength help to manage the uncertainty?', *Journal of Business Research*, 128, 31–44.

Weber, R. P. (1990) *Basic content analysis* (49th ed.). New York: Sage Publications.

Xiong, H., Wu, Z., Hou, F. and Zhang, J. (2020) 'Which firm-specific characteristics affect the market reaction of Chinese listed companies to the COVID-19 pandemic?', *Emerging Markets Finance and Trade*, 56(10), 2231–2242.

# Index